D0936317

THE GREAT NORTHWEST

THE
Great Northwest

A HISTORY

BY

OSCAR OSBURN WINTHER

SECOND EDITION,
REVISED AND ENLARGED

1952

ALFRED A. KNOPF   NEW YORK

THIS IS A BORZOI BOOK,
PUBLISHED BY ALFRED A. KNOPF, INC.

Copyright 1947, 1950 by Alfred A. Knopf, Inc. All rights reserved. No part of this book in excess of five hundred words may be reproduced in any form without permission in writing from the publisher, except by a reviewer who may quote brief passages and reproduce not more than three illustrations in a review to be printed in a magazine or newspaper. Manufactured in the United States of America. Published in Canada by McClelland & Stewart Limited.

Published September 22, 1947
Reprinted four times
Second Edition, Revised, September 1950
Reprinted, August 1952

IN MEMORY OF MY PARENTS

who found the good life
in the
Willamette Valley

PREFACE

TO REVISED EDITION

THE many reviews of the first edition of this book and the great number of letters from friends, general readers, and professional associates contributed much in the form of encouragement, friendly criticism, and suggestions. Even though most remarks on how to improve the first edition were excellent, not all could be incorporated here for the simple reason that a great many of them were in conflict with one another. One would suggest less material on the fur trade; another would say the space devoted to this subject was just the right amount. One would lament that more chapters were not devoted to Indians; another was happy that the Indian wars did not clutter up the pages of this book. Several critics would have liked more material on the missionaries; but at least one competent scholar in church history was happy to find the missionaries placed in their "proper setting."

Recurring was the suggestion that more space be devoted to the period since the passing of the frontier, even though, as Professor Herman J. Deutsch of Washington State College correctly states: "There simply has not been sufficient spadework" done to give "adequate insight into recent trends." In this revision I have expanded the period since about 1883 (completion of the Northern Pacific Railroad) so that the above date represents the approximate mid-point of the book. And while I have written this volume without specific leaning for either the region west of the Cascades or that lying east of those mountains, the material as it now stands is about equally divided so far as treatment of the two major sections of the Northwest is concerned.

Again I am under special obligation to those who gave specific aid: Mrs. Emmett Avery and Mr. Richard Whittemore, The State College of Washington; Professor Harold Barto, Central Washington College of Education; Professor Paul Glad, Hastings College; Professor Jonas A. Jonasson, Linfield College; Professor William D. Miner, Eastern Illinois

[v

State College; Mr. James Thompson, Indiana University; Professor Sidney Warren, University of Durham, England; and the personnel of industrial firms and government agencies.

O. O. W.

PREFACE

THIS book is a historical survey of the Pacific or — as I have entitled it — Great Northwest. The opening section explains the varying geographical limitations of the region. The early fur-trade-pioneer period has its setting in the expansive "Oregon Country" which lay west of the Continental Divide between present-day Alaska and California. The history since the settlement of the Oregon boundary question in 1846, on the other hand, has been focused upon what are today the states of Oregon, Washington, and Idaho, with scattered but related portions devoted to the regions now known as Montana and British Columbia.

The Great Northwest has come of age. Long an important hinterland, it has finally emerged as one of the very significant sections of the nation. Its influence in politics is, on the whole, progressive; in agriculture it has retained its high productive capacity; it is the gateway to Alaska and the Orient; and more recently its electrically powered industries have commanded attention and respect. Blessed with a rich, pioneer tradition, the Northwest is today exhibiting an ever-changing culture pattern that is rugged and vigorous. The forces that have brought this about, many having their roots in the remote past, comprise the major themes of this book.

I have personally consulted a quantity of basic source materials in local and outside archives, but a deep debt of gratitude is due many exacting scholars who have laboriously prepared the monographs, general books, and learned articles which have made the writing of this book possible. I likewise wish to express my sincere appreciation to a number of these specialists and scholars who provided me with materials, and generously read and criticized individual chapters of my manuscript before publication. Full responsibility for the validity and accuracy of statements made herein, nevertheless, rest with the author.

Those to whom I am indebted are: Mr. Raymond Allen, Bonneville Power Administration, Portland; Professor Thomas A. Bailey, Stanford University; Professor Read Bain, Miami University; Mr. Hu Blonk, United States Bureau of Reclamation, Regional Office, Boise; Dean Harold W. Bradley,

Claremont Colleges; Professor John W. Caughey, University of California at Los Angeles; Mr. Merrill J. Collett, Bonneville Power Administration, Portland; Professor Joseph W. Ellison, Oregon State College; Professor Otis W. Freeman, Eastern Washington College of Education, Cheney; Mr. John D. Galey, war-time Chairman of the West Coast Lumber Commission, Portland; Professor Charles M. Gates, University of Washington; Professor James B. Hedges, Brown University; the late Judge Frederic W. Howay, New Westminster, British Columbia; Professor Harold W. Innis, University of Toronto; Professor W. Turrentine Jackson, Iowa State College; Professor Melvin C. Jacobs, Whitman College; Professor Dorothy O. Johansen, Reed College; Miss A. M. Johnson, Hudson's Bay Company, Beaver House, London; Professor C. S. Kingston, Eastern Washington College of Education; Professor Richard G. Lillard, University of California at Los Angeles; Professor J. Orin Oliphant, Bucknell University; Professor Philip H. Overmeyer, Lewis and Clark College; Professor Frederic L. Paxson, University of California at Berkeley; Professor Walter N. Sage, University of British Columbia; Professor Waldo Schumacher, University of Oregon; and Professor Sophus K. Winther, University of Washington.

With special regard I add to this list Mary, my wife, who helped me in ways too numerous to specify. Dr. Erminie W. Voegelin, Editor, American Folklore Society, Bloomington, Indiana, generously made available her specialized knowledge of anthropology in the preparation of the sections on Indians in Chapter I. I owe much of my interest in Northwest history to the inspiring teaching of the late Professor Robert C. Clark of the University of Oregon, and to the continued encouragement of Professor Dan E. Clark at the same university. To Mrs. Marian Blackwell goes the credit for executing the pen and ink maps included in this book. And, finally, I wish to express my appreciation to the many libraries, historical societies, business firms, government agencies, and their personnel for courtesies and kindnesses extended me while collecting material.

                                        OSCAR OSBURN WINTHER
Indiana University

CONTENTS

PART ONE: THE FRONTIER PERIOD
[TO 1883]

CHAPTER I. WHEN THE WHITE MAN CAME

Introducing the Region 3
The Indian Tribes 6
Physical Characteristics of Pacific Northwest
    Indians 9
Native Tongues 11
Modes of Indian Life 12
White Intruders 19

CHAPTER II. THE SEA OTTER ERA

Clawing the Coastline. 21
British Explorations and the Establishment of a
    Sea Otter Trade 23
Yankee Triangle Trade 26

CHAPTER III. THE NORTH WEST COMPANY
    INVASION

When Fur Was King 33
Origin of the North West Company 34
British Dreams of Empire 35
Nor'westers Enter the Valley of the Columbia ... 36
Nor'westers in New Caledonia 39
Organization 40
In Search of Pelts 41
Communications 44
An Outlet to the Sea 46

CHAPTER IV. THE HONOURABLE HUDSON'S
    BAY COMPANY

A British Monopoly is Born 49
The Giant Merger 51

"Where Rolls the Oregon" 54
Outposts in the Wilderness 59

Chapter V. BRITISH MONOPOLY IN ACTION
In and Around the Posts 66
Fur Trading Cavalcades and Expeditions 67
"The Coasting Trade" 71
Fur Traders Turn to Agriculture 73
Company Herds and Flocks 77
The Puget's Sound Agricultural Company 79
Minor Subsidiaries 82

Chapter VI. AMERICAN VENTURES IN THE FUR TRADE
Captains Lewis and Clark 86
Precursors of Astor 89
Astor's Vision of Empire 90
Sagas of Endurance and Suffering 91
Astor's Achievements and Failures 94
The Jedediah Smith Disaster 98
The Adventurous Captain Bonneville 99
Nathaniel Wyeth — "A Visionary and a Failure" 102

Chapter VII. WENDING WESTWARD
"First Families" of the Willamette Valley 107
The Great Trail to Oregon 108
Missionary Settlers 113
Outbreak of Oregon Fever 120
Prairie Cavalcades 121
"Oh Susannah" 124

Chapter VIII. PROVISIONAL GOVERNMENT
A Prelude 127
Roots of Provisional Government 129
The Champoeg Meetings 132

The Immigrant Tide and Provisional Government   135
The Final Stage   137

CHAPTER IX. THE EAGLE SCREAMS
Joint Occupation   139
Watch Dogs of the Oregon Territory   141
Manifest Destiny   144
The Diplomatic Bout   146

CHAPTER X. OREGON AND WASHINGTON TERRITORIAL POLITICS
Significance of the Whitman Massacre   152
Creation of Oregon Territory   153
The Donation Land Law   157
Toward Statehood   158
Statehood and Impending Civil War   161
Washington Territory   162

CHAPTER XI. THE AGRICULTURAL FRONTIER
The Spread of Settlement   167
The Indian Menace   171
Blazing Roads Through the Wilderness   178
The Struggle for a Living   181
The Social Fabric   184

CHAPTER XII. THE STAGECOACH AND PADDLEWHEEL ERA
The Stagecoach Arrives   187
Mail Bags   188
Overland Stage and Mail Service   190
Express and Stagecoach Monopoly   193
Behind the Reins   198
Trials of the Wayfarer   200
Paddlewheel Days   202

CHAPTER XX. INDUSTRY AND COMMERCE

A Backward Glance 340
Northwest Manufactures: 1890 341
In the Wake of the Gold Rush 343
The Fishing Industry 346
Timber-r-r 352
The Spread of Industry 360
Gateway to the Pacific 361
The Tourist Business 363

CHAPTER XXI. HYDROELECTRICITY

Private Enterprise 366
Public Ownership: Local and National 373
Power Co-operatives and Public Utility Districts 376
Electrification of Industry 378
The Power Problem 382

CHAPTER XXII. POLITICO-ECONOMIC
FERMENT

Post-Civil War Attitudes, Behavior, and Trends
(1865–96) 384
First Call for Reform 389
The Grange 391
Populism 395
Local Elections: 1896–1916 403
The Oregon System 405
The Legislative Record 409
Local Politics Between Two Wars 411
The Nation and the Region 413

CHAPTER XXIII. THE SOCIAL FRONT

New Elements in the Population 417
"The Yellow Peril" 421

Persistence of the Westward Movement 426
Growing City Consciousness 431
The Labor Front 433

CHAPTER XXIV. THE REFINEMENTS OF LIFE
Literary Strivings 439
The Northwest Press 446
Theatrical and Musical Entertainment 449
Fine Arts and Architecture 453
Education 457

BIBLIOGRAPHY 463

INDEX *follows page* 491

ILLUSTRATIONS

Scenes of Oregon	10
Pacific Northwest Indian types	11
North fork of Payette River, Idaho	42
Dr. John McLoughlin, Chief Factor of the Columbia District for the Hudson's Bay Company	43
Fort Astoria	74
Crater Lake in Crater Lake National Park	75
Scenes of early day transportation	106
Chief Joseph	107
As Punch *saw the Oregon boundary dispute*	143
The Indian's portion	172
Railroads of the Northwest	264–5
Sheep breeding	296
Sawmill at Shelton, Washington	297
The Inland Empire	328
Northwest industries	329
Generating hydroelectricity	360
Washington-built airplanes	361
Before and after reclamation	392
The Coulee Dam by day and night	393
Seattle	424
Mount Rainier	425

MAPS AND CHARTS

Northwest Indian tribes	8
Principal fur trading posts	61
The Oregon Trail and route followed by Lewis and Clark	110
The Oregon boundary controversy	149
Principal wagon roads in the Pacific Northwest before 1870	179

[xvii

Political evolution of Northwest states (Oregon, Washington, Idaho) — 242–3
Major railroads in the Great Northwest — 267
Farms in Oregon, Washington, and Idaho — 337
Origin of tourists in Washington, 1949 — 364
Power generated by the principal electric utilities — 375
The Columbia River federal hydroelectric power system — 381
Population growth: Pacific Northwest and the United States — 429

PART ONE

THE FRONTIER PERIOD

(to 1883)

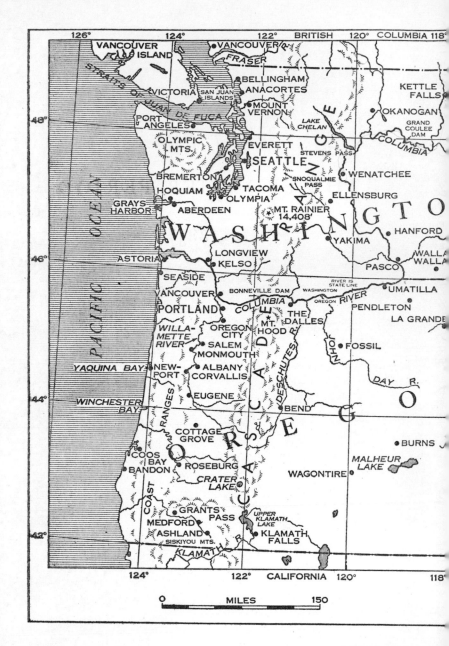

THE GREAT

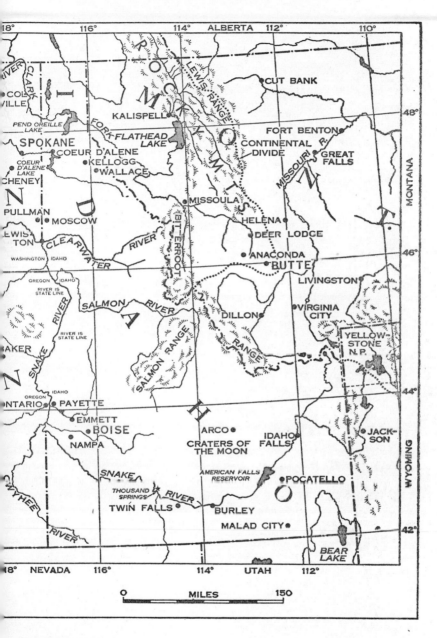

NORTHWEST

CHAPTER I

When the White Man Came

Introducing the Region

THE GREAT or Pacific Northwest has been variously defined. Today its narrowest limits are generally understood to embrace the states of Oregon, Washington, and Idaho. Those in a generous mood toss in British Columbia, Alaska, and the mountain counties of western Montana. Even three whole centuries after the discovery of America by Columbus only the coastline of this region was known to the white man. The interior was a mere geographical expression suitable for cartographers' sketches of imaginary rivers (especially the mythical "River of the West") on their New World maps. The term "Oregon Country" gained acceptance as a name for this region during the early years of the nineteenth century; but in the minds of many Americans bent on going there, "Oregon" meant the Willamette Valley.

By 1825, however, diplomatists and politicians had come to recognize the Oregon country as a region lying south of 54° 40′, north of the forty-second parallel, bounded on the west by the Pacific Ocean and on the east by the Continental Divide. Expressed in political terms, this area embraced present-day Oregon, Washington, Idaho, the western half of British Columbia, and the extreme western portions of Montana and Wyoming. Accepting these boundaries as the province of this history, the Great Northwest comprises an area roughly one-fifth the size of the present continental United States.

Physically, this is a region of contrasts. It is a land and water mass rich in natural history, a country amazingly varied in its geological formations, topography, soil, and climate. A range of rugged mountains named the Cascades extends like

[3

a protruding backbone through the middle of Oregon and Washington; and as the Pacific Coast Range of Canada it continues northward through western British Columbia into Alaska.

The region west of the Cascades possesses a diverse character. Its shoreline is fringed by the Coast Range and Olympic Mountains, which are separated from the Cascades by the low-lying Willamette-Puget Trough, better known as the Willamette and Cowlitz valleys and the Puget Sound area. Gentle westerly winds prevail, and during the course of a year deliver anywhere from 40 to more than 100 inches of rainfall except to leeward of the Olympics where rainfall may be less than 20 inches. This generous precipitation contributes to the productivity of the Willamette-Puget Trough and of numerous other valleys, such as those of the Umpqua and Rogue rivers in southern Oregon.

That portion of the Great Northwest lying east of the Cascades and west of the Rocky Mountains is popularly referred to either as the "Inland Empire" (the term generally used in this book) or the "Columbia Plateau." Geologically this region is called the Columbia Intermontane Province. It is an uneven inter-mountain area lying from one to five thousand feet above sea level, and is marked by innumerable mountains, hills, plateaus, and basins. At various times in its geologic past extensive portions of this region have been subjected to enormous lava flows (among the largest in the world) which today form the basis of the surface soil, along with local sediments and volcanic ash that drifted east from erupting craters in the Cascades. The Continental Divide which wanders from one range to another, including parts of the Rocky Mountains (and Canadian Rockies), and which separates the drainage of the continent, comprises the eastern boundary of the old Oregon country. Protruding westward from the Rockies are many mountainous spurs and highlands interspersed by valleys. In central Idaho this broad, ruggedly eroded highland is uncrossed by rail or practical highways. The climate east of the Cascades is dry and sunny, in contrast to the coastal area, and the extremes of heat and cold are more pronounced. Unlike the coast, the Inland Empire is frequently blanketed with snow during winter months; and welcome it is to the people living there who depend upon it as moisture for "dryland" wheat growing and as a source of water for irrigation and hydroelectric power.

This variation in topography and in climate, which becomes arid in central Washington and southeast Oregon, with increased rainfall as the Rockies are approached, accounts for the different types of soil and of natural vegetation, and the varied productivity of the land. Conifers blanket most mountain areas, and the whole western region constitutes one of the greatest commercial forests remaining in the world. The coastal valleys produce a great diversity of crops, while wheatfields, irrigated crops, orchards, and grazing lands are the proud possession of the Inland Empire. Coal occurs in western Washington, and numerous deposits of metals have been found in the Rockies and other ranges.

All streams west of this Continental Divide make up a vast drainage system which has for its ultimate outlet the Pacific Ocean. Mightiest of all the rivers of the West is the Columbia. It rises high in the ice fields of British Columbia and winds through that province for half of its 1,400-mile course. Then it makes a big bend in eastern Washington, gathers the waters of such formidable tributaries as the Snake, Spokane, Clark's Fork, Willamette, and Cowlitz, and rushes to the sea. Much of its long course is through rocky canyons, most notable of which is the Cascades Gorge. The Columbia drains an area 259,000 square miles in extent, and its mean water flow is eight times greater than that of the Colorado River. Before the construction of the Bonneville Dam and lock it was navigable for ocean-going vessels as far up as the Cascades (40 miles east of Portland). Such vessels can now proceed upstream to The Dalles, while barges ascend regularly to Wallula, just below the confluence with the Snake River. Portland, near the mouth of the Willamette River, remains the principal port in the Columbia system.

Important in the history of the Great Northwest is the turbulent Fraser which flows southward through western British Columbia and reaches ocean water near Vancouver. Cutting in through the Strait of Juan de Fuca, separating Vancouver

Island from the Olympic Peninsula, and forming a great irregular sea in western Washington is Puget Sound. Also separating Vancouver Island and the Canadian mainland is the Strait of Georgia. These deep water inlets have made possible the commodious ports of Seattle and Tacoma in Washington, Vancouver and Victoria in British Columbia, and smaller ones within Puget Sound. The coastal area of the Pacific Northwest is generally mountainous and lacks good harbors. Grays Harbor and Willapa Bay in Washington, and Coos Bay in Oregon are all three useful for the export of lumber, but too shallow for big ocean liners.

The Indian Tribes

Between twenty and forty thousand years ago, at the end of the last Ice Age, groups of northern Asiatic peoples began moving eastward. They crossed Bering Strait into the New World, which was then wholly unpopulated and totally unexplored. The eastward movement of these Old World peoples across the threshold of the Strait presumably continued for some time in a thin, irregular trickle. Probably among the last of the Asiatic groups to come to the New World were the ancestors of the Indians of the Pacific Northwest. Although late comers, some of them had, by the time Europeans rediscovered the Pacific coast, achieved a richness of culture unrivalled north of Mexico. The farther away from the coast these tribes moved, however, the more simple their lives became. Since Indians north of Mexico kept no written records, to anthropologists rather than to historians has fallen the difficult task of reconstructing the past of these Northwest tribes before white men found them.

At the end of the Indian period (i.e., before white men came) some one hundred twenty-five separate tribes lived in the Pacific Northwest.[1] Their total population has been

---

[1] Location of these groups prior to the period of white settlement is shown on the map (Figure 1). Designations for the various groups are those which are used most frequently today in the literature. Tribal names as used are derived from a variety of sources. Some are English approximations of native names, as for example Tlin' git, from Lingít, *people;* Haida, from Xa'aida, *people;* Takel'ma, from Dāglama'n, *those dwelling along a river.*

estimated at 180,000. Throughout North America the Indians were more densely settled along the seacoasts than in the interior, and this was true in the Pacific Northwest. Coast tribes such as the Tlingit and the Haida each numbered some 10,-000 persons; the Kwakiutl proper, 4,500; the Lower and Upper Chinook as a whole, 22,000; while the inland tribes ran from 500 for the Takelma of southern Oregon, to 4,000 and 5,000 for the Lillooet and Shuswap of interior British Columbia. Translated into terms of population density the figures for the Indians along the Northwest coast and approximately one hundred miles inland ranged from about one-third to a little less than one per square mile. East of the Cascades the density was less than one-sixth to the square mile. None of these densities seem impressive today, but when one reflects that the total continental population north of Mexico in native times was only 1,000,000 persons, or seven-tenths of one per cent of the present population, the figures begin to have a relative significance. Much of the Pacific Northwest was uninhabited, but not unclaimed and unexplored, by native tribes. Populations, especially in the coastal strip, tended to cluster in villages and to utilize the territory between villages chiefly for economic purposes.

After the early nineteenth century both the location and population figures for many tribes changed markedly. Some of the groups, such as the Tlingit, Tsimshian, Haida, Kwakiutl, Nootka, and many interior tribes of British Columbia, have

---

Others are Anglicized forms of the name one tribe used for another, as for example, Chinook from Tsinu'k, the Chehalis name; Sar'si from sa arsi, *not good*, the Blackfoot term for the Sarsi. A few tribal names refer to natural features, as We'natchi, which comes from the Yakima name, winltshi, *river issuing from a canyon.* The Thompson Indians were named for the English-named river which flows through their territory; the Lake Indians for the many lakes in their area. Some tribal names refer, either erroneously or correctly, to details of appearance of their bearers; for example, the Flathead are so called because early *voyageurs* dubbed them "Tetes-Plates," believing wrongly that this tribe practiced artificial head deformation, as did many of its neighbors. The Nez Percé were also erroneously named by French explorers; there is no evidence that either Nez Percé men or women pierced their nasal septums for nose ornaments. On the other hand, the name for the Carrier derives from an actual practice of widows carrying the bones of their dead husbands on their backs while mourning them. Several Pacific Northwest tribal names defy attempts at analysis; examples of such are Okinágen, Spokan', and Puy'allup.

been allowed by the white pre-emptors of Indian territory to occupy only a small part of their former area. Others, such as the coastal and some interior tribes of Washington and Oregon, have been removed to reservations, often at a dis-

Prepared by Dr. Erminie W. Voegelin.

NORTHWEST INDIAN TRIBES

tance from their original homes. Still other groups have become extinct during the past century and a half. After the beginning of the nineteenth century, Indian populations in the entire Pacific Northwest decreased rapidly, but those on or near the coast suffered the greatest losses. Epidemics of identifiable and unidentified diseases took an appalling toll. The Haida of Queen Charlotte Islands, once 10,000 strong, were by 1900 reduced through smallpox and other diseases for which they had built up no immunity, to some 1,000 persons. Chinook tribes of the lower Columbia, numbering in all approximately 22,000, suffered an epidemic of so-called "ague fever" in 1829, which in a single summer wiped out entire villages. In the course of three years it reduced the Chinook to one-tenth of their former numbers. A Hudson's Bay man described a Chinook village which he visited after a few days of the epidemic: "There were fires smoking, dogs barking, salmon drying on the racks. Only one thing was lacking, the cheerful sound of the human voice." He found only two people alive in the camp.

Enforced removals to reservations also cost the lives of many natives during the nineteenth century. But losses caused by these migrations, like those due to wars waged by some groups against white settlers, were relatively negligible in comparison to the ravages of diseases such as smallpox and measles brought by white traders and settlers.

Physical Characteristics of Pacific Northwest Indians

Natives of the Pacific Northwest belong to the New World subdivision of the Mongoloid (*Homo sapiens asiaticus*) race, one of the three major races of the world. Mongoloid peoples are distributed over Asia and both the Americas. They are distinguished from Negroids and Caucasoids by yellow to dark brown skin, straight black hair which is cylindrical in cross-section, a scant amount of body hair, and brown to black eyes. Within the Mongoloid race are numerous subgroups, both in Asia and in America, which can be distinguished on the basis of a combination of various common inherited physical features. Pacific Northwest tribes all belonged to one such group, referred to as the Pacifid subgroup (*Homo sapiens asiaticus*, var. *Pacifid*). The combination of physical traits which distinguishes the Pacifids are brachycephalism or broad headedness; [2] large, broad, rectangular, moderately flat faces; broad foreheads; straight, narrow noses with a high bridge; yellow skin color, especially among the coastal groups; head hair of medium coarseness; brown eyes. Stature of most of these tribes averaged 5′ 6″ for adult males and 5′ 1″ for females. Adults were thick set and powerful in appearance. There were some variations. For example, the Salish of Harrison Lake and Thompson River were of short stature (5′ 2″ to 5′ 4″ for adult males) while two or three southern groups, as the Chinook and Nez Percé, were relatively tall (5′ 6″ to 5′ 8″ for adult males). None of the peoples of this region, however, equalled in height such groups as the Northern Plains or the Colorado River Yuman tribes, in which male adults averaged 5′ 9″.

One non-inherited physical characteristic which seems strikingly peculiar to present-day Americans was the artificial head deformation practiced by many Pacific Northwest peoples in native times. Two kinds of intentional alteration of the shape of the skull during infancy were practiced, the so-called "flathead" and the less usual "Aymara" type. Flathead deformation was achieved by pressing the back of the baby's head against the cradle board, and pressing another, slanting board against the frontal part of the head. Since infants were rarely taken off the cradleboard except for baths, the pressure was kept constant and produced a head which was conical in profile. Such deformation was practiced on both males and females from southern Oregon to British Columbia, chiefly among tribes west of the Cascades, and especially by those along the Columbia River. The so-called "Aymara" type of intentional deformation, in which the skull was bound all around with small cushions or bandages to press it into an elongated, bag-like shape, was limited to the Kwakiutl groups on Vancouver Island. Among the peoples of the western half of the Pacific Northwest head deformation

---

[2] Cephalic indices (head breadth divided by head height and multiplied by 100) range from 80 to 84 for Pacific Northwest groups.

SCENES OF OREGON
(above) *The Columbia River Gorge* (below) *The Oregon Coast*
Courtesy Edward Weston and the Huntington Library

Bannock (medicine man)   *Flathead*

Couer d'Alene   *Spokane*

PACIFIC NORTHWEST INDIAN TYPES

From the Wanamaker Collection. Courtesy Indiana University Museum of Anthropology, Professor George K. Neumann, Director

had, through long practice, become a custom as fixed as bound feet formerly were for upper-class Chinese women. Deformed heads were regarded as a mark of distinction and superiority, while natural head forms were considered disgraceful, and permissible only for slaves.

Native Tongues

Areas of greatest linguistic diversity in native North America were California, the central part of the Gulf of Mexico coast, and the Pacific Northwest. In the last-named region twenty unrelated language families are represented by one or more languages. The total number of mutually unintelligible languages spoken in the Pacific Northwest amounted to at least fifty-six. Since no genetic relationship has as yet been established between any New and Old World language families, it is generally assumed that the many New World languages, including those of the Pacific Northwest, were developed in the New World. The multiplicity of New World languages plus their lack of relation to those of the Old World tends to serve as a check against hypotheses which are sometimes advanced that man entered the New World in relatively recent times, perhaps only a few thousand years ago.

Besides these native languages, a highly useful trade language, the Chinook Jargon, developed and was extensively used by all tribes on the coast and those on the Columbia River, where each year many groups met to trade at Celilo Falls and The Dalles. This Jargon was first detected by George Vancouver, famed British explorer, when he visited Grays Harbor near the mouth of the Columbia in 1792 and commented that the natives there were speaking a language that did not seem to be their native tongue. Early in the nineteenth century this speech, like the Mobilian speech of the central Gulf of Mexico coast, was established as a trade language. The foundation for the Jargon is Chinook proper, with words from Nootka and some of the Salish languages, as well as corrupted English, French, and possibly Russian words incorporated. Of 1,082 Chinook Jargon words noted in 1894, 23 were Nootka, 570 were English, 153 were French, and the remainder came from other languages. Although the Jargon is standardized to some extent over the area, nonetheless considerable local variation occurs. With the passing of the Lower Chinook and the great decrease in population of the Upper Chinook groups, this native trade language fell into disuse in the country of its origin, but around the turn of the century it took on new life farther north.

Modes of Indian Life

The mode of life of a Pacific Northwest Indian in aboriginal times depended to a large extent upon which part of this great region he called home — on or near the coast, in the interior intermontane plateau area, southern Oregon, or southern Idaho. Transplanted from any one of these areas to another, he not only would have been at a loss to talk to his new neighbors unless he and they knew Chinook Jargon, but he would probably have been quite surprised by their physical appearance, dress, food, and dwellings. The newcomer certainly would have been put to some trouble learning the different modes of life, in either their accustomed daily rounds or their more esoteric phases.

This diversity has led anthropologists to group Pacific Northwest Indian cultures into (1) those of the north Pacific coast; (2) those of the Plateau; and (3) those which are part of a Great Basin culture area. Bearers of the north Pacific coast culture lived along the coast and inland for about a hundred miles, from southern Oregon to and including parts of the Alaskan coast. Plateau peoples lived in the intermontane region of interior British Columbia, Washington, Oregon, and Idaho; Basin groups occupied southern Oregon and the southern half of Idaho. The latter peoples were the northern representatives of the Great Basin groups which extended over Nevada, Utah, and part of Colorado. In addition to all these were the Eskimos in the extreme northern Arctic zone. Lines dividing culture areas cannot be sharply drawn, because tribes situated near the edge of one area tended to share many traits with their neighbors living in the adjoining area.

North Pacific coast culture was the richest, most spectacular of all Pacific Northwest cultures. It was also the one culture in North America that was to an unusual degree reached by influences from Asia, some specific, others vague in character. Coast peoples lived on the beaches or along rivers, in large or small village groups. In the New World a sedentary mode of life usually meant that the main support of the people was agriculture, but the north Pacific coast was an exception to this. During the spring and summer Pacific coast tribes harvested from the sea and rivers, obtaining and storing food in such quantities that the winter months could largely be given over to leisure activities which had little or no direct connection with subsistence problems. Major sea foods were whales, which only the Makah, Quinault, and Quileute pursued and killed — all other groups contenting themselves with such stranded or dead animals as came their way, such as porpoises, seals, halibut, cod, and salmon — chief item of food for many of the tribes; olachen or candle-fish, an eight- or nine-inch, extremely oily fish from which grease was extracted in great quantities. Minor sea foods included shellfish — clams, mussels, crabs — eelgrass, and seaweed. Vegetable foods were quite varied, but not particularly abundant; fern, bracken and clover roots, berries, starchy bulbs such as camas, and the inner or cambium layer of hemlock, were gathered. Ducks were killed near the shores, but other meats were rare items of diet. Deer and elk were valued more for their skins than their flesh; black bears, which were plentiful on the coast, were sometimes hunted, despite their half-human appearance. As a whole the diet on the north Pacific coast was much richer in fats, protein, and minerals than in many other regions of native North America, but somewhat deficient in starch and other carbohydates.

The houses in which north Pacific coast people lived and held their feasts and dramatic winter ceremonies varied in details of construction, but everywhere were either rectangular or square in ground plan, with sloping or gabled roofs. They ranged in size from 20 by 30 feet, up to 60 by 500 feet. Basically, they consisted of a framework of upright posts and crossbeams enclosed by an outer shell of split cedar planks set vertically into the ground. Many tribes excavated the interiors of their houses; a firepit was set in the center of the house, with a smoke hole in the roof, and earthen terraces ran along the four sides of the excavated area. All houses were windowless, and had only one small entrance, in the front part. In villages along the coast or along interior rivers, houses stood in rows far enough back from the water for a wide street to run in front of them. Villages were occupied during winter and early spring; when the salmon began to run the village population removed to summer settlements. The outer planks of the houses in the village were removed, loaded on canoes and taken to the summer settlements, and then brought back and replaced in the fall.

Up and down the north Pacific coast travel, which was extensive, was almost entirely by water. Canoes, like houses, were fashioned from cedar, and varied in length from 16 feet to large seagoing craft 60 feet in length. They were usually propelled with paddles. Clothing was suitable for seagoing pursuits and for the damp climate; men and women usually went barefoot, and such everyday garments as they wore (capes, and for women, a knee-length skirt) were of shredded cedar bark. In their canoes at sea men wore conical wide-brimmed woven hats shaped like Chinese coolie hats. Blankets were woven from cedar bark, from the wool of a special breed of dog, and from that of mountain goats. The Chilkat, a Tlingit subgroup, carried weaving to a high development, producing goat wool blankets with tri-colored geometric designs which were bought and owned as objects of wealth by the nobility, and worn on ceremonial occasions. Salish blankets, woven of dog wool combined with feathers, sometimes had a simple black or brown pattern running through them, but were hardly comparable aesthetically to the striking Chilkat product.

The many aspects of the complex culture of the north Pacific coast peoples cannot be reviewed in detail here. As a whole it emphasized wealth, not in currency or precious metals but in goods such as olachen oil, blankets, boxes of dried salmon, chests, basketry trays, and other items. Such wealth brought prestige to its possessors when given away or consumed ostentatiously at large feasts or potlatches. Wealth lay in the hands of a noble or privileged class; commoners and slaves labored to produce it for their chiefs or headmen, who in turn were responsible for the support of their workers. Furthermore, everywhere along the coast and inland, trade in goods was active.

Not only were chiefs rich in material goods, but they also possessed immaterial rights and privileges, the claims to which had to be re-validated with lavish feasts by each new incumbent. Inherited rights included names and crests, ceremonial songs, origin myths, membership in religious societies, all of which were as much a measure of a man's prestige as his ownership of material property. In such a society, vigorous, stratified, relatively rich in material goods, and providing opportunity for specialization, art forms could be expected to develop. Art found a high form of expression in woodcarving and painting of utilitarian and decorative objects such as decorated boxes and chests, ingenious masks, graveposts, and a host of other items showing imagination and ingenuity and skill in workmanship.

In the Plateau area east of the coast a much more simple type of culture prevailed. Here the inhabitants made extensive use of salmon, deer, roots, and berries for food; their diet included on the whole more starch and berry sugars than did that of the coast peoples. House types showed considerable variation; some winter houses were circular in ground plan, with the interior excavated to form a round pit. The roof of this semi-subterranean house was conical, and entrance was by way of a smoke hole on the roof, then down a ladder or center-pole to the floor. Summer houses were movable mat- or rush-covered tents and single and double lean-tos.

Travel in the Plateau, which geographically was a land of mountains in the north and high rolling country in the south, was mainly overland instead of by water; such canoes as were used were crudely made dugouts or bark vessels. Large dogs serving some of the tribes as pack animals carried goods in small rawhide-covered panniers slung over their backs. Basketry containers and receptacles were widely used; woodwork was insignificant as compared with that of the north Pacific coast, and decorative art was simple and inconspicuous.

Tribal organization was loose. Often there was no head chief for the tribe. Band organization within the tribe was also loosely defined, being more fluid than that of a north Pacific coast village unit, for example. Social stratification into classes was only weakly developed; Plateau tribes had few slaves. However, definite distinctions in social position, based upon personal wealth, were made.

Individual questing for visions, begun during adolescence, was of extreme importance to the Plateau peoples. Practically every man undertook lone vision quests, hoping to make contact and gain the help of supernatural guardian spirits who, throughout his life, would be powerful allies whenever need for their help arose. In midwinter eight to ten weeks were given over to spirit dances in which all men who had guardian spirits participated. Impersonation of the spirits was part of the ceremonies and dancers even went so far, in many of the tribes, as to identify themselves with their spirits at this time, particularly with the Bluejay character. Winter was also a time for the telling of tales among the Plateau peoples; in their mythology stories about the creative and the foolish deeds of a double-sided character, the culture hero-trickster, are many, and command great interest.

Cultural influences from the coast tribes were of course strongest in the western half of the Plateau. In the eastern half, among such groups as the Upper Kootenai and the Nez Percé, intrusion of culture traits from the Plains area becomes apparent. There is reason to believe that this spread of Plains culture westward was of relatively late occurrence, after the horse had been introduced into the region. The Upper Kootenai and the Nez Percé both depended largely upon buffalo, rather than upon deer, for their staple food, and hunted bison in the open prairie country to the east of the mountains. They lived in conical skin tipis at least part of the year, and valued and used the horse for transport as the Plains people did. They dressed in Plains-type skin clothing, and in warfare used circular rawhide shields, like Plains warriors. Socially, they were organized into semi-nomadic bands; power and duties of leadership were entrusted to several men, rather than to one. Thus, among the Upper Kootenai there was a general chief for the group as a whole, a head or war chief, a guide or economic chief, and a hunting chief, as well as a Sun dance chief. The heads of the Crazy Dog and other societies were also called chief, likewise, those important personages, the coup-counting warriors. Various societies or lodges found among the Kootenai also reflect Plains influence, as does their performance of the Sun dance, which in the northern plains is the most important annual ceremony. However, the Plateau base of Kootenai and Nez Percé culture should not be overlooked. These tribes used semi-subterranean Plateau-type houses, either as sweat houses or living houses, in addition to using the tipi. They isolated girls upon arrival at puberty in huts at some distance from camp, and made them observe food and conduct taboos. Such a procedure was quite general in many parts of North America, including the Plateau, but was not practiced by the Plains people. In other practices, also, these eastern borderline tribes showed specific affiliations with the Plateau area.

The simple culture of the Great Basin peoples was represented in a modified way in the Pacific Northwest by five groups in southern Oregon and southern Idaho, namely, the Klamath, Modoc, Bannock, Snake or Northern Shoshone, and the Paviotso. Prior to their acquisition of the horse in the eighteenth century, these tribes seem to have been possessed of a simple culture, similar to that of the Basin peoples of Nevada and Utah. That is to say, they roamed about in small bands in what was mainly an arid, unproductive environment, hunting, fishing wherever possible, collecting seeds, roots, and bulbs. Large game animals — the bison and the deer — large fish such as the salmon, and vegetable foods like the acorn, which constituted the staple foods of the tribes to the north and west, were beyond access for most of the Basin tribes. They depended chiefly on antelope, rabbits, squirrels, gophers, doves, and other small game for meat, and piñons, grass seeds, small bulbs, and several kinds of roots for vegetable food. The gathering of such small foods took an interminable amount of time; to secure a sufficient quantity for day-to-day needs meant little leisure for the gatherers to practice any special arts and crafts.

The housetypes, dress, and social organization of Basin groups all reflect this. The usual house was a one-family, domed, mat-covered structure which took only a few hours to erect. Clothing was scanty and ornaments almost nil — knee-length front and back apron "skirts" of shredded sagebrush bark for women, a bark breechclout for men, rabbit fur blankets and moccasins for both sexes. The bilateral family consisting of parents, offspring, and an aged dependent or so, was the basic unit in the small bands which wandered about afoot within fairly delimited areas, on the move eight or nine months out of the year in order to gather the various wild food crops. Among such peoples there was little or no expression of any art forms. Religious interest centered on the supernatural powers of shamans to inflict and cure sickness, control the weather, and find lost objects, etc., and charm antelope and other game so that it could be easily caught by hunters.

Of the Pacific Northwest peoples of Basin culture, the Bannock, being the farthest east, were the most favorably situated to receive cultural stimulation from the Plains people. This was especially true after the horse was brought into southern Idaho around the middle of the eighteenth century, thereby affording such tribes as the Bannock a much quicker means of transport than foot travel, and enabling them to hunt such large game as the buffalo. With the horse came, then, the opportunity for a more assured food supply, and also wider contacts. Horses also enabled these Indians of the interior to acquire and utilize knowledge of Plains-type skin clothing for men and women, the tipi, and other items of Plains material culture. Such traits gradually spread westward, so that by the end of the eighteenth century the various Snake or Northern Shoshoni groups and the Paviotso had adopted them. In the early nineteenth century even the Modoc and the Klamath showed some Plains influence in their mode of life. If the whites had not followed hard on the heels of the horse in the region, more of Plains culture might have spread westward in the eighteenth and nineteenth centuries. With the advent of white settlers and the changed mode of life that the Plains tribes themselves were undergoing, westward diffusion of Plains culture stopped, once and for all.

White Intruders

With the coming of white explorers and traders (see ensuing chapters) contact was, of course, established between Indians and whites. Spanish, Russians, French, and Americans came to the north Pacific for the soft, lustrous furs of the sea otter, which for forty years or so were an important item in an international trade system. All up and down the coast sailing ships called; two favorite places of call were Nootka Sound, on the west coast of Vancouver Island, and the mouth of the Columbia River, which the Lower Chinook controlled. Furs in great quantities were brought by Indians to these spots, and paid for by white traders in beads, iron files, cloth, guns, ammunition, and other trade goods.

Under this system of trade a certain type of goods flowed out of the country, and useful goods flowed in — bright-colored cloth which suggested new designs to weavers, metal tools which enabled woodcarvers to develop their techniques and turn out finer-wrought products. And between visits of ships the Indians were left to follow their own pursuits. This they apparently did extremely well. Particularly during the first part of the fur trading period north Pacific coast culture expanded in content and gave many signs of being in a state of vigorous growth. But this happy condition did not last for more than a few decades. After Alexander Mackenzie proved that overland travel to the Pacific Northwest was possible, traders and trappers began to approach the region from the east. Whites who came by land established permanent trading posts and forts in the region; they took Indian women for wives, and became part of the local scene. Under the stimulation of rival fur companies the Indians over-trapped and over-killed the game, so that their resources for obtaining goods, including whiskey on which they had come to depend, rapidly dwindled.

With the advent of white settlers, however, conditions became much worse. In the fur trading period little effort was made to dispossess the Indians of their land, but as settlers began to flow in, tribe after tribe lost possession of its lands. In many cases Indians were removed, forcibly or otherwise, to unknown and for them totally unsuitable terrain.

All these changes occurred within the short span of a century. During the rapid transition from fur trade to settlement the Indians had insufficient time for adjustment. A few tribes waged short, unsuccessful wars against the settlers, but in each instance resistance by force was doomed to ultimate failure.

In its material achievements north Pacific coast culture vanished quickly and almost completely in the nineteenth century. Fragments of the non-material aspects of the culture may be found in the minds of older Indians, but as a functioning entity it has ceased to exist anywhere along the coast. Inland, some of the Plateau and Basin peoples of the Pacific Northwest still pursue their old life to some extent, but their present-day manner of living is a mixture of old and new, Indian and white, on a still-simple cultural level.

CHAPTER II

The Sea Otter Era

Clawing the Coastline

EXACTLY three centuries passed between the voyage of Columbus and the discovery of the Columbia River by the American Captain Robert Gray. These three centuries brought the rise of mighty European empires and the birth of the United States of America. During this time sailors of many nationalities acquired intimate knowledge of nearly all shore lines of the new world save those of the North Pacific. This does not mean that the northwest coast was unvisited by mariners. It may well be that occasional Spanish skippers, captains of the famous galleons that so regularly returned from the Philippines to Acapulco, Mexico, over the great circle route, came within sight of Washington's snow-capped Mount Olympus and the coastal range with its stately forests of fir, cedar, spruce, and hemlock. Veering a little closer, but too dangerously for comfort, daring seamen might on a clear day have observed the rugged shoreline, the many fjord-like coves and river mouths, sandy beaches, and knobby-looking dunes overgrown with dark green shrubs. Spaniards, based at New Spain (Mexico), were searching for a water passage through the North American mainland. To them any one of the many coastal indentations might have been the now-mythical Strait of Anían (the Spanish term for Northwest Passage).

During these first years of Pacific Ocean navigation Spanish galleons are known to have been blown ashore on the Oregon coast, their crews meeting disaster upon the rocks. But though the facts of such inadvertent contacts remain ob-

[21

scured, numerous early Spanish voyages come within the range of definitely recorded history. It is known for certain that in 1603 the Spanish pilot Martín de Aguilar, of the Vizcaíno expedition which had been driven north from Monterey Bay, saw Cape Blanco on the forty-third parallel. He is supposed to have seen an opening resembling that of a great river mouth at a point where the Columbia River actually flows into the Pacific.

During the period of English colonization in America, roughly from the founding of Jamestown to the close of the French and Indian War, the Spanish remained relatively inactive. Two nerve-racking nightmares, however, contrived to disturb the Spanish slumbers. One of these disturbances was Russia. Steadily, the Russians had been pushing eastward across the Steppes of Siberia. Then during 1728 the Danish navigator, Vitus Bering, flying the Russian flag, discovered and explored the strait which now carries his name. On a second expedition in 1741 Bering definitely discovered America from the East. And from then until the closing year of the century private subjects of the Czar crossed into what is today Alaska, and very actively and ruthlessly engaged in fur trade. In 1799 the Russian government chartered the Russian American Fur Company, which fortunately gave a certain amount of stability to the Muscovite operations in the New World. "When," asked suspicious Spaniards, "will the Russian Bear descend upon us?"

The other disturbance concerned England's sweeping victory in the French and Indian (Seven Years) War which, confirmed by the Peace of Paris in 1763, drove the French from North America and thereby upset the balance of power in the New World to the disadvantage of Spain. So, in 1769, the same year that Daniel Boone led settlers into Kentucky's wilderness, sons of Spain pushed northward into upper California and established missions, presidios, and pueblos in the region. Under the direction of the able Viceroy, Antonio Bucareli, Spanish exploration of the north Pacific coast was given renewed impetus. In 1773–74 Juan Pérez, a Spaniard, sailed up the Pacific coast as far as Alaska, a voyage during which he discovered and entered Nootka Sound and took note of several points along the Oregon coast. He was followed one year later (the year of the Battle of Lexington) by Bruno Heceta, who made added observations along the Oregon coast. He discovered, but did not investigate, the mouth of the Columbia River, dropped anchor at Point Grenville on the Washington coast thirty miles north of Grays Harbor, and went as far north as the forty-ninth parallel. In the same year, 1775, Juan Bodega sailed to the fifty-eighth parallel.

British Explorations and the Establishment of a Sea Otter Trade

In their tenacious search for a northwest passage the British also explored north Pacific waters, and hastened to exploit commercial opportunities offered by their discoveries. Most notable was the third voyage of Captain Cook in 1776. En route he discovered the Sandwich (Hawaiian) Islands and, following extensive maneuverings, which included Russo-American (Alaskan) waters, his ships *Resolution* and *Discovery* cast anchor in Nootka Sound during March, 1778, where Pérez had preceded him. While in these waters Cook's men took some sea otter skins aboard which, to the surprise of the English mariners, were in great demand at Canton when later the expedition called at this Chinese port.

The discovery by Cook's men, that a sea otter trade might well prove highly profitable, in time caused other English shipmasters to depart for these north Pacific waters. The first of such trading voyages was made in 1785 by Captain James Hanna with a crew of twenty in the sixty ton brig *Sea Otter*. The year following Hanna's voyage witnessed the entrance of eight English trading vessels in this new Pacific trade. Six of them returned safely with cargoes totaling $100,000 in value. Two of these vessels were outfitted at Bombay and sailed under the direction of Captain James Strange. The journal and letters of Strange are added evidence that he was engaged, as he phrased it, in a "lucrative branch of commerce."

Among other English sea captains prominently identified with this newborn trade was Captain Charles William Barkley, whose ship, the *Imperial Eagle,* in 1787 masqueraded under the Austrian flag. Important, too, was John Meares who arrived in the north Pacific in 1788, only to become involved with the Spanish in a jurisdictional dispute over Nootka Sound on the western side of Vancouver Island. Numerous as the British traders were, those not sailing under the jurisdiction of either the East India Company or the South Sea Company were placed at a grave disadvantage because of the monopolistic control exercised by those two powerful trading concerns. Rather than be regulated by these monopolies, many English shipmasters preferred operation under foreign flags to service under the Union Jack.

Captain John Meares, who was looked upon with suspicion by some of his contemporaries, left most lucid accounts of sea otter hunting. Particularly graphic is his picture of the catching of the mighty sea otter by skilled native hunters; the killing of this animal was a far more hazardous operation than whaling. "For this purpose," wrote Meares, "two very small canoes are prepared, in each of which are two expert hunters. The instruments they employ on this occasion are bows and arrows, and a small harpoon . . Thus equipped, the hunters proceed among the rocks in search of their prey. Sometimes they surprise him sleeping on his back, on the surface of the water; and, if they can get near the animal without awakening him, which requires infinite precaution, he is easily harpooned and dragged to the boat, when a fierce battle very often ensues between the otter and the hunters, who are frequently wounded by the claws and teeth of the animal." Often the animal was pursued for hours. Under such conditions the strategy was to maneuver the canoes to a position where the otter might be caught swimming below the surface of the water. When this was accomplished hunters stood in readiness with arrow and harpoon to shoot the very moment that the animal raised his head above the surface. A most dangerous situation existed if the otter happened to be overtaken at a time when it was caring for its young. ". . . the parental affection supersedes all sense of danger; and both the male and female defend their offspring with the most furious courage, tearing out the arrows and harpoons fixed in them with their teeth, and oftentimes even attacking the canoes." In this manner, then, the prize fur-bearing animals were killed, after which their skins soon found their way to trading vessels for eventual passage to China.

Not all British sea captains who called at the north Pacific coast during the quarter century following Cook's voyage were there for trade. One such exception was Captain George Vancouver, who came to look after British official interests and to make one final search for a northwest passage. English activities around Nootka Sound were regarded by Spain as an encroachment upon her territory, and in 1789 the viceroy of New Spain dispatched Captain Esteban José Martínez with a warship to Nootka with orders to protect Spanish interests. Upon arrival he took some British ships into his custody and ordered men ashore; they destroyed a small post operated by Meares. Aroused by these actions, the British government, in what is known as the Nootka Controversy, asked for restitution of the ships and reparations for Meares. The Nootka Sound Treaty of 1790 ended the dispute in England's favor; to accept formally the restored port of Nootka, Vancouver launched forth on his remarkable voyage. He reached the Pacific Northwest in 1792. Thereafter his explorations were extensive and detailed. His ships were the first to cruise the waters of Puget Sound; this great inlet Vancouver named in honor of his able Lieutenant, Peter Puget. Other places discovered by the navigator were given names which are retained to this day — Mount Baker, (observed from Juan de Fuca Strait), Mount Rainier, Hood Canal, Dungeness Point, Protection Island, Admiralty Inlet, Port Orchard, Port Townsend, Whidbey Island, Howe Sound. To Robert Gray, an American, goes the honor, if not for discovering the Columbia River, then certainly for being the first to enter and explore its mouth. Upon learning of its existence, Vancouver dispatched Lieutenant William R. Broughton to explore its waters. Broughton and his men sailed across the bar in his ship Chatham and then proceeded by rowboat upstream a distance of about one hundred miles.

As one looks back upon the numerous maritime adventures it is clearly revealed that three nations — Spain, Russia, and

England — did most of the exploring in the Northwest coast, and thereby established important claims to the region. Not until the very close of the eighteenth century did the Americans (then newly separated from England) make their entrance into this sphere of maritime operations.

Yankee Triangle Trade

As British subjects American colonists for generations had been skilled woodsmen, shipbuilders, and seamen; and the pursuit of trade, particularly in New England, had always been an essential part of their workaday life. Although Americans under the British crown had endured many regulations of their trade, they had also enjoyed important privileges and opportunities. When independence came the new United States found its commercial status greatly altered. No longer could Americans share as Englishmen in empire trade; they were obliged to look elsewhere for new markets. In the search for these new markets many an adventurous sea-thinking merchant of Salem, Newport, Boston, New York, and Philadelphia turned his thoughts first toward the Orient and then in the direction of the north Pacific.

Scarcely was the ink dry on the Treaty of Paris when Robert Morris wrote to John Jay: "I am sending some ships to China." On February 22, 1784, only eleven weeks after the last British warships cleared New York harbor, the first American ship, the *Empress of China*, sailed out past Staten Island, her sails squared, and her course set for China. She carried as supercargo, Major Samuel Shaw, and her hold was loaded with ginseng, a medicinal root of dubious value. Fifteen months later, the *Empress of China* returned safely to New York with a profit to the owners of $30,000.

Meanwhile, Elias Hasket Derby of Salem ordered his ship, the *Grand Turk*, to follow in the wake of the *Empress of China*. The youthful American republic was headed toward what was to become a brisk and profitable trade with the Orient, a trade that increased in volume with each passing year. So extensive did this commerce become that during the year 1789 alone no less than fifteen American vessels are purported to have called at the port of Canton.

Amidst alert and bustling sea life such as this, attention was directed to the words and writings of a young Connecticut Yankee, John Ledyard. After but four months at Dartmouth College, this none too diligent Groton-born lad set forth to see the world. He reached London at the time Captain Cook was making preparations for his third and last voyage of exploration. Ledyard accepted employment with the famous British sea captain, and was given the rating of corporal of the marines. In this capacity he sailed from London on July 12, 1776, around Good Hope to the Dutch East Indies, thence to New Zealand, starting point for the long cruise to the North Pacific. Captain Cook seemingly admired Ledyard and referred to him in the *Voyage* as "an intelligent man, [who joined the expedition] for the purpose of gaining information."

Like other members of Cook's crew, Ledyard had been impressed by the interest which Chinese merchants had shown in sea otter skins brought from the north Pacific. He returned to Huntington Bay aboard a British man-of-war at the close of 1782. The following year he published a journal supposedly based on his experiences. Ledyard then turned with bursting enthusiasm to his task of interesting American merchants in the great possibilities of the north Pacific-Chinese fur trade. He urged the merchants not to sail eastward to China as they were doing, but westward! His previous experience with Cook had convinced him that profits might well be made from a voyage fitted out expressly for this trade.

Ledyard found the Americans interested but not immediately willing to risk ships and capital necessary for such an undertaking. But scarcely had the disappointed Ledyard left America in the hope of finding some financial support when out of Boston came an important announcement — Joseph Barrell, Samuel Brown, and Charles Bulfinch of Boston, Crowell Hatch from near-by Cambridge, the already familiar and wealthy John Derby of Salem, and John M. Pintard of New York City had combined resources to enter the trans-Pacific fur trade. At a cost of $50,000 these gentlemen outfitted two vessels, the now famous *Columbia*, a fully rigged ship of 212 tons burden, and the sloop *Lady Washington*.

Under the command of John Kendrick and Robert Gray, respectively, the two vessels cleared Boston's harbor on September 30, 1787, less than two weeks after the adjournment of the Constitutional Convention at Philadelphia. In a public lecture on the north Pacific fur trade years later, the renowned William Sturgis vividly recalled to his audience this "extraordinary undertaking," and told that a medal commemorating the event had been struck off. On the one side of the medal were engraved the words "Columbia" and "Washington," while on the reverse appeared the names of the merchant adventurers who financed this pioneering enterprise.

A year elapsed before Kendrick and Gray arrived on the Pacific coast, where the two captains traded vessels. Both ships were used in the fur trade; although the course of the *Lady Washington* cannot be traced with certainty, she, like the *Columbia*, is believed to have reached Canton. Captain Gray resumed his westward course and in 1790 returned to Boston with a cargo of partially damaged tea. His sturdy vessel was the first to carry the American banner around the world.

Losses had been incurred in this first American venture into the fur trade, but with minor changes those backing the adventure were determined to try again. This time Gray was placed in full command, and with a cargo of trading goods valued at more than $25,000 the *Columbia* on September 28, 1790, sailed from Boston, once again bound for the north Pacific. The certificate shows that on board were 2,000 bricks, 135 barrels of beef, 60 barrels of pork, 1,500 pounds of gunpowder, 5 hogsheads of New England and West Indian rum, and quantities of tea, sugar, chocolate, and miscellaneous items, much of it for the Indian trade — copper sheets, "Barr Iron," "Iron Hoops," "Chissells," "blue duffil," "scarlet coating," buttons by the gross, and scores of other things.

The year 1791 was devoted to trade. Gray and his men wintered at Clayoquot Sound, Vancouver Island, during which time they built the sloop, *Adventure*. John Hoskins,

Robert Haswell, and John Boit, who were associated with the expedition, in their logs and narratives recorded much about this American enterprise. In Haswell's Second Log, for example, one reads for 1792 what might well be an exaggeration: "The ship during the cruise had collected upwards of 700 sea otter skins and 15 thousand skins of various other species."

Even though sea otter skins were singularly favored, Hoskins noted in his *Narrative:* "The skins are bears, wolves, foxes, rein, fallow and moose deers, land otters, raccoons, brown minks, martins, beavers, wild cats, grey rabbits, the large grey and small brown squirrels common in our country, and mice. The fallow deer, wolves, (which are grey) raccoons, squirrels, and martins are found in great abundance. . . ."

So much for the land fur-bearing animals. Equally important were the amphibious seals and sea otters, for as Hoskins correctly asserted, it was the traffic in the latter that "induced us to visit this coast." Hoskins described the sea otter:

. . . this animal when young is of a dirty white with long course hair which being hauled out leaves a short chestnut coloured fur its colours change through its natural gradation of life as it grows older the fur grows thicker blacker and longer with less hair till it arrives at its maturity having the belly and head at this time of a yellowish white after this as it still continues to grow older the longer hairs or fur are tipt with white until it becomes of a beautiful silver grey . . . this animal in shape much resembles the seal it has a very good set of teeth which are remarkably white and much valued by the natives the largest skin of this animal that I saw measured six feet two inches from the end of the nose to the tip of the tail. . . .

During the next spring, May 11, 1792, Captain Gray brought the sturdy little *Columbia* across the bar of the "Great River of the West" which Gray named after his ship. Important as was Gray's discovery, his job was to collect furs, and having secured his cargo he again sailed to China and on July 29, 1793, sea-conscious Boston witnessed the *Columbia* sailing into harbor.

"On her first voyage, the *Columbia* had solved the riddle

of the China trade," reflects Samuel Morison; "On her second, empire followed in the wake." In ever-increasing numbers American windjammers no larger than those commanded by Columbus three centuries before braved the perilous waters at the Horn and, always at the mercy of the elements, plowed their way to the Oregon coast. Their area of operation extended, in general, from the mouth of the Columbia to Cook's Inlet and out among the many islands that buttress the mainland.

Trade with the Indians was always carried on "alongside, or on board the ship, usually anchored near the shore," related Sturgis, who knew this business well. Because of the dangers involved, only native chiefs and otherwise important Indian personages were at first admitted on board. Since individual successes varied with the season and with the amount of competition, the time occupied on the coast was from one to three years. But once the captain was satisfied, off he sailed to Canton and there exchanged his cargo "for the productions of the Celestial Empire, to be brought home or taken to Europe, thus," to use again the words of Sturgis, "completing what may be called *a trading voyage.*"

This, to be sure, was a labor of excitement, if not of love. Men thrilled at the sight of beautiful furs being taken aboard ship; and with a nostalgia for those good old days, Sturgis later expressed the opinion that "excepting a beautiful woman and a lovely infant," he regarded the sea otter skin as the most attractive object that could ever be placed before him.

To describe every venture in this trans-Pacific trade would be pointless here. It remained large until about 1805 when a marked decline set in. During 1801–02, for example, fifteen vessels of all nationalities were operating in the north Pacific, and no less than 15,000 sea otter skins were collected. Returns on these operations naturally varied but recorded are instances in which $40,000 capital investment yielded $150,000 within the usual time allotted for a voyage, while still another investment of $50,000 gave a gross return of $284,000. By 1802, however, sea otter skins that once brought as much as $120 apiece sold in China for $20 each.

At first the sea otter trade was entirely British. But as noted, Americans entered the field in 1789, and within a decade had all but driven their British competitors from the field.[1] Most of the American vessels were from Boston, and in fact after 1800 that city may be said to have had a monopoly on the American north Pacific trade. To New Englanders this trade in furs became important because it provided them with a medium of exchange in Canton with which to buy oriental goods for sale on the American, or home, market. When sea otters became scarce in the north Pacific, traders focused their attention upon California, where, by special connivance with Mexican governmental officers, they could continue their operations along familiar lines. Most important of all in the history of the Pacific Northwest the sea otter trade established (along with the Sandwich Islands) this heretofore little known hinterland as an important commercial link in the trade of the world. Also out of this trade came a shift in the claims to the sovereignty over the Oregon country. Russia's claims were extended to Alaska, those of Spain all but vanished, while those of the United States and Great Britain became paramount.

The impact of the Napoleonic wars and the War of 1812 upon the trans-Pacific trade was very noticeable. British men-of-war roamed the high seas, and ships of nationalities at war with England were not safe. British and Russian vessels, however, continued to operate in Pacific waters, and until 1812 American merchantmen were there also. Particularly active were the trading houses of J. and T. H. Perkins, J. and Thomas Lamb, Edward Dorr and Sons, Boardman and Pope, George W. Lyman, and such individual traders as Captains Jonathan and Nathan Winship, Joseph O'Cain, and others. Contact between the Pacific Northwest and Canton was retained, and increasing in importance were the Sandwich Islands and, in a surreptitious manner, the coastal towns of

---

[1] F. W. Howay compiled a list of trading vessels operating in the North Pacific, 1785–1814, and these he classified as follows:

	British	American
1785–94	25	15
1795–1804	9	50
1805–14	3	40

Alta (Upper) California. News in 1812 of the outbreak of hostilities between the United States and England, however, dampened the spirits of Yankee traders, many of whom hastened to tie up in neutral ports to escape attacks by British fighting ships.

The inevitable revival of trade in the Pacific following the return of peace in 1815 brought many changes. The spotlight which previously had shone so brilliantly upon the coast of the northwest now shifted southward to California and southwestward to the Sandwich Islands. California sea otters, which prior to this date were being widely hunted, were thereafter slaughtered with greater intensity. After 1822 hides, tallow, and horns of the large and roaming California herds were in demand by Yankee traders in exchange for New England manufactures. Sandalwood from the mid-Pacific islands, which previously had been frowned upon by the Chinese as inferior, was also to enjoy a brief but booming market in Canton.

While these shifts transpired, a potentially great inland fur trade emerged from behind the scene in the old Oregon country. And for many years to come around this new and lucrative business much of the Pacific Northwest's history was to revolve.

Chapter III

The North West Company Invasion

When Fur Was King

IN THE VANGUARD of the westward march across North America was the fur trader. To every nation represented in New World expansion, fur trade was of some importance; to the French and British in Canada, traffic in pelts was the most lucrative of all enterprises. The Canadian trade, although at first carried on in a haphazard manner, very early began to operate on partnership arrangements and gradually emerged into a larger company organization. This was a logical development, since operations in the interior demanded a greater outlay of goods and equipment than could easily be provided by the average individual trader. In New France the state at an early date assumed considerable direct supervision over fur trading activities, whereas in the region of Hudson Bay the English Crown and Parliament delegated much of their authority to those who actually managed the trade. Thus, for example, on May 2, 1670, King Charles II gave his official approval to the articles of incorporation of the "Governor and Company of Adventurers of England Tradeing into Hudsons baye," now simply known as the Hudson's Bay Company.

The presence of both British and French companies in eastern Canada naturally resulted in international cutthroat competition and military strife that continued until the French were driven out of North America by war and the Peace of Paris in 1763. British political mastery of Canada soon led to Anglo-Saxon domination of the fur trade, as capital and supplies shifted from Paris to London, and businessmen were quick to extend their existing American operations to the Canadian West formerly in French hands. Employ-

[33

ment of men and the method of the trade in actual field operations after 1763 were fortunately left in the skillful hands of French Canadians.

Origin of the North West Company

To cope with the disrupting influences of the Seven Years' War powerful fur interests in the St. Lawrence Valley directed their attention to the Far West. The North West Company which they organized for this purpose probably began on a very informal basis in 1775, but by 1788 tangible agreements had been made. The company, operating as a simple partnership, included in its organization such already well-known men as Benjamin and Joseph Frobisher and Simon McTavish, Peter Pond, Alexander Mackenzie, David Thompson, and Simon Fraser. Peter Pond, an explorer and trader during 1775–8, was the first of the North West Company men to venture into the Lake Superior and Grand Portage region and to penetrate into northwestern Canada. It was Pond who first crossed Portage la Loche and who discovered Athabaska River and Lake Athabaska. Pond's significant work laid the foundation for the company's future operations in this strategic Athabaska area.

After Pond came a Scot, Mackenzie, also operating under the auspices of the North West Company. His extensive explorations in the Great Slave Lake region led him in 1789 to the Arctic mouth of the river now bearing his name. And again under the direction of the Company in 1792 Mackenzie, Alexander Mackay, six French Canadians, and two Indians set out from the Peace River for the Bella Coola, which they then followed to the Pacific during July, 1793.[1] Thus Mackenzie became the first white man to cross the North American continent, more than three centuries after its discovery. For this and other feats he was knighted by the King of England.

For several years the North West Company operated as a loose association of certain fur traders who agreed among themselves not to become connected with any other company, to establish at Montreal offices which would handle the

[1] Enroute the Mackenzie party traversed over 200 miles of the upper Fraser River, but failed to reach its mouth.

importation of essential supplies from England, and to market such bales of fur as drifted in from Grand Portage. This post would serve as a field depot for the area west of the Hudson Bay watershed, a region the company designed to pre-empt. For a time business ran smoothly, but in 1796, partly as a result of the Jay Treaty which called for British abandonment of Northwest posts, a rift occurred among the partners. So serious did the disagreements become that dissident elements withdrew to form, under the rebel leadership of Alexander Mackenzie, what has variously been called the New North West Company, Sir Alexander Mackenzie and Company, and, more popularly, the X Y Company.

Bitter and unrelenting rivalry grew out of this schism, as each group strove for supremacy. The loser, however, was neither contestant, but rather the impartial Indian on whom, during a two-year period, no less than 195,000 gallons of liquor were expended by the rivals in pursuance of the fur trade. Luckily for both whites and Indians, in 1804 the death of the obstreperous Simon McTavish made a reconciliation of contending factions possible. In 1821 the North West Company was merged with the Hudson's Bay Company to place under unified control the fur trade of half a continent.

British Dreams of Empire

To relate the complete history of the North West Company would be to go beyond the province of the present study. Suffice it to say that its march was a westward one that led unhesitatingly in the direction of the Oregon country which lay west of the Great Divide. Scarcely had the imaginative and industrious Mackenzie reached the Pacific in 1793 when he conjured up grandiose schemes for the early establishment of an ocean-to-ocean overland trade and for the eventual merging of the great fur business of Canada into one gigantic whole. Before the lapse of a year Mackenzie's brilliant ideas had found favor in official circles. Mackenzie was a good prognosticator, for within a quarter of a century his vision of overland trading routes and of unified management of the fur trade was to become a reality. Moreover, he foresaw the necessity of establishing posts in the Pacific Northwest. He wanted at least one on the Columbia River and another at the southerly limit of the British claims "which would probably secure the whole Traffic" for his company and, incidentally, strengthen his country's hold upon the Oregon territory.

Lieutenant Governor J. Graves Simcoe, who sponsored Mackenzie's plans before the British Privy Council for Trade and Plantations in London, had his own dreams of a new empire. Looking beyond the extension of fur operations to the Pacific coast, Simcoe envisaged a tie-up of the Columbia River trade with that of the already well established East India Company, "who possess the Privilege of the Chinese Market." Canada appeared to him a mighty portage stretching from Hudson Bay to the mouth of the Columbia River, and the necessity of tying together the British fur trade of Canada with that of the Far East was apparent. This he declared was a matter of "importance to Great Britain, as a maritime Power —& possibly, in the case of necessity, might be of consequence to the safety of Upper Canada."

To Duncan McGillivray, nephew of the recalcitrant Simon McTavish and clerk of the North West Company, must go some credit for turning dreams into reality by pushing field operations farther toward the Pacific area. Under his direction Fort Augusta on the Sturgeon River in Alberta was established in 1795. Four years later he set up Rocky Mountain House within the very view of the towering Rockies. From this place in 1800 David Thompson and McGillivray began explorations that led directly to the establishment of posts by the Nor'westers, as men of this concern were called, in the upper reaches of the Columbia River.

Nor'westers Enter the Valley of the Columbia

Leaving Rocky Mountain House in the autumn of 1800 Thompson and McGillivray explored a route which took them to a point twenty miles east of Banff. From there they returned to their base of operation, and the following year set forth in a different direction, finally reaching a spot in the

Rockies that satisfied them of the existence of practical trading routes to the Pacific slope.

Here matters rested until 1807 when the challenging news of the Lewis and Clark expedition reached British North West Company officials and stirred them to renewed action. Then it was that the meticulous David Thompson, still operating under instructions from McGillivray, journeyed farther westward. On this expedition Thompson went through what afterward was known as (Joseph) Howse Pass in the Rocky Mountains and located the headwaters of the Columbia and the North Saskatchewan rivers. From this point Thompson pioneered his way down upper Columbia and Kootenai (or Kootenay) rivers.

During the summer of 1807 David Thompson had begun construction on what became known as Kootenai House, one mile below the outlet of Lake Windermere in the southeastern part of present-day British Columbia. This post has the distinction of being the first within the area drained by the great Columbia River. In the locality Thompson set up his indispensable thermometer and spent the winter. But in April of the following year (1808) he set out with canoes and reached the portage of the Kootenai River. He descended that stream, and on May 6 was at Kootenai Falls, near present Libby, Montana. Here in October he sent his clerk, Finan McDonald, with men and canoes full of trading goods to establish a fort. When McDonald reached the designated place in November he began construction of leather lodges which were to become known as Fort Kootenai, or Kootenai House. McDonald, with James McMillan who joined him later, inaugurated a brisk trade with near-by Indians. Thus, by the end of 1808, Nor'westers had established two posts, both named Kootenai, and located on opposite sides of the present international boundary line.

During 1809 Thompson resumed his post-founding activities building Kullyspell House on the eastern shore of Lake Pend d'Oreille in present north Idaho, and Saleesh, or Flathead House, three miles above Thompson's Falls on Clark's Fork in present western Montana. The next year Spokane

House was established on the Spokane River, about ten miles northeast of the present city of Spokane. Built by Finan McDonald, it became the fifth North West Company post in the Columbia Department.

The energetic Thompson was disconcerted by the news in 1810 that the Piegan Indians had become belligerent and had blocked the Howse Pass over which his supplies were being sent. A substitute crossing of the Continental Divide, even better, was discovered about fifty miles farther north. This became known as the Athabaska Pass, and for years to come was to be important in commercial and transportation history of the Canadian West. Thus, in addition to having laid the foundation for the development by the Nor'westers of the fur trade of the Columbia Basin, Thompson, by his careful survey of the country through which he moved, had laid out a new and practical line of communication which in the future was to be vital to the Great Northwest fur trade.

Thompson's work did not end here. During the latter part of 1811 he returned to the Big Bend country where he busied himself at Spokane House. Meanwhile his fellow trader, David Stuart, moved north from Okanogan to the north branch of the Thompson River where in 1812 he established Fort Kamloops which provided a valuable and natural, as well as an only, link between the Columbia District and New Caledonia. Thompson next belatedly made his way down the Columbia River to its mouth in the hope that he might establish a post there ahead of the Astorians of whose plans he had been apprised. He arrived at the Pacific on July 15 or 16, 1811, only to find Americans on the scene. After a brief stay Thompson began his homeward journey. He reached Montreal in August, 1812, thanking "good Providence" for having brought him and his men safely past the dangers, not of the wilderness, but of enemy Americans with whom his country was now unhappily at war. The great surveyor, explorer, map maker, and fur trader had failed to outflank the Astorians, but the time was not far away when the fortunes of war would enable his company to acquire Fort Astoria and thus to realize his coveted dream, a fur trading post at the mouth of the mighty Columbia River.

Nor'westers in New Caledonia

While David Thompson was pushing interests of the North West Company deep into the Columbia River Basin, the equally audacious Simon Fraser and John Stuart were moving forward in a northwesterly direction. This was being done in order to accommodate the additional partners brought in by the amalgamation of the X Y and the North West companies. In 1805 the partners ordered these two men to proceed up the Peace River, cross over via the Parsnip and Pack rivers to the headwaters of what became the Fraser River (but then Jackanut), and there establish still other Company posts. This country, lying between the forty-ninth and fifty-eighth parallels, became known as New Caledonia, a region which, except for the Mackenzie expeditions and coastal sea otter operations, was hitherto very little known.

In the prosecution of his instructions Simon Fraser and his fellow officer, John Stuart, established a base at Rocky Mountain Portage on the Peace River. From that point they moved over the summit to McLeod Lake where in the fall of 1805 construction of Fort McLeod was begun. This was the first trading post to be built west of the Rocky Mountains and in what is now British Columbia. Fraser and Stuart returned to their base to winter, and in the spring of 1806, after first returning to Fort McLeod, they moved on to Stuart Lake where work on Fort Nakasleh (afterwards Fort St. James) was begun. They then proceeded to Fraser Lake where they founded Fort Natleh, or Fort Fraser. Anxious to thwart the Americans, Fraser and his men in 1807 moved on to the confluence of the Nechako and Fraser rivers (thinking the latter stream might be the Columbia) and established Fort George. From this point the courageous explorer and builder set forth the next year on his perilous trek down the turbulent Fraser River. To his everlasting chagrin he learned that the stream he followed was not the Columbia, but another which now bears his name. A trail was then cut extending from Fort McLeod to Fort St. James, and as such it became the first of its kind in the future British Columbia province.

In 1809 Fraser left New Caledonia, somewhat sick of his

western rambles. He had placed in charge John Stuart who with headquarters at Fort McLeod stayed on until the Hudson's Bay Company incorporated New Caledonia with the Columbia District. At the very time of Fraser's departure news reached the partners that John Jacob Astor planned to establish a post at the mouth of the Columbia. There is ample evidence that this created a stir among the New Caledonians. Accordingly John Stuart, assisted by the interesting and genial Daniel Harmon, lost no time in organizing the fur trade in this remote transmontane segment of the Northern Department and in making of this trade a profitable business venture.

Organization

Throughout the period of the operation of the North West Company prior to its merger with the Hudson's Bay Company no satisfactory intercommunication existed except between New Caledonia and the Columbia basin, the regions developed by Fraser and Thompson, respectively. Since each was approached through widely separated Rocky Mountain passes, the North West Company established separate administrations for the two regions. Fraser's New Caledonia remained a part of the contiguous Athabaska Department, the Company's choice and exclusive preserve. This enlarged the district to include the lands westward to the coast, bounded on the south by the watershed between the Fraser and the Columbia rivers and on the north by the Russians, whatever that could mean. Thompson's domain, on the other hand, became the separate Columbia Department, and in its ultimate area embraced the entire Columbia River watershed (including the Snake River), with the northern part of present day Utah tossed in for good measure. The country between the lower Columbia and Fraser rivers remained a sort of no man's land, but farther to the east at the confluence of the north and south branches of Thompson River the two sprawling administrative units were brought into contact by the establishment there of Fort Kamloops. At this point, too, the transcontinental trails converged to link the Company's entire Pacific operations with those east of the great Rocky

Mountains. During 1809 David Thompson was the sole clerk for the Columbia District, but the next year John McDonald was elevated to share that position.

Records of the Company are rather skimpy on matters pertaining to the Pacific Northwest region. Of special interest and importance, though are the references to the "purchase" of Fort Astoria, about which controversy was to ensue between British and American governments. On July 11, 1814, a meeting of the partners of the North West Company assembled at Fort William (old Kaministikwia). The Minutes read: ". . . the first Business introduced was the transactions in the Columbia last Winter & Fall, . . . no material objection was made to the terms on which the Purchase from the Pacific Fur Company had been made, except as to the Payments, the near period at which they are fixed being considered highly advantageous to the Concern. . . . The Advantages derived from the Arrangement were deemed considerable, by means of it the Posts were supplied for the Winter . . . and it greatly facilitated the getting out of the Country our Competitors the American Fur Company. . . ." The Minutes further revealed that at last plans could be made for the much desired sea approach. "If a favourable connection could be made with an American House — it was the general opinion — it should be adopted for facilitating the Business in China."

In Search of Pelts

Thompson's journal gives the earliest and best account of this pioneer fur trading venture in inland regions of the Pacific Northwest. Plans called for immediate action in order to forestall, not only American competition, but also that of the ever alert and ever encroaching Hudson's Bay Company. At first pelts and supplies were to be moved to and from supply bases east of the Rockies with the hope that the Pacific coast marine bases subsequently might be provided. With these considerations in mind, Oregon's first inland fur trading operations began.

From the very start David Thompson never overlooked a chance to trade, but not until the summer of 1809 did full-fledged operations get underway. The Saleesh Indians were selected as the best prospects and Thompson wrote on July 14, 1809, that, under the charge of Finan McDonald, he had sent forth a canoe, "its cargo four pieces of Merchandise: weighing 320 lbs. four, nine gallons kegs of greese (the melted fat of the Bison) and five bags of Pemmican, each of ninety pounds, with five men, a less number could not stem the courrent." In the process of these operations Kullyspell House was built — "a strong Log building for the Goods and Furrs, and for trading with the Natives."

By September trade was in full swing. Guns, ammunition, and iron-headed arrows that could pierce the thick-skinned bison and not break off as the stone ones did, were dispensed to the native hunters in exchange for hides and furs; iron objects, such as awls and needles, were demanded by the squaws who also came to the post to trade. Thompson's narrative for the winter of 1809–10 refers to constant trading of North West Company merchandise for furs, horses, and fresh and dried meats. He came to love the Saleesh and called them "a fine race of moral Indians." Thompson returned to Rainy Lake, presumably with his pelts, and there he and his men once again "made an assortment of goods, wherewith to load four Canoes for the furr trade of the interior country." They recrossed the summit and once again trade was resumed, although on this particular trip Thompson personally traveled on to the mouth of the Columbia River.

In New Caledonia trading began under similar circumstances. Here, as in the Columbia District, relations with the Indians began peacefully. Prospects for trade with them were from the outset good, although the Nor'westers found it difficult to induce the Indians to exert themselves beyond what was required for day-to-day living. Only as the natives developed a craving for liquor did the "incentive to industry" become increasingly noticeable.

The manner in which trade was conducted has been vividly recorded by Ross Cox who knew the business well. To the fort would come a party of Indians "loaded with the produce of their hunt." Having placed their skins upon the ground, the Indians would "squat themselves in a circle" and after their

NORTH FORK OF PAYETTE RIVER, IDAHO

DR. JOHN McLOUGHLIN

Chief Factor of the Columbia District for the Hudson's Bay Company

Courtesy Oregon Historical Society

chief or leader had lighted "the calumet of peace," and other ceremonies had been indulged in, the real business of trade began. Each Indian had his skins divided into piles or lots. For one pile he would demand a gun; for another he would ask for ammunition; for still a third, perhaps a copper kettle, an axe, a blanket, or a knife. "The trading business being over," adds Cox, "another general smoking match takes place; after which they retire to their village or encampment."

Friendly as relations between the Nor'westers and the Indians may have been, white traders continued to suffer from lack of supplies incurred by the great distances that separated them from the bases of supply. Traders could take with them only the bare necessities of life, utilizing most of the available space for trading truck, hence were compelled to live off the country.

Native fare consisted chiefly of salmon, fresh or dried, and the traders, too, became very dependent upon the annual run of delicious pink fish which to this day remains an important economic factor in the life of the region. Just how much the salmon meant to both the traders and Indians alike is well revealed in the instructive *Journal* of Daniel W. Harmon, long a Company clerk in New Caledonia. Writing on September 13, 1810, Harmon commented on the report that "salmon, this season, do not come up the rivers of that region, as usual. As this kind of fish forms the principal article of food, both for the Natives and white people, it is apprehended that they will all be under the necessity of proceeding towards the Pacific Ocean, until they find a people who have been more favoured by Providence." And again, writing from Fort McLeod, August 2, 1811, he expressed his concern over the delay of the salmon run. "Unless the salmon from the sea, soon make their appearance, our condition will be deplorable." This over-anxiety was probably conditioned more by shortage of food stores than their distrust in the salmon whose habits and antics are amazingly regular. And sure enough, on August 22nd the first salmon appeared: ". . . a joyous intelligence to us all." In addition to fish, berries of the region were gathered and some farming, or at least gardening, was done by the fur traders in order to make each post as self-sufficient as possible.

Not only were these first New Caledonians dependent upon native foods, but also upon a precarious line of communication with their home base. Not infrequently supply canoes failed to arrive, leaving the field men stranded in the trade for skins. On November 16, 1811, Harmon recorded that at Fort Stuart alone no less than seven thousand fish had been caught, but that supplies from the Peace River again failed to come through, making it necessary for him to cross the Rockies in December in an effort to recoup them.

Although life was hard, it was tempered with many successes. Stuart and Harmon continued their cordial relations with the Indians and Harmon at least demonstrated his sincerity by living happily with an Indian squaw who bore him several children. Years later he left his family to return to civilization, but not without writing: "I consider myself under a moral obligation not to dissolve the connexion, if she is willing to continue it."

Forts Stuart and McLeod continued for years to be the chief posts, with Rainy Lake as the unofficial headquarters or more correctly as an advance post for Fort William, to which Stuart went every summer with the annual catch of beavers, otters, lynxes, skunks, fishers, martens, muskrats, foxes, wolves, bison, and other kinds of skins and hides.

Communications

Self-sufficient as were these Pacific coast outposts their dependence upon Montreal and the East generally was inescapable. Difficulties involved in communication with home bases were almost unbelievable. To cover the distance from Montreal to Fort McLeod required at least a hundred days of steady and intensive canoe and foot travel. As a general thing travel was done by brigades of four large birch bark canoes, each carrying from three and one-half to four tons and manned by eight or nine skillful Canadian voyageurs. By paddling up the Ottawa and by cutting across to Lake Huron, the nine-hundred-mile jaunt to Sault Ste. Marie was made in thirty days; whereas an additional nine hundred miles to the general rendezvous at Fort William (replacing the Grand Portage after 1804) were covered in half that time. From Fort William the route varied, depending on whether one went to the Columbia River District or to New Caledonia, and from this point on west small canoes replaced the larger ones used in the East. But in any event, another six weeks to two months were employed in boating and portaging an additional three thousand miles, the added distance to the Pacific coast posts. The total distance, then, from Montreal to Fort McLeod was approximately 4,800 miles. The time involved was never exactly the same because the rate of travel depended on the weather. When crossing lakes, for instance, canoes were generally rigged with square sails, and a strong or favorable wind would greatly boost the speed. Goods making up the cargo were usually done up in bales of about ninety to one hundred pounds each, with from seventy to eighty bales in each boat. Canoes had to be portaged frequently. In the less severe rapids, in places where boats rather than canoes were used, the men would often walk along the bank and pull their heavily laden boats upstream by means of ropes. This method was known as "tracking."

Once on the Pacific slope, pack horses as well as canoes were employed for inter-post transit, but horses were not so readily available as might be supposed. For instance, the trader Alexander Ross stated that when reaching Fort Okanogan on his way upstream from Fort George following the Astoria purchase, "everything was at a dead stand for want of pack-horses to transport the goods inland, and as no horses were to be got nearer than the Eyakema [Yakima] Valley, some 200 miles south-west, it was resolved to proceed thither in quest of a supply: at that place all the Indians were rich in horses." Not until in the more advanced stages of the fur trade were horse or ox-drawn carts used rather widely to facilitate portaging and to transport goods across the plains.

Difficult and hazardous as were those extremely long hauls, some attempt was made at regularity and punctuality. In time west coast traders came to rely with confidence on the arrival of the winter express. And later when operations became even more routinized, light canoe service between Fort George, at the mouth of the Columbia River, and Montreal came to be referred to as the Hundred Day Express.

An Outlet to the Sea

Efficient as was the overland express, it early became apparent that direct access to and from the sea would be a condition for remaining in business in the Oregon country. Such an opening to the sea offered marvelous possibilities, the chief of which would be direct contact with both England and China. Toward this end the partners of the North West Company directed their efforts.

The War of 1812 provided the opportunity for which they had been waiting. The English government which heretofore had refused a request to forestall the Americans, namely the Astor enterprise, now hastened to order H.M.S. *Phoebe* at Portsmouth to escort the Company ship *Isaac Todd* and other merchant ships, and subsequently H. M. S. *Raccoon,* to proceed to the mouth of the Columbia River and there take possession of Astor's trading post. The *Raccoon,* being a faster sailing vessel, moved on ahead. Facing the prospect of encountering either armed attack, or at least a blockade by an overwhelming British force, the Astorians (among whom were many former North West Company partners), who already had experienced very hard luck, chose to accept an offer from the North West Company to buy Astoria. On October 16, 1813, the deal was consummated and the American post formally passed into the hands of the British fur trading company. Many questions were afterwards raised with regard to the validity of this transaction, but for all practical purposes the North West Company had its window to the sea. Meanwhile John Stuart at New Caledonia took steps to establish overland communication between his district far to the north and the Columbia River Valley.

Possession of such an outlet did not automatically establish trade connections with the Orient. Obstacles were the powerful East India Company and the South Sea Company, both monopolies which would levy serious impositions upon all British vessels not of their ownership that sought to venture into the China trade. All efforts on the part of the North West Company to reach an accord with its paternalistic British rivals failed, and finally in desperation the Canadian fur traders resorted to a subterfuge by making arrangements (following the Peace of Ghent) with the American firm, J. and T. H. Perkins Company of Boston, for handling the Columbia Department's outside trade. Not bound by the restrictions of the British monopolies, the Boston firm was free to carry goods at will to all ports of the world then open to American trade. Accordingly the Perkins firm undertook to carry North West Company supplies to Astoria where such cargoes were exchanged for furs. These in turn were carried from this Columbia River port to Canton where the money received from sales of furs was spent for teas and other Oriental goods taken back to Boston and sold on the American market. Thus it was that many furs from the Columbia Department henceforth moved westward to China instead, as formerly, eastward to England; and in contrast to the situation prior to 1813, this new trade proved to be extremely profitable, not only to the partners of the North West Company, but to the American consignees as well. Until the merger in 1821 this happy arrangement remained uninterrupted.

Although development of maritime trade was unquestionably the major change brought about by the purchase of Astoria, there is also evidence that the range of the inland trade was widened to include Willamette and Snake valleys, unexploited except for limited contacts which the Astorians may have had with Indians there.

A great variety of goods also reached the Columbia from England: wearing apparel, felt hats, butter, cheese, pickles, sauces, suet, candles, gunflints, gunpowder, guns, military stores, saddlery, fishing tackle, playing cards, stationery, tobacco pipes, wrought brass, copper, iron, etc. Each year brought more of the same kind of goods and many additions, including such articles as musical instruments, sails, carts, and wagons, having in 1818 an official value of well over the equivalent of $100,000.

The trouble, so far as the Columbia District was concerned, was that supplies shipped or packed into the Columbia District erased a desired balance of trade. Inefficiency in the Columbia District was on the increase after 1815, and not enough furs were secured to make the trade profitable. In 1821 the North West Company ceased to exist in name when it merged with the Hudson's Bay Company. The North West concern had much to contribute to this union by way of tangible assets, personnel, and business skill. The trade of New Caledonia had by then become profitable, and, if properly managed the Columbia District could be made a paying operation. This was brought about under Hudson's Bay Company management. From the larger and more lasting point of view, the North West Company must be credited with having opened the inland Oregon country to trade and settlement.

CHAPTER IV

The Honourable Hudson's Bay Company

A British Monopoly is Born

FROM OUT OF the American back country there arrived in England in the middle 1660s two intriguing French explorers. They were Pierre Esprit Radisson and Médard Chouart, known as Sieur des Groseilliers. They had been in the service of the French, had explored and traded in the upper Mississippi River region, and now had come to report to His Majesty, King Charles II's government, that a great area, rich in furs, lay north of Lake Superior and could be reached through Hudson Bay.

Enthusiastic reports of these men led to the formation on May 2, 1670, of the now famous and aged Hudson's Bay Company, or, as the charter reads: "The Governor and Company of Adventurers of England tradeing into Hudsons Bay." Granted by the direct patronage of the King, the charter gave these "adventurers" "the sole Trade and Commerce of all those Seas, Streightes, Bayes, Rivers, Lakes, Creekes, and Soundes, in whatsoever Latitude they shall bee, that lye within the entrance of the Streightes commonly called Hudsons Streightes." In addition to the foregoing rights and privileges, the company was empowered to pass laws, impose penalties and punishments, to sit in judgment on all civil and criminal cases in accordance with English law, and, moreover, it could employ armed force, appoint commanders, and build forts. And if need be, the Governor and Company could request the assistance of His Majesty's armed forces in the enforcement of the powers granted in the Charter.

Gay King Charles II of England personally handed the

[49

charter of this new company to his cousin, Prince Rupert, who accepted it for himself and seventeen other nobles, gentlemen, and London merchants, among whom was the powerful Duke of Albemarle, the Earl of Shaftesbury, and Sir George Carteret. Being in this manner born to the purple, it is fitting that through the years a heraldic coat-of-arms has been the symbol of the Hudson's Bay Company. This armorial insignia consists of an argent shield on which are surmounted the red cross of St. George and, fittingly enough, four black beavers. Further to accent the business in which the company has been engaged, at the crest of this shield is a cap with turned-up ermine, and sitting on the cap is a fox. On either side, and supporting the shield, are two elks. At the bottom is written the motto: *"Pro pelle cutem,"* which, when translated, reads: "A skin for a skin." The idea back of it is that fur traders literally risk their own skins in the procurement of the skins of animals.

At first the going was tough. In 1749 the Hudson's Bay Company could claim only four or five forts and about 120 employees. For that reason it faced, but nevertheless weathered, a severe attack in Parliament on the grounds that the company was a "non user" of its charter. So long as France was in control of Canada the company suffered many heavy losses; and when in 1763 England took possession, the door was opened for other encroachments, chiefly Montreal traders who were eventually to form the North West Company. Following the actual formation of the North West Company competition, especially along the boundary line west of Grand Portage, reached the point where indecencies were unbounded. Indians were demoralized with liquor, fur-bearing animals were killed without regard to future supply, and Nor'westers and Hudson's Bay men resorted to outright murder to further their respective ends.

Probably the most conspicuous instance of this life-and-death struggle was the Red River settlement feud. In 1811, the Hudson's Bay Company granted in fee simple to Lord Selkirk (then owning enough shares to control the parent company) 116,000 square miles on the Red River of the

North. This territory comprised parts of present-day Manitoba, Saskatchewan, Minnesota, and North Dakota. On this land Selkirk promptly founded a colony (1812) that lay athwart the main highway used by the Nor'westers in the conduct of their far western trade. That resistance to such a move would come was inevitable. During the summer of 1814, while the War of 1812 was still dragging on south of the border, bigwigs of the North West Company met at their usual western rendezvous, Fort William on Lake Superior. Their decision was that Selkirk's colonists must go. "Nothing but the complete downfall of the colony will satisfy some by fair means or foul," wrote Alexander Macdonell, a Nor'wester. During the summer of 1815 violence broke loose. Crops were destroyed, arson was committed, barns were destroyed. Then things reached the shooting stage. Macdonell was going to fight it out. Recriminations from the Selkirk men followed. In 1816 Selkirk, with a private army of about one hundred ex-soldiers, Swiss mercenaries, and colonials prepared to move against the Nor'westers, but not before the latter had succeeded in literally wiping out in cold blood twenty-one settlers who were still at their homes near the confluence of the Assiniboine and Red rivers.

The merciless slaughter of these settlers has become known as the Seven Oaks Massacre. This unhappy affair aroused British political circles, and investigations followed. Threat of official intervention — one which might have led to the revocation of company charters or licences — obligated these two rival concerns to do their own housecleaning.

The Giant Merger

Fights, kidnappings, highjackings, duellings, and other mutual recriminations continued for a while under their own momentum, but the final outcome of the Seven Oaks Massacre was a merger of the two rival concerns. At the urging of Lord Bathurst, the colonial secretary, negotiations for a merger were begun in London in 1820. On March 26, 1821, a final "deed of co-partnership," one built upon the original

Hudson's Bay Company charter, was agreed upon.[1] It was to be good for twenty-one years. The name Hudson's Bay Company was to be retained, that of the North West Company dropped. For the duration of this co-partnership the concern was to continue to be a monopoly guaranteed by an act of Parliament. But unlike the provision of the original charter of 1670, the area involved would not be limited to that draining into Hudson Bay, but would embrace as well the entire Canadian West, including the Oregon country. The vast territory over which the new Hudson's Bay Company would have administrative, as well as trading powers, included an area approximately equal in size to present continental United States. This territory would be divided into four great parts, namely: (1) the Northern Department of Rupert's Land, which up to 1825 included New Caledonia; (2) the Southern Department (the James Bay area, southward to provinces of Upper and Lower Canada); (3) the Montreal Department, embracing Upper and Lower Canada (and later Labrador); and, of special interest here, (4) the Columbia District (subject to the control of the Northern Department). At first the Columbia District comprised only the Columbia River Valley, but after 1825 New Caledonia was added.

Moreover, the new company provided that its shares would be prorated among respective proprietors, chief factors, and chief traders — a sort of share-in-the-profits plan. Total gains in any one year would be divided into one hundred shares, of which forty would go to the wintering partners in North America. These forty shares in turn were to be divided into eighty-five shares, fifty going to the former North West Company men and the remaining thirty-five going to Hudson's Bay men. Each factor was to receive two shares, each trader one share. In addition, all employees of the company re-

---

[1] As it developed, fifty-two shares went to the North West Company's wintering partners and thirty-three to the men of Hudson's Bay Company. Of these numbers the North West Company held three and the Hudson's Bay Company four shares for the use of retired servants. The Governors of the Northern and Southern departments, and all employees below the rank of Chief Trader, received fixed salaries. Chief Factors and Chief Traders only received a share of the profits, if any.

ceived regular annual salaries, which out of necessity included board and keep.

In an effort to prevent further violence, Parliament also passed in 1821 "An Act for regulating the Fur Trade, and establishing a Criminal and Civil Jurisdiction within certain Parts of *North America*." This Act called attention to the past misdeeds of the late rival concerns, showed how these companies were "productive of great Inconvenience and Loss," how they did "great injury to the native *Indians*," and committed "Breaches of the Peace, and Violence extending to the Loss of Lives, and considerable Destruction of Property." Henceforth the powers of the courts of Upper and Lower Canada would extend with certain reservations to the territories granted to the Hudson's Bay Company. The exception would be the Oregon country where British rights would be shared with the United States.

For all its compromises, reservations, and restrictions, the new merger turned out to be a fortunate one. It enabled the reorganized Hudson's Bay Company not only to retain most of its previous privileges, but to add new ones. It paved the way for expansion and for carrying on the fur trade with greater efficiency and profit over a much wider area than had hitherto been possible. More efficient machinery of management — which has lasted to this day — was established. Probably the most important organizational change made subsequent to the merger occurred in 1822 when two field governors were appointed to administer the four territories. William Williams received the appointment to the Southern and Montreal departments; George Simpson was assigned to the Northern Department and Columbia District. The two field governors were responsible to the Governor and Committee in London. In 1826 Williams was recalled and George Simpson was given the governorship of the Southern as well as of the Northern Department; and in 1839 was made Governor-in-Chief of the entire American operations of the Hudson's Bay Company, responsible, of course, to the Governor and Committee overseas.

George Simpson, whose birth in Scotland in 1787 was illegitimate, had been reared and well educated by a kinswoman. Employment with a London mercantile firm eventually led to his becoming associated with the Hudson's Bay Company, in which, thanks to his brilliance, his rise was meteoric. Simpson, writes Frederick Merk, "had the imaginative vision of a Clive; he drew his plans on a scale that was continental" and as such "he combined a grasp of detail that was extraordinary." Today as the Hudson's Bay House views its own history, Sir George Simpson still remains a pivotal personality in those critically transitional years. "In him," writes Hudson's Bay House at London, "a clear orderly mind and a driving ambition were sustained by a physical vitality which carried him buoyantly through life."

"Where Rolls the Oregon"

For three years following the merger George Simpson devoted most of his energies to the expansion of the fur trade east of the Rocky Mountains, but by no means did he ignore what to him was a great challenge — the development of a master plan with respect to the Columbia District. Before the merger the Hudson's Bay Company had done little but explore the possibilities of trade on the Pacific watershed. Representing the firm during 1810–11, Joseph Howse had crossed the Rocky Mountains at a pass now bearing his name. Howse had ventured as far west as the Flathead country, and returned with glowing accounts of his experiences. But with the exception of this isolated exploit, the new Hudson's Bay Company was obliged to draw upon the experiences of the former Nor'westers who had been in the region. Accordingly, the energetic Simpson began to form his plans of organization. A fact-finding committee of four men (three of whom had been partners of the North West Company) was appointed immediately to go to the Columbia River region and report back on the state of affairs existing there.

Reports from this and other sources were, on the whole, affirmative, and on July 12, 1823, Simpson stated in a memo dispatched to the authorities of the Columbia District that trade there "may not only defray its expenses, but yield moderate profits if strict economy and exertion are exercised and there is no opposition." No doubt contributing to the making of final plans and decisions was a London agreement entered into early in 1824 between the East India Company and the Hudson's Bay Company whereby the latter would sell the trading monopoly 20,000 beavers and 7,000 otter skins in 1824 and a similar number the following year. This deal would not only relieve the London market but would lessen dependency upon the American J. and T. H. Perkins Company which had acted as middleman for the North West Company.

In order to expedite communication between the Columbia District and the East, Norway House (north of Lake Winnipeg) was to replace Fort William as the scene of the annual council. Also definite plans were laid for sending John Work to Spokane House, and further arrangements were made for outfitting Alexander Ross to lead a trading brigade into the Snake River country during the summer of 1824. All this took place while diplomatic negotiations were going on relative to the political disposition of the territory; and although a final settlement was by no means reached, the withdrawal of Russia to 54° 40′ was encouraging.

The year 1824 was one of decision with respect to British interests in the Oregon country. Once having decided to carry on in the Columbia District the Governor and Committee at London acted with great promptness and dispatch. The company purchased the brig *William and Ann* and ordered it to proceed to the north Pacific waters; it ordered the construction of new headquarters somewhere on the north side of the Columbia River; it urged that the Snake River trade should be prosecuted with renewed vigor, lest Americans capture this trade; and, lastly, to Simpson the Company turned for a successful execution of the policies agreed upon.

August 15, 1824, found Simpson still at York Factory (the Company's great depot in Hudson Bay) where he had met with the Council and where final plans for the west coast operations had been mapped out. Extreme haste was necessary if he were to cross the Rocky Mountains before the heavy snows of winter would block his passage. He had hoped vainly for the arrival of another ship from London bearing additional instructions, but the deadline passed, and the voyage began. Traveling by canoe, Simpson was accompanied by James McMillan, chief trader and one familiar with the Columbia River region; also by eight *voyageurs*, an Indian guide, and a personal servant.

Twenty days earlier Simpson had dispatched his previously appointed Chief Factor for the Columbia District. This was Dr. John McLoughlin, a man whose dominant and vivid personality was to make a lasting imprint upon Oregon history. He was born October 19, 1784, on the south bank of the St. Lawrence River in the Province of Quebec (about 120 miles below the city of Quebec), and was a mixture of Irish, Scotch, and French Canadian blood. Little is known of his childhood except that he was baptized a Catholic, grew up on a farm, received training in medicine at Quebec, and at the still youthful age of nineteen was licensed by the Lieutenant-Governor of Lower Canada to practice medicine and surgery. Meanwhile the young M.D. had met influential persons, among them the old tyrant, Simon McTavish, who induced McLoughlin to enter the service of the North West Company which was then on the verge of reorganization. Until the merger eighteen years later, Dr. McLoughlin continued to serve the Nor'westers, first as physician and then as actual trader east of the Rocky Mountains. While he may have found it possible to combine the art of healing with that of fur trading, it was as a trader that McLoughlin showed great skill. In this capacity he acted until 1821 when as one of his company's representatives he was sent to London to arrange for the merger with the rival Hudson's Bay Company.

Not too much is known of McLoughlin's private life. Already the father of a son by an Indian squaw, McLoughlin, about 1812, married in fur trader fashion the half-breed widow of the hapless Alexander McKay. By her first husand this woman had borne four children; by her union with McLoughlin she bore an additional four.

Personally Dr. McLoughlin was of striking appearance. He was six feet, four inches tall, raw boned, well proportioned, and strong. His eyes were piercing; his flowing prematurely white hair hung down over his massive shoulders. He was dignified but impetuous, and to use the words of H. H. Bancroft, ". . . he was fitted to govern men both by awe and love." This, then is the man upon whom Governor Simpson pinned his hopes for the Columbia District, an area about which the Honourable Company had some misgivings.

Although McLoughlin was no dawdler, on September 26 the swiftly moving Simpson party overtook him near the Athabaska River. In writing in his Journal of this strange meeting in the wilderness Simpson described the unique Dr. McLoughlin as "such a figure as I should not like to meet in a dark Night in one of the bye lanes in the neighborhood of London dressed in Clothes that had once been fashionable, but now covered with a thousand patches of different Colors, his beard would do honor to the chin of a Grizzly Bear. . . . his own herculean dimensions forming a tout ensemble that would convey a good idea of the high way men of former Days."

By November 8, 1824 (having made the trans-Canadian jaunt from York Factory to Fort George at the mouth of the Columbia in eighty-four days), Simpson and McLoughlin were ready to revamp their Pacific coast domain. A new fort was to be built at Belle Vue Point on the north side of the Columbia River on what Simpson believed would permanently be British soil. The post to be erected there, to be named Fort Vancouver in honor of the great explorer, was to replace Fort George as headquarters for the District. Fort Nez Percé (Walla Walla) was to be shifted; Spokane House was to be abandoned, or rather replaced by what was to be Fort Colvile near Kettle Falls, seventy-five miles farther north; Kootenai House and many other posts were slated for a thorough revamping; and, as circumstances dictated, other new trading posts should be added to those already within that region.

Simpson was not slow to order a general streamlining of the administrative setup by eliminating excessive personnel and wasteful practices and by mapping out important expeditions such as those involving the Snake country. Moreover, the governor proposed that agriculture, stock raising, and salmon fishing should supplement the fur trade much more than they had previously; and it was his command that coastal and trans-Pacific trade should be made a very important part of the Company's operations in the Columbia District. Simpson personally remained in the District throughout the entire winter of 1824–25, helping Chief Factor McLoughlin to inaugurate the new regime. By March 19, 1825, the new Fort Vancouver (subsequently rebuilt on higher ground) had been completed, and in his journal for that day Simpson wrote:

At Sun rise mustered all the people to hoist the Flag Staff of the new Establishment and in presence of the Gentlemen, Servants, Chiefs & Indians I Baptised it by breaking a Bottle of Rum on the Flag Staff and repeating the following words in a loud voice, "In behalf of the Honble Hudsons Bay Co^y I hereby name this Establishment *Fort Vancouver* God Save King George the 4th" with three cheers. Gave a couple of Drams to the people and Indians on the occasion. The object of naming it after that distinguished navigator is to identify our claim to the Soil and Trade with his discovery of the River and Coast on behalf of G^t Britain. If the Honble Committee however do not approve the Name it can be altered. At 9 O'clock A. M. took leave of our Friend the D^r, embarked and continued our Voyage. Put up for the night about 20 miles below the Cascade Portage.[2]

Simpson's immediate task had been accomplished. He then returned east of the Rockies, en route visiting posts along the Columbia River — Walla Walla, Okanogan, and Spokane House. Plans with the chief traders were discussed further. Before he left, Simpson had ordered that the Columbia River Valley and New Caledonia, separate districts under the North West Company, were to be merged into one administrative and operating unit; the working out of this plan he placed in the hands of his capable Chief Factor McLoughlin. Under him were to serve many shrewd and brilliant traders, among them Peter Skene Ogden, James McMillan, James Douglas, Alexander R. McLeod, John Warren Dease, Archibald McDonald, Francis and Edward Ermatinger, and John

[2] Frederick Merk, ed., *Fur Trade and Empire: George Simpson's Journal, 1824–1825* (Cambridge, Mass., 1931), p. 124.

Work. These and several others were to be important in the early history of the old Oregon country.

Outposts in the Wilderness

For more than two decades McLoughlin remained the Chief Factor of the Columbia District, and not until the end of his services in 1846 did the Hudson's Bay Company retreat northward before the rising tide of the American immigrants. With great energy and perseverance the "White Headed Eagle" (for such did the Indians call McLoughlin) carried out the ambitious plans that the imaginative Governor Simpson had so courageously conceived.

Immediate steps were taken, first, to unite New Caledonia and the Columbia River basin into one co-ordinated administrative and trading unit, and second, to expand the fur trade. Toward these ends Chief Trader James McMillan set out to examine the heretofore unexploited lower Fraser River. And still further endeavors brought an opening, without hindrance from once hostile Indians, of trails which connected the new headquarters of Fort Vancouver with the potentially rich Puget Sound country.

Meanwhile the Company gave its attention to the important matter of the number, position, and character of fur trading posts. In this role the Fort Vancouver headquarters was made the hub toward which all trails led and in relation to which all other posts remained subsidiary. From Fort Vancouver brigades set forth; from it issued orders affecting operations in even the tiniest outpost in some isolated river valley hundreds of miles away. To Fort Vancouver flowed the coveted bales of furs; to it gravitated would-be settlers, visiting dignitaries, scientists, and travelers to whom the Fort offered relief and comfort. To the weary overland traveler, it was a haven; to those who came exhausted from a long sea voyage, it was a home.

Fort Vancouver continued to grow in physical proportions. At its fullest development in 1845 it consisted not only of stockaded areas, but of a sizeable village. The Fort proper shaped like a parallelogram, with dimensions of about 150 by

250 yards, was enclosed by a wooden wall made of pickets twenty feet high. The wall was strongly secured by inside buttresses. There was the customary bastion, in this case at the northwest corner where "twelve pounders" commanded not only the fort areas, but the entire village as well. Some "eighteen pounders" were located in the center of the stockade to support the main battery emplaced in the bastion. Within were numerous sturdy wooden buildings arranged around a central court. These served as offices, apartments for the clerks and other officers, and as warehouses for furs and imported English goods. Inside stood the governor's two-story residence with its popular dining hall and public sitting room. Both inside and outside of the stockade were workshops for the different mechanics — carpenters, blacksmiths, coopers, wheelwrights, and tinners. Immediately outside the Fort to the north was an orchard; and on the other three sides, cultivated fields. A road which passed by the southern side of the Fort was connected with others which reached the village a few yards to the west and the Columbia River a half mile to the south.

The village consisted of scattered, irregularly placed dwellings. Most of them were the homes of Company servants, but in the village were also located a Catholic church, a schoolhouse, and a stable. Along the river front southwest of the Fort was the wharf; also a pond surrounded by more servants' quarters, workshops, stables, pigsheds, storesheds, and, incidentally, a "hospital." Fort Vancouver was, as a contemporary observed, "the grand mart and rendezvous for the Company's trade and servants on the Pacific."

Lieutenant Charles Wilkes, commander of an American naval exploring expedition, called at Fort Vancouver in 1841 and was profoundly impressed. Later he wrote of McLoughlin's hospitality, of the long table in the large dining hall, and of the "abundance of good fare." Fort Vancouver, he wrote, "is a large manufacturing, agricultural, and commercial depôt, and there are few if any idlers, except the sick. Everybody seems to be in a hurry, whilst there appears to be no obvious reason for it." In the vicinity of the fort were also expansive farm lands devoted to a diversified agriculture and to the grazing of large herds of cattle, sheep, and horses. As will be shown later, agricultural activities were to become an important part of the Company's economy.

Outposts were less elaborate, although some of them con-

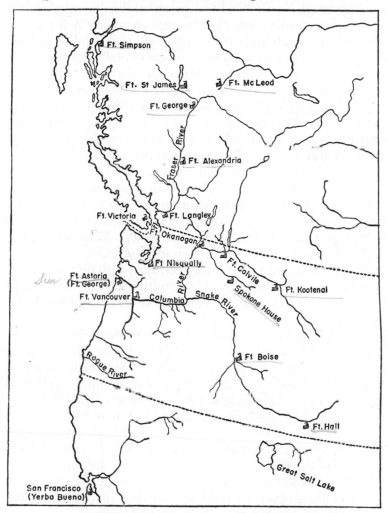

PRINCIPAL FUR TRADING POSTS

There were many other posts. The exact location of some cannot be determined, and several were rebuilt at different locations.

tained numerous structures within their outer walls. Many former North West Company posts were kept and improved. Forts McLeod, St. James, Fraser, George (B.C.), Kootenai, Flathead, Kamloops, Okanogan, and Nez Percé were among the important North West Company establishments retained in the new organization. Fort George (formerly Astoria) was allowed to operate only on a very small scale and to fall into disrepair, and Spokane House was completely abandoned.

To the number of posts retained the Company added, besides pivotal Fort Vancouver, many others. At Simpson's instigation Fort Colvile was founded in 1825 to replace Spokane House. This new post was located near Kettle Falls, about forty miles south of the present international boundary line and about the midway point on the 1,400-mile course of the Columbia River. John Work was detailed to supervise the construction of its first small unit, to which many buildings were subsequently added. When in 1846 an inventory of the Colvile properties was taken no less than nineteen separate buildings were listed, ranging from a store 25 by 60 feet to a pigeon house 9 by 9 feet. All were surrounded by a protective stockade. And like Fort Vancouver, Fort Colvile with its 340 acres under cultivation, its blacksmith and carpenter shops, flour mill, and bake house, was to all intents a self-sustaining unit.

Attention was also directed to the lower Fraser River where Dr. McLoughlin's trusted aide, James McMillan, arrived with a party on June 24, 1827, and began the construction of Fort Langley. McMillan chose a site on the left bank of the Fraser, twenty-eight miles upstream. It took but six weeks to build a stockaded structure 120 by 135 feet, according to the journal of Archibald McDonald who became the chief trader and whose duty was to develop the coastal trade. Because of the hasty workmanship, the post deteriorated rapidly, and in 1839 it was rebuilt two miles farther upstream, only to be destroyed by fire the following year. When it was again rebuilt it lasted as a post for a half century.

The next post of any importance was Fort Simpson, built in 1831 and located on the Nass River about twenty miles from its mouth. Three years later it, too, was relocated, this time at the north end of Tsimpsean Peninsula. For several decades to come Fort Simpson operated as a profitable trading establishment.

One such post followed another in the fulfillment of McLoughlin's dream of a network that would stretch from the Columbia River far north to Russian Alaska and east to the Continental Divide. In 1833 Fort McLoughlin was built on Milbanke Sound. The next year witnessed the building of Fort Boise on the Snake River a few miles from the mouth of the Boise River. Near it was Fort Hall on the big bend of the Snake River, which was acquired from Wyeth by the Hudson's Bay Company in 1837. Both these posts enhanced the Company's trade in a region hitherto reached by brigades only, and they also served to deter competing American traders from entering the Oregon country from the East. But ironically enough, the day was already at hand when both Forts Boise and Hall were to become important landmarks, not necessarily for American fur traders, but for long lines of westbound American immigrants.

To describe each post separately would be monotonous, for as the British Commander Richard C. Mayne observed: ". . . all Hudson Bay posts are much alike." Six to eight houses serving as lodgings for officers and men, mess halls, a trading store, workshop and storage places, were here compressed within the square wall from fifteen to twenty feet high. In two of the four corners, and rising above the walls, were wooden and usually octagonally shaped bastions. Openings on all sides were large enough to accommodate six and twelve pounders and thereby the entire surrounding countryside was within the range of cannon fire.

With respect to American immigration into the Willamette Valley, McLoughlin was a realist. He early became convinced that the future of the fur trade lay north of the Columbia. To be sure, the Chief Factor maintained a small establishment on the Umpqua River, he sent brigades far south into California, and he even sent W. G. Rae to Yerba Buena (San Francisco) to establish a post there which opened in May, 1841. But the advance of the Hudson's Bay Company in Old Oregon was predominantly northward.

This being so, the day would inevitably come when the interests of McLoughlin's company would clash with those of the Russians in Alaska. Even before the Hudson's Bay Company moved west of the Rocky Mountains, a Czarist ukase had declared that all lands north of the fifty-first parallel belonged to Russia, and he forbade foreigners to come within one hundred Italian miles of her coast. This led to the convention and agreements of 1824–25 involving Russia, Great Britain, and the United States, which established 54° 40' as the southern extent of Russian territorial claims.

Agreement in matters of sovereignty naturally brought with it limitations on trading companies of the countries involved. In view of such limitations Governor George Simpson and Rear Admiral Baron Ferdinand Wrangell of the Russian American Fur Company signed an important agreement at Hamburg, February 6, 1839, respecting trading operations in the border area of Alaska. Beginning in 1840 the Russians agreed to cede to the Hudson's Bay Company for exclusive trade for a period of ten years the waters and land from 54° 40' north to Cape Spencer. In return the British company agreed not to trade in the remaining Russian territory, and further agreed to pay annually to the Russian American Fur Company as rent 2,000 land otter skins. The Hudson's Bay Company further agreed to sell at specified prices to the Russians an additional 5,000 skins and quantities of agricultural produce such as flour, peas, barley, salted beef, butter, and hams.

This agreement led in 1840 to the establishment by James Douglas of Fort Taku (or Durham) on lands leased from the Russian American Fur Company. It also led to the leasing by the Hudson's Bay Company in the same year of Fort Stikine, also within this same area, and today the site of Wrangell, Alaska. Formerly this post had been called Redoubt St. Dionysius and had been built in 1834 to forestall British advances into the region.

The first American immigrant train arrived in the Willamette Valley in 1841. The Hudson's Bay Company saw this as the handwriting on the wall, and accordingly gave added impetus to its northern developments. Under the direction of

James Douglas, Fort Victoria was established on the southern tip of Vancouver Island in 1843. It was strategically located, and later replaced Fort Vancouver as headquarters for the Columbia District. In 1848 Fort Yale was founded at the head of navigation on the Fraser River, and during the following year Fort Hope was located twenty miles farther downstream. Also in 1849 Fort Rupert was established at the northern end of Vancouver Island; 1852 saw the founding of Nanaimo as a coal mining enterprise on the eastern shore of this large island. As time went on still other forts were established, and to this very day the Hudson's Bay Company maintains no less than two hundred trading posts in northern Canada, some of which are within the boundaries of what was once called the Oregon country. In addition to trading posts, the Company created agricultural establishments and other subsidiary industries.

Taken as a whole the Hudson's Bay Company posts in the Columbia District were strategically situated along rivers, bays, and the coast. In general these posts answered the requirements of the trade. The structures, varying in number at each fort, were sturdily built and in most cases were fortified and armed to meet the needs of the particular region in which they were located. The posts were stocked with a great variety of supplies, and were essential not only in the conduct of local trade but also in the operation of the Company brigades which covered a wide area. The posts were the physical instruments so necessary to fullest development of the fur trade.

CHAPTER V

British Monopoly in Action

In and Around the Posts

AROUND the individual Hudson's Bay Company posts much of the fur trade was carried on with natives of the region. Once a fur trading post had been constructed, adequately fortified, stocked with trading goods, and properly staffed, doors were cautiously opened for business. Company operators were careful not to admit too many Indians at one time (preferably only one or two), and once within the post, natives were carefully guarded. Actual trade, however, was preceded by an exchange of gifts. Pieces of wood or bronze, corresponding with the number of pelts delivered, served as money; these were good for the purchase of articles, the value of which was described in terms of a standard beaver skin.

Hudson's Bay blankets became favorite items of trade, but from available account books one learns that many other articles were placed on the store shelves — awls, needles, scissors, thread, Canton beads, buttons, combs, highly colored yard goods, flashy cock feathers, files, looking glasses, silk handkerchiefs, fish hooks, pocket knives, scalping knives, axes, and a limited assortment of groceries.

Conversely the same account books list the type, number, and estimated value of skins received. During one fiscal year, for example, Fort McLoughlin received the skins of no less than 1,111 beavers, 829 minks, 194 black, brown, and grizzly bears, 477 martens, 300 land and sea otters, 97 lynxes, and a smaller number of raccoons, fishers, rats, and wolverines, amounting in value to about $12,000 in American money. In some instances a limited amount of credit was allowed individual customers, but most frequently this was accorded only to Indians employed at or around the post.

66]

Everywhere the pattern for trade was very much the same, although in the far north interior — a region free from American competition — trading was done with a wider margin of profit than in the region penetrated by the Yankees. But even in the north, writes Walter N. Sage of the University of British Columbia, "The gathering of the peltries required much tact and ingenuity." At Fort Langley, for example, the extra precaution of transacting business along the river bank rather than within the stockade was taken; and only those Indians with beaver skins to trade were permitted within the walls of the fort. British warships were seldom in the north Pacific waters and since there was no standing army to offer protection, the Company forts had to rely upon their own strength whenever resistance was offered by the natives.

Fur Trading Cavalcades and Expeditions

The most certain way for the Hudson's Bay Company to be assured of a supply of skins was to send their traders and trappers to the real sources of supply — the streams, the valleys, and the hills of the hinterland. Less enterprising Indians could not be relied upon to put sufficient zest into their hunting and trapping. Neither could natives be depended upon to bring their pelts to the post for trade. Therefore, the Hudson's Bay Company organized bands of hunters, trappers, and traders who made periodic expeditions in search of furs. To make such expeditions into the hinterland feasible, brigades were organized to transport supplies from main depots, such as Fort Vancouver, to outlying posts. From these hinterland posts the trading expeditions set forth and returned; and again, from such places brigades conveyed the bales of fur back to the main depots for final shipment to London.

Most vital of all the brigade trails was one first established by the North West Company to connect its Fort St. James headquarters on Stuart Lake with its Montreal lifeline on the one hand, and with the Columbia River on the other. From Fort St. James in the north to Fort George (Astoria) at the mouth of the Columbia there accordingly emerged a route of commerce more than one thousand five hundred miles in length.[1] By several other trails, perhaps less sharply laid out, fur trading expeditions ventured into such areas as the Snake River country, the Thompson River country, the region of the Great Salt Lake, the Willamette and Umpqua valleys, the Oregon coast, and even far south into Spanish Alta California.

The number in a brigade varied anywhere from 50 to 400, with usually as many horses as people. Certain types of personnel were invariably present. The person running the show was ordinarily the chief trader, but at times the Chief Factor was personally in charge. As a mark of distinction the leader of the brigade was customarily dressed in a broadcloth suit, white shirt with high collar, and invariably a high beaver hat. The Chief Factor, or chief trader, carried with him a fire bag containing his flint and steel, touchwood, and tobacco. Then there were the hunters, trappers, traders, clerks, storekeepers, and an assorted number of Indians — whole families of them — whose job was to care for the horses, to handle provisions, trading goods, and other essential equipment.

"A beautiful sight," reminisced Malcolm McLeod, a veteran Company man, " was that horse brigade, with no broken hocks in the train, but every animal in his full beauty of form and colour, and all so tractable — more tractable than anything I ever knew in civilized life." Out ahead were the hunters in search of meat and the next camp where feed and water would be available. Next came the person in charge, followed by the indispensable piper who played on his bagpipes to the mile-long procession. A packer accompanied each horse, with a carefully loaded pack on the back of each animal, held properly in place by straps around the horse's belly and made tight with the diamond hitch. Trudging along in the rear were families of the packers.

Points of departure varied, depending upon the destination of a particular brigade. If a brigade left from Fort Vancouver for the inland, the first long stretch to Fort Okanogan

---

[1] The upper part of this route, from Fort St. James to Fort Alexandria, was traversed by water; from Fort Alexandria to Fort Okanogan the route was an overland trail; and from Okanogan to Fort George at the mouth of the Columbia, the course followed was the Columbia River. To this day it is referred to as the Hudson's Bay Brigade Trail.

(usually involving sixty days) was made in large klinker boats and canoes, whereas south bound troupes used horse transport. Very early spring was the time for leaving Fort Vancouver. Though on a smaller scale than previously described (about fifty to sixty in the party), the journey was not without its color and excitement, especially for those who had spent long, dreary, and monotonous winter months at some isolated post.

To many, like McLeod, the brigade was something romantic and exciting, but not to George Simpson. To him it was an absolute essential for the fur trade, but as a social entity people comprising the brigades were just bands of irresponsible human wretches, "the very scum of the country and generally outcasts from the Service. . . ." They were, he wrote, "the most unruly and troublesome gang to deal with in this or perhaps any other part of the World. . . ." Douglas was equally unflattering, commenting in a letter to Simpson on how "exceedingly riotous and unruly" the Fort Langley brigade had been during the summer of 1848. The group, he wrote, had caused "a great deal of trouble"; some had deserted and returned to the fort, where they had been punished. At best, life with the brigades was hard, cruel, and hazardous.

In the employment of both brigades and expeditions, the Hudson's Bay Company far outstripped its predecessors, although the Nor'westers had previously sent caravans into the Umpqua and Snake River valleys. Beginning with A. R. McLeod in 1826, however, the Hudson's Bay Company dispatched expeditions annually into the Umpqua Valley and subsequently across the Siskiyou Mountains into the great interior valley of California as far south as the Tulares. Very important was the trade in the country of the Snake Indians, and to it both Simpson and McLoughlin gave much attention. The first North West Company trading expedition had entered this Oregon back country in 1818, and for five years thereafter the region had been revisited by the Nor'westers. Following the reorganization, Peter Skene Ogden, son of a Quebec admiralty court judge and a United Empire Loyalist, was designated chief trader in charge of the Snake country trade. Simpson feared American penetration into this region, and believed that Ogden should pursue the trade there for all it was worth.

On December 20, 1824, Ogden left Flathead post with a formidable party of 75 men, mostly half-breeds, fully equipped with 25 tepees, 80 guns, 364 beaver traps, and 372 horses. The party moved eastward to the Missoula and Bitterroot rivers, across the Continental Divide to the very headwaters of the Missouri, and onto American soil. On its return the brigade struck the Salmon and Snake rivers, and subsequently moved so far southward as to become the probable discoverers of the Great Salt Lake. From this inland sea the Ogden party turned homeward. They moved northward in the general direction from which they had come, but ultimately returned to headquarters in November, 1825, by following the course of the Snake River. Ogden entered the region at a time when American traders were also there, but even so returns from this first year's catch amounted to 3,090 beaver skins, with profits encouraging enough to prompt Dr. McLoughlin to repeat the experiment. Ogden subsequently made four more expeditions into the Snake country. In so doing he put fur trading in this area on a very profitable footing for more than two decades. The sphere of Ogden's activities was gradually extended; in 1828 he cut far southward from the Snake River to the Great Salt Lake, the Humboldt River, and back by way of the Pitt River in northern California, with a catch of furs that netted him a profit of about $15,000.

Interior expeditions led by John McLeod, William Connolly, John Work, and other prominent traders, regularly penetrated the country of the Flathead, Cayuse, Nez Percé and the Blackfeet Indians. Such journeys were invariably dangerous, even though the Company took every reasonable precaution against Indian attack. Simpson once went so far as to suggest to McLoughlin that John Work would do well to marry a Cayuse squaw (expenses to be paid by the Company); that as a sort of goodwill messenger she should accompany him on his journey through the Cayuse country. That Work faced many dangers is revealed in a letter he wrote to his friend and fellow trader, Edward Ermatinger, following one of his expeditions: "I am happy in being able to inform you that I enjoy good health, and am yet blessed with the possession of my scalp which is rather more than I had reason to expect."

Available records of many expeditions indicate the number of furs gathered directly at numerous posts. The Fort Vancouver "Skin Book" (record book) gives the returns for all the Snake River expeditions from 1826 to 1852. The first party venturing into this region returned with 2,744 beaver skins, about equal the annual take in that year at Fort Colvile, and roughly two-thirds the number of beaver skins taken in at the Fort Vancouver headquarters. Two decades later the returns of the Snake River brigade were 1,454 beaver skins, as compared with only 962 at Fort Colvile, and 1,460 at Fort Vancouver. Other brigades did not do so well, but neither are the later returns from some of the small outlying trading posts impressive.

"The Coasting Trade"

A grand scheme for the rugged coastal area was evolved by Simpson and carried out by McLoughlin. Small craft operating along the coast in search of pelts were to make contact with posts accessible by water. Furs acquired by the smaller boats would be transferred to larger supply vessels which either carried the cargo to England or perchance to Canton and world markets. Arrangements for marketing furs at Canton were to be made through the East India Company. Although Yankee competition there would be a serious obstacle, it did not deter the Company.

McLoughlin meant to lose no time in the execution of the ready-made plans for the development of this coastal trade. Scarcely had the crude doors of Fort Vancouver swung open in 1825 when he received instructions to assign the supply ship *William and Ann*, then at Fort George, to coastal reconnaisance. Her captain, Henry Hanwell, was unfortunately both incompetent and dilatory, at least so said McLoughlin, and little or nothing was accomplished during this first season.

McLoughlin was not easily discouraged. He urged headquarters in London to send not one but two years' supply of goods. If sufficient materials were on hand at Fort Vancouver, McLoughlin argued, local trading operations could begin early in the spring without awaiting the arrival of the annual supply ship from abroad. Not until 1828 did the London office attempt to meet these demands by allocating three ships (about two hundred tons each) to the business of the Columbia Department — two to make annual voyages to and from London, the third to remain on the coast.

In addition, smaller vessels were built to be used exclusively in local river or coastal operations. One of these, the sixty-ton schooner *Vancouver* built at the fort for which it was named, was ready for service in 1828, and used until 1834. Then there was the seventy-ton schooner *Cadboro*, built in London but sent to the district with the *William and Ann* in 1827, which served as a permanent supply ship. Based first at Fort Langley, the sturdy little *Cadboro* was long familiar to nearly every coastal port. Also built at Fort Vancouver was the twenty-five to thirty-ton sloop *Broughton* used exculsively for river service. In a class by itself was the sturdy little steamer *Beaver,* launched in England in 1836. In spite of McLoughlin's initial objection to a steamer for the coastal trade this vessel (the first of its kind in Pacific waters), gave notable service to the Company for many years. On the whole, McLoughlin favored vessels of the two hundred-ton class for these coastal operations. Ships of this size, he believed, would command great respect from the natives during trading operations.

Forts were essential for coastal trade. Fort Vancouver, though located inland, was as much the central entrepôt for coastal operations as it was for those pertaining to the hinterland. Forts Stikine, Taku, Langley, Simpson, McLoughlin, and Nisqually were among the most important in a chain of forts established in proximity to coastal or Puget Sound waters between Russian Alaska and the mouth of the Columbia. So important were these land bases that in 1834 the Doctor ventured the statement, and gave figures to support it, that "we can carry on the trade of the coast to more advantage by establishing posts than by vessels and that four posts when established will be kept up at less expense than one Vessel. . . ."

This, then, comprised the physical arrangements for the Company's final push to the shores of the Pacific. It was a costly undertaking, but the "coasting trade" was soundly managed. Though carried at a loss at first, and never yielding tremendous profits, it had widespread ramifications. It facilitated expansion of salmon fishing and lumbering, future key industries of the Pacific Northwest; it threw open the gates to far-flung Pacific Ocean trade which, though carried on in limited volume, was to involve China, Russian America (Alaska), the Sandwich Islands, California, Mexico, and South America. It gave, moreover, renewed vision and greater zest to the Company as a whole.

Fur Traders Turn to Agriculture

When Simpson and McLoughlin first entered the Oregon country their thoughts were not confined strictly to fur trade, to the mere collection of pelts, but turned as well to ways and means of stocking the District's larder. Their writings betray a keen interest in what the soil might produce. They observed the thriving wild fruits and berries; they noted the green lush grasses blanketing the valleys west of the Cascades, the stately evergreens of "prodigious size" covering the lofty mountains; they even took cognizance of the fish abounding in the clear, sparkling streams. The problem of feeding their employees was an immediate one, and it was to Mother Nature that they turned for help. To think in such terms was not original, for it had long been customary for some farming, gardening, and fishing to be done around fur trading posts situated on arable soil and near either rivers or other bodies of water. Harmon, it is recalled, had a garden at Fort St. James in 1811, and thereby was the first white man in British Columbia to become a dirt farmer. At Fort Astoria, in the same year, men of the Pacific Fur Company planted a few wrinkly potatoes which grew and became the first white man's garden south of the Columbia River.

Later the farsighted Simpson made this entry in his journal: "The Post is agreeably situated . . . ; the Soil is much the same as at Spokane and produces the finest potatoes I have seen in the Country. Grain in any quantity might be raised here, but cultivation to any extent has never been attempted, indeed throughout the Columbia no pains have been taken to meet the demands of the trade in that way which was a great oversight. . . ." Then as if to justify his eagerness to develop agriculture, he added: "It has been said that Farming is no branch of the Fur Trade but I consider that every pursuit tending to leighten the Expence of the Trade is a branch thereof. . . ." In a letter of December 31, 1825, to the British Commissioner, Henry Addington, Governor Simpson even wrote that headquarters were being established at Belle Vue Point (Vancouver) rather than at Fort George in part because he thought the country thereabouts "capable of producing large quantities of grain of every kind"; and that "numerous herds of cattle" might be pastured there where the "nutritious roots are so abundant that almost any number of Hogs may be reared."

To Chief Factor McLoughlin such diversified responsibilities were accepted with evident pleasure, and his future supervision of the projects was done with meticulous and painstaking care. During the very first season at Fort Vancouver clearings were made and some wheat was grown; in the second season, barley, Indian corn, peas, and potatoes were added to what was to become an imposing list of produce. On September 1, 1826, McLoughlin reported to the London office with reservations: "Our farming goes on as well as we could Expect; . . ." Though not sharing Simpson's optimism as to the productivity of the soil, Chief Factor McLoughlin was confident that local requirements would be met within the next couple of years. Acres placed under cultivation increased steadily, and when Wilkes visited Fort Vancouver in 1841, the farms, according to this American observer, were nine miles square.

Impressive as the farms around Fort Vancouver had become, they scarcely overshadowed those at some of the subsidiary posts. On his first visit Simpson had left explicit instructions for farming at designated places, chiefly Fort Col-

FORT ASTORIA

This is taken from a woodcut by Charles Wilkes, and engraved by R. O'Brien, appearing in Wilkes, *Narrative,* vol. V.   Courtesy Huntington Library

Photo by George A. Grant. Courtesy U. S. National Park Service

CRATER LAKE
IN
CRATER LAKE
NATIONAL
PARK

This shows the eastern shore of the lake as seen from the rim.
The Phantom Ship (island) can be seen near the far shore, and Mt. Applegate is in the distance.

vile. In a letter dated April 16, 1825, to John Work, builder of that post, Simpson wrote: ". . . you will be so good as to take care of . . . seed *not ate* as next spring I expect that from 30 to 40 Bushels will be planted."

Orders were scrupulously carried out and with each passing year more and more fields were put under cultivation at this eastern Washington post. Wheat, barley, oats, Indian corn, Irish potatoes, peas, and garden vegetables of every description grew well at this up-river post, and were equal in quality to similar crops raised at Fort Vancouver. Farm products at Colvile soon increased in excess of local consumption, and surplus commodities were made available for export. Archibald McDonald, one of the men in charge of the fort, in 1837 described the farm as being then "on an extensive scale . . . upwards of 5000 bushels of grain . . . 3000 of wheat, 1000 of corn and more than 1200 of other grain." By 1841 total land then under cultivation was estimated to be about 130 acres. In addition to the production of staple commodities, wild strawberries, wild cherries, and hawthorn berries were harvested from the countryside.

At Cowlitz and at Nisqually (about which more will be said later) similar farming operations were put in motion. From Cowlitz Farm Wilkes wrote in 1841: "They have here six or seven hundred acres enclosed, and under cultivation, with several large granaries, a large farm-house, and numerous out-buildings to accommodate the dairy, workmen, cattle, etc. The grounds appear well prepared, and were covered with a luxuriant crop of wheat. At the farther end of the prairie," he continued, "was to be seen a settlement, with its orchards, etc., and between the trees, the chapel and parsonage of the Catholic Mission gave an air of civilization to the whole." Wilkes was reminded of the American frontier where nature seemed ever "ready for the plough."

Farther north was Fort Langley. There, too, gardening and limited farming activities were carried on under the direction of McMillan. He first specialized in potatoes, but also produced turnips, radishes, carrots, and red and white currants. Later McMillan obtained glass for devising a hotbed for seeding melons, cucumbers, pumpkins, gourds, and cabbages. By

1842 Fort Langley had also become a grain-raising center, yielding in that year 750 bushels of wheat, 500 bushels of oats, 250 bushels of barley, and 600 bushels of peas. Moreover, quantities of beef, pork, and butter were produced. From a larder such as this Fort Langley and neighboring posts made shipments of grain, flour, salted beef, hams, and butter to the Russians in Alaska; agriculture there became an important subsidiary business.

Elsewhere in New Caledonia some farming was done by the fur traders. From a grist mill erected on the upper Fraser flour was subsequently distributed to various northern posts — Kamloops, Alexandria, and St. James. Horticulture was not nearly so important, though here again a future key industry received its initial boost from the Hudson's Bay Company. "The first fruit tree grown on the Columbia sprang from the seeds of an apple eaten at a dinner-party in London," wrote the historian Bancroft. A lady had placed the seeds in Simpson's waistcoat pocket, so the story goes, and they were not discovered until the Governor again wore the coat at Fort Vancouver in 1827. Simpson thereupon gave the seeds to the gardener, who planted them. ". . . and thence within the territory of Oregon began the growth of apple-trees."

The Hudson's Bay Company was under contract to supply the Russians in Alaska with both meat and flour. To help meet both these demands and local needs, the Company was prompted to begin agriculture and cattle raising on Vancouver Island. Farming operations were started around Fort Victoria in 1845. Indians were used to clear the land for what was first known as Fort Farm, on a site corresponding with the present business section of the city of Victoria. Other farms in the vicinity of Fort Victoria during the fifties were Esquimalt, Craigflower (or Maple Point), Constance Cove, Viewpoint (or Viewfield), Beckley, North Dairy, and Uplands. Some of these were owned and operated by the Puget's Sound Agricultural Company (a subsidiary), others were managed either directly by the Hudson's Bay Company or by men associated with this concern. It is estimated that by 1860 the Hudson's Bay Company and its subsidiaries utilized about fifteen thousand acres of land on Vancouver Island for cultivation and grazing. A census of Vancouver Island for 1855 records the island's production of wheat for the preceding year at 4,715 bushels; oats, 1,730 bushels; peas, 1,567 bushels. In addition to its own farming operations the Hudson's Bay Company, by virtue of having received a royal grant to the island in 1849, was responsible for some general immigration from the United Kingdom. To push developments of this kind, however, was not to the best interest of the Company.

Company Herds and Flocks

Not until 1814 were cattle known to have been taken to the mainland of the Oregon country. At Fort George there were but 27 cattle (the largest single herd) when McLoughlin took charge. These — mostly Spanish in origin — he had driven to Fort Vancouver where others of better English breed were added to improve the strain. To McLoughlin nothing seemed so important as his precious herds of cattle that grazed in abundant pasture lands in the immediate vicinity of Fort Vancouver, and in the valleys of the Willamette and the Cowlitz.

Until such a time as cattle would become plentiful McLoughlin's policy was to increase and to preserve the herd. An occasional bull calf was killed for rennet used in cheesemaking, but with this exception slaughter was strictly forbidden until 1836. McLoughlin would willingly loan cows to American settlers, but under no circumstances would he sell them. McLoughlin was very eager to encourage the growth of his herds. By 1828 the number at Fort Vancouver was about two hundred; and although not champion milk producers, their yield by 1831 was in excess of local needs. By 1841 the number of cattle around Fort Vancouver, according to Wilkes, was near three thousand. Many were milch cows which provided the whole establishment with "most excellent milk." Best producers were those of a cross between the Spanish and the English varieties.

At some of the outlying posts the story is the same as at headquarters. Fort Colvile, for example, received its start when two bulls and two cows were brought there from Fort

Vancouver in 1825, and "from these have sprung," wrote Wilkes, "one hundred and nintey-six head of fine cattle." From the herds first arriving at Fort Langley in 1829 have come in part the thousands of cattle that are now raised in British Columbia Province.

These herds were not a direct part of the Hudson's Bay Company trade, but, like the grains they helped to stock the Company's larder and thereby simplified immeasurably the problem of food supply. The census of 1860, showing 182,-382 head of cattle in Oregon and the Territory of Washington alone (many, of course, having sprung from herds brought in directly by American settlers) is but one reminder of the Hudson's Bay Company's contribution to the development of ranching, dairying, and the cattle trade in that region. Large herds from this area, in addition, were driven to British Columbia, especially during and after 1859 when the gold rush brought thousands of prospectors into the Fraser, Cariboo, and Kamloops regions.

Important and extensive as was this early cattle breeding in the Oregon country, it was by no means carried on to the exclusion of other phases of livestock raising. Although horses, sheep, goats, and hogs were less numerous than cattle, they were nonetheless important. To fur traders, the horse and mule had proved indispensable both for the transportation of supplies and as a source of raw meat. Horses, as previously noted, had first been introduced to the Pacific Northwest Indians by their red brethren from east of the Rockies about 1734, perhaps earlier. They had multiplied considerably by the opening of the next century when additional numbers were brought in by white fur traders, particularly dependent upon pack animals wherever operations departed from navigable streams. Early traders, moreover, resorted to eating horse flesh whenever wild game was not readily available. French Canadians had no aversion to horse meat, and there were situations where Anglo Saxons and Latins alike regarded barbecued horse as a great delicacy. It was reported that during one winter alone no less than ninety horses were consumed at Fort Spokane; and in a three-year period at least seven hundred horses were eaten for food at Fort Walla Walla.

Hogs were also among the earliest arrivals in the Oregon country, and though some difficulties were encountered in raising them, McLoughlin reported "upwards of 250 Pigs" at the headquarters in 1831. With the passing of years pork greatly supplemented horse flesh as an item in diet.

Sheep raising also became an important part of the Hudson's Bay Company's ranching activities, contributing immeasurably to the future wool production in the region. Just when sheep came to the Northwest mainland is not known for certain. The Hudson's Bay Company is known to have imported sheep directly from California in 1829, with delivery made by the American Captain John Dominus. In 1834 Nathaniel Wyeth, another American, brought in additional numbers of sheep from the Sandwich Islands, where George Vancouver had transported sheep from California as early as 1792–94. The Company's interest in sheep was due partly to a desire to produce wool for export, and also to have mutton, always popular with Scots, on hand as an item of food. It was at Fort Nisqually and Cowlitz Farm, and upon the Vancouver Island farms, that sheep raising reached its fullest development under the auspices of the Company.

The Puget's Sound Agricultural Company

As the subsidiary enterprises of the Hudson's Bay Company increased in scope and volume of production, officials in London began raising questions concerning the wisdom and validity of such departures from the main business of the fur trade. A happy solution to the questions raised was found by none other than McLoughlin himself. When in London during 1838–39, the doctor proposed to the Governor and Committee meeting at Hudson's Bay House that there should be formed a separate concern devoted exclusively to agriculture. According to a prospectus describing the plan, such a concern would be styled Puget's Sound Agricultural Company; it would be capitalized at £200,000 (roughly one million dollars) and the stockholders of the Hudson's Bay Company would become stockholders of the new organization. John H. Pelly, Andrew Colvile (for whom Fort Colvile and subsequently the city of Colville [2] were named), and George Simpson were to be the governing agents, but it would be managed directly by McLoughlin at Fort Vancouver. Legally, therefore, the Puget's Sound Agricultural Company was to become what Simpson declared "an off-shoot of the Hudson's Bay Company," and what in the United States is termed a subsidiary. The prospectus specifically proposed that this new company was to be organized for "the raising of flocks and herds, with a view to the production of wool, hides and tallow, and also for the cultivation of other agricultural produce, . . ."

Its officers were not only to raise and distribute livestock and agricultural produce within the Columbia District but also to trade with Alaska, the Sandwich Islands, and possibly California. Hides, horns, tallow, and wool would be exported to England, to utilize available space in the Hudson's Bay Company supply ships returning to their home ports. Regardless of its objectives, official approval was given and Puget's Sound Agricultural Company was a going concern by the end of 1839.

The region selected for operations lay between the headwaters of the Cowlitz River and the southern tip of Puget Sound, an area measuring 167,040 acres. Choice of this baronial acreage was in many respects a happy one. The soil produced good grass, the region was accessible to sea-borne commerce; transecting the estate were important overland trails which connected Fort Vancouver headquarters with Puget Sound and many northern posts, and east-west trails extended across the Cascades to upper Columbia River posts. There was more than ample rainfall in this area; fresh water streams were abundant; thick evergreen forests covering the surrounding hills offered an unlimited supply of timber to those who were about to undertake this large-scale venture.

Two farms were to be established, one near the Cowlitz River Landing to be known as Cowlitz Farm, and the other

---

[2] Note that Americans changed the spelling of this place name.

to serve as headquarters for both, at or around the previously established Fort Nisqually, to be known as Nisqually Farm. Chosen to manage the Puget's Sound Agricultural Company under McLoughlin's general supervision was the capable and engaging Scot, Dr. William Fraser Tolmie, M.D., University of Glasgow, founder of and, at the time of his selection, the Chief Trader at Fort Nisqually. Amiability, courage, and resourcefulness were his dominant characteristics. A foreman, blacksmith, carpenter, several herdsmen, and a desired number of farm hands were hired to work for Dr. Tolmie. Some of the farm workers came directly from England, under terms which obliged them to be married, and to remain on the job for five years. Passage "out" was charged against the employees at the farms.

For stocking the farms, the Hudson's Bay Company simply transferred to the account of Puget's Sound Agricultural Company practically all of its livestock and farm implements. In short, the Hudson's Bay Company turned over to its new subsidiary lock, stock, and barrel its main farming business. In return the Puget's Sound Agricultural Company was not to engage in what was strictly speaking the fur trade.

Under Dr. Tolmie's direction the new undertaking developed with efficiency and speed. Buildings of "well-hewn" logs were constructed, soon giving to Cowlitz Farm the appearance of a sizeable village. Wilkes, who saw it in 1841, reported that the Company, though not without some difficulty, had met both its domestic obligations and the terms of its agreement to supply the Russians in Alaska with 15,000 bushels of grain and quantities of butter and cheese. During the summer of 1842 the farms packed 2,768 pounds of fine wool, 984 pounds of coarse wool, 72 pounds of black wool, 137 pounds of unclassified wool, and 78 pounds of Cheviot wool, all for exportation to England. In 1845 no less than 10,000 pounds of wool were sent to England. And to this were added hides, horns, and tallow.

Dr. Tolmie's "Journal of Occurrences" tells much about the everyday life at the establishments: how he got his "Cattle, horses, and Pigs . . . into order"; the plowing for "our Kitchen garden"; how "We now have for our new field near the small river 2000 fence poles"; the arrival from Vancouver of "the Express from the east of the Mountains"; how his men were "employed thrashing the pease — one busy at harrowing the new plowed field"; etc. These documents likewise allude to the repeated arrivals and departures of the Hudson's Bay ships, the *Beaver*, the *Mary Dare*, and the *Cadboro*.

At both Nisqually and Cowlitz profits from the sale of live-stock and produce were good and seldom if at all did losses exceed returns. The Puget's Sound Agricultural Company continued to operate, moreover, as was its right under the treaty, long after political sovereignty passed definitely into the hands of the United States. Americans, however, registered increasing protests against the concern; and as pressure for the liquidation of the Hudson's Bay Company property south of the forty-ninth parallel persistently increased, Puget's Sound Agricultural Company yielded to American pressure. In a settlement made between the American and British Governments in 1869 Hudson's Bay Company was awarded $650,000 for its holdings, $200,000 of which represented the value of the Puget's Sound Agricultural Company.

During the years that elapsed between the founding of Fort Vancouver and the passing of Nisqually from Company to private hands, the Hudson's Bay Company had contributed immeasurably to the future development of farming, ranching, and dairying in what is now the state of Washington. The concern cleared and improved hundreds of acres of land north of the Columbia River. It put crop raising beyond the experimental stage and made planting and sowing relatively easy for the Americans who followed. Fruit trees were introduced; cattle, sheep, and hogs were raised and new breeds, suitable to the area, were bred. By 1870 the Hudson's Bay Company gave reassurance to the 23,955 settlers then in Washington Territory that the region north of the Columbia was agriculturally rich.

Minor Subsidiaries

That Pacific Northwest waters teemed with huge, beautiful, and tasty red salmon was commonplace knowledge among mountain men. Nor did the fact that giant spruce, firs, cedars, and pines awaited the sharp blade of the woodsman's axe escape the attention of even the least imaginative of fur men who roamed this country. Here, indeed, were rich resources that were to become the area's principal sources of income.

It has been noted that Indians leaned very heavily on a fish diet, and that they also utilized available timber for both dwelling and canoe construction. From Indians Harmon and other Nor'westers learned how to dry and preserve salmon, although natives appeared not to distinguish between good and bad fish. By 1823 Hudson's Bay men at Fort George began to experiment with salmon as a possible article of export, and two years later Simpson favored adding it to the fur cargoes destined for Canton. With regard to lumber Simpson wrote to Captain Aemilius Simpson in 1828, that ". . . Timber Trade as a distinct branch of business would yield us large profits in proportion to the Tonnage employed therein." McLoughlin likewise favored experimenting in both salmon and lumber business, particularly in the California and Sandwich Island trade. Soon he planned the construction of a sawmill not far upstream from his Fort Vancouver headquarters.

The area near Fort Langley was regarded most suitable for catching and processing salmon. In 1827 the post's founder, McMillan, made his first large catch. As in the case of the fur trade, natives were inveigled into doing the actual work. For this purpose they used canoes, and boatloads of freshly caught salmon were taken to the beaches where still other Indians (usually women) cleaned, and often dried, the fish before delivery at the fort. In payment natives received commodities familiar to the fur trade.

So abundant were the salmon around Fort Langley that McMillan was prompted to boast: "We could trade at the door of our fort, I suppose, a million of dried salmon, if we chose — enough to feed all the people of Rupert's Land." Although this is perhaps an overstatement, in 1828 there were stored at Fort Langley 3,000 dried salmon and 16 tiers of salted salmon, and all told probably 20,000 fish had been acquired. By 1829 the salmon trade got under way, and each succeeding year showed a steady increase in this business. In 1830 nearly 300 barrels were prepared for shipment, and the peak was reached after 1845 when the annual salmon export from Fort Langley and other Fraser River fisheries is reported to have ranged between 1,000 and 2,000 barrels of salted and pickled salmon. In time this was supplemented by fishing done in the Columbia River where salmon was as abundant as in the Fraser River, but where the industry was not developed so rapidly. By the close of the period demand for this commodity existed in many parts of the world, including the Sandwich Islands, China, the United States, and England, with the best price for salted salmon being commanded in the Sandwich Islands. Since then the industry has enjoyed a remarkable growth. Always salmon has provided northwesterners with an important item in their diet, and to outsiders the popularity of this delectable-looking commodity has constantly increased.

Developments in the lumber business hinged mostly on the California market where 1,000 board feet brought from forty to fifty dollars. By 1828 McLoughlin had a small mill in operation about four to five miles above the Fort Vancouver headquarters. Ten years later this mill was completely rebuilt, and its capacity was so increased that its twenty-eight operators could turn out 2,400 feet of lumber daily. Writing to the London office in 1838, James Douglas declared that no less than 60,000 feet of one-inch boards were shipped to the Sandwich Islands with good profit. At best the market for lumber remained limited and output correspondingly small. And even at the Sandwich Islands, where prospects were once good, American and New Zealand competition lowered prices so much that the lumber trade, except in an exchange of boards for salt, became relatively negligible. At one time McLoughlin had taken steps toward the construction of a sawmill on the Willamette River, but the dismal foreign market caused him to abandon the project.

The list of Hudson's Bay Company subsidiary activities could well be expanded to include at least milling and distilling, the former playing an important role in meeting local needs for flour. But distilling McLoughlin gave up as a bad job after running off about 300 gallons of spirits. "I began to Distil in '33," he wrote, "but '36, finding the bad effects it had on our affairs I gave it over, and would recommend if possible never to attempt it again. . . ." All told, the total investments in agriculture, fishing, lumber, flour mills, and other subsidiaries to the fur trade amounted to nearly $200,000. By the late 1830s at least half the total investments of the Company in the Columbia District were charged to the account of industries and enterprises other than the fur trade. And to this one might append: these varied enterprises were in the long run of far greater importance to the continued growth and development of civilization in the Oregon country than the fur trade itself.

CHAPTER VI

American Ventures in the Fur Trade

Captains Lewis and Clark

NO HISTORY of the Oregon country would be complete without the story of the Lewis and Clark expedition. And no history of the American fur trade would have real meaning without inclusion of this famed journey to and from the mouth of the Columbia River, 1803–06. The idea of an expedition into the unknown, extreme western wilderness had long been a dream of the intellectually inquisitive Thomas Jefferson. He and his old friend and neighbor, Meriwether Lewis, discussed the possibility of just such a journey when the former was Secretary of State, but it was then considered inopportune.

The time for an expedition to the mouth of the Columbia River, however, seemed more propitious to Jefferson when as President on January 18, 1803, he asked Congress for, and was granted a niggardly $2,500 appropriation to extend the "geographical knowledge of our own continent." Although the expedition Jefferson had in mind was to be scientific in character, it was to be for the purpose of promoting American commerce, chiefly fur trade, with the Indians as far west as the Columbia basin.

With utmost confidence Jefferson turned to Lewis, at this time the President's private secretary, who with William Clark was to share the command of the exploring party. Meriwether Lewis was born near Charlottesville, Virginia, in 1774. He was well educated, had broad interests, and was not without considerable military experience and knowledge of the conditions of life on the frontier. William Clark, younger brother of George Rogers Clark, was born in 1770, also near

86]

Charlottesville in the President's native state. Both Clark and Lewis had known each other as youngsters; both had served with "Mad Anthony" Wayne in Indian campaigns; both had good, solid dependable qualities. Clark, more than Lewis, was intimately acquainted with western conditions. Each was a captain in the army.

The entire expedition, in fact, was in the nature of a military undertaking. Officers and men were to draw supplies and pay from the War Department (in this manner Jefferson found a way to supplement the small appropriation), and the men were to be subjected to strict military discipline imposed by the joint commanders, Lewis and Clark.

At a place in Illinois near St. Louis and the mouth of the Missouri River a winter encampment was established late in 1803. Recruits were given intensive training. Supplies and equipment were gathered during the winter months. On May 14, 1804, a party of forty-five persons [1] literally "hoisted sail" and began their long trek up the Missouri River by means of one large square-rigged flatboat, and two keel boats drawn by horses on the embankments. In a letter Lewis wrote to his mother from Fort Mandan, March 31, 1805, he described some of the difficulties experienced while ascending the muddy Missouri: "So far we have experienced more difficulties from the navigation of the Missouri than danger from the savages." He referred to falling banks, sand bars, partially concealed timbers, and the "turbid" quality of the water.

On board were many items useful as gifts for the Indians — red flannel, beads, brass wire, needles, handkerchiefs, silk ribbons, assorted fish hooks, and tobacco. Supplies for personal use of the party consisted of assorted foodstuffs, guns and ammunition, soap, and whiskey.

The Mandan Indian country (1,600 miles upstream) was reached by November, 1804, and there a winter encampment

---

[1] Membership of the party varied from time to time. Reuben G. Thwaites, editing the Lewis and Clark Journals, lists among those starting: Captains Lewis and Clark; Sergeants John Ordway, Nathaniel Pryor, Patrick Gass, and Charles Floyd; twenty-four privates, two of whom were sent back for misconduct; Clark's negro slave, York; and the remainder were *voyageurs* and frontiersmen. Later Sacajawea, an Indian woman, her husband, and her baby were added.

(near present Bismarck, North Dakota) was maintained until April, 1805, when the expedition again moved on toward the Pacific. During this encampment the party secured the services of a French Canadian named Charboneau, who understood the Hidatsa language, and his Indian wife, Sacajawea, who understood Shoshonean. Sacajawea had been born a Shoshonean on the west side of the Rockies. At an early age she had been taken east of these mountains to a place near the three forks of the Missouri River where she had been captured by enemy Indians who in turn had sold her to Charboneau. As a member of the Lewis and Clark expedition she performed many useful services. She had some familiarity with the country lying between the Mandans and her birthplace, and her help and ingenuity eased the problems connected with the march. There is, however, no reason for believing that Lewis and Clark could not have succeeded without her. Sacajawea must have been a woman of great endurance, for even though burdened by a child born to her shortly before the party left the Mandan camp, she was able to do well the tasks assigned to her. It is not necessary, as Professor C. S. Kingston has pointed out (see article listed in Recommended Readings), to embellish the facts concerning Sacajawea in order to accord her a high place among the women who helped to build the new United States.

In any event Captains Lewis and Clark and their intrepid party pushed through the Rocky and Bitterroot mountains following Clark's Fork of the Columbia (the most difficult part of the journey), and then finally down the lower Columbia River to its mouth. They reached the Pacific Ocean on November 15, 1805. Since leaving St. Louis the party had traveled four thousand miles.

The winter of 1805–06 was spent at a place near present Seaside, Oregon, where a crude fort, named Clatsop, was built for shelter from the continual coastal rains and for protection from the Indians. Only in the journals of Lewis and Clark can one catch the flavor of this epochal adventure, as for example in the following excerpt written by Captain Clark at Fort Clatsop on Christmas Eve, 1805: "hard rain at Different times last night and all this day without intermition. men all employed in finishing their huts and moveing into them. . . . Our Store of Meat entirely Spoiled, . . .

On Christmas Day he wrote:

Some rain at different times last night and showers of hail with intervales of fair starr light This morning at day we were saluted by all our party under our winders, a Shout and a Song. after brackfast we divided our tobacco which amounted to 2 Carrots, one half we gave to the party who used Tobacco those who did not we gave a Handkerchief as a present, The day proved showery all day, the Ind⁵ left us this evening. all our party moved into their huts. we dried some of our wet goods. I reved a present of a Fleeshe Hoserey [fleece hosiery] vest draws & socks of Capt Lewis, pᵣ Mockersons of Whitehouse, a small Indian basket of Guterich, & 2 Doz weasels tales of the Squar of Shabono, & some black roots of the Indians G. D. saw a Snake passing across the parth Our Diner to day consisted of pore Elk boiled, spilt [spoiled] fish & some roots, a bad Christmass diner worm day.

The return journey was begun March 23, 1806. The party returned along the route taken going west, with two exceptions. Having recrossed the Rocky Mountains, the party split while Lewis explored the Marias River and Clark the Yellowstone, and then reassembling, proceeded down the Missouri to St. Louis where they arrived September 23, 1806, having suffered but one death and one desertion.

An accurate and full appraisal of the Lewis and Clark expedition is difficult. Certainly it aroused the interest of Americans in the Oregon country; it strengthened the claims of the United States to this region; and it led, with very little delay, to an expansion of American fur trade in the direction of the Far West.

Precursors of Astor

Since Colonial days fur trade had been an important part of American economic life, and, as in Canada, the trader was always in the vanguard of westward expansion. Not, however, until the turn of the nineteenth century, did American fur traders begin a serious penetration of the trans-Mississippi West. And not until the return of the Lewis and Clark party in 1806 did the rich prospects from upper Missouri and the Oregon country trade whet the appetites of both eastern investors and western American Mountain Men.

Glowing as were the reports on the Lewis and Clark expedition, the fact remains that the overland trail to the valley of the Columbia was long and tortuous. It is therefore not surprising that the first approach to this valley was made by sea. The ship used was the *Albatross*, and her captain was Nathan Winship, one of three remarkable brothers interested in this venture. The *Albatross* had set her course from Boston; during May, 1810, her captain skillfully piloted his way over the perilous Columbia River bar.

Winship and his men sailed upstream about forty-five miles, and at an inviting meadow on the south bank they lashed the *Albatross* to trees and began to build a two-story log fort and to plant a garden. But a flood, doubtless caused by melting snow in the mountain hinterland, brought the river over its banks, inundated the garden, and caused the men to seek a new location for their fort. No sooner had this been done than the threats by the Indians caused Captain Winship to look for still another site. Before this could be found the much more ambitious, but similar, project of John Jacob Astor was under way, and caused the Winships to lose heart and give up their venture as a bad job.

Astor's Vision of Empire

Even while the Winship expedition was en route around the Horn (perhaps long before), Astor had his plans well laid. The famous New York merchant had long had an interest in the fur business, and had been irked greatly by the knowledge that such British firms as the North West Company and the Michilimackinac Company had powerful and strangling tentacles in his adopted United States. Astor knew that American furs flowed into Canada, and that at least seventy-five per cent of the furs purchased in the United States came from the British controlled province to the north. This proud, calculating merchant prince was especially humiliated to be obliged to buy his furs in Montreal at outlandish prices, and he thought the time had come to give battle. He would organize powerful American companies that he hoped in five years would extend their control of the United States fur trade to the very shores of the Pacific Ocean.

Astor was a man of great vision. He planned to do his job on a grand scale. New York, New Orleans, St. Louis, and, as plans unfolded, the mouth of the Columbia River would be important entrepôts. These would be connected by ocean, river, and overland routes of staggering lengths. He would have others share the risks, and thus it was that in 1808 Astor made known his plans to New York's Governor DeWitt Clinton, and in part to President Jefferson, with a view toward securing a charter. Jefferson approved Astor's plans (and, of course, they concerned the interests of the American government in the Oregon country); and with the blessings of the New York legislature and its chief executive, on April 6, 1808, Astor secured his charter. The organization was to be known as the American Fur Company; its capital stock was a million dollars.

Astor's next important move in the direction of his ultimate goal was to form the Pacific Fur Company in New York, June 23, 1810, to operate in the Oregon country. The articles of agreement of the Pacific Fur Company were numerous. Astor was to be the first partner, and associated with him were Alexander McKay, Donald McKenzie, Duncan McDougal, Wilson Price Hunt, David Stuart, Robert McLellan, John Clarke, and others. Funds advanced should not exceed $400,-000; there would be a hundred shares with Astor holding fifty which could, if Astor chose, be made over to the American Fur Company. Power was to rest with the founder, who in a step toward taking action on the northwest coast, chose Hunt to reside there as agent for the Pacific Fur Company.

Sagas of Endurance and Suffering

Astor's plans called for sending two expeditions, one by sea and one by land. These expeditions were before the end of 1810 to go to the Columbia River region, and establish a post. McDougal, Stuart, and McKay joined those going by sea aboard the ill-starred ship, the *Tonquin*, commanded by the stern and irascible Captain Jonathan Thorn, veteran of United States naval operations in Algiers. Thorn's ship set sail from New York on September 8th, and reached the mouth of the Columbia River on March 22, 1811, by way of the Horn and Hawaii. Unfortunately, the voyage had been filled with bickering and feuding between Captain Thorn, his crew, and his passengers.

A grim and tragic pall hovered over this ship. In his effort to find a passable channel across the Columbia Bar at Cape Disappointment, Thorn had lowered a "jolly-boat" with first mate Ebenezer D. Fox and four men aboard. High winds were whipping the waves to ominous heights, and soon the men vanished from view. On the following morning one of three boats lowered capsized and three additional men (one a Sandwich Islander) were lost. In due time, though, the 290-ton *Tonquin* bounced and tacked its way through the treacherous channel to a safe and protected cove midway between Tongue Point and Point George on the south bank of the Columbia where passengers and supplies were unloaded, and where Fort Astoria was presently to emerge.

Shortly after this precarious landing, Captain Thorn with 22 of his men aboard sailed northward. En route he took aboard Lamayzie, an Indian interpreter. He proceeded to Clayoquot Harbor (a few miles south of historic Nootka), Vancouver Island. Here in Templar Channel, Thorn made an ill-fated attempt to begin the coasting trade with the Indians. Scarcely had dealings begun when Thorn struck a chief with whom he had been in disagreement concerning the value of furs. Smarting from this "insult" the Indian planned to get vengeance by killing the crew and gaining possession of the ship. Subsequently when at least fifty of the Indians had been permitted aboard ship the slaughter began. Concealed knives were suddenly flashed by the natives and caught Thorn and his men unprepared to give battle. Lewis, a ship's clerk, was the first victim; then came the notable Alexander McKay, whose battered body was tossed overboard. Thorn's only weapon was a pocket knife with which (so say some of the accounts) he ripped open the bellies of four assailants before he too succumbed. Leaning in exhaustion over the tiller wheel Thorn was given a blow from behind and his lifeless body followed McKay's.

Escaping attack for the moment were seven sailors who were in the rigging above and who, fearing that their turn was imminent, made a desperate effort to reach the cabin where guns and ammunition were available. Two were killed in the attempt, and of the five who made it one was severely wounded. Gunfire through the skylight and companionway now raked the deck, and the Indians fled. Accounts as to what then happened vary. But sometime later four of the five sailors escaped from the *Tonquin*. Not until the following morning, however, did the cautious but eager savages return to the ship.

What next occurred was an explosion, and can best be told in the words of Lamayzic, the Indian interpreter, who during the attack jumped overboard and surrendered himself as a slave to Indian women standing by in their canoes. "I was on the shore when the explosion took place," said the Indian, whose words Franchère admits having rendered into "civilized expression," and "saw the great volume of smoke burst forth in the spot where the ship had been, and high in the air above, arms, legs, heads and bodies, flying in every direction." About two hundred Indians were killed; many others were wounded. "I have told you the truth," concluded the Indian interpreter, "and hope you will acquit me of having in any way participated in that bloody affair."

It was the opinion of Ross Cox, clerk and historian for the Company who later wrote about the event, that the barricaded crewmen deliberately planned to take this "terrible revenge," and others were of the opinion that since only four escaped (Cox says three), the fifth mortally wounded, decided to remain aboard to expend his life as dearly as possible by lighting the nine thousand pounds of powder in the ship's magazine. The truth will never be known, for those who escaped the *Tonquin* were subsequently found on a near-by beach and were put to death by wrathful Indian survivors.

The second act of this drama concerns the overland expedition led by Wilson Price Hunt. Departure from St. Louis had been delayed until March 12, 1811. The men ascended the Missouri to a point near the present North and South Dakota line, and then turned westward through present Wyoming until the Snake River was reached. From this point the course taken was not unlike that of the future Oregon Trail. They crossed barren and rugged stretches, did some needless meandering, and endured great suffering. Not until January, 1812, did the first contingent of the expedition straggle into Astoria. The coming of these reinforcements was welcomed by those already struggling against odds to erect a fort. The safe arrival in May, 1812, of the supply ship *Beaver* with both additional men and goods gave further encouragement. Bit by bit initial obstacles were being overcome. When, as previously stated, David Thompson of the North West Company paddled into view, he viewed the American flag flying above the crude yet defiant Fort Astoria. Thompson had feared as much, for it was by then apparent that Americans were making a strong bid for at least a share of Oregon's fur trade and perhaps for the ultimate control of the Oregon country itself.

Astor's Achievements and Failures

In their pursuit of the inland trade the Astorians met with both successes and disappointments. In keeping with custom, they made a beginning at gardening and at livestock raising. A small trading schooner, the *Dolly,* was built and launched. Partner Robert Stuart, and Donald McGillis, clerk, had begun trading operations by leading a party up the Willamette River in December, 1811; they were followed during April of the next year by Donald McKenzie and William Matthews, who probably reached the swiftly flowing tributary of the Willamette now bearing McKenzie's name. These parties were in turn followed (late in 1812) by William Wallace and J. C. Halsey, clerks, who are believed to have reached the source of the Willamette River; and again in 1813 by clerks John Reed and Alfred Seton. Reports on the Willamette Valley by these men were on the enthusiastic side, both with regard to the supply of beaver and to the abundance of wild game. No complete record of their accomplishments existed, but according to Franchère, whose duty was to keep records, Wallace and Halsey returned to Fort Astoria with 17 packs of furs and 32 bales of dried venison.

By March, 1812, Robert Stuart and McGillis had returned from the Willamette. New and important plans which Stuart was to execute without delay were awaiting his return. Before the end of March he was seen heading a party of seventeen men paddling up the Columbia. Three of these men, including Stuart, were to enter present-day Idaho in search of goods cached by Hunt's overlanders; a second party of six was to proceed to the East with messages for Astor; Stuart and the seven remaining would convey goods to Okanogan where David Stuart, uncle of Robert, had established Fort Okanogan during the preceding winter. An encounter with Indians, however, altered these plans, and the entire expedition continued in one body to Fort Okanogan; from there they returned to Astoria with David Stuart's winter catch of furs. Including the furs brought in by McKenzie, Franchère reported 140 packs.

On June 29, 1812, Robert Stuart again set out from Astoria. With six men, all veterans of Hunt's westward expedition, he proceeded directly toward the East, passing through the obscure South Pass by a course so much like that followed by future thousands of Oregon-bound immigrants. Robert Stuart has been called by some writers the discoverer of the South Pass. Actually, it required much subsequent investigation to determine the true nature of the terrain in the vicinity of the Pass and to establish it as the best place to cross the Continental Divide. Credit for "discovering" the South Pass must, therefore, be divided among many American fur traders. After considerable adventure, recounted in Stuart's own Narratives, the party arrived at St. Louis April 30, 1813. From there he went on to New York to report to Astor.

The list of achievements does not end here. In addition to Fort Okanogan (first American structure built in the present state of Washington) the trading posts of She Whaps was established at the junction of the branches of the Thompson River not far from Kamloops, B. C. In 1812 John Clarke, an

Astorian, built Fort Spokane (near the present city of Spokane, Washington) not far from the North West Company's Spokane House, built two years before.

Unfortunately, forces beyond the control of one man, even Astor, began to play havoc with a venture destined to failure. Before mid-year, 1812, Americans were once again at war with Great Britain. To the far-off Astorians the question henceforth was not competition with the Nor'westers, but the duration of time before the arrival of a British man-of-war. Astor did what he could to strengthen his Columbia outpost, even attempting to have supplies sent to it from England, but this plan failed to work. In spite of the risk of capture he dispatched the supply ship, the *Lark*, but this ship was lost. On land as well as at sea, the loss of life (ultimately sixty-five or more) was heavier than Astor could bear. As Hiram M. Chittenden, an authority on the fur trade, viewed it, "there was not a could-have-been in the whole transaction that did not turn out adversely. . . ."

News of war reached Fort Astoria early in 1813, at a time when Nor'westers had begun to make full use of their many advantages in their struggle with the American competitors. Now that war had come the British concern sought to strengthen its position by securing what the Astorians feared most — naval support. The British Admiralty acceded to this request and took appropriate steps to protect British interests in north Pacific waters. Though fully informed of the British intentions, neither Astor nor the Government of the United States was in any position to checkmate such a move. At Astoria mere news of the outbreak of war was enough to convince the partners that the post would have to be abandoned.

The summer of 1813 was set for abandonment, but as this deadline approached, the partners postponed the date and bargained with the Nor'westers (by now low on supplies and willing to negotiate) to divide the area between them. This, however, proved to be merely a postponement of the evil day, for when news reached the respective parties that a British man-of-war might arrive in Oregon waters at any time, liquidation proceedings were at once renewed. With the advantages then weighted heavily on the side of the Nor'westers the Astorians agreed to sell out, lock, stock, and barrel, to their rivals. The latter, on the other hand, were eager to buy, rather than await the actual arrival of the frigate, for fear that naval occupation of the fort might make of it a prize of war, and as such deprive the British fur trading company of ownership of the desperately needed supplies stored behind the log palisades of Fort Astoria.

By agreement reached in October, 1813, the Pacific Fur Company sold its various properties to the North West Company at prices to be worked out largely on the basis of prime cost. The amount finally paid the Pacific Fur Company was $58,291.02. Thus, as Kenneth Porter, Astor's biographer, aptly phrased it: "for all practical purposes, the careers of both the Pacific Fur Company and Astoria came to an end."

That the Pacific Fur Company suffered tremendous losses there is no doubt; that it sold out to the British under partial duress (a fact that gave the Astor interest a basis for subsequent claim) there is little room for doubt. On November 30, 1813, the armed British sloop *Raccoon* appeared at Astoria. She had been escorting the *Isaac Todd* (also assigned to the Columbia) and had raced ahead to take possession of Fort Astoria; formal occupation by the commander took place on December 13.

Chittenden remarked that "It is no flight of fancy . . . to say that if the Astorian enterprise had succeeded, the course of empire on the American continent would have been altogether different than it has been." He thought that had Astor succeeded, no part of the Oregon country would today be British. The Astor experiment in any event must not be regarded as entirely negative in its results. For one thing, not all was lost to the Americans. Under provisions of the Treaty of Ghent, American ownership of the property was recognized on October 6, 1818, and the whole adventure was to be one of many factors which strengthened American claims to Oregon. The Oregon country, moreover, became widely publicized, especially by the appearance of Washington Irving's *Astoria*.

The Jedediah Smith Disaster

Astor's west coast adventure was followed by a fifteen-year lull in American trading in the Oregon country, except for an occasional upper Missouri River party, such as those expeditions of General William H. Ashley, which for good measure pushed a little west across the Divide. The importance of this inadvertent penetration of the trans-Rocky Mountain area should not be minimized, for activity of this kind led to the discovery of suitable mountain passes, to the rounding out of the Oregon Trail, and to the conviction that good pelts were to be found abundantly in the valley of the Snake. This lull offered the British golden opportunity to consolidate their strength. But in the summer of 1828 there staggered up to the gates of Fort Vancouver one of the greatest of American Mountain Men, Jedediah Smith. He was followed soon after by three other distracted American traders.

Smith and his men had come for help, for a terrible calamity had occurred. Smith with a party of traders (successors to Ashley), had entered California from the Great Basin in 1826 and again in the following year. On his latter visit to California, however, Mexican officials ordered him out of the province. With a party of 19 men and about 300 horses and mules he made his departure through the northern exit. The party had followed up the Sacramento River, trapping as it went, and at the upper reaches of the river had turned westward through what are now Trinity, Humboldt, and Del Norte counties. When it reached the coast, the expedition followed the shore as far north as the Umpqua River in Oregon. At this point Smith planned to turn inland, strike the Willamette Valley, and then make his way to Fort Vancouver. But while thus encamped at the river mouth, the party was unexpectedly attacked by Kelawatset Indians. Only Smith and his three companions who came to Fort Vancouver for help survived the murderous assault, and after much privation reached the Hudson's Bay Company headquarters.

Large quantities of furs, said to number 780 beaver, more

than 50 large otter, and others which had been in possession of the party, were taken by the Indians, but these the Hudson's Bay Company recovered by means of a punitive expedition led by Alexander R. McLeod. This retaliatory raid, moreover, resulted in the death of twenty-one Indians, the destruction of two villages, forty-six canoes, and much other Indian property. Smith spent the winter of 1828–29 at the fort, where he sold his furs to McLeod, and when spring came he moved eastward with two checks from the doctor, totaling about $20,000, in his pocket.

The Adventurous Captain Bonneville

Smith's appearance in Oregon was at best an interlude, and it is doubtful whether he ever planned to establish his company even semi-permanently in the country. Not until the expedition of Captain Benjamin L. E. Bonneville, 1832–35, does another American figure at all conspicuously in affairs pertaining to the fur trade.

The Bonneville party consisted, according to his own count, of 121 men, who with a wide assortment of goods packed in twenty wagons left Fort Osage for the West April 30, 1832. The leader, Captain Bonneville ("Old Bonny," as his friends called him), had recently received a leave from the Army "for the purpose of . . . exploring the country to the Rocky Mountains and beyond." Just what the ulterior motive of the Bonneville expedition was is not and may never be known. He may have sought to explore for its own sake; but perhaps, too, for the sake of the army. Again, he may have had simply a yearning to carry on fur trade. At least it is in the capacity of a trader that he is considered here.

By late summer of 1832 Bonneville's adventurous band of Americans penetrated the Rockies, passed through Jackson's Hole and Pierre's Hole, crossed the Divide into Oregon Territory, and proceeded to a point three miles below the confluence of the Salmon River forks. There, on September 26, on the west bank of the Salmon, they began to erect their winter quarters, and by their presence on the outer perimeter of the Oregon country constituted a renewed challenge to British interests which by that time had become thoroughly entrenched.

During the autumn months Bonneville's hunters established friendly intercourse with the Nez Percé, Flathead, and Pend d'Oreille Indians, and decidedly unfriendly contacts with the ever-surly Blackfeet. Friendly tribes gladly assisted in the search for buffalo meat, which, reported Bonneville, natives brought into camp in great quantities. The generous natives were not, however, adverse to being ravens at the feast, and they remained merrily in the Bonneville camp until all food donations had been devoured. Through the winter, in fact at all times, Bonneville found it necessary to have his well-armed hunters constantly at work.

The party had come to this region, at least partly, for the purpose of trade, and through the spring and summer months of 1833 trappers and traders operated along the upper reaches of the Snake River. In this region the surprised and disappointed Bonneville men met a rival American party, led by Milton G. Sublette and J. B. Gervais of the Rocky Mountain Fur Company; on their way back East, they encountered Nathaniel Wyeth and a companion. All told, Bonneville spent three years in the mountains, operating on both sides of the Divide. During the summer of 1834 he and his men achieved the farthest penetration into the Oregon country. On March 4 the Bonneville party reached the Hudson's Bay Company post at Fort Walla Walla, managed at that time by Chief Trader Pierre C. Pambrun.

The British trader received the Americans very cordially — he even traded a roll of tobacco and some drygoods for furs (much to Dr. McLoughlin's regret) — but Pambrun refused, in fact, he did not have sufficient goods, to re-outfit his rivals. Pambrun was unduly maligned by Bonneville for this refusal. Explaining the encounter, Dr. McLoughlin wrote his home office that Pambrun had sold some goods to Bonneville at "Freemens prices," when they should have been sold at retail prices. Moreover, wrote McLoughlin: ". . . our Stores were low," and the goods on the shelves were sorely needed for the Indian trade. The thwarted Bonneville retraced his steps for a time, but the following July he and twenty-three of his men pushed across the Blue Mountains and reached the Columbia River about fifty miles below Fort Walla Walla. Bonneville had hoped to engage the Chinooks in trade, but found them loath to desert the Hudson's Bay Company for what was seemingly a fly-by-night affair. Reluctantly, therefore, he and his men turned back toward the Snake River Basin, spent the winter in the Bear River region of eastern Wyoming, and during the following spring returned to the states where his expedition ended in August of 1835.

Captain Bonneville and his men had been gone, in fact lost to the outside world, for three years and four months. "Old Bonny" had been AWOL for more than a year. Given up for dead, his name had been stricken from the army rolls, and only with the aid of Old Hickory was the supposed deceased taken back into active service. In 1852 Bonneville came to Oregon again. He was ordered to lay out and take command of Fort Vancouver Barracks. It is interesting to note that Captain Bonneville should be in command of a military post near the crumbling palisades of the once-powerful Hudson's Bay Company post which less than a score of years before had thwarted the efforts of this enterprising American trader and explorer.

As a leader of men Bonneville was a great success, but in other respects he was a failure. Throughout his experiences Bonneville showed himself earnestly interested in the fur trade (more so than in exploration), but in this respect his expedition was another American failure representing the loss of many thousands of dollars. His explorations were of little value, save perhaps the journey of his Lieutenant, Joseph R. Walker, who crossed the great interior basin and entered California. For years all that reminded the Oregon citizens of the adventures of Captain Bonneville was a railroad station on the south side of the famous Columbia River Cascades. But at this site there is now located the giant and magnificent United States Government dam bearing the explorer's name, an honor perhaps more generous than is deserved, yet one that is a lasting reminder of early American interest in Oregon.

Nathaniel Wyeth — "A Visionary and a Failure"

Within two weeks following Captain Bonneville's departure from Fort Osage, another trading party, led by Nathaniel Wyeth of Cambridge, Massachusetts, then twenty-nine years old, left Independence for the Columbia River Valley. Wyeth, by profession an ice merchant, was totally without experience in the fur trade. But this in no way deterred the man's unbounded determination and enthusiasm which had in part been fired by the imaginative pro-Oregon writings of Hall J. Kelley, who was then forming the Oregon Colonization Society. During the winter of 1831–32 Wyeth organized a joint-stock company for exploring, trading, trapping, and salmon fishing and processing in Oregon. Like Astor, Wyeth planned to dispatch a supply ship to the Columbia River by way of the Horn, and to have the main party proceed overland to the same river valley where a trading post would be established.

During this winter the brig *Sultana*, laden with Wyeth's supplies, set sail for the Columbia, while overlanders left Boston by mid-March, 1832. The latter proceeded to Baltimore where four men were added to make the total number about twenty-five. From there the party traveled westward to St. Louis, thence to Independence, Missouri, where they joined forces with a party then being formed by Captain William L. Sublette to go to the Rocky Mountain Fur Company's rendezvous at Pierre's Hole. The combined expeditions left Independence on May 12, following a westward course along the dreary, warm, muddy, and "foul" Platte River. The travelers suffered from lack of good water and shortages of food within the very sight, to use the words of Wyeth's cousin John, of "frightful droves" of buffalo. Along the trail no less than fourteen of Wyeth's men deserted. The remainder of the combined parties reached Pierre's Hole on July 8th. From here west through the country of the Blackfeet the Wyeth party, in company with one led by Milton G. Sublette, after savage encounters with Indians managed to reach the Snake River, cross the Blue Mountains, and descend to the Columbia River at Fort Walla Walla on October 14.

Wyeth was warmly received by Chief Trader Pambrun, and after a five-day stay moved on to Fort Vancouver where he arrived on the twenty-ninth. There he learned that the *Sultana* had not yet arrived; actually it had hit a reef along the coast of South America and had sunk. To Wyeth this meant at least temporary disaster to his entire scheme, and on November 19 he granted his men their request to be allowed to shift for themselves. Wyeth was, as he himself wrote, ". . . afloat on the great sea of life without stay or support." He spent the winter as a guest of Dr. John McLoughlin, with whom he was to have competed, and then made a trip up the Willamette River, and laid plans to re-establish his business. During the spring of 1833 he accompanied a Hudson's Bay Company brigade eastward, meeting Bonneville en route, and on November 7 reached his home at Cambridge.

Wyeth was not easily dismayed by his failure. He was eager to try again; he had, in fact, on his return home, made a definite contract with Milton G. Sublette and Thomas Fitzpatrick, agreeing to deliver to them during the following year $3,000 worth of supplies. Thus during the winter of 1833–34 Wyeth once again was making plans, which in addition to fur trade called for salmon fishing operations on the lower Columbia. And once again a supply ship, this time the *May Dacre,* was outfitted and in January, 1834, set sail for the Horn. At Boston he organized what was called the Columbia River Fishing and Trading Company, financed by Boston merchants. Seventy traders, hunters, trappers, the Philadelphia scientists Thomas Nuttall and John K. Townsend, and the missionaries Jason and Daniel Lee, along with 250 horses, made up the second overland expedition which Wyeth led westward from Independence on the following April 28th. When they reached the Green River rendezvous June 19th, they found a scene of wild disorder, with "whooping, and howling, and quarrelling," wrote the scientist Townsend. Mounted Indians dashed to and fro "yelling like fiends" and the "barking and baying of savage wolf-dogs, and the incessant cracking of rifles and carbines, render our camp a perfect bedlam." To the scientist and the missionaries this scene was revolting. To Wyeth, on the other hand, the rendezvous was simply an institution that was useful in the promotion of trade.

Fitzpatrick, however, broke his part of the bargain made during the previous summer; and Wyeth, left with a surplus of goods on hand, proceeded to build and man a trading post near the confluence of the Portneuf and Snake rivers, which he named Fort Hall. At this post, afterwards to become famous, he placed his goods on sale then went on to his main objective, the mouth of the Willamette River, where he arrived on September 14, 1834, one day ahead of the *May Dacre*, which had survived excruciating hardships at sea.

At last Wyeth had his one big chance to fulfill his many plans with respect to the Oregon country, even though the *May Dacre* arrived too late in the season to play much part in the anticipated salmon trade. Instead, the ship was sent out to the Sandwich Islands to trade with lumber forming part of her cargo. On Wapato Island (now Sauvies Island) in the mouth of the Willamette River, Wyeth built his second post, Fort William. With Dr. McLoughlin he apparently made a deal not to interfere with the Hudson's Bay Company trade, with the understanding that the English company would not interfere with Wyeth's fishing operations and horse trade. And ". . . I believe," wrote McLoughlin on September 30, 1835, "Captain Wyeth has most honourably Kept his word."

Wyeth did his best to succeed, but again misfortunes befell the eager and industrious New Englander. Desertions occurred, some goods were stolen, and his Fort Hall trader drank up his profits. Oregon rains seemingly disabled a third of the men, including Wyeth himself, and no less than seventeen died during the first winter. Although the Hudson's Bay Company lived up to its part of the bargain with Wyeth, it did not encourage American competition. By the very terms of the arrangement, McLoughlin wrote his home office, ". . . I prevented his [Wyeth's] Interfering with Us in Any place where we had no previous opposition and I did this without Actually giving up any thing as though we did not Raise the price of Salmon We opposed him as much as was Necessary." He adds, ". . . We may be certain Wyeths Losses are Great.

. . ." Many other factors combined to defeat Wyeth's most strenuous and praiseworthy efforts, not least of which were sickness and death. "I have been very sick," he wrote his wife from the Columbia River, September 22, 1835, "but have got well, and shall be on my way to the mountains, to winter at Fort Hall, in about six days. I expect to be home about the first of November, 1836. . . . We have lost by drowning, disease, and warfare seventeen persons up to this date, and fourteen now sick."

Thus defeated at every turn, broken in spirit and in health, Wyeth beat a final retreat. Fort William was leased and Fort Hall was sold to the Hudson's Bay Company; debts were paid and with a moderate number of pelts Wyeth returned to Cambridge where he successfully re-entered the ice business and lived until his death in 1856 in the house in which he had been born fifty-four years before.

Wyeth's failure, like that of his American predecessors, was due in part to inexperience, in part to his inability to compete with the more resourceful and better entrenched British rivals. Moreover, the American government failed to support Wyeth, as it failed to support Winship, Astor, and Bonneville; whereas the British government, by virtue of having granted a charter which created a monopoly, was in effect aiding the Honourable Company.

To dismiss Wyeth completely on this note of failure would be unfair. Like others before him, and like many who followed, this son of a Harvard graduate, this Cambridge ice dealer, did much to advertise the country west of the Rocky Mountains. Fully a decade before Frémont, the man who really only marked the road to Oregon, was hailed as the great pathfinder, Wyeth had traversed this already well-trodden trail four times. Although the self-effacing New Englanders scorned publicity, their experience was important to other immigrants who later came to the Willamette Valley. Moreover, some of Wyeth's men chose to remain in the valley of the Willamette, and several, unlike the Astorians who remained, turned their efforts toward tilling the deep, rich, dark soil that was theirs for the taking. On such developments alone Wyeth subsequently based the contention, and with considerable merit, that he was Oregon's first successful colonizer.

Wyeth's retirement from the region south of the Columbia River was soon to be followed by a general northward withdrawal of the Hudson's Bay Company. Thus south of the forty-ninth parallel the fur trade era was ending. In retrospect one notes that the Oregon country was the last frontier reached by fur traders who as early as the seventeenth century had begun to push westward across the broad North American continent. British inland fur traders, as represented by the Nor'westers, were the first to reach the Pacific Northwest. The North West Company was merged with the Hudson's Bay Company, and in this capacity British interests remained dominant in Oregon until the final settlement of the boundary question in 1846. American interests, as represented by Astor, Smith, Bonneville, and Wyeth, tried to compete with the British, but failed. The fur trade was immensely important in Pacific Northwest history. Aside from valuable resources extracted from the region, fur traders, notably Hudson's Bay men, were responsible for its agricultural and industrial beginnings. They attracted worldwide attention to the region, and, as will be discussed in the ensuing chapters, they paved the way for later settlement. And lastly, the fur trading era — rich in personalities and adventures — has a glamor and aura about it that have given to the old Oregon country a rich and exciting past.

The side-wheeler Lot Whitcomb

Cascades Portage Railroad. The locomotive was called the "Pony."

Portland Harbor scene in the nineties. Note the double Victorian spars on the sailing vessel in the foreground. These were introduced in England honoring Queen Victoria.

SCENES OF EARLY DAY TRANSPORTATION
Courtesy Donald Bates, Portland, Oregon

CHIEF JOSEPH

From a painting by J. H. Sharp (1902). Photo in the Wanamaker Collection, Indiana University Museum of Anthropology, Professor George K. Neumann, Director.

CHAPTER VII

Wending Westward

"First Families" of the Willamette Valley

FROM THE RANKS of fur traders came the first Oregon settlers. For reasons best known to themselves, several members of American fur trading parties and retiring servants of the North West Company and the Hudson's Bay Company established themselves as farmers. Most frequently they chose places in the fertile lower Willamette Valley, although the Walla Walla Valley, the Puget Sound area, the Rogue River Valley, and numerous other places became the residence of many.

When Astor's Pacific Fur Company ceased functioning, some of its servants remained for a while in the employ of the North West Company, and then they, too, became settlers; others simply shifted for themselves and sooner or later settled on the land. Three of these died too soon to be considered "permanent settlers," but the names of fifteen former Astorians have been so classified. One was William Cannon, a Pennsylvanian by birth, whose name appears on many important documents relative to Willamette Valley history until his death in 1854. Other early settlers were Joseph Gervais, also well known for his participation in the affairs of the Willamette Valley, also remembered is the heroine, Marie Dorion. The early presence of these settlers [1] (most of whom, to be sure, were French Canadians) emphasizes the fact that the missionaries did not, as one might be led to believe, constitute the first sizeable group of settlers in the Oregon country.

[1] Others in this list were Alexander Carson, John Coxe — a Hawaiian, Jean Baptiste Dubreuil, "Sailor Jack," Louis L. Bonte, Michel Laframbois, Etienne Lucier, Jean McKay, Francois Payette, and George Ramsey.

From the ranks of other American parties, such as those of Nathaniel Wyeth and Ewing Young, and from free traders came additional numbers. Young personally remained in Oregon and turned to farming. As was the custom on the frontier, most of these men had chosen Indian mates, and from these unions emerged the "first families" of the Willamette Valley.

The Great Trail to Oregon

Strictly speaking, no one person or party discovered the Oregon Trail. In 1805–06 Lewis and Clark covered the extreme western portion of what was to be the famous immigrant route leading from Independence to the Willamette Valley. As previously stated, the "discoverers" of the South Pass (a great gap in the Rocky Mountains, located in southwestern Wyoming) are not actually known; likewise, founders of still other portions of the Trail which came into general use have not been definitely established. Between the years 1832 and 1836 Bonneville and Wyeth led their expeditions to Oregon over this course, and not long thereafter the Oregon Trail became a household term in West-conscious America.

Actually, this route was not clearly defined. Unlike modern paved highways, with their elaborate system of signs directing traffic along fixed courses, the road to Oregon had a tendency to meander across the Plains in a manner determined by successive immigrant trains. Availability of water and grass for livestock, volume of traffic, and whims of travelers all had something to do with the day-to-day course that was followed. The trail, therefore, assumed the appearance of a series of parallel and interlaced wagon ruts several miles in width. It was joined at the eastern end by numerous feeder lines, while farther west short–cuts (such as the Lander cutoff and the Sublette cutoff) and the familiar turnoffs to California gave to the Oregon Trail a personality all of its own.

If one makes allowances for sufficient breadth and for certain deviations, the main outlines of the Oregon Trail can be drawn. The most important starting place was Independence, Missouri. From there the trail wormed its way northwestward across the Kansas and Blue rivers to the muddy Platte. For a long distance it hugged the south side of the Platte, then crossed over to follow the north fork of this river, passing en route such historic landmarks as Chimney Rock, Scott's Bluff, Old Fort Laramie, Independence Rock, and Devil's Gate. Of all the oddities of nature, none seems to have caught the fancy of the immigrant so much as that great dome-like, basaltic mound named Independence Rock. It was called by many people the Great Register, for here all comers paused to view the names of passers-by chiseled upon its surface, and to engrave their own. At this point the immigrants were 810 miles from their jumping-off place; they were at the approach to the Rocky Mountains; and South Pass lay about due westward. The ascent to the pass was gradual, and, surprisingly enough, one would scarcely realize that the great hump in the Continental Divide was being negotiated.

From South Pass the course was a steady descent in the direction of Fort Hall on the upper Snake River, 1,278 miles from Independence, and well within the limits of the Oregon country. For the wagon trains the route thus far had been a slow, dreary, steady, but relatively easy one. The stretch from Fort Hall westward following the swiftly flowing Snake River was through sage-covered desert, where travel became increasingly more hazardous and difficult. The trail passed Old Fort Boise, and then at Farewell Bend (near present Huntington, Oregon) it left the Snake River region and cut northwestward across a part of the difficult Blue Mountains and through the beautiful Grande Ronde until the Columbia River was reached.

At first the immigrants came upon the Columbia River by way of the Whitman Mission and Old Fort Walla Walla on the Walla Walla River, but by 1844 most of the caravans chose to reach the Columbia at its confluence with the Umatilla River. From there they would follow a slow but passable cutoff to The Dalles, where for the remaining sixty miles of their 2,000-mile trek to the Willamette Valley they were obliged to "take to water."

The earliest immigrant parties were not infrequently met at the main landings by servants of the Hudson's Bay Company who escorted them downstream to Fort Vancouver on bateaux. Later, when the migration became very heavy, immigrants built rafts on which persons, wagons, and other effects were precariously floated downstream. Livestock was usually driven over a mountain trail south of Mount Hood, which was at first too narrow for vehicles to pass. By taking to water at The Dalles a portage at Celilo Falls was averted, but at the Cascades — forty-one miles from Fort Vancouver — a portage was required of all who valued their lives and property.

Immigrants frequently arrived in a suffering, half–starved condition, and until the Hudson's Bay Company moved its headquarters to Fort Victoria some aid and comfort was given these Americans by this fur-trading firm. At other times Americans in the valley came to the rescue. Following a rest at Fort Vancouver, members of the parties usually headed for the ultimate destination, which most frequently was the Willamette Valley.

With a view toward eliminating this dangerous passage

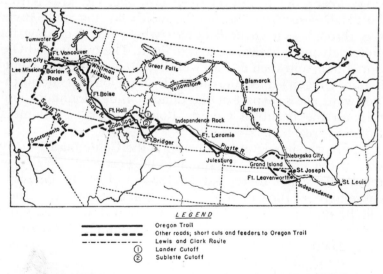

LEGEND
Oregon Trail
Other roads; short cuts and feeders to Oregon Trail
Lewis and Clark Route
① Lander Cutoff
② Sublette Cutoff

THE OREGON TRAIL AND ROUTE FOLLOWED
BY LEWIS AND CLARK

down the swirling Columbia River efforts were begun in 1845 to find an all-land wagon trail to Willamette Valley. Dr. Elijah White and some followers made a futile attempt to bring in the 1845 caravans by such a route. The Oregon Provisional Legislature also took a hand in the matter by authorizing projects that might lead to the finding of a successful route. Among the projects receiving an official blessing was one proposed to the Legislature by Captain Samuel K. Barlow, a newly arrived immigrant. During the summer of 1846 Barlow formed a partnership and organized a party which became the first to find a successful pass through the Cascade Mountains (at a point not far from the south side of Mt. Hood) and to construct a practicable wagon road leading from The Dalles to Oregon City. This road, which became known as the Barlow Road, was completed early enough in 1846 to enable 145 immigrant wagons and 1,559 head of livestock to pass over it during the fall of that year. Until 1912 the Barlow Road continued in operation as a toll road. Not only was its construction an important achievement in itself, but its existence brought to the Willamette Valley many settlers who might otherwise have gone to the north (or Washington side) side of the Columbia River.

As immigrant wagon trains arrived, choicest farm lands of the Willamette Valley were claimed. By 1846 several families had settled near what was to be Eugene City (later just Eugene) at the southern end of the valley floor, and the upper limit of steamship navigation. Large numbers chose to make their homes among the foothills above this future town site. Still others set their sights upon the less approachable Umpqua and Rouge River valleys that lay to the south. In an effort to open southern Oregon to settlement, and also to find another all-land route from Fort Hall into the Willamette Valley that could be used in the event of war with Great Britain, there was formed, during 1846, a road-building company, the exploits of which are fully as memorable as those associated with the Barlow Road.

Participating in this great new venture were Jesse and Lindsay Applegate, Levi and John Scott of the 1843 immigration, Moses "Black" Harris, a veteran mountain man, and ten others. They formed what is known as the South Road Company. Each of the fifteen men equipped himself with a saddle-horse and a pack-horse, a rifle, and other essential supplies, and as a group they planned to search for the new route. The men were to proceed in a southeastwardly direction until the Humboldt section of the Fort Hall-California road had been reached; then they were to follow this well-worn trail to Fort Hall where Oregon-bound immigrants would be induced to proceed along the new course laid out for them.

At great peril this party succeeded in its efforts, and late in 1846, more than one hundred wagons were piloted by Levi Scott into Oregon over the southern route. This route, however, had severe critics, the most outspoken of which was J. Quinn Thornton, one of the first to be persuaded by Applegate to try this road. "We had toiled on amidst great suffering," wrote Thornton, and at the place where a spring had been promised "We found a desert as dry and blasted, as if it had just been heaved upon from some infernal volcano." But neither the hardships endured by the Thorntons and their comrades, nor the gratuitous venom poured on Jesse Applegate, could erase the fact that a new route now linked the Willamette and southern valleys with the Oregon Trail. At the instigation of the Oregon legislature, Captain Levi Scott was subsequently appointed to supervise work leading to a shortening and an improvement of the road. In time this route found favor with immigrants, especially those whose destination was the Umpqua and Rogue River valleys. Discovery of a southern route in Oregon was a notable achievement by a group of stalwart men who had triumphed where one year before John C. Frémont had failed. Its existence, moreover, led to an improvement of the trail connecting Oregon with the Sacramento Valley over which many immigrants reached the Willamette Valley, and vice versa. Though immigrants at all times continued to trickle in by various land and sea routes, it was over the Oregon Trail — now a glorious tradition — that the great mass of Oregon-bound Americans traveled.

Missionary Settlers

Among the first settlers to make use of the Oregon Trail were, suprisingly enough, Methodist missionaries. They went West to convert the natives to Christianity, but some remained to establish the first integrated agricultural settlement in the Willamette Valley.

Factors explaining the reason for this important missionary venture are as numerous as they are involved. Christian missionaries had long been in the forefront of New World settlement, and seldom had the impulse to heed the "Macedonian call" been felt more keenly than during the first half of the nineteenth century. Of many places in the world where the missionaries might, and did, carry the Cross to the heathen, one was the Oregon country. Even as early as 1798 a project calling for the establishment of a Christian mission on the Pacific Northwest coast had been proposed by a German, Baron August von Schirnding. This nobleman even offered to co-operate with the London Missionary Society in order to bring his proposal into fulfillment. The Baron's plan never materialized, but projects calling for the spread of Christianity into the Northwest soon came from other sources. By 1810 or 1811 plans for just such a project were being formulated at Andover Theological Seminary. Also, in 1810–11, was founded the American Board of Commissioners for Foreign Missions (hereafter called the American Board) which represented the Presbyterian, Congregational, and Dutch Reformed denominations, and which, before long, was to direct its missionary zeal toward the Oregon country. Separate missionary societies were also started, among them a Baptist missionary society founded in 1813, and a Methodist society established in 1819. In the latter year the American Board dispatched its first missionaries to Hawaii. The island mission was established in 1820; and because of numerous maritime contacts between the Hawaiian Islands and the northwest coast, these American Board missionaries were not long in proposing to the home office in Boston that the Oregon country coast might be a suitable place for expansion. In 1829 the Prudential Committee of the American Board actually sent Reverend Jonathan S. Green from Hawaii to the northwest coast on a tour of reconnaissance. Green did not go inland, but he did visit some ports, and recommended that a mission be established near the mouth or lower part of the Columbia River.

Action on Green's proposal was delayed, and the first direct move to establish missions in Oregon was made neither by missionaries in Hawaii nor by any other decision of the American Board at Boston, but by the Methodist Missionary Society. A story printed in the Methodist *Christian Advocate and Journal* (New York) on March 1, 1833, and copied by *Zion's Herald* (Boston), greatly hastened the final decision. This item was a letter from G. P. Disosway, prominent Methodist layman and New York City merchant, in which was included another letter from William Walker, an interpreter and a member of the Wyandot tribe. The Walker letter related in a highly sentimentalized fashion a story, the known facts of which are as follows:

In 1831 four Nez Percé and Flathead Indians made a surprise visit to the St. Louis home of General William Clark, then Superintendent of Indian Affairs. Having had slight previous knowledge of Christianity, this Indian "deputation" had come to the famous explorer to ask for further enlightenment in the ways of the white man's worship. Two of the four Indians died while at St. Louis and were given a Catholic burial; a third is reputed to have died on his return trip; and the fourth, alone, may have made it safely back to his people.

The story as presented in the *Christian Advocate*, along with a drawing of a "flat" headed Indian, created widespread interest among its readers. Shortly thereafter the Methodist Missionary Board announced the appointment of Jason Lee, a youthful and fervent minister, as the person to be charged with founding a mission among the Flatheads.

Jason Lee came from a long line of New Englanders, although the northeast boundary as finally established had placed the family homestead on the Canadian side of the line. On a farm near the town of Stanstead, Quebec, Jason was born on June 28, 1803. He grew up to be a tall, athletic, and industrious young man with a leaning toward emotionalism and religion. His early years, he wrote in his diary, were spent "successively in business, in study, and in preaching." At the age of twenty-three he and his nephew, Daniel, were converted to Methodism, and later became ordained ministers. Both heeded a call published in the *Christian Advocate* by Dr. Wilbur Fisk, president of Wesleyan University (Middletown, Connecticut) for "two suitable men, unencumbered with families, and possessing the spirit of martyrs" to establish a mission among the Flatheads. Jason was given the title of Chief Missionary and Daniel that of Mission Associate and Junior Assistant.

Meetings designed to stir interest and to secure financial support for such a mission were subsequently held in Boston and vicinity. Speaking at one of these gatherings was Captain Nathaniel Wyeth; with him the Lee missionaries made arrangements to travel on what was Wyeth's second long trek over the Oregon Trail.

Jason and Daniel Lee and two lay assistants, Cyrus Shepard and Philip L. Edwards, joined the fur traders at St. Louis, and on the morning of April 28, 1834, the mixed party set out for Oregon. These God–fearing missionaries and the rather ungodly fur traders made an interesting study in contrasts, and it was not easy for the former to escape ridicule and embarrassment. From the Rocky Mountains Daniel Lee wrote: ". . . Capt. [Wyeth] is a perfect infidel as it respects revealed religion," but in all fairness Lee added that Wyeth "has acted in the part of a Gentleman toward us." On September 15 the missionaries completed the last leg of their journey when the barge was tied up on the gravelly beach below Fort Vancouver. The very next day, the *May Dacre*, Wyeth's brig which had been sent around the Horn with supplies, also arrived at the fort. The journey had been hard, but successful.

Dr. McLoughlin extended a warm welcome to the Lees and provided them with horses and guides to explore the lower Willamette Valley. More important, the crafty Chief Factor persuaded Jason Lee that the place to establish his Mission Headquarters should be among the friendly Indians of the Willamette Valley, instead of among the Nez Percés. This advice was accepted; he chose a spot on the east bank of the Willamette River near French Prairie where retired fur traders had built their cabins, and about ten miles north of present Salem. Telling of his initial efforts at this place, he later wrote: "We landed where we now are in October 1834 and pitched our tents, unloaded our canoes, and commenced building a house. The rainy season was approaching, and I did not like the idea of living in an Indian hut. We labored under disadvantages, for we were not carpenters. We however went into the woods and cut the timber. We took the green trees and split them, and hewed our boards for our floors." By a similar process a mission house was built, and thus was founded, late in 1834, the first Protestant mission in the Willamette Valley. Subsequently Lee established a branch mission at The Dalles, and another branch near Fort Nisqually.

Actual missionary work was begun as soon as possible, but with poor results. Lee despaired of the adult Indians, but held out some hope for the children who began attending a mission school. Despite hardships and misgivings he refused to give up, and pleaded with the Board of Missions in the East to send him more help. The Board responded by sending out reinforcements by sea in 1837. Among these new arrivals (the first reinforcement, it is called) was Miss Anna Maria Pittman, who later became the wife of Jason Lee. The next year Jason Lee returned East to seek still other reinforcements. From his farmer's background he recognized the agricultural possibilities of the valley to which he had come. Among 21 persons Lee induced to answer his call were 6 ministers, 4 young women teachers, a physician, a cabinet maker, a steward, and a number of farmers and mechanics. Many of these had families, and some had several children, thus making a total of 51. Together they were known as the "Great Reinforcement" which arrived by sea on the ship Lausanne in 1840. Moreover, Lee secured $42,000 for the purchase of essential equipment and supplies.

The coming of these reinforcements marks the turning point so far as the future of the Willamette mission was concerned. Cattle were increased; new acres were put to the plow; new homes arose. Herein lies the significance of the entire venture. As interest in the missionary work dwindled, that in the advancement of settlement increased. "As far as my personal observation went . . . ," wrote a visitor to the establishment in 1841, "they seem more occupied with the settlement of the country and in the agricultural pursuits than in the missionary labors." In time the Board realized this and sent Reverend George Gary to the mission to succeed Lee, and to attempt to disassociate the mission from much of its worldly activities. Both the Lees returned East where Jason died in 1845. Gary, who arrived in 1844, met with some rewards in his missionary activities, but from the long-time point of view the crowning success of the entire adventure was that the Lee mission became the nucleus of the American colonization as it also became the center of attraction for future settlers from all parts of the East and Middle West for whom the term Willamette Valley became synonymous with the word Oregon.

The American Board was likewise stirred to action, and followed very closely the example set by the Methodists. The services of Reverend Samuel Parker of Middlefield, Massachusetts, which had been willingly offered to the Board, were accepted. Accompanied by two others, Parker set out for the Oregon country in 1834, but not early enough to go with the west-bound fur trading caravans. He, therefore, soon returned to New York where his preachings netted him five volunteers, and acquaintanceship with Dr. Marcus Whitman and Narcissa Prentiss, both of whom had also offered to be at the bidding of the Board. Whitman, a physician with a yearning for the ministry, was a native of Rushville, New York, where he had been born September 4, 1802. During 1835 Parker and Whitman were sent to the West on reconnaissance and in the Green River region established contact with several Indian tribes.

From the Green River, Parker resumed his explorations while Whitman returned to Angelica, New York, and in February, 1836, he married Narcissa Prentiss. He secured the assistance of Reverend and Mrs. Henry Harman Spalding and William H. Gray, and shortly thereafter, a second mission founding party (this one sponsored by the American

Board) was heading west over the Oregon Trail. The wives of Whitman and Spalding bravely accompanied their husbands on the journey — the first time white women had traversed the Oregon Trail — and their achievement was widely acclaimed. The resourceful Whitman-Spalding party which accompanied American Fur Company traders on the Trail, had cattle driven with them, and used pack animals and wagons to carry supplies. Never before had wagons been taken so far west of the Green River as in this instance, and at Fort William (or Fort John) the determined Whitman had a wagon converted into a cart which was taken with difficulty as far west as Old Fort Boise. This served to bolster the hope that wagons might soon be taken all the way to the Willamette Valley. As the Lees before them had done, the party obtained supplies at Fort Vancouver. Meanwhile mission sites, in what today is called the Inland Empire, had been selected by Parker. To one — Waiilatpu on the Walla Walla River (Washington) in the Cayuse Indian country — went the Whitmans. To the other — at Lapwai on the Clearwater River (Idaho) in among the Nez Percé — went the Spaldings. Both missionary couples succeeded in erecting missionary establishments; both met with initial success in carrying on their Christian labors. In 1838 these courageous missionary pioneers of the Inland Empire were reinforced by the Reverends Cushing Eells, A. B. Smith and Elkanah Walker, their wives, and four others. This led to the establishment of a third mission, Tshimakain, on the north side of the Spokane River, about twenty-five miles north of present Spokane, Washington, and still a fourth at Kamiah, Idaho. But owing to tragic circumstances, to be told later, the final outcome, like that of the Methodists in the Willamette Valley, cannot be measured in terms of the number of Indians baptized into the Christian faith.

Active, too, were the Catholics, whose faith was embraced, though not too ardently, by practically all French Canadian fur traders in the region. This group was completely without official religious instruction and spiritual ministration. The presence of large numbers of company servants, many of whom were retiring at French Prairie, provided an opportunity to establish the Church among them, as well as to share with the Protestants in planting the faith among the Indians. To meet this challenge the Columbia region was officially recognized in 1836,[2] and in 1838 Father Francis N. Blanchet of the Montreal diocese, and the younger Father Modeste Demers from the Red River in Canada, were sent into the Oregon region. Like their Protestant colleagues, Fathers Blanchet and Demers suffered all the hardships of overland travel to Fort Vancouver where they arrived with a Hudson's Bay Company brigade on November 24, 1838, following a 5,325-mile trip which had required six months. Father Blanchet was made Vicar General to the Bishop of Quebec; Father Demers was sent to assist Blanchet in the Willamette Valley. The first Catholic mission was established on the Cowlitz River; a second, St. Paul, founded on the Willamette between present Oregon City and Salem, became the permanent residence of Father Blanchet who subsequently was elevated to Bishop. Though they were centered in the Willamette-Cowlitz area, their activities had a wide range, extending as far east as the Cayuse Indian country where Whitman's mission was located, and north to Vancouver Island where Demers eventually served as Bishop.

Also heeding the call were the black-robed Jesuits, and in the forefront of this spirited group was the Belgian, Father Pierre-Jean De Smet, who first came to the Oregon country from St. Louis in 1840. He established a mission among the Flatheads the following year; and before the lapse of six years, he had founded St. Ignatius Mission and Sacred Heart Mission in the Coeur d'Alene mountain region. Both physically and spiritually De Smet was a tower of strength. It is estimated that during his lifetime he traveled 180,000 miles, and certainly he gained great familiarity with the Oregon country. The Indians everywhere liked and respected him and in later years this Jesuit Father often served as me-

---

[2] The nearest ecclesiastical Superior was Bishop Provencher in what is now Manitoba, who in turn was an auxiliary to the Bishop of Quebec. It was to Bishop Provencher's Vicariate that the Columbia region was added in 1836.

diator between Indian and white man in times of trouble. In many places, and in other respects the Jesuits were, and still are, active in the Pacific Northwest.

On this missionary frontier rivalry between the Catholics and Protestants was keen, and at times bitter, but as viewed in retrospect many of the vile suspicions earlier entertained seem to be without foundation in fact. Taken in its entirety, the missionary influence cannot be totally ignored, either in the realm of the spirit, or in directing public attention to the rich agricultural potentialities of the Oregon country. As on other frontiers, missionaries were in the vanguard of western movement to the Oregon country. Just how many settlers may have come to Oregon at the direct instigation of the missionaries is a moot question, but as a group they constituted one of many elements who knowingly or unknowingly transformed the region south of the forty-ninth parallel from a fur empire to an agricultural frontier. Even as early as 1836 the astute McLoughlin saw the handwriting on the wall when he wrote to the Governor and Committee in London: ". . . Every One Knows who is acquainted with the Fur trade that as the country becomes settled the Fur trade Must Diminish. . . ."

Outbreak of Oregon Fever

It would be erroneous to assume that the missionary movement alone engendered excitement about Oregon. The region had as its champions in Congress men like Dr. John Floyd of Virginia, and Dr. Lewis F. Linn of Missouri. And never losing an opportunity to promote Oregon was Hall J. Kelley who in 1830 published at Boston *A Geographical Sketch of that Part of North America Called Oregon,* in which he described the country as one where "mountains are high and rough," but where also "the air is more salubrious, and the country better furnished with natural facilities for application of labour." Kelley urged his readers to go to Oregon, saying: "The settlement of the Oregon country, would conduce to a freer intercourse, and a more extensive and lucrative trade with the East Indias." The following year Kelley issued

A General Circular to All Persons of Good Character, Who Wish to Emigrate to the Oregon Territory, and this in turn was followed by other material. A letter to the Washington *Intelligencer,* 1848, appropriately said of Kelley: "It is the fate of men in advance of their times to be martyrs of the age for which they labor. . . . He has labored and others have reaped the harvest."

In 1836 Washington Irving's facile pen produced the two-volume work *Astoria,* which found a wide reading public. Other publications, such as Alphonso Wetmore's *Gazetteer Frontier Sketches* (1837), Zenas Leonard's *Narratives* (1838), C. A. Murray's *Travels in North America* (1838), were additions to an ever-growing body of literature which helped immensely to popularize Oregon.

John C. Frémont did much by way of describing Oregon; he kept interest in the West alive. Frémont's writings, though of not unquestioned accuracy and purpose, enjoyed wide popularity among those whose thoughts and interests had already been directed toward the West. Newspapers and magazines in both England and America, moreover, repeatedly carried sensational copy on Oregon; the great annual migration over the Trail brought the name "Oregon" to the lips of nearly every American man, woman, and child. As phrased by the Independence (Missouri) *Expositor* in 1845: "Whoo ha! Go it boys! We're in a perfect *Oregon fever.*" What was termed by contemporaries "the irresistible progress of our people" was in full operation. And the spirit thus exhibited — in many instances engendered by agrarian discontent in the Mississippi Valley — was that which Americans carried westward to the blue shores of the Pacific. "Their ploughs turn its sods, their axes level its timber," wrote *Hunt's Merchants' Magazine* in 1846 of those who had gone to the Willamette Valley; "no power on earth, nor all the powers of the earth, can check the swelling tide of the American population. . . ."

Prairie Cavalcades

Migration to Oregon and "Oregon Fever" went hand in hand. A small fragment of the so-called "Peoria Party" seemingly organized by Thomas J. Farnham for the self-appointed task of planting the American flag in Oregon — reached that region at varying times during 1839. In 1841 there came by covered wagon across the Oregon Trail as far as Soda Springs the Bidwell-Bartleson party. At Soda Springs the group, which numbered sixty-four, divided; one half set out for California, and the other half for Oregon. The latter took their wagons as far as Fort Hall where they were abandoned and belongings were taken on the backs of mules and horses for the remainder of the distance to the Columbia. The California-bound group managed to reach the Sacramento Valley, but not without great suffering.

The expedition of 1842 marked a definite step forward in organization and might well be thought of as marking the real beginning of the covered wagon migration to Oregon. A train of from sixteen to eighteen covered wagons and 107 persons set forth under the initial leadership of Dr. Elijah White, who had formerly been associated with the Lee mission and was returning to Oregon as a federal Indian sub-agent. Even though it was well organized, with various officials elected to assume the responsibilities of leadership, the journey appears to have been a quarrelsome one. The party left Elm Grove, near Independence, on May 16. White served as captain for a month, and thereafter Lansford W. Hastings took over the leadership until they reached the Little Sandy River where a split occurred concerning the further use of wagons. Some of the vehicles were taken as far as Fort Hall and were sold to the Hudson's Bay Company for a small consideration. From this post White and a few of his devoted followers moved on ahead, while Captain Hastings followed.

By mid-September the first of White's party reached the Whitman Mission, from which place water transportation was used to Fort Vancouver. To Dr. Whitman, White delivered letters from the Prudential Committee of the American Board which contained the startling instructions that the Waiilatpu and Lapwai missions were to be closed; Spalding was being recalled (an act later rescinded); and Whitman was to be transferred to the Spokane Indian area. Exactly what prompted Whitman to decide on the course he followed cannot be determined. All that is known for certain is that on the following October 3 (1842) he and a companion named Amos L. Lovejoy undertook to return East by horseback in the face of the oncoming winter. To posterity this courageous and successful undertaking has been known as "Whitman's Ride." From Fort Hall the two secured the services of a guide (later replaced) and a southern course was taken past Taos and to Bent's Fort; then, parting company with Lovejoy, Whitman hastened on to Westport and to the east coast where he visited Washington, New York, and Boston.

At the nation's capital Whitman called at the War Department; in New York he met Horace Greeley; and at Boston, of course, he reported to the American Board. Political motives designed to "save Oregon" from the British have been ascribed to Whitman's ride. Four and a half years later he personally wrote to the Board that he made the trip "to open a practical route and safe passage" for the immigrants he knew would be going to Oregon in 1843. Certain it is that Whitman caused no great wrinkle in official Washington; and even though he personally hastened West to join the migration of 1843 for a part of the way, the assertion made by some that Whitman was largely responsible for this migration is a part of what is now known as the Whitman Legend. The exact purpose of Whitman's ride has not been definitely established, but it may be presumed that pressing problems concerning the missions were important considerations.

The caravans making up the expeditions of 1843 have become known as the Great Migration. Although greater ones were to come, this one netted the Willamette Valley about 875 additions to its struggling settlements. This time the immigrants brought their wagons through to The Dalles on the Columbia River, albeit, as one of their party mildly phrased it, "over the roughest road I ever saw." From The Dalles the parties were floated down the Columbia to the mouth of the Willamette Valley on Hudson's Bay Company bateaux or on improvised rafts. In that same year of 1843, seven hundred head of cattle were driven over the trail alongside the caravans, and the safe arrival in Oregon of many of these was a clear sign to fur traders that the best trapping days were past, at least south of the Columbia. Each year had enlarged the size of the American population, estimated by Jason Lee to have been slightly more than one hundred in 1839, so that this migration of 1843 is believed to have raised the total population of the Willamette Valley (all American except for about sixty-one Canadian families living in the vicinity of French Prairie) to about one thousand five hundred.

The migration of 1843 inaugurated a new era in Oregon country history; it set the pattern for larger cavalcades which were to come regularly each year before the completion of the railroads. To settlers and fur men alike it was now clear that a transition was rapidly taking place. By 1845 the total population of the territory rose to about 6,000; and thanks to the first census taken in 1849 by General Joseph Lane as first territorial governor, it is known that 9,083 were in the Oregon Territory by that year. Of these, 8,785 were listed as citizens of the United States; 298 were foreigners (by then, most of the active Hudson's Bay servants had moved out); 5,410 were males, 3,673 were females. At mid-century the total had risen to 13,294, and prospects for the future growth and expansion continued to be bright. Manifest Destiny, so many people thought, had reached flood tide. At last, as Timothy Flint had long before envisaged: "the tide of the advancing backwoodsmen" had "met the surge of the Pacific." What had transpired in Oregon was what George Tucker of Virginia once called the unstoppable "progress of our civilization to the West."

"Oh Susannah"

To have crossed the Plains with a covered wagon train was to have participated in one of the most stirring episodes in American history. It was an experience that cannot be recaptured except vicariously, but in this latter respect all Americans indulge themselves to the fullest through the media of manuscripts, books, Westerns (magazines), songs, personal reminiscences, touring, the radio, and the silver screen.

Perhaps to a hardened and experienced guide the journey over the Oregon Trail was as routine as piloting a plane across the country would be to many aviators today. There was, after all, a rather fixed, or at least strongly recommended procedure for the cavalcades to follow. Variations from this endorsed pattern involved serious risks which only a few dared to take. This schedule called for winter and very early spring organization of emigrant companies and for assembling at some prearranged rendezvous, notably near Independence or St. Joseph, Missouri — "the jumping-off place" for Oregon. Often some enterprising person would advertise in newspapers saying in effect: "If interested in joining the 1843 Oregon Train, come equipped with wagon and animals to Sapling Grove during the month of March." At the rendezvous, officers were usually elected by the simple procedure of having the candidates start walking in a fixed direction, to be joined by each voting member of the party who would fall in line behind his choice for office. The candidate with the largest following (literally speaking) then was considered elected to the position of captain, sergeant, or whatever the post might have been.

With the aid of experienced guides (usually retired fur traders) covered wagon trains would form into brigades with separate arrangement made for handling the cattle and other livestock not used in pulling the wagons. The time for starting was about the first of May when the streams had receded sufficiently to permit fording and when grass would be plentiful for the animals. An average of ten miles per day was to be maintained in order to reach the Willamette Valley before the rainy season set in there during October.

Usually each family had one covered wagon, in which would ride driver, women, and small children. In it, too, would be the precious belongings, including a plow, some seed, bedding, and food. And then one wagon behind another began the dreary trek westward.

Capturing the spirit of this experience in unrivaled fashion was Jesse Applegate, member of the 1843 migration and author of "A Day With the Cow Column." In Applegate's group were sixty wagons, divided into fifteen platoons of four wagons each. Here then are snatches from Applegate's essay telling of a day on the Plains:

It is four o'clock A. M.; the sentinels on duty have discharged their rifles — the signal that the hours of sleep are over — and every wagon and tent is pouring forth its night's tenants, and slowly kindling smokes begin largely to rise and float away in the morning air. . . . breakfast is to be eaten, the tents struck, the wagons loaded and the teams yoked and brought up in readiness to be attached to their respective wagons. All know when, at seven o'clock, the signal to march sounds, that those not ready to take their proper places in the line of march must fall into the dusty rear for the day. . . .

It is on the stroke of seven; the rush to and fro, the cracking of whips, the loud command to oxen, and what seemed to be an inextricable confusion of the last ten minutes has ceased. Fortunately everyone has been found and every teamster is at his post. The clear notes of a trumpet sound in the front; the pilot and his guard mount their horses; the leading divisions of the wagons move out of the encampment, and take up the line of march; the rest fall into their places with the precision of clockwork, until the spot so lately full of life sinks back into that solitude that seems to reign over the broad plain and rushing river as the caravan draws its lazy length toward the distant El Dorado.[3]

It is no surprise that an experience such as this has not been dimmed with the passage of time.

[3] Alfred Powers, *History of Oregon Literature* (Portland, 1935), pp. 372–4.

Chapter VIII

Provisional Government

A Prelude

IF, AS WEBSTER SAYS, anarchy means the "absence of government," this word best describes the political status of the Americans in the Oregon country prior to about 1841. Article III of the Anglo-American treaty of 1818 provided in effect for occupation jointly, but no specific provision was made for government in the territory. Neither did the convention of 1827, extending the life of the foregoing treaty, make any provision for civil government. No steps could be taken by either government to establish a political framework, moreover, because such action would be construed as a definite violation of treaty obligation. Until measures were taken by residents themselves, early-day Oregon lacked a formal governmental structure. An American there, say in the 1820s, would have been bound by no restraints other than those dictated by his conscience or by fear of retribution on the part of fur trading companies, his fellow residents, or natives. Such a person could have committed murder, arson, and theft, or could have been "cruel and inhuman" to his wife, and no white person within the area would have had the constitutional and legal means for bringing him to justice.

So far as actual goings-on were concerned, Oregon never was without at least some extra-legal government. Long before white men came, each Indian tribe had worked out its own laws, mores, and folkways. Indians regarded these governmental paraphernalia as binding on outsiders. Explorers were subject to rules laid down by those responsible for the expeditions. Men in the Lewis and Clark expedition were in

[127]

the army, and thus had to submit to military rules and regulations.

British, American, and in the far north Russian, fur traders, by and large, were bound by the rules of the companies which they served. The exception would have been the lone mountain man who might have entered the region for trade without obligation to any employer. Employees of British fur companies — especially those of the Hudson's Bay Company — were under obligation to abide by company rules, and the companies in turn were responsible to the British Government. In 1835 a provisional, or extra-legal, jury at Wyeth's Fort William heard the homicide case of a man named Hubbard and exonerated him. At Astoria, in 1840, Americans and British took the law into their own hands and hanged an Indian murderer.

The Charter of 1821 gave to the Chief Factor limited judicial rights over British subjects in regions where His Majesty's courts had not been already organized, but the Hudson's Bay Company had no legal right whatsoever to govern or control in any way American subjects, and yet in actual practice McLoughlin exercised considerable influence, if not actual control, over many of them. Through astute business operations he kept Americans, both fur traders and settlers, from infiltrating, to any great extent, into the region north and west of the Columbia River. And through loans of cattle, grains, and other supplies the McLoughlin-dominated Hudson's Bay Company exercised a certain amount of power and control over American settlers in the Willamette and Walla Walla valleys.

American missionary leaders, such as Lee, Whitman, and De Smet, exercised actual authority over both those who worked with them and over the Indians. In turn the missionaries took their orders either from a home board or from high church authorities. Other examples of authority might be found. During 1838 the Methodist missions even went as far as to provide for a magistrate and constable for the dispensation of justice. Not without considerable conflict with Indians and Hudson's Bay Company officials did they perform their extra-legal duties. Only from the strictly legal standpoint was

Oregon ever without some kind of governing authority which in greater or less degree served as a control upon the inhabitants. Oregon, moreover, was not unlike several other frontier regions in America, for example East Tennessee (Watauga Association of 1772), Utah (Deseret), and Colorado where settlement came in advance of the establishment of civil government authorized by the laws of the United States.

Roots of Provisional Government or temporary

During the period of joint occupation British subjects were either content with, or acquiesced in, Company rule. American settlers, on the other hand, were desirous, first of the establishment of authority by the United States Government; this failing, then some kind of provisional government.

Even though John Floyd began his crusade for the establishment of an American government in Oregon as early as 1820, treaty obligations, domestic politics, and fear of what England might do caused the delay of any effective federal action until after the settlement of the Oregon boundary dispute. The only molehill produced by the mountain of Congressional debate before 1843 was the decision of the United States Government to authorize the appointment of a sub-Indian agent. Dr. Elijah White was chosen for this post, but not without mixed reactions from the settlers. With special instructions from President Jackson and Secretary of State John Forsyth not to excite British suspicions, William A. Slacum had visited the Willamette settlement in 1836; Lieutenant Charles Wilkes, United States Navy, led exploring parties into coastal areas in 1841; and a party led by Lieutenant John C. Frémont of the United States Topographical Engineers visited and explored portions of the Snake River and Eastern Oregon country. All these visits indicate official interest in Oregon, but none of these military expeditions led directly to the establishment of federal authority in the region.

Recognizing that federal action would be long in coming, American settlers took steps to form a provisional, or temporary government. Just who first thought of such action will never be known, but the idea appears to have originated among settlers and Methodist missionaries in the Willamette Valley. Encouraged by the Methodist missionary reinforcement of 1840 and prodded by the problem of how to dispose of the property of the deceased and, so far as was then known, heirless Ewing Young,[1] steps were taken leading to the establishment of a provisional government. The people were not averse to discussing worldly matters at funerals (after all, get-togethers were much too infrequent), and hence the burial of Young provided the occasion for selecting a committee on arrangements, and a mass meeting was called at the Methodist Mission near present-day Salem, for February 17, 1841.

Although not decisive in results, this meeting, deep in beautiful Willamette Valley, was the primary step leading to the final establishment of the provisional government. Those present were mostly persons associated with the mission, from among whom Jason Lee was chosen president, and Gustavus Hines secretary. A resolution was adopted calling for "drafting a constitution and code of laws for the government of the settlements south of the Columbia river," a government that would offer protection to settlers in that area who were not connected with the Hudson's Bay Company. Before the first day's session adjourned, candidates were nominated for governor, supreme judge, three constables, three road commissioners, attorney general, clerk of the court, public recorder, treasurer, and two overseers of the poor. It was recommended that the officers be chosen *viva voce*.

Meanwhile the equally numerous French settlers on the nearby prairie had held aloof. But on the second day, February 18th, they came out and joined the Americans in deliberations at the Lee Mission house. At this time David Leslie, member of the Methodist Mission group, was elected chairman. A secretary from each of the two national groups was chosen, and a committee was named to draft a plan for a provisional government and a code of laws. On this important committee were placed in balanced fashion three Methodist

---

[1] In later years it was discovered that Young had a son, Joaquin Young, to whom the value of this property — held by the state — was refunded.

ministers, one Catholic priest, three French Canadians, and two American settlers.[2] For political reasons the election of a governor was deferred, but a supreme judge, namely Dr. Ira L. Babcock, physician at the Methodist Mission, was chosen with probate powers to act according to the laws of New York State. A sheriff and two constables, a clerk and a recorder were also chosen and therewith the meeting adjourned.

This action was by no means evidence of unanimity of opinion. French, British, and American opinions clashed. Catholic-Protestant issues had been injected into the debate; after the meeting adjourned Committeeman Father Blanchet resigned (indicative of French Canadian non-participation), and his place was filled by Dr. William J. Bailey, an American Protestant settler. Nor had any constitution been drafted. Another meeting was held June 1, 1841, but no decisive action was reached regarding a constitution. Sentiments for a provisional government were nonetheless kept alive; arguments pro and con were debated in the Valley. Nevertheless, matters were allowed to drag on until 1843, when gatherings known as "Wolf Meetings" were held. At the first of these, on February 2, 1843, it was decided to call a second meeting on the following March 6 at the home of Joseph Gervais. To be sure, the subject of wolves — also bears and panthers — was discussed, and plans considered for "a defensive and destructive war" against all such animals. But "politicking" was also in order. It was resolved, according to the "Journal," [3] "That a committee be appointed to take into consideration the propriety of taking measures for civil and military protection of this colony." The next step was an important gathering at Champoeg, May, 1843. The purpose, according to official minutes kept by G. W. Le Breton, was "taking steps to organize themselves into a civil community, and provide themselves with protection, secured by the enforcement of law

[2] The members of this committee were: Father F. N. Blanchet, Reverend Jason Lee, David Donpierre, Reverend Gustavus Hines, M. Charlevon, Robert Moore, Reverend Josiah L. Parrish, Etienne Lucier, and William Johnson.

[3] La Fayette Grover, *The Oregon Archives* (Salem, 1853). Though scanty in information, it is the official record of these early sessions. It also is the most reliable printed source.

and order." The site of this meeting place, now well marked by a state monument and park, is on the bank of the Willamette River about midway between present Newberg and Butteville. At that time there was a Hudson's Bay warehouse at Champoeg, which was a shipping place for wheat produced in the Willamette Valley. Since it was accessible by both land and water, it was chosen.

The Champoeg Meetings

On the day set, May 2, 1843, a meeting was held as provided at Champoeg. It had been preceded by considerable excitement and argumentation among the approximately 160 men in the Valley concerning the conflicting views of French Canadians (former Hudson's Bay Company servants) and Americans. As in 1841, French Canadians in the Valley were largely ex-"company men," and tended to be influenced by the powerful English monopoly. In any event their Catholicism and French linguistic character tended to clash with that of their Protestant neighbors from the states. Marked differences in the two groups are very noticeable even to this day.

At the meeting a committee reported in favor of organizing a provisional government. For a time there was confusion on the manner of deciding the question. According to subsequent accounts, much of this confusion was caused by misunderstandings concerning the meaning and implications of the proposal — especially among the French Canadians. When taken, the vote was close with a slender majority [4] favoring organization of a provisional government, or as the "Journal" states, a "civil community." The importance of the May 2nd meeting at Champoeg has been exaggerated; but unlike previous ones, it chose and gave authority to acting public officers. Its deliberations led directly to the drawing up of the first code of laws for the Oregon country. And, finally, this body specified a place and date — Champoeg,

[4] The negative vote came from the French Canadians and the number is placed at 50. The affirmative vote has been believed by some to be 52, but the margin was probably not that narrow. The exact figure is not definitely known.

July 5, 1843 — [5] for "a public meeting" to decide upon acceptance or rejection of said code.

A constitution committee held six meetings prior to the July fifth assembly. These sessions were held in true frontier style since the meeting place was an unoccupied granary at Willamette Falls, and deliberations were open. Customary legal procedures were adhered to; other committees were appointed. Reports were prepared embodying proposed organic articles and laws, modeled upon the Northwest Ordinance of 1787 and the Statutes of Iowa Territory. Both the famous Ordinance and the Iowa laws undoubtedly fully satisfied the requirements of the committee, but their chance possession of these items (both bound in one volume, 1839 edition) — and no other law books being on hand — determined their use in forming Oregon's first constitution.

On July 5 settlers gathered at Champoeg. Hines was elected chairman, and he called for reports by committee spokesmen who presented their respective proposals. Each set of proposals was discussed and approved in its turn, and in that manner were organic laws or a constitution adopted by the assembled voters. Officers elected at the May meeting were thereafter sworn in,[6] and with this the government of Oregon's first written constitution was ready to function.

Considering the sources of this constitution it is not surprising that a Bill of Rights was included — a testimony to the democratic, freedom-loving, and essentially decent spirit of these Oregon pioneers. Freedom of religion; the right of habeas corpus and trial by jury; moderate fines; representative government; the maintenance and encouragement of schools, knowledge, and morality; fairness toward the Indians; and prohibition of slavery are the cherished ideals here

---

[5] In the meantime, another general meeting of the "citizens of the Willamette" was held at Champoeg, June 23, 1843, preparatory to the vote on July 5th. At this meeting a set of resolutions on the "feeling of the community" was passed. One resolution reads: "That it will give us the highest pleasure to be brought as soon as practicable, under the jurisdiction of our mother country." It was unanimously resolved that these resolutions should be transmitted to the United States government by Dr. Elijah White, the Indian Sub-Agent.

[6] As will be explained later, the constitution provided for an executive committee of three; those elected and sworn into office were David Hill, Alanson Beers, and Joseph Gale.

set forth. One novel feature was the vesting of the executive power in three persons rather than one. Provision for legislative and judicial branches of government and for subordinate officers were, however, in keeping with their models. They also provided, as was customary, for protection by a militia, namely, three companies of mounted riflemen, and for four administrative districts or counties.

Close to the heart of the Oregon pioneers, not excluding the Methodist missionaries, was the good earth — the rich soil they had come so far to acquire and till. Never did these squatters feel confident that the land they were farming would be theirs by title. It is not surprising that in an effort to strengthen their hold on their land claims provisions regarding possessory rights to land were included and emphasized. Here is the forerunner of the Homestead Act, signed by Lincoln nearly two decades later. Claimants of land were required by law to designate the boundaries of their land, and to have their claims recorded in the territorial recorder's office within twenty days after making a claim. If already in possession of the land at the time this constitution was adopted, a year was given to file at the recorder's office. A claimant could hold as much as one square mile (640 acres) of land in either square or oblong form, with the condition that he make improvements in the form of a "building or enclosing" within six months. One article, namely IV, forbade holding claims on town sites or extensive water privileges, and other sites needed for the transaction of manufacturing and trade. It appears that this foregoing article was inserted as a rider aimed at Dr. McLoughlin who claimed one of the best water power sites in Oregon — the falls at Oregon City.

To the same extent that these early constitution makers loved land did they hate and abhor taxes. For this reason, doubtlessly, no provision was made for taxation. There were to be no public buildings; expenses which might be involved could be met, so they thought at the time, by voluntary subscriptions. This, too, was a novel feature, yet one that unfortunately could not survive. Benjamin Franklin was right when he said that nothing in this life is so sure as death and taxes.

For all its virtues this constitution approved at Champoeg had many shortcomings, and it failed to provide that which was most earnestly sought — an orderly and stable government. "Its makers," in the opinion of R. C. Clark, "could not provide all the sanctions necessary for a strong government." The reasons for the weaknesses were these: perhaps an actual majority of the settlers did not recognize the government set-up; and no one was to be coerced into recognizing the authority of this government — least of all the Hudson's Bay Company and the French Canadians. For all its faults, it was better than anarchy, and improvements were fast in coming.

The Immigrant Tide and Provisional Government

The autumn of 1843 which brought the first great tide of American immigration into the Willamette Valley (approximately 875 in all), made revision of the code imperative. Modifications effected by the legislative committee of 1844 provided for a definition of the area to be governed, namely, the region south of the Columbia; for submitting a proposal to the electorate that, if passed, would reduce the executive branch from a committee of three to a single person; for the prohibition of the manufacture of distilled spirits; and, although having formerly gone on record as favoring abolition of slavery, provision was made (due to the arrival of many Southerners) for the expulsion of all Negroes and mulattoes.

This legislature also substituted a new land law for the one proclaimed in 1843. It limited 640-acre land claims to men who were free, over eighteen, entitled to vote, and to widows. Another land act authorized the taking of six hundred acres of prairie land and forty acres of timber land that were not of one piece.

Reluctantly recognizing the necessity of revenue for running the government, taxation was made legal. Since, as in all frontier communities, "hard" money was scarce, wheat was made legal tender for payment of taxes and all debts where no other form of payment was required by contract.

By 1845 — true to the American pattern — political parties were in evidence. Those who had led in the foregoing proceedings came to be known as Americans, or "Mission" Party; whereas those who were opposed to what had transpired, and who favored a new constitution to replace what was technically called the Organic Articles and Laws (and these were principally French Canadians), became known as the "Independent" Party. The first tended to be strongly anti-Hudson's Bay Company; the latter somewhat pro-Company in its sentiments.

Respective views of the parties were so strongly put forth in the legislative sessions of 1845 that, faced with doubts as to its own legality, the legislature decided to adjourn and call for a vote of the people. On the question of retaining the organic laws of July 5, 1843, with the amendments, the people gave a large majority vote in the affirmative. With this new vote of confidence the government resumed its functions, and Iowa's statutes, in so far as they would apply to Oregon, were formally accepted as the legal code for the country.

From this time forward the Provisional Government was successful. It met with no rebuffs from either the President of the United States or from Congress; neither was it condoned nor recognized by federal agencies. J. Quinn Thornton, an active participant in early political developments characterized the Oregon government as: "Strong without an army or navy, rich without a treasury."

There are those who thought that the action at Champoeg saved Oregon from the tentacles of the Hudson's Bay Company, if not from Great Britain itself.[7] Such assertions are gross over-statements. Taken as a whole the Company had more to fear from Americans not responsible to some authority — "desperate characters" from Missouri — than from a people bound by a body of laws, albeit of doubtful legality.

[7] An expression of this Oregon myth has been written by Peter H. D'Arcy, in an article entitled "Historical Review, Champoeg, the Plymouth Rock of the Northwest," *Oregon Historical Quarterly*, XXIX (1928), p. 221. D'Arcy's article was used by a Senate Committee in considering a joint resolution for authorizing the erection at Champoeg of a memorial to commemorate the winning of the Oregon country. It reads as follows: "Upon a count of the persons present [at the Champoeg Convention] it was found that 52 of them voted in favor of the report and 50 in opposition. Thus was organized the first American government west of the Rocky Mountains, and in consequence thereof, the whole 'Oregon country' was saved to the United States. . . ."

As it turned out, it was much easier for the Company to keep Americans off its preserves north of the Columbia River since that stream was explicitly specified as the northern limit of the territory over which the Provisional Government claimed jurisdiction. This limit was a recognition by the Americans of Company rights. For another thing, it provided legal machinery which the fur trading firm might use, if necessary, to collect $30,000 in debts owed by American settlers in the Willamette Valley.

During 1845 McLoughlin recognized in fact the Provisional Government by willingly contributing to its coffers $226.65 in taxes. Frederick Merk phrased it aptly when he wrote: "But the Hudson's Bay Company, much feared, was itself afraid. It is a phenomenon by no means new, two hostile elements facing and fearing each other. In Oregon this led, for once, not to war but to peace."

The Final Stage

The final period of the Provisional Government was to last from the settlement of the Oregon boundary dispute in 1846 to the actual establishment of a Territorial government in Oregon by the United States in March, 1849. During this period George Abernethy, of the Americans, or "Mission," Party, continued as governor, being re-elected by a narrow margin in 1847. Abernethy was the only single chief executive during the period of the Provisional Government (the committee of three having preceded him), and he was governor when the United States Government took over. Beginning in 1845, "districts" were designated as counties, and new ones were added to the original four. This last period was one of rapid increase in the number of American immigrants. It was a period of intense excitement over the question of settlement of the boundary dispute. And yet the Provisional Government did its work well, along Jeffersonian principles of having no more government than absolutely necessary. Joe Meek reported his headaches over failure in many cases to collect property and the fifty-cent poll taxes. But even so, as Congress debated the future status of Oregon, the Provisional

Government was able to maintain a great degree of law and order in the territory, to lay out and construct, or provide for, roads, ferries, and bridges, and to pass laws for the general good of the community.

Legislative sessions were conducted in a semi-formal manner, and rules were frequently suspended to take care of unexpected situations as they arose. For example, early in the 1845 session, Jesse Applegate is reputed to have rushed breathlessly into the legislative chamber, and promptly asked that rules be suspended to permit him to introduce a bill to prohibit duelling. Applegate wished to prevent a duel that appeared imminent between Dr. White and Samuel M. Holderness. The house put aside its rules; a bill was read once for information and twice simply by title, and then passed. Within one hour from the time Applegate rushed onto the floor a bill had become a law, and the duel averted. During the August, 1845, session an act was adopted which incorporated the circulating library at Oregon City. Business firms were incorporated; a law respecting legal tender was enacted. The latter provided that wheat, hides, tallow, beef, pork, butter, lard, peas, lumber, and other articles of export were to be legal tender. During the December session of this year the legislature passed a prohibition law, but the bill received the governor's veto. At this session a post office was created at Oregon City, and William G. T'Vault, editor of the *Oregon Spectator* was named the first postmaster of Oregon.

No attempt is made here to enumerate all the laws passed by the Provisional Government. Suffice it to say that the wheels of government were put into motion and that the new machinery worked well. Perhaps the greatest compliment paid the Provisional Government was the Act of Congress on August 14, 1848, providing for territorial government that was to be proclaimed during March of the following year. The Act provided that the existing laws of the Provisional Government then in force, (except those having to do with land grants), were to continue in force if not unconstitutional.

Chapter IX

The Eagle Screams

Joint Occupation

UNTIL 1819 the governments of Spain, Russia, Great Britain, and the United States claimed a stake in the Oregon country. Boundaries of the region remained vague, but to diplomats they were generally understood to be the southern boundary of present-day Alaska, the northern boundary of Alta (Upper) California, the "Great Stony" Mountains, and the Pacific Ocean. As yet no one nation had been so bold as to claim an exclusive title to the entire region. And not wishing to commit themselves, the United States and Great Britain, in 1818, agreed by treaty to continue for ten years the status quo. Neither country would attempt to preclude the other.

Also in 1818, and again six years later, the forty–ninth parallel was proposed by the United States as a possible line dividing American and British territory in Oregon. England rejected the offer and in 1824 proposed instead the Columbia River as the boundary. Then two years later this proposition was amended by England to grant to the United States in addition a triangle of land between Puget Sound and Grays Harbor which would, however, not be contiguous to the proposed American territory south of the Columbia River. This offer was rejected by the United States, but in view of the near termination of the ten-year treaty, it was mutually agreed in 1827 to extend occupation jointly for an indefinite period with the understanding that it could be abrogated by either party upon giving one year's notice.

Spain was the first country to withdraw reluctantly from this exclusive circle of interested parties. By the terms of a treaty dated 1819, she agreed not only to transfer the Floridas

[139

to the United States, but also to recognize the forty-second parallel as the northern limit of Alta California, and to transfer all claims north of that line to the Americans. Russia also made an exit when in treaties with the United States and Great Britain, 1824 and 1825 respectively, the line of fifty-four forty was recognized as the southern boundary of Russia's North American holdings. By these three treaties Oregon at last became accepted as exclusively Anglo–American territory lying west of the Rockies between the forty-second parallel and fifty-four forty.[1] Henceforth it remained for the two English speaking claimants either to stay merged, to divide, or to conquer. Which would it be?

To begin with, the British, while not jumping the gun, were leading the race by the time the aforementioned treaties were completed in 1827. It will be recalled from preceding chapters that the great fur trading merger had been made, and that Governor Simpson and Chief Factor McLoughlin had organized the Columbia District with Fort Vancouver as headquarters. Many new Hudson's Bay Company posts were either in blueprint or under actual construction north of the Columbia River, and the coasting trade was being given serious attention by McLoughlin. Fur trading cavalcades were combing for pelts not only in all of Oregon but for good measure were crossing the Rockies into United States territory and were penetrating southward into California. Operations established prior to 1827 continued to gain such momentum that for nearly another two score years Americans were all but excluded from the region north of the Columbia River.

Politically Great Britain did nothing to violate the treaty of 1818, for no effort was made on her part to establish an official government in Oregon, although in some ways Company rule served as an effective political agency. The British government continued to support Hudson's Bay Company interests, and the English foreign office showed no disposition

---

[1] Formal names and respective dates of these treaties or conventions are as follows: (1) Anglo-American Convention, October 20, 1818; (2) Spanish-American Treaty, February 22, 1819; (3) Russian-American Convention, April 17, 1824; and (4) Anglo-Russian Convention, Februray 28, 1825.

to relinquish any of its claims to Oregon so long as the Company prospered. The British foreign minister, George Canning, moreover, saw a great commercial advantage in his country's ownership of the north Pacific coastline between the mouth of the Columbia River and the Straits of Juan de Fuca. Canning, unlike Simpson, looked beyond the region itself, and dreamed of a day when Oregon, as in the sea otter era, might become an important link in trans–Pacific trade.

For its part the American government likewise exhibited a sustained guardian interest in Oregon, although this attention was not at first very obvious. It developed slowly, but once fully awakened it took on the aspect of a "Blue Norther" racing at accelerated velocity across the Texan plains. President Jefferson had shown official interest in Oregon by dispatching Lewis and Clark to the region; by the Treaty of Ghent ending the War of 1812 the United States secured British recognition of American rights in Oregon (although the Pacific Fur Company property at Fort Astoria was never returned to its American owners); and finally, treaties with Great Britain, Spain, and Russia respecting joint occupation and boundaries were all evidence of early American official recognition of Oregon.

Watch Dogs of the Oregon Territory

In Congress, too, Oregon had its early advocates. One was Dr. John Floyd from western Virginia. Floyd first entered Congress in 1817, and during his early years in the lower House he was a voice shouting in the wilderness for the development of the Far West. On December 20, 1820, he exploded his first bombshell by asking in Congress that a committee be appointed "to inquire into the situation of the settlements upon the Pacific Ocean, and the expediency of occupying the Columbia River." The House approved, and Floyd became chairman of the new committee which one month later (January 25, 1821) reported a bill authorizing occupation by the United States of the Columbia River Valley. The committee based its claims to the region upon rights acquired under the Louisiana Purchase. Not one speech was made in defense of the bill, and it was left to die on the calendar. A year later

Floyd again introduced his measure; and though he spoke in its behalf, Congress declined further consideration.

Floyd had been rebuffed, but he had sown a seed which, fertilized and nursed by subsequent events, was to grow. In time it was to become a topic which was to require the fervent attention of every Congressman. Just such a situation arose in December, 1837, when President Martin Van Buren submitted a report on Oregon. Congress's attention was belatedly directed to the fact that British interests were still in control of Fort Astoria; a growing number of expansionists, both within and outside of Congress, directed their attention to the whole question of Oregon.

Senator Lewis F. Linn, Missouri, began wielding the cudgel February 7, 1838, when he introduced a bill in the Senate authorizing not only the military occupation of the Columbia River, but also the erection of an army fort on its bank. Obviously the passage of such a measure would mean the end of joint occupation. Linn followed up his proposal by introducing memorials from the people in Oregon and by submitting numerous resolutions which asserted American claims to the whole of Oregon, and which called for the abrogation of the Anglo-American agreement of 1818, the extension of Federal laws to Oregon, and the granting of one section of land free to American settlers in the region.

If Floyd had been tenacious in pursuing the Oregon problem, Senator Linn was nothing short of rabid. Time and time again he served notice on his colleagues that he would again present his bill, memorials, and more resolutions respecting Oregon. He was a man possessed of a great and abiding faith in the future of a region which should not be forsaken in the interests of Anglo-American amity. If for no other reason, the commercial advantages alone offered sufficient "inducements for the government of the United States to take formal and speedy possession," he said to the Senate on January 28, 1839. He became increasingly belligerent in his attitude toward Great Britain, and in a Senate speech, January 8, 1841, complained that the settlers of Oregon "would be numbered with the dead before the British Government would amicably settle a question of this nature." If the United States had a just right to the territory (and he believed it had), then "he was not the man to say it should be abandoned to any power on earth." There should be no appeasing of either the Hudson's Bay Company or the British government, for the only way they would be appeased would be to have "undisputed possession of the Northwest Territory." And should the United States go that far? Heaven forbid!

Punch, X, p. 201 (London, 1846)

AS *PUNCH* SAW THE OREGON BOUNDARY DISPUTE

"*Ridiculous Exhibition; or, Yankee-Noodle Putting His Head into the British Lion's Mouth*"

Slowly Linn gained supporters for his almost holy cause, and by 1842 Congress was the scene of increasing discussions on a bill (not unlike earlier ones) to erect forts on the Oregon Trail and to grant land in Oregon to private individuals. Thomas Hart Benton of Missouri and John C. Calhoun of South Carolina — both towering figures in the Senate — were among those who by that time were speakng vigorously for this bill.

"If Great Britain has a better claim, let her show it," said

Benton. "There was nothing to be ashamed of in this matter, if it was an honest claim." When in 1842 the Washington (Webster-Ashburton) Treaty, which settled the Maine-New Brunswick boundary dispute, failed to settle the Oregon boundary, too, debate in Congress became more heated. Since Daniel Webster was a Whig, it was to Democrat Benton's political advantage in his home state of Missouri to attack the treaty. Probably at no other time was the expression of Congressional opinion more bitter than on January 12, 1843, when Benton said: "They [the British] have crossed the 49th degree, come down upon the Columbia, taken possession of it from the head to the mouth, fortified it and colonized it, monopolized the fur trade, driven all our traders across the mountains, killed more than a thousand of them [by the Indians]. . . ." Reminiscent of Patrick Henry's "Give me liberty or give me death" speech, Benton concluded by saying: "Peace is our policy. War is the policy of England, and war with us is now her favorite policy. Let it come rather than dishonor!" Calhoun was not for relinquishing American claims by any manner or means, but he believed that the United States would over–extend itself if it attempted a military occupation of a region so distant from the sources of supply.

Debate on the bill (calling for forts and sale of land in Oregon) continued in the Senate until February 3, 1843, when it passed that body by the narrow margin of a twenty-four to twenty-two vote. The western Senators contributed the largest share of the ayes. Fortunately, so far as Anglo-American relations were concerned, the measure failed to pass in the House, and the bill was allowed to die.

Manifest Destiny

Usually the press, the pulpit, and other media of public expression provide a sounding board for Congressmen. In this controversy, timid lawmakers would have found strong support from the home front — especially in the West. Resolutions presented in Congress cried out for the establishment of United States authority in Oregon. Military occupation is necessary, argued Missiourian memorialists, to protect the settlers from Indians and Britishers.

When the American public, which had already begun its migration to the Willamette Valley, heard of Webster's failure to settle the Oregon question, sentiment, especially in the West, became aroused. People foregathered in groups and passed more resolutions and drew up more petitions and memorials. The Democratic editor found in the Oregon question a source of "hot copy" for the newspapers. "Let the whole West rouse up as one man, and her voice will not be unheeded," said Madison, Indiana's, *Courier and Constitutional Advocate*. And wrote one boastful Southerner to the New Orleans *Picayune:* "Some skeery folks talk about the navy of England; but who cares for the navy? Others say that she is the *mistress* of the ocean. Suppose she is — aint we the *master* of it? . . . Who's afeerd?"

Excitement over Oregon, and also Texas, continued to rise steadily throughout 1844, and when the Democrats met in convention that year they were in an expansionist mood. Nothing short of the Alaskan boundary would satisfy the convention, and the battle cry became "Fifty-four forty or fight." And into the platform was nailed the plank: "That our title to the whole of the Territory of Oregon is clear and unquestionable; that no portion of the same ought to be ceded to England or to any other power. . . ." On a platform such as this, the Democrats nominated as their presidential standard bearer James K. Polk, a "dark horse" from the South. So far as the Democrats were concerned, the battleflags had been hoisted and throughout the country defiance was hurled at the British cousins. It was "Oregon — Every foot or not an inch." It was the "re-occupation of Oregon and the re-annexation of Texas." And when the victorious Polk took office he was reminded by Senator E. A. Hannegan of Indiana that to fall short of fifty-four forty would be "a fall so profound — a damnation so deep that the hand of resurrection could not reach him."

Even at the Hermitage, old Andrew Jackson added his advice and admonition to those of others, about "Oragogon":

". . . expose England's perfidy to the whole civilized wor[l]d," wrote Old Hickory to Polk. "To prevent war with England a bold & undaunted front must be exposed. England with all her Boast dare not go to war."

The Diplomatic Bout

Meanwhile the diplomats kept their ears close to the ground, and despite the heat on the American sideline, channels of negotiations were kept open. Not through oversight had Webster failed to settle the Oregon boundary question in 1842. During that very year he had given attention to, and actually sounded out, the British, on a plan for a three-way division of the Pacific coast whereby Great Britain would come into possession of all territory north of the Columbia River, the United States would possess the land from that river to the thirty-sixth parallel, and from there on south the land would be Mexican. This division would have given the United States joint use of the Columbia, and ownership of San Francisco Bay and Monterey. Nothing came of this plan. Also, on repeated occasions the United States had offered as a compromise the present forty-ninth parallel as an international dividing line. For her part, Great Britain had more than once offered to accept the Columbia River as the boundary line. When Simpson and McLoughlin first established Fort Vancouver in 1825, they thought in those terms.

As the situation stood when the victorious Polk took office in 1845, the only area actually in dispute (diplomatically speaking) was the territory that lay between the forty-ninth parallel and north and west of the bending Columbia River. Despairing of a settlement, the British Minister Pakenham had recommended arbitration, but the proposal had been flatly refused by the American Secretary of State. To be sure, President Polk had been nominated on a platform claiming title to the "whole" of Oregon, but it is equally true that in his inaugural address on March 4, 1845, Polk left out the word "whole" and simply said: "Our title to the country of Oregon is 'clear and unquestionable.' " The word Oregon in this sense might mean anything. Moreover, the narrow margin by which

Polk had won his election gave him no clear mandate to push out John Bull and thereby start a war with him.

What, after all, was the English climate of opinion? How well had the British accepted this great popular upsurge against them? Was the British public likewise clamoring for all of Oregon or another fight?

In traditional manner the English were slow to become aroused, but when Polk's inaugural address reached the British public, war talk swept their country. The semi-official *Times* declared for a while that Great Britain was "unwilling to incur the ridicule of attaching importance to mere displays of ignorant rancor. . . . We are prepared to defend the claims of this country to the utmost, wherever they are seriously challenged." Said *Wilmer and Smith's Times* in referring to Polk's address: "About whatever savors, even remotely, of intimidation, John Bull is characteristically thin-skinned. There are certain animals that may be lead, but won't be driven — John Bull is one of them. . . . The new president's peremptory style has stirred up his bile. . . ." Very heated, indeed, was the *London Colonial Magazine* when it went so far as to say that "a war with America cannot but be productive of good." The magazine argued that "Never before were the states of the union in a worse condition for carrying on a war; never . . . was England better fitted. . . ." To appease the United States would be merely "to pave the way for fresh insults" from a country on which "little reliance is to be placed."

Officially the British government was willing to write off American campaign speech-making as designed for local, rather than foreign, consumption. Polk's inaugural address was another matter; it was taken as "official," and the British government circles were perturbed. In Parliament both parties presented a common front. John Bull's face was stern and determined, but it hid a secret desire for peace. If peace could be maintained with honor, Lord Aberdeen, conservative foreign minister in Sir Robert Peel's government, was even willing to yield the triangle in dispute. It was not worth a war. The cabinet, on the other hand, was less generous, because it feared the political consequences of capitulation. To win over his cabinet and the nation to his point of view without loss of national pride was the course followed by Aberdeen. By resorting to clever use of propaganda he succeeded in convincing his party and countrymen that trade and prosperity, nourished by international goodwill, was more important to England than what he thought was a pine swamp, a semi-navigable river, and a region threatened by American settlers ("border ruffians") and therefore no longer profitable to the fur trade. By successfully pursuing this policy the way was being paved for the road that led ultimately to solution by diplomacy.

For political reasons Senator James Buchanan had ridden on the fifty-four forty bandwagon, with the result that he was chosen as Secretary of State by President Polk. Even though deeply committed to his party, he preferred peace to war. His first attempt to solve the Oregon question occurred on July 12, 1845, when with Polk's acquiescence, he made a secret offer of compromise at the forty-ninth parallel to Richard Pakenham, the British minister to Washington. Rather than communicate this information to the compromise-minded Lord Aberdeen, Pakenham flatly refused the offer.

The situation became even more complicated when Polk withdrew the offer rather than to re-offer it to Great Britain through Louis McLane, the American minister at the Court of St. James. It was then up to the British to make the next move, and the astute Polk had learned enough to conclude that such a move would eventually come. For reasons given (namely Aberdeen's educational, or propaganda program), months elapsed before such another came. By January, 1846, Aberdeen had secured a pledge of support from the opposition Whig party, led by Lord John Russell. On April 23 following, the Senate voted to terminate the joint occupation (effective one year later), and upon receiving the President's signature four days later England was formally notified of this action. It appears that serving this notice broke the deadlock (not at all a surprise within informed circles), for on June 6 the British proposed a compromise which called for the mutual acceptance of the forty-ninth parallel, the line so frequently proposed by the United States. On June 10, Polk made a clever political move by sending this proposal to the Senate for advice; and two days later, by a vote of thirty-eight to twelve, the upper house advised its acceptance. Polk on June 15 signed the treaty, and the following day, June 16, the Senate, without even sending it to the committee on Foreign Relations, gave its final approval by a vote of forty-one to fourteen. Ratified by Great Britain on June 17, it was proclaimed August 5, 1846. 49th parallel agreemen

The instrument thus concluded was known officially as the Oregon Treaty. It contains five articles, which in summary provide: 1. As a boundary line between the United States and

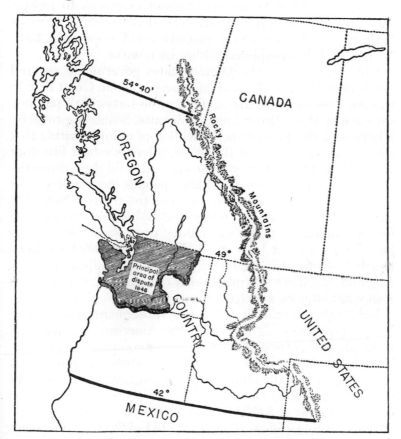

THE OREGON BOUNDARY CONTROVERSY

Canada, the forty-ninth parallel shall be continued westward from the summit of the Rocky Mountains to the middle channel separating the mainland from Vancouver Island; thence southward along the middle channel, through the Juan de Fuca Strait to the Pacific ocean; 2. The American portion of the Columbia River (the lower half) "shall be free and open to the Hudson's Bay Company and to all British subjects trading with the same. . . . 3. The possessory rights of the Hudson's Bay Company and all British subjects, as of the date of this treaty, shall be respected; 4. The possessory rights of the Puget's Sound Agricultural Company shall also be respected. Should the United States government ever seek to possess such property, both parties involved shall mutually agree as to the proper valuation to be placed on said property; 5. Ratification shall be completed within six months.

Out of this treaty the United States government secured the territory to which it had laid specific claim. Great Britain was the loser because, by accepting the forty-ninth parallel, she gave up the entire triangle in dispute. Senate approval by a large majority gives some indication of opinion within that ratifying body. Some of the more ardent western fifty-four forty men felt that their government had "sold them down the river." Most easterners and many people the country over were pleased about the ratification of the treaty. "Now that this question is settled," wrote the Baltimore *Patriot,* "we should not forget that this country owes something of acknowledgement, at least, to those senators who have been chiefly instrumental in effecting its amicable adjustment." In England, too, there was great relief that another Anglo-American war had been averted.

Relatively minor difficulties arose subsequently concerning British possessory rights within the American territory. By terms of another treaty between the two countries, signed July 1, 1863, a Joint Commission decided in 1869 that the United States should pay the Hudson's Bay Company and the Puget's Sound Agricultural Company for said possessory rights the respective sums of $450,000 and $200,000.

Some dispute also arose over Article I of the Oregon Treaty relative to the exact course of the boundary line to be drawn southward around Vancouver Island. It was difficult to agree upon which of two important channels was the principal one; and since the strategically important San Juan Islands lay between the two disputed channels, the point of argument was not without importance. One of the terms of the Treaty of Washington (1871) provided that this San Juan boundary dispute should be referred to Germany's Emperor as arbitrator. On October 21, 1872, the Emperor decided on the western, rather than the eastern, channel, which meant that the United States acquired the island area in dispute.

Chapter X

Oregon and Washington Territorial Politics

Significance of the Whitman Massacre

ALL THROUGH the spring and summer months of 1847 an ominous air enshrouded life at Whitman's mission at Waiilatpu. Dr. Whitman was discouraged; and as early as April he had thought seriously of terminating his Christian work among the Cayuse Indians. At Lapwai, his colleague Spalding also had misgivings. Everywhere in that inland area natives had apparently become surly and resentful. They had their reasons, of course. They believed that the whites — whites of various types — were gaining possession of their lands, were outsmarting them at trade, and were probably responsible for the horrible measles epidemic which had been taking a heavy toll of Indian lives. Many Indians thought Dr. Whitman, the recognized leader in those parts, was personally responsible for this life-taking scourge.

Whitman's apprehension was, in fact, well founded, for in the camp of Tilaukait, a Cayuse, a general massacre of the entire mission personnel was being plotted.

On November 29, 1847, the blow, as planned, was struck. That morning Cayuse Indians sauntered unobtrusively onto the mission grounds. But hidden beneath their blankets were their weapons. Casually Tilaukait, with Tamsuky, inquired at the mission kitchen for Whitman. The doctor entered, closed the door; as he conversed with Tilaukait, Tamsuky approached from behind and struck Whitman a fatal blow upon the head. This was the signal for the other conspirators to begin a general massacre. Out of 72 persons then present at or near the mission, the Indians slaughtered 14, including both

152]

Whitman and his wife Narcissa. About 53 women and children, many of whom were abused, were held captive until finally ransomed by the Hudson's Bay Company, while the remainder escaped.

This atrocity brought about two happenings of significance to the Oregon country. First, public indignation throughout the whole nation was so aroused that legislative action in making Oregon a territory was speeded up. Second, the Oregon Provisional Government, headed by Governor Abernethy, lost no time in ordering the military against the Cayuse, which, in turn, began the Cayuse War. More will be said later about this war, but for the present, the spotlight might be turned on the national capital.

Creation of Oregon Territory

Settlement of the boundary dispute in 1846 had removed all international barriers to the establishment of a territorial government for the Oregon country. Americans in Oregon, moreover, by means of memorials to the national lawmakers in Washington, had kept the territorial issue alive. But in spite of this, Congress had exhibited a lethargy irking to action-minded settlers in the Oregon country. Not until the arrival at the national capital of Joe Meek, ragged and dirty from his overland journey, and bearing the bad tidings of the Whitman Massacre,[1] did Congressmen seem to awaken and turn seriously to the territorial question. Prior to the massacre, Governor Abernethy had sent able J. Quinn Thornton to Washington, D. C., to look after Oregon's interests. His presence there at the time of the bizarre Meek's arrival was of added help in winning support on the Oregon territorial bill.

Although President Polk had previously recommended territorial status for Oregon, Southern senators delayed action, thinking that by so doing they might open Oregon to slavery. But during May, 1848, the President tossed into the lap of Congress the news of the Cayuse War, with a request for speedy action. Even so, heartbreaking delays occurred,

[1] Meek had left Walla Walla the first week in March, 1848, and arrived at Washington, D. C., the last week of May.

though not so deliberate as before. Stephen A. Douglas's bill to prohibit slavery in Oregon was introduced in the Senate and passed. The House, on the other hand, deliberated at great length, but finally approved the measure with amendments which the Senate accepted after an all-night session on August 13. The bill, excluding slavery from the proposed Oregon Territory, received the President's signature on the following day.

The territory was to comprise that part of the old Oregon country lying south of the forty-ninth parallel which by the treaty of 1846 was determined to belong to the United States. An initial appropriation of $26,500 was allowed for public buildings, a territorial library, lighthouses, and contingent expenses, and in addition, salaries for the territorial officers, including members of the legislature. Disappointing, though, were the omissions. A much hoped-for land donations provision was not included, although there were indications that a separate land act would follow. Urgently needed troops and munitions of war were not mentioned, even though the Secretary of War was believed to have sufficient authority to provide the military requirement of the Territory.

Oregon had in President Polk a staunch supporter, who wished to place the new territory on a solid working basis before he retired from office in March, 1849. No time could be lost, for if presidential appointments to office were delayed, such appointees would have slight opportunity to leave for the West before approaching winter.

As Territorial Governor of Oregon Polk appointed General Joseph Lane, called by many "the Marion of Indiana." A native of North Carolina, Lane as a youth had moved westward through Kentucky and into southern Indiana where in those years the struggle for life was not easy. His was an eloquent tongue, early applied to Indiana politics. Lane was elected to the State Assembly, and when the Mexican War broke out, he was one of the first in his state to enlist as a private in the 2nd Indiana Regiment of Volunteers. Before the close of the war he had been made a general and was one of the few performing distinguished service in the Battle of Buena Vista. Because of his notable war record and his loyal Democratic party affiliation Lane ("Jo" Lane to all who knew him) was offered the post as Territorial Governor of Oregon. To Joe Meek, who, with his picturesque appearance and backwoods mannerisms, had become a much-discussed personality in Washington, went the appointment as United States Marshal.[2]

The approach of winter weather in the Rocky Mountains was no deterrent to these two rugged men, who within one week after passage of the territorial act were on their way to Fort Leavenworth where a military escort, a surgeon, teamsters and servants numbering about fifty men were to join the officials on the long trail to Oregon. The party traveled a southern route through Santa Fe, Tucson, and the Gila River to San Pedro, California. One by one the escort deserted until the party was reduced to six. Upon reaching San Pedro, Lane and Meek boarded a sailing ship which carried them to San Francisco just in time to witness the first mad round of the California Gold Rush in the spring of 1849. Some of the men Meek saw milling around in San Francisco were his old Oregon acquaintances who had already been at the mines and had either made their stake or had given it up as a bad venture. Tempted though they may have been to try their own luck at the diggings, the two officers remained faithful to their trust, and boarded the ship *Janet* which took them to the Columbia. The last lap was by canoe, up the Columbia and then up the Willamette to Oregon City, where they arrived March 2, 1849, just two days before President Polk was to go out of office.[3] Lane, losing no time in putting the governmental machinery into motion, on the very next day, March 3, published a proclamation which officially declared Oregon a territory.

Governor Lane was an able administrator. One of his first acts as governor was to order a population census taken in the

[2] Other appointees were: Knitzing Pritchett, secretary; William P. Bryant, chief justice; O. C. Pratt and William Strong, associate justices; Amory Holbrook, United States Attorney; John Adair, collector of customs for the district of Oregon.

[3] News that Oregon Territory had been created reached Oregon by way of the Hawaiian Islands February 5, 1849, roughly a month before Lane's arrival.

Territory. He dealt with Indian uprisings in an adroit manner, and as speedily and forcefully as military resources would permit. And until the federal government acted, he declared the land law of the Provisional Government to be substantially in force. At Oregon City the first territorial legislature met during the summer of 1849. Legislation was enacted which, showing the community bias, forbade Negroes and mulattoes from residing in the territory. A law was passed assuring public support of schools, and another providing for the construction of roads.

Zachary Taylor, a Whig, succeeded the Democratic Polk as President of the United States in March, 1849. The new administration offered the post of Governor of Oregon Territory to the then young and little-known Illinois party worker, Abraham Lincoln. When Lincoln declined the honor, General John P. Gaines was appointed to replace Lane. Under Gaines the work of organizing the territorial government continued, although not without heated opposition from a Democratic majority which looked with considerable suspicion upon a Whig administration. Lane, meanwhile, as delegate to Congress for the Oregon electorate, directed his energies for the passage of an appropriate land law for Oregon Territory.

During the territorial period political party organizations began to crystallize and take form. The roots of such parties go far back into the American heritage. Americans have always exhibited an inclination to be politically minded, and experience in Oregon was not unlike that in other parts of the West: political activity was quick in coming. One has only to recall the so-called mission group or "party" which was active in forming the Provisional Government. But these earlier alignments were local in character and in scope of activity. Then, too, during the early fifties a group emerged in Jackson Country which adopted the label Peoples' Party, — another way of saying Whig. This group in 1854 threw its support to the newly born national Republican Party. A regular old-line Democratic Party, newly organized in Oregon in 1852, placed a party ticket before the voters. A Democratic machine was also not long in coming — one made up of politically prominent individuals soon to become known as the "Salem

Clique." [4] In spite of growing opposition from Republicans, the Democratic Party had the upper hand in the territory until the eve of the Civil War.

Oregon's first newspaper, *The Spectator* (Oregon City), edited by W. G. T'Vault, became a staunch supporter of Democracy, as did the *Oregon Statesman,* founded by the Methodist Democrat Samuel R. Thurston. The *Statesman* was first published at Oregon City and later was moved to Salem where it was controlled by Asahel Bush, the belligerent leader of the "Salem Clique," whose vituperative spirit created what became known as the "Oregon style of journalism" best described as "storm-and-stress" composition. The Portland *Oregonian*, edited by Thomas J. Dryer, was founded as a Whig organ and was first issued as a weekly, December 4, 1850. Later it became the leading Republican newspaper in Oregon, a position which it still maintains. To Bush, the *Oregonian* was just an enemy at which to throw invectives. "There is not a brothel in the land," wrote Bush, "that would not have been disgraced by the presence of the *Oregonian.* . . ." and if "the editor of the Spectator don't like to be called 'bullethead', 'blockhead,' etc., he should blame Nature for giving him a thick skull." Other Oregon newspapers taking an active part in politics during the fifties were those strongly opposed to the "Salem Clique," namely, the Eugene *Democratic Herald* and the *Oregon Argus,* a Republican newspaper.

The Donation Land Law

By all odds the most important piece of federal legislation affecting the Pacific Northwest during the formative years was the Donation Land Law passed by Congress September 27, 1850. Before its passage settlers lacked any real sense of security in regard to their land claims. To men and women who had endured the hardships of the long trek to Oregon and who had with great expenditure of energy cleared the forests and tilled the soil, an irrevocable title to their land claims was

[4] Among the prominent members of this group were L. F. Grover, Ben Harding, R. P. Boise, J. W. Nesmith, M. P. Deady, George L. Curry, William Tichenor, S. F. Chadwick and Joseph Lane.

a matter of utmost importance. Along with a number of minor matters the Donation Land Law provided that: (1) A survey would be made of the public lands of Oregon. (2) To every resident white, or half-breed settler over eighteen years of age, who was either a citizen or who had or would declare an intention of becoming so before December 1, 1851, a grant of 320 acres of land would be made. If married, the man and wife would each in his or her own right be entitled to 320 acres, or together a total of 640 acres. (3) Final title, or patent, would be issued after four years of residence on said land. (4) Heirs to claimants would be recognized under the law.

In 1853 an amendment to the Donation Land Law enabled persons unwilling to wait the full four years required for the patent to buy their lands outright for $1.25 per acre after two years' residence on said land. One year later, preemption privileges were extended to any unclaimed lands. In 1855 the donation privileges expired. Taken in its entirety the law was what settlers in the Oregon country had wanted, and it proved to be a great boon to agricultural settlement. But it was not without faults. In reflecting upon it, the historian Bancroft said: "It developed rapacity in some places, and encouraged slothful habits among some by giving them more than they could care for, and allowing them to hope for riches from the sale of their unused acres." To this one might add that the law encouraged agriculture at the expense of industrial and commercial developments in the territory.

Toward Statehood

Throughout the territorial period Oregon politics were controlled by Democrats whose most powerful stronghold was in the Willamette Valley. Whig and Know Nothing opposition was present, especially in southern Oregon where Republicanism was later to find its most verdant growth. When in 1856 the Republican Party put its first national ticket before the people, response in Oregon was lively and offered for the first time a potential threat to the Democratic machine. Even after the election zealous followers of this newborn organization continued their work in Oregon, calling a convention at Albany during February 1857, to unify their organization under the banner "Free State Republican Party of Oregon." Like groups in other parts of the country the party announced its opposition to the further extension of slavery into territories, and its approval of the construction of a railroad to the Pacific. But of apparently even greater significance was the party's demand for admission of Oregon into the union as a free state.

Meanwhile Lane, still Territorial delegate to Congress, was also working for Oregon's admission into the Union, though without reference to slavery. In 1856 he personally brought a bill for admission before Congress, but the lawmakers failed to act because of complicated reasons that were soon to become more evident. Lane's dogged perseverance kept him at the heels of Congress, and in its following session the House went so far as to pass a measure designed to invite Oregon to draw up a constitution preparatory for admittance into the Union.

Nor was the road to statehood in Oregon a smooth one. Until 1857 efforts by the Democrats to secure authority for calling a constitutional convention were sidestepped by anti-Democratic elements. Public opinion, however, during 1857 suddenly changed to favor such action, and by August 17 a convention, held at Salem, had prepared a constitution to be submitted to the territorial electorate for their approval. Headed by Matthew P. Deady, Oregon's distinguished pioneer jurist, for nearly a month this body deliberated on a desired form of government. Although slavery was discussed, at no time was this issue allowed to disrupt normal proceedings. On the question of whether or not Negroes and slavery should be allowed in Oregon, the Convention finally decided that the matter should be left to a vote by the people. In any case, the bill of rights specifically prohibited Negroes, mulattoes, and Chinese from exercising the right to vote. With the exceptions noted, the constitutional framework adopted by the Convention followed in most respects precedents established by western states that had been previously admitted into the Union.

Boundaries prescribed were those now existing, with the addition of Walla Walla Valley, a portion which Congress retained as a part of Washington Territory. At the polls in November 10,410 voters cast ballots on the question of approving the constitution, with or without the two amended stipulations regarding Negroes. The vote was apportioned as follows: for the constitution — 7,195; against it, 3,215; for slavery in Oregon — 2,645; opposed to slavery, 7,727; for admittance into Oregon of free Negroes — 1,081; opposed, 8,640. (Not until November 2, 1926, was this latter provision repealed). The results of this election demonstrated clearly the presence in Oregon of a strong Southern element (especially in Lane and Jackson counties), but it also revealed the overwhelming strength of the regular, old-line Democratic Party. Final decision rested with the Congress of the United States.

Within the grayish walls of Congress the political thermometer fluttered, rose, and fell with each passing day during the hectic prelude to the Civil War. For this reason there was no predicting the outcome at the national capital, and as it turned out, the question of the admission of Oregon became a political football used by teams not too clearly designated as to the color of jersey and headgear. Sectional advantages were clearly sought. "Bleeding Kansas" was a factor disrupting proceedings on the Oregon admission, as were also the Negro and slave clauses in the Oregon constitution.

In the Senate discussion centered on the number of people residing in the Territory and on the clause prohibiting "free Negroes" in the region. After some heated debate, the Senate passed the bill by a vote of 35 to 17. Debate in the lower house, coming after action in the Senate,was more heated. Ironically the measure there was sponsored by Alexander H. Stephens, a pro-slavery Congressman from Georgia, and it was opposed by Galusha Grow, an anti-slavery exponent from Pennsylvania. Several Republicans held that Democrats failed to apply to Oregon the rules that were applied to Kansas; they were also keenly aware of a fact (not known at the time of the Senate debate) that two Democrats had been elected to represent Oregon in the Congress. In the vote taken February 12, 1859,

114 favored admission, 103 opposed it.[5] The measure received the signature of President James Buchanan, and Oregon was thereby declared to be a state in the Union. Upon receipt of this news, the United States Marine Band led a joyous crowd first to the White House where the President made an address, then to the residence of Vice-President John C. Breckinridge, who also made a speech. Then serenades of Senators-elect Joseph Lane and Delazon Smith gave a final festive touch to the occasion in Washington, D. C.

Statehood and Impending Civil War

John Whiteaker, Democrat, was the first governor of the state. To him fell the responsibility of organizing the new governmental machinery. The first break in the solid Democratic front came in 1860 when Senator Lane revealed his secessionist leanings by accepting the nomination as the running-mate of John C. Breckinridge on the Southern Democratic, pro-slavery ticket which was to oppose the Republican slate, headed by Lincoln, and that of the Northern Democrats, headed by Douglas. It was even rumored that Lane with other west coast senators, notably William M. Gwin of California, favored the creation of a Pacific Republic which would support the South in the event of Civil War.[6] The new Republican Party, on the other hand, was gaining steadily in popularity. Pre-convention Republican politics in Oregon regarded William H. Seward as first choice for the party's standard bearer, but at the famous Chicago Wigwam Convention, Oregon's support went to Lincoln. With the actual outbreak of hostilities many Democrats gave their support to the administration, the Union (Republican) Party, but throughout the war years many Southern sympathizers remained in Oregon. The fact,

---

[5] A breakdown of this vote shows that on the affirmative side were 14 Republicans, 59 Northern Democrats, and 41 Southern Democrats; on the negative side were 73 Republicans, 4 Northern Democrats and 26 Southern Democrats.

[6] Nothing came of this move for the creation of a Pacific Republic, and with the outbreak of the Civil War, Lane personally returned to Oregon and lived out his life in the southern part of the state, considerably in disrepute for having supported a losing cause. He died at Roseburg, Oregon, in 1881.

however, that many Democrats did desert their own party in favor of the administration party was enjoyed by the Republicans who thereby gained the balance of power previously held by their opponents. Wrote Dryer of the *Oregonian:* "Have at you then, ye bullying Disunionists and ye time-serving Doughfaces! We need not the cowardly threats of one or the servile whinings of the other." Political happenings in Oregon follow very closely trends in other parts of the North.

In the critical November election the Oregon vote was close, with Lincoln receiving a slim plurality of 270 votes over his Democratic opponents. The actual count was: Lincoln, 5,344; Breckinridge, 5,074; Douglas, 4,131; Bell, 212. Oregon was the only Northern state to give a larger popular Democratic vote for Breckinridge than for Douglas. This situation is perhaps explained by the presence of many pro-slavery Missourians in the state, and by persisting loyalty of these elements to Lane, who shared the secessionist ticket with Breckinridge.

The fall of Fort Sumter caused a great stir throughout the Pacific Northwest, and many sons of this last frontier returned East to offer their services — some to the North, others to the Confederacy. Since the draft of 1863 did not apply to this area, for the war period as a whole the total number who saw service from both Oregon and Washington was relatively small.

In the election of 1864 Lincoln again carried the state by a rather narrow margin, and shortly after Appomattox old party groups reasserted themselves. By 1868 the cry of "Save the Union" was no longer a heavy vote-getter, and the political status tended to return to what it had been a decade earlier, with the Democrats bagging a majority of the offices. Not until the eighties did the Republicans once again control Oregon politics, a hold which was retained until early in the present century.

Washington Territory

Early settlers who crossed to the north side of the Columbia River and made their home at Tumwater and on Elliott Bay were of the same stock that chose the Willamette Valley as their western abode. And yet no sooner had there been this physical parting of the ways than differences arose. The Columbia River in those days was too mighty a barrier. Settlers in the Willamette Valley soon became too absorbed in their own local affairs to think of the strays who had entered present Washington; and, conversely, the latter were quick in thinking themselves neglected by the government seated on the bank of the Willamette. The situation did not necessarily stunt the growth of the Puget Sound communities. Except for the retarding effects of the Whitman massacre in 1847 and the California gold discovery one year later, the population there increased steadily in numbers. By the close of 1850 the number of inhabitants exceeded 1,000, and by an actual count in 1853, the white population north of the Columbia was placed at 3,965 whites.

On July 4, 1851, the first signal was sounded for separation from Oregon Territory. In an Independence Day oration at Olympia, John B. Chapman called for action which led to a convention at Cowlitz on the following August 29. At the Cowlitz Convention (for by such name it is known) reasons for separation were set forth; geographical isolation was the recurrent argument advanced. At this convention Seth Catlin, known to many as the "Sage of Monticello" (Washington, not Virginia), was elected president, and it was agreed that another meeting should be called for May, 1852, to draft a constitution preparatory to admission into the Union as a state. Why, so they thought, should they bother with territorial status?

Although the scheduled meeting was never held, one convened at Monticello on October 25, 1852, which with more modesty than might have been anticipated, memorialized Congress for the establishment of a separate territory to be named "Columbia." On November 4 the Oregon Legislature voiced its concurrence by adopting a similar memorial. And then, as if Congress were possessed of a sudden zest for speed, this joint request was approved by the lower house on February 8. Representative Richard H. Stanton, Kentucky, preferred the name "Washington" to "Columbia." The proposal thus to honor the Father of the country was gladly accepted.

Boundaries of the territory were fixed: west, the Pacific Ocean; north, the forty-ninth parallel; east, the summit of the Rocky Mountains; south, the forty-sixth parallel from the Rockies to the Columbia River, and thence along the Columbia to the ocean. Senate approval came March 2, 1853, and on the very same day President Millard Fillmore, a Whig, signed the bill. This act became known as the Organic Law, which with amendments served as a constitution for Washington Territory until statehood in 1889. When Oregon became a state in 1859, boundaries of Washington Territory were altered to embrace all of the original Oregon Territory (1849), excepting the confines of Oregon state. And when Idaho Territory was created in 1863, the boundaries of Washington Territory were made to correspond with those of the present State of Washington.

Since President Fillmore retired from office two days after the enactment of the Organic Law, to his successor, President Franklin Pierce, a Democrat, came the duty of appointing first officers for Washington Territory. Pierce selected Major Isaac Ingall Stevens as Governor, and J. Patton Anderson as United States Marshal. The new governor's first move, to order surveys made of possible railroad and wagon routes leading through the Cascades directly into the new Territory, shows, perhaps, that the demands of the Cowlitz Convention were not to go unheeded. To implement this project Congress appropriated funds, one item being $20,000 for the construction of a "military road from Walla-Walla to Steilacomb [Steilacoom], Puget's Sound." Among those assigned to do the actual surveying under the direction of Stevens was the future Civil War General, George B. McClellan, who at this time was a captain in the United States Army. McClellan was ordered to "use every exertion" to rush his work through to completion in time for 1853 fall immigration to use the road. Another assigned to make road surveys through the mountains was Captain John Mullan, about whom more will be said later.

When the party, which had left Washington, D. C., May 9, crossed the summit of the Rocky Mountains on September 24, Governor Stevens proclaimed the new territorial government to be in operation. Leaving Captain McClellan in the mountain wilderness with 40 men and 173 horses and mules with which to conduct the surveying and road operations, the governor, by means of canoe, hastened down the Columbia and up the Cowlitz rivers to his capital at Olympia. On November 25 he reached Olympia — described by a contemporary as a "rain-drenched mudhole." (Mrs. Stevens, arriving at Olympia the following year, recorded as her first impressions of this frontier capital: "Below us, in deep mud, were a few low, wooden houses, at the head of Puget Sound. My heart sank, for the first time in my life, at the prospect.") The new government was officially organized during February, 1854. In his first message to the legislature Stevens stressed the urgency for road building. A look at the Territorial Statutes for those first years is evidence enough that proposals of this nature were popular with the lawmakers.

Governor Stevens was born March 25, 1818, in Andover, Massachusetts. He was a West Point graduate (first in his class of 1839) and had received special training as an engineer. Like Lane of Oregon, Stevens was a man of great courage, energy, and capacity for getting things done. He faced the Indian problems with perhaps too much bluntness, but since his business was to negotiate treaties, negotiate them he did. Under his direction a force of army engineers and scientists totalling 243 men scoured the mountains for suitable passes, and finally demonstrated the feasibility of constructing a railroad line to Puget Sound along a northern route. Today three main railroad lines cross Washington's Cascade Mountains: the Northern Pacific over Stampede Pass, the Milwaukee Line over Snoqualmie Pass, and the Great Northern over Stevens Pass.

Less brilliant was the performance of Stevens's road-maker, McClellan. When McClellan examined Naches Pass, over which his road to Fort Steilacoom was to go, he gave up the project as a bad job and failed to carry out his military instructions. Only through the determined efforts of settlers themselves was a wagon road over Naches Pass completed during 1853, and in time for use by those immigrants who that year chose to go to the Puget Sound country rather than to the Willamette Valley as their precursors had done.

Aside from transportation and Indians, such important items as land legislation and the settlement of Hudson's Bay Company claims occupied the attention of Governor Stevens. Party politics was in full swing by 1855. By that time Stevens was considered a strong "anti-Indian man," and his followers, though opposed, were numerous and strong enough to secure the governor's election as Territorial delegate to Congress in 1856. Congressman Stevens worked diligently for the best interests of the territory he had so efficiently organized. Stevens, like Lane, was a pro-slave Democrat; but unlike his colleague, gave his loyalty and his life to the cause of the Union. He was appointed Colonel of the 79th New York Regiment in 1861 and took part that year in the defense of the national capital. Later he was elevated to Brigadier General, and in the Battle of Chantilly, 1862, met death while personally leading his troops against the enemy.

During the Civil War and for a decade thereafter Washington's territorial history parallels in many respects that of her neighbor to the south. There was the proverbial fight over location of the capital and the University. Olympia retained the honor as the seat of government, and Seattle clung successfully to its institution of higher learning, the University of Washington, founded 1861. Each decade witnessed a steady upward climb in population. From the 1853 figures (3,965 whites), the population rose to 11,594 in 1860, and by 1870 to 23,995. Politically-minded Washingtonians waited impatiently and unnecessarily long for their admission into the Union, which came in 1889.[7]

[7] For a discussion of political transition from territorial to statehood status in Washington, see Chapter XV.

Chapter XI

The Agricultural Frontier

The Spread of Settlement

SETTLEMENT of the Oregon boundary question, establishment of territorial governments, and passage by Congress of the Donation Land Law were all political acts which boosted American settlement in what are today the Northwest states.[1]

The United States Census reveals that the population by 1860 was well represented by merchants, professional men (especially clergymen), mechanics, teamsters, fishermen, and by men and women following many other professions and occupations. Typical of frontier communities, farmers or farm laborers made up one-half of the total population. Today less than one-fifth of the people in the United States are so classified. It may also be presumed that in a frontier society such as existed in the Pacific Northwest many who may have been labeled by the census taker as following trades also did some farming. A man who, for instance, called himself a blacksmith, or a clergyman, might actually have done more farming than either mechanical or professional work. The presence of large numbers of farmers is not surprising when one realizes that under the terms of the Donation Land Law good farm land could be had almost for the asking.

Immigrants first hastened to settle in all parts of the Willamette Valley. The region below the Willamette River Falls, an area where land was fair and transportation was simplified

---

[1] Governor Lane's census, it is recalled, placed the population of all the Oregon Territory at 9,083 in 1849. Following this year the increase was very rapid, with Oregon alone claiming a population of 52,465 in 1860, one year after statehood. When Washington Territory was created in 1853 its population was estimated at 3,965, but by 1860 this figure had risen to 11,594.

[167

by river navigation, became a favorite of many early American settlers. Moreover, it attracted the attention of prospective industrialists who saw in this portion of the Willamette Valley favorite sites for sawmills, gristmills, and shipyards. This area, therefore, was the first to witness, in addition to its agricultural development, a lively urban growth. Oregon City, at the site of the falls, stole the march on its rivals. It had served as the capital of the provisional government and also as the territorial capital until 1850 when that honor began to be passed around, first to Salem, then to Corvallis, and finally back to Salem again. The townsite of Portland was surveyed in 1844–45. Although its initial growth was slow, by 1850 the tiny village began to show signs of leadership. As both agriculture and commerce (primarily in agricultural commodities) began, communities in the Tualatin Plains southwest of Portland, Linnton, Milwaukie, St. Johns, St. Helens, Hillsboro, and many other lower Willamette Valley towns, emerged.

The region above the Willamette Falls early had been the choice of French Canadians who began to settle at French Prairie in the late twenties, and of those Americans who were attracted by Jason Lee's Methodist Mission. Surveys made in 1846 led to the establishment of Salem as the center of this farming community. Corvallis, first called Marysville, was originally settled in 1846, and by mid-century had become a thriving community of more than a hundred people. Simultaneously settlers began spreading out into the most attractive parts of present Linn, Lane, Benton, and Polk counties. Construction of the South Road brought many settlers into the Willamette Valley from the south. A considerable number of these found the region around the junction of the Willamette and McKenzie rivers to their liking, and therefore chose to remain in the vicinity of what are now Eugene (site of the Eugene Skinner land claim of 1846), Albany, Thurston, Pleasant Hill, and Cottage Grove.

The South Road also opened the way to ultimate settlement in southern Oregon. After 1850 agricultural communities emerged in the Umpqua Valley, as did also such towns as Umpqua City, Scottsburg, Elkton, Winchester, and Roseburg, the county seat of Douglas County. The discovery of gold in southern Oregon helped to boom the Rogue River area, especially Jacksonville, but farming settlements also emerged in this narrow but fertile valley where the cities of Grants Pass, Ashland, and later Medford, emerged.[2]

Discovery of gold in California in 1848 had created great stir and excitement among the people throughout the Northwest, and a large number of men left for the diggings in search of fortune. This exodus turned out to be temporary, and after about 1853 the spread of settlement and growth in population continued steadily. Except for numerous price fluctuations induced by an unsteady California market, the Gold Rush proved to be beneficial to the Oregon country. Although the Hudson's Bay Company managed to garner a considerable amount of California gold that flowed northward, much of this precious metal was brought into general circulation. Moreover, miners who had not yet been in Oregon abandoned their pursuit of uncertain fortune for something much more sure — free land in the Willamette Valley and the region of Puget Sound.

Not until after the settlement of the Oregon boundary dispute and the withdrawal of the Hudson's Bay Company headquarters from Fort Vancouver to Fort Victoria did Americans push north of the Columbia River in considerable numbers. As in the Willamette Valley or elsewhere in the Oregon country, land claims in future Washington were respected by fellow settlers and recognized under the pre-emption laws or Donation Land Law of 1850. Michael T. Simmons of Ken-

[2] These towns were very small. The 1850 Census places the population of Oregon City, the largest in the Territory, at 697. The bulk of the population was rural, and, listed by counties, was given by the government numeration as follows: Benton, 814; Clackamas, 1,859; Clatsop, 462; Linn, 994; Marion, 2,749; Polk, 1,051; Yamhill, 1,512.

A decade later, 1860, the Oregon towns had grown sufficiently to be officially noticed, and the most populous ones listed in the Census included: Portland, 2,874; Oregon City, 889; Salem, 625; Corvallis, 700; Eugene City, 1,183; Roseburg, 835; Jacksonville, 892; Ashland, 327; and Winchester, 412. Meanwhile county populations had climbed speedily upward. Benton by that time had 3,074; Clackamas, 3,466; Clatsop, with very little gain, had 498; Linn, 6,772; Marion, 4,150; Polk, 3,625; Yamhill, 3,245. Meanwhile Multnomah County with Portland as its seat of government had appeared in the list with 4,150; also eleven new counties with populations ranging from 95 in Tillamook on the coast (later to be famous for its cheese) to 1,689 inhabitants in Wasco east of the Cascades.

tucky and eight companions comprised the first group of Americans to settle north of the Columbia River. After considerable exploration they began a settlement at the southern tip of Puget Sound in 1845. Their settlement was first called New Market, but the name was later changed to Tumwater. Olympia which soon emerged near-by was destined to become the future capital of Washington Territory and State. Long and narrow Whidbey Island was also favored by American settlers, and Port Townsend was designated by the United States government as headquarters for the Puget Sound customs district. In 1850 settlers led by Alfred A. Plummer began filing claims in that part of the Sound. John C. Holgate selected a land claim in Elliott Bay — site of the present city of Seattle. Others came the following year and filed claims on land along the Duwamish River. Then in November, 1851, at Alki Point arrived a group now considered the Pilgrim fathers of Seattle — Arthur A. Denny, William Bell, and Carson D. Boren, who promptly staked out claims; during ensuing months Dr. David S. Maynard, Henry L. Yesler, and others came. Thanks to the friendly help of the Indian Chief Seattle there was born a small but determined community which today is Washington's leading metropolis, the city of Seattle.

To name all the noted pioneers who came to Elliott Bay would be tedious, but suffice it to list among the arrivals of 1853 Thomas Mercer (who brought the first wagon), Dexter Horton, and Edward and Seymour Hanford, who took up claims and became included in the roster of well known first families of Seattle.

During the early fifties many claims were filed on lands on the south shore of Juan de Fuca Strait near New Dungeness. And many of those who entered Washington over the newly constructed Naches Pass road found the land in Puyallup Valley to their liking and chose to file claims there. Two arrivals on the Chehalis River — Corydon F. Porter and J. L. Scammon — settled where Montesano is now. C. W. Stuart became the first to settle on the north shore of Grays Harbor, present site of Hoquiam; Shoalwater Bay was chosen by others.

Taken as a whole, most settlers showed a preference for,

and filed claims on, lands along the lower Columbia, the Cowlitz, in or about Olympia and Fort Nisqually, Elliott Bay, and some of the islands or lesser inlets of Puget Sound. As in Oregon, towns emerged.[3]

Throughout the decade of the fifties the Donation Land Law had been chiefly responsible for this rapid increase of population, especially rural growth, in the Willamette Valley. In Washington Territory, during the same decade, this was not the case, for by 1859 only twenty-four claims had been filed under the Donation Act; whereas forty-nine had been filed under pre-emption laws. The Donation Land Law, however, was important in the ultimate development of the entire Northwest, if not the entire West, for it was the slip from which the homestead law took root. On May 20, 1862, the homestead bill, receiving President Lincoln's signature, became a law. It gave to "any person who is the head of a family, or who had arrived at the age of twenty-one years, and is a citizen of the United States, or who has filed his declaration of intent to become such" the privilege of obtaining a quarter section of land from the government domain by paying a nominal filing fee, by residing on the land for five years, and by making certain specified improvements. For all its faults, and it had many, the Homestead Act, like arid land laws which followed, stepped up the agricultural expansion wherever free land was available.

The Indian Menace

The arrival of settlers was at no time good news to the Indians. To those Indians of the Pacific Northwest it meant exactly what it had meant to the aborigines in other parts of America: the gradual loss of their hunting grounds, and therewith deprivation of the means of livelihood. At times fur traders had been confronted with attacks and atrocities and very early settlers had suffered minor disturbances, but not until

---

[3] The Census for 1860 fails to state urban populations for Washington Territory, but it does give those of its nineteen counties. Clark County led with 2,384, followed by Thurston with 1,507, and Walla Walla County with 1,318. King, of which Seattle is the county seat, registered only 302 inhabitants.

the Whitman massacre in 1847 (previously related), did the Indians appear as a general threat to settlers everywhere. The forces which culminated in the Whitman massacre continued to swell in proportions thereafter, and finally culminated in the Cayuse War. (1847–50).

Without waiting for establishment of a territorial government, the provisional legislature took steps to raise troops

Courtesy Huntington Library

THE INDIAN'S PORTION

A *cartoon by F. Opper*, Puck, *March 20, 1880.*

and to seek out the enemy — in particular the Whitman murderers. A peace commission headed by General Joel Palmer, United States Superintendent of Indian Affairs for Oregon, was also appointed with powers to act in the event negotiations were possible, while at the same time Joe Meek was being sent overland to Washington, D. C., to seek help from the federal government.

Field operations were extremely difficult in view of the remoteness of the Cayuse country from the Willamette Valley, the seat of government and of settlement. A military base was established at the Cascades on the Columbia River, however, with Colonel Cornelius Gilliam in charge. The first attack was launched on January 8, 1848, at The Dalles by a detachment of fifty men led by Major H. A. G. Lee. Subsequently, commanded by Gilliam and Lee, were launched dual attacks which carried the fighting as far east as the Deschutes River where the Indians were beaten and dispersed. After some delay caused by orders concerning peace commissioners, Gilliam, with a force of five hundred men, marched without incident to Fort Walla Walla. Throughout the remainder of 1848 the skirmishes between American settler-soldiers and the Cayuse occurred without any decisive action, and without the murderers of the Whitmans having been surrendered. Fortunately the autumn emigration of that year came through without molestation. Not until after the establishment of the Territorial Government by Governor Joseph Lane in March, 1849, was peace in sight. With United States regulars at his command, Lane (after suppressing some Indian disturbances in the lower Columbia) made preparations for a fresh attack. At this juncture the Cayuse Indians, realizing that further resistance would be futile, acceded to the negotiators' demands by offering to surrender the murderers. The culprits, five in number, were placed in the custody of federal officers at The Dalles, then taken to Oregon City where they were tried and convicted of murder and then hanged in 1850. With this act the Cayuse War may be considered over, although to assert that white people were henceforth safe in the Cayuse country would be an exaggeration. Congress subsequently appropriated $100,000 to help defray the cost incurred by the campaign, and the remaining Cayuse were placed on reservations.

Pacification of the Cayuse did not by any means end Indian disorders. The heavy overland traffic occasioned by the Gold Rush in California precipitated clashes with the never-too-friendly Rogue River Indians. Southern Oregon settlers were obliged to absorb the brunt of these attacks, with heavy loss in lives and property, in what has been called the Rogue River Indian War, 1850–55. In dealing with this uprising Governor Lane displayed his soldier-like qualities. Without the slightest hesitation he faced his wily enemies. Councils were held with a remarkable display of courage. One council took place in the Rogue River Valley without success in 1850. Three years later Lane and his force returned with the added authority of a howitzer (always looked upon with respect by the Indians), and even though the situation there was precarious, another council was held. The place of meeting was Table Rock, one of the prominent mesa formations near present Medford, Oregon. Table Rock Treaty, ratified by the Senate one year later, was the outcome of the conference, and by its terms the Indians were placed on a reservation. As was frequently the case, not all remained within the confines of the reservation, and during 1855 fresh disturbances broke out in the Valley. Regulars once again appeared, and after several skirmishes in which settlers participated, peace was finally restored in Southern Oregon.

Simultaneously, new Indian uprisings occurred in the newly created Washington Territory. Following Lane's technique, Governor Stevens called a council at Walla Walla in 1855 to which the Yakima, Walla Walla, and the Cayuse Indians were invited. With the aid of Joel Palmer, Superintendent of Indian Affairs, negotiations were entered into with Chief Lawyer of the Nez Percé and many other chiefs and sub-chiefs, including Chief Garry of the Spokanes, who attended the meeting as a spectator. Peu-peu-mox-mox was also there representing the Walla Wallas, Yakimas, and Cayuse, but his mood was surly. Agreements, or treaties, were finally concluded whereby the Indians agreed to make land cessions amounting to 60,000 acres, and accept life on reservations in return for payments totaling $750,000. The Nez Percé obtained a reservation of 5,000 square miles and $200,000 for improvements; the Yakimas received two reservations, at Simcoe and Wenatchee, with similar payments; and the Walla Wallas, Cayuse, and Umatillas received the Umatilla reservation of 800 square miles and a sum slightly less than did the foregoing. In addition, allotments in the form of chiefs' salaries were made.

The Indians, however, were not satisfied with their treaties. Dissenting groups refused to comply with these arrangements; and even during negotiations plots were formulated for renewal of hostilities. Since the leading rebels were Yakima chiefs, the combat which ensued has been known as the Yakima War, 1855–59. Plans to attack at Naches Pass an American army unit led by Lieutenant W. A. Slaughter fortunately failed to materialize, but thereafter the situation throughout eastern Washington remained tense.

In January, 1856, a band of red men composed of Yakima, Klikitat, and Cascade tribesmen planned a bold onslaught, not only upon white settlers living near the Cascades, but upon river steamers as well. At the opportune moment, when steamers from both below and above the Rapids were at the Chenoweth portage, the concerted attack upon settlers and ships was launched. Fortunately all did not go well for the Indians; for one thing they failed to capture the steamships. The *Mary*, had a sufficiently large number of armed men on board to stave off the marauders long enough to get up steam and make an escape. One white man drowned during the encounter, and two were wounded. The other ship at the scene of the attack, the *Wasco*, also got away, with all of its crew aboard.

The escaped vessels spread news of the attack to the besieged settlers left at the Cascades and brought help from Lieutenant Phil Sheridan, of later Civil War fame, and forty dragoons stationed at Fort Vancouver. The steamer *Belle*, after landing the dragoons, hastened downstream for additional reinforcements, but the timely arrival of Sheridan and his men had prevented a wholesale massacre and brought about a restoration of normal navigation on the river. Late in April Colonel George Wright led a unit of regular troops into the Yakima country. These men, reinforced by other troops commanded by Colonel Edward J. Steptoe, either dispersed the Indians or effected their submission to instructions from American officers. Colonel Wright then as a means of maintaining peace ordered the construction of Fort Simcoe midway between present Yakima and The Dalles.

Chief Seattle, of the Duwamish league on Puget Sound, and his daughter, Angeline (for years to come a picturesque character in Seattle), remained doggedly faithful to the settlers at Elliott Bay. But neither Chief Seattle nor his loyal followers could offer assurance against individual Indians, in particular Chiefs Leschi and Patkanim, who smarted under injustices both real and imaginary. And neither were there assurances that the Yakimas east of the Cascades and vengeful Haidas from the north would not swoop down upon the struggling shanty town of Seattle. Governor Stevens took what precaution he could. He built military roads, erected blockhouses, organized a militia, and even secured some support of the United States Navy which stationed the sloop-of-war *Decatur* in Elliott Bay. When in 1856 an attack came, it was not without forewarning. The engagements which ensued were fierce, but decisively in favor of the whites.

Victories seemed empty so long as the Indians remained dissatisfied. In 1858 trouble broke out again in eastern Washington. There were rumors of Indian trouble in the vicinity of Colville where American miners were still searching for gold. During May of that year Colonel Steptoe with 158 dragoons and 2 howitzers left Fort Walla Walla for the scene of trouble. But on the detachment's leisurely ride northward war-painted Spokanes at a place called Pine Creek offered the first protest. Brushing the threat aside, Colonel Steptoe ordered his men to push on, only to be encountered with a running battle which involved not only the Spokanes but Coeur d'Alenes, Yakimas, and Palouse Indians as well. The engagement all but exhausted the American supply of ammunition and compelled a retreat, first to Pine Creek, and then under cover of darkness back to home base. The regulars had suffered a severe defeat, if not, as some call it, a "Steptoe disaster."

Smarting under this humiliation, Colonel George Wright, with six hundred well-armed regulars, hastened to go forth to seek revenge and to restore the shattered prestige of the Army. This overwhelming display of force, and the use of superior long-range rifles, proved too much for the embattled red men. At Four Lakes, on the Spokane Plains, the Indians suffered devastating blows which included the loss of eight hundred horses killed by the Americans to prevent recapture. On September 12 came the surrender and severe terms of peace.

By an order of the War Department, the Pacific area was

divided into two military districts, the Department of California which included the Umpqua region, and the Department of Oregon, embracing Washington Territory, with its headquarters at Fort Vancouver. Over the first was placed General Newman S. Clarke, and over the second General William S. Harney. Following this final pacification of the Indians, General Harney reopened the Walla Walla country to settlement. During 1859 Congress finally ratified the half score of treaties which four years earlier had been negotiated by Governor Stevens.

For the next thirteen years a semblance of peace prevailed between Indians and whites. But in 1872 the Modoc War broke out. In the lava beds near Tule Lake in northern California — a first class natural fortification — Modoc Jack and about fifty followers resisted a force of one thousand soldiers led by General Edward R. S. Canby in their efforts to confine the Modocs to their reservation. During a peace conference Jack treacherously shot and killed General Canby and another commissioner, and during engagements numerous soldiers were either killed or wounded by the well concealed Indians. The Modocs eventually ran out of ammunition and surrendered. Jack and three of his men were hanged; the rest were removed to Quapay agency in Indian Territory.

The final chapter in serious Indian warfare in the Pacific Northwest came in 1877 when Chief Joseph and his nonreservation Nez Percé (of which more will be said later) made a brilliant but unsuccessful dash toward Canada.

In summary, five major Indian wars occurred in the Pacific Northwest between 1847 and 1877: the Cayuse War, 1847–50; the Rogue River War, 1850–56; the Yakima War, 1855–59; the Modoc War, 1872; and Chief Joseph's War, 1877. In addition there were numerous Indian skirmishes in western Washington, including the attack on Seattle in 1856, and desultory raids by Indians which led either directly or indirectly to the wars previously discussed. By 1883 the Northwest Indians, for the most part, were on reservations either within or outside of the Pacific Northwest states. The largest of the reservations in the region were the Columbia and Colville on the upper Columbia River (south of the Canadian boundary); the Yakima and Coeur d'Alene in the places so designated today; the Klamath by the lakes which bear that name in southern Oregon; and the Lapwai reservation in west-central Idaho. Numerous small reservations were scattered throughout western Washington and Oregon. The reservation policy of the United States government was not a solution for the Indian problem; in fact, no solution for the Indian problem has been found to this day. Only through superior force, corruption, intimidation, and sheer weight of numbers have white people secured their desired ends.

Blazing Roads Through the Wilderness

Though much thought and attention had been given to roads and transportation during the period of the Provisional government, accomplishments were negligible. New roads had to be built, and old ones needed improvement. During the fifties much effort was expended in surfacing the roads for all-season use. Planking, or corduroy, was at first the most practical and most widely used method, because timber was abundant and sawmills already were numerous. Newspaper references to this type of road construction began to appear in 1850. One notes, for instance, in the *Oregon Spectator*, December 26, 1850, that the citizens of Salem and vicinity met to consider "the practicability of a Plank Road from Milwaukie up the valley to Albany," and after but a few minutes' consideration a committee resolved: "That, in our opinion, a Plank Road for general public use, is of far more utility to the people of the country, than rail roads." Further, plank roads would not be so monopolistic as railroads and would give every man, rich or poor, an opportunity to do his own trading.

By the middle of 1851 plank roads received the blessing of the territorial legislature, a signal for nearly all cities and towns to jockey for advantage. During August, 1851, the Portland and Valley Plank Road Company was formed, which actually began construction of a plank toll road from Portland over what is now the frequently traveled Canyon Road. A month later the road had been "commenced with skill" and would be completed with "unflinching energy." By September

27 enough grading had been done to permit inaugural ceremonies. Colonel William M. King of Portland, president and
superintendent of the company, placed the first plank into
position but not until the assembled group had listened to at
least five fervidly patriotic orations. All were conscious of
their pioneering venture in road building, for it was empha-

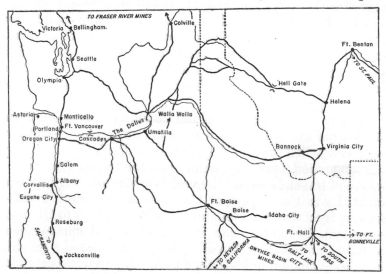

PRINCIPAL WAGON ROADS IN THE PACIFIC
NORTHWEST BEFORE 1870

sized that this was to be the first plank road on the Pacific
shores. The ladies lent their support by serving a barbecue
dinner spread upon the newly laid planks.

One serious drawback during the territorial period was that
such enterprises were left largely to private effort. The legislature did little more than direct territorial road commissioners
to indicate the general course of projected routes and to require from every male person between twenty-one and fifty
years of age a day's work a year on roads. The condition of
Oregon's roads varied, of course, with the season. For the most
part they were impassable during the rainy period, but by
1856 fairly good roads during dry weather were reported.

Not until Oregon became a state in 1859 did the first real

boon to road building come. By an act of Congress the new commonwealth was required to use five per cent of the net proceeds from public land sales for road building and other internal improvements. During the first three decades of statehood the Oregon legislature lent an attentive ear to the popular demand for roads, private road companies, reminiscent of earlier days, continued to function.

When in 1844 settlers advanced northward into what is now the commonwealth of Washington, the problem of roads moved along with them. So serious did it seem to the first Washingtonians that even then they considered separation from Oregon on the ground that no transportation facilities had been provided.

Prior to 1851 — the year of the Cowlitz Convention, when steps were taken to form a separate government — settlers were compelled to rely solely, as the Hudson's Bay Company has long relied, upon the streams and the trappers' trails as a means of travel. Not until the year Washington Territory was created was the important Cascade, or Emigrant, Road — leading from over the mountains via Naches Pass to Olympia — opened. Governor Isaac Stevens took road improvement seriously, and each session of the legislature passed a steadily increasing amount of legislation pertaining to transportation. Provisions were made for the location, establishment, and operation of ferries, but apparently nothing was done about bridge construction.

Throughout the whole period before 1890 there was a persistent effort to improve lines of communication between the Pacific Northwest and the states, especially by finding a better way to cross the Cascade barrier. Federal aid for this was sought and at the time secured. By 1859 a pass known as Walker's Road had been cut through the mountains north of Mount Hood, but there appears to be some doubt of its usability. This was likewise true of the McKenzie Pass and the Willamette Pass, which were not considered practical routes during the territorial period.

Back of this vigorous road activity was, quite naturally, the general desire to relieve the isolation in which the Oregon pioneers found themselves. People needed to find better and quicker ways to reach the market; they wanted to move with more speed and facility from one place to another. The greater increase and spread of settlement that came with passing years accentuated, on the one hand, this problem of communication, and, on the other hand, helped to heighten the cry that was ultimately to bring some relief.

The Struggle for a Living

Fur companies had made some provision for the livelihood of their trappers and traders. But no company nor outside agency assumed any responsibility for the pioneer farmers whose very living had to be extracted from the soil. "Wheat," wrote an early local historian, "is the staple product of the Willamette Valley. Its suitableness has ever been recognized since the arts of agriculture began in the northwest, and the first rude attempts at cultivation were made." Wheat, however, was not the sole article of production during these early years. Quantities of oats, potatoes, hay for the livestock, poultry, eggs, and a variety of fruits such as apples, peaches, pears, and vegetables — beans and peas — were also produced. Families in those days did most of their own processing. They dried their fruit, made cider, rendered lard, cured bacon and beef, salted pork, dried and smoked fish, and made cheese. Wool was at first spun, woven, and made into garments in the home. Pioneer farmers, moreover, were adept at tanning hides, forging tools, tinkering, and building homes. In these and other respects pioneer life in the Oregon country was not unlike that experienced by numerous other American frontier areas that had existed before the Pacific was at last reached.

Oregon pioneers, like other pioneers before them, were on the whole industrious, resourceful, and self-reliant, but not entirely self-sufficient. Many things were needed from the outside, articles that could best be secured by trade. The people were greatly in need of more and better farm machinery; they were eager to increase by outside trade or purchase their small but growing numbers of horses, cattle, and sheep. Before boarding the covered wagons pioneer mothers had sacrificed precious pieces of furniture in order that room might be made for seed, grain, and essential farm equipment. In their new homes in the Far West they hoped to replace these articles.

One step toward the fulfillment of these needs was taken as early as 1837 when the Methodist Mission group, in conjunction with the Hudson's Bay Company, had organized the Willamette Cattle Company. Formed at the instigation of Lieutenant William A. Slacum, U. S. N., then visiting the Pacific Northwest in an official capacity, the company planned to buy a herd of wild, but inexpensive slim-flanked Spanish cattle in California and drive them overland to the Willamette Valley along the route followed by Ewing Young and Hall J. Kelley (in 1834 they had driven 120 horses and mules into the Valley from California). No less than 630 head of cattle reached the Valley in one big drive engineered by the Willamete Cattle Company. Though somewhat the worse for wear, these cattle soon thrived and increased in the Willamette Valley where grass was plentiful. Difficult as these experimental cattle drives were, they demonstrated, a full quarter century before the much publicized Texan drives began, that large herds of cattle could be rounded up and driven hundreds of miles over open country and across rugged and wooded mountain ranges. These cattle, supplemented by others driven across the Plains and by bulls imported from England by the Hudson's Bay Company, gave the region its start in the cattle business.

Ordinary transportation of goods within the farming area was much less spectacular and exciting than the long drives. It was done by means of slow, lumbering Conestoga wagons, and water craft of varying types. Here again, in the matter of delivering produce to the nearest market, the pioneer farmer relied upon himself. In all probability he still had on hand the reliable Conestoga wagon, or prairie schooner, that had taken him and his family across the Plains; this served well for hauling grain and other produce destined for the market. Commercial wagon freighting, such as was so familiar to the Great Plains, never became extensive west of the Cascades. It was in the Rogue River Valley, rather than in the Willamette Valley, that wagon freighting enjoyed its fullest development so far as this western fringe was concerned. Local farmers were unable to meet the demands of gold miners who stormed into the region during the early 1850s; and, since the Rogue River was not navigable for coastal vessels, great quantities of goods had either to be packed in or freighted in from outside sources.

Lines of Conestogas and pack trains converged on Jacksonville from both the Willamette Valley and from California. Crescent City, for instance, a California seaport 120 miles from Jacksonville, supplied not only local agricultural produce, but much other merchandise shipped there by water from San Francisco. Pack trains were used exclusively on the mountain trail from Crescent City, and freight rates were accordingly very high. The distance from Portland to Jacksonville was almost 325 miles, but the greater distance was offset by the presence of at least the semblance of a wagon road which teamsters could use during dry seasons. At first freight moved but one way, from Portland south, and the chief commodities shipped to the southern Oregon mining camps were groceries. The emergence of farming communities in the Rogue and Umpqua river valleys made a two-way trade possible by about 1870. By that time surplus farm goods produced in southern Oregon, namely bacon, lard, butter, cheese, and hides, were sent to Portland for export trade in exchange for dry goods received from Portland.

Ocean commerce depended upon the casual comings and goings of sailing vessels and "steam schooners" which worked their way up and down the California and Oregon coasts. These craft were well adapted for maneuvering into what skippers called "dog holes" — small coves and rudely improvised harbors — where cargoes of lumber and other commodities could be taken aboard for delivery in many parts of the world.

Lumber led the list of exportable commodities; flour was second in importance. One mill alone, the Standard Mills of Milwaukie, which were built at the close of the fifties, produced more than 250 barrels of flour daily. Although the salmon industry had enjoyed a continuous increase since its humble beginning during the Hudson's Bay Company days, the export of canned salmon did not begin until 1871. A woolen mill was erected in 1856 to take care of the local wool, which according to the figures for 1860 had reached 200,000 pounds.[4] Trade with foreign countries was as yet very small. In return for outgo the Pacific Northwest imported liquors, glass, iron, tin, and such foodstuffs as rice, sugar, molasses, ore, and other items.

This already-thriving ocean commerce was greatly augmented in 1857 by the discovery of gold in the upper Fraser River country. It is estimated that in the year 1858 no less than 23,000 miners left California to seek new fortunes in the wilds of Canada. Shipping interests profited from both this passenger service and the shipment of supplies. In spite of disasters and reverses the ocean shipping business of the Pacific Northwest emerged from the fifties with a firm footing. It was meeting very definite needs which, in the absence of railroads, could hardly have been met in any other way.

The Social Fabric

Pioneer society of the Pacific Northwest, if not complex, was at least segmented. French Canadians distinguished themselves from other groups linguistically, religiously, and socially. Their spoken French was of the form retained by their ancestors in Quebec following their migration from France during the seventeenth century. It had become modified in many ways during the preceding two centuries, but it remained basically the vernacular French of the age of Louis XIV. French Canadians were, of course, Catholic; their loyalty to the Church, and in some degree to the Hudson's Bay Company, set them apart from American elements. Many had Indian or half-breed wives, but that was no mark of distinction in a region where such practice was widespread. Most were illiterate. By the 1840s many French Canadians had retired from the fur trade and had turned to farming. But fol-

4 With reference to actual exports and imports H. H. Bancroft asserts: "In 1857 Oregon had 60,000 inhabitants, and shipped 60,000 barrels of flour, 3,000,000 pounds of bacon and pork, 250,000 pounds of butter, 25,000 bushels of apples, $40,000 worth of chickens and eggs, $200,000 worth of lumber, $75,000 worth of fruit-trees, $20,000 worth of garden-stuff, and 52,000 head of cattle, the total value of which was $3,200,000."

lowing the plowed furrow seemed dull compared with the thrilling and carefree existence of the *voyageur*.

Nor did all the Americans love the restraining life of the farm or the bourgeois existence of the merchant. Many Americans in the Northwest before 1860 were Mountain Men, or free traders. Robert C. Clark, in his book on the history of the Willamette Valley, characterized the Mountain Men as a rough, tough, and boisterous type, and very naive. As an example, Clark cites "Uncle Joe" Meek, first United States Marshal in Oregon, who, when asked to account for $40,000 due the United States Government from the sale of a smuggling ship, replied, "Why thar war barly enough for the officers of the court!" As a group these restless, semi-literate, pseudo-agricultural people were of the type that in Oregon and elsewhere were always in the advance of the westward march. They were the squatters who came into a new area, made little clearings in the wilderness, built cabins, then moved on. In Oregon, however, they had reached the farthest West, and were obliged either to remain or "hit the back trail."

Seldom on any frontier was there a more respectable or more substantial group of immigrants than those who comprised the membership of the great caravans that arrived annually from over the Oregon Trail. Down-and-outers found no place of welcome in Oregon caravans. A considerable outlay of hard-earned cash was needed before going over the Trail, to outfit oneself with essential equipment — wagon, livestock, foodstuffs, tools. The shiftless and indolent classes of mid-nineteenth century America found it difficult to raise the capital necessary for such a venture. People of the dependable classes were to constitute the bulk of home builders, settlers, and trades people throughout the Willamette-Puget trough and in southern Oregon. From their ranks, many originally from New England, came the political, educational, and moral leadership.

Reference has been made to industries in and out of the home. Each farmer tried to make himself as self-sufficient as possible. Work was hard, hours long, but life was not without gaiety. There were picnics, weddings, and other get-togethers; church-going was for most people a cherished weekly event; and then there were such practical sports as hunting and fishing which made for welcome diversions and provided variation to the otherwise monotonous diet of potatoes, bread, salted pork, and dairy products. During the long, rainy winter months settlers remained indoors a good part of the time. It was here within the home that the cultural flame (see Chapter XVI) was not only kept aglow, but was gently fanned.

CHAPTER XII

The Stagecoach and Paddlewheel Era

The Stagecoach Arrives

NOTHING so distressed the settlers as being isolated — isolated from one another and from the outside world. For this reason the coming of regular transportation, the establishment of postal system (inadequate though it was), of express service, and finally the scheduled arrivals of splashing paddlewheelers were important events in the progress of frontier society. The sight of the first stagecoach in the Pacific Northwest was to most settlers like seeing an old friend once again. In the East, from whence most of the people in the Oregon country had come, stagecoaches had been in general use for nearly a century. Scarcely had the Provisional Government, with the help of a few commercially-minded and public-spirited individuals, begun the building of crude roads when stagecoach service in Oregon began. The first mention of a commercial stage line appeared in the Oregon City *Spectator*, November 29, 1846, when S. H. L. Meek, proprietor, announced that the "Telegraph Line" with "Eight Ox Power" would operate on a semi-weekly basis between Oregon City and the Tualatin settlement, "rain or no rain — mud or no mud — load or no load — *but not without pay.*"

Progress was slow at first, but within a decade after Meek's inauguratory venture stagecoach service was widespread. One firm, calling itself the Pioneer Line, maintained a tri-weekly route between Oregon City and Corvallis. "The Stages are of Concord manufacture," is the assurance of this proprietor, "comfortable and safe. The horses are capable, and make good time, and the drivers are reliable." Soon thereafter B. and E. W. Davis pushed stagecoach transportation farther southward by establishing weekly service between Corvallis,

[187

Eugene City, and Winchester on the Umpqua. During the rainy season roads between Eugene City and Winchester were such that the Davis concern had to convey mails and passengers by horseback. In each instance the best of service was assured the traveling public. The speed of the coaches operated by the Oregon Stage Company suggested to its owners a "head-swim" pace. But not to be outdone, H. C. Riggs boasted:

. . . The word 'FAIL', has never been written or printed in his [Riggs'] 'Lexicon!' 'Live or Die, Sink or Swim, Survive or Perish,' he is determined to keep up with the improvements of the day and age. — In the swift progress The Great American People are making in the direction of Universal Empire, should horse-flesh prove too tardy, he *may* avail himself of the breezes of heaven, as *indicated above,* and meet the wishes of a generous, go-aheaditive public.

N. B. This notice is merely 'annunciatory.' The *Horses will be hitched on at the expiration of the twenty days.*

North of the Columbia River development of the stagecoach business followed a similar pattern. The very first passenger service out of Olympia was in 1854, and it appears to have been offered in connection with wagon freighting. It was the custom for freighting concerns in Olympia to meet Cowlitz River boats, and, with an eye for extra business, the freighters offered to transport passengers to and from the river landing. Regular stages, however, came as soon as business warranted the establishment of a line. The first regular stage vehicles used in Washington Territory were the mudwagons, and the selection was an admirable one. Ezra Meeker, a prominent pioneer, recounted how the unhappy travelers in and out of Olympia were "conveyed . . . over either the roughest corduroy or deepest mud, the one bruising the muscles the other straining the nerves in the anticipation of being dumped into the bottomless pit of mud."

Mail Bags

Throughout the entire pre-statehood period mail service remained abominable. Complaints were constant, bitter, and many. "What has become of the Post-office agent for Oregon and California?"; "Oregon has been sadly neglected"; "Just think of it; the citizens of Oregon are required to pay *four* times the amount of postage, on all correspondence, that is ex-acted from Utah, Deseret, and Minnesota"; "Our suffering is intolerable!"; "We cannot account for the neglect. . . ." These are some of the running comments on the United States mail service in Oregon before statehood. "Job, who 'rests in Paradise,' is reported to have been a very patient man when upon the earth," said *The Oregon Statesman,* "but we question whether he had enough of that amiable virtue to have enabled him to preserve his equanimity if he had been a 'sufferer' from the mail arrangements or *dis*-arrangements in Oregon."

Action of the federal government in establishing adequate mail service had been slow in coming, at least to the minds of the people who made up such communities. If, before 1850, letters were to be sent to the states, one simply waited for someone who might be going East and who would be willing to deposit the letter in a box upon reaching Missouri. The need for a post road was stressed alongside the argument that the government should build immigrant and military roads in the region. In 1846 Congress, after deciding against the establishment of a post road between Missouri and the Columbia, appropriated $100,000 to provide bi-monthly service between the states and Astoria via the Isthmus of Panama. The next year federal mail actually reached this distant outpost at the mouth of the Columbia, but only after the provisional government had tried to establish a mail system of its own during the previous year.

Not until three years following the first delivery of United States mails at Astoria did the government, again after more memorials had been sent, establish definite post roads in the Oregon Territory. The first was from Astoria up the Columbia to the mouth of the Cowlitz; from there on up the Columbia to the Willamette, and southward to the Umpqua. The second was to run between the mouth of the Cowlitz River and Nisqually. Mail up the Pacific coast was to be carried by the Pacific Mail Steamship Company boats, but the service of this Company left much to be desired. One of the Company's ships, the S. S. *Caroline,* first sailed up the Columbia River with mail in 1850. The service turned out to be very irregular, and the press continued to rage against "the provoking irregularity, and wanton disregard of the public accommodation" of the Pacific Mail Steamship Company and against the "reckless and almost ruthless manner in which the service is performed." Settlers in the Puget Sound area, moreover, felt left out, and so the clamor continued until 1855 when Congress authorized direct semi-monthly service between San Francisco and the head of Puget Sound.

Overland Stage and Mail Service

In 1854 at Sacramento was formed the California Stage Company, a giant merger, which soon brought the Oregon country into direct and regular communication with the outside. This consolidation, directed by prominent staging proprietors in California, absorbed at least five-sixths of all the staging lines in California. The capital stock was fixed at one million dollars, and Sacramento became the headquarters for 170 stations scattered over 14 separate routes. At the time of the merger, the California Stage Company was the largest organization of its kind in the United States.

With this organization, and with ample equipment on hand, this new company soon began to expand, especially in the direction of Oregon. From its original northern terminus at Shasta City, the firm stocked the road to Yreka via the Pitt River, making use of an old immigrant road. In spite of many difficulties, the California Stage Company was determined to push its line as far north as Portland. In order to do so it was necessary to combat an Indian menace and to construct long stretches of road in northern California. By 1860 the road was opened from Sacramento to Jacksonville, Oregon. From this place there existed a stage road all the way to Portland. At last four- or six-horse stage and mail service between Sacramento and Portland, a distance of about 710 miles, could be offered with comparative safety, comfort, and speed. Service was formally inaugurated September 15, 1860. Stages left Portland and Sacramento, respectively, every morning at six o'clock. South from Portland the route passed through Oregon City, Dutch Town, Salem, Albany, Corvallis, Eugene, Oakland, Roseburg, Canyonville, and Jacksonville. Along the entire route were 60 stations, 14 district agents, 75 hostlers, and 35 drivers. To stock the road required 28 coaches, 30 stage wagons, and 500 head of horses. Although seven days were allowed by the mail contract for this run, the actual scheduled time was six days, seven hours. Now at last, wrote a Sacramento correspondent, one need not "risk his life on the rough coast of Oregon." Instead he "can take a quiet seat in the stage, pass through a most interesting section of country, and reach Portland at his leisure."

Through this period of rapid growth on the Pacific Coast the United States government could not disregard the clamor of the West for rapid overland mail service. The first of several feeble steps to establish such operations was taken by the federal government when a contract to Absalom Woodward and George Chorpenning to carry mails monthly between Sacramento and Salt Lake City was confirmed on October 16, 1851. In 1857, following a long dispute in Congress in which sectional interests manifested themselves, Postmaster-General Aaron V. Brown at length determined to establish a temporary stage and mail line between San Antonio, Texas, and San Diego, California — a line which was too slow and too far south to help the Pacific Northwest in the slightest.

Of much more importance to the West than the foregoing half-hearted measures was the passage by Congress on March 3, 1857, of the Post Office Appropriations Act providing funds for a stagecoach and postal service that was really commensurate with the needs of the people in the West. Among other things this act authorized the letting of contracts for the "conveyance of the entire letter mail" from some point on the Mississippi River to and from San Francisco for a period of six years "with good four-horse coaches on spring wagons." Said service "shall be performed within twenty-five days for each trip." On July 2, 1857, the contract was awarded to John Butterfield, William G. Fargo, William B. Dinsmore, and others. In accordance with the terms, the Post Office Department selected a route about 2,700 miles long, to start from St. Louis,

Missouri, and Memphis, Tennessee, and to converge at Little Rock, Arkansas; "thence, *via* Preston, Texas, . . . to Fort Yuma, California; thence, through the best passes . . . to San Francisco." For this semi-weekly service the contractors were to receive $600,000 annually.

Service over the Butterfield route began on September 15, 1858. Successful completion of the first trip from East to West, made in 24 days, 18 hours, 35 minutes, was regarded everywhere with pride and approbation. So elated was President Buchanan when he heard that the first journey had been made that he wired John Butterfield: "I cordially congratulate you upon the result. It is a glorious triumph for civilization and the Union."

Inauguration of the Butterfield service between the East and California had an immediate effect upon the Pacific Northwest situation. It not only meant that the California Stage Company stages could connect with those of the Butterfield Company (which they did) but, as has been shown, within two more years this combined network of mail and postal service was pushed north to Portland. In 1860 mail and passenger service was offered between St. Louis and Portland, a distance of more than 3,400 miles via El Paso and over what must have seemed to the northwesterners a tremendous detour, in thirty-two days' time.

The Civil War brought about changes too numerous to relate here in detail. Overland service between the Pacific coast and the East, of course, had to be shifted from the southern route to one that followed roughly the old California-Oregon Trail. Butterfield and Wells Fargo interests gained control over the section west of Salt Lake City; the well known freighting firm of Russell, Majors and Waddell served the area east of the Mormon capital.

At the close of the war the California Stage Company went into eclipse due to its failure to secure favorable mail contracts. Thereupon, the mail contract for the California-Oregon route was granted to a Portland man, Henry W. Corbett, one of the publishers of the Portland *Oregonian,* and a person whose personality and business success soon won for him a seat in the United States Senate.

Corbett gave his new line a good send-off, July 1, 1866. Many reorganizations were made; there were personnel changes, and large varicolored placards were posted to advertise the "Oregon Line Stages" which go "Through [from Portland] in Six Days to Sacramento." A traveler on the line wrote Corbett August 14, 1866, praising the organization very highly. "The Hostlers all seemed to be on hand, . . . the Stock on the whole route in good order; in fact there was but little . . . that could be complained of except bad bridges. . . ." Although changes were subsequently made in organization, the Oregon Stage Company continued to control the stagecoach business between California and Oregon until these two states were linked by rail in 1887.

Express and Stagecoach Monopoly

Until about the middle of the nineteenth century methods of transporting freight were as inefficient as the proverbially tedious modes of passenger transportation. Freight, for the most part, was either moved aboard leisurely windjammers, in lumbering Conestogas, or on the backs of phlegmatic pack mules. Transmission of news and of the mails was fast only in relation to the snail's pace set by the freighters. If parcels were very valuable and extraordinary haste were needed, special messengers might be employed or delivery might be entrusted to a stage driver who as a favor, or for a consideration, would personally transact such special business if it could be done along his prescribed route of travel. Not until about the 1830s did it occur to anyone that profitable business, even great fortunes, might be made out of the speedy delivery of certain types of goods, namely small packages of high value — gold dust, bullion, jewelry securities, or perishable commodities. The transportation of such items has come to be termed "express."

Organized express companies first appeared on the Atlantic coast, where for a long time stage drivers and shipping agents had in a measure fulfilled the duties of expressmen. Sending money or parcels by mail was at first not thought of, and, as Alvin Harlow has written, a "business man's contemplated journey to another city would be noised about days in advance, and his acquaintances not only burdened him with letters and commissions, but pointed him out to others." Just who was the first expressman is therefore difficult to tell. B. D. and L. B. Earle are known to have been bank messengers over the Boston and Providence Railroad when this road opened late in 1834, and, after serving in this capacity for a period of years, to have organized Earle's Express. Other names, notably that of William F. Harnden, are also associated with the earliest beginnings of the express business. Also pioneers in this field were Alvin Adams, Henry Wells, and William G. Fargo, who, though beginning their operations on the Atlantic seaboard, eventually expanded their lines to California and the Pacific Northwest.

It was in California that the express business first appeared on the West coast in anything like a permanent and well-organized business. There scores of individual express operators began offering their services as postmen and pseudo-bankers for the gold miners whose contacts with the outside world were at best very restricted. Alexander H. Todd, who claimed to be California's first regular expressman, related in a dictated statement how he began his business: "I took the names of the miners, charging them a dollar apiece for recording their names, came to San Francisco, got the letters from the Post Office, and took them back to the mines, charging an ounce a letter for taking them up." Todd had no sooner begun his letter-carrying business than he was asked to convey gold dust to San Francisco depositories, and thereafter service after service was added to Todd's list. One small express operator then another began business, until by 1860 no less than 264 such concerns existed in California, and many of them extended their operations into Oregon. In 1851, for instance, Todd and Company announced: "AGENTS IN OREGON — Abernethy & Clark, Oregon City; Hopkins & Donald, Milwaukie; Capt. Samuel E. May, Portland; Sutler's Store, Vancouver; W. H. Tappan, St. Helens [;] Hensil & Co., Astoria." Other early express concerns were Newell and Company's Express; Gregory and Company; Cram, Rogers and Company.

One must not conclude that all express companies in Oregon and Washington during the fifties originated in California. An exception, certainly, is W. G. T'Vault, in 1846 Oregon's first postmaster, and later editor of the *Oregon Spectator*. T'Vault combined express and postal service. His first system failed, but in 1852 this pioneer in Oregon transportation established T'Vault & Co.'s Oregon and Shasta Express, with offices at Oregon City, Winchester, Rogue River Indian Agency, Josephine Creek, Minersville on Humbug Creek, Humbug City, and Shasta City, California.

A firm named Stuart's Express, in operation by 1854, appears to have been strictly regional in character in that it operated between Portland and Olympia. Between these two places it forwarded and received express through Adams and Company. On August 12 of that year it boasted that, even with "stoppages" its messenger had covered the 180-mile distance between these two cities *within thirty-six hours!* Then continuing: "This is a feat that we believe has never before been accomplished." In order to set this record the messenger had to avail himself of three modes of transportation — steamboat, canoe, and land travel. When the gold rush to Colville took place in 1855 proprietor A. B. Stuart apparently extended his services to that place. Adams then having failed, the Stuart firm switched its connections to that of Wells, Fargo and Company. By 1856 Stuart extended regular stops to include St. Helens, Rainier, Monticello, Cowlitz Landing, Steilacoom, Seattle, Port Townsend, and Vancouver Island; in the year following its sphere of service extended southward to Champoeg, Salem, Albany, and Corvallis. Toward the close of the decade Stuart's greatest competitor in Oregon appears to have been Tracy and Company. E. W. Tracy, proprietor, offered regular service to Fort Vancouver, Cascades, The Dalles, Walla Walla, Colville, Oregon City, Salem, Albany, Corvallis, Dayton, Butteville, Champoeg, and Eugene City. Such places as Butteville, Fairfield, Independence, Thurston, Dayton, Eugene City, and Lafayette were served by the firm of Levinson and Company's Express.

The Washington side of the Columbia, as has been noted, was served by express companies with head offices in Portland. With headquarters in Olympia, however, was the firm of Parker, Colter and Company's Express, founded in 1853, which forwarded parcels to and from Portland. It was later succeeded by Stuart's Express. Also at Olympia were Webber and Slater's Express, Johnson's Express, and Smith's Express, subsequently Lambert and Smith's Express, also organized in 1853 to carry on local package business between the capital and Alki Point on Puget Sound.

These minor express companies performed many services. Their very existence is sufficient evidence that they satisfied a great need by helping Oregon's territorial population to break down in a measure the isolated life in which it found itself. "Were our citizens dependent on the mails, as now managed on the coast, especially in Oregon," said the *Pacific Christian Advocate* in 1856, ". . . they would soon become veritable Rip Van Winkles, and bankrupt besides." The article then pointed out how the express service had saved the day.

When express companies became numerous a tendency to consolidate and to compete for mastery in a given area became noticeable. By 1853 Adams and Company and Wells, Fargo and Company were leaders in California, and both extended their services into the north Pacific region. Their chief Oregon connections were with Todd and Company and the Stuart Express, and an agreement with Colter's Express enabled the firm to serve Olympia, Washington, and the Puget Sound region. The great success of Adams and Company was due to the dispatch with which it could collect and deliver mail and light freight — "not only days," wrote Olympia's *Pioneer and Democrat,* "but actually *weeks* in advance of the mails at this place. Was it not for the express, we should be in a sorry condition indeed." Unfortunately, a financial panic — often referred to as the "Express Panic" — struck the West in 1855, and as a result western branches of Adams and Company failed.

Following this failure, leadership was assumed by its competitor, Wells, Fargo and Company, which in 1852 had made San Francisco the focal point of its far-flung operations. Unlike Adams, the Wells Fargo firm survived the panic and thereafter held mastery in the field.

In 1860 the Company maintained 147 express offices in California, and had established offices at Portland, Port Orford, Umpqua City, and Prairie City in Oregon; Seattle, Olympia, Steilacoom, Port Townsend, and Whatcom in Washington; and at Victoria and Fraser River in British Columbia. A financial statement published by the Company in 1860 shows a gross revenue of $395,187.70 and a net income on express operations of $151,128.47.

Through the sixties and seventies Wells, Fargo and Company continued to expand its activities in the Pacific Northwest, noticeably so when the mining frontier advanced into the Inland Empire. In the absence of special express offices, the firm continued to follow a practice, long tried in California, of appointing local stagecoach operators as its agents. In nearly every town to which there were stagecoach connections advertisements regarding passenger service usually also carried the words: "and Wells, Fargo & Co.'s Express." Before mail facilities could be established in towns that suddenly emerged as a result of gold discoveries in southern Oregon and the Inland Empire, Wells Fargo messengers were on the spot offering their services. Were it not for this institution, wrote the Portland *Oregonian,* "we could not hear from the Capital, or any interior town on the overland route." The Wells, Fargo and Company office came to be regarded as much a part of any western town as the billiard saloon and restaurant.

As the express and stagecoach business entered its final pre-rail phase, there arose on the transportation scene a man whose personality, energy, and ruthlessness won him the titles of "Stagecoach King" and the "Napoleon of the West." This person, Ben Holladay, had dabbled in many western business ventures and in 1862 he had gained control of the Russell, Majors and Waddell interests, namely the Salt Lake-Atchison line. Then capitalizing upon the flow of miners into the Inland Empire (the subject of the next chapter) Holladay secured mail contracts which enabled him to extend his lines from Salt Lake City to Virginia City, Montana; to Boise; and then ultimately to Walla Walla, Umatilla, and The Dalles where connections with Columbia steamers were made. Although local lines existed in this area, competition was no deterrent. As finally organized, the Holladay network (2,000 miles in length) extended from Atchison on the Missouri River to Salt Lake City and The Dalles, thus, at last, providing direct contact between the Pacific Northwest and the East; detours via California were no longer necessary for eastbound passengers.

It soon became apparent that the two giant transportation systems — Wells, Fargo and Company and the Holladay Overland Mail and Express Company — could not work harmoniously together. After jockeying for position for a while, Holladay sold out his entire interest to his competitor for $1,500,000 in cash, $300,000 of Wells Fargo stock, and a directorship in the latter firm. Holladay was to reappear later in connection with railroads and steamship lines, but his departure from the stagecoach business left Wells, Fargo and Company with a monopoly in the stagecoach and express field.

Behind the Reins

Although mud wagons and other types of vehicles were used, the best and the standard one for stage travel was the Concord coach. The Concord was marvelously well made by the Abbott-Downing Company in New Hampshire. The running gear was strongly held together with parts of iron, and the body was made of well-seasoned ash. The body of the coach rested upon two thick and equally strong thoroughbraces, straps which extended from curved arms joining the front and rear axles. This construction enabled the passenger compartment to roll rather than bounce and jerk whenever the vehicle hit the countless holes and ruts in the roads. Since the center of gravity was lower than on many other makes of coaches, the Concord was less subject to tipping. Nine persons could be accommodated inside, two on the driver's seat, and a dozen or more could find places on the top. In the rear was the "boot," which in transportation parlance meant a leather-covered triangular-shaped rack.

To drive a stagecoach over the corduroy and dirt roads of

the plains or of the Pacific Northwest was a matter requiring dexterity and skill. Not just anyone could do it, and, as one writer put it, "Time was . . . when the man who held the ribbons over a six-horse team on the summits of the Sierra and in the cañons of the Coast and Cascade ranges was more highly esteemed than the millionaire or the statesman who rode behind him." These drivers were variously popularly known as "jehus," "knights of the lash," and "whips." With reference to drivers of the Oregon country, Brigadier General James F. Rusling, an extensive traveler in the region, remarked that the drivers were close-lipped when on the box, but loquacious when off. Rusling believed they were extremely fond of both tobacco and whiskey, and also of "pondrous oaths." Coming upon a wagon freight, their greeting was something like this: "Clar the road! Get out of the way thar with your bull teams!" Stories no end, many of them tall, have been told about these jehus, stories that are now a valued body of western lore. There was, for example, "Geyser" Bob who drove in and out of Yellowstone and was called "Geyser" because he had apparently convinced some Englishmen whom he felt were too inquisitive that he had on many occasions driven down into Old Faithful and had come out at the Beehive. Passengers, often a source of annoyance, were variously dealt with. Should the ladies get out of hand, the driver could, of course, shout "Indians!" and "that," said one old Idaho jehu, "quieted them quicker than 40-rod whiskey does a man."

Charlie McConnell drove on the California and Oregon Stage Line, and is referred to as the "prince of drivers." Wallis Nash, who sat in the box beside him on his way to Portland, wrote: "He handled his horses, and worked the heavy brake, and smoked cigars, and chatted unceasingly to his two box-seat passengers, doing all equally well." Famous, too, in the annals of the Pacific Northwest staging is Henry C. Ward who began his career in September, 1849, as one of the very first drivers in California. Then in 1860 Ward came to Portland to operate stages over the Oregon-California Line. Later his name became connected with pioneer staging into Idaho.

Toward the end of his life Ward was the Portland stable superintendent for the Wells, Fargo and Company Express; this company cared for him until his death in 1904.

Trials of the Wayfarer

Reactions to stagecoach transportation varied greatly. Some enjoyed it; some thought it a "serious matter" to be traveling in a stage from San Francisco to Portland "when one knows what a stage is, and what the roads are." One riding in a box on the top was always subject to the fear of dozing and falling off the stage. And "riding inside was no better," wrote Nash. On the inside "your head strikes against the wooden supports of the leather sides." Legs, too, appear to have been in the way, for there was never quite room enough for them. Then, "just as you can hold up no longer, and sleep is stealing over you, creak, gur-r-r, crack go the hind wheels just under you, as the brake comes violently into play down hill, and the stones fly. And the dust!"

During the winter months the roads were, as one correspondent aptly wrote in 1866, "inconceivably bad, for winter in Oregon means rain, not frost." This same correspondent believed that in winter travelers in Oregon really paid "for the privilege of being jounced in mud-wagons, or dislocated on horseback, or mired on foot." Even at this early date Oregonians were satirically referred to by their light-hearted neighbors to the south as "Webfeet." Stagecoach passengers were even rumored to have died of old age during their winter journeys from Sacramento to Portland. During mid-winter no traffic over the California road occurred at all, and it was about the middle of April before the first California Stage Company coach came through to Portland.

Transportation by stagecoach in Washington Territory was for a long time subordinate to inland waterway travel. In going from Portland to points in the Puget Sound area, the traveler almost invariably started by boat. He would sail down the Willamette River to its mouth, then on down the Columbia to the entrance of the Cowlitz River and up that river to Cowlitz Landing, or some other desired point. With the beginning of railroad developments in the Puget Sound area, this procedure was gradually modified so that one could go by boat from Portland to Kalama (laid out in 1870 as headquarters for the future Northern Pacific Railroad) where one could entrain for Puget Sound. ". . . but when I first wended my weary way in that direction," recollected a traveler of the seventies, "I was forced to travel by canoe up rapid rivers, and by stage over heart-breaking corduroy roads, through mud several feet deep, and through trackless forests. . . ."

The extent of the discomfort endured by early day travelers in Washington Territory may be deduced from the following letter written in Monticello, Washington, December 23, 1866, and addressed to Horace Greeley's *New York Tribune:*

I'm in great luck sure, for I'm here alive. . . . And if human nature ever gets into a condition to appreciate and properly value a soft clean bed, or a clean cloth bountifully spread with everything good, it is at this end of the stage line from Olympia. . . . At every step of his progress, the question arises, how is relief of this intolerable suffering to be obtained. . . . The great want of the Territory is the want of roads, and *the road* of all other roads most needed is this from Olympia to the Columbia river. . . .

In the Inland Empire travelers endure desert conditions in many places; and though the route was generally free from mud, travel through long stretches of sagebrush was not always a delight.

Stagecoach travel whetted the appetite and contributed to enjoyment of a good night's sleep. Usually at ten- to fifteen-mile intervals along the country roads were stations. At some of these stops were made only long enough for a hasty exchange of horses, but frequently these places passed for what in old New England would have been cozy taverns and inns. In the Far West simple, often rude, farmhouses where overworked housewives "took in boarders" served the purpose. At such places passengers hastened to get off to stretch their cramped legs, and if it were at meal time or late at night they partook of whatever services such places had to offer. Here the hungry and much bounced-about traveler was, to quote one person, "fed chiefly on small, square bits of tough, fried meat, with fried potatoes, and sometimes pie. (This last you would eat of more freely were it not for the legions of house-flies, which dispute with you every mouthful!) He admitted that there were exceptions to bad fare and that at times the meals were even very good.

In Montana Helen F. Sanders observed that stage stations were conspicuous for their lack of accommodations, and such a name as "Dirty Woman's Ranch" was not uncommonly applied by facetious stage drivers. At one station when Colonel Wilbur Fisk Sanders, a Montana pioneer, looked somewhat disgruntled, the proprietor blurted out:

"Colonel, ain't your egg hard enough?"

Replied the Colonel: "The whole d—— breakfast is hard enough."

Some of the more courageous and long-suffering souls made no stopovers for the night, choosing to continue their journey without interruption until the welcome end was reached. These passengers had to make the most of their opportunities. Sometimes the mail bags were piled high enough in the bottom of the coach for travelers to stretch out and catch a few hours of uneasy sleep.

Much of the clamor and drama associated with stagecoach travel is a fiction of the modern mind, heedless of the bruises and strain which the traveler of an earlier age had to endure. There were, nevertheless, those who were loath to give up the Concord, willing to take the jolts rather than submit to the greater monotony aboard the steamer and rail train. "Railroads and steam-boats are all very well, if a person wants to be rushed through on business," to use the words of one old timer, "but for comfort and pleasure give me the old Coach, when the day is fine, and the road is hard, . . . and the horses go to their collars with a will. . . ."

Paddlewheel Days

The first steamship ever to ply the waters of the Pacific was the S. S. *Beaver*. This small but sturdy vessel was built on the Thames in England for the Hudson's Bay Company in Oregon, and was delivered to Dr. John McLoughlin at Fort Vancouver in 1836.

The "Old Steamer *Beaver*," as pioneers fondly came to call her, had a long and varied life. No Hudson's Bay Company post within reach failed to transact business with this ship. She proved highly satisfactory in the conduct of the Company's Russian trade. Fur and a countless variety of supplies were hauled by her crew. She had four brass cannons mounted on her deck; and with muskets, cutlasses, and hand grenades within easy reach, the *Beaver* greatly facilitated the maintenance of order among the coastal Indians. For exploratory work in and out of hundreds of Northwest coast inlets this faithful little steamship proved indispensable. By the middle seventies the *Beaver's* usefulness to the Hudson's Bay Company appeared to have dwindled, and she was sold to a businessman in Victoria who for another fourteen years used her to tow log booms, ships, and the like. Finally on July 26, 1888, the S. S. *Beaver* reached her journey's end when she ran aground at Prospect Point at the entrance to the Vancouver, B. C., Harbor and later sank.

The *Beaver* was not the only steamship operated by the Hudson's Bay Company, although not until 1853 did a second one, the 220-ton *Otter* make its appearance in northwest waters.

Only at mid-century did Americans in Oregon turn their attention to steamship transportation, but then they did so with their customary zest. In 1850 the way was opened by a group of Astoria businessmen who launched the ninety-foot sidewheeler, *Columbia*. The operations of this ship between Astoria and Portland may be regarded as the first regular steamship service on the river for which the steamer was named.

In its early stages steamship building became identified with municipal pride. One group of promoters, wishing to outdo another, began to stress the importance of steamship building as a way of bringing trade to their own town. Into this pattern fell Lot Whitcomb of Milwaukie, who with others in 1850 built a 150-foot paddlewheeler bearing the promoter's name. For several years the *Lot Whitcomb* plied the lower Columbia River waters.

Meanwhile the trade of the Willamette Valley continued to grow, and during 1851–52 at least a half-dozen steamships were launched to serve either above or below the Willamette River Falls. For a brief period Oregon's territorial capital (Oregon City) became the center of considerable maritime activity. From the high bluffs overlooking the town, people could have watched this steadily growing number of steam-propelled vessels that churned in and out of their slips. One of these was the *Wallamet;* another was the *Multnomah* which on August 18, 1851, made its first trip to Salem. Between 1850–57 Willamette River service was extended as far up as Eugene City, a development which might possibly be explained by the appearance, during the last half of the fifties, of a new type of steamer. This was the keelboat, or flat-bottomed stern-wheeler, which drew less water and had more power against rapids than any other steam-propelled vessel then in use. It could skim across the many shallow rapids of the river, avoid many of the snags that lurked treacherously below the surface of the water, and due to its low water line operate far into the dry season of the year.

Paddlewheel operations on the Washington side paralleled those on the Willamette. From Cowlitz Landing restive settlers at Tumwater maintained contact with the Willamette Valley and Astoria. In 1850 F. A. Chenoweth on the Washington side paved the way for steamer service up to The Dalles by establishing a horse-drawn tramcar portage service at the Cascades, and the next year saw at least three steamers on the middle Columbia between the Cascades and The Dalles. Steamer service above The Dalles began in 1859, when the sternwheeler *Colonel Wright* coursed the far inland stretch of water between the Falls of Celilo and Fort Walla Walla.

The plight of American settlers at Tumwater, disturbed about their isolation from the larger and thriving settlements in the Willamette Valley, was as nothing when compared with the suffering of courageous American pioneers who settled at the present site of Seattle. Rarely, during the first critical stages, did these families have contact with the outside world. "In early times," reminisced pioneer Arthur Denny, "we occasionally saw the Hudson Bay steamer, 'Beaver' and 'Otter,' passing to and from the station at Nisqually. . . ." In 1853 Captain Warren Gove, with his little steamer *Fairy,* initiated a distinctly lame steamer service in the Sound. The coming of the well-built *Major Tompkins* a year later was an occasion for "patriotic joy" and the "blowing up of stumps" for struggling American pioneers at Elliott Bay and on the islands of the Sound.

As in stagecoach operations in the steamship business the trend was toward monopoly. During the early sixties was formed the Oregon Steam Navigation Company which gained mastery of the steamship business on the Columbia River and its tributaries. During the Inland Empire gold rush this concern enjoyed a capacity patronage, and its founders, chief among whom were Simeon G. Reed, John C. Ainsworth, R. R. Thompson, Daniel F. Bradford, and Benjamin Stark, accumulated sizeable personal fortunes.[1]

[1] Reference to the Oregon Steam Navigation Company will be made again in connection with the coming of railroads to the Pacific Northwest.

Chapter XIII

The Cultural Quest

Carrying the Gospel and Learning to the Natives

THE SPANIARDS conquered by means of the combined use of the sword and the cross. Spreading of the gospel to all native peoples brought under the Spanish banner was begun in the New World by Columbus, and remained the established practice when Esteban Martínez came to Nootka Sound nearly three centuries later. In the Martínez expedition in 1789 were four Catholic fathers, all instructed to spread the Word of God to the natives of what is now Vancouver Island. So far as is known this marks the inception of an instructional program in the Pacific Northwest.

Overland fur men who came afterwards were not, as a rule, interested in either the religious or cultural development of the natives, unless practical and selfish purposes were thereby enhanced. To be sure, an occasional individual trader deviated from his absorption with practical affairs and gave thought and expression to things philosophical; at times such a person even conveyed some of his thoughts (few though they were) to the none too inquisitive Indians. The first established trader to stress the practical need for missionary work in the Northwest was Ross Cox, the clerk and historian at Fort Astoria. Cox believed that Indians had a capacity for knowledge and that it was the duty of the missionary to carry the torch of learning and religion westward. As he phrased it: "proclaim to the benighted savages 'glory to God in the highest. . . .'"

The North West Company, however, was little interested in Indian reform, and of the Hudson's Bay Company it may at best be said that the great monopoly was indifferent, but not strongly opposed, to the presence of missionaries within its

206]

fur empire. Simpson at first saw no great good in educated Indians, for in his opinion some that he knew were "blackguards of the worst description" who appear to "pick up the vices of the Whites upon which they improve but retain those of the Indian in their utmost extent." (This position he later modified in the interest of expediency.) Dr. McLoughlin was generous to the missionaries, though anxious, as in the case of American ones, to encourage their operations south and east of the Columbia River where the Company entertained few hopes for permanent occupation. Before the Company's withdrawal north of the forty-ninth parallel missions and mission schools under the management of chaplains were established by the Hudson's Bay Company in the Columbia District.

In spite of the Company's somewhat indifferent attitude in matters pertaining to church and school, it is worth noting that the first school organized in the Oregon country was operated within the palisades of Fort Vancouver, and that the teacher who ran this school at Dr. McLoughlin's request was John Ball, a member of the first Wyeth expedition. Ball's classes began November 19, 1832, and continued until March 1, 1833. Ball was then succeeded by Solomon H. Smith, also a member of the Wyeth expedition, who carried on as teacher until amorous involvements necessitated a shift in position. Smith fell in love with — and married — the wife of the fort baker. Removing to French Prairie, he began, in the home of Joseph Gervais, the first non-mission school in what is now Oregon state. Back at Fort Vancouver, Cyrus Shepard, one of the Methodist group, continued the work of his predecessors, teaching Indians, half-breeds, and an occasional child of white immigrants who remained for a time at the hospitable "Big House."

The role of missionaries in westward migration has been told. Of equal importance is the part played by these God-fearing men and women as trail blazers in the educational life on the old Oregon frontier. Reputedly, a call for learning — a call for the white man's "Book" — had urged the Lees, Whitmans, Spaldings, and others to go west to found their missions. Even though the Lee (Methodist) group became deeply interested in farming and in colonization, they gave some attention to the education of natives. Until he was faced with discouragement about the aptitude of the Calapooya Indians, Jason Lee was a believer in the improvement of natives by means of manual training schools. Indian children, moreover, needed some instruction in understanding the English language. A school was in operation at the Lee Mission by the winter of 1834–35; its first student body consisted of three lazy Indians. By November of that year the official record book refers to daily instruction to as many as twenty, and states that "several of the children are making laudable improvement." Within two years, Lee's ideas of saving the Indians through manual training had taken definite shape, and a school officially known as the Indian Mission Manual Labor School had been formed. Out of these educational beginnings came eventually Willamette University, chartered in 1853.

The printing press has long been regarded as a symbol of culture. The missionary Henry Spalding of the American Board introduced the press into the Pacific Northwest. Sent originally from Boston to Honolulu, it arrived at Fort Vancouver in 1839, and was delivered to Spalding at Lapwai Mission. There it was set up, and the first book run off (still 1839), a Nez Percé primer — *Nez Perces First Book,* Clear Water: Mission Press, 1839.[1]

Quite apart from the press, all the American Board missions placed considerable emphasis upon schooling as a means of achieving their Christian ideals. Cushing Eells opened a school for Indians at his mission in 1839; he found the native children able but not eager to learn. Teachers were present in the area, and at Waiilatpu the Whitmans undertook to give schooling to not only Indians but white children, most of them orphans whose parents had died on the Oregon Trail. As a recognition of this accent on learning, Whitman College at Walla Walla now stands as a monument to the missionary doctor and his associates. The Catholic missionaries in the Oregon coun-

---

[1] Actually the first book issued was chiefly a repair job. In 1843 a primer prepared in the Flathead language was printed by Spalding and Elkanah Walker.

try placed less emphasis upon the three "R's" in dealing with the natives, although schools for both boys and girls were conducted as early as 1844. With the help of the "Catholic Ladder," [2] much was done to spread Catholicism among the natives. Considerable effort was lost in trying to educate and Christianize certain tribes, and in some instances the results were a complete and tragic failure. In the Flathead country the Jesuit Father Adrian Hoecken, working under the direction of Father De Smet, took steps to establish Indian mission schools in 1855. Headway was slow, but in 1864 four sisters arrived at the St. Ignatius Mission (western Montana) to offer their services as teachers. By then Father Urban Grassi was constructing a school building; but even without waiting for the completion of the structure, the sisters began their work in October. The school curriculum was described as a "plain common English education—spelling, reading, and writing with the rudiments of arithmetic." Anything beyond that was thought to "encourage his [the Indian's] natural indolence."

To the missionaries must go credit for establishing schools in the Pacific Northwest, and placing emphasis upon the cultural and religious aspects of life.

Education in the Rough

As the various denominations shied away from the natives and toward white settlers, the desire to foster parochial education developed rapidly. Elementary "Term Schools," as they were called, began to appear. The first was organized by John E. Lyle in 1846, and was dignified by the name Jefferson Institute. The school structure was a log house, located in Polk County. In a memoir published in 1929 Harriet Nesmith McArthur recalled that her mother and other relatives had attended Lyle's school. "The institute," she wrote, "was a log building on the donation land claim of Carey Embree."

---

[2] Ladders were charts, about six feet long and eighteen inches wide, on which illustrations and parallel bars were painted. They were first devised by Father Blanchet at Cowlitz Mission, 1842, as a means of illustrating for the natives his talks on the four millennial periods, heretics, heaven, hell, and other concepts of the church. The best explanation of the meaning of the Catholic Ladder is given by Clarence B. Bagley, *Early Catholic Mission* (Seattle, 1932), II, pp. 119–22.

Benches made of long planks were placed near the walls. The children, however, sat facing the walls, with wide boards set on props against the walls for desks. Pupils usually wrote with goose quills which Lyle kept in condition, and the only pencils ever used were pointed lead bullets. The writing paper was blue, and is believed to have been purchased from the Hudson's Bay Company. School books were those which pioneers had brought with them, and indispensable was the Bible from which each child read a verse at the beginning of the school day. In all, twenty-five students, including three Applegates, attended the first year, and the experiment was considered a success.

Others of this type soon followed, and after 1850 were prevalent in the settled part of the Northwest. No sooner had settlers come to Tumwater at Puget Sound (1852) than A. W. Moore, the community's first postmaster, also became the first schoolmaster. Cowlitz Landing became the seat of a school during the following year, followed by similar schools at Port Townsend and Seattle. They were conducted on a private basis, usually under the auspices of some denomination, and a fee ranging from eight to ten dollars per term was charged each pupil. These schools had their counterparts on other American frontiers. Teachers were frequently itinerant, surroundings were crude, and instruction was simple. Webster's *Spelling Book*, Sanders's readers, and McGuffey's *Eclectic Reader* (a separate one for each grade), Thompson's or Smith's *Arithmetic,* and Smith's and Clark's grammars were among the textbooks used. Some of the private schools, especially in the larger cities, gradually improved their standard and never entirely lost vogue, particularly for families with some means.

The physical structure of most of these early schools was not unlike Lyle's Institute — crude at best. A pioneer teacher, Joseph H. Sharp, described early Lane County, Oregon, schools: "The houses were either log, frame, or box, principally log. . . . Some had huge fireplaces where red hot coals assisted the teacher's switch to keep the outer boy and girl warm while he stored away his ABC's or fed his mind on ab, ib, ob."

The system of grades in the first schools was not strictly adhered to, and even in schools with grades many exercises, such as spelling and arithmetic matches, and piece-speaking, were carried on by the "scholars" of all ages. Teachers were at first men, and not until the middle fifties was a woman known to have taught school in Oregon Territory. Salaries were miserly, and often consisted in part of board and keep.

The age of Andrew Jackson had given strength to the movement for free public (common) schools. This ideal the pioneers carried with them to the Oregon country. The first legislative session of Oregon Territory held in Oregon City, 1849, enacted an organic act conferring 1,280 acres of land upon every township (the sixteenth and thirty-sixth sections of each township); the interest of the money coming from the sale of these lands was to be used to support public schools. This act also made free education compulsory. Since the money thus derived was insufficient to support the common schools, in 1853–54 the law was revised to provide that a two-mill tax levy in every county should be added to the school fund, together with money secured from fines imposed for breaking the laws of the Territory. When Oregon became a state this law, with modifications, was retained. When Washington became a territory, its legislature enacted almost identical school legislation during 1854, and in 1864 the Idaho legislature passed a law which gave one per cent of gross receipts from all toll-roads, bridges, ferries, and all other franchises to the school fund.

Thus the clear intention of these pioneer societies was to establish and support education. But in practice many drawbacks existed. Instruction was largely confined to elementary grades; and in the long absence of normal schools, the standards of teacher training and teacher qualifications were necessarily very low. Equally inadequate were the school buildings and the equipment that went into them. Not until the eighties was any attempt at required school attendance made, and only well along in the present century (with certain exceptions) did compulsory education on the nine-month, rather than a three- to six-month, basis, become a reality. To say that the products of these schools were educated would be most generous.

The normal school movement begun by Horace Mann early in the nineteenth century did not bear fruit in Oregon until 1882 when the Oregon State Legislature provided for the establishment of normal schools at Monmouth and Ashland.

Pioneers were interested in higher education and made provision for it when the time came. But not always fully conscious of what higher education might entail, those same founding fathers seemingly ignored the secondary, and especially college preparatory, training. In this respect the Pacific Northwest was not unlike other frontier societies. High schools were not much a part of public thinking until after the Civil War, and even then developed very slowly.

Until the present century, the Pacific Northwest leaned heavily upon church endowed schools — variously called institutes, colleges, seminaries, or academies — and upon special departments within the universities preparing youth for higher learning. The *Biennial Report* by the president of Oregon State College reflects the sad state of affairs in 1874: ". . . young men are received here who are really in the primary studies, . . . and even some who could not read have been taught here." Academies and colleges took their responsibilities seriously, in fact very seriously, and present-day Joe College informalities were strictly banned. Until 1869 segregation of the sexes was the policy, and no student could leave town without permission, and then never on the Sabbath. At Oregon State College "All communication between ladies and gentlemen on the college premises are expressly forbidden," while at Umpqua Academy (Douglas County) "No uncouth noises are allowed by students especially such as hooting, screaming or vulgar salutations." Even so an indictment against the Umpqua student body states that "The campus rang with strange sounds at night, and sometimes in day light all manner of loafish gestures and waggish ways disgraced the social intercourse of some of the students."

Most of the prominent denominations founded their own academies, of which there were no less than twenty-eight in Oregon alone by 1878. In Washington academies were also established at Vancouver, Olympia, Seattle, Ellensburg, and other towns.

No attempt will be made here to name them all. Vying for ascendancy were Methodists and Catholics. The former controlled the Oregon Institute, established in 1844 at Salem (succeeded in 1853 by Willamette University). As a university it was correlated with Methodist academies including the above-mentioned Umpqua Academy and others at Wilbur, Sheridan, Santiam, and Dallas, Oregon. Corvallis Academy, also Methodist, eventually became Oregon State College. Clackamas Seminary for ladies was a joint Methodist and Congregationalist enterprise. In Washington, Wesleyan Institute was established midway between Olympia and Tumwater in 1856. At Portland the Catholics established, in 1859, St. Mary's Academy, which was the oldest denominational school in the town. It was founded by the Sisters of the Most Holy Name of Jesus and Mary, and opened with six pupils. Also founded there as a Catholic school was St. Michael's College; at Jacksonville, St. Mary's Academy; by 1876 four other academies had been set up by the Church in Oregon.

The Episcopal Church school goes back to 1852 when Reverend William Richmond came to Oregon from New York and established a mission school near Yamhill. Two years later an Episcopal Missionary Diocese of Oregon and Washington was created with Bishop Thomas F. Scott in charge. Under Scott's direction Trinity School was founded on the west bank of the Willamette River where Oswego now stands. Bishop Scott Academy at Portland, St. Helen's Hall, and other Episcopal schools followed.

The Baptist Home Mission Society in the East helped their brethren in the Far West to organize, in 1848, a school at Oregon City which struggled along first under the name of Oregon City College, then Oregon City University. Hope for this institution appears to have dimmed when the territorial capital moved to Corvallis in 1855. During the following year an unfinished school building begun by the Christian Church at McMinnville was offered the Baptists who thereupon founded McMinnville College to replace their Oregon City institution.

Schools of this character, all struggling against poverty,

managed to keep learning alive until the period when public high schools were organized to prepare students for advanced university work, and, in fact, to replace the academies.[3] They offered courses in religion and moral philosophy — all denominational to be sure — but they also gave a limited grounding in the arts and sciences so essential for a grasp of advanced university studies. Instructors were generally men and women who had been trained in the East for missionary work. Some were very able teachers, some were poor; nearly all had their hearts in the work they were performing.

Adequate libraries, without which schools do not function well today, were unknown during the academy era. During the fifties in the Portland area were a few Sunday School libraries of from 100 to 200 volumes. No libraries, private or institutional, were reported in the Washington counties of Lewis and Clark for that decade. The Oregon Territorial Library at Oregon City for which federal funds had been appropriated, with 1,500 volumes was by far the best in the region. During the sixties some private libraries ranging from 200 to 1,000 volumes are known to have existed, but as for school libraries, Pacific University, a school founded by the Congregationalists at Forest Grove, with 1,500 volumes, appears to have been outstanding. In 1870, Albany College (a Presbyterian School) reported a 1,000-volume library, and by that time Pacific University had forged ahead with 3,000 books on its shelves. A majority of the books dealt with religion and Free Masonry; apparently no attempt to secure a balance among studies in the various academic disciplines was made. Newspapers, previously discussed in connection with politics, were numerous, and provided entertainment and information on other matters besides political candidates and principles.

The Rise of State Universities

Founding of universities did not in itself mean that the golden age of learning had come. Quite to the contrary, uni-

[3] It should be borne in mind that a distinction existed between these academies and strictly private schools, of which there were some, although a few academies were eventually transformed from academies into private educational institutions.

versities endured heartbreaking handicaps at first, due more to the public inability rather than unwillingness to support higher education.

This growing willingness to support education at all levels — perhaps prematurely — was shown by Washington's Territorial legislature which on January 29, 1855, in the second year of the government's existence, made provision for a university. The 1860–61 legislature voted to locate the territorial University of Washington at Seattle, and selected as members of the first Board of Commissioners Daniel Bagley, John Webster, and Edmund Carr. A ten-acre wooded lot in "downtown" Seattle was donated as a university site by Arthur A. Denny, C. C. Terry, and Judge Edward Lander, and the first cornerstone was laid May 26, 1861. On November 4 of this year the academic doors were opened for instruction by President and sole Professor Asa S. Mercer, but without even one solitary university student on hand. About thirty children were there, and for a year Mercer operated the "university" as a term school. The great day came October 10, 1862, when the first university student appeared with sufficient preparation for advanced work. Even by 1892 (thirty-two years later) when Washington State College opened at Pullman, the University of Washington faculty numbered but ten, the regular university enrollment was only forty-two (271 preparatory or normal students were enrolled), and the university budget was $5,000 for that year.

In Oregon the plethora of denominational colleges [4] made demand for a state university slow, and establishment was accordingly delayed. Then when the time for a university appeared to be at hand, the fight for its location reminds one of earlier battles over the location of state capitals. At the propitious time, the Lane County forces were best organized and promised a $50,000 building. The legislature in 1872 there-

[4] By 1876 the following were chartered denominational colleges and universities in Oregon, each offering work beyond that of the academies: Willamette University at Salem, Methodist; Pacific University at Forest Grove, Congregationalist; McMinnville College (now Linfield College) at McMinnville, Baptist; Christian College at Monmouth, Disciples of Christ; Methodist College at Corvallis, Southern Methodist; Philomath College at Philomath, United Brethren; and Albany College at Albany, Presbyterian. The latter is now Lewis and Clark College at Portland.

fore chose Eugene as their site for the University, and also appointed a board of regents headed by Matthew P. Deady. The Lane County-Eugene group found itself hard pressed to raise the funds pledged. At a time when prospects looked most gloomy Judge Joshua J. Walton, also a member of the first board, pushed the campaign for funds to a requisite goal. The first building, Deady Hall, mortgaged though it was, proved acceptable, and during July, 1876, the University of Oregon began with a faculty of five, eighty regular university students, ninety-seven preparatory students, and no library.

The first president of the University of Oregon was John W. Johnson, a rugged frontier educator who had crossed the plains with a covered wagon caravan as so many of his fellow citizens had done. Later he had returned to Yale to complete his college course. Johnson was a tower of intellectual strength and an inspiration in a state where academic discipline had heretofore been sidetracked for the more immediate needs of making a livelihood. Former University of Oregon Dean Henry Sheldon said of President Johnson: "He had always been a hard worker, who so completely mastered the Latin classics that he seldom had occasion to refer to the textbook when engaged in instruction. He was a driver in the classroom, with a contempt for shoddiness and laziness. . . . He won the respect of the abler students and the fear of the shiftless members of the group."

With a mortgage hanging over its head, the University rested insecurely, and the crisis came in 1881 when there was fear of foreclosure on Deady Hall for $4,000. The total university indebtedness amounted to nearly double this amount, but at the critical moment Oregon's famed railroad builder, Henry Villard, saved the day by donating $7,000 to liquidate the indebtedness. Other bequests followed from Villard. In 1883 he made a donation of $50,000 in Northern Pacific Railroad Company bonds, with the stipulation that $400 of the annual income from these securities should be used for the purchase of library books. Villard was truly the angel who enabled this institution to overcome its infant maladies.

Oregon State College grew out of Corvallis College which had been established as a Southern Methodist institution in

1865. Following passage of the Morrill Act, July 2, 1862, under which the state received the income from the sale of 90,000 acres of federal lands, Oregon took steps to organize an agricultural college. It was formally established in 1869 with two professors and twenty-eight students, and courses in geology, "vegetable economics," and basic sciences were offered. Later, civil engineering, forestry, and other expansions in the curriculum were made.

The University of Idaho was founded at Moscow in 1892, later in point of time when compared with its sister institutions, but not late in the development of community life in that territory. From tax funds the young state raised $125,000 for the erection of its first building, and a $6,000 to $7,000 budget for the maintenance of the University. The University of Idaho, like Oregon State College, also opened its doors with a faculty of two, but with a regular university enrollment of forty-two students. It, too, followed the general procedure of admitting students to do work preparatory to admittance on university standing. The university made no pretense of trying to imitate too closely practices followed in older eastern universities, but felt obligated to meet, first of all, problems peculiar to a society still youthful at the close of the nineteenth century.

Religious and Social Life

Apart from their educational operations, religious organizations had a civilizing influence upon the rugged pioneers. Doffing their work clothes after chore time on Sunday morning, hitching the team to the wagon (later the buggy), and driving off to the meeting house for services provided the families with momentary relief from the drudgery of the farm. Apart from religious implications, going to church in pioneer days gave isolated people a chance for a little social intercourse. Ladies could compare notes on homemade bonnets whenever the sermon became dry, men and women shook hands after the services and briefly exchanged words about the crops, and restless children might slip out before the final singing time and prayers for a little rough play where the teams were tied. In the course of time church socials became more frequent, Ladies Aid societies were formed, marriage and funeral services became more elaborate, camp meeting revivals were held, and in many other ways the churches played an important role in the emotional and cultural life of the people.

Apart from the churches were other social diversions. In rural communities debating societies, annual picnics, and school programs provided entertainments, and, if folks were not "agin it," there were dances for the young. Towns took on a certain amount of sophistication, as for example Oregon City, which lost no time boasting of its Lyceum society — the first in the Northwest — as other towns were privileged to do before the close of the century. Free Masonry and other secret and semi-secret societies, or lodges, made their appearance in the towns and found an appeal for a social-hungry population about to become somewhat class conscious. To many of the male population the saloon provided a social and, unfortunately, a financial outlet.

From Cabin to Pseudo-Gothic

Architecture, like any other aspect of society, passed through different phases. The true frontier building types belong to the fur trade-Indian-mission era. These were followed by different types brought in by early farmers and townspeople. Common to both fur traders and many of the early settlers were the rude log cabins. Trees were plentiful at first and the log structure was comparatively simple to erect. Logs, too, some hewn or ripsawed, some rounded and notched, were used in the construction of many of the early blockhouses, forts, or posts and palisades; also, they found their place in the church missions. In the public park at Dayton stands today one of the best preserved examples of blockhouses of the early days. It was known as Fort Yamhill and was used as a protection against the Indians in the Grande Ronde Valley. Like many blockhouses, it has two stories; but unlike many which had a larger top story overhanging the lower in parallel lines, the top story of Fort Yamhill is placed diagonally across the lower. This was a functional creation which enabled defenders to fire in eight rather than in four directions. The houses at the Hudson's Bay posts, and the missions betray, like Fort Yamhill, a close adherence to practical needs rather than to architectural styles and adornments prevalent at the moment. Sawmills came early and both town and country houses quickly graduated from log cabins and entered the frame building stage. Some, in fact most, of these were ugly — nothing but rude shack dwellings and stores with false fronts. Gradually people of means became more numerous, and some houses with beauty of design began to appear.

Many of the first settlers in the Pacific Northwest were either southerners or were from the southern fringe of the Middle West (Missouri). Those who could afford to do so built houses which show their southern (neo-classic) origin — low-pitched roofs, high ceilings, small window panes, and one- and two-decker porches supported by slender columns. In some respects such houses in Oregon were an improvement over those in the South, for much of the heaviness and clumsiness had disappeared in the westward transition. During and after the Civil War the Victorian Gothic style began to replace the southern, neo-classic type. The ornate character of the Gothic, or perhaps neo-Gothic house, had little besides spaciousness and durability to commend it.

Except for the occasional piece brought across the plains, house furnishings were at first crude makeshifts. Gradually substantial, quality merchandise began to appear on the market with the result that homes in the Northwest became increasingly more comfortable and gracious. Then when large private fortunes were made, such as those coming from steamship transportation, there appeared the elegant, flamboyant era of the *nouveau riche*. Taken as whole, though, pioneer culture was as simple as it was genuine. This was a period of struggle for survival, yet one filled with optimism and hope that an easier and richer life would some day come to all who were industrious and thrifty.

CHAPTER XIV

The Mineral Frontier and Commerce
of the Inland Empire

The Forty-Niners

ON JANUARY 24, 1848, the wild-eyed James W. Marshall gazed into the tailrace of John Sutter's sawmill at Coloma, California, and saw yellowish particles that turned out to be gold. Despite Sutter's feeble attempts to keep this a secret, the news spread. Lack of telegraphic and rail facilities for communication in the Far West, nevertheless, prevented the news from reaching most parts of the United States before September. A high point in the excitement was reached when on December 5, 1848, President James K. Polk gave the discovery an official verification in his annual message to Congress: "The accounts of the abundance of gold in that territory are of such an extraordinary character as would scarcely command belief were they not corroborated by the authentic reports of officers in the public service, who have visited the mineral district. . . ." The mad rush that followed is well known. Nearly 100,000 gold seekers reached California before the end of 1849, and additional thousands came during the early fifties.

A remarkably large number of the California Argonauts were lucky at the diggings. Some of them acquired large fortunes; nearly all were able to pan some gold dust if they worked hard enough at the job. Gold in Oregon was first found by some shipwrecked sailors who landed at Crescent City, California, and worked their way northward across the Oregon line to what is now Waldo. At this place, in the very southwestern corner of Oregon, so the story goes, they prospected and "washed" a considerable amount of gold. News of

220]

their discovery spread, and in 1851 a stampede from California to what became Sailor Diggings ensued. The town of Waldo which presently emerged soon reached a population of 2,500. Near-by Browntown Camp sprang into being, as did also the rough-and-tough gold mining town of Kerbyville which by 1855 became the center of southern Oregon mining.

Following the California pattern, prospecting in Oregon spread rapidly to other places, and in 1858 the site of the present town of Jacksonville yielded many gold nuggets ranging from six to as much as seventy ounces in weight. Discoveries in Applegate Creek and Rogue River soon followed, and despite many individual setbacks, present Jackson County, during the Civil War years, produced an average of $1,000,000 in gold per month. Gold was also found at Coos Bay, and on the Santiam River (not far from Portland), but the amount removed from these two places was negligible. On the whole, gold mines west of the Cascades were of an untrustworthy type for they tended to become exhausted when least expected. It is to the region known as the Inland Empire, and not the coastal area, that one must turn for the central theme concerning the Pacific Northwest's mineral frontier.

The Gold Rush to the Inland Empire

The Inland Empire, as defined in the opening chapter, embraces what is now southeastern British Columbia, eastern Oregon and Washington, Idaho, and western Montana. Into this region came first explorers, fur traders, and then missionaries, and across its heart was to pass the Oregon Trail over which thousands of immigrants moved west. But to the first Willamette-bound pioneers this country held no special charm. Little did the early Oregon pioneers realize that its mountains and its sparkling streams held treasures of gold, and little did they know that before many years thousands of fortune seekers were to cross and recross its terrain, sift its stream beds from mouth to source, explore minutely even its remotest mountainsides and ravines, and build mining camps and boom towns fed by an elaborate transportation network. And little could these early Oregon pioneers realize that at some distant day the Inland Empire was to become one of the richest wheat-producing areas of the entire United States, an area important for its cattle raising, and an area where irrigation would transform much of the desert into luxuriantly productive fields of alfalfa, sugar beets, (Idaho) potatoes, and other profitable crops.

In 1855 around Fort Colvile, the region between the Spokane and Pend d'Oreille rivers, the first significant discovery of gold was made in this interior region of the old Oregon country. For twenty-nine years Fort Colvile had been a Hudson's Bay Company trading post, but the French-speaking inhabitants at the establishment had failed to observe (at least they did not advertise it) the precious "dust" over which they must have walked. Who, exactly, discovered the gold at this place is not known to history, but word of such a find passed among the people of the Pacific Northwest and in the Fall of 1855 the first searchers rushed to the Fort Colvile region.

Grave difficulties soon presented themselves. The region was rather hard to reach, and the absence of adequate transportation facilities restricted the flow of supplies to the miners. Gold found here was not abundant and it proved difficult to mine without sluice boxes and other equipment not available to the prospectors who had come merely with their simple picks, shovels and pans. Moreover, the Indians, particularly Shoshones and Yakimas proved openly hostile to the miners. This factor, along with others previously alluded to, brought on the costly Indian wars of 1855–59, which virtually halted gold mining in many parts of the Inland Empire. The Indians continued a menace, from the white man's point of view, until 1858, when, it will be recalled, Colonel George Wright threw his full strength against the inland tribes, bringing peace for several years.

Scarcely had peace come when a series of rich gold discoveries were made in what are now the states of Idaho, Oregon, and Montana. In Idaho these discoveries were made on the tributaries of the Snake River. On Oro Fino Creek, a branch of the Clearwater which empties into the Snake River at Lewiston, in the year 1860 a small party of prospectors led by "Captain" E. D. Pierce made the first gold discovery in Idaho.

News of Pierce's success soon spread, and during the winter of 1860–61 diggings on the Oro Fino became extensive. In 1861 deposits were also found on the south fork of the Clearwater in what is known as the Elk City district, and this in turn was followed by rich discoveries in the Salmon River and the Boise River country in 1862. Lewiston, Florence, Pierce City, and Oro Fino City came into being in this Clearwater-Salmon River region. Then in 1864, far to the south, the entire Boise Valley became the scene of great mining activity. In this area Boise City, Idaho City, Centreville, Placerville, Eagle City, Pioneer City, and other towns emerged. Farther to the south-west, in what is called the Owyhee district, mining activity likewise boomed, and there the towns of Ruby City and Silver City grew up. Still later gold discoveries were made in the Coeur d'Alene Mountains, well up in the Idaho panhandle, and such towns as Coeur d'Alene, Beaver City, and Murray arose to accommodate the people who concentrated there.

The manner of life in each of these successive districts followed the pattern already so familiar to California, to Nevada, and to Colorado. As soon as news of a new and rich discovery reached the ears of prospectors whose luck had been none too good, off they would go to the new diggings. A mining population was very fluid. Thomas C. Donaldson, a prominent Idaho pioneer, has described this condition very well:

The meaning of the phrase "transient population" struck me forcibly one day in 1870 when the Loon Creek "strike" was announced. Loon Creek was a point fifty miles northeast of Idaho City. An honest (?) miner had come into Boise one night with a ten-pound sack of nuggets which, he said, had been panned out of Loon Creek. "Ten dollars a day easy," said this honest miner, "plenty of ground, and they ain't two people out there." He further stated that he had entered Boise from the east and the news had not reached Idaho City. Well, in an hour's time Boise was bustle and confusion. New diggings at Loon Creek! Great news! Millions in it! Volunteers came forward who knew, so they said, every speck of dust out there. Before daylight came, one hundred men were riding or trailing northward.

In this particular instance Loon Creek turned out to be "ordinary diggings for Chinamen, four dollars a day at most," so the miners either returned to Boise or moved on to some other place. But wherever a discovery offered adequate rewards a mining town came into being. William J. McConnell, Idaho pioneer and once an Idaho governor and United States senator, related how "Houses had sprung up like magic in the town named 'Orofino,' and before the end of the summer of 1861, the newly-fledged metropolis was supplied with stores, hotels and saloons, the last outnumbering the others."

But by the end of 1861 miners all but deserted Oro Fino on the Clearwater for Baboon Gulch where two men had produced $1,800 of yellow gold in three hours, where one man had taken out seventy-five pounds of gold, where another removed forty-five pounds of ore. By the spring of 1863 the towns of Pioneer City (Hogem), Placerville, and Centreville had been built where had stood an "undefiled pine forest" six months before, where, as an old timer phrased it, "the foot of civilized man rarely if ever had trod."

Then as each new discovery occurred there was a stampede, not alone for a mining claim, but for the most favored town sites as well. But when miners moved on to greener pastures, what had once been booming urban centers became ghost towns, whose deserted, wobbly, board sidewalks and empty buildings were to be silent reminders of a once-bustling past. Throughout the sixties and seventies gold mining, nevertheless, remained active. With the introduction of machine methods of mining, silver and copper gained the ascendancy and in 1940 Idaho ranked first in silver production. Since 1860 no less than $1,300,000,000 worth of minerals have been produced in the Gem State.

Gold in Montana

Another region which attracted great numbers of fortune seekers was what is now western Montana, the region bounded on the west by the Bitterroot Mountains (the eastern boundary of present Idaho) and the Rockies. Gold had been found in Montana as early as 1852. On February 15 of that year Major John Owen wrote in his diary "Gold Hunting found some." But not until the arrival of the James and Granville Stuart party in 1858 was prospecting taken seriously. Gradually excitement and interest spread until between 1862–64 fever height was reached with the development of extremely rich placer and quartz mines at Bannack (Montana's first mining town), Gold Creek (especially Grasshopper Diggings), Alder Gulch (served by Virginia City), Confederate Gulch, Deer Lodge, Last Chance Gulch (Helena), and many other places.

The stampede to Montana and its feverish gold mining caused Rossiter W. Raymond, the United States Commissioner of Mining Statistics, to declare in 1870: "The progress of the [Montana] Territory during the short period of her existence is only equalled by that of California after the days of 1849." Continued Raymond: "The wonderful gold deposits developed by the early pioneers, while adding largely to the world's stock of precious metals, have carried population, industry, wealth, and civilization to a country before unknown beyond the meagre accounts of adventurers, trappers, and explorers."

Population growth of the individual mining towns was tremendous. In 1863 Bannack's inhabitants had reached, according to some estimates, 2,000 to 3,000; Virginia City had a population of 10,000. By 1870 the census population of Montana was 20,595, and most of these people were in the southwestern part of the present state, literally hundreds of miles away from the source of supplies. And since, as Dr. Robert E. Albright has pointed out in his dissertation, "practically nothing was being produced within the Territory in agricultural, stockraising or industrial lines almost the entire demand was met from the outside." Bannack and Virginia City lay 400 miles from Salt Lake, 1,400 from Omaha, 1,000 from Portland, 600 from navigation on the Columbia River, and 200 miles from Fort Benton.

Commissioner Raymond observed with reference to Montana what so frequently happened in Idaho, Oregon, and other mineral frontiers: "Their exploitation seems to travel in a circle." Gold Creek was deserted for Bannack, Bannack for Alder Gulch, and then the miners went back to Bannack. The towns of Montana were like those of Idaho: their growth was rapid, their buildings rough, rude, and flimsy, and their population boisterous. Again like Idaho, the quantity of the mineral production of Montana was great. Recent estimates of gold production for 1862–69 alone amount to $94,000,000; and the yield of silver and copper (subsequently developed) added more millions.

The dry plateau region of eastern Oregon lying within the Inland Empire also had its gold stampede, but it was on a small scale. Immigrants who passed through Meek's Cutoff in 1845 are known to have found some gold in present Malheur County. But not until 1861 were gold seekers in that region adequately rewarded. The Malheur, John Day, and Powder rivers then became the scene of panning activities, and individual finds of from $20 to $50 per day were common (one man took out $6,000 in four days), stamp mills were subsequently erected, and Baker City owes its founding to this eastern Oregon rush.

Fraser River and the Cariboo

The mineral exploitation of British Columbia is a story so interwoven with the rest of the Pacific Northwest that it cannot properly be omitted from this discussion. During the spring of 1858 the Hudson's Bay Company's steamer, the *Otter*, tied up at the San Francisco docks with a cargo which included some gold dug along the banks of the far-off Fraser River. As on other frontiers, gold had been found north of the forty-ninth parallel at earlier dates (some had been found on Queen Charlotte's Islands in 1851), but not until 1858 did news of substantial discoveries come to the attention of a transient American mining population anxious to find some new El Dorado.

Leaving at once for the Canadian mines were hundreds of Californians. To the host of hardened and experienced Argonauts one "might add," wrote the Britisher Alfred Waddington, "a good stock of gamblers, pickpockets, swindlers, . . . thieves, drunkards, and jail birds, let loose by the governors of California for the benefit of all mankind besides the halt, lame, blind and mad." At San Francisco on June 4, 1858, John

Domer, another Britisher, wrote: "From California the exodus of miners continues. Some thousands have left by sea, and great numbers are going overland, . . . travelling through Oregon to the new El Dorado." Oregonians were likewise stirred by this news. Dr. Carl Friesach, reported from Portland in August, 1858 "the whole population in the greatest state of excitement on account of the news of the discovery of gold fields on the Fraser River; it was the only topic of conversation in the whole town." In the Puget Sound area large numbers of the settlers, ships' crews, soldiers stationed at Forts Steilacoom, Townsend, and Bellingham, cast duty and responsibility to the winds and headed north to the diggings.

The sudden inrush of these tough and hardened California miners upon the once quiet and peaceful fur-trading post of Victoria was over-awing. James Douglas, who had by this time become governor of Vancouver Island, sought to regulate the stampede since stopping it would be impossible. He ordered that permits for mining would have to be secured from British authorities, and a fee of about five dollars (twenty-one shillings) per month paid for the privilege of digging gold on British soil. Moreover, any craft operating in British waters, even though it be a canoe, would have to be licensed at from six to twelve dollars per month. Governor Douglas, in imposing these and other restrictions, overstepped the bounds of his authority (limited to Vancouver Island) by applying his regulations to the mainland.

Such restrictions were not enough to discourage gold seekers, who were eager to get to new diggings, although vigorous protests and evasions were made. In June, 1858, no less than 7,147 left San Francisco for Canada, while still others poured in from Oregon, and, indeed, from Great Britain as well.

The open seaport of Victoria became the unquestioned entrepôt for the Fraser River diggings. The excitement at Victoria during the summer of 1858 was what the British Commander Richard C. Mayne of the Royal Navy termed "indescribable." "To anyone who had known San Francisco or Melbourne under similar circumstances, the condition at Victoria was not surprising;" wrote Mayne, "but to those hitherto unacquainted with the earliest febrile symptoms attending the discovery of gold, the change in its aspect and prospects might well seem magical." He recounted the customary land boom, the hiking of prices, docks jammed with ships, and the steady arrival of miners with their varied assortment of supplies. "Victoria," he wrote, "appeared to have leapt at once from the site of a promising settlement into a full-grown town."

The story of how miners moved on from Victoria, across ninety miles of treacherous Sound to Fort Langley at the mouth of the Fraser, and how they managed to reach the many upstream bars, among them Forts Hope and Yale and Lytton, will be told in the following chapter. Suffice it to say here that in British Columbia the mining population ran true to form — forever on the go. The total number of this population certainly did not exceed 30,000, and the figure might well have been lower. Some bars proved to be very productive; $25 for a man's hard-day's labor was not uncommon. Some men made $150, and some as little as $2.50. Varying reports caused the future seekers to gravitate, as was noted with regard to the American frontier, toward the better paying bars.

In time some of the more adventurous miners managed to surmount the physical obstacle offered by Fraser River Canyon (a feat of no small magnitude), and drifted north into Cariboo. Here gold was found in added abundance, and by 1863 no less than 4,000 had reached the distant British Columbia hinterland, when the shack towns of Barkerville and Cariboo sprang up as a result. As this population peak was reached so was that of gold production. But just as the Cariboo output began to decline, came news of a rich discovery at Kootenai, followed in 1865 by discoveries in the upper Columbia River region between Cariboo and Kootenai. Taken as a whole, the British Columbia Gold Rush of the late fifties and early sixties was extremely spectacular, but like those in southern Oregon the mines proved to be rather short-lived.

Several mines which were developed two to three decades later, for example those in the Rossland district, were more lasting. Much mining is still being done in British Columbia, but in accordance with trends ore is now being extracted largely by means of heavy industrial equipment. While the gold rush history of British Columbia is remarkably similar to that of the Inland Empire, Montana, California, Nevada, Colorado, and other American mineral areas, there is one marked difference, namely, it is less tainted with lawlessness. Writing on this subject, three British Columbia historians say: "The whole training of the Americans had been along the lines of independence and self-reliance; the British had been trained to refer every question to their superiors." This law-and-order attitude, constantly fostered and insisted upon by Governor Douglas, had a quieting effect upon the American guests of the British government. "The rowdyism of San Francisco," wrote this trio, "was absent." Victoria was a boom town, but the miners were "well-behaved" and the "same obedience to law is found in the [British Columbia] gold fields."

The history of events in nearly all of these mining camps seems to follow a given pattern. First would be discovery of precious ore, announcement of which was usually followed by a mad rush to the new diggings. Close upon the heels of the gold-seekers were such groups as the merchants, traders, hostlers, gamblers, barkeepers, and the "hurdy-gurdy" girls, all intent upon exploiting the business possibilities associated with a new "strike."

People could get to a new gold field relatively easily, but the bonanza towns created by a gold rush presented difficult problems of supply. An individual miner could and did carry with him certain essential mining equipment and foodstuff to see him through the first few days, or, at most, weeks. Beyond that time he was obliged to rely upon the merchant and the transport operation for the replenishment of his larder. In the more remote mining camps the task of bringing supplies proved to be as enormous as it was hazardous, and to the packers and wagon freighters goes the credit for overcoming all difficulties.

The Pack Train Era

Like water transportation, pack animal transportation is nearly as old as civilization itself. It was certainly the most representative of the transportation systems of New Spain where for more than three centuries mules had trudged faithfully over winding mountain trails. Pack mules had enabled the Spaniards to push northward into Mexico and ultimately into Alta California. Almost immediately after the mining frontier moved into the Oregon country those familiar strings of lazy, slow, lumbering, yet dependable "Mexican mules" could be seen winding their way across the Siskiyou Mountains into the area.

Driving mules was obviously no task for amateurs whose clumsiness the animals would not be long in detecting — and exploiting. Mules had to be well looked after if satisfactory service was to be expected from them. Care had to be exercised to prevent galling; the best insurance was to keep the animal fairly fat. Tough and strong as were the Mexican mules, difficulties were experienced with them in the Pacific Northwest where climatic conditions were so unlike those of Mexico and the Southwest. Many mules died during the cold and rainy seasons. In order to shelter the animals, muleteers were obliged to build sheds. In the Fraser River country, where snowfalls were frequently heavy, the problem of forage, solved in warmer climates by simply turning the animals loose to graze, had to be dealt with. In the early stages of gold digging very little hay was available and the hungry mules were often obliged to subsist on dried foliage. Similarly, in Idaho and Montana pack animals suffered severely during the cold seasons. The *Montana Post* relates that in the vicinity of Lake Pend d'Oreille these beasts were "perishing in great numbers, from want of feed and extreme cold combined."

In addition to the wide use of pack animals, then as now, individual miners or prospectors used the burro to carry personal belongings, such as blankets, tools (including a shovel, pick, axe, gold-pan, mortar and pestle), a canteen filled with water, cooking utensils, food, and tobacco. It was advisable never to overload or push a pack animal; at least a proverb reads: "Never crowd a burro if you are in a hurry!"

In the absence of practical, all-season wagon roads pack trains were first organized to transport goods from such northern California supply depots as Shasta City, Crescent City, and Humboldt Bay across the narrow and winding mountain trails into Rogue River Valley, where placer miners and settlers alike came during and after 1850. During 1851 one hundred mules were said to have left Union (Humboldt Bay) weekly for the north California mines, carrying $4,000 to $5,000 worth of goods. The chief seat of this Oregon trade was Jacksonville, but Illinois Valley, Sailor Diggings, New Orleans Bar, Applegate Creek, and many other places were served by the Crescent City entrepôt. Packers usually took ten days to cover the 120-mile stretch from Crescent City to Jacksonville.

In Montana and Idaho the packing business experienced its greatest growth. Before wagon freight lines could be organized to operate between Fort Benton (the upper Missouri River port reached by St. Louis shippers) and Montana mining camps, pack animals were placed in service. Throughout the gold rush era Portland was the leading depot in Oregon for the interior areas. Goods were first shipped from Portland by steamers to such prominent river towns and landings as Umatilla, Wallula, Walla Walla, and The Dalles. From these points goods were then trans-shipped by pack trains over numerous mountainous trails to the mining communities of Idaho and Montana. Boise, Idaho, alone had an estimated population of from 15,000 to 20,000 in 1863. At first everything had to be packed into the Boise Basin, except for a small quantity hauled in by wagon from Salt Lake City. Hundreds of pack animals were needed to handle this work, for in addition to taking care of immediate demands merchants and miners had to store up supplies for winter months when travel virtually ceased. "Packing was quite a good business," relates the veteran Hailey, "freight ranging from sixteen to twenty-five cents per pound." Idaho City, Centreville (or Centerville), Placerville, Pioneer City, and Granite Creek were served by packers during the early sixties.

An interesting but relatively unimportant aspect of the packing business in the Pacific Northwest was the use of camels. These animals had been brought into the Southwest by the United States Army during the middle of the nineteenth century, very largely at the instigation of Secretary of War Jefferson Davis, in the belief that they could be used on the American deserts of southern California, Arizona, and

New Mexico, very much as they had been used in Africa, Asia, and other parts of the world, as valuable and efficient pack animals. Imaginative as it was, this army experiment failed.

The army's experience with camels stirred private interests, and in 1859 there had been formed the California and Utah Camel Association which imported an additional herd from Asia with less favorable results. After an unsuccessful effort by the War Department to sell the camels at auction at a minimum price of $1,200, they were sold separately. Some were ultimately placed in service on the Cariboo Road in British Columbia, and others in Idaho and Montana. Two camel trains made trips over the Umatilla-Boise-Bannack City trail but not with great success. Still another train of about six camels was used over the Mullan route, but one by one the animals disappeared. One, for instance, was shot for a moose; another drowned.

The Mullan Road

Many were the trails and crude roads that stretched the length and breadth of the Inland Empire. A number were Indian trails quickly adopted for use by the mining population. Space does not permit a description of these, save one — the Mullan Road, which was another of the numerous engineering accomplishments carried out under the direction of Governor Isaac I. Stevens. The Mullan Road bears the name of the army lieutenant who built it. Upon his arrival in Washington Territory in 1853, Stevens left Lieutenant John Mullan with thirteen men at Fort Owen, an outpost in the upper reaches of Clark's Fork and the Coeur d'Alene Mountains, where they began work on a wagon road which when completed would link together the two great river basins of the Columbia and the Missouri. The following year Congress appropriated $30,000 for the execution of the project, and specified that the road should run from Fort Benton on the upper Missouri to Wallula, the site of Old Fort Walla Walla, where connections could be established with other emigrant routes leading to the Puget Sound and the Willamette Valley. Factors beyond the control of Mullan necessitated delays, but in 1859 Congress increased its appropriation by $100,000 for the completion of the project.

Work proceeded at great speed. At one time 150 men were at work cutting a 25-foot swath through heavy timberland for a distance of 120 miles, through the Bitterroot and Coeur d'Alene mountains, making grades across open country, building hundreds of bridges, and establishing many ferry boats until August, 1860, when the road was completed with a total length of 624 miles. Almost immediately after its completion an army unit pased over its full length, a feat which was accomplished in 57 days.

It must, however, be remembered that what passed for a road in those early days would scarcely be graced with the name today. Mullan had in reality provided a route over which vehicles might be conveyed during the dry seasons of the year. But even this proved questionable since the builder had failed to anticipate the full damage of the heavy spring rains of the region. Mullan had to remain in the field until May 23, 1862, during which time improvements on the road were constantly made. At that time the road, which by then was generally known as the Mullan Road, represented seven years of effort on the part of its maker, less time for scores of other men, and a total expenditure of $230,000. The Mullan Road was ostensibly designed for military purposes, but it was hoped by those who originally petitioned Congress for it that immigrants might use it extensively. Mullan personally anticipating this, made provision for supplies for the immigrants and at given places along the route left memorandum notes regarding suitable camp sites.

By 1862 the military usefulness of the road was greatly diminished in view of an apparently marked quiescent state among the Oregon Indians. More important, therefore, for meeting immediate needs, was the fact that Montana, already enjoying a fur trade, was on the verge of what was destined to be a great and historic gold rush. And in no small measure the Mullan Road was to play a significant role in the early history of Montana, first as an important route of commerce, and second as an avenue for immigration.

The opening of the Missouri River freighter service at a time coinciding with the completion of the Mullan Road had far-reaching effect. Not only was there opened up an entirely new transcontinental line of communication via Montana, but immediately a keen awareness of competition for the Montana trade emerged between St. Louis, Missouri, and Portland, Oregon. During the gold rush period wagon traffic was heaviest over the eastern end, and at best the western portion reverted into a mule trail along which improved detours were worked out by the packers. Even so, either in whole or in part, the Mullan Road had great usefulness for the widely scattered mining population of the sixties. It must be regarded, moreover, as a monument to Lieutenant Mullan who at this early date had the vision and the courage even to conceive, let alone build, a road through 624 miles of undeveloped country. Today a broad paved highway (U. S. No. 10) winds its way along much of Mullan's original route, through scenic Idaho and western Montana. Once in after years Mullan reflected how "Night after night I have laid out in the unbeaten forests, or in the pathless prairies with no bed but a few pine leaves (needles), with no pillow but my saddle, and in my imagination heard the whistle of the engine, the whirr of the machinery, the paddle of the steamboat wheels, as they plowed the waters of the sound. In my enthusiasm," he added, "I saw the country thickly populated, thousands pouring over the borders to make homes in this far western land." For John Mullan all these dreams came true.

Wagon Freight Commerce

Wagon freighting gradually replaced packing during the dry season in regions where something answering the description of roads appeared. There was, of course, nothing new about commercial wagon freighting. The famous Conestoga wagon had been developed in colonial Pennsylvania, and had flourished in communities not easily supplied by water routes. During the fifties and the Civil War period Russell, Majors and Waddell had put into operation an elaborate wagon freighting system which connected the plains area with western railroad termini. Similar freighting companies operated in Texas; and Nevada was almost entirely dependent upon the long freighting trains from California which brought into the Wasatch region most of the necessities of life.

West of the Cascade Mountains, it was in the Rogue River Valley — cut off as it was from the navigable water routes — that wagon freighting enjoyed its earliest and busiest life. Just as pack trains in the early days brought goods into the Rogue Valley from California and from the Willamette Valley, so too did wagon freighters come to deliver quantities of goods from those same sources. From Crescent City came not only local agricultural goods, but much other merchandise shipped in by water from San Francisco. Freighting between Portland and Jacksonville also took on importance during southern Oregon's Gold Rush. This traffic operated two ways. Farmers in Douglas County in the South would haul bacon, lard, butter, cheese, and hides to Portland in exchange for dry goods and groceries.

Extensive wagon freighting into the Fraser River and Cariboo districts began in 1858 with the feverish mining activity there, and continued on a large scale until the middle eighties. There, as elsewhere on the mining frontier, pack trains were the first freight carriers to appear. This situation changed when in 1863 construction began on a wagon road between Yale (which succeeded Hope as the upper limit of river navigation on the Fraser) and Cariboo. This ambitious project had the approval of Governor James Douglas of British Columbia who, as he wrote to the home government, wished to secure "the whole trade of the colony for Fraser's River" and defeat "all attempts at competition from Oregon." This thoroughfare became known as the Cariboo Wagon Road, and from the point of view of sheer daring and human ingenuity was a signal achievement in frontier roadmaking.

In 1864 important strides were made in road construction between the Inland Empire and California. In an effort to connect the Boise Basin with the Sacramento Valley on February 6, 1864, was organized the Idaho and California Wagon-Road Company with a capital of $50,000. Beginning at the Snake River Ferry near Old Fort Boise, this concern proceeded to lay out a road southward to Ruby City (Owyhee district) through the Pitt River Valley, and finally coming out at Red Bluff, California.

Soon other California groups became interested in the Boise trade, and in 1865 a second road was marked out. It connected the Sacramento and Boise valleys by cutting through the northern passes across the Sierra Nevada Mountains, then turning northward to Boise Valley. At a later date still other roads connected Idaho with the Sacramento Valley.

This importation of goods from California did much to relieve the food shortage in Idaho which at times was acute. Even so, during the unusually severe winter of 1864–65 — following the first season of the California trade — the shortage of food essentials was so great that serious privation occurred; in the more isolated Idaho settlements flour is said to have sold for as much as $5.00 per pound and potatoes for 45¢ a pound. Resumption of wagon freighting in the spring soon restored prices to a more reasonable figure.

The Oregon-Idaho freighting business, unlike the California trade, was intricately combined with water transit concerns, and in particular the Oregon Steam Navigation Company. The laying out of passable wagon roads enabled freight companies to take over the service, previously carried on by pack trains, of connecting river steamship routes. The old Oregon Trail — in places altered and improved — which connected with The Dalles-Walla Walla Road was now also used in the Oregon-Idaho trade. Maps of the late sixties show no less than four wagon trails extending from the Columbia River through the Blue Mountains to the Boise Valley.

Wagon freighting over these various Oregon-Idaho routes was confined to the summer season, the months of July, August, and September, when the volume of freight was very heavy.

It is practically impossible to divorce Idaho freighting from that of Montana. Mineral developments in the two regions were simultaneous, and even though separated by the Continental Divide, Idaho and Montana were nonetheless bound together by many common lines of communication with the outside world. Oregon-Montana freighters reached their destination by following the same roads used in the Idaho trade as far inland as Boise. From Boise they followed the Oregon Trail, which connected with Fort Hall. At this key point a road ran northward to serve Virginia City, Bannack City, Deer Lodge, and numerous other Montana mining towns. The distance from the Umatilla landing to Virginia City, Montana, was estimated at from 850 to 900 miles.

Montana was also served by Californians, and one important avenue was that previously described which connected northern California with Boise. From Boise, Montana-bound Californians followed the route via Fort Hall that was also taken by their Oregon competitors. The distance between upper Sacramento River points and the Montana mining districts was also from 800 to 900 miles.

From the vital junction of Fort Hall a road extended southward, through Utah's famous freighting town of Corinne, to Salt Lake City. Here was the terminus of still another wagon road to Los Angeles by way of the Mojave Desert.

From Fort Benton westward to Helena (a distance of 135 miles), and to the lower Montana mining camps (about 200 miles), the Mullan Road was a satisfactory route for wagon travel and as such enabled wagon freighters to participate in the St. Louis — upper Missouri River trade. St. Louis steamboat companies engaging in the upper Missouri trade usually established wagon freighting connections at Fort Benton to assure their eastern and midwestern customers safe delivery "to all points in the mines." The time involved in such a shipment was thirty-five to forty days from St. Louis to Fort Benton by steamer, then ten to fifteen days by wagon freight from the dock to the camps. Grasses around Fort Benton were good the year round, which proved a great boon to the bullwhackers to whom feed for the animals was a constant problem. Helena, more than any other Montana city, was the beneficiary of this Missouri River trade. Figures of the volume of the Inland Empire trade are scarce, but it is estimated that, in 1866 alone, more than 6,000 tons, valued at $6,000,000, were conveyed by 3,000 wagons and 20,000 oxen and mules from Fort Benton to the Montana towns. Completion of the first transcontinental railroad in 1869 greatly altered the entire commercial structure of the Pacific, and the completion of the Northern Pacific Railroad all but ended the pack mule-wagon freight business.

Those who engaged in the work of freighting became accomplished in their art, and fabulous tales have been told about the skill of teamsters in handling their animals, in dealing with smug stage drivers as they hurried past a freight train, in modifying the King's English, and most of all, in wielding the whip. Teamsters were not known for their modesty and often gave added support to stories which extolled a mule skinner's or bullwhacker's accomplishments. At least one agreement was common to all of the class: one never admitted hauling less freight for the size of his wagon and the number of draft animals than any competitor. Wagon freighting, wherever it was done, was hard, dirty, tedious, and dangerous business. It was work which tried men's patience and only the toughest of the tough ever made bullwhacking or mule skinning his life's work. An immense part in the building of the West was played by the wagon freighter, and especially so in the Inland Empire.

CHAPTER XV

Government and Lawlessness in the Inland Empire

Creation of Idaho Territory

EVEN THOUGH Washington Territory as created in 1853 was too big and unwieldly to be a desirable administrative unit, so it remained until the population in outlying districts began voicing its dissatisfaction at being ruled from far distant Olympia. To meet this objection the Washington territorial government created Nez Percé, Idaho, and Boise counties (as parts of Washington Territory), and efforts were made to provide transportation facilities within these populated areas. When these steps failed to appease inland elements, steps were taken to bring about the establishment of a separate territorial government. The Washington legislature was petitioned for such action as early as 1861; other attempts followed, but not until the problem came to the direct attention of Congress at Washington, D. C., were positive steps taken.

A federal law creating Idaho Territory was signed by President Abraham Lincoln March 3, 1863. By this Organic Law Washington was shrunk to its present size; Dakota and Nebraska territories were sliced to establish the boundaries of Idaho Territory which included the areas of the present states of Idaho, Montana, and Wyoming. These boundaries remained in effect only a short time, for on May 26, 1864, Montana Territory was organized with its present dimensions, and four years later Wyoming Territory was created. This reduced Idaho to its present irregular shape with its elongated, mountainous panhandle sandwiched between Washington and Montana and with the sprawling Snake River Plain and the

[239

Owyhee Plateaus. On the other hand, those portions of the Organic Law pertaining to government, rather than boundaries of Idaho, remained intact throughout Idaho's prolonged territorial period. They provided that the President appoint a governor, secretary, three supreme court justices, and an attorney-general, and the inevitable United States Marshal. As was the custom, the Law provided for a law-making body, in this instance with a council of seven and a legislature of thirteen, elected by popular vote.

President Lincoln's choice of a governor for Idaho was William H. Wallace, an old friend of his, and an uncle of the more illustrious Lew Wallace, author of *Ben Hur*. Wallace had already served as governor and Congressional delegate of Washington Territory, and at the time of his appointment was a practicing attorney in Pierce County, Washington Territory. So strictly speaking he was not an importation as both Lane and Stevens had been.

Idaho's territorial legislature met first in Lewiston, then a typically crude, mining-shack town. By comparison, Oregon City was a center of culture and refinement. Some of the legislators rode horseback several hundred miles to attend the session of the legislature. It is no wonder that this first inland empire body of lawmakers discussed railroads, telegraph, and roads — not to mention some more centrally located permanent capital, preferably Boise. Decision on the latter question was partly solved by the pro-Boise faction who stole the seal and legislative records and carried them off to Boise where a crude frame building was to be designated the capitol of Idaho Territory in 1864.

During her territorial existence Idaho witnessed the end of her mining boom, though by no means the end of mining, for Idaho is today the "Gem State" of the Union. Valleys of volcanic ash that at first appeared barren and worthless for agriculture proved to be otherwise. Cattle and sheep thrived upon the nutritious grasses. The western side of the panhandle was excellent for farming. Idaho and Owyhee valleys were especially good for grazing. Lands in the Snake River region lent themselves to irrigation, and once watered proved to be amazingly fertile and productive. Dirt farmers steadily increased in numbers. They came from all parts of the country, but the most important single element were Mormons who found southeastern Idaho a natural area for expanding from their Utah base. Beginning in 1860 with the founding of Franklin, a succession of Mormon settlements was established and became, as in Utah, prosperous communities.

The political life of Idaho came to reflect these varied interests, and conflicts arose chiefly between the cattle and sheep men over use of the "free" grazing lands. Miners in the panhandle — feeling their isolation after the removal of the capital from Lewiston to Boise — sought vainly to re-annex themselves to Washington Territory.

The political record of the Idaho territorial government left much to be desired. Territorial governors — all Republican except one — were not conspicuous for their statesmanship, and the early Democratic legislatures were not above reproach. In February, 1864, Wallace took his seat as Congressional delegate from Idaho, an office to which he had been elected shortly after his appointment as Governor. To fill the governorship, President Lincoln blunderingly appointed Caleb Lyon, a "deserving" party man and art and literary connoisseur from New York. Lyon has been described as "a polished misfit in a country of mining camps." The people of Idaho failed to appreciate his debonair manners, his literary terminology, and his insistence on formal dress, but they did have a realistic understanding of the disappearance of $50,000 of public funds.

Lyon left Idaho before the expiration of his term, and affairs of government were left in the hands of Secretary C. DeWitt Smith, a lawyer, who, though a "young man of promise," to quote Bancroft, "could not withstand the temptations with which he found himself surrounded in Idaho." He drank heavily, and died from the effects of dissipation in 1865, six months after his arrival in Idaho. Governor Lyon continued his absence from Idaho, and following the death of Secretary Smith, acting Secretary Horace C. Gilson, at one time resident of Ohio, served technically as the territorial executive. But he, too, was dishonest, absconding to China with $30,000 of federal funds appropriated to Idaho. Since incompetence

POLITICAL EVOLUTION OF NORTHWEST STATES
(Raised portions represent present state areas.)

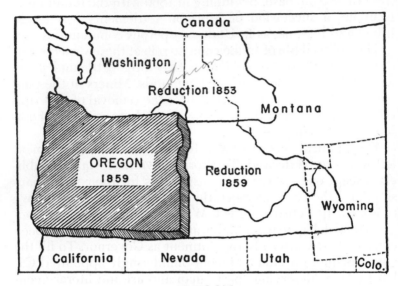

OREGON

OREGON:

The 1853 reduction of Oregon Territory became Washington Territory, to which was added the further reduction in 1859.

WASHINGTON:

The 1859 addition comprised lands which later became southern Idaho and part of western Wyoming. The 1863 reduction of Washington Territory was the equivalent of present-day Idaho, western Montana, and Wyoming.

IDAHO:

The 1864 reduction of Idaho Territory included present-day Montana; that of 1868, Wyoming.

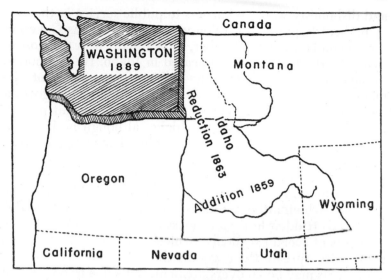

WASHINGTON

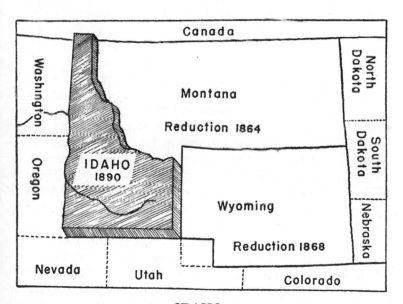

IDAHO

and dishonesty were no barriers to public service in the eyes of Radical Republicans, Lyon was reappointed as Governor for a second term in September, 1865. Finally near the close of that year the Governor reappeared in Idaho. He is reported to have spent most of his time looking for non-existent diamonds in Owyhee County, instead of running the government. Before the first year of his second term had passed, Lyon permanently abandoned Idaho; although he lived for several years thereafter, death saved him from Congressional investigation and public disgrace.

Fortunately the later period saw an improvement in Idaho's political morality and, according to Bancroft: "Most of the disorders which attended its infancy as a territory soon disappeared. Hidden in a great mass of sin and folly were the elements of social excellence, which, with an opportunity to germinate, spread their goodly branches throughout the land." This may be an overstatement, but some improvement did come. In June, 1886, David W. Ballard, an Oregon physician, became governor of Idaho Territory. Instead of absconding with funds (although he was later accused of doing so), Ballard reported that the federal government carried a $65,000 indebtedness on Idaho, but local records showed that less than $10,000 had been spent for the benefit of the Territory since its formation. Ballard, however, was a Republican, and the strongly Democratic legislature fought him at every turn. A turbulent Indian situation, moreover, heaped coals upon the fire. President Andrew Johnson, after four failures to secure Senate approval of a successor to Ballard, proceeded to dismiss him on grounds of incompetence. The Senate, however, refused to accept the removal, and there matters stood when Ulysses S. Grant assumed the presidency in 1869. In 1870 when the term expired, President Grant appointed Gilman Marston of New Hampshire to take Ballard's place. Eighteen months elapsed before Marston arrived in the Territory to assume office. Professor W. Turrentine Jackson has aptly summed up this period in Idaho: "In tracing the political difficulties of the Idaho Territory between 1863 and 1870, another case study has been presented to demonstrate the unfitness of many men appointed to federal positions in the territories during the era of Civil War and Reconstruction. Too often corrupt partisans sought and received territorial appointments for the sole purpose of exploiting the resources of the territory." In this case Idaho suffered, and there is reason to believe that her development was greatly stunted by mismanagement of public affairs.

Montana Territory

Only the western portion of present Montana directly concerns the Pacific Northwest, and during the gold rush period this Rocky Mountain area was part and parcel of the mineral empire. On May 26, 1864, Congress created Montana Territory (a comfortable feeling, after having been, at one time or another, a part of six different territories). Sidney Edgerton of Ohio was appointed by President Lincoln to be the first governor. A government was organized with Bannack as the first place of meeting for the legislature. The lawmakers nevertheless chose near-by Virginia City to be the territorial capital; in 1875 it was moved to Helena, the present site. Montana, like Idaho, passed through a period of political uncertainty and unrest. From the start Montana Territory was politically rocky. Prospectors who made up the bulk of its boisterous population came from both North and South, areas then engaged in the last bloody phases of Civil War. Montana's executive and judiciary branches were staunchly loyal to the Union, but the legislature leaned heavily toward the party of Democracy. The friction engendered by this political rift was fearful, and might well explain why certain elements preferred the verdicts of "Judge Lynch" to the decrees in spired by the federal government.

In both Idaho and Montana — in fact throughout the mineral frontier — respect for constituted authority was not deepseated, and the outlaw, though unwanted, became a very familiar figure.

Desperadoes and the Mountain Code

In 1862 the Salmon River region, scene of early mining activities, was plagued by bad men until vigilantes stamped them out either by hanging or ostracism. The same happened at Lewiston, where Lloyd Magruder, a prominent citizen, and five others in a party were murdered for money supposedly in their possession. This bloody affair has since been referred to as the Magruder massacre.

Describing the situation at Boise in 1864, Thomas Donaldson, an Idaho pioneer, reminisced: "Boise contained at that time a splendid assortment of murderers, robbers, and tinhorn gamblers. They were offscourings of all the abandoned and worn-out mining camps in the territory." Most notorious of that fraternity were the Updyke and Dixon gangs. For a period of about three years they robbed at will in and around Boise, but in 1866 vigilantes went to work with a vengeance. Then it was that the leader, Dave Updyke, was, to use a popular expression, "strung up." His body was found in an old shed bearing a sign which read: "Dave Updyke, the aider of murderers and horse thieves. XXX." James Dixon was next, and on his lifeless body was pinned a list of crimes attributed to him.

Favorite targets for outlaws were pack trains and stagecoaches; attacks continued at intervals in Idaho through the territorial period, and exploits of "road agents" were, to say the least, daring. For instance, in 1880 the Salisbury, Gilmore and Company stage, carrying Wells Fargo treasure, was robbed at Glenn's Snake River Ferry near Boise. It was after dark and the southbound stage was overdue. The hostler had just hung out a lantern when into the station jumped two armed men. They bound and gagged the hostler and threw him into a stable. When the stage arrived the road agents ordered the driver and one sole passenger from their seats and then proceeded to loot the express box, mail bags, and the station. Their job accomplished, the two highwaymen vanished into the darkness as mysteriously as they had come. Wells, Fargo and Company lost no time going in pursuit. They had such a good description of the men that within one week the guilty ones were hailed into Judge H. E. Prickett's federal court at Boise. The trial was expeditious; the men were found guilty of robbing the mails and jeopardizing human lives. The sentence was for life in the penitentiary.

Unfortunately, legal justice was not always attained with such dispatch in Idaho, and most frequently it was left to popular tribunals to dispense justice. Not infrequently a simple statement such as the following would appear in local newspapers: "David English, Nelson Scott and Wm. Peoples who were arrested here a week or two since on charges of highway robbery were hung by the citizens of Lewiston, on Saturday night last." Then, as if a moral justification were needed, the newspaper added: "If guilty the retribution was just — that they were guilty there was not the remotest doubt."

In no place were desperadoes so well organized, so vicious and bold, as in Montana. Established governmental machinery failed to cope with the crime wave that swept along Montana's many lonely, mountain trails. A series of holdups and slayings began in October, 1863. It was not at first known who committed these acts, and to what extent they were a part of an organized scheme of operations. But as the holdups continued in such methodical fashion without anyone's being brought to justice, suspicion belatedly turned upon Henry Plummer, the Sheriff of the Bannack and Virginia City districts. Distrust of the Sheriff was amply justified. He was actually the evil genius under whose businesslike direction a gang of about one hundred highwaymen, cattle rustlers, horse thieves, and murderers operated with precision, deftness, and skill. Plummer was an easterner by birth and rearing, but no one seems to know his native state. Although it was not at first known to the citizens of Bannack, this outwardly respectable man had behind him a long list of crimes, including murder, committed in New England, Nevada, California, and Idaho. During 1861 he had lived in Lewiston with a woman erroneously thought to be his wife. The two had moved freely in respected social circles of this city, while he had been establishing leadership in a band of outlaws that terrorized the mining camps of Idaho.

Finally two of the Lewiston culprits were hanged. This grim act proved sufficient warning to the rest who moved on to new pastures. Plummer, together with several of his intimates, went to mining camps of Montana where with added recruits he formed the notorious gang of "The Innocents." The organization of this group was amazingly intricate. There were various grades of officers, each office being filled according to the capability and criminal aptitude of each man. Plummer was naturally first in command, with "Billy" Bunton probably as gangster Number Two. George Ives, Ned Ray, Buck Stinson held high ratings by their chiefs; "Clubfoot George" Lane, "Long John" Franck, "Gad" Moore, "Old Tex" Crowell, "Dutch John" Wagner, and the rest had their special assignments. Men of another type sought and achieved key positions in public life, as for example Plummer, as Sheriff at Bannack, and Jack Gallagher, his Deputy Sheriff, at Virginia City. Several served as stool pigeons; others were given jobs of marking the stages which were known to have treasure aboard. Only the most dexterous gunmen were assigned to actual highway operations. The most daring and brutal of the gunmen were Ives and Crowell. Ives was cold-blooded. Once when his sawed-off shotgun failed to kill his victim, Ives stepped over to the injured man, and while talking calmly of this and that, drew his revolver and finished the job. Not all were known to each other, but members wore a special sailor's tie-knot as identification. From the "inside" Plummer kept in personal touch with his men by going frequently to the gang's rendezvous, "Robbers' Roost," and gave as his favorite excuse for leaving town inspection of his "silver deposits."

Suspicion of Sheriff Plummer reached a climax with his lassitude in what was called the Thomas Caldwell robbery. Immediately following this event a group of about twenty-five irate citizens gathered at Virginia City and then set forth in search of "Robbers' Roost." Early the next morning the place was found and approached. Shortly they encountered a man answering the description of the suspect George Ives. At the time it was not known that a large number of the gang were present at the hideout, although George Hilderman and "Long John" Franck were among those brought in with Ives. On their way back to town Ives attempted to escape, but was recaptured. Once in Virginia City, the three prisoners were bound together by a logging chain to await a vengeful trial before a vigilante court.

Ives's trial came first. It was held outdoors and the public was free to attend. After all witnesses were heard, as well as the arguments of the counsels of defense and prosecution, the judge, seated upon a wagon, gave the case to a jury consisting of twenty-four men. Within thirty minutes a verdict was returned. Twenty-three jurors declared Ives guilty of murder and robbery; one dissented. It was then moved as an alternative that the assembly adopt the verdict of the vigilantes that Ives was guilty. This motion carried, and after some haggling among the crowd, Ives was led ten yards from the scene of trial and hanged. The trial of Hilderman was brief and ended differently from that of Ives. Because he turned state's evidence, and because of his advanced age, the robust vigilantes took pity on Hilderman and allowed him to leave the Territory with his life.

Out of these incidents came the more formal organization of a Vigilance Committee which served notice on the outlaws, and brought most of them to their doom at the end of a rope. The climax came early when Plummer was caught unarmed. He begged for mercy, but was told: "It is useless for you to beg for your life; . . . You are to be hanged." They took him to a scaffold where two of his comrades, Ned Ray and Buck Stinson, were swinging by the hemp. Plummer requested that he be given a "good drop" and this was granted so far as possible. The noose was placed around Plummer's neck and the vigilantes lifted him with their arms as high as they could reach, and then let go. The date was January 10, 1864.

Between the hanging of Ives in 1863, and that of James Daniel in 1866, thirty-two road agents felt in similar fashion the increasing activity of the Montana vigilantes. Others were banned, so that no doubt remained that the Plummer gang, probably the most vicious in the West, was thoroughly and effectively stamped out. Before that time came, however, lawlessness had cost the lives of at least 102 persons killed by this organized gang of cutthroats. With the most vicious of the outlaws either hanged or exiled, the Vigilance Committee had little reason for being, and did, in fact, cease to function. Constituted authorities came to assume, more fully, the requisites of their offices. This was made easier by the gradual passing of the most rugged of frontier conditions and the steady immigration into the inland areas of conservative agriculturists, who believed in the functioning of law through constituted government, and whose peaceful, quiet lives made their influence felt upon the social body as a whole.

Chief Joseph and the Non-Reservation Nez Percé

Lamentable is the story of Chief Joseph and his Nez Percé followers, whose forebears had lived peaceably in the Grande Ronde country, in northeastern Oregon, as far back as the memory of man could go. Never had these peace-loving cousins of the Idaho Nez Percé been known to draw the blood of a single white man until, in 1877, when war was — at least from their point of view — made inevitable.

By treaty in 1855 large portions of Nez Percé lands were ceded to the whites; and again in 1863 a treaty was signed which required that all the Nez Percé should live on the Lapwai Reservation in Idaho. Some obeyed and retired to the reservation, but Chief Joseph, a distant cousin of the Idaho Nez Percé, and his followers living in the Grande Ronde did not consider themselves signators of the pact, and therefore refused to go to the Reservation. For thirteen years nothing was done. Then in 1876 President Grant, pressured by white squatters who wanted the Indian lands, ordered that the treaty of 1863 be promptly enforced. General O. O. Howard, of Civil War notoriety, was in command of the district involved, and upon him fell the onerous responsibility of enforcing the presidential order. Negotiations were opened with Chief Joseph, and unfortunate incidents occurred. Squatters began committing outrages on the Indians, and these brought retaliations from some hot-tempered Nez Percé braves who, seeking vengeance, killed twenty whites.

The braves forced the issue, and reluctantly Chief Joseph decided not to fight, but to flee toward Canada with two hundred warriors and six hundred women and children. The retreat toward Canada is one of the most amazing stories in Indian history. When Joseph and his band of refugees began their flight, they were faced by the forces of General John

Gibbon at Fort Shaw, pursued by those of General Howard, and flanked by numerous mobile units within easy reach of telegraphic instructions designed to spring a trap on the over-burdened Indians. Well planned as this strategy was, General Howard failed to anticipate the brilliant countermoves of the wily Chief Joseph. The Indians managed to elude the pursuing forces of General Howard, but they encountered those of General Gibbon at Big Hole River, Montana, on August 9, 1877. Gibbon's forces were repulsed, and the Nez Percé resumed their flight.

For a distance of more than one thousand miles the Indians continued their circuitous retreat through southwestern Montana, Idaho, the Yellowstone Park, along the Clarke's Fork to the Yellowstone River in Wyoming. Along the latter stream they encountered a force of United States troops commanded by General S. D. Sturgis, fought them off, and then pushed northward into the Bear Mountain within thirty miles of the Canadian border. They committed no atrocities along the route of flight; they paid farmers for supplies; and all the while they outwitted the American regulars who pursued them.

At this point, thinking they were safe from attack the exhausted, starved, wounded, and frozen Nez Percé paused to rest, only to be spotted by the troops of General Miles who had made a speedy cross-country movement designed to overtake the enemy before it passed outside the jurisdiction of the United States. On September 30, after a seventy-five day search, Howard, the "Christian soldier," moved in for battle. Facing a choice of three alternatives — to flee with his warriors, leaving women, children and wounded behind; to surrender; or to fight from cleverly prepared positions — Chief Joseph chose to fight it out. For five days there was bitter skirmishing, but on October 4th the noble chief surrendered with this remark: "I am tired of fighting. Our chiefs are all killed. . . . The little children are freezing to death. My people, some of them, have run away and have no blankets, no food. . . . My heart is sick and sad."

The surviving Nez Percé were placed on a reservation in Kansas until 1885 when they were permitted to return to the region they loved, to Colville Reservation, but not to the

Grande Ronde. At Colville, Joseph lived among his people, and not without honor, until his death in 1904. The episode here described was the last serious Indian disturbance in the Pacific Northwest. The manner in which it was handled was widely criticized by an American people grown tired of abusing Indians. To most people Chief Joseph is regarded as a brilliant hero, and his people as good Indians who had been brutally mistreated.

Omnibus States

Today one refers to Washington, Idaho, Montana, Wyoming, North Dakota, and South Dakota as the "omnibus" states. In their struggle for statehood they encountered common problems and all joined the Union within a period of two years, 1889–90. It is therefore difficult to discuss the admission of the Pacific Northwest omnibus states without referring to those belonging to the North Central area.

It will be recalled that Washington Territory had been created as far back as 1853, but even as early as 1868 all of the above-mentioned areas had been similarly organized. Why then, was there such a long delay in achieving statehood?

The answer to this question has many ramifications, chiefly political. During the earlier territorial periods the main deterrent was the absence of a sufficiently large population of the type that showed a disposition to remain in the territories. With the exception of western Washington, the largest percentage of the inhabitants were miners who drifted about from one camp to another and, certainly in many instances, wound up their gold hunting exploits by returning to their former homes outside the states. The steady, more permanent farmer — ranching-merchant type of population — was slow to arrive in numbers sufficient to impress Congress, which had assumed the right to lay down conditions for admission of states into the Union. The territories in question, moreover, were almost completely isolated before the completion of the Northern Pacific Railroad in 1883. They were skirted by the Oregon Trail and by the Union Pacific Railroad, and to the American people they remained the wild and woolly West where, and with some truth, the scalping knife was still used with reckless abandon.

Statehood was a favorite subject of conversation in the territorial Northwest, and an organized movement aimed at acquiring state membership in the Union began in Washington Territory during 1878 when an unauthorized constitutional Convention met at Walla Walla. Elsewhere in the region the issue of statehood was soon to become prominent.

Outstanding as were the economic and social factors, the most important reason for protracted delay of admission was national politics. For four years following the disputed Tilden-Hayes election of 1876 Republicans, who might then have looked with favor upon increasing their strength by admitting what would doubtless have become G. O. P. states, were faced with an adverse Democratic House. The election of 1880 gave the Republicans a clean sweep in national politics for two years (a position not again to be enjoyed until 1897), but efforts in 1882 to admit their first try, Dakota, failed of passage in the Senate through party defection of a Republican senator from Maine. Then in 1885 when the Senate was finally ready to admit Dakota (and probably the Northwest territories as well), Grover Cleveland, a Democrat, assumed office as Chief Executive and thwarted Republican efforts.

So the political tug-of-war continued until completion of the Northern Pacific Railroad and the ever-rising tide of permanent residents in the great area made further denial extremely embarrassing. The population of Washington in 1880 was 75,116; in 1890, it numbered 349,390 — the most striking increase in the nation during that ten-year interval. The population of Idaho in 1880 was 32,610; in 1890 it was 84,385; and that of Montana was 39,159 and 132,159 in 1880 and 1890, respectively. Neighboring territories of Dakota and Wyoming registered similar sharp increases.

Election of Republican Benjamin Harrison as President, November, 1888, plus the realization that Republicans in the ensuing Congress would probably secure passage of enabling acts, brought to an end the long delaying action of the Democrats. If passage of such acts was inevitable, so the Democrats thought, why not now be the ones to support such measures and secure political credit for it? Perhaps, too, Democratic New Mexico could be included among the states to be admitted. An omnibus bill (but as finally voted upon, a bill stripped of its Democratic features) inviting Washington, Montana, North and South Dakota to draw up constitutions preparatory to admission, was passed, and signed by President Cleveland, February 22, 1889.[1] The measure, among other provisions, asked for certain "irrevocable" pledges, namely, religious toleration, renunciation of claims on public lands, assumption of territorial debts, provision for public schools "free from sectarian control," a republican form of government, equality of races in the matter of civil rights, and, of course, constitutions not repugnant to the Declaration of Independence and the Constitution of the United States.

In accordance with the enabling act, Washington Territory representatives met at Olympia and on Independence Day began proceedings to form a constitution. They drew up a document providing for a representative government with executive officers to hold office on four-year terms, bicameral legislature, state supreme court, county superior courts, and county and township governments. It also made ample provision for educating all children residing within its borders, regardless of race, color, caste, or sex. As in Oregon, certain controversial provisions were submitted to a vote by the people. One of these was woman suffrage, which was defeated by more than a two–to–one vote; another was prohibition, defeated by 31,487 to 19,546; and the last and most heated question of all — permanent location of the capital — resulted in a plurality vote for Olympia, which remains the capital to this day. The constitution itself was also voted upon at the same balloting (October 1, 1889), and was approved 40,152 to 11,879. At the same election officers were chosen — all Republican. Elisha P. Ferry, previously territorial governor, was elected to be the first governor of the state. John L. Wilson won the first seat to the national House of Representatives;

---

[1] In their maneuverings Democrats had hoped to include Democratic New Mexico in the omnibus bill, but Republicans defeated this measure in Committee.

and when the state legislature convened, it chose as senators John B. Allen, Walla Walla, and Watson C. Squire, Seattle. On November 11, 1889, President Benjamin Harrison proclaimed Washington to be a state.

Nine days previously, November 2, 1889, North Dakota and South Dakota had come into the Union, and, only three days before, Montana was admitted.

Idaho and Wyoming had been left out of the omnibus bills, but they refused to be sidetracked. In Idaho the question of what to do about the ever-increasing number of Mormons evoked spirited controversy. The 1884–85 legislature favored disfranchisement of the Saints, who then reportedly numbered about 25,000. For reasons related to the Mormon question, the same body went on record favoring annexation of the Idaho panhandle to Washington, and made such a recommendation in a memorial to Congress. During 1886 both houses of Congress passed a bill calling for such annexation, but Grover Cleveland, the veto-President, pocketed the measure.

During the following year (1887) the territorial legislature, realizing that Idaho might cease to exist, made an about face, and this time petitioned Congress to retain the panhandle and thereby keep Idaho intact. Following this line of reasoning a constitutional convention assembled in 1889 without the blessings of an enabling act, and prepared a liberal constitution not unlike that of her neighboring states. Congress gave its approval, and by presidential proclamation Idaho became a state on July 3, 1890. George L. Shoup, last of the territorial governors, was elected as the first chief executive of the Gem State. One week later, July 10th, Wyoming was admitted. Within no previous twelve-month period had so many states become a part of the Union.

PART TWO

THE POST–FRONTIER PERIOD

(1883–1950)

Chapter XVI

Bands of Steel

Surveys and Projections

THE NORTHERN PACIFIC Railroad completed in 1883 and the Canadian Pacific two years later, followed by the Great Northern in 1893, were truly symbolic of a century of material progress in the Pacific Northwest. Yet to most pioneers of the Pacific Northwest the sight of a railroad train simply meant reunion with old friends. To many persons traveling by rail in the East before going to the west coast, completion of the Northern Pacific Railroad was an accomplishment long overdue. After all, as far back as 1845 the proposals of Asa Whitney and George Wilkes for such a road had first been laid before the deaf ears of Congress. John C. Frémont had lent support to similar plans, as had also Senator Thomas Hart Benton, Calvin Colton, and many other friends of the Far West.

Finally in 1853 Congress authorized the Secretary of War to make explorations and surveys to determine the most practical route for a railroad to the Pacific. Five such routes were staked out, with Isaac I. Stevens, Washington's first territorial governor, surveying a northern route with proposed terminals at Puget Sound and the Great Lakes. The heightening sectional conflict brought additional delays. Not until 1864, and then through the leadership of Josiah Perham, did Congress pass an act authorizing the construction of a railroad to Puget Sound. It was to follow a route west from Lake Superior to Puget Sound and the Columbia River Valley. This measure was known as the Northern Pacific Act. Simultaneously Congress passed a revised Union Pacific Act, and both received the signature of President Lincoln on July 4 of the year the Act was introduced.

Even though Congress had agreed to a most liberal grant of 44,000,000 acres of public land in its Northern Pacific Act, no provision was made for government cash subsidy or loan. Thus future financing of the road remained very much in doubt. Not, in fact, until the banker Jay Cooke cast his lot with the enterprise in 1869 could full-scale construction work begin.

At both ends of the projected route, out of Kalama, Washington, and from near Lake Superior in Minnesota, track was actually being laid during 1870. Greatest strides were made from the East. Although Jay Cooke and Company failed in 1873, by that date the westward construction had reached Bismarck, North Dakota. From Kalama on, at the western end, construction reached Commencement Bay where the official terminal city of Tacoma had been laid out. Here operations came to a halt, and two years later the Northern Pacific Railroad Company defaulted the interest on its bonds and became insolvent.

Local Short-line Railroads

Back of this national undertaking were numerous regional developments. Before construction on the Northern Pacific Railroad began some local railroad building had been done as a means of serving the principal waterways. Bradford and Company began work in 1851 on a wooden portage tramway along the north bank of the Columbia River Cascades. Four years later, Colonel Joseph S. Ruckel started a portage wagon road on the south bank of the Cascades. On this roadbed the Oregon Portage Railroad later operated. These portage lines were controlled by the Oregon Steam Navigation Company. In 1863 this concern completed an iron-railed road along what had previously been known as Thompson's Portage, on The Dalles-Celilo portage railroad. Added improvements were made on this vital portage, most notable of which was the transfer from the Oregon Portage line of the compact little steam locomotive, the "Oregon Pony," and for three years this engine operated along the banks of the Columbia River.

The first railroad in the Inland Empire was the Walla Walla

and Columbia, about thirty-two miles long, built by the in-genious Dr. Dorsey S. Baker, one of the early Oregon pio-neers. It was very much a homemade road. The rails were of fir, spiked to mortised ties. Later the rails were reinforced with iron straps. The rolling stock was of the crudest type, including a locomotive imported from Pittsburgh in 1872. This line, because of its spirited builder and singularity, was variously called "Dr. Baker's road," the "strap iron road," and the "rawhide road." In 1875 it was completed. Staggering profits were made from the enterprise, but this is not surpris-ing when one observes that the freight rates on the thirty-two mile line were from $4.50 to $6.00 per ton. In 1878 Dr. Baker sold his fortune-making railroad to the Oregon Steam Naviga-tion Company for $321,132.00.

Some indication of the number and size of scattered rail-road lines in the Columbia River region was revealed when in 1879 the Oregon Steam Navigation Company agreed to sell its properties to Henry Villard. The famous steamship firm listed among its assets: (1) the Cascade Portage Railroad. Washington Territory, 6 miles of roadbed and track, along with sidings, turntables, shops, etc., 3 locomotives, 3 passen-ger cars, and 35 box cars, all valued at $300,000; (2) the Ore-gon Portage Railroad, 5 miles of grading and trestle, 7 miles of telegraph line, and miscellaneous other equipment with a total value of $75,000; (3) The Dalles and Celilo Railroad, 14½ miles of roadbed, track and sidings, turntables, 3 loco-motives, 27 box cars, 19 flatcars, 2 passenger cars, etc., valued at $700,000; (4) the Walla Walla and Columbia Railroad, formerly Dr. Baker's, with new steel rails added and valued at $600,000; (5) miscellaneous equipment necessary for rail operations, such as 250 miles of telegraph line between Walla Walla and Portland, valued at $25,000, and machine shops and equipment worth $15,000.

Strivings in the Willamette Valley

Early settlers in the Willamette Valley who clamored so vociferously for railroad construction were without financial means to bring their wishes to fruition. Help was needed from outside sources, and such was to come, not from Wall Street, but from financial interests in California. During the sixties in California numerous "bonanza railroads" were under construction. The "Big Four," Leland Stanford, Collis P. Huntington, Charles Crocker, and Mark Hopkins, had organized the Central Pacific Railroad, and in 1864 construction of the first transcontinental rail line had begun. Among the multitude of projected routes was one which would connect California with Portland, Oregon.

Taking the initiative in this move for a California-Oregon railroad was an energetic surveying engineer from California named Simon G. Elliott. Supporting Elliott were several lawyers, businessmen, and politicans from both California and Oregon, men who stood to gain from such a project. In all about seventy individuals were financially interested, and at the once-bustling boom town of Jacksonville, Oregon, on October 13, 1863, the California and Columbia River Railroad Company was incorporated. A rift soon developed in this concern, and before the year was out one faction led by Elliott formed a second company called the California and Oregon Railroad Company; control of the old group passed to Joseph Gaston of Portland.

Both companies proceeded to make surveys. The survey for the older concern called for a railroad beginning at Jacksonville and going north through the Umpqua Mountains and Valley, across the Calapooya Mountains at Applegate Pass and thence along the west side of the Willamette River to Portland. The survey for the second company proposed a route through northern California which followed the Sacramento and Shasta rivers, passed through the thriving mining town of Yreka, followed Willow Creek until crossing the Klamath River, and then went over the Siskiyou Mountains; thence through Oregon via Bear Creek Valley to Jacksonville, along the Rogue and Umpqua rivers to Roseburg, and finally down the Willamette Valley; through Eugene City, Corvallis, Albany, Jefferson, Salem, to Portland.

Unlike its competitor, the California and Oregon Company looked for aid from the federal government rather than from the Oregon legislature. To facilitate this procedure there was formed on July 13, 1865, what might be called a sister organization, with the name reversed to read Oregon and California Railroad Company. Accordingly, in 1866, Congress passed a measure which gave to the California and Oregon Railroad Company and to whatever concern the Oregon legislature might designate, twenty alternate sections of public land for each mile of railroad to be constructed. This liberal Congressional act left no doubt as to the recipient of the grant within California, but the door was still left wide open as to who would get it in Oregon. Which company would the Oregon legislature designate? That was the question. Would it be the Oregon and California Railroad Company? The Californa and Columbia River Company? Or would it be another company as yet unformed?

These questions became subjects of torrid controversy in Oregon political circles. As it turned out, Gaston's California and Columbia River concern ceased to exist, but during October, 1866, there emerged in its place (again under Gaston's leadership) a new organization known as the Oregon Central Railroad Company. To the surprise of many the Oregon legislature chose to recognize this new concern as the one eligible to receive the liberal land grant proffered by the federal government. There followed a scramble for power within the victor's camp. One group rallied around Gaston, long a supporter of Barry and the so-called "west side route." Opponents of Gaston joined I. R. Moores, who favored a union with Elliott's Californians and the adoption of the Elliott route, projected to follow the east side (or bank) of the Willamette River. Thenceforth the two concerns became known, respectively, as the West Side Company and the East Side Company. Each considered itself the legitimate successor of the Oregon Central Railroad Company, and as such rightful heir to the land grant. During April, 1868, both companies began construction of a railroad out of Portland, each thinking that this evidence of good deeds would further strengthen claim with the state lawmakers.

What happened was a race for survival between two concerns, each greatly handicapped by lack of funds. For a while it looked as if the West Siders would win. In the nick of time, however, the rival East Siders were saved by the arrival of the audacious and, according to his enemies, villainous Ben Holladay. A partnership was formed between Holladay and Elliott, and from this point on the question as to which of the two contesting companies was legally and legitimately entitled to official recognition was purely academic. To the ruthless Holladay such quibbling was a waste of time when lavish entertainment, bribery, and bullying proved infinitely more expeditious as a means of attaining desired ends.

When in 1868 Ben Holladay arrived in Oregon, he was not only the undisputed "Stagecoach King" of America, but also a powerful figure in Pacific coast steamship circles. He was a personality not easily pushed aside, and it is not surprising that in October, 1868, the Oregon legislature granted to the East Side Company, Holladay's group the coveted plum of 3,800,000 acres of public land.

In the face of such utter humiliation nothing was left for Gaston's West Side Company but to capitulate. During August, 1870, the West Siders transferred their control to Holladay, who proceeded to merge the two Willamette railroad projects into one. To his reorganized and reincorporated concern Holladay gave the familiar name of Oregon and California Railroad Company.

Leadership under Holladay left much to be desired, from the standpoint of both investors and Oregon public as a whole. Holladay soon quarreled with Elliott, and removed him from his position as superintendent of construction. According to Henry Villard, however, "this riddance did not really improve his situation." Financial problems multiplied for Holladay as work on the roadbed and the laying of new track proceeded. By January, 1870, about $800,000 had already been spent on the project and much more would be needed to complete the road to Eugene City, at the upper end of the Willamette Valley. To secure needed funds Holladay recklessly sold bonds at sixty to seventy-five per cent of par value, largely to German investors. With funds thus secured, though at ruinous discount rates, Holladay plunged ahead.

Railroad construction was stepped up. In order to eliminate river competition, Holladay bought out at least nine small local steamship lines as well as the Oregon City portage.

Bold as the entire scheme was — a plan which would certainly give to the Oregon and California Railroad Company monopolistic control over Willamette Valley transportation — the race with time was a losing one. Profitable freight business failed to materialize; bond sales slackened; the German security-holders became increasingly restive when in 1873 interest payment failed to materialize. The affairs of Holladay had reached their crest, and the panic of 1873 started this swashbuckling American rugged individualist on his way out. As the fortunes of Holladay waned, those of Henry Villard were definitely in the ascendancy.

Henry Villard's Northwest Triumphs

The saga of fastidious Henry Villard is an entrancing one. Like that of Holladay, it is the story of a self-made man whose meteoric rise to a position of power in the fields of finance and western transportation has epic qualities. About his arrival in the United States in 1853, Henry Villard, a native of Bavaria, remarked in his memoirs: "I was utterly destitute of money, had but a limited supply of wearing apparel, and that not suited to the approaching cold season, and I literally did not know a single person in New York or elsewhere in the Eastern States to whom I could apply for help and counsel. To crown all, I could not speak a word of English."

He came from a reputable background, with good native endowments and, for his age (eighteen years), had a thorough educational training. His early experiences in the land of his adoption were in the fields of teaching and journalism, and not until the seventies did he become actively interested in banking and railroads.

When in 1871 Villard's health began to fail, he left for Germany. In Heidelberg, where he had gone in 1872 to rest and to visit relatives, he suffered an apoplectic stroke. During his convalescence at the then gay old Heidelberg, Villard was approached by an acquaintance "regarding an unfortunate investment he had made in American railroad bonds." Out of this chance inquiry came an agreement whereby Villard would represent the German stockholders of the Oregon and California Railroad Company upon his return to the states. In 1874 Villard, with Richard Koehler from Germany, arrived in Oregon. "What I saw of Oregon on that trip to Portland," wrote Villard, "filled me with the greatest enthusiasm."

Villard planned to proceed slowly, eliminating Holladay when the time was ripe — if he could. Since the panic of 1873 had greatly weakened Holladay, his deposition was merely a matter of choosing the most desirable time. That time came in April, 1878. Holladay, unable to meet his obligations, was compelled to transfer his stocks to Villard and to withdraw as an active figure in Oregon railroading.

Villard and his associates thereupon proceeded to reorganize their extensive holdings as they saw fit. Villard soon became president of both a revamped Oregon Steamship Company and of the Oregon and California Railroad Company. The finances of both these concerns were merged. Koehler became vice-president of the latter company, and such figures as T. R. Cornelius, A. G. Cunningham, and G. W. Weidler were elected to prominent positions.

Good fortune, combined with sagacity, had catapulted a German-born journalist into the ranks of American tycoons. A chance situation suddenly boosted him to the head of an important transportation system. As an executive officer, Villard was quick to see both the limitations and the golden opportunities for his newly re-formed companies. If combined with the extensive facilities of the Oregon Steam Navigation Company, and if in turn direct railroad connections could be established between California and the East, then a great future was in store for the entire network. Toward this end Villard next directed his energies. Times were improving. ". . . the approach of the resumption of specie payments had started a 'boom' in Wall Street," relates Villard, "the like of which was never witnessed before. . . ." He formulated his plans well, and as a first step he proposed to buy out the extensive holdings of the Oregon Steam Navigation Company. John C. Ainsworth, president of the steamship concern, asked $5,000,000, fifty per cent to be paid in cash, the rest in stocks and bonds. "He [Villard] wasn't an hour coming to terms," according to Ainsworth, and the deal was completed May 23, 1879. Being in possession of these new holdings, Villard, on June 13, 1879, organized and became president of the Oregon Railway and Navigation Company, for all intents and purposes the old Oregon Steam Navigation Company. Plans called for the building of a trunk line along the south bank of the Columbia River with "fan-like" feeder lines extending into eastern Oregon and eastern Washington Territory. During 1880 construction on these lines began. By 1883 the Oregon Railway and Navigation Company had spent more than $20,000,000 in building some five hundred miles of standard-gauge road; moreover, this investment was well made, for in 1883 the Oregon Railway and Navigation Company was one of the most profitable lines in the United States.

Villard Completes the Northern Pacific Railroad

Although immediate returns of the Oregon Railway and Navigation Company exceeded expectations, Villard saw danger signals ahead. Again, as many times before, Portland interests, now including those of Villard, feared developments at Puget Sound, western terminus for the Northern Pacific Railroad. With the revival of activity in Northern Pacific Railroad circles during the late seventies, Villard's Portland coterie suspected, and rightly so, that if the Northern Pacific Railroad Company intended to complete its line to the Pacific, with Tacoma as its official western terminus, interests of Puget Sound were destined to be aided to the detriment of Portland and the lower Columbia River Valley in general, and the Oregon Railway and Navigation Company in particular. Villard knew that his existing transportation system, good as it appeared to be, was not sufficient; that either Portland must become the main terminus of a transcontinental railroad [1] or Tacoma must be hampered in achieving this goal. The commercial prestige of Portland should, at all costs, be main-

[1] There had been earlier schemes to make Portland a terminus of a transcontinental system, but prior to 1880 none promised to be successful.

Courtesy Norfolk and Western Railroad

A locomotive in use on the Northern Pacific Railway in 1870

Courtesy Northern Pacific Railroad

En route to Northern Pacific "Last Spike" celebration, held at Gold Creek, Montana, September 8, 1883. This was one of four special trains carrying notables, including General U. S. Grant, to the celebration.

RAILROADS OF THE NORTHWEST

Courtesy Great Northern Railroad

A Great Northern Diesel-powered freight train on Two Medicine Bridge approaching Glacier National Park.

Courtesy Chicago, Milwaukee, St. Paul and Pacific Railroad

"The Olympian" of the Milwaukee Road in the mountains, Washington. West of Harlowton, Montana, this line is partly electric.

RAILROADS OF THE NORTHWEST

tained. To strengthen his position, Villard began to extend his system east from The Dalles with the object of connecting far eastward with either the rival Northern Pacific or the Oregon Short Line extension of the Union Pacific. He hoped that such a move would prevent the construction of a competing line in the lower Columbia basin which Villard regarded as his private preserve.

Meanwhile, Villard evolved a much more magnificent scheme whereby he might gain control of the entire Northern Pacific system rather than try to head it off. He kept his own counsel on this matter until December 1880, when he was prepared to act. Two distinct lines of approach were outlined. The first of these demanded the organization of what he called the Oregon and Transcontinental Company, which would be the "financing concern." Through two close friends whom he could trust and to whom he revealed his plans, he bought Northern Pacific securities. To raise additional funds for such purchases, he created what is now known as the "Blind Pool." In "an act of greatest boldness" (to use Villard's own words), he appealed on Wall Street for cash without divulging the purpose for which the money was to be spent — an action without precedent in Wall Street history.

By this method, one which revealed remarkable confidence in the honesty and ability of Villard, no less than $8,000,000 was subscribed. With these resources at his command, Villard, popularly known from this time on as "The 'Blind Pool' Man," and as the most-discussed person in financial circles, demanded and received recognition in the management of the Northern Pacific Railroad Company. By October 1881 he was elected president of this giant concern.

It was now possible for this remarkable financier to complete the construction of the Northern Pacific Railroad and link it with the elaborate transportation network already in operation in the Pacific Northwest.[2] The last costly stretch

[2] The line was built to connect with the Oregon Railway and Navigation system, with Portland regarded as the western terminus. The route followed was by way of Wallula, across the Inland Empire, and into Montana where connection with the Northern Pacific line was made. Connections, however, were later made with the Kalama-Tacoma branch so that Puget Sound was also served; in fact, the western end of the Northern Pacific system took the

separating East from West followed the rugged Clark's Fork Valley through the Bitterroot Mountains, a route early familiar to the fur traders of the North West Company. Most difficult of all was construction through the Hell Gate Canyon. On September 8, 1883, near Gold Creek, seven miles west of Garrison, Montana, this gap was closed and the last spike driven.

The Columbia and Willamette valleys, as well as Puget Sound, thereby became a part of the intricate Northern Pacific system. To Villard personally, and to the Pacific Northwest, the driving of the last spike was a great and memorable occasion. Nearly four decades had elapsed since Asa Whitney had first dreamed of such an undertaking. Now, after the expenditure of vast sums of money and of physical and mental effort, Whitney's dream had come true.

In order to complete the Northern Pacific, Villard's expenditures exceeded by $7,986,508 his $40,000,000 in receipts. By October this deficit swelled to $9,459,921 and the end was not in sight. To meet these expenditures, second-mortgage bonds were issued to the extent of $20,000,000, with the result that Northern Pacific securities depreciated in value. In the face of these adversities, caused by unexpected construction costs, Villard, by January 4, 1884, had resigned as president of the Northern Pacific, the Oregon and Transcontinental Company, and of the Oregon Railway and Navigation Company. This shift in management did not halt operations. Steps were soon taken to build the Cascade branch of the line, which, with the cutting of Stampede Tunnel in the Cascade Mountains, made the completion of this important segment possible in 1888. Once again old regional and city rivalries flared to new heights.

Completion of the Oregon and California Railroad

Railroad construction south from Portland, which had reached Roseburg in 1872, for the next eleven years remained

---

form of a large elliptical loop, beginning at Pasco, Washington, following the south side of the Columbia River to Portland, thence north to Tacoma, east via Ellensburg, and back to Pasco. From Tacoma a line was built to Seattle.

at a standstill. During this entire period the earning remained low.

Under Villard's direction construction toward the Oregon-California boundary was resumed in 1883. By May of the following year the line was completed as far south as Ashland and some additional work had been done beyond the city before Villard's insolvency brought operations to a stop. For a while the Oregon and California Railroad staved off bankruptcy, but in 1885 the company went into receivership, and two years thereafter control of the line passed into the hands of the Southern Pacific Railroad Company.

Previously, the Southern Pacific Company had acquired

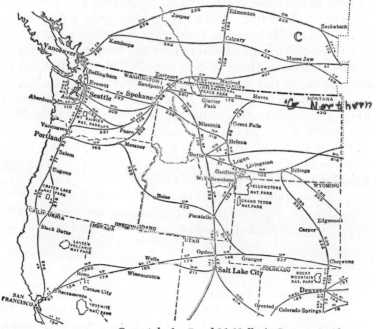

Copyright by Rand McNally & Company, Chicago

MAJOR RAILROADS IN THE GREAT NORTHWEST

For complete railroad maps of each state, see Rand McNally's Handy Railroad Maps of the United States (Chicago, 1937).

control of the old California and Oregon Railroad, and had completed construction of this line north to the Oregon border. With both Oregon and California lines under Southern Pacific control, the remaining gap was hastily closed. A tunnel for 3,700 feet through a part of the Siskiyou Mountains near Ashland was the last piece of construction. But, according to the Ashland *Tidings,* rail connections were established on December 17, 1887, and a northbound construction train "was run upon the Oregon and California road." A formal celebration at Ashland followed later in the day during which Charles Crocker, one of California's "Big Four," drove the traditional golden spike.

The hour was getting late, relates the Ashland *Tidings,* and Crocker executed his part of the program with dispatch. "I hold in my hand the last spike," said Crocker. There were cries of "Hold it up!" "With this golden spike I propose now to unite the rails between California and Oregon, and I hope it will be the means of cementing the friendship of the two States and make them as one people." He pointed out how the driving of this spike would unite Portland with New Orleans and how Oregon had by this act become a part of the longest railroad system in the world, controlled by the Southern Pacific Railroad Company.

This line was 3,336 miles in length, with branches totaling 5,000 miles. Crocker neglected to say that by the driving of this last spike at Ashland the entire United States of America was encircled by rails, that the Pacific Northwest now ceased to be an isolated frontier region and was at last an important segment of this mammoth band of iron and steel.

Oregon Short Line Railroad

It would appear that developments such as those described above would have discouraged other railroad companies from entering what appeared at best to be a limited transportation market. But not wishing to be shut out from the Pacific Northwest, the Union Pacific (which railroad, along with the Central Pacific, had completed, in 1869, the first transcontinental line by building west of Omaha to Sacramento) took steps to extend its network to Portland. In 1881 the Union Pacific secured from Congress the incorporation of the Oregon Short Line Railroad which was designed to run from Granger, Wyoming, a point on the main Union Pacific line, to Huntington, Oregon. At Huntington connections would be made with the Oregon Railway and Navigation Company for trackage down the Columbia River gorge to Portland. Three years later (1884), the Oregon Short Line was completed, thus providing the Northwest with direct service over Union Pacific facilities.

Canadians Build to Pacific

Not without importance to western American railroad developments was the construction in Canada of the Canadian Pacific Railroad. The government of the Dominion of Canada likewise faced the problem of establishing adequate transportation facilities with its prairie territories and its Pacific coast population in the province of British Columbia. Location of the Canadian Pacific was decided upon in 1879, and the following year a company or syndicate was formed and given the privilege of completing the line to the Pacific within a ten-year period. Actually, it was completed, via Kicking Horse Pass in the Rockies, within five years (November 7, 1885), and much of the credit for this engineering achievement goes to Donald A. Smith, later Lord Strathcona. In 1887 the line opened to Vancouver, British Columbia, which has since been its western terminus. In 1891 a branch was completed south from Vancouver, where connections were made with American lines. Also, in 1903, the Dominion took steps which led to completion in 1915 of what is now called the Canadian National Railroad (an amalgamation of the Grand Trunk and the Canadian Northern), extending from Moncton, New Brunswick, to Prince Rupert, British Columbia. Connections are made with Vancouver from Fort George, and in turn with American railroads. Failure to build would have given strength to the American annexation movement in British Columbia; their construction, on the other hand, cemented the Canadian West to the Canadian

East, at the same time strengthening the commercial ties traversing the international border.

James J. Hill and the Great Northern

In many respects different from the general pattern of railroad building in the Far West is the story of the Great Northern Railroad. Rather than being nursed into being by generous government land grants and subsidies, this railroad company worked its own way to the Pacific, and on a pay-as-you-go basis. Builder of this road was the astute Canadian-born James Jerome Hill. "Jim" Hill, as he was called, was once quoted as saying: "Give me enough Swedes and whiskey and I'll build a railroad to Hell." This saying, apocryphal or not, at least exemplifies the rugged spirit of the builder. Hill began his career in St. Paul at the age of eighteen. After working ten years as a shipping clerk, he started his own storage, transfer, and express business in 1866. To this he added a fuel business the following year. His enterprises brought him into contact with the important Red River trade and this in turn aroused his desire to acquire what was his first railroad — the St. Paul and Pacific, a bankrupt line.

Dutch investors were eager to rid themselves of this derelict, and Hill was presented with an opportunity calling for his peculiar foresight and ability. He and three other men came to realize the intrinsic values of the road, and in 1878 took steps to gain control of it. Hill's associates were Norman Kittson, his partner in the Red River Transportation Company; Donald Smith (later builder of the Canadian Pacific); and George Stephen, later Lord Mount Stephen, president of the Bank of Montreal. Failing to get financial aid for immediate purchase, the three agreed to buy the road on credit and in May, 1879, organized the St. Paul, Minneapolis and Manitoba Railroad Company. For a time Hill gave his chief attention to the Manitoba (he became president in 1882), but from 1880–83 he also assisted in the organization and building of the Canadian Pacific.

Despite the warnings of pessimists and the critical condition of Hill's first railroad at the time of purchase, the investment was, as Hill had predicted, extremely fortunate. Within the first five years of the Manitoba's existence, the mileage had doubled, net earnings trebled, and equipment quadrupled. But by 1883 Hill was confronted with the necessity of extending his line westward, since it faced increasing competition from the Canadian Pacific to the north and from the Northern Pacific to the south.

Hill decided to build westward, but to do it slowly at first. From 1883 to 1886 extensions were confined to a few additional miles in feeders, some principally in Dakota, and to the leasing of scattered small lines. By 1887, however, Hill had placed over 300 miles in operation on the Dakota Territory extension and the road was completed to Great Falls, Montana Territory. At this point the Hill line met a local road, the Montana Central, organized the previous year with the plan in mind to build from Great Falls to Helena and Butte. Hill made the Montana Central an offer. He agreed to furnish the capital necessary to construct and equip this line in return for the stock and bonds of the company. His purpose was apparently to use this line, not only as a means of extending trackage, but as a buffer against competition. During 1888–89 there was a lull in the extension of the Manitoba system. Its builders were uncertain whether to construct a new road or join with one of the completed transcontinentals. Finally, in September, 1889, the Manitoba group decided definitely to extend its own line to the Pacific coast; in preparation for this move, the company organization was juggled, and out of this reorganization emerged the Great Northern Railway Company. The new company was created on the basis of a liberal charter granted to the Minneapolis and St. Cloud Company, one of Manitoba's subsidiaries, and the old Manitoba was officially transferred to the new Great Northern on February 1, 1890. In its lease the Manitoba agreed to construct an extension from Fort Assiniboin in Montana to Puget Sound.

Active work on the Pacific extension commenced in August, 1890, and went ahead without interruptions. It proceeded along a line south of and parallel to the international boundary that was sandwiched in between the Northern Pacific and the Canadian Pacific System. Once past the Rocky Mountains, the far western extension dropped southward to Spokane and over the Cascades to Everett. Then, following the usual period of jockeying for terminal honors, the decision was made to go on to Seattle.[3] The last rail of the 834-mile stretch from Fort Assiniboin was in place January 5, 1893.

By June 30, 1893, the Great Northern system was operating 3,765 miles of road, and in that year of financial panic the company paid five per cent in dividends and showed a surplus in excess of one million dollars. Hill had demonstrated the soundness of his great venture.

One of the secrets of "Jim" Hill's striking success with his western extension was the method by which it was constructed. Hill had a theory that it was always best to find the route which would make long hauls easy and economical — in other words the most level route possible. He built his road with the idea of keeping down the operating costs and of showing a larger margin of profit than others. From the very start the Great Northern was noted for its low ratio of operating expenses and its comparatively long trains and heavy trainloads.

After 1894 the Hill system was gradually increased, so that by 1904 the total mileage was 5,622. But this increase in mileage was overshadowed by another development in those years: the consolidation of the Great Northern, Northern Pacific, and Burlington. The bankruptcy of the Northern Pacific had meant reorganization of the company and J. P. Morgan was placed in charge. The story of the formation of a Hill-Morgan coalition and establishment of control over the

[3] The Stevens Pass carried the road to a 4,059-foot elevation. In 1900 a 2.63-mile tunnel was cut through the Cascades which reduced the elevation 677 feet; maximum grade from 4% to 2.2%. Great Northern engineers were not satisfied, and in 1925 surveys were made which resulted in the construction of a 7.79-mile tunnel between Berne and Scenic. This new tunnel, completed in 1928, reduced the summit to 2,881 feet and kept the maximum grade at 2.2%. The economies of operation were greatly improved by this new tunnel, and train time was equally reduced. This was one of the major engineering feats of the decade and won commendation from President Calvin Coolidge.

Northern Pacific and Burlington is too long and complicated to be told here. However, it should be mentioned that an attempt was made to organize formally the three roads under the Northern Securities Company. In the famous Northern Securities case of 1904, the Supreme Court handed down a five-to-four decision compelling the dissolution of the corporation. One should hasten to add here that dissolution of the giant holding company did not mean the end of community of interests among the three railroads involved in the case. In the period after 1904, three developments in the history of the road are prominent: the constant expansion and reaching out for traffic; the failure of plans for stimulating Oriental commerce; and the consolidation of the Great Northern by the assimilation of subsidiary companies. During the twenties, the Great Northern, like other northwest roads, complained of hard times. One of the problems it faced was the possible disruption of the Hill system by action of the Interstate Commerce Commision. The plan was dropped in 1931 because of conditions arising out of the depression.

Meanwhile the Hill interests remained active on the west coast. One of the major achievements there was the building (1905 and after), jointly with the Northern Pacific, the so-called "North Bank Road," officially the Spokane, Portland and Seattle Railroad. The line was laid out from Spokane; it reached and followed the north bank of the Columbia to Vancouver, Washington, where it crossed over into Portland, and where connection was also made with Seattle. Important additions and extensions to this line were also made. In 1907 it acquired the Astoria and Columbia River Railroad; the following year it purchased a line between Lyle and Goldendale known as the Columbia River and Northern Railway; and in 1910 it purchased controlling interest in the Oregon Electric (see below).

Through the efforts of Robert E. Strahorn, known as the mystery man of the railroads, the Hill interests were further extended. After Strahorn's operating with great secrecy, and paying out huge sums of money in personally signed checks for construction in eastern Washington, it was finally revealed that he had been building an extension to the Oregon Railway and Navigation Company lines. The extension, known as the North Coast Railroad, reached Spokane, thereby connecting the Inland Empire capital with the Union Pacific system. After 1915 Strahorn was active in other railroad developments east of the Cascades which in 1927 were sold to the Great Northern Railroad. These, combined with previous holdings, gave Hill interests a railroad branch extending southward through Bend to Klamath Falls. Three years later, approval was given for extending this eastern Oregon line southward into California, where, by joint use of Southern Pacific roadbed and by connection with the Western Pacific, an entrance was made to San Francisco — much to the resentment of the Southern Pacific Company.

Finally the Willamette Valley witnessed some extensions of the Hill interests as well as others made by the Southern Pacific, the latter out of fear of what the Great Northern might do in western Oregon. Thus, in 1912, Hill built the now defunct Oregon Electric from Portland to Eugene. Shortly thereafter the Southern Pacific acquired the defunct Yaquina (Oregon Pacific) Railroad originally constructed to Yaquina Bay by T. Egenton Hogg; and also built an extension from Eugene west to the coast of Florence. Still another line, the narrow-gauge Oregon Railway with tracks on both sides of the Willamette River (the tracks converged at Portland), was taken over by the Southern Pacific Company, made standard gauge, and was linked with the network of the latter. In 1926, following a protracted feud with the Great Northern, the Southern Pacific Company also completed the Natron Cut-Off from Eugene to Weed via Oakland and Klamath Falls, now known as the Cascade Route. The Cascade Route offers a very even grade and thereby considerably reduces operation costs between Portland and San Francisco. The route by-passes Roseburg, Grants Pass, Medford, Ashland, and other southern Oregon communities, which now feel themselves sadly neglected by the Southern Pacific Railroad Company. In spite of complaints of southern Oregon, emphasis has been placed on improved speed and service.

The Milwaukee Road

In 1909 the last of the American trunk lines to reach the Pacific Northwest coast was the Chicago, Milwaukee, St. Paul and Pacific Railroad, or as it is usually called, "The Milwaukee Road." The history of this railroad is not greatly unlike other large American rail systems in that it emerged out of local needs, passed through stages of financial reorganization, and meanwhile became a trunk line.

By the late 1840s, the portion of Wisconsin bordering on Lake Michigan, with Milwaukee as its commercial center, was thickly settled. But west of this concentration of population with its easy access to lake shipping was an undeveloped hinterland. Obviously, cheap transportation was needed in the back country. On February 11, 1847, the Milwaukee and Waukesha Railroad Company obtained a charter marking the origin of the network now known as the Milwaukee Road. By difficult piecemeal financing and contracting, a railroad from Milwaukee to La Crosse was completed in 1858. Failure followed, but out of the ruins came, in 1863, the organization of the Milwaukee and St. Paul Railway Company. The new company looked toward the immediate extension of the road to St. Paul, but entry into that city was blocked by other lines. It therefore became necessary for the officers of the organization to purchase their way. In 1865, the Milwaukee by an exchange of stock secured control of the Prairie du Chien with its railhead on the Mississippi. The Prairie road then obtained a 999-year lease on an Iowa road, and in 1866 the Milwaukee purchased the Minnesota Central. Thus by 1867 the Milwaukee owned and operated 835 miles of railroad, roughly forming a triangle between Milwaukee, St. Paul, and Mason City, Iowa. In the next quarter-century the Milwaukee became a regional system or network of roads. In 1873 it built into Chicago, and striking westward reached Kansas City in 1887. Meanwhile the Milwaukee secured, by construction and purchase, a large system of feeder lines which reached into northern Wisconsin, northwestern Minnesota, and the Dakotas. By June, 1891, the Milwaukee's lines totaled 6,083 miles.

The period from 1891 to 1905 saw the rise of the Milwaukee to a stable and powerful position, for the policy of its leaders had become one of internal improvement and development. Double tracking was completed between Chicago and Milwaukee and Chicago and the Mississippi. The replacement of iron rails with steel was so rapid that by 1898 there remained only 517 miles of iron rails. The Milwaukee was one of the first roads to adopt the system of shipping grain in bulk, which in turn led to the further development of its own grain elevator system. It was the only American railroad operating its own sleeping cars in 1905. In line with its policy of physical improvement, it built its own locomotives and cars. Readiness to experiment was shown in the sixteen years' struggle to perfect the lighting of passenger trains by electricity. The road was not only the first to apply electricity to train lighting, but was also the first to achieve satisfactory results. By 1905 it led all American railroads with some 3,000 electrically lighted cars. Although the years prior to 1900 were marked by severe business depressions, it may be said that the Milwaukee was able to survive them all. At the turn of the century this road was regarded as one of the best in the country. The Milwaukee may be thought of as having had a strong progressive individuality and a hatred of outside dominance. But that individuality was to be challenged and outside interests were to become weighty factors in shaping future policy.

In contrast to this earlier prosperous era, the period after 1900 became one beset with many financial problems, not least of which was westward extension. As early as 1901 the road was considering the idea of building to the Pacific Coast. In writing to President Albert J. Earling on March 29, Roswell Miller, acting chairman of the Board of Directors, referred to a conversation with E. H. Harriman of the Union Pacific in which Miller had expressed dissatisfaction with existing arrangements for the interchange of business between his road and the Union Pacific. The Chicago Northwestern, he felt, was treated more favorably, and Miller told Harriman that because of this situation, the Milwaukee would be compelled to build to the Pacific coast. Harriman replied that he could start the next day if he liked. In the meantime, James J. Hill and J. P. Morgan had shown an interest in the Milwaukee. The Great Northern and the Northern Pacific, controlled by the Hill-Morgan coalition, stood in need of a connection with Chicago and considered the purchase of the Milwaukee. Finally a treaty was projected between the Milwaukee and the Missouri Pacific. This brought Harriman to terms and in October, 1902, the Union Pacific and the Milwaukee arrived at an agreement. But the alliance was far from conclusive, for before the end of the year, Miller wrote that "if we do not make it [the extension to the Coast] we will be bottled up by a combination between the Union Pacific, the Great Northern, and the Northern Pacific."

Rivalry between powerful transportation interests had apparently become intense. The directors of the Milwaukee, fearful of being caught in a nutcracker with the Hill lines to the north controlling the Burlington, and the Harriman lines to the south working in harmony with the Northwestern, decided to push on to the Pacific in the belief that the western division could be constructed for a fraction of the cost of older lines. Finally, there was a real estate and industrial boom in the Pacific Northwest at this time and it was expected that the Milwaukee would benefit from such a development. Potential competition of the Panama Canal does not seem to have been considered by the executives.

In 1905, steps were taken to secure a right of way; Miller advised Earling to proceed with arrangements for construction; on November 28 the board formally authorized a line to Seattle and Tacoma. The Pacific Railroad Company was incorporated in Washington in the interest of the Milwaukee. Within a year three more companies had been incorporated in Montana, Idaho, and South Dakota to build the extension through these states; all drew upon the Milwaukee Road for money to aid in construction.

In the fall of 1906, with construction moving along at a rapid pace, the proposed route of the extension was made public. The line was to run from Glenham, South Dakota, in a northwestern direction across the Missouri River and the southwest corner of North Dakota to a junction with the Yellowstone River at Terry, Montana. It was to proceed thence up the Yellowstone, on through Three Forks to Butte, and taking the logical route proceed down Clark's Fork to the Idaho-Montana line near Mullan, Idaho. It would then move on through Coeur d'Alene to Spokane. From Spokane to Seattle the road was to describe an arc to the southward, crossing the Cascade Range via Snoqualmie Pass. From Chicago to Seattle the distance was estimated to be 2,305 miles, about 150 miles shorter than by way of the Burlington and Northern Pacific, and 80 miles shorter than the Burlington-Great Northern route (for details see map).

Proportionally, the construction of the western extension did not take as long as the preliminary explorations and surveys. The construction was a highly organized work, for the line was advanced on several divisions of the route simultaneously. The Milwaukee Road, however, faced a problem in the Musselshell River sector of the 800-mile division between Glenham and Butte. The Jawbone Railroad operated here along the projected line of route and it was necessary to make either a detour or some arrangement with its owner, Richard A. Harlow. Difficulties were magnified by the fact that James J. Hill held a mortgage on the Jawbone. A lease was the only possible solution at the moment; it was entered into in 1907, and the construction of the road continued with such speed that by August, 1908, the line to Butte was opened for operation. In view of its status, the Jawbone was the object of considerable speculation. If Harlow defaulted on his mortgage payments and Hill foreclosed, the Great Northern magnate would acquire part of the main line of the Milwaukee Road. Fortunately for that organization, Hill went to England in 1909 and the Milwaukee secretly advanced to Harlow sufficient money to pay off his mortgage. Once Harlow had accomplished this, the Milwaukee through its Washington subsidiary bought the Jawbone.

On April 1, 1909, the last rail was laid on the main line and by August the extension had been opened for through passengers and freight. The cost of the extension had been about sixty million dollars; more feeder lines were needed for successful operations.

As construction on the main line neared completion, the subsidiary organizations of Montana, Idaho, and South Dakota were consolidated under the Washington Company, and given the name Chicago, Milwaukee, and Puget Sound Railway Company. By the close of 1912, unification of the extension with the Milwaukee Road had become desirable and on January 1, 1913, the accounts were merged — in keeping with what appears to have been rather standard practices of American interstate railroads.

Merging of the accounts, however, could not erase the fact that heavier-than-expected building costs and insufficient revenue from operations began to give the Milwaukee Road financial headaches. Failure to make satisfactory distinctions between operational costs and constructional costs brought the Company into dispute with the Interstate Commerce Commission. It would appear that those responsible for the great expansion of this line had failed to exercise caution at a time when it was badly needed.

Early in 1913, there were rumors that the Milwaukee was planning the electrification of about 450 miles of the Company's lines through the mountains in Montana and Idaho. Such a progressive move seemed to present many advantages. The usual braking on descending grades would be eliminated by means of electric motors so operated that they would act as generators, returning current to the line, and controlling the speed of trains. More speed could be attained on ascending grades by electricity than by steam. Greater comfort to passengers resulted from the elimination of smoke, and the reduction of delays in coaling, taking on water, and the like constituted additional advantages. The management felt that costs would be lowered through improved service and heavier patronage would result from attention drawn to the project. Furthermore, among the directors of the Milwaukee at this time were men who had a special interest in the electrification of the Milwaukee Road.

One of these men interested in electrification was John D.

Ryan, who became director of the Milwaukee Road upon the request of another director, William Rockefeller. Ryan was president of the Anaconda Mining Company; he also controlled water power in Montana and northern Idaho. The project to electrify part of the road would provide a new and valuable outlet for Ryan's undeveloped hydroelectric resources. While it had been President Earling's original intention to establish the road's own power stations, it appears that Ryan convinced Milwaukee officials of the greater advantages of purchased power, especially if purchased from companies in which Ryan had financial interests. Accordingly, in 1912, the Milwaukee Road made a 99-year contract with the Great Falls Power Company in which Ryan owned half interest. The next year a similar contract was entered into between the Milwaukee Road and the Thompson Falls Company, also controlled by Ryan. The two power companies then merged in 1913 with the Montana Power Company, but with no loss of control by Ryan. Then in 1917, in order to secure power for the coast division, another long-term contract was awarded the Intermountain Power Company (also controlled by Ryan interests), which in turn was incorporated with the Washington Power Company.

Armed with these contracts, the Milwaukee Road proceeded (1914–15) to electrify two divisions extending from Harlowtown, Montana, to Avery, Idaho, a distance of 438 miles. The Company next (1917) electrified 207 miles on the western slope. A total, then, of 645 miles of the Milwaukee Line was electrified at a cost of $22,990,254. Even though the contracts made for purchase of hydroelectric power were disadvantageous, the annual savings to the Milwaukee Road are estimated at over twelve million dollars annually.

World War I years gave the company a guaranteed annual compensation. But the postwar years were so difficult that on March 25, 1925, the Milwaukee Road passed into the hands of a receiver. Two years later it was reorganized as the Chicago, Milwaukee, St. Paul and Pacific. The reorganization was not sufficiently drastic to meet the difficult thirties. The road's income suffered from the general depression, from the loss of the export grain market, from several years of extreme drought in its area, and from the increasing competition of motor transport. By 1935 the finances of the Milwaukee were in a serious way. In June the road was given permission to reorganize; and on July 1 it defaulted on interest on its general mortgage bonds. After consulting with the Reconstruction Finance Corporation and representatives of the bondholders, the directors accepted a plan of reorganization. The Federal Court appointed trustees to manage the road, and the Interstate Commerce Commission took the reorganization plan under consideration. More than a decade of bankruptcy and reorganization proceedings ensued, but finally in 1945 a court decision directed consummation of the reorganization of the Chicago, Milwaukee, St. Paul and Pacific Railroad.

The experiences of the Milwaukee during World War II were similar to those of other railroads. Generally speaking, it might be said that the road served the war effort with distinction. Prosperity had definitely arrived, although the scarcity of matériel for upkeep hampered operation. The Milwaukee ended 1945 with road and equipment valuation of $799,137,296.12, capital stock of $324,495,400, and a funded debt of $191,155,833.74. The net income for the year stood at $14,077,911. Thus the Milwaukee Road could face the future with greater confidence than at any time since 1905.

CHAPTER XVII

On the Open Ranges

The Range Cattle Business

IMPORTANT AS LIVESTOCK had been to the Hudson's Bay Company and to pioneer settlers (see pp. 77–82, 182), it was not until the Civil War period and after that cattle and sheep raising in the Pacific Northwest emerged as large-scale enterprises similar to those on the Great Plains. Then, as demand arose for new grazing areas, attention was directed to previously ignored areas east of the Cascade Mountains. In eastern Oregon (notably Wasco, Umatilla, and Union counties in the northeast, and Baker, Grant, and Lake counties in the southeast) bunch grass was abundant and nutritious. Similar grazing resources existed in eastern Washington (namely east of Lake Chelan on into Okanogan county; Yakima and Klickitat counties), and in the Spokane-Columbia-Snake River triangle embracing part of southern Idaho. There duck grass, also some bluegrass, was found in addition to bunch grass, and not to be ignored as good feed for livestock was the coarse sage of the desert. Moreover, the grassy inter-mountain valleys lying between the Cascades and the Continental Divide and prairies of Wyoming may also be considered part of the great ranges that for the years 1860–90 were to be the unfenced feeding grounds, first for cattle of the Pacific Northwest, and then also for sheep.

The business of handling livestock on the open ranges, especially cattle, was peculiarly western. For one thing, it was an industry requiring the handling of exceedingly large herds under rather primitive conditions. Also associated with this unique enterprise was the cowboy, a new type of westerner, and the emergence on the plains of such phenomena

282]

as round-ups, large-scale herding, long drives, and social patterns unfamiliar to the dirt-farming areas elsewhere in the United States. The range cattle business had its earliest roots in New Spain; but on the great plains of Texas and the Middle West, on the valley floors of California, and in the semiarid Inland Empire, full-scale developments occurred. Each of these regions has its own special operations, its own range history; but the cattle business, at least as it emerged in the Inland Empire, was greatly influenced by developments on neighboring ranges.

Livestock was, of course, known to the Inland Empire prior to the Civil War. Cattle traders, missionaries, freighters, and other individuals living in the open range country prior to 1860 account for the first importations of cattle there. These beginnings were augmented by the California gold rush which created the first marked expansion in beef production. The large mining populations in California brought about heavy demands for meat; and Californians, faced for a time with devastating droughts, looked to the Oregon country, notably the Inland Empire, as a suitable area into which to expand livestock production. This situation was shortly overshadowed by the northward advance of the mineral frontier which in turn brought into the Inland Empire thousands of gold seekers, who were eager to buy fresh meat at almost any price. The result was what one might expect: the arrival of cattle from many parts of the country, especially western Oregon and Washington, California (by then recovered from the effects of drought and in good supply), and from the Great Plains. The first cattle brought to the Inland Empire were of varying breeds and quality. Spanish-California black cattle introduced into Idaho in the early sixties were not of the best; neither were the Texas longhorns which arrived in Idaho and western Montana by way of the great Texas cattle trails. Livestock from western Oregon and Washington were, on the other hand, of relatively improved breeds. There the Hudson's Bay Company had done much to raise the quality of its herds by the importation of thoroughbred bulls from the British Isles. Settlers from the farming areas of the East brought with them the best specimens from their farmyard herds, which multiplied and became another source of supply for the Inland Empire. And even though the emphasis was at first upon quantity rather than quality, there an effort was constantly made to improve the quality of cattle on the ranges.[1] In any event, a good initial market, prevalence of grass on available government land, suitable climate, and the gradual diminution of Indian depredations contributed to an amazingly rapid growth of the range cattle business in the Inland Empire from 1860 until the middle 1880s, when decline was pronounced.

Within this broad framework of growth, one observes varied, complex, and interacting forces. A special census report for 1880 [2] calls attention to regional subdivisions, each with its own special pattern of development. The Columbia Basin was one such region; southeastern Oregon, southern Idaho, and northern Nevada (otherwise referred to as the Winnemucca Province), a second; western Montana, a third; and, if one may stretch boundaries, Wyoming was yet a fourth distinctive area. First to enjoy a really lush growth of range cattle operations was the Columbia Basin. But it was also this division which experienced the first marked decline. The second of these areas, slower to start, was destined to be a region which to this day remains an important beef-producing area. Western Montana, by virtue of its inter-mountain position and its exposure to direct influences of the Great Plains, had its own little cattle kingdom, as, of course, did Wyoming. Geographically, Wyoming was a part of the Great Plains, but its location gave it an interlocking position between those plains and the Pacific Northwest. Across Wyoming wound the Oregon Trail (later important in cattle and sheep drives), and across Wyoming, too, stretched the Union Pacific Railroad, so important as the first major outlet for

[1] W. S. Ladd, Ben Holladay, S. G. Reed were among those who imported such superior breeds as Durhams, Dutch shorthorns, Devons, Ayrshires, shorthorns. These men laid the foundation for a later phase of cattle raising which placed a premium on quality rather than quantity.

[2] Clarence W. Gordon, "Report on Cattle, Sheep, and Swine Supplementary to Enumeration of Livestock on Farms in 1880," *Tenth Census of the United States* (1880), Vol. III.

Pacific Northwest livestock. For these reasons Wyoming is included here as at least a subsidiary division of the range cattle orbit of the Northwest.

A detailed discussion of each of these subdivisions is impossible here, but general trends may be noted. By 1870 local markets were saturated and overproduction was in evidence. Prospects then existing for outside markets were dimmed by the national financial panic of 1873 and meat prices were further depressed. Hard times continued and the ranges became overstocked. Some indication as to number may be had from the *United States Census* which for 1880 credits Oregon with 352,561 cattle not listed as milch cows; Washington, 103,111; and Idaho, 71,292; and for Western Montana, an estimated 15,000.[3] By 1880, decisive changes began to occur. Most overstocked was the Columbia Basin, and the situation there was greatly aggravated by the invasion of sheepmen and dirt farmers. In many places in the Columbia Basin the open range began giving way to ranch-type (fenced-in), semi-agricultural operations. In all but the southeastern Oregon division the situation remained grave until the revival of eastern slaughter-house business and the opening of the northern plains (particularly Wyoming) provided outlets for surplus Northwest cattle. By 1880 these new developments were in full swing, and great herds were then driven East.

Important to this eastward movement of Oregon and Washington cattle was the Union Pacific-Central Railroad which established Cheyenne and Granger, Wyoming, as important shipping junctions, and indirectly enhanced the importance of Wyoming, notably Laramie Valley, as a profitable grazing area. Still another influential factor was the formation, in 1873, of the Wyoming Stock Growers' Association which in time largely determined the scope and nature of cattle business in the northern plains area. This Association frowned upon the importation of diseased Texas long-

---

[3] Even though these are official figures, they are at best rough estimates. No rancher knew for sure how many cattle he had; not all were willing to tell the truth. The actual number probably exceeds the Census figures.

horns, but instead looked with favor upon stocking the Wyoming ranges with healthy, low-priced cattle from the Pacific Northwest.

Cheyenne became the great mecca for Northwest cattle during the 1880s, and the "Old Wyoming Trail" (this trail closely followed the northwest extension of Holladay's stagecoach route, which in turn followed in parts the Oregon Trail) became the route of the massive eastward drives. Perhaps there is more truth than poetry in the song:

> Whoopee ti yi yo, git along, little dogies,
> It's your misfortune and none of my own,
> Whoopee ti yi yo, git along, little dogies,
> For you know Wyoming will be your new home.

During the year 1880, 200,000 head of Oregon, Washington, and Idaho cattle are reported to have moved eastward over the trails.

By 1885 the range cattle business was in decline. By then the Great Plains, too, had become overstocked and production costs were greatly increased. The beef market declined again. Inland Empire wheat farming ushered in by the newly completed Northern Pacific Railroad reduced the size of the open ranges, and on remaining pasture lands came the invasion of sheep. Except for the Winnemucca Province, cattlemen were compelled to restrict their herds largely to privately owned and fenced-in ranches. When, by 1890, this state of affairs was reached, a new era in the cattle business was at hand. It meant that the range cattle business was in transition from the free and open range phase to what the Gordon Report in the Census for 1880 calls "a condition of agriculture." Today the history of this range cattle business of the Inland Empire is a reminder that the Pacific Northwest shared in that remarkable process of handling cattle that emerged in the Far West after the Civil War.

Life on the Range

The range cattle business was anything but drab. It gave rise to types of life laden with action and possessed of social experiences unknown to the Atlantic seaboard and the trans-Allegheny West. Western cowmen became distinctive personalities; some became known as "cattle kings," respected for their wealth measured by the size of their herds; others remained poor, but nonetheless spirited, cowpunchers. Even though the use of land for grazing purposes was free to first comers (prior occupation) it was not easy to become an honest, well-to-do stockman without first having capital to invest in cattle. And to become even the humblest of cowhands demanded graduation from the hard school of experience.

Providing one had the necessary capital, the steps taken in establishing a unit of operation were rather simple. Once a herd had become established in a given range area, a stockman usually acquired title to a section or more of land to serve as a base of operation. On this land would be constructed a dwelling, usually a crude shack or cabin, to house all hands. On this land would also be built a stable for a dozen or more saddle horses and even some work horses, corrals for branding stock, and often widely scattered stock pens to facilitate supplementary feeding when heavy snow and ice would not permit grazing on the open ranges. Hay for this special feeding was secured by fencing in meadows to allow the natural grasses to mature for cutting and stacking. A stockman also had to provide wages of $30–$40 per month plus food for all hands hired, which included a foreman, cook, farm boys, and cowboys. Other essential equipment included wagons, guns, and wearing apparel.

Only those possessing exceptionally large herds were called "cattle kings." Such individuals were found in all sections of the open range country, but privately owned herds of over 25,000 head were few. Benjamin E. Snipes, The Dalles, who in 1881 purchased 12,000 head of cattle from the Phelps and Wadleigh Company of Okanogan, was a rare and much-discussed cattle dealer. Peter French in southeastern Oregon was the owner of the famed "P" and Diamond ranches and possessed "king"-sized herds until he was shot and killed in 1897. Other cattle kings were (W. B.) Todhunter and Devine, owners of the Whitehorse Ranch in Harvey County; also Baron de Bonnemain, Conrad Kohrs, and the owners of

The Swan Land and Cattle Company, Montana. Kohrs, although associated with the Great Plains area, had the crowning title of "Cattle King of the Northwest." His cattle roamed thousands of acres claimed by prior occupation, and it was Kohrs who was the originator of the Montana Stock Growers' Association.

The principal operations were carried on by the hired cowboys whose lives, perhaps a little dull during the winters, were intensely active during the spring, summer, and autumn months. In parts of the Columbia Basin stock was herded the year 'round, but elsewhere cattle usually roamed freely much of the time. Rules for handling the cattle were made either by informal meetings of stockmen within the respective locales or by formal stock growers' associations which often represented an entire territory, as in the case of the Wyoming Stock Growers' Association. Most often these rules, or established practices, called for annual early-spring roundups to be held on scheduled dates. Cowboys would proceed to round up and sort cattle according to brands; and the branding irons would be put to calves seemingly attached to mother cows within the respective herds.[4]

After the roundups came individual drives to market or drives from winter to summer pastures. All this was hard work, but once a herd had been assembled it was possible for twelve to fifteen cowboys, bossed by a foreman, served by a horse wrangler, and fed by a cook, to handle anywhere from 1,200 to 2,500 head of cattle on long drives.

For the first two days, or until a herd appeared tired and well adjusted to the trail, the driving was incessant. Thereafter a regular and leisurely routine was established. As the song goes: "before daylight," the cattle were on the hoof and grazing, and the wrangler was busy rounding up horses for the day. Then after a hastily gulped breakfast of perhaps bacon, coffee, and sour dough biscuits prepared by the usually tyrannical cook at his well-stocked chuck wagon, the long day's drive began. Usually two men rode ahead of the herd; the rest on the flanks, and in the rear. At noon there

---

[4] Unbranded animals whose ownership could not be readily determined were handled according to rules laid down by the cattlemen's associations.

was a pause — if possible by a stream where the cattle partook of water and again indulged in leisurely grazing. Nearby would be the indispensable chuck wagon with noonday fare in readiness — perhaps fresh roast beef and more coffee and biscuits. The afternoon drive usually seemed hot, tedious, and relentless. And then came night when the cattle, full of feed, watered, and tired, lay down for rest. The cowboys ate their suppers, chatted about the day's drive, smoked cigarettes, and sang and told stories. Night guards often pacified the drowsing animals with songs and chatter; and except for an occasional stampede caused from sudden fright, the starry nights remained peaceful until, once again around the clock, the cook and the horse wrangler gave timely warning that another day was about to begin.

Cowboys in the Pacific Northwest were predominantly American, with the exception of southeastern Oregon, where Mexican vaqueros drifting in from California and Mexico were numerous. Mexicans there were regarded as more skillful than the Americans in the use of the riata (lasso), and in all ways were expert cowhands. The cowboy population of the Pacific Northwest was not unlike that of either Texas or the Great Plains of the Middle West. Mexican vaqueros were the product of four centuries of cattle herding on New Spain's northern frontier. The American cowboy emerged in great numbers after the Civil War when herds of Texas longhorns were driven north to market. He learned much of his art of handling large herds of cattle in open country, refinements in rope throwing, branding, and riding from his Mexican neighbors. And from them, too, came not only many ideas for suitable wearing apparel, but much of the cowboy vocabulary. In fact, most objects and institutions borrowed from the Mexicans retained, at least partially, their Spanish pronunciations. Hoosegow, meaning jail, came from the Spanish *juzgado*, ranch from *rancho*, cinch from *cincha*, mustang from *mesteño*, lariat from *la reata*, and many American words of the range were similarly derived from the Spanish-speaking Mexicans.

The Americans, of course, were not just copiers, for they too contributed much that was original to their newly acquired art. The Colt 45 six-shooting revolver was as American as Bull Durham tobacco for roll-your-own cigarettes. Americans developed their own types of saddles, among them the single-cinch saddle distinctive to Oregon and Idaho, and the double-cinch saddle common to Texas and Wyoming. Still other practices were peculiar to one or more parts of the Northwest. In Montana and Wyoming riders often rode hackamore(halter)-broken, well-reined ponies and thus dispensed with bridles and bits. Saddle blankets varied with the region, as did chaps, spurs, ropes, and assorted paraphernalia. As cowboys drifted into the Pacific Northwest they exhibited varying or special talents. Some were specialists in horsebreaking; some were bucking-horse riders; others were expert ropers — so essential in roundup work; and still others were skilled at herding young cattle, catching strays, and so on. To become a skilled, all-round cowhand took years of experience, and to quote John K. Rollinson, who knew the Oregon-Wyoming cattle country well, "Having attended that hard and exacting college of range lore, there were few indeed of these men who could ever say that they had graduated from their school of learning. . . . They well knew that the man who 'learned too quick' in this exacting trade was generally a failure at his work."

Cowboys as *species homo* have been credited by some with all human virtues; by others as the embodiment of wickedness. In the words of Mrs. Nat Collins, Montana's "Cattle Queen" (1894): "The cowboys, as a rule, are bright, active, intelligent young men, generous and liberal to a fault, and withal possessed of many noble qualities. True it is there are some worthless, low and degraded men among their number, but those of this character constitute but a small minority." She classified the Montana cowboys as easterners with "good educations" whom the force of adverse circumstances brought West. Some drank heavily, but this may have been in self-defense, as a Montana bartender observed: "If a man quits drinking here, he will be dead in a month." But for all their roughness Mrs. Collins "would rather be 'Aunty,' 'Mother,' or 'Cattle Queen' of the Montana cowboys than sit upon the throne of Queen Victoria."

Due to the absence of transcontinental railroads prior to 1883, the region developed no important cowtowns such as emerged at rail junctions on the Great Plains. Cattlemen shared with miners, farmers, and sheepmen the local markets afforded by such towns or places as Virginia City (Montana), Bannock, Helena, Colvile, and Forts Benton, Walla Walla, and the many "camps" scattered through the Inland Empire. The most important cowtown to Northwesterners was, as stated, Cheyenne — a Union Pacific terminal outside the narrow limits of the region. When in the middle seventies the long drives to Wyoming began, cowboys from the Pacific Northwest often shared with their cohorts from the Great Plains in the indulgences which this gay western town had to offer. Saloons, with and without the "painted ladies," were numerous and well-patronized in Cheyenne; but the favorite gathering place of cattlemen — a place where the mention of sheep was taboo — was the famous Cheyenne Club.

The range cattle business had passed its peak before the Northern Pacific Railroad was completed. By the early nineties important transformations were far along. Wrote Julian Ralph, traveling the Northern Pacific line (1893): "Towns are growing up on their [the cattlemen's] pasture-lands; irrigation schemes of a dozen sorts threaten to turn bunch-grass scenery into farmland views; farmers are pre-empting valleys and the sides of waterways; and the day is not too far distant when stock-raising must be done mainly in small herds, with winter corrals, and then the cowboy's day will end."

Sheep Move Westward

In 1940 the Northwest produced over 7,000,000 sheep and lambs valued at over $20,000,000. A century of assiduous attention to sheep raising had made these impressive figures possible. Sheep had long been a part of the American economic system and particularly that of the frontier. As early as 1609 sheep had been introduced into Jamestown and a half century later the Virginia Colony boasted 3,000 of these woolly creatures. During the first half of the seventeenth century the other English colonies, as well as the Dutch of New York and the Swedes on the Delaware, imported sheep and promoted sheep raising. Then as migrations moved westward, sheep followed the frontier. The presence of cheap lands for pasturage, the existence of transportation barriers making it difficult to move agricultural goods to markets, and the need for a home supply of wool were a few of the factors that influenced sheep growing in western frontier areas.

Prior to 1800, sheep raising was done almost exclusively for production of wool for home use; thereafter attempts were made to expand the industry. The importation of the improved merino breed, effects of the War of 1812, and the introduction and growth of industrial weaving of woolens in the United States, all contributed to this expansion. Even so, the general rise in midwest agricultural prices caused sheep raising to give way to more profitable pursuits, and one notes a continued tendency of sheep raisers to push farther and farther west. By 1850 sheep in the Middle West were on the decline; on the other hand, flocks in the trans-Mississippi West were on the increase.

Not only were sheep moved into the far western regions from the older, established settlements of the East, but they were introduced from various other sources as well. The Spanish had first brought sheep into the Southwest at the time of the conquistadores, and they had been reintroduced on various subsequent occasions, as for example into Alta California when that province was founded in 1769. As indicated earlier (see pp. 78–9) sheep were brought into the old Oregon country by various and sundry individuals and flocks had been tenderly nurtured by the Hudson's Bay Company, which was eager to build up its livestock resources as a support to its far-flung fur trade. In attempts at improving their stock both Dr. McLoughlin and Dr. Tolmie of the Puget's Sound Agricultural Company imported pure breeds from England, and as such made distinct contributions to the industry's progress in the Northwest. Later, the Company sold sheep to settlers, who in turn made distinct contributions to the sheep industry in Old Oregon. The part played by the

Hudson's Bay Company was not an unmixed blessing since diseases among some of the flocks spread to animals not their own.

The missionaries also did their part. Very early, Whitman had sheep brought to his mission from the Sandwich Islands. By 1840 he had a flock of eighty sheep. He taught the Indians how to herd the sheep, and despite losses from the severe cold, dogs, coyotes, Indian raids, and the killing of sheep for food, his herd continued to grow. It is also known that when representatives of the Willamette Valley Cattle Company went to California to buy cattle (1837), these men met Jacob Lease, a sheepman, whom they persuaded to drive his flock north for sale to Jason Lee's group of missionary settlers. Also, in 1841, settlers in the Willamette Valley pooled their resources and built a 48-foot schooner, the *Star of Oregon*, which was taken to California to be sold there, and the proceeds used to buy livestock to be driven to Oregon. From this transaction no less than 3,000 sheep (also many cattle and horses) were acquired and driven north. The drive was hard and long, taking seventy-five days, but it helped end what Americans thought of as the Hudson's Bay Company monopoly; it laid more firmly the foundations for many new flocks of sheep in the old Oregon country.

Still other American settlers, namely those who continued to pour in from across the Great Plains, trailed sheep (that is, those not eaten en route) to new homes in the Willamette Valley. Joseph Watt was one of the earliest pioneers to drive sheep over the Oregon Trail for the express purpose of establishing flocks in the Northwest. Watt had gone to Oregon in 1844 and then returned to Missouri. He had been convinced by his short stay in Oregon that sheep raising could be made profitable, and he surmised correctly that sheep could be driven across the Plains with ease. Accordingly, he and his family assembled a herd of 435 sheep in St. Joseph, and in 1848 joined a wagon train headed for the Willamette Valley. The whole family helped in the care of the sheep. While on the trail they had to keep the flock from wandering and they had to keep it moving with the train. Finally they reached their destination with a loss of only 100 sheep. Here Watt's services did not end. He attempted to set up a woolen mill in Oregon; and even though misfortunes ruined his efforts, Watt pioneered in behalf of the woolen industry in this area. Moreover, Watt pointed the way for other sheep importers who in the future brought in ever-increasing numbers of sheep.

As sheep drives into Oregon increased in number and in size, both from the South and from the East, the Northwest began to place added emphasis on commercial wool production.[5] Attempts were constantly being made to improve the breeds. The driving of sheep to the California gold fields helped in this respect since it enabled Oregonians to purge their flocks of poor animals. Pure-blooded specimens continued to be imported from England; also from Australia and New Zealand. State and county fairs did their part to stimulate interest in better breeds by offering prizes.

So far, special attention has been focused on the Willamette Valley. After Washington Territory was created in 1853, one notes that numerous flocks were driven north from Oregon into the Puget Sound region. Sheep there, as in Oregon, had to be protected in the winter. They were raised mainly for wool, but from time to time mutton was exported via Puget Sound to California.

Sheep raising in the Northwest followed two distinct but corresponding patterns. West of the Cascade Mountains where sheep first thrived, the industry tended to become identified with small, privately owned farms. Flocks there would average from about 75 to 100. Much of the winter feed was raised on the farms, and owners kept the sheep principally for wool. As time went on, wheat became more profitable than sheep, and farmers began to reduce their flocks. Sheep were still kept, however, for in the summer months they were used as scavengers to glean the stubble and weeds from the fields. With a decrease in the number of sheep went also a decline in the type of breeds. After 1880 the sheep declined rapidly in the area west of the Cascades;

---

[5] During the gold rush days in California, however, the Oregon drives were reversed and sheep were driven southward from Oregon to California to supply the mining areas with food.

but this decline was offset by marked increases east of this range of mountains.

In contrast to this situation along the coast, the free and open ranges of the Inland Empire (cattlemen notwithstanding) allowed for the development of large flocks that ranged in number from about 1,500 and upward.[6] Ample space did not mean adequate protection; each operator usually had to shift for himself; local protective laws did not, as a rule, exist; and conflict with the cattlemen was an ever-present possibility. As one cattleman wrote: "We came here [to Okanogan] first. . . . We will not give it up to the sheepmen." Moreover, the open ranges offered little natural protection, and since barns and sheds were very scarce, shepherds found it necessary to seek out sheltered river valleys during winter months. In such places sheep were usually kept until after lambing and until the spring shearing and marking had been completed. This over with, the flocks moved out upon the pastures in the foothills and open ranges. And in summer, as snows receded, the moves were made toward higher ground.

Sheep raising in the Inland Empire country was largely carried on through a system of absentee ownership, although some of the smaller operators did supervise many of the tasks such as packing, selection of new pastures, and helping to avoid clashes with cowmen and with other sheep men.

Very seldom did the owners do their own herding; this job was done by professionals who drifted in from Mexico, from the Southwest, and even from Australia. Actually shepherds were an international lot; their nationalities were often Basque, French, Indian, Mexican, Portuguese, Scottish, and American. In the hands of the dime novelists and Hollywood, the herder has fared badly. Little or no romance has been allowed to surround this figure even though his role in western development has been about equal to that of the

---

[6] It must, of course, be kept in mind that in many parts of the Inland Empire, especially Idaho, small farms existed and on them sheep raising differed very little from the system in vogue west of the Cascades. As early as 1850, for instance, Mormon settlers in southern Idaho brought sheep with them and they were raised along with other livestock on the Mormon farms. Irrigation, sheep, and wheat were not unknown combinations in the Payette Valley.

glamourized cowboy. The herder's task was to see that the sheep stayed together and were properly fed. He used a loose system of herding which allowed the animals a wide range of roaming, but which in turn involved a problem of holding the strong sheep down to the pace of the weaker animals. The herder stayed with his flock at all times, and therefore had to have supplies brought to him. The shepherd's day began at sunrise, when he would put his flock out to feed. The sheep would feed until about nine and rest until midafternoon, when they would feed again until time to be driven back to camp by sundown. Not until then could the shepherd prepare and eat his supper, and lay out rations for a quick breakfast and lunch for the next day for himself and his faithful dog. The main diet was fried meat. hardtack, and coffee.

The Great Sheep Drives

Following the Civil War the sheep industry had its ups and downs. Cessation of hostilities brought about sharp retrenchments, followed by national expansion during the 1870s, and then again a tapering off. In the wake of these changes wool prices fluctuated, sheep population on the ranges varied, and one observes that in places where railroad transportation was readily available and where urban markets were not too distant there occurred a general shift from wool breeds to mutton breeds.

So far as the West, in particular, is concerned, the sheep industry, after 1865, changed and shifted constantly in response to major economic developments. The world wheat market had its effect in that when wheat prices were good, this commodity again was produced for export rather than as feed for livestock. The steady advance of the homesteader tended to restrict the range of moving flocks.

In response to these dynamic forces there occurred — not unlike those of the range cattle industry — large movements, or drives, of sheep from one place to another. After 1865, for instance, sheep were being driven eastward from the coastal farming areas of Oregon and Washington and into the Inland Empire; and in turn, as the frontier closed in, sheep

Courtesy Wide World Photos

SHEEP BREEDING

Every fall these Idaho flocks make the slow trek from summer mountain pastures to the valleys. Sheep breeding in the Northwest has declined since 1900.

SAWMILL AT SHELTON, WASHINGTON

Courtesy of Look Magazine

were taken from the open ranges and into the mountainous, but semi-wooded, pasture areas. Then as the emphasis shifted heavily from wool to mutton, as it did from 1885 to 1890, there occurred the greatest movements of all — the driving of band upon band from the Northwest eastward to such middlewestern feeding grounds as those in Kansas and Nebraska and thence to the great Omaha stockyards for slaughter. Drives that originated in Oregon often started from such towns as Prineville, Heppner, and Pendleton; in Washington, Walla Walla became a taking-off place; in Idaho, Boise. These drives often involved 5,000 to 7,000 sheep at a time. The flocks moved eastward over a course (ten to forty miles in width) that corresponded closely to the old Oregon Trail. Still other bands were taken slowly along the upper reaches of the Missouri River and then east across Montana, with St. Paul as the ultimate market destination. Variations along these general, broad trails were constantly made. Feeding places often differed from year to year, and seasonal fluctuations in weather often necessitated changes in the course.

In preparing for the long trail drive, great caution had to be exercised in finding the right persons to conduct the drive. The men had to understand and know not only the trail but sheep as well; they had to be responsible and willing to take care of the flocks. They had to be in good physical condition to be able to stand the life on the trail. In preparation for the drive, the sheep were first sheared, then dipped in a chemical solution to rid them of vermin and skin disease. Life on the trail was hard and routine. The drivers would get their flocks under way at sunrise, and the men were often obliged to eat on the move. Distances covered in a day averaged about eight or ten miles. One of the tasks, in addition to finding proper pasturage for the sheep and keeping the sheep from straying, was to find adequate water supply. Sheep do not like to drink from pools; they prefer running water, and this presented special problems, especially in dry areas.

Because of the shorter growing season, the trails that emanated from Oregon were harder and more difficult than those that started from California. However, the Oregon area had an advantage over California in that it was closer to the markets. Oftentimes cattle and horses were driven along with the sheep. In such cases the sheep would follow the other animals. However, when the heavier animals tired, the sheep would often push on ahead and reach the destination first. The time involved in covering the trail was about seven months.

The trails were fraught with danger for both sheep and herders, who might encounter any of the following: flooded rivers, stampedes, outlaws, Indians, poisonous herbage, wolves and other beasts of prey, and stretches of alkali land. Also, unfriendly cattlemen and homesteaders might be met, whereupon range wars would result. Generally, however, the bitterness of the range wars was not so keen in the Northwest, and the unrest and bloodshed caused by these clashes were not so severe as in the Southwest.

The pattern thus established continued, with variations, through the 1880s. The coming of the railroads helped to boom the sheep industry, since their arrival made the costly long drives unnecessary. The McKinley tariff of 1890 (supported in the West by an unusual combination of woolgrowers and silver producers) seemed to bolster wool prices for a while, but the election of 1892 with its threat to free trade is believed to have again depressed the industry. In any event, the sheep prices dropped in 1893, and a general period of decline set in — a decline contributed to by the advance of homesteaders and dry farming and overproduction of wool and mutton. By 1900 most of the trails were closed to cattle and sheep alike, and an interesting and exciting phase of western life was gone. But apart from the social implications, the sheepmen, with their great drives to the markets had, by 1900, been able to shift the center of the wool-mutton-producing industry from the eastern farm areas to the transmountain West.

Chapter XVIII

Irrigating the Wastelands

Irrigation Through Private Initiative

SUITABLE SOIL, climate, and moisture are prerequisites for agriculture. Without irrigation, an annual rainfall of about twenty inches is normally required for satisfactory crop production. West of the one hundredth meridian are 740,000,000 acres (one-third of the United States) receiving subrequisite precipitation. And large areas of the Pacific Northwest east of the Cascades, blessed with good soil and sufficient sunshine, are without this necessary moisture. Recognizing this deficiency many early settlers in these arid or semi-arid portions of the old Oregon country turned to irrigation, while still others resorted to dry farming.

The Indians may well have been the first to irrigate in the Pacific Northwest, as was true in the Northwest. In any event, it is known that the Yakimas carried on irrigation. The Whitmans at Waiilatpu Mission and the Spaldings at Lapwai Mission were certainly pioneers in such activity, and they were probably first among the whites to divert water from streams for purposes of irrigation — in their case for growing vegetable gardens. Mrs. Whitman was rightly proud of their produce, which included muskmelons, potatoes, beets, cabbage, corn, and turnips. And if the Indians did not earlier resort to irrigation, it is known that Dr. Whitman prevailed upon his proselytes to begin doing so. Lieutenant Charles Wilkes, who visited this mission, wrote: "The Indians have learned the necessity of irrigating their crops, by finding that Dr. Whitman's succeeded better than their own." Wilkes then went on to say, however, that rather than dig their own ditches the Indians tried to help themselves to the doctor's

[299

water supply. Thus, quarrels over water rights were not long in coming. Wilkes, furthermore, publicized what later settlers came to realize: that "all cultivation has to be more or less carried on by irrigation." One might add that the Catholics, namely, the Oblate Fathers, also did some irrigating.

First to undertake rather extensive irrigation enterprises in the Columbia Basin were the Mormons. When on July 24, 1847, the Mormons began their City Creek project near present Salt Lake City, they became the first Anglo-Saxons to establish a permanent irrigation project in the arid west. Moreover, the Mormons early were willing to recognize that successful operation of irrigation projects necessitated modification of, but by no means complete discarding of, the English common-law views regarding water rights. The Mormons drew up practical codes respecting the creation of water districts, for construction of irrigation works, and for fair distribution of water. Among other things their code provided for financing by those directly benefited; assessment in ratio to acreages reclaimed; and public control over distribution; it also provided for penalties, condemnations, and the appointment of district trustees. This pattern established by the Mormons was of far-reaching significance to the Pacific Northwest inasmuch as the Saints migrated into the Snake River region, to which place they brought with them and made use of the irrigation codes and methods of operation successfully devised in the Great Salt Lake region.

By 1890 there were in the Mormon-occupied counties of southern Idaho [1] three score or more locally owned and operated irrigation canals tapping the upper reaches of the Snake River. Co-operative ownership of the larger ditches was preferred over corporate ownership. "The feeling of the farmers toward the corporations owning and renting the water," reads the 1890 *United States Census*, ". . . is not always friendly." Failure on the part of individual users to meet payments to private companies often resulted in foreclosure and tenantry. In addition to these co-operatively owned canals, a large number of settlers had constructed small private ditches. It is estimated that by 1890 there was

---

[1] These counties were Bear Lake, Brigham, Cassia, and Oneida.

one such independent ditch for every 385 acres under irrigation in Idaho. It should also be noted here that placing land under irrigation did not necessarily mean efficient or effective use of water. "Great disparity is to be seen between crops on adjacent farms where all the physical conditions are similar," reported the *Eleventh Census* (1890). Every conceivable method of irrigation was then employed. At one extreme, some farmers simply turned water out upon open and unleveled fields and relied upon the water finding its own way for good or bad; at the other extreme, very refined methods involving leveling and systematic methods of applying water were also employed — and with excellent results.

Important as were the relative contributions of these pioneers, irrigation in Idaho was still in its experimental stage when the transitional decade of the nineties began. Idaho, with 4,323 irrigators, led in reclamation attainments among the Northwest states. Statistically speaking, less than half the farm area then existing (a total of 217,005 acres) was under irrigation and the total population did not exceed one person per square mile.[2]

Progress during the 1890s was very rapid. In spite of prevailing dislike for private corporations, one notes the introduction of considerable outside capital being invested in Idaho irrigation projects. By the opening of the twentieth century no less than 608,718 acres in Idaho were being irrigated from more than 13,000 miles of ditches. Although many of the ditches were owned co-operatively by small groups of farmers, some of the largest ones were the property of outside private corporations, principally New York and Salt Lake City concerns. Even after the Federal Reclamation Service began its work early in the present century, private irrigation continued to expand; for example, a 200,000-acre project undertaken in the Twin Falls area by the Buhl-Kimberly Corporation.

The early history of irrigation in Oregon varies in many respects from that of Idaho. In contrast to Idaho's Snake River Valley where cereal crops could not be grown without

---

[2] The counties by then experiencing irrigation were Ada, Alturas, Bear Lake, Brigham, Boise, Cassia, Custer, Elmore, and Idaho.

irrigation, many parts of Oregon's semi-arid eastern portion (east of the Cascades) offered opportunities for dry farming. Farmers there could count on sufficient moisture to produce about two to three crops out of every five years, so irrigation was not considered absolutely necessary. Even so, irrigation quietly moved into eastern Oregon, and in 1890 the *Census* reported 3,150 irrigators and 177,944 acres under irrigation. Again, unlike the Saints on the upper Snake, the Oregon ranchers relied more heavily upon their own individual enterprise than upon co-operative efforts. In Oregon the first irrigation methods were extremely simple. Each farmer attempted to build his own ditch; and if the undertaking proved too imposing for one person, two or more would join efforts. Irrigation in Oregon was not absolutely confined to the eastern counties, since fruit and vegetable growers in both southern Oregon and in the Willamette Valley had by then introduced irrigation to help equalize the application of water to their land.[3] By 1900 Oregon had increased her irrigated acreage to 387,095.

Washington was least advanced in an irrigation program by 1890; only 1,046 irrigators were counted by the *Census,* and lands under irrigation totaled only 48,799 acres. In Washington, as in Oregon, much of the semi-arid land east of the Cascades was being successfully dry-farmed. In one respect, Washington faced a unique problem; the water supply in the regions suitable for irrigation was not, except in a few favored spots, readily accessible. An inconsiderate Columbia River carrying enormous quantities of water to the sea was so unobliging as to run far below the level of the arable lands of the Big Bend country, and the places where water could be economically diverted on a small scale for irrigation purposes were relatively few. For this reason pioneer settlers in eastern Washington very early put aside their individual and local partnership efforts in favor of large-scale (either private, semi-private, or co-operative) projects. The larger the projects entertained, the more local farmers be-

[3] Oregon counties having irrigation in 1890 were: Baker, Crook, Gilliam, Grant, Harney, Jackson, Josephine, Klamath, Lake, Malheur, Morrow, Sherman, Umatilla, Union, Wallowa, and Wasco.

came dependent upon outside promoters and irrigation companies which either possessed or were capable of raising more capital than the growers were able to provide for reclamation development. In Kittitas and Yakima counties, where rainfall was negligible, one notes the first of Washington's large-scale projects put into operation. The largest private project in Washington was a continuation of what was known as the Sunnyside Canal (later absorbed by the Reclamation Bureau). In 1889 was organized the Yakima Canal Company, capitalized at one million dollars. Option on land was received from the Northern Pacific Railroad Company, and that concern subsequently advanced capital for the project in exchange for two-thirds of the stock.[4] The reorganized company greatly expanded the scope of operations; it undertook to construct seven reservoirs, one canal in Kittitas County and two more in Yakima County. By 1902 the firm had brought 64,000 acres under irrigation at an expenditure of a million dollars. In addition to the above, there were other sizeable private irrigation firms in Washington during this formative period.[5] The Yakima Irrigation and Improvement Company was one such concern; the James J. Hill interests sponsored still another, which built the Gunn Ditch in Wenatchee. The Spokane Falls Irrigation Company was still another. Of the various private projects Robert C. Nesbit and Professor Charles M. Gates, who have written upon agriculture in eastern Washington, have this to say: "Yet irrigation companies like these were far from successful. Ambitious projects were undertaken with insufficient capital or without adequate realization of the engineering difficulties involved." They indicate that several of these projects folded up in the panic of 1893 and still others remained unused because of speculation.

The next important move in behalf of reclamation came not from private sources, but from the federal government.

[4] As a result of this reorganization, the name Yakima Canal Company was changed to Northern Pacific, Yakima, and Kittitas Irrigation Company.

[5] In 1900 Washington had 135,470 acres under irrigation. In addition to the counties mentioned above, those of Adams, Asotin, Columbia, Franklin, Garfield, Klickitat, Spokane, Stevens, and Walla Walla shared in these operations.

But first something must be said about the growth of general public interest which stirred the federal government into action.[6]

Public Interest in Reclamation

So long as land in humid areas was available, Americans generally gave little thought to reclamation in the great arid West. As farmers saw their last frontier vanish, and vanish rapidly, during the post-Civil War decades, public interest in reclamation and in the conservation of the country's natural resources was awakened. As far back as 1873 there had been enacted the Timber Culture Act, which was a sort of liberalized amendment to the Homestead Act, enabling homesteaders to apply for a second 160 acres, providing trees would be planted on one-fourth of the new acreage. Then in 1877 came the Desert Land Act providing that a settler could buy a whole section of land at $1.25 per acre providing he irrigated part of it. The Desert Land Act proved to be a colossal failure so far as reclamation was concerned. Recognizing this, Congress in 1890 limited individual entries to 320 acres and in 1891 amended the law to require the expenditure by the settler of $3.00 per acre before title would be granted. Three dollars per acre, however, would not go far toward irrigating an acre of land, and so the Desert Land Act continued to encourage fraud and to defeat what were at least the ostensible purposes of this act. The act did, however, promote the interests of well-to-do cattle- and sheepmen who wished to gain title to grazing lands.

In 1894 came the Carey Act. The measure provided that the government would donate to each western arid state a quantity of desert land (not exceeding one million acres to any one state) on the condition that the states would cause said lands to be settled, irrigated, and cultivated. No one settler could secure more than 160 acres. Although great hopes were held out for this act, not unlike the Desert Land Act it resulted in extensive fraud in which the participating

---

[6] State governments played a relatively small role in reclamation although state legislation respecting water rights and transfer of land was passed.

states became involved. By 1910 less than ten per cent of the land granted under the Carey Act was actually under irrigation.

Failure of the federal enactments did not mean failure of the federal government to promote the cause of irrigation. Established in 1879 to replace the United States Geographical and Geological Survey of the Rocky Mountain Region was the United States Geological Survey. The work of this new subdivision of the Department of the Interior was, after a brief interim period, carried forward with distinction by J. W. Powell. Heading up hydrography in this set-up was Frederick H. Newell, who in addition to his many other duties, instituted an important training program for his men. In 1902 Newell became Chief Engineer of the Reclamation Service, and under his direction much pioneering work was carried on in the field of water resources and conservation. Congress charged the new Geologic Survey with the responsibility of looking into feasible irrigation projects; in short, it wanted to know what part of the arid West could be reclaimed. A sum of $350,000 was appropriated for this survey, which work, incidentally, was hindered by the grazing interests. Then in 1889 there was also appointed from the Senate the Select Committee on Irrigation and Reclamation of Arid Lands. This body sought information on the best methods of reclaiming arid lands. The same year the Bureau of Census gathered information concerning irrigation, namely, on costs, areas, conditions, and crops. Meanwhile the press kept the subject of reclamation constantly before the public.

Throughout the nineties, Congressional committees heard testimonies on irrigation, and what were known as irrigation congresses, or meetings, were held at various places. One such congress was held at Salt Lake City in 1891; a second, called the International Congress, was held at Los Angeles in 1893. Another important one was the seventeenth held at Spokane in 1909. These conclaves aroused public interest in reclamation of the arid West, and called for effective, honest, and not fraudulent action. By 1900 the country had become sufficiently aroused to cause both major political parties to include reclamation in their platforms.

Heading reclamation forces in the Congress of the United States was Francis G. Newlands, Representative from the arid state of Nevada and Chairman of the National Irrigation Association. Toward him were routed various proposals for federal support of irrigation projects that were too large for private enterprise. With the expert technical assistance of Newell, Newlands framed a bill which passed Congress on June 3, 1902. Two weeks later it was enthusiastically approved by reclamation-minded Theodore Roosevelt as the National Reclamation Act. This measure provided for the creation of a Reclamation Fund to be derived from the sale of public lands in sixteen western states which, of course, included Oregon, Washington, and Idaho. Funds thus accrued were to be used for surveys and construction and maintenance of irrigation projects. Projects of this kind called principally for the construction of dams and irrigation canals in designated arid areas. The law further provided that settlers, who could acquire from the government not less than 40 and not more than 160 acres under the terms of the Homestead Act, would make repayments to the Fund for the cost of constructing the necessary irrigation works. This could be done in ten annual installments, at no interest. Thus was created a revolving sum of money which could be used for the development of additional irrigation projects.

The plan worked as well as could be expected. After 1907 Newell was head of Reclamation Service, then separated from the Geological Survey. Through federal enactment additional sums of money have since become available for similar projects. Revenue from oil and mineral royalties, sale of federal power licenses, sale of surplus water, and outright appropriations are sources from which these funds are received. During early days the work undertaken resulted in no great clash with private enterprise. Concerning this matter, Arthur P. Davis, Chief Engineer, and later head of the Service, wrote in 1917: "Practically all of the projects undertaken by the Reclamation Service had been abandoned after unsuccessful attempts to finance them as private projects, or else were new projects so difficult as not to attract even the attention of promoters." Government engineers working for the Service took great pride in their projects and carried on their work conservatively, economically, and with the least possible (though never avoidable) politics. Numerous large projects undertaken by the Service were widely scattered throughout the Far West, and all three of the Pacific Northwest states were benefited. In 1923 the Reclamation Service was granted full bureau status; and in 1939 Congress passed the Reclamation Projects Act which further adjusted the problems facing water users. By 1944 the Bureau had developed no less than fifty-two operating projects which served 4,055,329 acres. Moreover, the area for which the Bureau was prepared to supply water totaled 4,885,251 acres.

Reclamation Service in Operation

The first undertaking in the Pacific Northwest by the Reclamation Service is known as the Boise Project. As early as 1864 the right to divert water from the Boise River, a tributary of the Snake, had been granted. This water was used to irrigate the town site of Boise and to furnish Fort Boise with water. Several private developments followed, but after passage of the Reclamation Act in 1902 landowners petitioned for government participation. Engineers found that it was possible to capture an abundant supply of water from the Boise River, which has its source in the western slopes of the Sawtooth Range. Once controlled behind dams, it could then be distributed through artificially constructed canals over no less than 200,000 acres of land in the Boise Valley. The Reclamation Service undertook to construct reservoirs at Deer Flat and at Arrowrock. The Deer Flat reservoir, one covering 9,835 acres, was made possible by the erection of two earthen dams. The intake for this reservoir was placed eight miles above the present city of Boise; the outlet canal system fed water to 120,000 acres of land below this town which was once desert. In order not to interfere with lumbering in the area, a log way was constructed at Arrowrock Dam to allow passing of logs over the dam. A powerhouse and more than seven hundred miles of canals were constructed in the initial government project of Idaho, completed in

1910. Seepage loss from the dam gave the engineers considerable worry at first. During 1909 seventy-five per cent of the amount of water admitted was lost through seepage, but gradually the rate of seepage was reduced and the reservoir filled to capacity.

The Arrowrock Dam, about fifteen airline miles east of Boise, was built of concrete, wedged in between the high perpendicular walls of the canyon. The dam is 354 feet high (for several years the highest dam in the world) and is 1,100 feet across at the top. When filled, the reservoir back of the dam covers 3,100 acres, a total of 286,500 acre-feet of water. The dam was completed in 1915. Its canal system was first made to serve an additional 112,000 acres of land. In 1930 there was completed the Deadwood Dam on a river by that name, and its water was directed into the Boise system. And actually under construction are the Cascades Dam on the North fork of the Payette with a capacity of 700,000 acre-feet, and the Anderson Dam, which will have a 500,000 acre-feet capacity. The Anderson Dam will be a multiple-purpose structure and will be the key unit in the Bureau's whole southwest Idaho project. The entire Boise project, including privately developed districts which receive a full or supplemental supply from the federal government, totals about 320,000 acres of land.

The main stream of the Snake was also captured, and hydroelectric power harnessed by constructing, early in the century, a dam about six miles south of Minidoka. This made possible the irrigation of 70,000 more acres of thirsty but rich desert land in southern Idaho in the vicinity of Acequia, Rupert, and Burley. The 1911 enlargement of Jackson Lake at the northwest corner of Wyoming affected both Idaho and Wyoming and yielded still other acres to the settler's plow. Then in 1923 there was undertaken, through federal and private co-operation, the large American Falls Reservoir Project which brought about the erection of a mile-long dam below the town of American Falls, Idaho. Operations necessitated removal of the entire town, and when completed placed 120,000 more acres under irrigation. This entire massive federal development in eastern Idaho, including reservoirs in addition to those heretofore mentioned, provides a full or partial supply of water for 1,000,000 irrigable acres. The projects are known as the Minidoka Project and the Upper Snake River Storage Project.

Scheduled for the future is the Palisades Dam on the Snake eight miles west of the Wyoming border. Being completed in the spring of 1946 was the 3,500-acre Post Falls unit near Coeur d'Alene, Idaho. About 30,000 acres are irrigated in Idaho through the Owyhee Project, which straddles the Idaho-Oregon border. Seventy thousand acres of this development lie in Oregon.

So, either separately or jointly, the Bureau of Reclamation and private enterprise in Idaho had by 1940 brought under irrigation and fruitful production 1,895,048 acres of what was once bleak, desolate, arid land covered by sagebrush. Out of this reclaimed area had come into production (by 1940) 42,343 farms representing an investment of more than one hundred million dollars. Idaho is exceeded only by California and Colorado in the number of acres under irrigation.

Oregon took action in 1905 by passing its own irrigation act which provided for the appointment of a State Engineer and for co-operation with the national Reclamation Service. During that same year steps were taken leading to the construction of the Umatilla Project on the Umatilla River, a tributary of the Columbia. The following year a diversion, or weir, dam was constructed across this river and a feed canal was built to convey water from the river to Cold Springs Canyon. From there it was distributed to 25,000 acres which had been owned partly by the federal government and partly by private individuals. Good as the project appeared on paper to local interests, troubles mounted after the water began flowing. Leakage from the canals raised the water table, or level, to such an extent that some of the farm lands became mere bogs, even ponds. There was no natural drainage to eliminate this surface water except back to the river through the subsoil. Drainage canals, therefore, had to be constructed at considerable cost, but not without success. Settlers were slow in coming to the Umatilla Valley, and many of those who did come left without making any improvement. Not despairing, backers of the project made a 10,000-acre extension in 1912, and to offset seepage the main canals were lined with concrete. Progress of the entire project then followed. Hermiston, the town of the reclaimed area, began to grow; more settlers came, alfalfa hay was raised for dairy cattle, and vegetables, fruits, and berries were successfully grown. By 1917 this project was at last coming out of the red.

The second Oregon project was even more of a gamble for the Reclamation Service. It called for entering the tule marsh lands of Klamath County in southern Oregon and northern California, inland from the ocean about 150 miles, where it was found that at least a portion of the 300,000 acres of land was reclaimable. Here the project called for use of Upper Klamath, Clear, and Horse Fly lakes as natural storage reservoirs with very little construction necessary. These waters (the surplus of which normally drained into Klamath River) were tapped for irrigating a strip of land about fifty miles long running northward from the California line, and for development of power at the outlet of the Upper Klamath Lake. The plan was sound because the lakes held large quantities of water and were fed from a sufficiently large watershed which would enable discharge by gravity of the water requirements for irrigating an eventual total of 236,401 acres.

Troubles resulted, not with the engineering phase of the irrigation project, but over riparian rights of individuals and of the states of Oregon and California. Also, use of the water on some of the lands proved none too successful because of the unproductive quality of the soil. Moreover, drainage of the marshes offered difficulties; when they were drained the tule mat of the marsh beds was found to be extremely tough and not tractable to the ordinary means of cultivation then in vogue. With great difficulty these tule marsh lands were prepared for planting and seeding, only to produce disappointing results. Plants began well, but some never reached maturity because of the heavy salt, alkaline content of the soil. Leaching was tried but without much success. There matters have rested so far as reclaiming the tule marshes was concerned. Farmers could not make a profit from their efforts. The dry lands, on the other hand, have yielded well in the production of grasses, clover, alfalfa, sugar beets, and potatoes.

The prosperity of the region was further boosted by the coming of railroads which made possible exploitation of the region's timber resources. Klamath Falls, urban center of the area, responded to these various stimuli and grew from a tiny village of 400 in 1904 to 16,497 in 1940.

By 1940 the Bureau of Reclamation practically completed in Oregon and Idaho combined what is called the Vale and Owyhee projects near Vale and Ontario, Oregon. More than 120,000 acres which have been reclaimed are being given over to the raising of clover, alfalfa, sugar beets, potatoes, and cattle.

On May 18, 1946, the inhabitants of Jefferson County, Oregon (north of Bend), gathered to celebrate initial delivery of water to the 50,000-acre north unit of the Deschutes Project. Its completion was regarded as a milestone in the development of central Oregon. The project called for the completion by 1948 of all facilities required to serve the whole project. This development makes feasible the future success of agricultural production. In previous dry-cycle years, wheat production had been a failure.

All told, Oregon had by 1940 placed under public and private irrigation 19,389 farms totaling over one million acres in which more than fifty million dollars had been invested.

In Washington federal reclamation activities began in Okanogan County. Created in 1887, this county was a part of the Colville Indian Reservation. The year before, it had been opened for general settlement, and with it beginnings in irrigation were made by diverting water from Salmon Creek. These miniature individual projects at least proved the practicability as well as the need for reclaiming this portion of the Big Bend (east-central Washington) district where the average rainfall was less than thirteen inches annually. Farmers, finding that irrigation there was too big an undertaking for private individuals, petitioned the Reclamation Service for assistance.

The Service found it practical to include Okanogan in its program. A storage water dam was built on the Salmon River below Conconully, Washington, and additional use was made of Salmon Lake by draining into the reservoir, named the Conconully. Twelve miles below the reservoir, water is diverted by a second dam in the Salmon River bed and is sent forth through tunnels and canals to more than 3,000 acres in Okanogan Valley between the city of Okanogan and Riverside, Washington — not far from the Canadian border. Under irrigation the soil proved to be especially good for alfalfa and fruit-tree production, especially apples. By 1910 no less than 19,000 acres were reclaimed in Okanogan and Stevens counties by federal and private enterprise. Since then, expansion of irrigation projects has been relatively slight in northeastern Washington.

Another, and far more important, project undertaken by the Reclamation Service in Washington was in the 200-mile-long and 50-mile-wide Yakima Valley in Central Washington — an arid region which lay between the productive wheat lands and the Cascade Mountains. Individual, partnership, and co-operative enterprises to reclaim the Valley had begun as early as 1867, the largest private project being the Sunnyside Canal. Many of these projects failed financially during the panic of 1893; but even so, by 1900 they had brought water artificially from the well-fed Yakima River to no less than 120,000 acres.

Much more needed to be done, and the possibilities of a federal reclamation project were apparent. Results achieved there by the Service overshadowed all previous projects. Water supply was so plentiful and farming potentialities so great that the engineers saw the possibility of irrigating an eventual total of 670,000 acres of rich, volcanic-ash soil blessed with plenty of summer heat. Railroad communications were already established, and preceding agricultural success made the situation ideal for further expansion at low cost. The Service purchased the Sunnyside Canal, improvements were made, and work was begun in 1905 on two of at least five projected reservoirs on the various tributaries of the Yakima River. After that time, the work progressed rapidly, and in

1944, 412,000 acres were served by the Yakima system, which includes six reservoirs. The project as blueprinted, however, was so large that developments are as yet uncompleted. Under construction up to date is what is called the 72,000 Roza Division in parts of Yakima, Kittitas, and Benton counties. Water distribution in future developments will be strictly regulated under the laws governing reclamation, and deliv-

Region I Projects — $4,792,377,000 Postwar Inventory.

	Idaho	Washington	Oregon	Western Montana	Grand Total
Number of Projects	18	5	20	4	47
New Lands *	299,680	1,116,000	468,515	86,000	1,970,195
Supplemental Water †	1,067,155	252,000	167,500	66,200	1,552,855
Installation Authorized Projects *	90,500	852,000		142,000	1,084,500
Est. Firm * Projects Under Study *	123,620	622,000	7,800		753,420
Est. Total Cost (1940 prices)	$170,443,200	$411,488,000	$97,353,200	$47,998,000	$727,282,400

* Acres.
† Acre feet.

ery will in no case be made to more than 160 acres in ownership of one person.

The foregoing has been a summary of major irrigation developments Reclamation has had, and will continue to have, a profound effect upon agriculture in the Northwest. The change from semi-arid to irrigated farming represents much greater capitalization, specialization, intensification, productivity, and variety; it has caused population to increase sharply and cities to rise where sagebrush once stood. It has, in short, brought to once arid areas a new way of life.

It must also be borne in mind that almost all of the projects described have a multiple purpose. Most dams have been designed to aid in the generation of hydroelectric power which has a direct relationship to reclamation work, to facilitate flood control, improve navigation, and in many instances provide for wild-life refuges and for recreational developments — also operated under the control of the United States Bureau of Reclamation. The Bureau has already prepared its blueprint for the future; the table on page 313 indicates what may be in store for the Pacific Northwest, including western Montana.

Overtures toward the Big Bend

Not all plans considered by the federal agencies for the Northwest came to fruition. One such plan was the Priest Rapids Project in which the Northern Pacific Railroad had shown interest in 1897 and on which the Reclamation Service made a report seven years later. It called for irrigation of a large tract of land in the Pasco region by pumping water from the Columbia to canals several hundred feet above the River. The scheme was feasible but nothing was done. Another turn-of-the-century plan involving the same area was named the Palouse Project, which called for damming and taking water from the Palouse River for irrigation around Pasco and Connell. The cost was considered too great and the project was tabled, reopened and tabled again by the Reclamation Service. In 1912 local advocates directed their pleas to the Washington State Legislature, which authorized study of the plan. The result was a joint federal-state investigation, but once again the plan was put aside for reason of high costs involved. Still a third proposal that never materialized was the Quincy Valley project involving Quincy and Beverly Plains in southern Grant County, Washington. A proposal emanating from the settlers themselves was that of pumping water from the Columbia River in natural depressions (reservoirs) for release in irrigation canals. The land had been first used slightly by stockmen; and although subsequently homesteaded, farmers experienced repeated crop failures because of insufficient rainfall. In 1907 the Reclamation Service was asked by local inhabitants to investigate irrigation possibilities. It did so and reported unfavorable results so far as costs were involved. The Quincy

Project illustrates well the politics involved in all government irrigation projects. The inhabitants objected to a negative answer and all interested organized groups and individuals proceeded to high-pressure Washington, including the President, Theodore Roosevelt, to whom politicians wrote: "The settlers in this Quincy Valley, Washington, desire through its committee to call your attention to . . . the enclosed Resolutions. . . . We wished to have this Valley surveyed by the Reclamation Service, to find out if it is feasible as all the settlers believe. . . . Hoping you will use your influence in our behalf. . . ."

In spite of all importunities, the Service turned a deaf ear. Then in 1909 Quincy farmers formed a water users' association for promotion of private capital. After all efforts and considerable funds had been expended on the proposed project, the settlers in 1909 came to realize reluctantly that the Quincy project would be a much too costly undertaking. The grim fact remained that the people of the Big Bend country were for all intents and purposes without irrigation.

The Grand Coulee Dam — "Eighth Wonder of the World"

Impressive as are the projects described above, none can compare with the tremendous developments involving completed construction of the Grand Coulee Dam on the Big Bend of the Columbia River in eastern Washington; nor with construction of subsidiary dams, essential irrigation works, and power distribution systems. These gigantic engineering projects involve not only irrigation but also flood control, production of hydroelectric power (see Chapter XXI), improvement in river navigation, and provide added wild-life refuges and recreational facilities as well. They were, one may assume, a logical culmination of previous work undertaken by the Bureau of Reclamation, but contributing to them was a persistent public interest and pressure coming from not only the Northwest (in particular the Inland Empire), but also from reclamation-minded people throughout the nation.

Steps leading ultimately to construction of the Grand Coulee project were taken in 1893 when, under the direction of United States Geological Survey, Israel C. Russell surveyed the Big Bend area, presumably for the purpose "of ascertaining to what extent the conditions there existing favor the project of obtaining artesian water for irrigation." Russell produced a negative report regarding the artesian water supply, but he came forth with a positive plan for diverting water from the Columbia into an irrigation ditch beginning in the Saddle Mountains. Subsequent surveys followed Russell's lead in that they attempted to show the practicability of harnessing either the Columbia River or a tributary at some point that would provide irrigation for the rich but arid lands in the Big Bend area. Such surveys included one by another Geological Survey conducted by T. A. Noble in 1903. The one big problem involved in all proposed plans was that of conveying water across an elevated basaltic mass separating the intake point from the lands to be irrigated. Surveys led to two major alternative plans, each with detailed variations. One called for tunneling through the high obstruction to provide gravity flow from behind a dam. The other provided (1903) for diverting water from far up the Columbia into the Grand Coulee, a giant canyon, from which water could then flow unobstructed to desired areas.[7]

During the first two decades of the present century, interest in the proposed Big Bend project heightened, and opinions as to the desirability of such a project varied in accordance with special interests. The master plan, involving development of hydroelectric power and irrigation, was completed by the Bureau of Reclamation during the early months of Franklin D. Roosevelt's first administration. It called first for the construction of a dam across the Columbia River at the upper bend directly north of the dry canyon. When completed, this dam would be 4,300 feet long at the crest and

[7] The Grand Coulee is 52 miles long, about 600 feet deep, and ranges from 2 to 6 miles in width. During the Ice Age the Grand Coulee had been the course through which the Columbia had traveled. With the recession of continental glaciers the river changed its course and left this great gulch literally high and dry.

550 feet high. At this height a lake, 151 miles long and covering 82,000 acres, would be formed behind the dam reaching all the way back to the Canadian border. Installed in powerhouses on the face of the dam would be eighteen generators with a combined capacity of 2,280,000 kilowatts.

The Grand Coulee Dam, as it is named, is now completed. By all odds the most massive structure ever made by man, this is, of course, the most stupendous undertaking of the Bureau of Reclamation. Americans love big things, and writers have gloried in comparing the dam's size with that of other man-made objects. For instance, four liners the size of the *Queen Mary* could be placed end for end and would not extend across the crest of the dam. The 22,500,000 tons of concrete in its construction could make an obelisk a city block square that would reach skyward two and seven-tenths times higher than the Empire State Building. It would pave a 32-foot modern highway running from Seattle to New York City, or it would make a pyramid more than three times the size of the Great Pyramid of Cheops. The brilliant United States government engineers and their private contractors employed an average of about four thousand workers over a six-year period to build the Grand Coulee Dam and power plant — and at a cost to taxpayers budgeted at $181,101,000.

So much for the dam and the power project. The other, and more costly, aspect of the undertaking has to do with reclamation. From the lake behind the dam (filled at the present time), water is to be lifted 280 feet and dumped into the dry canyon, now officially named the Grand Coulee Reservoir. This is to be done by means of electrically powered pumps, capable of lifting five hundred tons of water per second. Its purpose will be to regulate pumping and water consumption for the million acres to be served. Plans call for the construction of two main canals leading southward from the reservoir to a million-acre tract of rich volcanic-ash soil lying above the junction of the Columbia and Snake rivers. From these main ditches will be constructed a network of feeders requisite for conveying the water to the individual acreages. It has been estimated that at least 15,000 farming families will occupy this new area, almost next door to the previously developed Yakima Valley. The reclamation project calls for the final expenditure of $380,000,000.

During the first years of construction there were many who doubted the wisdom of this entire project. Writing in 1937, the magazine *Fortune* made this statement: "Grand Coulee is a magnificent gesture of either faith or foolishness, depending on the years to come." Since electricity could not be conveyed to the industrial centers of America, would industries ever go to this new source of power? World War II provided the unexpected affirmative answer to this question. And again, in view of the Great Depression (during which period the dam was being built, and during which time crops were plowed under), was it wise to provide for increased production of agricultural commodities? The world scarcity of foods following World War II might also provide an affirmative answer to this query. Laying aside politics and economic theories and practices, there is universal respect and admiration for Frank A. Banks, the government supervising engineer, for John L. Savage, chief designing engineer, and for the private contractors and the thousands of workers who built the "Eighth Wonder of the World" in the state of Washington. "No American," as Stuart Chase phrased it, "can stand below the spillways of the Grand Coulee and not be proud to belong to a nation which could rear this mighty thing."

It remains for the future to determine the husbandry of the million-acre-plus Columbia Basin to be fed with water from the Grand Coulee. The scramble for land in this as yet unprepared oasis has already begun. Fortunately, the United States government has taken steps to curb land speculation. Even so, significant developments are under way in anticipation of future occupation. Business transactions are in evidence at the long forlorn village of Moses Lake, where a restaurant and a couple of service stations made up the business district. Now new business buildings are in the making. The Milwaukee Railroad has purchased seventy-two acres there and plans erection of such railroad facilities — freight yards, refrigeration plants — as can best serve the area. Long a place of about 350 people, by now it has multiplied many fold. Like booms, preparatory to the coming of water to the Basin, the old, long-desolate towns of Coulee City, Ephrata, Quincy, and other places are beginning a mushroom growth. "Today the population of Ephrata is 3,000," wrote a visiting correspondent in 1947, "and anyone will tell you that it will go to 15,000" (a new sewer system has recently been completed to take care of that many people). With true western optimism, some local Ephratians think the population will exceed 50,000 when the desert begins to bloom. Pasco, by no means a ghost town before these operations began, has already profited greatly by the enlargement of its agricultural hinterland. According to recently retired Secretary of the Interior J. A. Krug: "The increase in farm income alone, made possible by irrigation, will average about $46,000,000 annually, based on prewar farm prices. Power from the world's largest generators at Coulee Dam will not only provide the energy needed for irrigation pumping and other farm uses, but will spark the establishment of new industries and stimulate development of mineral, timber, and other resources."

And what about the markets for the new produce? The answer in part is the home market — the new growing West. Barges will assist in carrying goods downstream to Portland; railroad and truck lines will help serve a population still hungry for fruits, vegetables, and dairy products.

The Reclamation Timetable

During World War II plans for the future continued and in December, 1947, the United States Department of the Interior issued *The Reclamation Program: 1948–54.* This was its blueprint for the future. This master plan for seventeen arid and semi-arid states west of the Mississippi is based upon both physical and human geography and is a good example of long-range planning. Upon the basis of assembled data an attempt is made to predict society's needs for water and power by 1954.

So far as the Pacific Northwest is concerned (Region I to the Reclamation Bureau), the overall water resources situation offers great opportunities for future development. Out of 179,000,000 acres of land in the region, 8,050,000 acres are within reach of available water supply and are regarded as susceptible to irrigation.[8] This is about twice the number of acres already under irrigation in 1947, namely, 4,100,000 acres. Of this enormous acreage the Bureau of Reclamation (Congress's purse strings permitting) would, between the years 1949–54, either reclaim or provide supplemental water to 1,520,000 acres. Thus the reclamation planning proceeds at an accelerated pace. If fully financed, the public investment for the period 1949–54 would almost equal the entire amount invested in reclamation projects in the Northwest up to and including 1947. The annual increase in income over that of the above date is estimated to be about fifty per cent.

To what extent is progress being made in fulfillment of this master plan? A Bureau of Reclamation release dated November 4, 1949, indicates that work is proceeding on several fronts.

In Idaho, work was continuing on the Anderson Ranch Dam on the south fork of Boise River; clearing operations were under way in the Payette Division preparatory for irrigating 6,000 new acres. A Lewiston Orchard Project was about ready to add 3,838 new acres to the roster; Minidoka, 4,500 acres; Preston Bench, 4,050 acres.

In Oregon work was proceeding on several dams and reservoirs in the Deschutes area; expansion and repair was under way on the Klamath Project. Then on the Oregon-Idaho Owyhee project a main canal and lateral system was completed for watering 1,686 farms with 103,499 acres.

Most impressive was the work in progress in Washington State where $79,000,000 were currently being spent on the Grand Coulee Dam project. Under construction were the pumping plant, the O'Sullivan and South Coulee Dams, continued work on the North Dam. Also under construction were canals and generating plants identified with this huge irrigation project. Yakima projects in the Roza and Kenne-

---

[8] Out of this total acreage forests cover ninety million acres (1947); thirty-two million are grazing lands and sixteen million acres are suitable for dry farming.

wick Divisions were likewise showing evidence of improvement work. To what extent the Northwest will realize the goal set for it by the Department of the Interior's Reclamation Bureau depends entirely upon the generosity of Congress.

Chapter XIX

Husbandry: Post-Frontier

The Agricultural Revolution

THE PHENOMENAL EXTENSION of the reclamation program was but one phase of a multiple agricultural revolution that swept across America, especially the West, during the half century following Appomattox. Farms tripled in number during these years, and more new acres yielded to the plow than had been brought under cultivation during the entire pre-Civil War era. It was an age, to quote Charles A. Beard and Mary Beard, that "marked the absorption of agriculture into the industrial vortex, endlessly sustained by capitalism, science, and machinery." Not least of this trinity was machinery. Many new and improved farm tools and machines then made their appearance. These devices contributed greatly toward revolutionizing agricultural methods in previously settled areas, but they also contributed greatly toward the rapid opening of the western plains country to the farmer.

During the decades following the Civil War this process of intensified mechanization of agricultural operations moved in upon the Pacific Northwest. Many new and improved sulky plows (first single, then multiple) appeared on the western ranges. Improved discers, spring-toothed harrows, corrugators, press drills, improved hay stackers, mowers, binders, and threshers were but a few of the tools and machines which opened the West to large-scale farming. Joseph F. Glidden's discovery of a high-speed method for manufacturing barbed wire, thus making great quantities available at low cost, helped immeasurably in transforming the ranges from grazing lands into wheat fields. Also, during

322]

the late nineteenth century, horse power began to give way to steam power where large-scale operations were involved; and after the turn of the century the internal combustion engine opened the door to what today amounts to intensive motorization and mechanization on large and small farms alike.

Moreover, the impact of twentieth-century reclamation (chiefly irrigation) augmented this agricultural revolution. Irrigation on a large scale posed many new problems for the farmers. New and untried methods of husbandry were called for. New crops could and should be raised to prevent glutting the market with the old and familiar staple commodities. Irrigation more than doubled the per-acre cost of farming and increased outlays calling for refinancing on an enlarged scale which in turn required more able and more aggressive methods of marketing as a means of maintaining a new agricultural economy. Scientific researches in agricultural methods and in soil analysis likewise contributed their share toward widening, and in places intensifying, farming processes on more profitable bases.

Making the Desert Bloom

Of all these breath-taking changes none was more significant than the introduction of irrigation into the arid and semi-arid regions of the West. Most of the early pioneers in the old Oregon country knew nothing whatever about irrigation methods; scarcely any of them had associated reclamation of any kind with the word Oregon. Then when settlers did begin to move into the region east of the Cascades, and irrigation was either required or highly desirable, the required techniques seemed strangely foreign. Even tho simple act of diverting water from a stream to adjacent land was a new American experience to many. To prepare land properly for maximum utilization of water, to regulate the flow of water, and to till the flooded areas in proper manner required new learning processes.

Proper preparation of desert soil for irrigation called first for cleaning the land of rocks, sagebrush, junipers, and other obstructive desert growth. Next, the land had to be properly surveyed, leveled, plowed, and planted. Then, depending somewhat on methods desired, lateral furrows had to be made in order finally to bring the water to the field crops. Among the various methods developed for applying water in the Northwest are wild flooding, strip border flooding, furrows, and corrugations. Smaller irrigation systems, especially those used west of the Cascades, provide either for submerged pipe distribution or for overhead sprinkling.[1] Proper drainage to prevent alkalization was also a requisite for proper irrigation. Moreover, experimentation within the region was necessary in order to discover how much and how frequently water should be applied to the respective crops being produced. Types of soil, lengths of the growing season, temperature, humidity, use of fertilizers, and many other factors had to be checked upon as bases for determining water requirements. For instance, it was discovered that in southern Idaho thirty inches of water per season produced the maximum amount of alfalfa, while only eighteen inches produced the most potatoes and cereal crops. In Oregon, strangely enough, water requirements were relatively less than those of the panhandle state.

Out of scientific experimentation, both institutional and private, and as a result of much trial and error, specialized crop farming gradually emerged in the reclaimed areas. In areas below 3,000-foot elevation, diversified farming — production of alfalfa, clover, and vegetables — can be carried on very successfully. On elevations above 3,000 feet, forage and cereal crops thrive best, and also more livestock is produced in such regions.

In Idaho the raising of sugar beets has gained steadily. However, potatoes — "Idaho bakers," as they are known throughout the country — constitute the chief Idaho crop. On both irrigated and non-irrigated lands Idaho produces at least one-half of all potatoes raised in the Northwest. Actually there is a great variety of crops in Idaho — alfalfa hay and seed, clover hay and seed, corn (chiefly for fodder),

---

[1] See Howard T. Lewis and Stephen I. Miller, *The Economic Resources of the Pacific Northwest* (Seattle, 1923), pp. 112–14.

oats, barley, beans, onions, celery, lettuce, and berries. Some apples are produced, but not to the same degree of specialization as in Wenatchee Valley, Washington.

Today eastern Washington has become a heavy producer of peaches, potatoes, nationally advertised apples (especially Wenatchee apples), and varieties of hay, grains, livestock, and dairy products. The coming in of irrigation methods caused land values to rise perceptibly. In eastern Washington, for example, one notes that within two decades after water was turned onto the soil, good raw land (land without special plantings on it) rose from an average of about $50 an acre to an average of about $200 per acre. Improved and planted lands commanded even higher prices. Orchard lands in 1910 often sold for more than $2,000 per acre. This increased capitalization meant in turn that irrigation farming required greater financial resources than did many other types of western farming. And even those who undertook irrigation farming had, in most cases, to be content at first with from ten to fifty acres of land. Then, if all went well, and profits were made, the holdings could be increased in the future. Under ordinary circumstances, one hundred acres of irrigated land was about the maximum that one operator could manage efficiently.

As scientific knowledge of irrigation farming advanced, and as farmers gained in experience with methods and in knowledge about markets, specialization developed. At the turn of the century, Wenatchee, Washington, farmers began to experiment vigorously and extensively in apple growing.[2] While trees were maturing, berries and other crops were raised between the rows. Results from apple growing were at first good. But by 1910 Wenatchee had expanded its acreages so much that, without adequately developed markets, the region experienced financial stringencies of an intensity not experienced in many other irrigated areas. Since then Wenatchee apple growers have had their good times

[2] Apple growing, of course, did not actually begin in Wenatchee; neither was it confined to reclaimed areas. The Willamette and Rogue river valleys not only shared in this development but often led. More recently, growers in the coastal valleys have turned to irrigation.

and bad ones. During each of the two world wars returns on apples were very profitable, but during the Great Depression, even with apples being sold on the best of the nation's street corners, apple growing proved to be unprofitable.

In places where irrigated lands were not so highly capitalized and where climate permitted, such as in Kittitas County, lower Yakima Valley, and the Big Bend of Washington, in Klamath Falls, Oregon, and in parts of the Boise Valley, Idaho, the trend was toward diversified farming of a type less costly than fruit raising. A standard and usually profitable crop was alfalfa hay. Alfalfa, if sufficiently watered, would yield three and four cuttings annually, and at a profit, especially to those who used their own hay as feed for livestock. But as a rule, only a few farmers limited themselves to raising alfalfa; instead, they developed systems of crop rotations which, depending somewhat on the area, involved the raising of sugar beets, fruits, berries, some cereals, and an abundance of potatoes. Then, as urban markets emerged, a great variety of vegetables (especially celery, onions, lettuce, beans, and beets) were produced to meet the needs of the city populations. Expansion of the canning industry likewise increased the demand for diverse varieties of vegetables and fruits. More recently the introduction of quick-freezing techniques have greatly altered the crop planning, as in the case of new techniques developed to harvest and quick-freeze peas and other vegetables and fruits in the field.

Dry Farming

Reclaimed lands comprise but a very small portion of the total number of acres under cultivation in the Inland Empire. In fact, long before irrigation had been resorted to on a sizeable scale, the prevailing agricultural system was one termed "dry farming" or dry-land agriculture. It is a system of agriculture peculiar to the semi-arid regions of the "high country," and one not very well understood by the early settlers who moved to the plains west of the 100th meridian and into semi-arid parts of the Oregon country and California. Their immediate problem was how to farm in marginal rainfall areas without resorting to irrigation. Techniques for dry farming were evolved by those who first ventured in the semi-arid areas, but newer and better techniques are constantly forthcoming as a result, not only of experience, but of scientific experimentation by local and federal agricultural agencies.

Without technical refinements, the basic system known as dry farming is one that calls for summer fallowing. It was found that if farmers in semi-arid regions would plow their land in the summer and allow from one-third to one-half of their plowed field to lie fallow, then grain (this usually meant wheat) seeded in the late summer would have sufficient moisture to bring it to maturity. Promotion literature, of which there was plenty, did much to advertise this method of farming throughout the United States and abroad. Refinements and variations in the general pattern were numerous but the basic procedure called for plowing to a depth of twelve inches; this was followed by thorough pulverization; then there was to be regular alternation between the fields to be seeded and those to be left idle. Credit for devising one of the most widely used formulas goes to Hardy W. Campbell of Dakota Territory; it became known as the Campbell system, and was formalized in a publication by Campbell entitled *Soil Culture Manual*, dated 1902. This manual called for: (1) deep plowing; (2) cultivation both before and after seeding; (3) light seeding; (4) alternate summer fallowing; (5) cultivation of the land during the fallow season as well as in the year of seeding.

Of great aid in publicizing dry-farming methods were the Northern Pacific and Great Northern railroad companies, both of which stood to gain directly by utilization of land suitable to this method of agriculture, as so much of that land lay in areas served by these railroad lines. Notably active was Professor Thomas Shaw, who was not only the agricultural expert for both the Great Northern and Northern Pacific lines, but also author of *Dry Land Farming* (St. Paul, 1901). Shaw favored taking liberties with the Campbell system by adjusting to local situations, and he was, among other things, a staunch advocate of winter wheat for the Northwest. Later, dry-farming congresses (one of which was held at Spokane in 1910) and other groups and agencies not only contributed to knowledge about dry farming, but assisted in the propagation of information to the regions engaged in it.

So far as the Inland Empire was concerned, development of dry farming was enhanced not only by learning the "know how," and having the necessary farm machinery on hand, but also by the availability of railroads for transportation of crops. By 1890 these conditions had been met, and the result was a radical transformation. A region which before this date had been the scene of open range grazing, re-emerged as a gigantic checkerboard of alternating fields of golden wheat and black fallow soil.[3] Tiny villages that formerly lay astride cattle trails now became the bases for dry-farming operations, and arising in many places along the railroad tracks were new wheat towns. Likewise open range cattlemen gave way to homesteaders; and land purchasers (predominantly native American stock) arrived in ever increasing numbers. The latter, being richer than the homesteaders, often brought with them new capital in the form of heavy farm machinery and other equipment needed for large-scale dry-farming operations. Combines were introduced for harvesting wheat crops, and in time the motor truck became an indispensable adjunct to an Inland Empire wheat farm. In eastern Washington alone, by 1890, more than one and a half million acres of land were under cultivation, and thereafter the growth in the number of farms and in population continued rapidly.

Taken as a whole, the success of dry farming was depend-

[3] Specifically, the wheat producing sub-areas within the Inland Empire were: (1) the Palouse country, south of Spokane, Spokane and Whitman counties; east Adams and north Walla Walla counties; Columbia and Garfield counties. (2) The Big Bend, west and southeast of the Columbia River; Lincoln and north Adams counties; Grant and Douglas counties. (3) Districts in Idaho, namely, Benewah and Latah counties (extension of the Palouse area); the region north and east of Lewiston, including Nez Perce, Lewis, Clearwater, and Idaho counties. (4) Then finally, the Grande Ronde and the Deschutes river (Wasco) area in the north central portions of Oregon.

Harvesting wheat in eastern Washington. A "Caterpillar" Diesel is pulling a 16½ foot combine which can harvest 40 acres of wheat in 10 hours.

Sunset entrance to Spokane, "Capital" of the Inland Empire

THE INLAND EMPIRE
Courtesy Spokane Chamber of Commerce

NORTHWEST INDUSTRIES (above) *A modern sawmill* (center) *A tug towing a log raft through Lake Washington Canal, Seattle* (below) *Trentwood Rolling Mill near Spokane*

Courtesy Seattle and Spokane Chambers of Commerce

ent upon new techniques, liquid capital, adequate machinery, an available labor supply,[4] and land. At least in the early stages, land was plentiful and relatively inexpensive. Size of individual farms, however, depended largely upon an operator's available capital. In 1890, farms in Adams County, Washington, for example, averaged 352 acres with a capital investment of about $2,500. In 1910, on the other hand, the average farm had increased to 775 acres, and the average capital investment had bounded to $20,000. To this day the trend has been toward bigness, with ever-increasing capital investment.

As the basis for an article in *Harper's Magazine*, Oscar Lewis of Washington University, St. Louis,[5] has selected Franklin County in the state of Washington to show what has finally come from dry-farming techniques in an area where rainfall is less than nine inches. In 1945, he pointed out, 150 farm families produced 500,000 bushels of wheat on 450,000 acres. Individual farms averaged from about 2,000 to 3,000 acres, although some individual farms comprised 8,000 acres. Every phase is mechanized, and the per-farm investment for machinery ranges from $10 to $35,000. The gross annual income is $20,000 to $40,000 per farmer.

Mechanics and knowledge not available in Campbell's day have brought changes in techniques. Although fallowing persists, a system of stubble mulching (preparing a mulch out of the stubbles and straw) has replaced plowing under the straw and stubbles. New rotating weeders and other machines have come; so, too, an almost complete shift from horse and other older sources of power to diesel power ("cats"), which means speedier operations and economy in labor. With present-day machinery one man can now till 60 acres in twelve hours, and by changing operators, 120 acres in twenty-four hours; whereas with horses, one man could plow at most only 15 acres per day. Mechanical revolutions such as this have brought an inevitable decrease in the rela-

---

[4] Much of the labor was supplied by transient, or migratory, workers who followed the harvests by working their way northward as the season advanced.

[5] Oscar Lewis, "Bumper Crops in the Desert," *Harper's Magazine*, CXCIII (Dec., 1946), 525–28.

tive number of dry-farming operators of the Inland Empire; only the most capable have survived.

Diversified, or General, Farming

Early pioneers, many of them steeped in the agricultural traditions of New England and the Ohio Valley, preferred to engage in what is known as diversified, or general, farming. It was the kind of farming they knew best; and, dictated by peculiar circumstances brought on by isolation and favored by the geography of the coast regions of Oregon and Washington, emphasis was placed by the early settler upon diversification. These settlers produced many crops, and their farmyards gave evidence of raising a variety of livestock.

For the early years the choice was a wise one, and even now, with economic self-sufficiency of individual farming units less essential, general farming prevails. Moreover, there has been a spread of this system from the coastal valleys to many portions of the Inland Empire. The diversity of crops raised varies with the community. As a rule, individual farms are small, many twenty acres each and under.[6] In the Puget Sound area farms average less than fifty acres; in the Willamette Valley they range from about fifty to one hundred acres; and east of the Cascades (not counting irrigated farms discussed above) the farms averaged about a quarter section (120 acres) in size. On these farms one individual operator may produce a variety of grains and use his cereal for raising hogs and chickens; another may raise a variety of hay crops and use his produce as feed for dairy cattle. Good pasturage is generally available in all seasons. Still others combine horticulture with diversified farming. The combinations are endless. More recently, individual producers have shown a disposition to do more crop-specialty farming, but within a given community great diversity continues.

One of the most important developments in areas generally associated with diversified farming has been dairying.

---

[6] The 1940 census reveals that out of 187,178 farms in the Northwest at that time, there were 55,287 farms under twenty acres in size.

Very early the pioneer farmers realized the need for dairy cattle, and references have been made previously to their efforts at importation and development of dairy herds in the Oregon country. Very early the "general-purpose cow," as it was called, was recognized as essential to a self-sustaining community. It was, wrote *The Rural Spirit*, one of the region's farm journals: ". . . the one that makes butter in winter, cheese in summer, fine veal once a year and obligingly does service as a beef animal when oleomargarine or filled cheese injures the market for dairy products or old age begins to steal upon her."

The general-purpose cow had her day, but she was incapable of competing with her more specialized descendant, the thoroughbred. Thoroughbred dairy cattle made their debut early in the Oregon country, but it was not until the present century that the farm journals began to plead with their readers to enlarge the numbers of highly selected cattle. The particular breed acquired by farmers depended upon the local market for dairy products.

Growth in urban population in the Northwest brought a correspondingly increased demand for fresh bottled milk and butter. With this demand present, dairymen tended to enlarge their herds with such heavy milk-producers as Holsteins and, to a slightly less degree, Guernseys and Ayrshires. In cheese-making, Tillamook County, Oregon — "the dairyman's paradise" — farmers likewise increased the number of heavy-milking breeds. On the other hand, dairymen who found demand greatest for cream tended to favor Jersey cows, whose milk makes up in richness what it lacks in bulk. To the dairy farmer this meant not only increased specialization, but also increased capitalization. Even as early as 1908 the Seattle *Post Intelligencer* observed: "The day of cheap farms has passed." Since then the trend toward more and more scientific operation is in evidence on the region's dairy farms with correspondingly greater capitalization. Producers' co-operatives and competitive demands on the part of the dairy-products manufacturers have added greatly to the farmers' profits, which in turn have been an added incentive to place dairy-farm operations upon a sanitary, efficient, and highly productive basis. Technological advances have helped to make these developments possible. Rural electrification has now reached the dairy barn; machines now do the milking; refrigeration helps to safeguard the product; and motorized transportation speeds up daily collections. The largest of these means of transportation, the huge glass-lined and refrigerated tankers, make possible enlargement of metropolitan milksheds, which in turn stimulates the dairying interests in regions formerly shut out from the large city fresh-milk markets. Today dairying, centered though it is in the Willamette-Puget Sound trough, has also become established in the irrigated lands of Yakima, Kittitas, and Walla Walla counties of eastern Washington, in the reclaimed valleys of Umatilla County in eastern Oregon, and in the western parts of the Snake River Valley and Bear Lake districts of Idaho.

Everywhere, then, are found modern dairy plants. And from the assembly lines of large dairy plants now come standardized Grade-A milk, powdered milk, buttermilk of various kinds, processed cheeses of many scents and colors, and ice creams ranging in flavor from exotic pistachio to old-time vanilla, packaged in many shapes and colors. To this array of dairy products must be added powdered milk and evaporated, or condensed, milk. The manufacture of these commodities, now produced in great quantities, contributes toward stability in an industry affected by seasonal fluctuations in milk production. When excesses of raw milk occur, surpluses may either be powdered or canned in condensed form. Not only is the preservation of milk in these forms extended, but world-wide distribution and increased uses for this vital product are possible.

Horticulture has likewise experienced remarkable changes and developments during the present century. Reference has already been made to specialized apple growing in Wenatchee, but its development in the Willamette, Hood River, Umpqua, and Rogue River valleys was also very rapid during the first decade of this century. Contributing to this rapid development of apple culture was a rising demand for the fruit, which in turn influenced easterners, attracted also by the mild climate and scenery, to migrate to the coastal portions of the Northwest for the purpose of planting apple orchards. By 1910, the market began to be glutted, but many growers felt that the problem was one not of production, but of marketing, and so apple raising continued on an ever-increasing scale.[7]

Southern Oregon, especially the region around Medford, has become a heavy producer of pears. In the Willamette Valley prunes, cherries, nuts (especially Lamberts and English walnuts), and a great variety of fruits and berries are produced. Truck farming, especially in regions near such large cities as Seattle and Portland, has long been active. And in various spots there are grown, in addition to specialty crops already mentioned, soybeans, hops, flax, flowers, seeds, bulbs, and many other commodities. The story of bulbs helps to illustrate how specialty crops made their way into this section of the country. Early in the present century George Gibbs, a native of England and then a resident of Whatcom County, Washington, challenged the Dutch monopoly of the bulb industry by producing bulbs commercially. It was found that the sandy loam of Puyallup Valley and the Bellingham Bay and Fargo Lake areas were suitable for narcissus and tulip bulbs. Restrictions on Holland bulbs during the last war boomed this already well-established industry to the point where 150 to 175 carloads of bulbs were being shipped out of Washington annually. Oregon, too, has placed bulb raising on a profitable commercial basis.

Development of canning, quick freezing (notably of pears), scientific agriculture, irrigation, experimentation, increased mechanization, and improved marketing methods by both private and fruit growers' associations have in one way or another contributed to the steady enlargement of diversified farming in the Northwest.

Livestock

The passing of the frontier, and with it the demise of the range cattle and sheep industries, did not mean to the Northwest the end of beef and mutton production — far from it.

---

[7] Efforts at solving the marketing problems are discussed below.

The passing of the open range meant in most instances (see Chapter XVII) a shift from relatively unrestricted grazing either to regulated unfenced, government-owned grazing areas, or to fenced-in privately owned ranges. It should, of course, be noted that the carrying capacity of the grazing lands declined rapidly due to over-exploitation. In some cases over-grazing actually destroyed native roots, and land became worthless for grazing purposes. To quote Willis B. Merriam: "Where formerly two or three acres of virgin grazing land per month sufficed to feed one cow, now [1942] five to eight acres are needed." Designed, at least in part, to offset this depletion was the passage of the [Edward] Taylor Grazing Act of 1934 and its 1936 amendment. This Act put an end to unrestricted grazing, a carryover from the days of the "Long Drive." Under the terms of this act, grazing fees are charged by the government for use of the Domain, with the idea of preventing over-grazing. Seventy-five per cent of the fees thus collected are returned to local communities for range improvements, which might take the form of increasing water supply, reseeding, or fighting rodents. Charging of a grazing fee under this act did much to hasten the extermination of wild horses on the Public Domain and in this way made room for more suitable forms of livestock. As a result of these developments grazing continued over wide areas in the Inland Empire where, as geographers say, the dry, moderate temperature is conducive to livestock raising.[8] Not only are there more beef cattle and sheep in the Northwest today than there were at the height of the open range period, but both beef cattle and sheep are of incomparably better grade.

In addition, the present methods of feeding cattle are a great improvement over the old open range methods. Supplementary feeding of grazing cattle, especially in the winter, has been found to pay dividends to cattle raisers. In some instances full feeding of cattle from late December to March, and sheep for a briefer period, has been found profit-

[8] Grazing areas at present are as follows: Idaho — 20,750,000 acres, or 39 per cent of total acreage, is classified as grazing; Washington has 6,000,-000 acres or about 13 per cent grazing; Oregon, about 23,000,000 acres or 38 per cent. Including western Montana, about 70,000,000 acres of grazing exist.

able. An example of dramatic government assistance in mitigating disasters occurred during the 1948–49 winter blizzards. Federal government agencies conducted "Operations Haylift"; in other words, hay was distributed to stranded and frozen cattle by means of airplanes. Also, the severity of the 1949–50 winter in the Northwest called for much special care of the livestock.

One of the most significant trends in the livestock business of the Northwest, one greatly aided and abetted by the United States Department of Agriculture, the farm journals, and the livestock associations, is the continued improvement in the breeds of cattle and sheep. As previously indicated, thoroughbred bulls and rams were early brought to the open ranges. At the turn of the century it was boasted that among the thoroughbred strains in the Northwest were Hereford, shorthorn, Galloway, and Red Polled cattle; Shropshire, Hampshire, Oxforddowns, Lincoln, Cotswold, and Angora sheep; Berkshire, Duroc, Poland China, Hampshire, and Chester White hogs; and to round out the list, Percheron and Belgian draft horses.

Then, too, control of summer grazing land has provided more limited grazing, but it also has been more rewarding. Public demand for improved and standardized grades of meat has also contributed to an improvement in the meat-producing business. Stockyards and packing houses, catering to the public tastes, have been able, through control over buying, to bring about many improvements in livestock raising. More systematic marketing has also curbed glutting with its consequent breaking of price levels.

All this does not mean that stockmen have enjoyed steady prosperity since the passing of the open ranges. Seeded crop and grass fluctuations have caused corresponding variations in productions and in income. During World War I and again during and after World War II (to 1950) meat prices rose and maintained high levels, and large profits were made. But during the Great Depression stockmen suffered reverses as did everyone else. In spite of these market fluctuations and continuous changes in the processes of producing livestock, it is apparent that natural conditions, at least, favor a continued existence of this particular phase of agriculture. The 1940 *Census* (giving figures for the preceding year) placed the value of livestock in the three Northwest states at $157,300,218. Interestingly enough, value of livestock was about the same in each individual state. The total of livestock products for 1939 was placed at about one-third the value of the livestock itself.

Marketing Problems and Producers' Co-operatives

For the most part, agricultural producers of the Northwest have relied upon the operation of the traditional law of supply and demand to facilitate disposal of their produce at a profit. Some, of course, have pleaded since pioneer days for government-imposed protective tariffs, still others for federal support of transcontinental railroads and intercession by the Interstate Commerce Commission in behalf of special lower rates for crop transportation. Some groups have, since early times, launched out in their attacks upon "monopolies," and still others, facing ruinous prices, took steps to effect co-operative buying and marketing.

In the Pacific Northwest, as elsewhere, during the hard post-Civil War times, the Farmers' Union (descendant of the Farmers' Alliance) emerged, along with other agricultural societies and co-operatives. The organization of the Fruit Growers' Union (1892), the Ritzville Warehouse Company (1893), "Choeg" (an important egg co-operative) in Washington, and the Hood River Apple Growers' Association (1892) in Oregon, indicates the beginning of marketing co-operatives. From the outset these co-operatives took the view that their problem was one of finding better ways of marketing their produce, not one seeking curtailment of production. Idaho producers' groups likewise strove to market baking potatoes of ten- to fourteen-ounce sizes rather than of very uneven sizes. The apple growers began grading their apples and packing them in uniform sizes throughout the boxes rather than having the big beautiful ones on top and small worm-eaten ones at the bottom. To place its stamp of approval on its products the Hood River Apple Growers' Association developed a standard product which it called the "Diamond Brand," and soon the Washington Fruit Growers' Association produced its famed "Big Y" brand; others followed.

As the next step came the emulation of the California growers in the organization of both privately owned and co-operatively owned fruit growers' exchanges; one such was

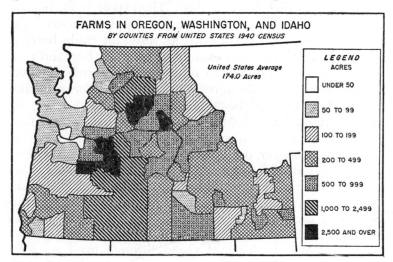

FARMS IN OREGON, WASHINGTON, AND IDAHO
BY COUNTIES FROM UNITED STATES 1940 CENSUS

United States Average 174.0 Acres

LEGEND
ACRES
UNDER 50
50 TO 99
100 TO 199
200 TO 499
500 TO 999
1,000 TO 2,499
2,500 AND OVER

the Pacific Northwest Fruit Distributors, a co-operative founded about 1912, to: (1) establish an orderly market; (2) distribute fruit; and (3) maintain prices. The road ahead was rocky, and this as well as many other fruit exchanges and co-operatives failed.

Perhaps the vicissitudes of co-operative marketing can best be illustrated by noting what has happened in the Oregon apple industry. Prior to the 1890s the Northwest, leaning heavily upon a precarious overseas market, faced overproduction. The coming of the transcontinental railroads eased this situation slightly, especially as growers devised improved methods of packaging and selling in competition with other growing areas within the United States. The outbreak of World War I choked off the foreign market, but demands at home were such as to put the apple industry upon a very profitable basis. Then, after this war, the foreign market rebounded dramatically and the Northwest shared heavily in these foreign shipments; the three states were able to export twenty-five per cent of their commercial crop. At one point Oregon exported abroad seventy per cent of her commercial crop. And in view of this roseate prospect, planting increased. Writes Professor Joseph W. Ellison, who has made a special study of this: "The export trade became the safety valve of the Northwestern apple industry." But then came the 1929 crash with its resultant trade barriers. By the middle thirties, for example, exports to England were sliced in half; shipments to other countries suffered even more. Reciprocal trade agreements offered some remedies, and the turn upward began in 1936. A corresponding decrease (after a bitter battle with railroads) in freight rates eased the situation with respect to the United States market.

Growers, however, did not sit idly by with hopes that government aid would solve their marketing problems. They knew there was much for them to do for themselves, besides raising beautiful apples, and most obvious was the fact that they must keep pace with crop-moving methods and the selling practices devised by their alert California neighbors. This could only be brought about through even more cooperative efforts than had been exercised heretofore. In 1936 a new super association of growers emerged out of the old and most representative of such existing local organizations as the Hood River Apple Growers' Association, Yakima Fruit Growers' Association, the Skookum Packers' Association, and the Wenatchee-Okanogan Co-operative Association. The name given this new organization was the Pacific Northwest Fruits, Inc. Reminiscent of the California Fruit Growers' Association with its famous Sunkist label, Pacific Northwest Fruits adopted "Doc Apple" as its premium brand, and proceeded to introduce uniform packing and to devise controlled shipping and pricing and advertising methods. There was, as in the early days of the California Fruit Growers' experience, resistance to heavy advertising expenditures, but with leadership from the state of Washington, the Association has demonstrated its soundness. It has been a success. World

War II, of course, provided new and unlimited marketing opportunities and the postwar years to 1950 were good ones.[9] In general it may be said that co-operative buying and selling is on the increase.[10]

[9] The best treatment of this subject is Joseph W. Ellison, "Marketing of Northwestern Apples, 1929–1940," *Agricultural History*, XVI (April, 1942), 103–15.

[10] Comparative figures on co-operative buying and selling are as follows:

	Oregon	*Washington*	*Idaho*
1919	9.6	11.2	8.9
1939	31.2	33.5	33.8

CHAPTER XX

Industry and Commerce

A Backward Glance

DOMINANT AS WERE agricultural pursuits in pioneer days, it is well to recall that the history of Pacific Northwest industry has its roots in Indian culture. From the aborigines the first white immigrants learned more about industry than about husbandry. From them the fur traders garnered information about processing salmon; they learned how to make pemmican, and how best to catch sea otter; and from the Indians, early settlers learned something about canoe making, housebuilding, weaving, basketmaking, and design. Even today the influence of Indian design in the arts and crafts is readily apparent, and traces of native culture are revealed in some modern architectural designs. In any event, industry was an integral part of the region's aboriginal culture.

The fur age likewise made its contribution to manufacturing, for it will be recalled that lumbering, catching and processing of salmon, the manufacture of dairy products, milling, and even distilling were subsidiary activities of the Hudson's Bay Company. And even though pioneer settlers placed emphasis upon farming, their frontier requirements called for industrial activity ranging from farmyard tinkering and blacksmithing to lumbering, milling, and shipbuilding on an export or commercial basis.

Not until the close of the nineteenth century, however, did the region become fully aware of its industrial potentials. Remarks not unlike the following in the *Oregonian* (August 21, 1880) then began to recur in the local press: "Nothing short of the wonderful resources of the [Northwest] country would have kept up the rate of progress which the

340]

country has enjoyed. . . ." Boastful as was the Northwest of its great stands of timber, wealth in fish, minerals, and agriculture, it is nonetheless clear that the people who were industrially and commercially minded were painfully aware of their dependence upon eastern manufacturers for many finished goods and were also aware of their dependence upon eastern capitalists for funds with which to buy eastern-made commodities. Moreover, this new corner of the country was obliged to invite "foreign" industrialists to share in the exploitation of the region's rich natural harvest. A distinction, however, was made between the eastern capitalists who reinvested in the region the profits they made in Northwest business ventures, and those, on the other hand, who made fortunes in the Oregon country and proceeded to spend their profits in other places. The former were looked upon as sort of industrial or financial pioneers and were favored; the latter were merely tolerated for the reason that money, good or bad, was sorely needed. Northwesterners resented being "colonists" of the East in much the same way that early American colonials smarted from being producers of raw materials but not also unrestricted manufacturers in the British mercantile system.

Northwest Manufactures: 1890

The year 1890 is a suitable one for inventory purposes, since it offered the United States census takers their first opportunity to collect data in the Pacific Northwest on a statewide basis.[1] The cold figures appearing in the *Eleventh Census: 1890* clearly reveal that by the time the frontier conditions had all but vanished, the states of Oregon and Washington were clearly well along on the road to industrialization. Idaho and Montana continued to lag.[2] Note the following chart:

---

[1] Hereafter political boundaries remain fixed and it is possible to make periodical comparisons that are more valid than those relating to territorial eras when political boundaries were frequently redrawn.

[2] While noting the industrial data for 1890, recall that the respective state populations were: Washington, 349,390; Oregon, 313,767; Montana, 132,159; Idaho, 84,385.

NORTHWEST MANUFACTURES: 1890 [3]

	No. of Establishments	Capitalization	Value of Products
Washington	1,543	$34,369,735	$41,768,022
Oregon	1,523	32,122,051	41,432,174
Montana	289	4,293,794	5,507,573
Idaho	140	1,048,916	1,396,096
TOTALS	3,495	$71,834,496	$90,103,865

As we might expect, lumber mills (lumbering is discussed separately in this chapter) were far out ahead in the list of industrial establishments. In Washington there were operating, in 1890, no less than 501 sawmills (roughly a third of the total number of establishments in Washington) and various types of factories producing timber products. In Oregon there were 340 such enterprises; whereas in Idaho there were only 44, and in Montana, 30. Oregon with 86 gristmills clearly monopolized the cereal manufacturing field. Prevalent in all of the Northwest states were the traditional blacksmith shops, carpentering (as distinguished from milling) shops, masonry, tile making, boot and saddlery establishments; and also men's and women's tailoring houses. And considering the widespread interest in newspapers and other reading materials, it is not surprising to find in Washington 145 printing and publishing firms; in Oregon, 130; in Montana, 41; in Idaho, 27.

No one state appears to have manufactured certain items to the exclusion of its sister states, although for obvious reasons the two coastal states did most of the shipbuilding, just as the two inland commonwealths far outdistanced their maritime neighbors in the production of metals. Iron foundries, woolen mills, malt liquor plants, smelters, sheet-metal factories, and others too numerous to mention dotted the region's industrial landscape in 1890.

Industries then were widespread and by no means confined to the larger towns, although it is to be noted that the three cities having the largest populations — Portland (46,-

[3] Report on Manufacturing Industries in the United States at the Eleventh Census: 1890 (Washington, D. C., 1895). Mining is treated separately in the Census, and also in this chapter.

385), Seattle (42,837), and Tacoma (36,006) — were likewise the leading manufacturing centers. Portland led in the number of establishments with 569. Carpentering, boot- and shoemaking, publishing and printing, custom millinery work, lumbering, millwork, carriage and wagon making, and shipbuilding were but part of the industrial activities then current at Oregon's river metropolis. Tacoma, second to Seattle in population, led her rival in industrial establishments; Tacoma had 570, Seattle, 546. In no special way did these Washington port cities differ from Portland in types of establishments except that Tacoma was alone in having eleven plumbing and gas-fitting establishments. In Portland the capital invested in industries and the total value of its industrial products were, respectively, sixteen and twenty-five millions; whereas the corresponding amounts for Tacoma were seven and ten millions; for Seattle, four and ten millions.

In the Wake of the Gold Rush

Long important to the general industrial growth of the Pacific Northwest is mining (see Chapter XIV). Except in certain sections such as those of southern Oregon and eastern Washington, where mineral deposits proved to be limited and insufficiently rich for continued exploitation, the regions previously designated as mineral frontiers of the 1850s and '60s tended to develop into significant long range mining areas. Notably sustained in gold and silver productivity have been mountain segments of northern Idaho and western Montana. More recent than the gold-rush period of the sixties, the region in and around Butte, Montana, has turned out to be the world's greatest copper-producing center; and the region in and around Kellogg, Idaho, now produces about eighty-five per cent of the region's lead and zinc. The recent search for light and rare metals has once again brought the entire Northwest under the scrutinous eyes of prospectors.

Whatever the general trends may have been, mineral production in 1889 (as recorded in the 1890 Census) was as follows: in gold the Montana production was $3,139,327; Idaho,

$1,984,159. Oregon produced slightly less than a million dollars' worth of gold, and Washington almost ceased to count with its contribution of less than $200,000. In silver production Montana again far outstripped the Gem State of Idaho with a phenomenal production of $17,468,960 as compared with $4,395,959 for Idaho. There was almost no silver production in the two coastal states. Also in 1889, Montana produced nearly a hundred million pounds of copper and a little less than a half-million dollars' worth in lead and zinc, whereas Idaho produced about a hundred and fifty thousand pounds of copper and over one million dollars' worth of zinc and lead.

The total production of these metallic ores is impressive. Since gold was first discovered in the Northwest, roughly a half-billion dollars' worth of it has been extracted within the four named states, and much of the nearly one billion dollars' worth of this precious metal taken out of Alaska and the Klondike since 1895 has been handled within the Northwest. Idaho has led all states in the Union in the production of silver, and Montana has ranked third. And since silver mining in those states has been associated with the extraction of nonferrous metallic ores, silver mining has influenced production of lead and zinc and, to a lesser extent, copper. In the case of copper, of which Montana is a heavy producer, the reverse situation has existed in that much of the silver produced has come directly from the mining of copper.

While some copper is produced in all the Northwest states, the greatest single producer is Montana, with the spotlight on Butte. In 1878, an Irish immigrant named Marcus Daly purchased what he thought was a silver mine for $30,000; it became the Anaconda, the largest and most famous copper mine in the world. In 1881 the Anaconda Silver Mining Company was founded, and this also dates the discovery of a copper seam fifty feet wide. In 1882 the name became the Anaconda Copper Mining Company. Subsequently, a firm known as the Amalgamated Copper Company purchased the mine for $39,000,000 and promptly capitalized it for almost twice this amount. Marcus Daly retained an interest in the company, and with him became associated William A. Clark and Frederick A. Heinz, thereafter known as the "copper kings." Not only did Amalgamated Copper take millions of dollars' worth of ore out of the famed "mile high, a mile deep" hill (or Hell) at Butte, but the company gained a powerful hold upon the political structure of the entire state of Montana. Today the company also operates large smelting plants at Great Falls and Anaconda, Montana.

Butte became known by the cynics as the "Black Heart of Montana"; by the boosters as "the richest hill on earth." It merited both names. By 1884 production was in full swing. Over 5,000 men were at work for Anaconda; the payroll was about $600,000 per month; and production in copper and silver in that year was about $14,000,000. Ten years later these figures were multiplied by four, and by 1900 a quarter of all the copper in the world came out of the bowels of the "Hill." And as for Butte being anything but a model community, Montana's own writers (under sponsorship of the Montana State Department of Agriculture, Labor and Industry) have this to say:

Small wonder that Butte grew overnight and that she developed some rare characteristics. . . . Few were "family men" in those days. Home was where the single man hung his hat. Fights were numerous. The city jail was never without occupants. The black wagon of the police roamed the streets night after night looking for customers and business was always good.[4]

Or expressed in local doggerel:

> First came the miners to work in the mine,
> Then came the ladies who lived on the line.

Modern industrial production, especially during World War II, has placed a premium on nonferrous metals, many of which are produced in the Northwest. Most important of these is bauxite, the principal ore from which aluminum is made.

On the whole, ore production in the Northwest, as elsewhere, has been somewhat erratic. Statistics on amounts and values of production show variations from year to year. For

---

4 [Federal Writers' Project], *Copper Camp* (New York, 1943), pp. 20–21.

all its fluctuations, the region continues to be an important mineral producer as indicated in the *Sixteenth Census* . . . : *1940*. Note the following statistical summary on value of total production of the major nonferrous metallic ores:

TOTAL VALUE OF THE PRODUCTION OF NONFERROUS
METALLIC ORES IN PACIFIC NORTHWEST, 1939 [5]

	Gold	Silver	Copper	Lead	Zinc
Oregon	$ 2,839,371				
Washington	1,297,204	$ 2,599,334			
Idaho	3,401,149	6,104,451		$9,198,146	$2,308,171
Montana	7,382,788	1,683,709		339,584	
TOTAL	$14,920,512	$10,387,494	$24,821,722	$9,537,730	$2,308,171

The latest reports available, those for 1947 in the 1950 *World Almanac,* indicate that Idaho still leads in the nation's silver production, with Montana ranking third. In lead production, Idaho is second in the nation. But as for copper, Montana. has yielded leadership to southwestern states and is now in fourth place. Coal, too, is mined in the Northwest, with Washington the leading producer. It was found in Renton in 1852 and production began at Bellingham Bay, and the area has maintained a lead to this day. (For mention of steel and light metals, see next chapter.)

The Fishing Industry

The ocean, Puget Sound, other coastal inlets, and the extensive river systems — these, coupled with a favorable marine environment — have made possible in the Northwest a supply of sea life unexcelled elsewhere in the world. As has been shown previously, seafood sustained numerous Indian tribes. Sea otter first attracted the commercial interests of the Europeans and Americans in the north Pacific waters. And again, fur traders relied to a great extent upon fish to supplement their diet, and upon the fur-bearing animals inhabiting the streams as a source for their pelts.

Salmon has long provided the basis for the Northwest's fishing industry. Since this fish is caught along the entire

[5] Figures for individual states not given; Montana was the biggest producer of copper.

north Pacific watershed (as far south as Monterey, and north to Bering Strait), one is not surprised to find that the salmon-fishing industry has a long and varied history. As a matter of fact, salmon are also found in Asiatic waters, for example, off the Japanese coast, but American runs far exceed those on the opposite Pacific shores. Today Alaska has the greatest salmon reserve and produces sixty per cent of the world salmon pack; but the Columbia River and Puget Sound areas are also heavy producers.

A discussion of salmon necessitates reference to the habits and peculiarities of this fish which never cease to amaze and intrigue the ichthyologists, sportsmen, and even veteran commercial fishermen. Salmon are anadromous; they spend most of their life in the ocean but ascend rivers to spawn. During spring and summer months salmon aged from two to six years, depending upon the variety, come to their fresh-water spawning beds — the places where they were hatched. These salmon birthplaces may be near the ocean, but again they may be, as in the case of the Columbia River, over a thousand miles upstream. In making upstream runs the salmon overcome imposing obstacles such as swift rapids, waterfalls, and more recently such man-made fish ladders and elevators as those at the sixty-five-foot Bonneville Dam.[6] Salmon are at their very best at the time they reach the coast and begin their often difficult swim to spawning grounds. From the standpoint of best commercial operations, these fish should really be caught before they enter fresh water, at which time they stop eating and then gradually become flabby and begin to disintegrate. By the time they finally reach their spawning grounds and have laid their eggs, they have become completely exhausted, and soon thereafter die.[7]

[6] On this point politicians became interested. Supporters of the New Deal administration, which built Bonneville Dam, expressed confidence that the salmon would ascend the ladders; opponents of the New Deal had their doubts. Reports indicate that the salmon made the grade and thereby saved the Democratic Party from disgrace.

[7] The eggs, usually laid in ground beds, hatch in about two months; the young salmon often linger many months in fresh water before taking off for their two-to-three-year ocean cycle.

The species of salmon best known and fished commercially in the Pacific Northwest (including Alaska) number five. They are the Chinook, or King; Sockeye, or Red Salmon; Coho, or Silver; Humpback, or Pink Salmon; and Chum, or Keta. In addition there are steelhead trout, and many other varieties of fresh-water salmon eagerly baited by sportsmen. Of all, the Chinook, or King, are most sought and are most valuable. They are large (often weighing from forty to sixty pounds) and the meat is deep pink and very delicious to those who enjoy eating fish.

As explained previously, salmon constituted an important part of Indian diet, and early British and American fur traders likewise made use of both fresh and processed salmon for local consumption and for export. Development of the canning industry in the United States offered newer and greater opportunities for commercial fishing, which in turn led to the adoption of various contrivances for snaring salmon in commercial quantities. Indians at The Dalles continued with success the use of old-fashioned dip nets and spears. On the lower Columbia, however, American fishermen employed the rather dangerous use of gill nets in midstream and purse seines on the bars. Various types of fish wheels (some stationary, others on scows) and traps were also used.[8] Trolling with hook and line was also a favorite method of salmon fishing.

In any event, the rapid increase in fishing went hand in hand with development of the commercial salmon canning industry which actually began on the Sacramento River, California, in 1864, in a small cannery established by Hapgood, Hume and Company. Two years later this same firm established the first salmon cannery in the Pacific Northwest; the location was at Eagle Cliff on the south side of the Columbia River. At first canning was slow and rather clumsy business. Each tin can needed soldering by hand, and assembly-line methods had not become well-established.

---

[8] Today there are restrictions imposed on fishing methods in behalf of conservation. For a detailed discussion of salmon-fishing methods, see John N. Cobb, *Pacific Salmon Fisheries*, Appendix I to the *Report of the United States Commissioner of Fisheries for 1921* (Washington, 1921).

During this first year in Oregon, the company packed 4,000 cases (forty-eight pounds each); the second year (1867), the pack was 18,000 cases. Thereafter, salmon canning in the Pacific Northwest developed rapidly. By 1880 there were fifty-five canneries in Oregon packing annually one-half million cases valued at about two million dollars. By then canneries had also appeared on Puget Sound and in Alaska. By then, too, salmon had become established as an important food item in a world market which centered first in Australia, next in England, and then, after completion of the Northern Pacific Railroad, in the United States.

Much of the fishing was done by Finns and Scandinavians, but Chinese, Japanese, Filipinos, Mexicans, Negroes, Puerto Ricans, as well as white native Americans, were, and are, employed in this fishing industry. Traditionally, pay has been on a per-fish basis. Most of the work done within the canneries was at first done by Chinese laborers but many of them were displaced early in the present century when salmon canning was revolutionized by the invention of a machine called the "Iron Chink." This device automatically decapitates the fish; removes tails, fins, and entrails; and cuts the meat to order. Other devices developed in the canning industry made possible automatic filling, sealing, steam pressure cooking, and labeling of the cans. Moreover, not all salmon canneries are stationary. Floating canneries exist today, and all the aforementioned processes can be done at or near the fishing grounds.

The rapid expansion of salmon canning was a great boon to industrial growth and expansion of the Pacific Northwest. But even in the 1880s it was realized that the supply of salmon was not limitless and that legislative enactments were necessary to regulate fishing and to insure propagation. Accordingly, federal and state laws have been passed from time to time and interstate agreements made which have provided for the establishment of federal and state fish-and-game commissions, regulation of fishing methods (such as the use of traps, explosives, and drugs); laws passed establishing and providing for the operation of fish hatcheries, and for the gathering of vital statistical data. In addition, international conventions have brought about further controls.

Annoying though many of the regulations have been, they have done much to save the salmon industry from extinction. In more recent years Alaska has become the largest producer. During the year 1940, there were canned in Alaska 5,028,378 cases of salmon; 386,999 on the Columbia River; 121,428 in Puget Sound; 1,445,101 in neighboring British Columbia.[9]

In addition, much of the salmon catch is handled fresh. More recent developments in quick freezing have revolutionized marketing aspects of this industry. Quick-frozen fresh salmon either is or can be made available at all times in every grocery store in which deep-freeze refrigeration is provided. Also available to the consumer is smoked, mild-cured, kippered, pickled, dried, "jerked," and dry-salted salmon; and among the numerous by-products are caviar, meal, oil, eggs, and fertilizer.

Large as this industry has become, and relatively inexpensive as it is to operate the business, one observes that a very large fraction of the total volume is handled by a small number of firms. Consolidations began at the turn of the century and this process continues. Even so, the small operator continues to occupy a marginal position in the industry, and competition is extremely keen. The business is precarious, and failures are frequent.

While salmon overshadows all fish in the Northwest, other species figure in commercial operations. Among them is the whale-like halibut, caught on North Pacific (American and Canadian) banks in the amount of about twenty-five million pounds annually. Cod, not easily distinguished from its more famous New England cousin, is found throughout the North Pacific, especially so off Kodiak Island and in the Bering Sea. Eastern cod processors have, however, controlled the cod business since colonial days and have had no thought of re-

---

9 Earlier comparative figures on production by the case are as follows:

	Alaska	U. S.
1910	2,438,000	3,555,623
1920	4,395,509	5,101,705
1930	6,791,544	7,274,209

linquishing it to west coast upstarts. For this reason, Pacific cod has not enjoyed the popularity accorded Pacific salmon, for which no serious rival exists.

The Columbia River, and areas north, are also bountifully supplied with a small, oily fish called smelt. The smelt run comes early in the year; during this time the rivers and streams are almost choked with these little fishes. They are easily caught, and commercial and noncommercial fishermen (oldsters and youngsters) take part in the annual catch.

More recently, tuna fish, normally caught in waters of southern California, have made an appearance off the Oregon coast and have opened up new possibilities in the fishing industry. Sharks are also caught off the Oregon coast. Shark meat is edible, but at present the livers of this man-eating fish have a premium value in the preparation of vitamin products.

Some varieties of oysters are native to the Northwest and best among them is the tiny Olympic. Artificial transplantation of a large variety of Japanese oysters (*Ostreagigas*) was begun in 1905. In the form of tiny "seeds" they were planted in Puget Sound waters where growth was at first slow and where the oyster at first failed to reproduce. Then in 1928 began considerable expansion due to greatly increased "seed" production in Japan at prices much lower than had been the case earlier. Willapa Bay became an area of extensive development of this business, and a new and highly acceptable item (worth about one million dollars annually) was added to the list of Northwest-produced shellfish which also includes clam and shrimp.

No attempt is made here to name all the commercially exploited species of aquatic life found in Northwest waters such as cod, flounder, and sole; the list runs into the hundreds. Over one hundred and fifty varieties, more or less, are consumed, and these include reptiles and mammals. Altogether, Washington, Oregon, and Alaska produce about forty per cent of all fish and by-products of fish marketed in the United States and her possessions. Moreover, nearly one-half of the net tonnage of the nation's fishing fleet operates in the North Pacific. Figures for 1945 (the latest available) indicate that in this final year of the war the Pacific Northwest states operated more fishing vessels (2,142), had more active, commercial fishermen (34,028), processed more fish (1,428,278 pounds), valued at more dollars ($62,694,-000) than any other section of the United States, including Alaska and New England

Timber-r-r

Today the Pacific Northwest possesses more than one-third of the board feet of standing timber in the United States. More than half of all the acreage in this entire region is classified officially as forest area. This does not mean that all of this timber (most of which is soft wood) could now, or in the foreseeable future, be sawed into lumber for commercial use. Much of it in the higher altitudes will never attain an adequate size; much of it is growing on remote, inaccessibly high mountainsides beyond the reach of the woodsman's axe, and beyond the ends of truck roads and railroads over which such timber could be hauled to mills. Even so, forty-six million acres out of approximately fifty-three million acres of timber in the Pacific Northwest are labeled as commercial forests, suitable for being cut into lumber, or used for woodpulp, fuel, pilings, or for the manufacture of furniture, plastics, clothing, and multitudinous other products. The forests, commercial and noncommercial, moreover, are of value in flood and erosion control and for recreational purposes.

The species existing in greatest quantities are Douglas fir, west of the Cascades; ponderosa (yellow) pine and western white pine, east of the Cascades. Immediately before the outbreak of World War II, these forests made possible an industry which employed directly about 120,000 persons, additional tens of thousands indirectly, and annually produced about five hundred million dollars' worth of wood products of all description. Not all facts are available relative to the role played by the forests in the late war, but during 1943, a near-peak-production year, the lumber output of the three northwest states was eleven and three-fourths billion board feet, enough to build a five-foot board sidewalk fifteen times around the world at the Equator. It is amazing to observe that by 1947, a year when many expected a post-war slump, the high level of 1943 was maintained almost exactly.[10]

Back of this colossal enterprise lies a long history closely interwoven with the economic, political, and social life of the inhabitants. The forests provided hunting grounds for Indians, as well as materials for weapons, foods, medicines, canoes, and dwellings. Wild forest life provided pelts and partial subsistence for fur hunters. Fur traders and pioneer farmers alike used logs for their first dwellings, although to many of the first settlers trees were regarded as obstacles to be cleared away in preparation for tilling of the soil. It is recalled (see Chapter V) that Chief Factor John McLough-lin of the Hudson's Bay Company built and operated the first sawmill in the old Oregon country; that from this mill on the Columbia above Fort Vancouver lumber was sawed for both domestic use and for export. Thereafter, other small mills, privately owned and operated, began to emerge at several places, especially on the Puget Sound coastline and along the Willamette River and its tributaries where settle-ments were most numerous and where there was easy access to water transportation. Cutting timbers for pilings, and for masts and spars so essential to the windjammers which plied the northern waters in early days, was also done so close to river banks and shores that logs could be slid directly into the water by means of flumes.

A group of early pioneers, including Michael T. Simmons, Jesse Ferguson, Frank Shaw, Edmund Sylvester, and others, organized in the Olympia area the Puget Sound Milling Company, and in 1847 established a sawmill at Tumwater, the first north of the Columbia River. Names still remem-bered in the Seattle vicinity of some of those connected with pioneer lumbering are: Henry L. Yesler, Dexter Horton, Captain William Renton, A. A. Denny, George A. Meigs.

[10] The output for each state in 1943 was as follows: Oregon, 6,501,424,-000; Washington, 4,490,088,000; Idaho, 889,748,000 board feet. The output for 1947 was: Oregon, 7,102,410; Washington, 3,705,401; Idaho, 950,791 board feet.

Common as log cabins were in Old Oregon, settlers early made the transition from these simple, crude dwellings to homes and business structures built with lumber. With the coming of sawmills, slabs were used in road construction. Plank roads, as previously noted, early revolutionized transportation. By the 1890s the Pacific Northwest, always conscious of its great stands of timber, began to promote large-scale forest exploitation as a means of stepping up industrial activity. Early settlers in the area had shown no inclination to conserve this resource. At the close of the century the attitude appears to have been: Why conserve? Does not the Pacific Northwest possess five times the total amount of timber found in the United States east of the Rocky Mountains? The Portland *Oregonian's Handbook,* published in 1894, set the tone for that day: "Nowhere else in the world are forests which compare, in extent and in the quantity of valuable timber contained, with the vast timber reserves of the Pacific Northwest." The value placed upon this natural wealth was seven-hundred million dollars. And in answer to those who might have urged caution, the *Handbook* boldly said: "Many generations will yet come and pass away before the mighty forests here are felled to the ground. It is not unreasonable to hope that the forests of the Pacific Northwest will in the near future be the chief source of supply of the world for lumber."

National post-Civil War legislation did much to facilitate the kind of aggressive exploitation favored by those who either viewed the forests as limitless or who worried little about the distant future. In general, the federal and state governments, by far the largest proprietors of the region's forests, pursued liberal policies in the transfer of forest-land use and ownership into private hands. Among federal legislative enactments so contributing were the Swamp Land Act of 1850, the Homestead Act of 1862, the Timber Culture Act of 1873, numerous land grants to railroad companies and public schools, and the liquidation of Indian titles. By and large, the first beneficiaries of such transfers were large companies and resourceful individuals engaged in large-scale timber and milling operations. To them the timber resources of the Pacific Northwest looked especially tempting, and pincer-like raids occurred from northern California by numerous concerns operating there; from the north-central Middle West, chiefly by the Weyerhaeuser interests; and from the deep South, especially the Long Bell Lumber Company.

In all parts of the country, men, or families, rose to great wealth and prominence as possessors and exploiters of enormous tracts of forest lands, but overshadowing all in the Pacific Northwest, if not in the whole United States, and cited here as an example, is the Weyerhaeuser family. The founding father of this dynasty was Frederick Weyerhaeuser, who first operated in Wisconsin and Minnesota during the post-Civil War years. Though shunning public notoriety, Frederick Weyerhaeuser's companies at one time dominated the lumber business in at least six states. For all his activities in the world of forests and finances, Weyerhaeuser found time to raise to his liking seven timber-minded children who contributed much to the expansion of the family activities into the Pacific Northwest, where their holdings in the form of standing timber, sawmills, and lumber by-products industries are presently dominant. Writes Professor Richard G. Lillard: "For three generations and more the family has been as consistent in its way as the Boston Lowells in theirs. Today over ninety corporations are affiliated in the Weyerhaeuser's decentralized lumber empire." But, regardless of what private source acquired control, relinquishment by the federal government of forest-land controls tended to open the door to wholesale spoliation.

It was not long before public reaction to such practices arose, and the federal government, by passage of restraining legislation, took steps to check the wanton engrossing and exploitation of the remaining national forests. Government efforts, however, proved to be feeble. One act imposed a "stumpage fee," in the form of a $2.50 charge for each thousand feet of lumber cut on public land. In 1878 the Timber and Stone Act was passed whereby timberland unfit for farming could be sold to private citizens at $2.50 per acre (thus making such lands more difficult to acquire than under the much-abused Homestead Act) and making it unlawful to cut timber on government property. This failed to halt spoliation, because large private timber interests proceeded to purchase great holdings.

The national conservation program augmented by President Theodore Roosevelt checked this process to some extent. Muckrakers of the "Square Deal" era made the country aware of wasteful practices of lumber barons, and as recently as 1927 the late Professor Robert C. Clark made the following admonishment regarding the situation in his own state of Oregon: "The lumber industry is one of Oregon's greatest and most valuable resources; but this resource will become, unless our methods radically change, a vanishing one, a wasted and waning asset which if the destructive exploitation goes on unchecked, will lead to serious changes in our environment and economic life in general."

At present only one-half of the commercial forest lands in the Pacific Northwest remain a possession of the federal government; the remainder are owned by state, county, and private citizens.[11] In many instances, however, ownership, because of tax delinquency and other factors, is not too clear. To quote Stephen N. Wyckoff, Director (1942), Pacific Northwest Forest and Range Station: "This condition of mixed ownership, with the attendant impossibility of effective management and protection, constitutes one of the serious impediments to the orderly use of forest lands of the Pacific Northwest for continued production of forest products." Concentration of lumber-mill and private forest ownership into the hands of relatively few individuals and concerns was the logical outcome of the foregoing processes. Ownership by the "barons," as they have been called, did not halt the ruthless and wasteful methods of timber utilization begun by pioneer settlers. Until the turn of the century, and in some cases continuing to the present time, great

---

[11] According to *American Forests*, official journal of the American Forestry Association, September, 1946, p. 416, the acres as classified are: National forests, 17,341,000; other federal, 2,856,000; Indian forests, 2,815,-000; state and county, 3,435,000; farm woodlands, 3,334,000; industrial and other, 16,423,000.

mountainsides were stripped of their timber stands, along with which went root mats essential to flood control.

Quite apart from the social question of timber ownership and production wastes is the record of enormous lumber productivity in the Northwest. Such centers as Tacoma, Seattle, and Portland owe much of their economic growth to the lumber industry. Roughly one-half the men employed in Tacoma are engaged in wood-processing industries. Tacoma is the center for the manufacture of shingles, plywood, and veneer, sash and doors, matches, furniture, and wood novelties. The making of plywood has become an important adjunct of the lumber industry. The first plywood plant was built at St. Johns, Oregon, in 1905. Then during World War I the manufacture of plywood received its first significant boost; during World War II annual production exceeded one and a half million square feet from widely distributed plants such as those at Bellingham, Anacortes, Everett, Seattle, Longview, and Olympia, Washington; Albany, Lebanon, Springfield, and Coquille, Oregon. The Pacific Northwest is one of the leading pulp and paper areas in the United States. It possesses thirty or more mills engaged in the manufacture of sulphite pulp out of the coastal region's hemlock, Sitka spruce, balsam, Douglas fir, and black cottonwood. From this product comes much of the nation's newsprint, high-quality paper, rayon, and the now endless array of cellulose goods.

Complete data on logging and lumbering are not readily available. Many of the hundreds of small, individual operators who log and cut timber at their tiny mills, and who cut and sell cord wood and the like give no accurate accounting of themselves. Logging and lumbering industries valued at or in excess of $5,000 have provided the census taker with figures which for 1939 (a year which felt the first demands of war, but before full production was reached) are given on the following page.

Some indication of the relative importance of the lumbering industry is indicated by the fact that in 1939 no less than forty per cent of the value of all products shipped out of the

Northwest was represented by forest products. Then with America's entry into the war, wartime production required indiscriminate cutting. Mature and immature trees alike were felled; the finest, along with the poorer, grades of timber were sawed for crating the war machines that were shipped overseas. Newer and improved devices and methods, such as mechanically felling trees, and the "skyline" or overhead system of conveying logs across ravines to truck-

LOGGING AND LUMBERING DATA ON INDUSTRIES VALUED AT OR IN EXCESS OF $5,000 FOR THE YEAR 1939 [12]

	No. of Logging Outfits	No. of Sawmills	Value of Logging	Value of Sawmills
Oregon	239	429	$23,363,038	$108,663,140
Washington	231	419	16,322,586	123,604,988
Idaho	11	11	1,298,030	21,062,468
Montana	11	53	914,453	6,429,983
TOTAL			$41,898,107	$259,760,579

Combined Value = $300,658,786

ing routes, were widely substituted for flumes and skidroads characteristic of early-day lumber-camp operations. Forests that were formerly believed beyond the reach of woodsmen were therefore consumed in the great war effort. Meanwhile, fires continued to take their annual toll of trees. Simultaneously, improved methods at mills were devised for expediting sawing and shipping of lumber. Electrical power has been applied more extensively to the entire industry. The Weyerhaeuser mill at Klamath Falls, Oregon, is, for example, an all-electric plant. Movable cranes with ever-increasing reaching and lifting capacity are being employed while the latest-model straddle bugs flit speedily to and fro with their loads of freshly processed stacks of aromatic lumber.

In wartime the forests are expendable, and the result is a renewed threat of depletion of the forests of the Northwest. The social effects of this process are also apparent. No less than seventy-six towns that once relied upon lumber for their

[12] Sixteenth Census of the United States: 1940. Manufactures: 1939 (Washington, D. C., 1942), Vol. III, passim.

existence have now completely disappeared; in other cut-over areas, populations have declined; and such large and presently significant areas as those of Grays Harbor, Aberdeen, South Bend, Longview, and Sweet Home are threatened. The idea of maintaining a sustained yield of timber is old; it has for generations past been a system known to Europeans. Not, however, until World War I did at least some northwesterners look with favor upon the adoption of a system whereby there could be continuous cutting at a rate equal to the rate of tree maturity. Writing in the University of Oregon's *Commonwealth Review* in 1918, Burt P. Kirkland called attention to additional factors relative to unrestricted cutting. An unhealthy social situation was one such factor. Ninety per cent of lumber camps were, he said, "womanless, voteless, and jobless." The annual turnover in lumber camps was then about six hundred per cent. Kirkland argued that as long as the industry was interested only in destroying the forests there would be no stable labor. He therefore proposed a program which would: (1) require forest land to be reforested to at least seventy-five per cent following cutting; (2) protect young growth; (3) place ownership in economical hands; (4) strive for a continuous yield.

The present problem is, therefore, how best to restore forests for future peaceful usage and for future national defense. Ideas on this differ, but in a stimulating article in *Harper's Magazine* (August, 1945), Roy A. H. Thompson, a veteran timber expert, makes a positive suggestion. He advises private commercial, as well as government, reforestation in cut-over or damaged areas. Tree farming can be done on a profitable basis, although in the case of private operations some government assistance will be needed to facilitate this process. He proposes continued ownership by federal, state, and local government of existing public forests, and that additional lands should be acquired and administered by the three governmental agencies. Cutting should be carefully regulated to prevent waste in order to stabilize tree population and the milling industry. The program thus proposed is enormous in scope. In addition to the foregoing suggestions, it calls for extensive road and fire-trail building, for additional telephone and radio communications, establishment of air fields for patrol operations, and the utilization of trained personnel to replant and regulate this vitally important commodity. The lumber industry program is now: "Stay and grow"; not "Cut out and go."

The Spread of Industry

Those living in close proximity to the ocean and its large rivers flowing into the Pacific have, as in the case of fishing, exhibited a lusty seagoing spirit not unlike their New England forebears. And in the realm of industry, northwesterners have also shown from the start an interest in, and a capacity for, the building of ships. During World War I, and again during World War II, shipbuilding reached the proportions of a leading war industry. And in the shipyards of Henry J. Kaiser, the West's most prominent and successful industrialist, the Northwest established an enviable record of achievement during the recent conflict. Other important industries of long standing are those based directly or indirectly upon agriculture. Manufacturing establishments include textile mills, principally woolen but some flax; sugar-beet factories; fruit and vegetable canneries; dairy plants, manufacturing especially butter, cheese, and ice cream; plants which manufacture preserves; and flour mills. Newspaper publishing and printing, as in 1890, are still important businesses. More recent, but nonetheless thriving, additions to this group are establishments in which are processed the quick-frozen foods, malt liquors, and dog-food products made largely from wild horse meat. Out of the list the dairy industry is preeminently important, with an annual output of about $75,-000,000. And looming on the industrial horizon is the sheet-glass industry, so long concentrated in the East. Surveys point to an ever-widening range of manufacturing in this still youthful economy.

Most spectacular has been the advance made in manufactures in Washington and Oregon during the boom decade of the 1940s. Contributing in no small way to an increased outlet for local manufactures has been the rapid rise in the

GENERATING HYDROELECTRICITY

The Bonneville Dam and Bonneville Dam generator room

Courtesy U. S. Dept. of the Interior. Bonneville Power Administration, Portland, Oregon

Courtesy Boeing Airplane Company

WASHINGTON-BUILT AIRPLANES FLY AROUND THE WORLD

Stratocruisers and B-50 bombers are in production in this Boeing Airplane Factory at Seattle in November, 1947.

region's population resulting largely from wartime immigration. Using figures for 1940 and those for 1947 (latest available), one observes some of these increases as indicated below (Ohio was used as a basis of comparison with an industrial Middlewestern state):

MANUFACTURING STATISTICS COMPARED

	No. of Estab. 1940	No. of Estab. 1947	Wage Earners 1940	Wage Earners 1947	Value of Mfg. 1940	Value of Mfg. 1947
Wash.	3,240	3,412	90,324	144,305	$ 286,647,263	$ 874,072,000
Oregon	2,248	3,075	63,622	105,591	172,174,744	675,817,000
Idaho	549	664	10,877	16,907	31,770,204	109,694,000
Mont.	585	652	9,171	16,092	39,790,182	92,258,000
Ohio	10,070	12,303	598,397	1,194,603	2,125,474,003	6,359,006,000

Gateway to the Pacific

Normal trade channels were so badly disrupted by the war that one must return to the decade of the thirties for any worthwhile analysis of this phase of the economic life. In 1939 both wholesale and retail trade had recovered considerably from the depression low. In that year in Oregon, Washington, and Idaho, no less than 172,000 men and women were employed in wholesale and retail operations, whereas sales in each of the two categories were roughly one and one-third billion dollars. During the war, sales reached all-time highs with stores maintaining their inventory positions only with extreme difficulty.

With two northwest states facing the Pacific Ocean, coastwise and transoceanic trade has since the earliest days been of importance. The Pacific coast, as stated at the outset, is not blessed with many good harbors, but of the few it has, those of Seattle, Tacoma, and Portland are among the world's leading ports. Until the turn of the present century San Francisco enjoyed an envied position, not only as the metropolis of the Northwest, but as the main port of trade with the Far East. Construction of transcontinental railroad lines into the Northwest, establishment of oceanic steamship lines, and improvement of port facilities gradually enabled the Northwest to overcome its commercial dependence upon the city by the Golden Gate. By capitalizing upon their closer proximity to the Far East, Seattle, Tacoma, and Portland also earned the right to be called Gateways to the Orient. Ocean liners plying the Great Circle Route and connecting with transcontinental railroad lines, and in turn with trans-Atlantic lines, established the northwest port cities as vital transshipment points on what were the shortest lines of transit between such Far Eastern trading centers as Yokohama, Osaka, Shanghai, and Vladivostok on the one side of the world; New York, London, and places on the continent of Europe on the other side.[13]

The Northwest, moreover, has shared in the commerce with Canada; and ever since the Klondike Gold Rush, Seattle has been the chief outfitting place for Alaskan operations. The latter now include handling of the huge annual Alaskan fishing pack, shipment of mining and agricultural equipment and supplies, servicing of military establishments, and conducting an ever-increasing tourist business in this sprawling northern territory. In fact, Alaska is to a large extent an economic appendage of Washington and Oregon.

Back in the heyday of peacetime oceanborne commerce, the Pacific coast, with four per cent of the nation's harbors, handled twenty-seven per cent of the goods moved in ocean transport. Los Angeles and San Francisco were both far out in the lead, but in 1929 the Port of Seattle handled 445,000 tons of imports and 718,000 tons of exports; Tacoma, 391,000 and 667,000, respectively; and Portland, 109,000 and 1,377,-000 tons of the respective categories. Portland's huge export total is largely accounted for by her pre-eminent position as a wheat export center. Washington exports in prewar years were chiefly fish, processed dairy products, wheat, lumber, fresh fruits, and motor cars; her chief imports, coffee, silk, paper, and copper. Oregon exported chiefly wheat, as stated, fresh fruits, and wood and wood manufactures, while her imports were principally sugar, copper, vegetable oils, jute, iron, steel, and paper.

During World War II, northwest ports were extremely

[13] Important as the "Gateway" concept is, writers on the Northwest have overstressed it.

important; Seattle as an important embarkation point; Portland as a chief port for Russian lend-lease. The latest figures available for 1947 show Seattle has taken second place to Portland in tonnage carried through their respective harbors. These figures show that Tacoma ranks a weak third, Everett fourth, and Coos Bay, Oregon, a close fifth.[14] Important and growing shipping points are Olympia, Bellingham, Port Angeles, Washington, and St. Helens, Oregon.

Large and important as Northwest trade is, a close analysis reveals that the region continues, as in early days, to survive on its capital resources which to a large degree are being marketed locally and exported in either raw or processed conditions in order to provide incomes. In other words, there is a dependence upon the exchange of such native raw resources as forest, agriculture, and mines for needed manufactures produced in other regions. Prewar figures showed that agriculture and the forests constituted about ninety-five per cent of the region's exports; manufactured goods represented eighty per cent of its imports. As the region's Planning Commission has revealed, the economy needs more diversification inasmuch as the forests, the arable land, and the minerals are not inexhaustible. The boost given manufacturing by the development of hydroelectricity on a large scale and by the recent war has done much to produce local industries to offset the exhilarated rate of forest depletion.

The Tourist Business

California is the tourist capital of the West. Los Angeles lives and thrives to a large extent upon the influx of its thousands upon thousands of visitors. California tourist agencies have been known to suggest that among the interesting sights to see while in the Golden State is Crater Lake, the scenic pearl of Oregon. Fortunately, many of these tourists also find time to swing through Oregon, Washington, Idaho,

---

[14] The harbor tonnage figures for 1947 are as follows: Portland, 11,591,-262; Seattle, 10,627,198; Tacoma, 4,464,370; Everett, 3,754,118; Coos Bay, 3,178,316. See *The World Almanac and Book of Facts for 1950* (New York, 1950), pp. 641–42.

as well as British Columbia, while on their western tour, and the Californians rank first as to number of Northwest visitors. Approximately one-third of the region's guests come from the State of California. A special tourist survey for the State of Washington for 1949 reveals, as indicated on the following

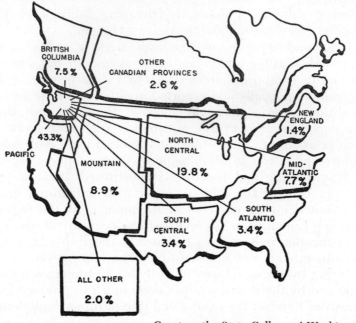

Courtesy the State College of Washington

ORIGIN OF TOURISTS IN WASHINGTON, 1949

chart, the respective regional contributions to this state's two million visitors and its $123,200,000 tourist business for this one year.[15]

Among important tourist attractions is, as mentioned, Crater Lake in southern Oregon. Embedded as it is one thousand feet below the rim of an old volcanic crater (Mount Mazama), its deep, usually placid waters are of a magnificent, unmatched dark-blue color. Also interesting to tourists

[15] Donald Greenaway and Robert F. Lanzillotti, *The Washington Tourist Survey: 1949* (Pullman, 1950). This survey was made under the auspices of the School of Economics and Business, The State College of Washington.

in southern Oregon are the Oregon Caves which, though not as gigantic as those at Carlsbad in New Mexico, exhibit many fascinating feats of nature, among them colorful stalagmite and stalactite column formations. Southern Oregon, and especially wild Rogue River, is one of the region's most popular fishing spots. Snowcapped peaks, among them the Three Sisters, Mount Hood, Mount St. Helens, Mount Rainier (altitude 14,408 feet, and the second highest in the United States), and Mount Baker are strung along the summit of the Cascades and provide the proper settings for recreational resorts. The coastal Roosevelt Highway, the Columbia River Highway, the Olympic Peninsula, Crater of the Moon, Dry Falls of the Columbia, Sun Valley, myriads of lakes (especially Chelan, Pend Oreille,[16] Crescent, Coeur d'Alene, and, as mentioned, Crater), hundreds of streams well-stocked with trout, and lately the man-made Grand Coulee and Bonneville dams, are among the attractions around which the lucrative tourist business has developed. In addition to all these, Portland has made a commercial success of its annual Rose Festival, while Seattle has done likewise with its Potlatch, Pendleton with its roundup, and Eugene with its period pageant.

In view of these overall industrial and business developments, the Pacific Northwest looks with some pride to its past record. But both in the fields of industry and commerce it has suffered from what might be termed economic colonialism. It has not as yet been able to cut itself completely loose from controls exercised by eastern financial and industrial institutions. Until this umbilical cord has been severed, many are of the opinion that a full-scale development of the regional resources belongs to the indefinite future.

16 This is the modern spelling for Lake Pend d'Orcille.

Chapter XXI

Hydroelectricity

Private Enterprise

THE PACIFIC NORTHWEST is hydroelectric-minded. Giant hydroelectric power projects built and being built by the United States government, often overshadowing private projects in this field, have contributed to public awareness as to what goes on in this important field of activity. Forgotten or unknown to many is the pioneering role assumed by private enterprise. The first ventures in the field of hydroelectric development in the Pacific Northwest were made through private initiative and with private capital. It should also be recognized that hydroelectrical development is not an afterthought to the people of the Northwest. The region's record of activity in the field of commercial power production is one closely identified with the very earliest experiments in this field in America.

One recalls that it was in 1879 an astounded world learned that Thomas A. Edison had manufactured the first incandescent lamp for commercial use. This very same year also marks the beginning of the electrical industry in the Pacific Northwest. In Portland in that year a circuit of exposed copper wire was strung from the engine room of the steamer *State of California* to an arc light hung at a city street intersection. With electrical power generated by this ship's Brush arc-light dynamo the street corner was illuminated, to the delight and amazement of Portland's 20,000 inhabitants. Then during July of 1880 Portland was given a second opportunity to view this improved form of lighting aboard Henry Villard's steamer *Columbia,* which was equipped with four sixty-lamp Edison dynamos. The city was again impressed and pleased, and it had not long to wait for the first commercial installation of electrical lighting. During September, 1880, George W. Weidler installed a dynamo for arc lighting in his sawmill and a couple of years later the Ainsworth Dock was lighted electrically. And on the occasion of celebrating the completion of the Northern Pacific Railroad in 1883 there came from Villard the announcement that surveys showed that hydroelectrical power on a quantity basis could be produced from the Willamette Falls. These events provided the backdrop to corporate enterprises formed to harness this wizard-like power and distribute it to the public on a commercially profitable basis.

The Portland General Electric Company, a private power concern which now serves Portland and much of the lower Willamette Valley, claims for its original ancestor Portland's first electric company, called the United States Electric Lighting and Power Company. Its first president was P. F. Morey, and other founders included Fred V. Holman, of future prominence. Morey had come earlier to Portland from San Francisco to install and operate a hydraulic elevator plant in which structure the new electric company's equipment was first installed. In 1885 operations were begun in the form of street lighting service. Under Morey's leadership, expansion came fast. He was one of the first to envisage the use of the Willamette Falls at Oregon City in generating power for Portland, fourteen miles distant. With this end in view Morey, in 1888, helped to form a second organization which was called The Willamette Falls Electric Company. The latter began at once to build a power house, or as it was then called, a "dynamo house," on the east side of the Falls. In this structure was placed some of the equipment first used in the hydraulic elevator plant in Portland, and on June 3, 1889, the lights in a street circuit in Portland were illuminated with direct hydroelectric current generated at the Falls at Oregon City. The company now contends that, as far as is known, this long-distance transmission of electricity was the first of its kind in the entire United States.

Success was instantaneous; the next day, June 4, the Portland *Oregonian* made the following comment:

The Willamette Falls Electric Company started up one of their Brush arc dynamos last evening, and the electricity was sent from Oregon City for lighting one of their 10:00 o'clock circuits in this city. It worked magnificently and conclusively demonstrated the fact that our city can be lighted successfully from the Falls. The result was a pleasing surprise to the company, the percentage of loss of electricity by transmission being much less than their most sanguine expectations. The work of removing the machinery from the station here to the Falls will be carried on as expeditiously as possible. Another large dynamo will be moved up today.

Follow-up activities took the form of increasing the load capacity by installation of new generators, adding new and more lighting equipment to Portland's streets. Then, about 1890, the transmission of alternating, as well as direct, current was introduced. Meanwhile, Oregon City had witnessed the formation of a small company which proceeded to establish a generating plant on the west side of the Willamette Falls for local consumption. Again, through the influence of Morey, a merger of the two Oregon City power concerns with the ship and lock company at the Falls was brought about. The merger was incorporated in 1892 as the Portland General Electric Company. Since that date the company has been variously known as the Portland Railway Light and Power Company, Portland Electric Power Company, the Pacific Northwest Public Service Company, and now again (as in the beginning) it is the Portland General Electric Company. As this privately owned power company looks back upon its own history, certain milestones stand out. There are: the supplying of power for the Lewis and Clark Centennial Exposition in 1905; World War I, which gave marked impetus to expansion; completion of the Bonneville Dam in 1939, which brought about a contract with the Bonneville Power Administration for the privilege of distributing electricity generated at the federal dams; and then the almost simultaneous outbreak of World War II, which called for maximum production. Today the Portland General Electric system serves 2,300 square miles of rural and urban territory in the heart of the Willamette Valley. The company now asserts that it serves forty-four cities and towns; in all, 191,000 homes, farms, and industries. Most of the power distributed by this concern is now purchased from the Bonneville Power Administration.[1]

The Puget Sound area experienced an electrical power history not unlike that of the Portland area. Actually, the first user of electric power for industrial purposes is believed to have been the Tacoma Mill Company, which in 1882 installed a fire-generated dynamo for illuminating the mill and lumber yard. The next year a Port Blakely sawmill concern on Bainbridge Island installed a similar unit. Seattle's electric illumination began with the organization of The Seattle Electric Lighting Company in 1885. This concern had secured a franchise from the city of Seattle "to erect poles and stretch wires for electrical purposes." Under the direction of its president, George D. Hill, the concern proceeded to fulfill its obligations by building a power plant near the foot of Jackson Street, and on March 22, 1886, lights from the "wires" were turned on. To the amazement of a reporter for the Seattle *Post-Intelligencer*, who, on this occasion, was at the power plant: ". . . when the dynamo was started, instantly the room was made brilliant with a clear white light." The Seattle Electric Lighting Company also became the first to install Edison incandescent lighting, with central station service.

At the present time the leading private power utility in western Washington, one rivaling the Portland General Electric Company, is the Puget Sound Power and Light — whose first progenitor was the Seattle Electric Lighting Company. The latter had battled its early years through much cutthroat competition. Largely through the influence of Stone and Webster, an eastern engineering concern, a merger of several firms into one was brought about in 1899. And to this consolidation was given the name Seattle Electric Company. During the first decade of this century the Stone and Webster interests began to invest heavily in hydroelectric powerplant development. Their first dam and plant was completed

---

[1] For the fiscal year ending June 30, 1948, the Bonneville Power Administration delivered 1,034,997,308 kilowatt hours to this concern, roughly one-tenth of Bonneville's total sales.

at Electron on the Puyallup River in 1904. Known as the Puget Sound Power Company, it was operated as a subsidiary to the Seattle Electric. Successful as the Seattle Electric was in serving the city of Seattle, severe competition arose from a Chicago concern called the Snoqualmie Falls Power Company, which constructed and operated a hydroelectric plant at the Falls which name it bore. Meanwhile the city of Seattle became interested in municipal power development, constructed a plant at Cedar Falls in 1905, and proceeded to take over its own street lighting. Seattle offered direct competitive service to individual private users within the municipality.

The second decade, however, opened new outlets for the Seattle Electric Company, and in 1912 a consolidation resulted in another change of name to Puget Sound Traction, Light, and Power Company. The word "traction" suggests one of the most profitable outlets for power development during the early years of this century. It took the form of establishing electrically powered interurban railroad service between Seattle and such neighbors as Tacoma, Everett, Mount Vernon, and Bellingham. After 1910, decline in the traction business set in, and by 1920 the automobile had made it a thing of the past.

To meet this decline, Puget Sound Power and Light (dropping "Traction" from its name) expanded into interurban and even rural power service. To meet these new demands, additional and more widely scattered dam and plant developments were made during and after the twenties. So extensively did the Company spread itself that at present it has no less than five separate operating divisions. Its service reaches out to such places as Whidbey Island, Clear Lake, Acme, Anacortes, Rockport, Grays Harbor, and east of the Cascades into Ellensburg and Wenatchee. One of the company's latest projects is the Rock Island Power Plant, located on the Columbia River just twelve miles below Wenatchee. This privately owned power dam is 3,800 feet long and has an average height of 162 feet. In so expanding, the Puget Sound Power and Light Company has continued to acquire many small western and central Washington power plants. The company justifies this consolidation and expansion on the theory that the bigger the system is, the better the service will be and the lower the cost will be to consumers. The company has, says its own spokesman: ". . . rebuilt the distribution system in nearly every community served, standardizing poles and construction, increasing copper and providing voltage regulation." At present, 4,100 square miles of area are served by Puget Sound Power and Light.

The Company now faces a critical problem in trying to compete with the public-owned Bonneville Power Administration. Against this agency, Frank McLaughlin, president of the Puget Sound Power and Light, is waging a bitter, last-ditch fight. Even so, steps have already been taken to sell these extensive holdings to public-utility districts tied in with Bonneville. A portion was so disposed of in Snohomish County in 1949, and similar steps are being taken in the Seattle-Tacoma areas. "The early demise" of this $135,000,000 system was forecast by the *New York Times*, March 12, 1950; it was viewed as an inevitable and "best solution" in face of public power competition.

Electric service in eastern Washington began in 1885 when the enterprising George A. Fitch of Spokane purchased a small dynamo that had been used by the steamer *Columbia*. The dynamo was delivered to Spokane Falls and there installed in the basement of a flour mill owned by Fitch. Then, upon securing a franchise to distribute power to the city of Spokane, Fitch's public service began in the form of operating twelve arc lamps on the city streets. The next year, 1886, some Spokane businessmen pooled their resources and formed what became known as the Spokane Falls Water Power Company and proceeded to purchase Fitch's plant and to lease the site for water power. From this small beginning emerged the Washington Power Company, which eventually built additional power plants at Little Falls, Long Lake, Lake Chelan, and other places in the area. During the 1920s the Washington Power Company had become an important power company in the Spokane area and was about to harness the Columbia River at Kettle Falls when federal plans for the Grand Coulee project made the private project unfeasible.

In Idaho the history of electric power development is not unlike that of Washington and Oregon. In 1887 the Gem state saw its first electric works, a plant established near Boise. Two fifteen-kilowatt-capacity generators then lighted Boise's streets, and out of this development emerged, by 1916, the important Idaho Power Company which in 1930 established an eight-plant interconnection for service over a wide area in the state.

In addition to those singled out for discussion from each of the major areas, there are other privately owned utilities such as the Mountain States Power Company, Washington Water Power Company, Idaho Power Company, Montana Power Company, and Pacific Power and Light Company (Astoria). There are others, but suffice it to say, by way of summary, that private companies were the pioneers; they were the ones which gained public acceptance of electricity; they made extensive outlays, carried on experimentation, and took risks. Mortality among private concerns was at first high. Those that survived commanded high and often exorbitant rates for their services to municipalities, private industries, and homes. But quite apart from public criticism of private power companies — and there has been a tremendous amount of it — the fact remains that to them goes much of the credit for doing the groundwork that gave the Pacific Northwest leadership in hydroelectric development.

Private electrical utilities had, and still have, public responsibilities, and in view of this, state legislation has emerged to create departments of public works designed to regulate the power industry. During World War I federal government curtailments were imposed, and during World War II the arm of the federal government again reached out to form a power pool out of both private and public producers in Oregon, Washington, Idaho, and western Montana (the Montana Power Company). Actually, this action paved the way for closer co-operation among producers to make possible more efficient use of power; it also pointed the way to greater future opportunities for private producers in the field of rural, as well as urban, electrification.

Public Ownership: Local and National

Privately owned utilities did not have the field to themselves indefinitely. In the Pacific Northwest, steps were taken early by municipalities to build, own, and operate electrical plants. The two leading Washington municipalities, Seattle and Tacoma, entered the power-producing field very early. Tacoma City Light and Seattle City Light (as noted above) early took over street and home lighting, and now offer power to industry in direct competition with private utilities. The Skagit River developments of Seattle City Light have been on a large scale and have attracted nation-wide attention. The City of Eugene, City of Idaho Falls, City of Bonner Ferry, and City of McMinnville are but a few of the city-owned hydro-, diesel, or steam electric plants in the Northwest.

Impressive as the private and municipal power developments have been, there was room left for the federal government. The program of the United States Bureau of Reclamation, which at first placed its emphasis upon irrigation projects, had a vital interest in hydroelectric power development. In many instances federal dams were constructed as much for power production as for irrigation, flood-control, or river-navigation purposes. For instance, the early plans for the federal Coulee Dam called for development of hydroelectric power to be used in part for giant water-pumping operations at the dam site and for power distribution in the region.

Much of the groundwork for federal government power development in the Columbia River system, therefore, had been laid in the early part of the century, but it took the depression-born National Industrial Recovery Act of 1933 to pave the way for full-dress federal government action. Implementation of this act, so far as the Pacific Northwest was concerned, came about through passage of the Rivers and Harbors Act in 1935, and through much supplementary legislation. These laws have brought about the construction of Bonneville and Grand Coulee dams and such interlocking dams and power projects now generally known as the Columbia Basin Project.[2]

To deal with generation, distribution, and sale of hydroelectric power the federal government has created (apart from reclamation and other phases of the entire Columbia Basin Project) a special management set-up technically called the Bonneville Power Administration. Out of an estimated total repayment obligation representing capital costs of $505,459,180 for the entire Columbia Basin Project, repayment obligations totaling $382,547,068 have been assumed by the Bonneville Power Administration. This investment of public money in power development will be represented at the Grand Coulee Dam by 1951 by fifteen power units (ultimately eighteen). During the war six of these units, plus two smaller ones borrowed from the California Central Valley Project, were turning out power for the war effort.

The Bonneville Power Administration includes also the power plant at Bonneville Dam, located 42 miles upstream from Portland and 140 miles from the mouth of the Columbia River. The concrete dam has an overall length of 1,090 feet, and a height of 170 feet from its lowest foundations, raising the reservoir depth to 72 feet. The power house, located near the lower end of a once well-known landmark, Bradford Island, contains ten huge generators.[3]

Generation of electricity by the Bonneville Power Administration first began at the Bonneville Dam in 1939. In that

[2] Description of the Grand Coulee Dam and the Reclamation features of the project have been included in Chapter XVIII. The principal purpose of the Columbia Basin Project is reclamation, but power, flood control, and improved navigation are important aspects of the enterprise.

[3] Another important feature of the Bonneville Dam Project includes a shiplock which is 76 feet wide and 500 feet long with a vertical lift of 59 feet — the greatest lock lift in the world. And here too are located the fishways (or ladders) discussed in connection with the salmon industry. Two types of fishways have been installed; one is a fishpool ladder, the other is called a fishlock which works very much like a shiplock. And, not least, flood control and improved navigation on the Columbia River have been brought about by the construction of the dam and spillway systems. Ocean-going vessels can now reach The Dalles.

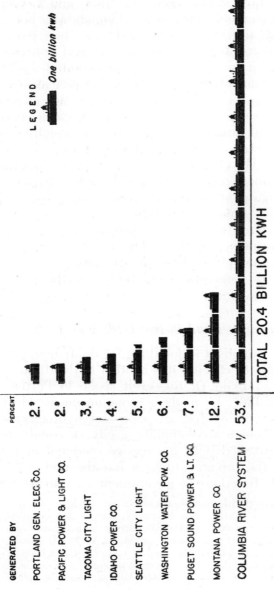

GENERATED BY	PERCENT
PORTLAND GEN. ELEC. CO.	2.⁹
PACIFIC POWER & LIGHT CO.	2.⁹
TACOMA CITY LIGHT	3.⁹
IDAHO POWER CO.	4.⁴
SEATTLE CITY LIGHT	5.⁴
WASHINGTON WATER POW. CO.	6.⁴
PUGET SOUND POWER & LT. CO.	7.⁹
MONTANA POWER CO.	12.⁸
COLUMBIA RIVER SYSTEM 1/	53.⁴

LEGEND

One billion kwh

TOTAL 20.4 BILLION KWH

THE ABOVE UTILITIES ARE MEMBERS OF THE NORTHWEST POWER POOL. UTAH POWER & LIGHT IS ALSO A MEMBER OF THE POOL BUT IS NOT INCLUDED BECAUSE ITS MAJOR SERVICE AREA IS OUTSIDE THE COLUMBIA RIVER BASIN.

1/ BONNEVILLE AND GRAND COULEE POWER PLANTS OPERATED BY THE CORPS OF ENGINEERS AND BUREAU OF RECLAMATION RESPECTIVELY

SOURCE: WEEKLY OPERATING REPORTS OF NORTHWEST POWER POOL.

POWER GENERATED BY THE PRINCIPAL ELECTRIC UTILITIES
YEAR ENDED JUNE 30, 1948

year, 34,874,138 kilowatt hours of power were produced. Two years later, production began at the Grand Coulee Dam and production reached nearly a million kilowatt hours. Then, as more and more dynamos whirled into action, power output was augmented annually; and for the fiscal year ending June 30, 1948, the two plants generated a combined total of 10,885,907,000 kilowatt hours.[4] In order to increase output further during the war, there occurred the above-mentioned hookup to form a giant power pool which made possible a combined output two times that of the Bonneville Power Administration; the overall efficiency of all units was also increased. The chart on the preceding page lists the names of the members of the pool and the kilowatt power which each of them generated in the year ending June 30, 1948. The pool has proved its usefulness and is still being maintained. According to a précis of propaganda issued in 1949 by local business interests: "The Pacific Northwest power pool is an example of how all agencies, public and private, can and do cooperate voluntarily for the public good. . . ."

Power Co-operatives and Public Utility Districts

In many people's minds it is one thing for the federal government to generate electricity; it is another to distribute it. When candidate Franklin D. Roosevelt spoke in Portland on September 21, 1932, he made a pronouncement which foreshadowed the coming federal policy on hydroelectric power. He said: "Where a community, a city, or county, or a district, is not satisfied with the service rendered or the rates charged by the private utility, it has the undeniable right as one of its functions of government . . . to set up

---

[4] The Bonneville Power Administration's official news release, *Currents*, IV (January 18, 1950), 1–2, states that Bonneville Dam is now completed with ten generators which produce 564,000 kilowatts at normal peak capacity; the Coulee Dam has twelve generators producing 1,440,000 kilowatts at normal peak capacity. Combined the total is now 2,004,000 kilowatts. Coulee is scheduled to have the six remaining generators in operation by 1951. These will increase the capacity 720,000 kilowatts and the total to 2,724,000 kilowatts.

. . . its own governmentally owned and operated service."
As the time came when the Coulee and Bonneville dams
neared completion, it was on this original Roosevelt principle that policies were laid down for distribution. The Bonneville Project Act (1937) states: "To preserve and protect the
preferential rights and public bodies and cooperatives . . .
there shall be available for sale to public bodies and cooperatives not less than fifty per centum of the electrical energy
produced at the Bonneville Project. . . ."

As already indicated, the Bonneville Power Administration
has and is delivering power to private utilities for distribution to consumers and to private manufacturing establishments. But as for ways of further implementing the Bonneville Project Act as pertains to "sale to public bodies," there
were at least three avenues opened. One called for delivery
of power wholesale to municipally owned utilities such, for
example, as Seattle City Light, Tacoma City Light, and
Eugene City Light. In the year ending June 30, 1948, the
Bonneville Power Administration sold 647,066,584 kilowatt
hours to municipalities. A second possible outlet was to sell
to co-operatives. During the same fiscal year twenty-three
co-operatives purchased 156,564,291 kilowatt hours. These
organizations were rural in character and were widely
scattered. Among them were the Big Bend Electric Co-
operative, Coos-Curry Electric Co-operative, Inland Empire
Rural Electric Association, and Lane County Electric Co-
operative. The third possibility was to organize rural state-
controlled Public Utility Districts which would also buy
power. To facilitate and encourage the formation of these
public organizations, especially the latter, financial aid was
given by the federally controlled Rural Electrification Administration. The utility districts, like the co-operatives, have
gradually increased in number. They are now popularly
known as "PUDs" (Public Utility Districts), and for the
1948 fiscal year eighteen widely scattered ones purchased
733,845,282 kilowatt hours from the Bonneville Administration. The history of the formation, growth, and functions of
the PUDs, and the storm of controversy surrounding them

(legal and otherwise), is, of course, a major aspect of the public utilities movement in the Pacific Northwest.[5]

Electrification of Industry

World War II greatly accelerated both the manufacture and use of hydroelectric power from all sources in the Pacific Northwest. In addition to ordinary prewar uses, the new power serviced the government's highly secret atomic bomb (Manhattan) project at Hanford, Washington. One-third of the nation's reduction and rolling of aluminum during the war was accomplished with electrical power in northwest factories located at Vancouver, Spokane, Tacoma, and Longview in Washington, and at Troutdale, Oregon. The annual aluminum capacity of Northwest plants by 1944 totaled 18,000 tons. Lumber mills which long had made extensive use of electrically driven machines greatly increased their use during the war. Airplane factories, notably the mam-

[5] Views within and outside the Northwest vary greatly on the subject of public ownership of utilities. In the Northwest a heated controversy has raged, not so much over the receipt of federal appropriations for power development in the region, but over questions involving the disposal of generated power. In the February 2, 1950, issue of the Bonneville Power Administration's house organ, *Currents*, the Administration's position is well summed up in an excerpt republished from the *Longview Daily News* as of January 11, 1950:

. . . In the case of one of the biggest public enterprises in the Northwest — the Bonneville Power Administration — there is something of a substitute for competition that keeps that vast business striving for a good record. That something is the necessity for congressional approval of its annual budget and the expenditures it makes for improvements and extensions to the power distribution system.

As a result Bonneville is not above tooting its own horn when it has something to toot about and we do not blame it in the least. Bonneville points with some pride to the fact that it recently paid a $2 million surplus into the treasury, thereby advancing repayments on its indebtedness about 10 years ahead of date due.

Bonneville Dam itself cost $87,500,000 and $59,000,000 of that was to be repaid from power revenues. Already power has paid back on that indebtedness $31,208,000 including interest and operating expenses. The huge network of transmission lines cost $133,000,000. And power revenues have paid back on that indebtedness $27,400,000.

Keeping ahead of its debt payments has been possible for Bonneville despite the fact that its wholesale rate of $17.50 per kilowatt year — the lowest in the nation — has not been increased.

moth Boeing plant at Seattle, which turned out the B-17 Flying Fortress and the B-29 Superfortress, were electrically powered. Also electrified were shipyards at Seattle, Portland, Bremerton, and elsewhere. Other war industries used electric power, among them chemical plants producing vitally needed magnesium (at Spokane), ferrosilicon (at Wenatchee), manganese (at Hoodsport), ferrochrome, calcium carbide, chlorates, and steel in widely scattered areas. These new plants, most of them exploiting for the first time certain mineral resources contained in the region, represented a total investment of about $160,000,000, and most of these establishments were powered largely from the Bonneville Power Administration. In Seattle the Bethlehem Steel Company plant alone has an annual capacity of 180,000 tons, while the Oregon Electric Steel Rolling Mills has 35,000-ton capacity. Bellingham and Concrete in Washington, and Oswego, Oregon, are heavy producers of another important item — cement.[6]

Many of these materials have already found their way into peacetime uses. But a regional survey, conducted by the Bonneville Power Administration, of the varied physical resources of the Pacific Northwest, reveals greater opportunities for future industrial expansion that can be brought about by delivering essential power to the places of operation. This survey and other carefully conducted surveys reveal the feasibility of future exploitation of the large deposits of phosphate rock in Idaho and western Montana suitable for the manufacture of phosphorus and phosphate fertilizers; manufacture of electric furnace iron and electrolytic zinc; production of abrasives, nitrogen and nitrates, coke, charcoal, and numerous other items that have been and are becoming essential to present-day industrial output.

[6] For the year ending June 30, 1940, the biggest industrial customers of the Bonneville Power Administration were the Aluminum Company of America (1,502,248,000 kilowatt hours); Permanente Metals Corporation with subsidiaries, Spokane Aluminum Fabrication (193,830,000), Spokane Aluminum Reduction Company (1,725,180,000), Tacoma Aluminum Reduction Company (229,855,000); the Reynolds Metals Company with plants at Longview (106,632,000) and Troutdale (1,144,720,000); also other industries, making a total of 5,551,999,270 kilowatt hours. This is roughly one-half of Bonneville's production.

Moreover, the Pacific Northwest may now look forward to the actual manufacturing of finished parts (in many instances begun during the war), for example, the making of aluminum castings, steel alloy parts, and industrial acids essential to the making of ships, automobiles, airplanes, and other modern machines and devices. Added to this are opportunities for further expansion of the region's already important pulp and paper industries, and the manufacture of other cellulose derivatives which include rayon, nylon, certain types of ceramics, industrial gases, and wood-waste products. In 1944 there were no less than twenty-seven separate pulp mills in the region, and in 1941 these produced over two million tons of pulp commodities of all sorts.

Imposing as the list is, the Pacific Northwest is not without industrial limitations. In many instances the region possesses merely important segments of the major nonferrous metals industries. For this reason only parts essential to the completed products of such items as automobiles, building hardware, and plumbing fixtures are made in Oregon, Washington, and Idaho, while finishing continues to be done in the East.

The wide distribution of low-cost hydroelectric power has already revolutionized farm life in many sections. In 1943 farms in Oregon, Washington, and Idaho totaled 187,178; and out of this number 143,300 were serviced through central electrical stations. Only 32,800 farms were without such service, and an unknown number of these were equipped with privately owned electrical plants. Among electrically powered or operated conveniences are milking machines, water pumps for home use and for individual irrigation operations, incubators and brooders, dairy ventilating fans, bottle washers, cream separators, fodder choppers, and many other devices. They all either ease or supplement the labors of the farmers whose means permit investment in such equipment. Rural electrification has offered corresponding labor-saving opportunities and conveniences to housewives, as well as many comforts and pleasures to the entire family. Products, in addition to the familiar electric lights and electrical appliances, might in the future include individual

Courtesy Bonneville Power Administration

THE COLUMBIA RIVER FEDERAL HYDRO–ELECTRIC POWER SYSTEM

quick-freezing units to replace the time-honored Mason jar, as well as dehydrators and television sets.

The Power Problem

This remarkable industrial growth (see also Chapter XX), stimulated by hydroelectric developments and general increase of public consumption of electricity, has by now created demands for power that far exceed the present rate of production. In the years 1948 and 1949 an acute power shortage was experienced; in fact, the regional requirements (doubled since 1940) have not been available since World War II. Great as has been power development, it has not kept pace with the region's growth in general, and industrial growth in particular.

Plans call for expansion in both private and public utilities in the immediate future, although the extent of publicly owned plants depends upon the voters and Congress. In the words of Paul J. Raver, Bonneville Administrator, the situation ahead looks bleak. "For several years in the future there will be practically no reserves of generating capacity, major transmission lines, or substation equipment," he writes. He predicts a critical shortage until 1954 "at the earliest." To take care of this acute situation the Bonneville Power Administration has prepared its plans for future expansion. These plans call for construction of many new dams and installation of additional generating equipment, providing, of course, public funds become available.

In order to meet these requirements more adequately and in order also to integrate better all phases of conservation development in the Northwest, there are many who favor the creation of a Columbia Valley Authority similar to the Tennessee Valley Authority. The staunchest advocate of a CVA is President Harry S. Truman, who specifically asked for it in his annual message to Congress, January, 1950. On the other hand, Senator Wayne L. Morse, Oregon liberal Republican, has expressed himself in opposition to the plan.

Private and other public utilities also have their blueprints for the future and many of these, including numerous business and lay organizations, such as Chambers of Commerce, favor development along present lines. They argue through an Inter-Agency Committee: ". . . we already have a giant, coordinated program of development well under way [one calling for an outlay of two and one-half billion dollars]. No CVA could ever be as democratic or make any faster progress than the present system. . . ." In any event the region boasts of these accomplishments:

1. Eighty-six major hydroelectric projects. Per-capita installation within the region is twice the installation for the average American.
2. Thirty-two major irrigation dams; 3,800,000 acres under irrigation in the Columbia Basin.
3. Twelve multipurpose dams (in addition to the above eighty-six).
4. Thirteen thousand miles of high-voltage transmission lines.
5. Electric rates of the Pacific Northwest are one-half the national average.
6. Ninety-five per cent of all farms in the Columbia Basin are electrified whereas only 72.8 per cent of the farms in the United States are electrified.

The region can look back upon nearly three-quarters of a century of remarkable progress in the field of hydroelectrical development; it looks forward to a future even more spectacular.

CHAPTER XXII

Politico-Economic Ferment

Post-Civil War Attitudes, Behavior, and Trends (1865–96)

PIONEER WAYS OF LIFE withered fast before the onslaught of steel rails, steam engines, irrigation ditches, dams, and factories. In 1890 the frontier imprint was still visible in many places; but one generation later, a new, more distinctly native and modern civilization had emerged. This swift transformation, so apparent in the physical environment, was reflected, sharply and profoundly, in the political, economic, and social life. Before the 1890s the political clamor was for such things as transcontinental railroads, steamboats, wagon roads, and improved mail service, land cessions, pacification of the Indians and, as has been noted, statehood for the territories. And so far as private business operations were concerned, the prevailing political viewpoint (adhered to in both theory and practice) was laissez faire.

To cite illustrations of the political state of mind of the post-Civil War generation one might turn to the region's executive and legislative handiwork. In what one might have thought of as a critical postwar year, 1866, Oregon's Governor Addison C. Gibbs felt impelled to say to the Legislature: "The passing year has been one of general health and prosperity, for which we should be grateful to Almighty God. . . . It appears to me that there is not very much legislation needed at this session of the Legislature, and I have but few recommendations to make." The Governor did, however, recommend chastisement of the Indians. To ex-

384]

pect a state lawmaking body to refrain entirely from legislative enactments was asking much, and the session was chiefly productive of statutes pertaining to licensing of Chinese, or "Kanaka" prospectors and peddlers, declaring Harrisburg a "body politic," and improving ways and means of collecting, rather than imposing, taxes. Similarly, in the territories the let-things-alone note prevailed. William Pickering, Territorial Governor of Washington, not unlike the Oregon chief executive, extended his thanks to "Almighty God, for his . . . manifold blessings" and then devoted himself to quoting real-estate values and reviewing population growth in the Territory. Likewise, the political utterances and legislative enactments in Idaho Territory were concerned with anything but matters either of social reform or restrictions. In short, the prevailing attitude appears to have been: the Civil War was over; the Northwest had sacrificed little in the struggle; and since peace had come, let governments aid rather than hamper economic processes. The modern term used to describe this bygone age is "rugged individualism."

In the field of politics it is not surprising, in 1865, to find the party that had led the Union to victory was eager to remain in power. The Republican hold on the political reins was, however, shaky, and the years to 1890 witnessed a somewhat erratic return of Democratic strength in this region where in antebellum days Lady Democracy had once been sovereign. Oregon alone voted in presidential elections prior to 1892. There the popular votes in the presidential elections were often close. In 1868 Oregon gave her three electoral votes to Democrat Horatio Seymour rather than to Republican Ulysses S. Grant, but four years later (1872) the hero of Appomattox was favored over the Democratic candidate Horace Greeley. Republicans won by a narrow margin in the disputed Tilden (Democrat)-Hayes (Republican) election of 1876, and also carried the state for James A. Garfield, James G. Blaine, and Benjamin Harrison in the succeeding three presidential elections. But while the Republicans held the edge in elections of the president, Oregon's governors (1862–95) were thrice Republican and four times Democratic.[1] In the 1868 state election Oregon Democrats won a 13-to-9 superiority over the Republicans in the State Senate and 30-to-17 ratio in the House, and for the period under review managed, by and large, to maintain control.

The party affiliations of governors of Washington and Idaho Territories were those of the presidents who made the appointments to their offices. With the exception of Grover Cleveland, the presidents of the United States during this territorial period were all Republican. The members of the respective territorial legislatures were, however, chosen in general elections which produced Republican superiority in the Washington territorial legislature; and a changing control in the Idaho territorial legislature. In the 1868 election in Idaho, the Democrats won a 7-to-3 superiority over the Republicans in the Council; and a 17-to-3 control in the House. But in 1888 the Republicans gained a 9-to-3 dominance in the Council, with one of 21-to-1 in the House. And, as will be discussed later, this situation was again reversed in the election of 1892. In general it may be said that the post-Civil War generation experienced both the blessings and the aggravations of the two-party system.

The operation of the established political system offered no guarantees either of efficiency or honesty in government. Unfortunately, the Pacific Northwest came in for many of the political abuses then common to the nation. New York's Tweed Ring, the Salary Grab, Crédit Mobilier, and Orville Babcock's Whiskey Ring were but symbols of widespread political corruption in the United States during the "Grant Era." In Oregon the nadir of political corruption was reached in the above-mentioned Tilden-Hayes election of 1876 when Oregon's electoral votes, vital to the election of a president,

---

[1] Oregon's governors (1862–95), their party affiliations, and their terms in office were, as follows:

    Addison C. Gibbs, 1862–66 — Republican
    George L. Woods, 1866–70 — Republican
    LaFayette Grover, 1870–77 — Democrat
    Stephen F. Chadwick, 1877–78 (not elected) — Democrat
    W. W. Thayer, 1878–82 — Democrat
    Z. F. Moody, 1882–87 — Republican
    Sylvester Pennoyer, 1887–95 — Democrat (People's Party)

were involved in low political chicanery. In this election, a double set of returns was forwarded from Oregon, even though the Republican candidate, Rutherford B. Hayes, had won at the state polls a clear, undisputed majority over the Democratic opponent, Samuel J. Tilden. This irregularity in reporting the Oregon vote came about when it was discovered that one of the Republican electors, John W. Watts of Yamhill, was found to be ineligible; and being eager to take advantage of this opportunity, Governor LaFayette Grover, Democrat, sought to replace Watts with a Democrat who would cast that one desperately needed electoral vote to secure a victory for Tilden. Even though Governor Grover's powers did not extend beyond being present when the Oregon Secretary of State (the legal "returning officer") canvassed the election returns and granted certificates of election to the three persons having received the highest votes, Grover (in defiance of the clear intent of the law, which provided that eligible electors fill unexpected vacancies) proceeded to deliver to Stephen F. Chadwick, Secretary of State, three certificates, one of which contained the name of E. A. Cronin in place of that of the disqualified Watts. Governor Grover justified this action on the specious theory that Watts' ineligibility meant that the Democratic selectee, Cronin, would win by default. Then the Secretary of State signed these certificates and delivered all three of them to Cronin who, to make matters even more farcical, declared the other two Republican electors ineligible. They had refused to "act with me," said Cronin, whose next move was to present his two extra certificates to fellow party (Democratic) members. The three Democrats thereupon met and cast their votes. Since but one vote was needed to assure Tilden's election, the electors made a show of restraint; they cast one electoral vote for Tilden and Vice-Presidential candidate Thomas A. Hendricks, and two for Hayes' running mate, William A. Wheeler. Cronin later carried the returns to Washington, for which performance he received $3,000 from the democratic managers.

In the face of this situation the three ousted Republicans could hardly be expected to remain inactive. They too met as a "College" and cast all three of their votes for Hayes and Wheeler. Both sets of Oregon returns, along with disputed returns from other states, were eventually lodged with a special Electoral Commission created by Congress. And, important to the final outcome, the Republicans had secured from the Oregon Secretary of State a statement specifying the popular vote in the election; this document was forwarded to Washington along with the electoral vote. The Democratic return sent to Washington did not, on the other hand, contain such certification of the popular vote; it contained, as stated above, the Governor's certificates on appointment of electors, signed by the Secretary of State. In the end, the Electoral Commission decided unanimously that the Democratic (Cronin) return did not contain the vote of Oregon; and voted 8 to 7 to accept the Republican return on the ground that the election commission could not inquire as to what lay back of the election results as certified by the Secretary of State, whom the Commission regarded as the proper certifying officer. Hayes was made president and a disturbed nation accepted the outcome.

Meanwhile, the processes of living moved on in the Pacific Northwest, though not without troubles. The passing of the frontier stage of life and the coming of the modern era did not necessarily bring bountiful prosperity, least of all to agriculture. Farmers there were slow in finding a ready market for many of their crops, and for this reason proceeded to concentrate on the most negotiable commodity, wheat. This cereal most farmers knew how to raise; it grew luxuriantly in the Northwest; it was not very perishable; and it was a staple product for which there usually existed outside markets, provided, of course, these markets could be reached. This heavy dependence on one crop, however, had serious drawbacks. Prices fluctuated greatly on the world wheat markets and, moreover, emphasis placed on wheat production throughout other newly opened areas in the West tended to depress prices still further. Export wheat prices had remained fairly high, 1866–74, but a sharp break came in 1875 and, with fluctuations, the price curve was downward until

1895,[2] when the export price fell to fifty-seven cents per bushel. Pacific Northwest farmers were favored with direct access to river and ocean shipping, but, unfortunately, the shipping companies charged freight rates offsetting this advantage. It might well have been hoped that the coming of transcontinental railroads would have produced competition for the wheat-carrying business and in this way lower freight charges, but interlocking ownership of rail and water transportation facilities, and also of grain elevators, prevented this from happening to any great extent. Summed up, the carriers charged about what the traffic would bear, and for the period 1880–95 the record reveals a sharp drop in wheat purchasing power. In the face of lowering political standards and economic stringencies, climaxed by the decline in wheat prices, public and official sentiment became aroused. Throughout the entire West there arose a fervid demand for regulation and reform.

First Call for Reform

The first and most convenient object for attack was the common carriers. It will be recalled that in the post-Civil War era official and public clamor had been for linking the East and West with rails. Generous gifts of public lands were offered to induce railroad construction, and no legislative obstacles were placed upon this important path to progress. But scarcely had the railroads been reassured when sentiment turned against them. Even as early as 1874 Oregon's Governor Grover proposed state regulation of common carriers, saying: "In several of the other States of this Union, where such public control has not before been established, there is now going on a struggle between the people and these corporations, testing the very elements of the right of sovereignty and of the law making power." The governor believed Oregon to be the only state without legal

---

[2] In 1874, the export price of wheat was $1.43; in 1875 it dropped to $1.12; in 1879, to $1.07; and after a rebound, 1880–84, it fell to $.86 in 1885. A bottom of $.57 was reached in 1895.

regulation of railroads, and he believed it remarkable if, "feeling the impulse of new-grown power, and incited by the keen energy of private interest," the railroads would not "trample upon the people's rights. . . ." He proposed the regulation of common carriers, advocating that railroads be "limited to the purposes of their incorporation," namely, carriers of passengers and freight. He favored reasonable maximum rates, allocation of additional stations, fencing in of the right-of-ways, and the facilitation of direct legal actions by injured persons. Steamship lines, long subject to popular criticism for charging exorbitant rates, now also came within the orbit of gubernatorial scrutiny. Five million bushels of wheat were in the Willamette Valley granaries, and it was pointed out that a five-per-cent decrease per bushel in the river steamer rates would mean a quarter of a million dollars to hard-pressed Oregon farmers. In Washington Territory the trend was similar. Scarcely had the Northern Pacific Railroad been completed there when the territorial governor, Eugene Semple, suggested railroad regulation. To his legislature in 1887, the governor said: "On my recent trip to the eastern part of the Territory, I heard many complaints of exorbitant charges on the part of railway companies for carrying crops to the seaboard. The people . . . are looking to the Legislature for some kind of relief." Governor Semple went on to say that "rights of the Legislature to regulate freights and fares should not be doubted," that this body should "exercise" this right, and that trial regulatory legislation should be devised.

Doubtless influencing this altered official tone was pressure from the electorate. Hard-pressed farmers had begun to organize, and as their strength increased through organized effort, so too did their influence in political circles. For farmers to organize was not at all a new experience. Farmer organizations existed in the eastern seaboard during the eighteenth century; in the Northwest farmers had local organizations, and, in a nebulous sort of way, state-wide associations before the rise of the troubles alluded to. As early as 1853 farmers of Yamhill County had formed a local union. Idaho's earliest pioneers and early settlers in eastern Washington had united to promote local irrigation projects. In 1860 there was formed the Oregon Agricultural Society, and one year later Oregon had its first state fair, the culmination of considerable planning and co-operation by earlier county-fair groups in which farmers took an active part. Though not overtly dedicated to taking political action, all the former agrarian organizations had within themselves the germs that could, and often did, produce political action. Some of these "Farmers' Clubs," as they were called, were specifically formed to fight the familiar transportation monopolies which controlled the strategic Cascades portages on the lower Columbia River, and also the transfer facilities at the Willamette River Falls. In 1873 the Farmers' Clubs of Oregon united into a state-wide organization and called themselves the Farmers' Union. With a new feeling of strength, delegates assembled and adopted resolutions calling for the building of their own warehouses to withstand "oppressions and extortions of the railroad monopoly." And as a further means of combating railroad increases, the Farmers' Union resolved to build its own boats, and also resolved somehow to wrest from the "monopolies" control of the vital Willamette River Falls and Cascade portages.

The territories experienced a similar emergence of Farmers' Clubs during the early seventies, as, in fact, did the entire West. Washington, for instance, had sixty-one such clubs, and an undetermined number of farmer organizations arose in Idaho and Montana territories. Clearly, the groundwork was laid for what was coming next, namely, a tie-up with national organizations, the chief one of which was the Patrons of Husbandry, or the Grange.

The Grange

The Grange had been founded in 1867 by Oliver H. Kelley, a Washington, D. C., postal clerk. Kelley was distressed by the plight of Southern farmers, and sought first to reform prevailing methods of agriculture. His ideas spread like thistle weeds, not only throughout the South, but all over the West. A secret ritual evolved within the Grange, and this seemed to have an appeal to farmers just as ceremony had appealed to city dwellers who joined such societies as the Masons, Elks (B.P.O.E.), Odd Fellows (I.O.O.F.), Knights of Pythias, and similar fraternal orders. Chief emphasis was upon reform, and a positive twofold program of action soon developed within the Grange. One phase of this program called for the exercise of political pressures aimed at forcing down railroad rates, and further restriction of monopolies; the other pointed toward co-operative ownership of farm-machinery factories, elevators, and warehouses. The local farmers' press generally gave support to the movement, and even opened its papers to verse not yet classed among the nation's best. Read one stanza addressed to the farmers:

> You are oppressed on every side
> By those infernal moneyed men
> They take your wheat for less than cost
> And crush you to the earth again.

The peak of success was reached by 1874, when the Grange claimed no less than 800,000 members and 20,000 units. One year earlier the Grangers had swept into the Northwest. The first group was organized in Clackamas County, Oregon, and by the end of the year, thirty-seven chapters had been formed in Polk, Linn, Lane, Yamhill, and other Oregon counties. Four counties in Washington Territory also formed Granger locals. On September 23, 1873, representatives of the locals met at Salem and formed the Oregon State Grange. The Washington locals, and those formed in Idaho the following years, were included with the Oregon State Grange. Daniel Clark, who headed the Farmers' Union of Oregon, was, and deservingly so, elected the first Grange Master of Oregon, and others active in farm organization work were accorded such offices as Overseer, Lecturer, Steward, Gate Keeper, and Lady Assistant Steward.

The growth of the Grange in the Pacific Northwest was as fantastic as was the mushrooming rise and expansion of this organization in other parts of the West and South. The peak year in the Northwest was 1875; there were then 10,885 members in 181 locals in Oregon, 61 in Washington Territory, and

BEFORE AND AFTER RECLAMATION

(above) *Sagebrush-covered land near Boise, Idaho. This land is to be developed by the U. S. Bureau of Reclamation.* (below) *Irrigating potatoes on the 320,000-acre Boise, Idaho, project.*

Courtesy U. S. Bureau of Reclamation, Boise, Idaho

Courtesy U. S. Dept. of the Interior. Bonneville Power Administration, Portland, Oregon

Photo by U. S. Bureau of Reclamation. Courtesy Spokane Chamber of Commerce

THE COULEE DAM BY DAY AND BY NIGHT

17 in Idaho Territory.[3] No one escaped this surge toward a union banner. With respect to Oregon one notes on the list of units such diverse and widespread communities as Newport, Canby, Astoria, Yoncalla, Ashland, Monmouth, Pendleton, Sheridan; in Washington there were Elma, Vancouver, Ellensburg, Olympia, Walla Walla, Cowperville; and on the Idaho roster were Boise City, Falk's Store, Weiser, Mount Idaho, and Salubria.

The Grange had a threefold purpose: (1) to improve the economic lot of the farming classes; (2) to further education; and (3) to ameliorate the social life of agrarian peoples. In order to promote the first objective (and the most vital), committees were formed to facilitate more direct purchase of farm implements from the producers, and to take steps leading ultimately to manufacture, by the Grange itself, of farm implements. And again, as in the case of the Farmers' Clubs, direct shipment of grains "in bulk" was desired, as was also the establishment of Grange stores. For purpose two, better common schools were sought. And third, but probably most significant and lasting, was the Grange social program which led to erection of Grange halls (forerunners of rural community centers in the West) where folks gathered for good times. Picnics, box socials, singing, general oratory, and debates were all popular events in Grange Halls. Was this "God's Country," or the "Landlord's Country"? one stalwart orator would ask, and the fireworks would begin.

The Grange was not intended to be a political party, but political movements were inevitable. It was the opinion of the Portland *Oregonian* that such national scandals as the Crédit Mobilier contributed to the disorganization of both the Democratic and Republican parties, and that the Grange "forced" the major parties to become more subservient to the popular will. Moreover, the Grange was political in the sense that national, state, and local units did not hesitate to pass politically colored resolutions. Some of the more outspoken local resolves indicated that Grange members were

---

[3] A complete listing of subordinate granges by county, post office, and with respective dignitaries, appears in Ezra S. Carr, *The Patrons of Husbandry on the Pacific Coast* (San Francisco, 1875), pp. 283–89.

in favor of such things as a curb on "transportation monopolies," tariff reductions, and establishment of income taxes.

Nationally and locally the Grange failed to solve either the economic or the social problems besetting the farmers during the post-Civil War years, even though some lasting benefits were derived from the organization. For the farmers to maintain the high pitch of enthusiasm and devotion exhibited in 1875 was also more than could be expected, and thereafter membership began to decline. Many Grange units even ceased to exist. By 1881 membership in the Oregon (Northwest) Grange dropped to 1,440; the member granges, to 53. The panic of 1893 and the rise of Populists infused some new life into the Grange during the early nineties, and the Northwest membership began to rise again. In 1889 there was organized a separate State Grange of Washington, which has remained active and which has continued its political fight against such things as absentee landlordism, trusts, and the railroads. The Washington Grange has favored lower transportation rates, woman's suffrage, and prohibition, and at the same time it has placed an accent on nativism, or "Englishness." An exception is made for the Scandinavians.

During the middle 1920s some of the Grangers deserted their organization to join the new Farm Bureau movement which took an active part in supporting Robert La Follette, the Progressive Republican candidate for the presidency in 1924. Some of the old fire of the Grange was rekindled during the Great Depression of the 1930s, however. It is well expressed in a letter written by Ervin E. King, Master of the Washington State Grange, to President Franklin D. Roosevelt, October 29, 1939 (the letter appears in Harriet Ann Crawford's *The Washington State Grange*), saying: "Farmers want a price; they don't want subsidies or doles. They want to work hard, then get decent wages for their toil."

Today Grangerism is still a force in the Pacific Northwest, at least in a negative way. In Oregon the Grange has had a large hand in the defeat of the sales tax and in imposing tax limitations of one sort or another. This shows how a belligerent minority can at times prevail over a lukewarm majority. Now, as in 1873, the Grangers support the simple ideal first voiced by Postal Clerk Kelley: "The greatest good for the greatest number." The Grange did not bring in the millenium; it did not even restore what farmers considered to be a fair price for their wheat. The Grange failed as a co-operative, the result in part of lack of both capital and experience. Much, though, was learned from experience, and the social values derived from closer community associations were wholesome and important to a society emerging from its frontier stage of development.

The fact that the Grange did not become an official political party did not mean that the farming people of either the nation as a whole or of the Northwest were unwilling to break with the major parties in order to form a political organization of their own. Actually, what first developed in Oregon was a fusion of reform elements (labor, prohibitionists, and farmers) into what in 1890 became the Union Party, with candidates on state and national tickets and a platform designed to please all groups of malcontents. Then, also on July 11, 1891, there was formed at Portland the Oregon Farmers' Alliance which was a segment of a large body known as the Northern Alliance.[4] Then next came the organization of the Peoples', or the Populist, Party in 1892.

Populism

Populism was by far the most prominent of the political movements in the half-century following the Civil War, and as such was the culmination of agrarian movements voicing protest against the established order of things. In a specific sense, Populism was a movement that grew out of the deflation of the 1880s, but as a political movement it voiced

---

[4] The Alliance movement, like the Grange, had its first rapid growth in the South and Middle West. Beginning in Texas in the middle seventies it emerged into the Texas Grand State Alliance in 1878; later it merged with another important organization in Arkansas, the Agricultural Wheel. Alliances spread into the northern plains where there was formed the National Farmers' Alliance, or Northwestern Alliance. By 1890 the Alliances had spread into the West Coast states, and as indicated there was formed the above-mentioned organization in Portland. The relationship between the Northern Alliance and the Knights of Labor was often close.

protest not only against low prices (or reversely, scarce money), but also against trusts, public land policies, the prevailing tax system, and many other aspects of nineteenth-century capitalism and the federal government.

The Populist movement assumed a definite political form when, in July, 1892, members of the Farmers' Alliance, one of the most prominent agricultural societies in the Middle West and South, and elements in the Granger and other organizations took steps to meet in convention at Omaha. At this sensational gathering a Populist organization was formed, a full-fledged platform was approved, and candidates for the presidency and vice-presidency were nominated. This Party, like preceding ones, bemoaned the plight of the farmers and laborers. It formally demanded: (1) free and unlimited coinage of silver; (2) increase by not less than fifty per cent of the circulating medium; (3) a graduated federal income tax; (4) greater economy in the federal government; and (5) a postal savings bank. Failure to endorse the eight-hour day and trade-union movement caused such labor groups as the Knights of Labor to stay out of the Populist Party in 1892. Subsequently many labor elements did join with the Populists in order to form a popular front. Chosen to head the national ticket was James B. Weaver, of Ohio. Weaver had come up the hard way. He had become a general during the Civil War; he had taken an active part first in the Democratic Party and then in the relatively new Republican Party. He became a congressman and in this role became classified as a soft-money man, or Greenbacker. As the Greenback Party dwindled, Weaver slipped easily into the growing Farmers' Alliance, emerging finally from that organization as the choice of the Populist Party.

Populists in the Northwest, as elsewhere, drew their strength from the discontented farmer (and, to a certain extent, labor) groups which had been organized previously, but which somehow had failed to reach the goals they set for themselves. In Populism they saw a new ray of hope through the amalgamation of many, if not all, of the discontented and "oppressed" factions. As if anticipating the formal organization of the Populist Party, there had been held at Salem, Oregon, August 10, 1889, a convention of Grangers, Prohibitionists, the Union Labor Party, and the Knights of Labor. Though each group of delegates had its own special objectives, the convention as a body voiced the common grievances as follows: "The power of the saloon in politics is continually increasing, . . . The power of trusts and corporations has become an intolerable tyranny, the encroachments of landgrabbers have almost exhausted the public domain, and the corruption of the ballot has rendered our elections little less than a disgraceful farce." Other meetings followed, resolutions were passed designed to bring about an end to the abuses, and then out of these sessions there emerged a formal political organization known as the Union Party.

When in 1892 Populism swept into the Northwest, the backlog of protest already had been laid by the Union Party and by numerous other discontented farmer and labor organizations. It cannot be said categorically that Populism in the Northwest sprang directly from local organizations, but their presence in the area and their similarity of objectives had paved the way for Populist organizers when they entered Oregon, Washington, and Idaho. In any event, People's Party, or Populist, Clubs emerged throughout the area during 1892 through the direct efforts of national organizers. Populist newspapers appeared with equal rapidity. Then came the state party organizations and the placing of Populist candidates before an excited electorate. Never before had the people of the Northwest witnessed so powerful a third-party movement as they did from 1892 to 1896.

State platforms were in many ways identical with the national platform issued by the Omaha convention, but planks respecting local situations were added in each of the Northwest states. For instance, the Oregon platform contained a plank calling for improved Columbia River navigation and for a government-owned railroad paralleling that stream. Also called for by the Oregon Populists were state-operated liquor stores in place of saloons, state publication of textbooks, and prohibition of the use of private detectives by corporations.

The effect of the People's, or Populist, party on the two

major parties in the Northwest was apparent. Both came out for free and unlimited coinage of silver in Idaho, and in Washington the Democrats adopted this plank at their state convention. In Oregon both Democrats and Republicans declared for bimetallism. Both major parties tried hard to capitalize as best they could on Populist enthusiasm, and the Democrats, in particular, tried hard to fuse with the Weaver forces so far as the national ticket was concerned. A pseudo-fusion was achieved in Oregon when one I. Nathan Pierce, a Populist elector, was endorsed by Oregon's Democratic Central Committee. The Populists, however, refused to endorse the Democratic fusion slate, and the result was complete capitulation of the state Democratic committee to the Populists. The electorate, however, failed to support the committee's action and thereby a Republican victory was assured. In Washington there was no attempt at fusion of the national ticket and none was achieved in Idaho. In view of this situation in Idaho, Democrats there who favored Weaver did the next best thing: they "scratched" their own party ticket by casting their votes for Weaver.

The campaign was exciting. During May, 1892, General Weaver appeared personally in Washington and Oregon and gave encouragement to the new movement. The older and more established newspapers with either Democratic or Republican affiliations tended to ignore the movement. The *Oregonian* had earlier pointed to the folly of the farmers in trying to hold their wheat for higher markets in face of a national, even a world, wheat surplus. And then, with the actual appearance of Weaver (he made fifteen to twenty appearances) within the state borders, this newspaper on May 11, 1892, said reporters had given little heed to this "original calamity man of the country," this "apostle of the worst." Moreover, the *Oregonian* frowned upon Weaver's being joined by the "Hell"-evoking Mary Elizabeth Lease,[5] that "shrewish Lysistrata of Kansas." And the fact that the Populists of Oregon accepted, as they did, a fusion ticket with the Democrats aroused the Republican press. Republicans

[5] Mrs. Lease is especially remembered for having said: "What you farmers need to do is raise less corn and more *Hell*."

consoled themselves with the thought that, since a fusion ticket allowed party members no choice, voters would refuse to accept the fusion ticket altogether. Most of the established Idaho newspapers were then vitally interested in the silver issue of 1892, but even so they said little about Weaver and the Populists.

The new party, however, developed its own press. *The People's Call*, a Populist newspaper of Seattle, called for "cool, deliberate thought" in adjusting economic conditions, but, characteristic of the national movement, this party organ warned against physical revolution. It contended that violence, should it break out, would create "destruction which would appall the dark ages." This did not mean, however, that the *Call* softened its blows. One of its correspondents, who signed himself Skookum the Trapper, declared that "Over-production of blood-suckers, money lenders, boodlers and knaves, vote buyers, ward heelers and ignorant politicians" were at the source of the evil.

Nationally, Weaver polled more than one million votes in the 1892 election, an amazing achievement for a third party. In the Electoral College he gained twenty-two votes. In the Pacific Northwest the General received 54.66 per cent of the popular vote of Idaho, which won for him the state's full complement of three electoral votes; in Oregon 16.24 per cent of the popular votes and one in the Electoral College; and in Washington 21.79 per cent of the popular vote, but no electoral votes.

Likewise of great local significance were the election returns for state offices. In Idaho, local Populists did not win a clean sweep, but nevertheless won 4 seats in the state Senate, compared with 6 Republican and 8 Democratic seats. In the House of Representatives they won 7 seats; to the Republicans and Democrats went 20 and 9, respectively. The governor remained, as before, Republican. In Oregon the fusionists won the governorship and but 1 senator, as compared with 16 for the Republicans and 11 for the Democrats. In the House 2 Populists, 38 Republicans, and 17 Democrats were chosen. In Washington the Republicans won all the state executive offices, but in the legislature the results were:

Senate, 25 Republicans, 9 Democrats, and 0 Populist; in the House, 50 Republicans, 20 Democrats, and 8 Populists. Thus the overall picture was one offering some encouragement for the Populists in the Northwest, and they chose to keep their organization alive with the hope of eventually achieving complete victory.

In the meantime the economic situation became worse, intensified by the financial crash of 1893. On the Oregon political front Governor Sylvester Pennoyer, elected in 1888 as a Democrat, and re-elected in 1892 on the fusionist ticket, broke completely with his major party during his second term. Pennoyer's independence was clearly revealed when wheat in Oregon sank to forty-three cents per bushel, for then it was that he bolted his party, and "went over bag and baggage to the Populists." He declared that "social needs always outrun social provision for them"; the Democratic Party had "abandoned its principles and now ought by right to abandon its name." To those who refused to call this new attack "Populism," the name "Pennoyerism" was applied. Thus, while Oregon did not officially elect a Populist, it in reality had one from 1895–97. By 1896 the Pacific Northwest was experiencing a sharp depression, as was the rest of the nation. The approach of the 1896 campaign offered two alternatives: one, to retain the cohesion of the Populist Party; the other, to merge with free-silver Democrats, and by fusion increase chances of a Republican defeat. The nomination by the Democrats of William Jennings Bryan, a bimetallist and an eloquent spokesman for the discontented Westerners, turned the tide in favor of a fusion ticket. At this convention the Populists accordingly nominated Bryan as their presidential candidate; but they extended the vice-presidential nomination to Thomas Watson, a member of their own party. Other compromises on candidates were worked out and several local candidates appeared on the ballot as Populists.

The 1896 platform declared itself opposed to a single-money standard; instead, bimetallism demanded free and unlimited coinage of silver at a ratio of 16-to-1. The campaign nationally and locally was one of the most heated in

American political history. It was also crucial, because in its final analysis it represented a clearly drawn battle between the forces of capital and industry on the one hand, and agrarianism on the other. Once again General Weaver, in support of Bryan, appeared in the Northwest pleading the cause of free and unlimited coinage of silver, and in return Republicans dubbed the opposition "Popocrats," intent upon wrecking the sound, free economy of America. William Mc-Kinley, Republican standard bearer, was hailed as the "advance agent of prosperity." In Idaho, the "Gem State," the silver issue assumed major prominence; in Oregon and Washington transportation and wheat prices were paramount issues. As never before, newspapers of varying political views came to grips with this clear-cut, major issue of bimetallism.

The Republican *Oregonian*, by then the leading metropolitan newspaper in the region, began early in January, 1896, the work of educating its readers on the falsities of proposals of this silver element. For the most part editorials were directed to the labor vote, pointing out that if labor were to be paid in cheap dollars (the inevitable result of bimetallism), the purchasing power of the dollar would be cheapened correspondingly. "Put our working people on this basis," said the *Oregonian*, "and we may be able to compete with such countries as China, Japan, India, and Argentina. But this would mean lowering the standard of living of the American working man." The paper further argued editorially, on January 10, 1869, that the sixteen-to-one formula was fraudulent, that it was a "standing wonder" that any of the workers could be misled by appeals which "carry with them their own condemnation when looked at with the eye of common sense." During the early spring there was a lull, and it was thought the "silver craze" was actually dying down. But when in April the Oregon Democrat leaders met at Salem, the silver issue was again hot. Said P. H. D'Arcy, addressing the state convention: ". . . the democratic party of Oregon is called upon to make a stand upon the vital question [of silver]. . . . If the democratic party wishes to survive, it must declare itself in favor of the free coinage of silver and gold." Then throughout the summer, especially following the Chicago Convention which nominated Bryan, little but heat was generated from either side. The Republican press referred to the silver Democrats as "conspirators," "Silver Highwaymen," and "the Silver hold-up"; and it spoke of "Bryan's Hallucinations . . . sufficient to call his mental soundness in question."

In Idaho the campaign interest centered on the money question. But here, as in 1892, the Republican meeting at Pocatello re-elected delegates to the national convention and favored silver as "primary money." But when the Republican Convention which nominated McKinley came out strongly for gold, the Idaho Republicans split into pro- and anti-gold factions; each claimed to be the regular official party, but in the state convention at Boise, August 26, 1896, the pro-gold group, of course, supported the Republican standard bearers, William McKinley and Garret A. Hobart. The bolters, namely the anti-gold Republicans, met after the state Democratic Convention had been held and threw their support to the Democrats, who had again fused with the Populists to form what was called the People's Democratic Party.

As election day approached, it was quite clear that the Republican ticket would win, but, said the *Oregonian,* October 31: "the bare and remote possibility of his [Bryan's] election sends the chill through the social body like the fatal rigor of a fever patient." The result at the polls was a complete national triumph for McKinley and his party. In its broader implications McKinley's victory meant industrial domination of America. For about a decade the people were given ample opportunity to observe what untrammeled corporate interests could actually perform. During a mere two-year period, 1898–1900, industrial combinations with capitalization of ten or more million dollars jumped from twenty to seventy-three. The United States Steel Corporation became the first organization of its kind to exceed a one-billion-dollar capitalization. It was shortly followed by the Northern Securities Company, the American Tobacco Company, the Bethlehem Steel Company, and others of this giant character. Free competitive enterprise, as Americans had known it, all but ceased to exist in some fields of operation. Conservatism in politics became the order of the McKinley era so far as the nation was concerned, but not in the Pacific Northwest.

At no time did the Pacific Northwest conform to these general trends. In the election of 1896 both Idaho and Washington were carried by Bryan on the Democratic (fusion) ticket and by large majorities. McKinley carried Oregon by the narrow plurality of 1,972 votes. Democrats and Populists also won a majority of the seats in the Idaho and Washington legislatures, but in Oregon, Republicans gained substantial control of state politics. From this point Populism was on its way out, locally and nationally. But it did not pass without having made some gains. Many of the reforms for which the Populists stood, though bimetallism was not one of them, were in time embodied in both local and national government agencies.

Local Elections: 1896–1916

The local political record [6] since 1896 is one marked by many fluctuations and irregularities; especially is this the case during the era beginning with the election of McKinley (1896) and ending in 1916 on the eve of American participation in World War I. Oregon, popularly thought of as staunchly Republican since Civil War times, showed marked vacillation in its state elections. In 1898, Oregon elected T. T. Geer, Republican, as Governor in a landslide victory which netted fifty-three per cent of the vote as compared with forty per cent for his fusionist opponent. Four years later (1902) the pendulum swung the other way; the Democrats won the gubernatorial race in the following three tries by electing George E. Chamberlain twice in succession and Oswald West once. Then, in 1914, the Republicans once again won the governorship by electing James Withycombe. Throughout this period of alternating governorships, the Republicans maintained overwhelming control of the state legislature. Moreover, the Populist vote was negligible after 1896. A detailed analysis of the county returns of these state elections reveals, however, no radical shifts in voting on state

[6] National election data will be treated separately in this chapter.

officers except in the one case of Multnomah County, the political division in which Portland is located. Of this populous and important county one can say with regard to gubernatorial elections that: as Multnomah County went, so went the State. In the elections reviewed above, Multnomah County's plurality was in each case on the side of the victor.

The state of Washington has pursued its own distinctive course in matters of politics. In Washington, John R. Rogers, the Fusionist (Populist) candidate who had been elected governer in 1896, was re-elected in 1900. Rogers, admired for his courage and "rugged honesty," was the only candidate who survived the Republican landslide of the latter year. But in the 1904 and 1908 elections, Republicans Alter E. Mead and Samuel G. Cosgrove, respectively, were chosen chief executives, only to be succeeded in 1912 and again in 1916 by a Democrat, Ernest Lister. Equally erratic was the state's legislative makeup. In the 1896 election the Populists and Democrats combined to gain control of the Senate, but the Republicans swept the House. In 1900 the Republicans carried both houses, but, as stated, not the governorship; and this party retained its control until the end of the period under review. As in the case of Multnomah County in Oregon, the counties in which Seattle and Tacoma are located, namely, King and Pierce, respectively, exhibited a vacillating voting record for this period.

Idaho gubernatorial elections, 1896–1916, produced the following results: in 1896 Frank Steunenberg, Democrat, was elected; in 1900, Frank W. Hunt, Democrat; 1902, John T. Morrison, Republican; 1904, Frank R. Gooding, Republican; 1908, James H. Brady, Republican; 1910, James H. Hawley, Democrat; 1912, John M. Haines, Republican; 1914, Moses Alexander, Democrat. The same seesaw pattern best describes the situation in the state legislature. In that body, the Fusionists (Populists and Democrats) and a segment calling themselves Silver Republicans (one of which was young William E. Borah) gained control in both houses in 1896 and retained it for twelve years. After this time the schism within the Republican ranks was healed and the silver issue ceased to retain its magic hold upon the Idaho voters. In 1916, however, the balance in the legislature swung back to the Democrats.

The Oregon System

So much for election results. The most important aspects of politics are those which concern legislative enactments. The constant change in state party balance appears to have been but a minor deterrent to the fulfillment of the basic trends of the period ushered in by President Theodore Roosevelt, namely, political reform. The (Theodore) Roosevelt administration, followed by the initial two years of Woodrow Wilson's first term in office, may properly be called the "Progressive Era." It may be distinguished from the early Populist era in that the latter was largely a native agrarian eruption (and largely western), whereas the Progressive Era was one not entirely free from foreign ideologies and one which produced much social legislation that affected all elements of American society.

The most notable example of this accent upon legislative reform is what happened in Oregon. There an outstanding political leader named William S. U'Ren, a staunch single-tax advocate of the Henry George school, became an effective advocate of the direct method of nominations and elections as a means of achieving his tax goal. As early as 1892, perhaps even earlier, U'Ren had begun his agitation for more popular participation in the political affairs than had been provided in Oregon's 1859 constitution. He proposed as a means of overcoming what he regarded as long-standing fraud and cunning in Oregon politics, the adoption of constitutional amendments which would provide for initiative and referendum action in legislative procedures. A direct Legislation League (forerunner of the People's Power League) was organized, and a reform campaign was begun to make "every man his own legislature." Measures were submitted to the Oregon legislature in 1899 asking for the above-mentioned amendments, and in 1902 initiative and referendum features were actually embodied as Article 4, section 1, of the Oregon constitution.[7] This measure, sponsored, one might say, by minority groups, was formally endorsed by both the major political parties. In 1904 this new feature of government was used for the first time in securing enactment of a direct-primary law, and in 1906 another constitutional amendment further extended the initiative and referendum to all state districts and municipalities.

The Oregon electorate continued to take a direct part in establishing, widening, and increasing the power of the electorate. In 1904 the above-mentioned Oregon Primary Law was enacted, as a substitution for the usually well-oiled political party-convention machinery in matters of selecting candidates for public office. Perhaps the most appealing aspect of this law was that it paved the way for the popular election of United States Senators. It provided for placing the names of candidates for the United States Senate on the ballot in the same manner that other candidates' names would appear. Also embodied in this Direct Primary Law was a pledge, called Statement No. 1, which candidates for the Oregon Legislature could sign. It read in part:

. . . I will always vote for that candidate for United States Senator in Congress who has received the highest number of the people's votes for that position in the general election next preceding the election of the Senator in Congress without regard of my individual preference.

By using this pledge method, it was possible to assure popular election of senators without amending the Constitution of Oregon, which called for election of these officials by the legislature without specified mandate from the people as to who should be chosen. Since not all candidates for the legislature signed Statement No. 1, the system was not considered sufficiently water-tight until 1910, at which time the voters passed a Compulsory Statement Bill.

In 1908 a constitutional amendment was approved which gave the Oregon electors the power to recall public officials.

---

[7] The initiative and referendum amendment measure was submitted by the legislature to the voters in 1901 and was approved by an overwhelming vote of 60,024 to 5,668.

And in this same year the voters passed what was called the Corrupt Practices Act, a law which limited the amount of money that candidates and other persons may contribute or spend in election campaigns, and which declared what constitutes corruption in the form of undue influence or use of money. The law was especially aimed at political "heelers" who had heretofore hovered around voting booths for the purpose of bribing or in other ways influencing voters.

Reforms continued to mount. In 1910 the state passed the Presidential Preference Primary Law: an act "to amend the Direct Primary Law by extending its provisions to presidential nominations, allowing voters to designate their choice for their party candidates for President and Vice-President. . . ." Still other reform measures provided for Women's Suffrage (1912) and for Workmen's Compensation (1913).

The lead taken by Oregon was in many instances followed by other states. In Washington and Idaho the legislative pattern was not quite as extreme as that of Oregon, but reform along similar lines occurred during the opening years of the present century. As early as 1896, Idaho put into effect a Women's Suffrage Act following a long bitter fight which had brought the famed suffragette, Mrs. Carrie Chapman Catt, to the scene of action in support of the measure.[8] In 1908 Idaho had also secured a Direct Primary Law; and two years later this state passed a Presidential Primary Law "allowing voters to designate their choice for President and Vice-President." Also in 1908, a Direct Primary Law went into effect in Washington where two years later the Women's Suffrage Amendment was ratified. In 1911 Washington also placed an Initiative, Referendum, and Recall Amendment before the people for a three-to-one approval.

[8] The idea of woman suffrage was not original to the West. It was first embodied in the New Jersey constitution of 1776. But this law was voided in 1807, and it was not until 1848, in Seneca Falls, New York, that the issue was again put before a wary public by a convention of women. There it was that Lucretia Mott, Elizabeth Cady Stanton, and others sponsored their "Declaration of Sentiments," and a resolution was passed favoring woman suffrage. Wyoming in 1890, however, became the first state in the Union (e.g., after adoption of the Constitution of the United States) to give the ballot to women, and this was done by providing for woman suffrage in the state's constitution.

To what extent did all this reform legislation actually reform politics? Critical studies of the now nationally famous "Oregon System" have been made by political scientists and sociologists. In 1915 Professor James D. Barnett ("Stiffy" to all his students) of the University of Oregon published an elaborate and penetrating analysis of the System: *The Operation of the Initiative, Referendum, and Recall in Oregon* (see Bibliography), from which the following summary remark is taken:

Some of the opposition is doubtless due, partly to objections to direct government upon general principles, and partly to the natural objections of interests whose policies have been thwarted by the system; but probably it is due, at least as much, to the abuses which the system has suffered in practice. However, all the opposition together is probably comparatively insignificant and the general popularity of the system well established. It is universally admitted that there are faults in the system, but the principle of the system is very generally accepted.

The *Oregonian* took this view in 1912: "The Oregon System is not in the balance. It is here to stay."

A study by Waldo Schumacher, also a professor of political science at the University of Oregon, takes a somewhat more reserved view on popular government as practiced in his state. He has attempted to show (see Bibliography) that, democratic as the initiative and referendum are, the existence of this machinery has not in itself made for better government in Oregon. On the basis of voter performance over a thirty-year period the electorate has revealed a disheartening lack of interest and lack of ability in voting on measures in contrast to voting on men. "Devices and organization constitute the form," says Schumacher, "interest and vigilance are the essentials of democracy." Still another study, a doctoral dissertation of 1941 by Paul T. Culbertson, bears on this subject, e.g., the iniative and referendum in Oregon. Concludes Dr. Culbertson: "As one views Oregon's experience with direct legislation in its broader aspects, it is immediately obvious that the initiative and referendum have been used frequently. . . . Many, if not most, of the objectives . . . were intangible in character and not easily measured or evaluated." It is Dr. Culbertson's opinion that the public expected "utopian results" from mere governmental machinery, and people have overlooked the "fundamental importance of an intelligent, alert, informed electorate."

The Legislative Record

In view of these far-reaching extensions of the democratic processes of government, it is of significance to inquire into the political and, more specifically, the legislative record that accompanied the adoption of the Oregon System. With reference to the legislative climate of opinion as viewed by memorials and resolutions, it would appear, first of all, that the Northwest legislators favored strongly the imposition of controls on large businesses.

In the *General Laws of Oregon* for as early as 1901 one notes in a Senate Joint Resolution respecting a proposed amendment to the state Constitution that "Corporations must be formed under general laws, but shall not be created by special laws." Another Oregon Senate Resolution asks the United States Congress for passage of a pure-food law. In 1903, a resolution from this same lawmaking body declared that trusts and monopolies threatened "Common welfare, the peace of society, and the prosperity of our social and governmental society, and the perpetuity of our social and governmental system." The Senate even asked the Congress of the United States to support President Theodore Roosevelt in his trust-busting campaign. To this list one might also add a Board of (Tax) Equalization Law, laws regulating storage of grain, regulating fishing, requiring land registration, prohibiting slot machines, and regulating "imitation" butter (oleomargarine). In Washington, where control of corporations was provided for in the state Constitution (1889), the legislature passed, not only concurrent resolutions imploring the federal Congress to pass an amendment providing direct election of Senators and one conferring the elective franchise on women, but also one favoring the strengthening of the Interstate Commerce Commission. In

Idaho's legislature were passed many memorials asking not only for passage of laws for "the free coinage of silver" but also for passage of laws designed to keep mineral lands out of the grasp of the railroad companies.

More pertinent is the enactment of this philosophy into law. During this period Oregon and Washington created public service commissions and, after some vacillations, special railroad commissions. The former were empowered to control public-service corporations such as those offering electric, telephone, gas, and water service. The latter were designed especially to control railroads, with the end purpose of attaining such things as better service, more comfortable stations, sanitary stockyards, uniform rates, and protection of employees. The first *Report* of Oregon's Railroad Commission (1908) indicates that it had settled many cases of complaints in an informal way by bringing the complainants and operators together. These complaints concerned such matters as demands for more railroad sidings, having freight cars available at times when needed, a demand for toilet facilities for men in the Salem station, and a demand by southern Oregon apple growers that freight rates on their fruit be lowered. The Public Service Commission heard similar cases, but not, as a rule, those pertaining to railroads.

Laws similar in character and in interest were passed in all the Northwest states up to about 1916. For Oregon the following are examples: acts "to prohibit the selling of adulterous candy"; "to prevent sale of unwholesome milk and dairy products"; "providing that railroad corporations are responsible for injuries to their employees in cases of wrongful act, neglect, or default." Other acts included a child-labor law; the creation of a bureau of labor statistics and inspector of workshops; a law prescribing how railroad tickets should be sold; laws limiting hours of labor for women and mine workers; and others of similar character. Washington statutes contain many similar acts: "creating a Bureau of Labor"; "requiring streetcar companies to demand only a 10 hour day"; establishing definite and uniform railroad rates; prohibiting blacklisting of labor; providing for an eight-hour day for state contracts; creating sanitary codes; providing safety devices in machines. Idaho laws of the character described were not so numerous, but among them was an act limiting miners and smelters to an eight-hour day; an act establishing mine inspection; and another to give employees the right to organize without interference.

Local Politics Between Two Wars

At the close of World War I the Pacific Northwest shared in the general swing away from the Democratic Party in favor of solid Republicanism. Spearheaded by Oregon, which in 1915 had replaced the dynamic Democratic Governor Oswald West with Republican James Withycombe, the electorate of this state chose to continue Republican control of the governorship by re-electing Withycombe in 1918. This governor died the following year and Ben W. Olcott, Republican and former Secretary of State, succeeded to the office of Chief Executive. In 1922, however, the eastern Oregon Democrat Walter M. Pierce captured this office, only to have it regained by the Republican I. L. Patterson. Oregon's Republican governors seem to have a habit of dying in office, as was the case also with Patterson; A. W. Norblad (Republican), who had been president of the Senate, took over the governorship; and, later on, Republican Carl Snell.

In 1930, Julius L. Meier, prominent Portland merchant (co-owner of Meier and Frank Department Store) ran for the governorship as an Independent and won. The vote in this out-of-the-ordinary election was as follows: Republicans, 46,840; Democrats, 62,438; Independents, 135,608. Four years later (1934), with a depression under way, a Democrat, Charles H. Martin, was elected, only to have the office return to the Republican fold in the next three successive elections, namely, Charles Sprague, for one term, and Earl Snell, who was re-elected for a second term in 1946. When Snell lost his life in an airplane accident, Douglas McKay, Republican, was brought into the governor's chair.

In contrast to the erratic political situation respecting the governorship, the Oregon State Legislature presents a record of almost unbroken Republican control from World War I to the present time. At one time, 1934, the Democrats gained a majority in the House. This, in view of the nation-wide adherence to President Franklin D. Roosevelt during the depression years, is remarkable.

The Washington political picture, so far as the governorship is concerned, is similar to that of Oregon. It runs as follows: 1919, Louis F. Hart (succeeded Lister, who died), Democrat; Roland H. Hartley, 1924, Republican; Clarence D. Martin, 1932, Republican; Arthur B. Langlie, 1940, Republican; then in 1944, William C. Wallgren, a Democrat; and again, in 1948, back to a Republican, Arthur B. Langlie. Washington's State Legislature, in contrast to that of Oregon, corresponded more closely to the national tide. Following World War I, the Republicans dominated; with the coming of the depression in 1932, the Democrats swept in, and held control in both the 1936 and 1940 elections. Even overshadowing Washington's gubernatorial campaigns during this era was the election as Lieutenant Governor of Seattle's jazz-band leader, Victor ("Vic") A. Meyers, in 1932 and again four years later. In the 1936 election, the electorate gave Meyers the largest vote ever bestowed upon the second-highest officer of the State.

During between-the-wars period, the State of Washington took another step in behalf of what it thought was more democracy in government by adopting a blanket primary law in 1935. Its predecessor, the closed-primary act of 1907, had been an improvement over the old party convention system, but there were those, Senator Homer T. Bone and the Washington State Grange in particular, who favored and secured passage of the blanket primary act. Instead of limiting voters in primary elections to marking ballots in behalf of candidates of one political party only (the one preferred at time of registration), the blanket primary law gives voters the opportunity to mark ballots containing the names of all candidates regardless of party. Political scientists are not wholly agreed that this law will accomplish the ends sought by its sponsors, but it is still rather early to expect a definite judgment.

In Idaho the election of governors since World War I has been as follows: D. W. Davis, 1918; Charles C. Moore, 1922; and H. C. Baldridge, 1926 (all Republicans); then C. B. Ross, 1930; C. A. Clark, 1934; Charles C. Gossett, 1938 and 1942 (all Democrats); then C. A. Bottelfsen, 1946; and C. A. Robins, 1948 (both Republicans).

In looking back over the region's local political history it would appear that no prevailing pattern has existed. In Washington and Idaho no one political party has maintained itself in power. Not since 1878, however, have the Democrats controlled Oregon's legislature. The region as a whole, and each individual state, has exhibited at times distinct leanings toward reform legislation; at other times the pendulum has swung in an opposite direction. James Farley's quip, "There are forty-seven states and the Soviet of Washington," could have been applied to all three states. All have exhibited a stubborn resistance to uniformity, though on the whole the region's legislative record has been fairly progressive.

The Nation and the Region

Lack of space prevents a complete report here on this vital question: To what extent have the Northwest states tagged along with the winning parties in national presidential elections?

In the stirring election of 1896 resulting in the election of Republican William McKinley over the Democratic William Jennings Bryan, the Republicans carried Oregon by a narrow margin; the Democrats swept Washington and Idaho (every county in this latter state). In the three following Republican elections — 1900, 1904, and 1908 — the winning party won straight major victories in both Oregon and Washington; in Idaho the winning party was Democratic again in 1900, Republican in 1904 and 1908. In the three-way race in 1912, involving Woodrow Wilson, William H. Taft, and Theodore Roosevelt, Wilson, the Democrat, was favored by the Republican split and carried all three of the Northwest states. From Wilson's war election in 1916 to the election of Hoover in 1928, Oregon stayed in the Republican column; both Washington and Idaho went Democratic in 1916, and thereafter voted overwhelmingly Republican. In choosing its national representatives, Oregon since 1880 has sent only four Democrats to Congress; and not since it returned George E. Chamberlain, Democrat, to the Senate for a second term in 1914 has it favored the Democratic party in its selection of Senators. On the other hand, Oregon's sister states have been anything but consistent in the political label of their representatives at the national capital.

Oregon, Washington, and Idaho suffered with the rest of the nation during the Great Depression which was in the making during the carefree era of Calvin Coolidge, and which was heralded by the sudden collapse of the stock market in October, 1929. This latter catastrophe came early in the administration of Herbert Hoover. During nearly all four years of his presidency, the economic situation grew increasingly worse. The Hoover administration, faced by a hostile Congress, made belated and feeble attempts at recovery, especially in 1932 when there was created a Reconstruction Finance Corporation with a two-billion-dollar fund for emergency loans to financial and semifinancial institutions. Federal funds were also allocated for loans to states and municipalities for use in relieving unemployment. But nothing that was done by the Hoover administration ended the Depression (it was actually world-wide in scope), and in the national elections of 1932 the Republicans suffered an overwhelming defeat at the hands of the Democrats. The Pacific Northwest states shared in administering this complete Republican rout.

The man elected to the office of the presidency of the United States in 1932 was Franklin Delano Roosevelt, who at the time was the popular governor of New York. In the weeks preceding his election Roosevelt had carried on a record-breaking campaign which carried him into all three of the Pacific Northwest states, and the Governor's magnetic personality, his buoyant, yet defiant, spirit seemed to offer some hope to Americans who had become discouraged and demoralized by the Depression.

The plan of attack by the Roosevelt administration was termed by the President himself the "New Deal." The program inaugurated in March, 1933, was threefold: relief, recovery, and reform. Congress responded to the President's bidding with unprecedented speed; and measures, one after the other, were enacted. Not all the measures survived the Supreme Court test, but in spite of this a substantial part of the New Deal program was put into operation. Federal funds were quickly made available for direct federal relief under the Works Progress Administration (W.P.A.); federal agencies, notably the Public Works Administration (P.W.A.), the Republican-enacted Reconstruction Finance Corporation (R.F.C.), the National Recovery Administration (N.R.A), and the Agricultural Adjustment Administration (A.A.A.), were inaugurated to bring about economic recovery. Innumerable reform acts designed to regulate banking, the Stock Exchange, and corporations were passed at Roosevelt's request to help bring back prosperity. Of all the New Deal measures, none were to affect the future of the Pacific Northwest so much as those providing for power, reclamation, flood control, and navigation developments previously discussed. The measures leading to the creation of the Bonneville Power Administration and scattered reclamation developments were supported not only by New Dealers, but by such Republican leaders as Charles L. McNary, long admired as a moderately progressive senator from Oregon.

Contrary to tradition, the people in four successive elections chose Roosevelt as their president. In each election, results were decisive. A general swing-back to Republicanism came in the local Oregon elections of 1944, but Roosevelt again carried this state over Thomas E. Dewey, the Republican standard bearer. The mid-term elections of November, 1946, brought further sweeping gains for the Republicans, who garnered control of both houses of Congress. But this control was short-lived in view of Harry S. Truman's victory over Dewey in 1948 and a return of Democratic control of both houses of Congress by that election.[9]

[9] The following is a tabulation of election returns in the Pacific Northwest states, 1896–1948. The figures are those presented in Edgar E. Robinson, *Presidential Vote, 1896–1932* (Stanford, 1934), *passim; The Presidential Vote, 1936* (Stanford, 1940), *passim; World Almanac and Book of Facts for 1950* (New York, 1950), the last for elections since 1936.

	1896	1900	1904	1908	1912	1916	1920
Oregon							
Dem.	46,739	33,385	17,521	38,049	47,064	120,087	80,019
Rep.	48,779	46,526	60,455	62,530	34,673	126,813	143,592
Others	1,896	4,305	12,178	10,310	55,303	14,750	14,911
Wash.							
Dem.	51,646	44,823	28,098	58,383	86,840	183,388	84,298
Rep.	39,153	57,456	101,540	106,062	70,445	167,208	223,137
Others	2,784	5,322	15,513	19,187	164,575	30,398	91,280
Idaho							
Dem.	23,189	29,414	18,480	36,195	34,017	70,054	46,579
Rep.	6,324	27,237	47,792	52,654	32,972	55,368	88,975
Others	173	1,330	6,314	8,536	39,056	9,193	70

	1924	1928	1932	1936	1940	1944	1948
Oregon							
Dem.	67,589	109,223	213,871	266,733	258,415	248,635	238,861
Rep.	142,579	205,341	136,019	122,706	219,555	225,365	258,216
Others	69,320	5,378	18,861	24,582	3,230	6,147	18,743
Wash.							
Dem.	42,842	156,772	353,260	459,579	462,145	486,744	462,781
Rep.	220,224	335,844	208,645	206,892	322,123	361,689	376,277
Others	158,483	8,224	52,909	25,867	9,565	7,865	44,785
Idaho							
Dem.	24,256	53,271	109,479	125,683	127,849	107,399	107,370
Rep.	69,879	99,848	71,312	66,256	106,553	100,137	101,514
Others	54,160	1,329	5,729	7,678	773	785	5,932

CHAPTER XXIII

The Social Front

New Elements in the Population

AS THE NINETEENTH CENTURY neared its close, critical observers were impressed by the rapidly changing scene in the Pacific Northwest. The frontier was fast vanishing in many, though by no means in all, portions of the region. Stagecoach lines were rapidly giving way to railroads; new cities arose, and grew; the wilderness still yielded rapidly to the settler's axe and saw. Deserts, as Brigham Young had predicted for Utah, were being made "to blossom as the rose."

Even more significant than the altering physical scene was the striking social metamorphosis experienced by the three Northwest states. By 1890 the population of the oldest commonwealth, Oregon, was 317,704; that of the two newly created states of Washington and Idaho, 357,232 and 88,548, respectively. The rate of growth thereafter continued to exceed the rate for the nation as a whole; in fact, the rate of increase was approximating what might be termed boom proportions.[1] During World War II, Washington and Oregon continued to boom, but Idaho joined the North Central states in suffering a loss.

No longer was this bulging population made up of "just plain American folks" from "back East" and from "down South." The much-trumpeted railroads and low-fare steam-

[1] Population figures for the twentieth century are as follows:

	1900	1910	1920	1930	1940
Oregon	413,536	672,765	783,389	953,786	1,089,684
Washington	518,103	1,141,990	1,356,621	1,563,396	1,736,191
Idaho	161,772	325,594	413,866	445,032	524,873

For estimated figures for 1949, see below in this chapter.

[417

ship lines had swung open the floodgates to immigrants, not only from other parts of the nation, but from Canada, Europe, and to a lesser extent from the Orient.

Attracted by the rich and abundant resources of the region and by ballyhoo circulated by the transportation companies, foreigners began arriving in ever-increasing numbers after 1883 — the date of the completion of the Northern Pacific Railroad. In that year the Northern Pacific Railroad Company maintained no less than 124 agents in Norway, Sweden, Denmark, and other places in northern Europe. Hundreds of thousands of copies of promotion literature reached the hands of distressed peoples eager to go to the New World, especially the West.[2]

Unlike the nation at large, which by 1890 experienced a shift in the origin of its immigrants from the north of Europe to the south of Europe, the Pacific Northwest continued to draw most heavily from Canada, Germany, the Scandinavian countries, and the British Isles. In that year it contained nearly 30,000 Germans, most of them in Oregon and Washington.

At first Germans gravitated toward communities such as those at Aurora and in Clackamas County in Oregon. The settlement at Aurora dates back to 1856, when it was founded by a group of religious Germans from Bethel, Missouri. The community was started and operated for a while on a semi-Utopian communistic basis. Later the Germans spread widely to both rural and urban areas, and they have taken an active part in community life.

One of the largest foreign groups to enter the Northwest, especially after 1890, was the Scandinavian. By 1910 more than 90,000 had come, and arrivals continued, though at a reduced rate, until 1924 when the gates were all but slammed shut on immigrants from all parts of the world. The concentration point of Norwegian immigrants in the United States was on the north central plains. From there they pushed westward into northeastern Montana and on

---

[2] By 1890 Washington was far out in the lead with 90,005 foreign-born residents, while Oregon had 57,317, and Idaho 17,456, inhabitants born outside the United States.

to the coast. They established numerous island settlements on the rich farm land of Puget Sound and in the Willamette Valley; a few settled in eastern Washington, while others went to the mining camps of western Montana and Idaho. They began arriving in the 1880s and continued to come on into the present century. King County with Seattle, Pierce County with Tacoma, and the farming and fishing counties of Snohomish, Skagit, Whatcom, and Kitsap in Washington are present-day Norwegian concentration points. Swedish immigration was contemporaneous with that of the Norwegians. They, too, pushed into the Pacific Northwest, but unlike their Scandinavian brethren, the Swedes favored working on the railroads and in lumber camps, where the mythical character Paul Bunyan and his blue ox were doing great deeds. The Swedes became close friends with Paul and taught him to swear with a Swedish accent. Ballard, a section of Seattle, is a present-day Swedish concentration point. The third contingent of the Scandinavian trio, the Danes, came a bit later. Many of them settled in farming communities established by themselves, as, for example, those at Danebo, west of Eugene, and at Junction City, Oregon. Others found their way into cities where the dairying industry, with which the Danes have considerable acquaintance, attracted many of them.

Although representing a new element in social pattern, Scandinavians were never unwelcome. They, and especially the second and succeeding generations, adapted themselves to the mores of the older established population. They were highly literate, and, though much of their Old World culture (especially their Lutheranism and their love of Selskab, coffee and layer cake) was retained, they rapidly became Americanized. They possessed independence of spirit, worshiped enterprise, and believed in democracy — all traits relished by the old pioneer stock.

Finns, erroneously associated with the Scandinavians so far as racial and linguistic traits are concerned, have drifted into the fishing towns and villages, especially Astoria, where much of the fishing industry is carried on by them. The Canadians have settled mostly in Washington, and like their kinsfolk from the British Isles, have participated in all phases of the community life, so much so that little distinction is made between these groups and the old American inhabitants.

Settling along both sides of the Idaho-Oregon Snake River line in the Malheur County area of Oregon and the Jordan River Valley, Idaho, were the Basques. This is range country and the Basques who entered this region in the 1890s have, in spite of their Spanish seafaring traditions, become adept at cattle and sheep raising. The Basques are a distinctive people and live peacefully and honestly by themselves. Their love of old-country traditions is at least outwardly evidenced by their partiality for red- and blue-roofed houses, and, at least on ceremonial occasions, by their appearance in native costume — black beret, scarf, silk shirt, and canvas shoes with straw soles. It is recorded that only two Basques applied for relief in Malheur County prior to 1938, and out of 200 applicants for old-age pensions in this county, not one was a Basque.

With the growth of urban centers the present century witnessed the coming of many immigrants from south and east Europe, although, as previously stated, in relatively fewer numbers than in the eastern states. These included the familiar Greek restaurateurs, Italian small shopkeepers, and Polish industrial workers. The Bolshevik Revolution caused White Russian émigrés also to take up residence in Seattle and Portland after 1917. Very few Mexicans, in fact, very few Latin Americans of any kind, have come to the Northwest to remain. Some transient Mexican laborers have done work as section hands on the railroads, and more recently as temporary farm laborers, but those who have become permanent residents of the United States seem to select the sunny Southwest rather than the dampish Northwest as a permanent abode. Many of the foreigners were Jews, who, reinforced by native-born Jews from other parts of the United States, also gravitated toward urban areas, where many of them achieved prominence in professional, financial, and business affairs.[3]

[3] In 1937 there were in Oregon 11,649 Jews; in Washington 18,422;

The Negro problem arose early. It will be recalled that the Negroes brought into the old Oregon country by early settlers from the South were not welcomed and that the Oregon constitution specifically excluded the immigration of free Negroes into the state of Oregon (see Chapter X). This measure has since become a dead letter. By 1940 there were 2,565 Negroes in Oregon; 7,424 in Washington; and only 595 in Idaho. They had settled chiefly in Seattle and Portland, and dwelt in districts of their own. During World War II the Negro population increased sharply in the large coastal towns. While a new complete census is awaited to determine the full extent of this growth, a partial count reveals that in one area alone, the Portland-Vanport-Vancouver region, the Negroes increased from approximately 2,000 in 1940 to 15,000 in 1944. In another spot, the Richmond-Hanford area, Negroes now comprise an important minority group.) Not all remained after the war was over, but large numbers of them have indicated a desire to make the Pacific Northwest their permanent home. What the effects of postwar dislocations will be upon the Negro population and upon the ecology of affected communities remains to be seen.

"The Yellow Peril"

Chinese began arriving on the West Coast during 1850. Like others throughout the world, Chinese men were stirred by the news of fabulous discoveries of gold in California. It was early observed that Chinese coolies were excellent workers; and in the face of an acute labor shortage, they were imported in large numbers by the Central Pacific Railroad Company to do construction work. When the Central Pacific line was completed in 1869 many of the unemployed Chinese drifted north, principally to Portland, where they competed with white workers for jobs. Anti-Chinese sentiment arose at once, and this was heightened by the financial

---

in Idaho 1,138. This is slightly more than 1 per cent of the total population of the first two states; less than .23 of 1 per cent in Idaho; whereas the percentage of Jews in the United States is 3.69.

panic of 1873. Still they came. By 1880 there were in Oregon 9,510 Chinese; in Washington, 3,186; and in Idaho, 3,379; but in California there were 75,132. In Northwest cities, as on the sand lots of San Francisco where Dennis Kearney carried on his antiyellow agitation, demonstrations were made against the Chinese. Passage of the Chinese Exclusion Act in 1882 brought only temporary abatement of the anticoolie sentiment, for in the Northwest the belief prevailed that illegal entry from Canada was constant and heavy, and the only solution, some thought, was mob action.

The Portland *Oregonian* took a vigorous stand against the Chinese, while at the same time it pointed out why the Chinese were being accepted in some quarters. They were useful to industry, which thrived by their economy. Poor people on the other hand complained, saying Chinese would secure many jobs not too lowly for Americans; or to use one expression appearing in the *Oregonian,* March 3, 1880: they put "our girls 'above' cooking and housework." Said this newspaper, January 1, 1880: "the smell of the drug is upon him, and he harbors the courtezan and plies the gamblers' trade, and by this threefold art entices and ruins our youth of both sexes, besides enslaving his own people."

Some local legal restraints were added to those already present from the time of statehood. For instance, laws were enacted prohibiting Chinese from mining without license or peddling without special licenses.

Passage of the Chinese Exclusion Act in 1882 pacified some critics, but not for long. By 1885–86 prejudices mounted and pointed toward violence. Through Portland's streets cries of "Kill the Chinks" and "Chase out the foreigners" were often heard. Many trade union members were inclined toward taking overt action. On one occasion Sylvester Pennoyer was credited with preventing violence by means of his persuasive oratory. Trouble was not confined to friction between whites and Chinese. The latter were organized by tongs, and rioting (usually over gambling) often broke out among what Americans called "Highbinder Societies," bearing such names as Hip Sing Hong, Sue Sing Hong, Hup Sing Hong, and so forth. "The Highbinders must Go," said the *Oregonian*, December 5, 1888. On September 5, 1885, Indians in Squak Valley (twenty miles north of Seattle) staged a massacre of some sleeping Chinese workers who had come there to pick hops, killing three and wounding three more. A month later a mass meeting held at the Northern Pacific Railroad town of Tacoma resulted in a decision to give the hapless Chinese there (most of whom had helped to build the Northern Pacific) thirty days to "git outa town or know the reason why." When the time was up, the Chinese were still there, but a mob of three hundred men escorted the coolies to the station in a driving rain and shipped them off to Portland. The day after, the Chinese quarter of Tacoma was burned and the "peaceful expulsion" was thus completed.

Seattle faced a similar situation. Aroused by the general storm of resentment toward the Chinese growing out of a depressed local employment situation, and also out of a prevailing racial prejudice, action first took the form of mass meetings in which certain elements demanded eviction by mob action. This sentiment was in no way allayed by the Seattle press, especially William R. Hearst's *Post-Intelligencer* and the Seattle *Call*, whose editorials also cried out for the scalps of "the treacherous almond-eyed sons of Confucius." To forestall violent mob action, some leading citizens took steps to organize "Home Guards." Things moved toward a climax when on February 7, 1886, the forces of expulsion (angered by failure of drastic legislation to be passed at Olympia) moved in on the Chinese quarters, loaded 350 occupants on wagons, and escorted them without any police interference to the dock at the foot of Main Street, where it was intended to place the unhappy Chinese aboard the S. S. *Queen of the Pacific* scheduled to depart for San Francisco. At this juncture the captain of the *Queen*, willing enough to take paying customers, threatened the mob with a hot-water hose. The result was that 196 Chinese, whose fares were paid and who wished to leave Seattle, departed for San Francisco on the delayed steamer. The rest were informed of their legal rights, but not without some skirmishing between the forces of law and order on the one hand, vigilante elements — including the Knights of Labor — on the other, and frightened Chinese in between. Further intervention of two units of the Home Guards — the Seattle Rifles and the University Cadets — served to restore order.

Hearing what had taken place, Governor Squire hastened to declare martial law, and soldiers were assigned guard duty in all parts of Seattle. Still further action was taken: President Cleveland ordered the Fourteenth United States Infantry to Seattle to augment the local police forces. Quiet returned to Seattle on the 8th of February, and the developments growing out of the affair took the form chiefly of legal conspiracy proceedings which resulted in no convictions.

In 1834 a Japanese junk washed ashore near Cape Flattery. Three Japanese men were rescued and brought to Fort Vancouver where they remained for a while before being taken to England and thence back to the Orient. Fifty years later the first Japanese woman arrived. She was Miyo Iwakoshi, and she took up residence in Portland. Six years later she married another Japanese immigrant, S. Takagi, and the two began to operate a Japanese restaurant. This was the beginning of what eventually became a heavy immigration of Japanese into the Northwest. The tide had reached a crest and had leveled off by 1930; at that time there were 17,837 Japanese in Washington; 4,958 in Oregon; and a mere 1,421 in Idaho. As a basis of comparison, there were then in California no less than 97,456 Japanese.

Early in the century this group of Orientals tended to move into agriculture, although many showed a preference for railroad and household work. Later there was a tendency to congregate in cities such as Portland, Seattle, and Tacoma (nearest ports of entry), but Japanese families early pushed up the Columbia River into the Hood River apple region. They did gardening and farming, and carried on small businesses with remarkable success; and more so than the Chinese and the Negroes, the Japanese mixed rather freely with the white population. Until the passage, 1921–23, of more stringent antialien land laws in all three northwest states, many Japanese purchased farms. Prior to the outbreak of war between the United States and Japan, relations between

SEATTLE (above) *Elliott Bay is in the foreground. Part of Lake Washington is visible in the right background, and in the far left snow-capped Mount Baker can be seen.* (below) *A Seattle fishing fleet. Oregon and Washington operate 13,000 such craft.*

Courtesy Seattle Chamber of Commerce

MOUNT RAINIER

the Japanese and white residents were rather friendly; especially was this true in Oregon, which state had been spared severe riots at the time of the anti-Chinese crusade. Instances of anti-Japanese sentiment did, however, exist. In the Hood River Valley an Anti-Alien League was organized which opposed selling and leasing of land to sons of Nippon. "We certainly do not intend to permit this essentially American valley to become a Japanese colony as have some sections of California," said the League's secretary in 1919. This year, which marked the beginning of the post-World War I era, witnessed an intensification of anti-Japanese sentiment and, as will be recalled, this contributed to the passage first of state anti-Japanese legislation, then to Japanese exclusion in the United States Immigration Act of 1924, an act which in turn strained Japanese-American diplomatic relations.

The Hood River region, and more particularly the Hood River American Legion Post, led in the anti-Japanese agitation following World War I, and again revealed a contemptuous attitude toward its Japanese residents during World War II. The Hood River Post carried its prejudices first to the state and ultimately to the National Legion Convention, which in turn influenced the passage of the Immigration Act of 1924 excluding Japanese from further immigration into the United States. Shortly after the outbreak of war with Japan on December 7, 1941, all Japanese were removed from the immediate coastal area. Most of them were placed in relocation camps scattered throughout the inland regions, and were under the supervision of the War Relocation Authority. Their property was held for them by the United States Alien Property Custodian and in most cases was given back soon after V-J Day to the Japanese loyal to America. At this time, too, these same loyal Japanese were permitted to return to the Coast, many to their former homes. Some Japanese evacuees, however, have chosen not to return to their former west coast homes because they have found more tolerance in the Middle West, where large numbers have secured postwar employment and where wartime prejudices subsided more quickly than in some areas on the coast.

Today most of the first-generation immigrants in the

Northwest are dead. The ratio of foreign-born to the total population is therefore less than it was prior to 1924, a ratio which, especially in Idaho, has always been small.[4] Except for Orientals, second- and third-generation foreigners have either blended through marriage with the older American stock, or have in other ways lost much of their identity as outsiders.

Persistence of the Westward Movement

Immigration was not confined to Europeans and Orientals, for the passing of the frontier by 1890 did not end the westward migration of Americans into the Northwest. Great numbers of Americans continue to this day to pull up stakes and move West, where, they hope, life holds new possibilities for them.

Of interest is the movement of individual American cultural groups from other areas of the United States to the Pacific Northwest. A conspicuous example has been the migration during the present century of more than 14,000 Appalachian Highlanders to western Washington. One group coming from the Kentucky-West Virginia-Virginia section

[4] In 1919 there were 411,955 foreign-born persons in the three Northwest states. The 1940 Census reveals the following number of European-born in the three Northwest states:

	Oregon	Washington	Idaho
Austria	2,097	4,373	542
Czechoslovakia	1,169	1,424	373
Denmark	3,013	5,424	1,244
England	6,385	16,206	2,252
Finland	4,343	9,199	658
France	799	1,482	271
Germany	9,883	15,470	2,533
Greece	1,267	2,476	345
Hungary	512	637	102
Ireland	2,194	3,758	466
Italy	4,083	8,853	892
Norway	6,129	26,489	1,637
Poland	1,431	3,119	166
Russia	5,981	8,598	1,113
Sweden	8,498	26,993	2,974
Totals	57,784	134,501	15,567

Grand Total 207,852

of the Appalachians settled in the hilly parts of Lewis and Cowlitz counties. Others from the southern Appalachians of North Carolina and Tennessee removed themselves to the Puget Sound lowlands of Skagit and Snohomish counties in Washington. Their coming, after generations of residence in the hill country of the upper South, seems to be explained by railroad and other developments which resulted in exploitation of their homelands and at the same time made movement elsewhere relatively easy. Environmental shifts have meant in many cases a change of types of work pursued, but to a striking degree old cultural traits, language peculiarities, folk music, and attitude toward work have been retained in Washington.

The terrific drought which hit the west central plains during the middle 1930s created a Dust Bowl from which large numbers were compelled to flee. John Steinbeck's book, *Grapes of Wrath*, focused public attention on but one phase of this westward exodus, the Okie-Arkie "jalopy" migration to California. Actually, about a half million of these unfortunate Dust Bowl refugees moved into the Inland Empire and settled, as did pioneers of an earlier day, on cheap lands available to them. These modern "dusted out" immigrants came not so much from Oklahoma and Arkansas as from the previously productive wheat and corn belt of the Dakotas, Nebraska, and Kansas, and from Wyoming, eastern Colorado, and eastern Montana, areas which were also badly affected by the protracted drought.

In hitherto sparsely settled areas, as, for example, the Bonner's Ferry, Idaho, district near the Canadian line, cutover timberlands could be bought cheaply and on easy terms, and clearing the ground of stumps could be done with modern equipment for about ten dollars per acre. Simple dwellings befitting a pioneer venture could be erected cheaply, and a yearly income of $400 to $600 from the land enabled the families to survive the depression. Others found their way into reclaimed areas; still others went into urban areas where little or no industrial employment could then be obtained. About 200,000 immigrants streamed into Oregon between 1930 and 1937, although not all of these were Dust Bowl evacuees. Some were described as a remnant of the general westward movement drift, some as seekers of a milder climate, as migratory laborers, and as people who normally like to move to neighboring states. While there was also an exodus, the net turnover has been determined as one person leaving for every two entering.

A more detailed analysis of the modern migrant families suggests additional comparisons with those who nearly a century before came across the Plains to Oregon in covered wagons. Families in both cases were large — larger than the average present resident family; single male migrants were numerous; the dominant age group was from twenty to forty-four. Just as the early arrivals came to a large extent from rural backgrounds, but were jacks of all trades, likewise a very high percentage of modern "On to Oregon" migrants were unskilled laborers, farm hands, truck farmers, and salesmen; some also were skilled carpenters and mechanics. Remembering that there is always present a large number of drifters ("bindle stiffs") and migrant workers, it is not surprising, in view of the Depression, that only about one half of those who came chose to remain. Figures for the other Northwest states are about the same as those for Oregon.

Unlike the covered-wagon days when new arrivals were given a thumping welcome, and also unlike the 1890s when foreigners were eagerly sought, the immigrants of the trying thirties, generally speaking, were not wanted. Wrote the *Oregonian,* February 6, 1936: "Certainly if California piles up the transients on its borders, and Washington does the same, Oregon cannot but do likewise, and then such action would swell across the mountains like a wave."

Who was to blame for this great pouring of transients into the Pacific Northwest? What should be done? Northwest planners met in search of answers. The regional Chambers of Commerce were largely to blame because they had over-advertised the region. Industry, especially the lumber industry, was criticized for offering no stabilization. Professor Philip A. Parsons, head of the Oregon State Planning Board, made these pertinent observations: the Northwest in 1938 should recognize that "new residents . . . are now existing

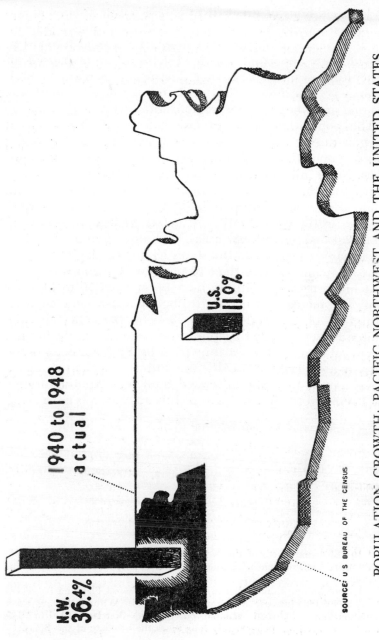

1940 to 1948 actual

N.W. 36.4%

U.S. 11.0%

SOURCE: U S BUREAU OF THE CENSUS

POPULATION GROWTH: PACIFIC NORTHWEST AND THE UNITED STATES

under conditions of great distress and political danger." Information should be gathered; industries should be developed; a conservation program should be carried forward to provide new opportunities. At best the future expansion of agriculture (quite apart from the steady increase in farm tenancy) [5] was limited. Future industrial development was the one great hope for the region,[6] the Board held.

The population boom experienced by Washington and Oregon during the 1940–45 period, and the corresponding loss of population in Idaho, was brought on by war conditions. More military installations were placed in the coastal states than in Idaho, and military personnel, drained from other areas, was correspondingly large. Moreover, war industries in the coastal cities attracted civilian workers from the rural and small-town areas, including Idaho. Washington became classed with the states having the highest rate of increase, namely, more than 15 per cent. Oregon was in the next highest group, with an increase of from 10 to 14.9 per cent. The increase turned out to be modest when compared with that of the period 1946–50. The prediction by the United States Census that the trends established during the war would exceed the wartime peak by 1950 has been borne out. In a special release by the Bureau of Census, dated November 4, 1949, the estimated total population figure for the Pacific Northwest states as of July 1, 1949, was as follows:

POPULATION FIGURES FOR THE PACIFIC NORTHWEST, 1949

	July 1, 1949	1940	Increase (+) or Decease (−) 1940–49	Per Cent
Washington	2,582,000	1,736,191	+ 846,000	+ 48.7
Oregon	1,736,000	1,089,684	+ 647,000	+ 59.3
Idaho	592,000	559,456	− 39,000	− 6.9
Totals	4,910,000	3,385,331	+1,454,000	+101.1

[5] In 1885, one-fourth of the Northwest farmers were tenants; in 1935, according to the President's Commission on Tenancy, one-half were in this category.

[6] It is of interest to note that in 1938 the Northwest Planning Board expected a 400,000 increase in population by 1950. Without having exact population figures for 1938 available, one observes that from 1940 to 1949 the increase was 1,524,669 — nearly four times the estimate of the Board.

Since the war's end Oregon has not only stepped ahead of Washington in rate of increase, but for the years 1940–49 it leads the nation with its 59.3 per cent increase. The Pacific Northwest is therefore anything but static in its population makeup. It is constantly being refreshed from the outside; it is forever undergoing a reshuffling from within.

Growing City Consciousness

The rise of an industrial America was inescapably accompanied by the rise of cities. As industries pushed westward during the decades following the Civil War, places that once were classed as small country towns began to take on the aspects of urban centers, and new industrial cities came into being. As large modern sawmills, cement factories, slaughter houses, canneries, railroad shops, iron works, shipyards, commercial establishments, and innumerable other industrial plants sprang up, rural families, and especially farmers' sons, began drifting toward the cities in the belief that factory wages would be more remunerative than the slim returns from long hours of farm labor. And as previously noted, many immigrants gravitated toward the cities to seek similar employment.

During the half-century from 1890 to 1940 the population of Seattle increased from 42,837 to 368,302, with a metropolitan population of 452,639; near-by and competitive Tacoma saw its population increased from 36,006 to 109,408, with a metropolitan area numbering 156,018. Spokane, erroneously regarded by Seattle as its "inland outpost," jumped during the same period from a small country cattle and wheat town of 19,922 into second place in Washington with 122,001 inhabitants and a metropolitan population placed at 141,370. Oregon's largest city, Portland, numbered 46,385 in 1890, and in its determined race to keep abreast of bumptious Seattle registered 305,394, and a metropolitan population of 406,406, in 1940. In Idaho this cityward shift has not been so pronounced, for in 1940 Boise City, Idaho's largest urban center, had but 26,130 inhabitants, and Pocatello, next in size, 18,133.

The war greatly augmented the growth of the cities, but exact figures are not at present available. Too, war industries stepped up the population of such smaller cities as Vancouver, Klamath Falls, Everett, and Longview. Between 1940 and 1943, the Seattle metropolitan area increased 18.2 per cent; the Portland metropolitan area increased 24 per cent. These rates were considerably greater than that of the Los Angeles metropolitan area, which was 13 per cent.

In addition to injecting new growth and activity into established cities, the late war created new cities. Most spectacular was the mushrooming emergence of Hanford (near Richland), Washington, as a place to produce fissionable materials in connection with the making of atomic bombs. This city was selected for its proximity to the needed cooling waters of the Columbia and availability of hydroelectric power in sufficient quantity. Hanford, near the turn of the century, had been the center of an ambitious, but weakly financed, irrigation system serving the northern half of Benton County. It had prospered only briefly, and by 1942 was engaged only in small truck-farming, chiefly asparagus and cherries. In the early months of 1943, a 200-mile tract was acquired by lease or purchase through the Real Estate Division of the Office of the Chief of Engineers. Eventually, nearly one thousand square miles were brought under government control. Only a few farms and the villages of Hanford and Pasco were on the site of the project. On April 6, 1943, ground was broken for the construction camp at Hanford, which at the peak of construction activity for what was then known as the "White Bluffs Military Project," had a population of 60,000, making it the fourth-largest city in the state of Washington. Pasco boomed from 4,000 to 10,000 almost overnight. The Richland population had taken ill their eviction, until the circumstances, but not the nature, of the project had been explained to them by Lieutenant Colonel Harry Kadlec, himself a native of Washington. The decision to continue building up an atomic stockpile has caused the Hanford area to flourish in the postwar era.

Another city, Vanport, emerged on the swampy ground between Portland and Vancouver, Washington. A city of hastily constructed prefabricated dwellings, it served mainly as a residence for war workers. A disastrous flood in the winter of 1947–48 did not enhance Vanport as a city for homemakers.

The Labor Front

A normal accompaniment of industrial urban population is the strengthening of labor unions. As observed by the *Oregonian*, "Labor unions came with pioneers." The first in Oregon and Washington was the Typographical Society in Portland (1862). It was followed, for example, by the Brotherhood of Locomotive Engineers (1867) and the Longshoremen's Protective Union (1868). The seventies and eighties saw the rise of many more unions throughout the Northwest — notably the Knights of Labor, succeeded by the American Federation of Labor. As has been pointed out, these labor organizations became identified with political upsurges during the closing decade of the nineteenth century. Prevalent as the labor organizations were, their growth and strength were at first stunted by the rather shifting character of Northwest labor, the moving about freely from one job to another. This did not make for stability of the labor market. The first strike in the region was in 1869. It, like most other early demonstrations and walkouts, brought no noticeable gains. The first successful strike of significance was the carpenters' strike in 1890.

During the 1880s the mining areas of Idaho and western Montana experienced sporadic but violent labor troubles. Union organizers from the copper mines at Butte spread their activities into the Coeur d'Alene district of northern Idaho. The first labor disputes to occur there were at Bellevue and Bullion in 1884. These assumed ominous proportions when armed action was threatened by both mine owners and workers; and while agreement was reached without bloodshed, it set a pattern for subsequent strikes which did result in rioting and killing. At Gem, Idaho, near Wallace, in July, 1892, a pitched battle occurred between miners and guards imported by the operators. The workers scored a victory when the guards surrendered, but there were six dead and many wounded. Matters did not rest here. Subsequently, many miners were arrested, placed in a "bull pen" near Wallace, and tried for conspiracy and murder. None of the 140 miners charged with murder were convicted, and convictions for conspiracy were not sustained by higher courts.

Meanwhile the Western Federation of Miners was formed, and labor troubles in this region continued until the turn of the century. At Kellogg, Idaho, in April, 1899, another violent flare-up occurred when the miners asked for $3.50 per day in wages, and for a union shop. The demands were refused, the belligerent workers commandeered a Northern Pacific Railroad train serving the Shoshone County area, and proceeded to Kellogg, where rioting resulted. At this point Governor Frank Steunenberg intervened by asking President McKinley for, and receiving, federal forces to cope with this situation. The governor also declared martial law on May 3, 1899, and in turn came the arrest of about one thousand miners. The ensuing court proceedings, the State of Idaho vs. the Western Federation of Miners in which the future senator, William E. Borah, served as prosecutor, were long and bitter. The prisoners, after about a year of incarceration pending a decision, staged a mass escape and the prosecution failed by default. In resentment, a tragic anticlimax to this event came in 1905 when a disgruntled labor agitator and self-confessed criminal named Harry Orchard placed a bomb on Steunenberg's gate; the explosion of the bomb killed the capable ex-governor.

In making his confession Orchard declared that he had been chiefly influenced in committing this act by none other than William D. Haywood, then an active national officer of the Western Federation of Miners. Haywood was promptly arrested in Salt Lake City and was brought to Idaho for trial. Interest in this case became nation-wide, and many doubts were held regarding the probable complicity of Haywood in the treacherous murder. Haywood's trial, held in 1907, ended in his acquittal.

The entrance of Haywood into the Steunenberg murder case spotlighted a personality whose political and economic views, and whose subsequent radical labor-organizing activities, were destined to arouse the public temper as never before. In 1905 it was "Big Bill" Haywood who was largely instrumental in founding an organization built upon the Marxian concept of the class struggle, namely, the Industrial Workers of the World. Its members, popularly known as the I.W.W.s, or Wobblies, found the Northwest lumber camps, mines, and farming areas a fruitful climate for operation. The I.W.W. favored the uniting of all industrial workers of the world into one body and the pursuance of a radical course of action that would hasten the demise of the capitalist system. The Preamble to the I.W.W. statement of principles refuted the old American slogan: "A fair day's wage for a fair day's work." Instead, the watchword of the I.W.W.s was the "Abolition of the wage system." Although its appeal was world-wide, membership came largely from western miners, metal workers, railroad men, and migratory workers. Organization followed the lines of the present-day Congress of Industrial Organizations in that it formed industrial unions on a nation-wide scope, as, for example, the Marine Transport Workers' Industrial Union.

Trouble followed in the wake of the I.W.W.s. In the Pacific Northwest many were arrested on a great variety of charges, especially during World War I. Among those arrested in 1918 was Haywood, who had advocated violence. He was charged with committing seditious acts, was this time convicted, and given a twenty-year sentence and a $10,000 fine. While out on bail awaiting a new trial in 1921, he fled to the U.S.S.R., where he lived until his death seven years later. In opposition to arrests such as those of Haywood and others, came bitter denouncements that the I.W.W.s had been "denied the right of free press, free speech and free assemblage," as guaranteed by the Bill of Rights.

The contemporary literature for and against the I.W.W.s is highly colored. One of the most interesting accounts of them was given in a series of articles written in 1918 by Robert W. Bruère, reporter for the New York *Evening Post*, entitled "Following the Trail of the I.W.W." Bruère estimated that in this crucial war year there were about 7,000 members in the Northwest forests, that for the most part the men who felled the trees for the war effort were Wobblies. Bruère, in a report to the National Institute of Social Sciences (1918), took the serious view that "The problem is not one of the malice or wickedness of individuals, either among the employers or the workers. The country," he said, "is facing a serious psychological situation" which was likely to spread if not handled intelligently. Bruère held the view that the incidents of mistreatment of the I.W.W.s was basically wrong. He said: "In the face of such incidents is there any wonder that the I.W.W. preaches a doctrine of revolution . . . ?"

Apart from the conflicting views, the fact remains that the I.W.W.s were powerful enough to tie up periodically much of the Northwest logging operations during and immediately after World War I. Much as the general public hated the "Wobblies," there were many who sympathized with their 1917 wartime demands: an eight-hour day, $60 per month and board, wholesome food served on porcelain dishes, and sanitary sleeping quarters with a maximum of twelve men to each shack.

The most tantalizing feature of an I.W.W. wartime strike was clearly stated in the Union's Northwest organ, *The Industrial Worker*, published in Seattle. Wrote its editor, May 12, 1923: "Fellow Workers, the I.W.W. believes in striking on the job. . . . Fellow Workers, it is up to you. . . . Organized crews can use the strike on the job with terrible effect — with great injury to the profits of the boss. . . . Put the fear of the Wobblies into the boss."

The climax of I.W.W. disturbances came at Centralia, Washington, on Armistice Day, 1919, when some American legionnaires broke rank in the parade and without legal right tried to oust I.W.W. members — including Wesley Everest, who was also a veteran — from their own hall. Shooting resulted, and four legionnaires were killed. During the mob violence which followed, the organized veterans seized Everest and first emasculated and then lynched him. More than a thousand arrests of I.W.W. members and other suspected radicals were made; one of these, a boy of nineteen, lost his sanity while in jail. Nine workmen were accused of killing the legionnaires, and upon conflicting evidence were convicted of second-degree murder. Church and other groups who became aroused and investigated the case succeeded in obtaining clemency for the convicts. Only one served a long prison term; he was released in 1939 by Governor Martin. Following this event, or at least following a lumber strike in 1923, the I.W.W. all but vanished, as did also the conservative and ineffectual Loyal Legion of Loggers and Lumbermen.

In general the post-World War I labor problems were not unlike those of the present postwar period; labor's chief objective was the maintenance of the war period gains. During the period from 1919 to the middle twenties the chief bargaining agents were the state federations of labor (the A.F. of L.), which demanded retention of the eight-hour day and wages to meet the inflationary prices following the war. The vicious spiral of wage boosts and price increases continued until 1922, when a sharp recession set in. Even so, in 1921 seamen were asked to accept a wage cut; and, notwithstanding efforts of the United States Shipping Board, an eighty-one-day marine strike ensued. And even before the return of the railroads by the federal government (in which hands they had been during the war) to owners in 1920, rumblings of discontent were heard from railroad workmen. Many left their jobs in open defiance of the National Transportation Act. The various federal wartime labor relations boards did what they could to maintain industrial peace, but by 1923 most of these emergency organizations had passed out of existence. In concluding a review of this period (see Bibliography), Harry Elmer Tobie says: "In this period of extreme price and wage adjustments, nothing was definitely settled as to which principle should prevail in the settlement of industrial disputes: the principle of the living wage, or the principle of reasonable and equitable profits."

The depression administered a telling blow to organized labor, although the N.R.A. offered some resuscitation. In the

1934 marine union strike, organized labor showed surprising strength; and with the upswing in business there emerged the now powerful C.I.O. Surveys show that for the period 1927–40 the Pacific Northwest was no more seriously affected by labor troubles than was the United States as a whole; basing calculations on annual averages, less than two per cent of the gainfully employed went out on strike during those years. One observes, however, that for the period 1927–33 there was very little strike activity; for the years 1933–40, the tide of strikes was rising. The top year was 1935, when 51,000 Northwest workers went out on strike and 1,600,000 man-days of work were lost due to that cause. It is also of interest to note that during this period of more than a decade, nearly one-half of "idle man-days" due to strikes could be charged to the lumber industry; and in order of corresponding strike employment came the longshore business and then mining.

During the past decade, 1940–50, the Northwest, and more particularly the Seattle A.F. of L. Teamsters' Union, has found in the person of David W. Beck a remarkable and outstanding labor leader. As head of the Teamsters' Union, Beck has gradually gained control of nearly all organized, and, in effect, unorganized labor in Seattle. Through "Dave" Beck's efforts Seattle is today regarded as one of the most tightly closed-shop cities in the entire country. In accomplishing this, Beck, who believes in the profit system, has gone far toward stabilizing the industrial-labor setup. His election, first to membership, then, in April, 1950, to the presidency, of the University of Washington Board of Regents is an indication of the present influence of organized labor in the life of the larger community.

There was what amounted to a moratorium on strikes during World War II. Immediately thereafter labor began to strike for higher wages to meet the rapidly rising costs of living.

Chapter XXIV

The Refinements of Life

Literary Strivings

UNTIL THE ADVENT of high-speed modern communication, the Pacific Northwest had been considered remote from the large population centers of the world where culture and learning had flourished. But at no time was this far-western civilization devoid of what might be termed the refinements of life. Settlers brought with them to the West their assorted cultural baggage, and never allowed this heritage to become lost. Fur traders, covered-wagon migrants, cowhands, and the immigrants from across the seas all loved their respective folk songs and folktales. In almost all groups there was someone who could play a "fiddle" or an accordion, sing the old favorites, and spin old yarns, however tall these tales might have been. More difficult to the pioneers was the problem of securing access to the printed word when, and if, that was desired. Reading matter was always scarce. Relatively few books had been accorded space in covered wagons, and reading material of all kinds — books, magazines, newspapers and the like — was slow in finding widespread circulation (see Chapter XIII). An exception was the Bible.

There was also a dearth of literary production, at least of merit, during the pioneer period. Students of Northwest literature point only with antiquarian pride to *The Prairie Flower; or Adventures in the Far West*, published in Cincinnati in 1849, as the region's first novel, but somehow fail to agree as to who wrote the book. To be sure, Joaquin Miller lived and wrote in Oregon, but many other states and countries were host to this wandering, imaginative lyricist

[439

who had crossed the Plains from his native state of Indiana in 1852. Sizing up the literary situation in 1889, the late Professor Edmond S. Meany said: "No, Puget Sound has no literature but this region has plenty of real estate, timber, coal, iron and fish, and at present the inhabitants are scrambling over each other in their efforts to become rich out of the natural wealth of the land. . . . Literature will be fostered by and by." Meany was right in the sense that little of what might be called *belles-lettres* had, by 1889, been produced by northwestern writers.

What Professor Meany did not fully realize at the time was that the region he loved so much was about ready to burst forth with a considerable output of literary effusions. The year 1890 produced the Reverend Frederick Homer Balch's *The Bridge of the Gods*, a book not great as a literary masterpiece but one which as an authentic and sympathetic portrayal of Indian life in the Northwest was to enjoy, in time, a prolonged national popularity. The book has gone through thirty or more printings, and it is still being read. Balch, a native of Lebanon, Oregon, and a resident of Lyle, Washington, died, at the age of thirty, six months after the first publication of his book.

Although not a native of Idaho, Mary Hallock Foote lived there long enough to be affected by her environment. She related her impressions in several novels dealing with mining society, which she had come to know was the wife of a mining engineer. Her prose contributions were highly romanticized versions of a period of mining history characterized by bloody labor warfare, and her view of the militant labor unions was distinctly unsympathetic. Mrs. Foote's numerous novels, all published in the East, were popular both in and out of the region — *The Chosen Valley* (1892), *Coeur D'Alène* (1894), *The Desert and the Sown* (1902), and *A Picked Company* (1912).

Ella R. Higginson of Washington was another writer of some distinction in this period, which was dominated by female authors. While her creative efforts were confined mostly to poetry, she also achieved considerable success in her only novel, *Mariella; of Out West*, published by Macmillan in 1904. It portrayed realistically the conditions of pioneer life during the "boom" years of settlement. Her short stories and poems (her favorite form of expression) dealing with rural pioneer life also met with a warm response from her readers who, pioneers themselves, were able to recognize their prototypes in the pages. Also writing in the local-color tradition and primarily a poet, too, was Herbert Bashford. His *Nature Stories of the Northwest* were sensitive impressions in prose of his physical surroundings. There were other lesser literary figures writing in the same vein during this period. One was Orville Adams, whose novel, *The Cruiser*, was published in Spokane in 1909. All of them drew on the pioneer era with which they were familiar. The emphasis was always on events and problems peculiar to the area, with the result that with a few exceptions their works lacked universal appeal.

Probably the most widely read novels in the Northwest during the first decade of the century were those written by Eva Emery Dye, who, like her literary predecessors, drew upon the region's past for her materials. As she wrote for a market which demanded tales of heroic exploits and epical achievements, she altered history to suit her purposes. *McLoughlin and Old Oregon* (1900), *Stories of Oregon* (1900), *The Conquest* (1902), and *McDonald of Oregon: A Tale of Two Shores* (1906) all glorified early events in Northwestern history. Most of her books were published by A. C. McClurg and Company of Chicago, which concern had also brought out the Balch book. Her novel, *The Conquest*, reached Broadway, where it was presented in dramatic form.

Mrs. Dye provides the easy transition from historical fiction to regional nonfiction; in this field the writings (here again of a woman) of Frances Fuller Victor of Oregon are outstanding. Mrs. Victor is now best known as a historian, and a fairly good one. But in her early career as a writer, trying to assist her naval engineer husband in supplementing a meager income, she performed editorial and general newspaper work in San Francisco. In 1865 she and her husband moved to Oregon and from then on began a steady outpouring of writing on the Northwest — *River of the West* (1870),

Oregon and Washington (1872), and many articles. Then in 1878 Mrs. Victor joined the staff of the historian Hubert Howe Bancroft, who at the time was beginning the writing and compiling of his thirty-nine-volume historical work. Acting in the capacity of "ghost writer," Mrs. Victor wrote several of Bancroft's histories.[1] To this day Mrs. Victor's parts of the Bancroft volumes are considered excellent reference material.

Much less reliable and much more slanted as to emphasis and personal opinion was Mrs. Victor's contemporary, the journalist, poet, and historian, Samuel A. Clarker, whose *Pioneer Days of Oregon History* (1905) tends to romanticize pioneer life and to confuse legends with facts.

Early in the present century the state university and college assumed leadership in historical writing, and with mixed results. The late Professor John B. Horner, Oregon State College, continued to glorify the Northwest's pioneer past as did also Professor Meany, for a long time head of University of Washington's history department. Meany was a living embodiment of Washington's traditions, and a student's course at the University was not complete without exposure to Professor Meany's lectures. Not only did the trustees show their esteem by naming the campus auditorium Meany Hall, but today's imposing and modern hostelry in University District is named the Meany Hotel. Meany's best work (see Bibliography for other references) is his *History of Washington* (1910). At the University of Oregon, the late Professor Joseph Schafer wrote *A History of the Pacific Northwest* (1905), the first standard textbook on the region; and at the University of Idaho, Professor Cornelius J. Bros-

---

[1] John W. Caughey in his biography *Hubert Howe Bancroft: Historian of the West* (Berkeley, 1946), pp. 262–63, accords Mrs. Victor authorship of the following of Bancroft's *Works* published between 1884–90: All of the *History of Oregon*, Vols. I and II; all of *Washington, Idaho, and Montana;* all of *Alaska;* all of *British Columbia;* and of the *History of California,* one-third of Vol. VI, five-eights of Vol. VII; *Nevada, Colorado, and Wyoming,* sixteen-seventeenths; *Northwest Coast,* roughly one-eighth; *California Inter Pocula,* one-tenth. Alfred Powers, *History of Oregon Literature* (Portland, 1935), p. 308, credits Mrs. Victor with authorship of more of Bancroft's works than does Caughey.

nan has written on the history of his·state (see also Bibliography).

A remarkable mixture, and not only of fictional and nonfictional writing, was Charles Erskine Scott Wood, whose work straddles the preceding and present century. To quote Sidney Warren, *Farthest Frontier* (New York, 1949), Wood was "one of the most unusual and complex personalities this country has produced. . . . He was dubbed 'The Philosophic Anarchist,' and for the major part of his life he was in the forefront of any movement aimed at the amelioration of human misery." Wood contributed to the periodicals of his day, wrote many short stories, and also produced some poetry. Wood was in the vanguard of social critics, since become numerous, whose views have often incurred the scorn of the local press.

Most notable of such figures was the one-time Professor J. Allen Smith, University of Washington political scientist, who had come to the University following dismissal from Marietta College (Ohio) for having supported the candidacy of William Jennings Bryan in the 1896 election. His book, *The Spirit of American Government* (1907), won him a national reputation as a scholar and critic of modern society. Because of liberal leanings, his dismissal from the University of Washington was sought, but was not obtained.

During the 1920s and 1930s Pacific Northwest writers, especially creative writers, aligned themselves with two separate and opposing camps. One group preferred to carry on in the academic tradition; to imitate in style, form, and technique the classical masters whose worth had withstood the critics and time. Opposed to these were writers who, to borrow a term, were "toting the banner of 'regional culture.'" Much writing and publishing has been done by each group. Not all of it is likely to become immortal; but from the pens of a number of Northwest writers has come what might be the basis for a genuine regional literature. Examples of this could be numerous, but suffice it to say that *Honey in the Horn*, by H. L. Davis, a prize-winning novel with pioneer Oregon as its setting, was an ably executed regional study.

Davis, unlike earlier romanticists of the Northwest, portrays pioneer homesteading life in eastern Oregon as being anything but pleasant and heroic. Archie Binns has done both fictional and nonfictional writing, and among others his novel, *The Laurels Are Cut Down,* uses the local backdrop and with telling effect creates characters that belong in this setting. So, too, do James Stevens in *Paul Bunyan* and Nard Jones in *Oregon Detour, Swift Flows the River,* and his other writings. Publishing houses have come to recognize that creative writing in the Northwest has great vitality and promise, and seek with eagerness the best of the writing that is now being produced. Vardis Fisher is perhaps associated with a region somewhat larger than the Northwest, but his one-time attachment to Idaho gives that state a claim to him. Fisher is a very able writer and rightly belongs to the so-called school of the "new regionalism." Largely autobiographical, some of his novels deal with life in the Antelope Hills where he had grown up. During the depression years, 1931–37, Fisher brought out seven novels, all published at Caldwell, Idaho. His best known book, *Children of God,* however, deals with the life of the Prophet Joseph Smith, who was never in Idaho.

Not all Northwest authors are regionalists in the strict meaning of the term, and many who happen to live in Oregon, Washington, or Idaho have preferred to write about subject matter and scenes far removed from those physically closest to them. Michael Foster was one of these and his novels, *American Dream* and *Forgive Adam,* won him recognition among readers in many lands. The first three novels by Sophus Keith Winther, long a resident of Oregon and Washington, have their setting not in the Northwest but in Cass County, Nebraska, where the author grew up. This trilogy, *Take All to Nebraska, Mortgage Your Heart,* and *This Passion Never Dies,* has also been published in both Denmark and Sweden, and in recognition of his work the author was decorated by King Christian X of Denmark with the Medal of Freedom. The setting for his novel *Beyond the Garden Gate* is, however, placed in Eugene, Oregon. Clara Weatherwax was most representative of a growing group of so-called proletarian novelists during the thirties, when that type of fiction was not unfashionable. Her *Marching, Marching* has Washington as its background, but that fact is only incidental, for what she portrayed were the intensified class antagonisms, the injustices of class oppression, and the experience of workers in labor's struggle. The Seattle situation, therefore, was merely a case study of a general and widespread condition. Robert Cantrel may also be regarded as another member of the proletarian school of writers from the Northwest.

At the present there is no dearth of literary production in the Northwest. Stewart Holbrook, having returned from his native Vermont to make his home in Portland, frequently writes magazine articles and books on obscure aspects and characters in history. Ernest Haycox has published more than a score of novels dealing with the highly romantic aspects of western life. Also prolific is the short-story writer, Robert Ormond Case.

From the very beginning, poetry and verse have been a favorite form of literary expression. Even the first issues of the first newspaper in the entire land beyond the Rocky Mountains, the *Oregon Spectator*, included rhymes on a variety of themes. Almost everyone, it seemed, wrote poetry, although during the early period only one frontier poet, Joaquin Miller, achieved any reputation beyond his native region. Samuel Simpson was another of the early poets to achieve considerable popularity among his fellow Oregonians, but neither his fame nor that of his "epic" poem, *Beautiful Willamette*, has endured to any appreciable extent. Both Ella R. Higginson and Herbert Bashford published their first volumes of poetry in 1898, and their collections deal almost entirely with the scenery and nature of the Northwest. Their poetry extolled the changing beauty of the seasons, the grandeur and majesty of the mountains, and the alternately turbulent and pacific sea. *Songs of the Olympics,* by Alice Harriman, was another well-known book of poetry which continued in the descriptive vein. Florence Ashley Beeler was the first of the Washington poets to inaugurate a new approach, for the range of her subjects was much wider.

Charles Erskine Scott Wood also wrote poetry, the appeal of which was based largely on the ideas it conveyed. Stoddard King of Spokane became, for a while, one of the most widely quoted versifiers in the country with the publication during the twenties of two volumes of light and humorous rhymes, *What the Queen Said* and *Grand Right and Left*. And in 1931 Audrey Wurdemann, a Seattle girl, won the Pulitzer prize for her second volume of poetry, *Bright Ambush*. She was the youngest writer ever to be so honored. She remains today one of the most widely recognized of American poets. Two other Washingtonians, Mary Carolyn Davies and Genevieve Taggard, have also achieved some degree of fame since leaving their native environment. Poets have been more numerous than either novelists or short-story writers. Their verse has appeared in local newspapers and magazines as well as national periodicals, and they have had their work issued in book form by local presses in Portland, Oregon, and Caldwell, Idaho.

There is probably a greater proportion of writers from the Northwest whose stories and articles appear in national publications than from any other region, aside from the publishing centers themselves. Recently Ben Hibbs, editor of the *Saturday Evening Post*, stated that "I don't know another city the size of Portland that can boast as many top writers." Ernest Haycox is doubtless in a class by himself, for he has had more than four hundred stories published since 1922, but others, too, from the state of Oregon are receiving a wide hearing in national weeklies and monthlies such as the *Saturday Evening Post*, *Collier's*, *McCall's*, *Atlantic Monthly*, and *American Mercury*. Among the more successful have been Richard L. Neuberger, able critic of Northwest affairs; the brother-and-sister team, Victoria and Robert Ormond Case; John and Ward Hawkins; Stewart Holbrook; Ben Hur Lampman; and Roderick Lull.

The Northwest Press

The pattern of journalistic development in the Pacific Northwest paralleled that of other parts of the country. The impact of technological changes in transportation and communication exerted the same influence on newspaper growth here as elsewhere. Until the influx of population and the end of isolation on the frontier, the pioneer newspaper exhibited the characteristics common to all the newspapers of that era. Prior to the 1880s, almost all the papers in the Northwest were either political, religious, or so-called literary organs. They were founded invariably to satisfy an editor's own need to express his views and to publish an organ in which he might indulge in special pleading. The early pioneer newspaper was almost always the unique product of an editor whose individuality was clearly discernible on all of its pages. By present-day standards, the contents were dull and unrelieved by any of the now familiar media used to entertain the modern reader — cartoons, comic strips, sports columns, Sunday pictorial supplements, and so forth. The life of the average newspaper was a brief one: newspapers would mushroom and in many instances soon disappear.

The *Oregon Spectator* (started in 1845) enjoys the distinction of being the first newspaper founded west of the Rocky Mountains (see p. 157). It survived longer than most of the other papers issued during that early period, but it did not last even a decade. As was to be expected, the great majority of journals were weeklies, and it was as a weekly that the famous *Oregonian* (founded in 1850) of Portland had its beginnings (see again p. 157). No other newspaper expressed in a more classic way the era of personal journalism. For more than forty years, until his death in 1910, Harvey Scott was its moving spirit. He shaped its policies, he set its editorial tone, and he lifted it from the level of just another paper to the position of pre-eminence which it has continued to occupy.

Other important newspapers were also intimately associated with the names of persons who founded them. The *Washington Standard* at Olympia was started by John Miller Murphy in 1860; for half a century he was its dominant influence. By the time its career was terminated in 1922, the newspaper had enjoyed a longer period of uninterrupted service than any other established during that early period in Washington Territory. Another outstanding example was the *Seattle Times,* which, until it was taken over by Colonel Alden J. Blethen in 1896, experienced hard times as a result of numerous changes in ownership and lack of funds. Under Blethen's guidance, the paper became, and has remained, one of the leading journals in the Northwest. Sam Jackson launched the *Oregon Journal* in Portland in 1902 and made it a success. It is today one of the leading afternoon dailies in the state of Oregon. And there were many lesser and less-enduring papers whose destinies were inextricably linked with that of their editor or publishers. But by the turn of the century, the era of personal journalism was well on its way out. The newspaper became primarily a news-disseminating medium, reflecting more generally the larger public issues than the personal ambitions and views of the editor. The tendency for newspaper chains to supplant individual proprietorships became more pronounced. Seattle, for instance, eventually became fertile ground for the Hearst chain as represented by the *Seattle Post-Intelligencer.* Newspapers had their faces lifted, and the modern touch was in evidence throughout their columns. The comic strips, sport pages, society columns, musical and literary sections — all of the features by which modern newspapers are recognized — made their appearance at the beginning of the present century. And influenced by the chain newspapers, the remaining privately owned ones have either been obliged or have sought to imitate their more powerful competitors. Even the once stately format of the *Oregonian* has given way to banner headlines on its front page.

A further indication of the power and influence of the metropolitan press is that as population has increased, there has been a relatively smaller increase in the number of newspapers. Even though the daily newspaper was becoming more and more influential, more weekly newspapers continued to outnumber the dailies. Not even the miracle of modern science and technology could diminish the demand for small-town weeklies, serving as they do the needs of a purely local population. However, lacking the greater financial resources of the metropolitan dailies, the weeklies were naturally worse hit by the ravages of the depression. Almost one-third of these in the state of Washington, for example, were compelled to abandon publication. This was, though, a temporary setback, and many have since returned to their work with renewed vigor.

After 1890, a so-called specialized press began to develop. In Washington, Oregon, and Idaho, language newspapers and those devoted to the interests of the professions and of various callings such as lumbering, mining, fishing, and farming were increasing in number, and during World War II the "House Journals" circulated among respective employee groups. In recent years about fifty such "trade," "class," and "business house" publications have appeared in Portland alone.

Fortunately the vituperative era of "Oregon Journalism" — the kind devoted largely to personal abuse — has vanished. Continued progress has brought with it a measure of stability and prosperity. That Northwestern journalism has made great strides and has taken its place in the front ranks of the nation's press can be seen by citing a few distinctions which were bestowed on newspapermen in Oregon in the course of one year. In 1939, R. G. Gallvert of the *Oregonian* won the Pulitzer prize for his outstanding editorials; Donald J. Sterling of the *Oregon Journal* was elected president of the American Society of Newspaper Editors; the *McMinnville Telephone-Register* was cited by the National Editorial Association as being the best all-around weekly newspaper in the United States; and the *Hood River News* was awarded a trophy by the same organization for the weekly having the best editorial page.

Theatrical and Musical Entertainment

People on the Northwest frontier did not differ greatly with respect to reading matter nor with respect to other forms of entertainment and diversions. With the rise of towns came performing artists of every kind — magicians, ventriloquists, singers, dancers, monologists, and lyceum and other lecturers. So far as is known, the first theatrical performance in Old Oregon, *Three Weeks of Marriage,* was given in 1846 by the crew of the British ship *Modeste,* which was then anchored off Fort Vancouver. From then on Portland and, less often, the Willamette Valley and Puget Sound towns were treated to performances by traveling artists and troubadours who found in the frontiersmen their most appreciative audiences. Lotta Crabtree failed to reach Portland, but in 1855 she treated the hardened miners of Browntown to the fanciest dancing on record in the southern part of the territory. In the same year Stephen C. Masset, an impersonator, singer, and all-around troubadour, cheered many a farmer audience in the Willamette Valley by his versatile performances. At the Willamette Theatre in Portland, 1864, appeared Julia Dean Hayes in productions of Shakespeare and as a lead in *The Man with the Iron Mask.* With equal enthusiasm this community later received a performance of William W. Pratt's stirring melodrama and stockshow favorite, *Ten Nights in a Bar Room;* also *Rip Van Winkle, Ben Hur, The Count of Monte Cristo,* and other assorted shows. Seattle in 1870 welcomed Anna Bishop, singer, and Camelia Urso, violinist. Urso displayed the first Stradivarius violin seen in the Pacific Northwest. Two years later, David W. Nesfield, baritone, and Mlle Marie Gaugain, danseuse, appeared. They were followed by Louise Irving, "mockingbird vocalist"; Ilma de Mirska, the Hungarian nightingale; and Maggie, the colored nightingale. And so the assortment of talent passed either lightly or heavily on the frontier stage. Too often, though, the Northwest has been by-passed or overlooked by concert artists and road shows, whose New York managers have become painfully aware that the Columbia is not a tributary of the Hudson River, and that Puget Sound is not an estuary on lower Manhattan Island.

As the population of the region grew, the roadshow theatres no longer sufficed. Theatres were springing up to house stock or resident companies, which performed a different play weekly and often stayed on in a theatre for years. The 1890s will long be remembered in theatre history as the decade of the Gibson and the Floradora girls. It was also a decade during which the classics enjoyed unusual popularity.

Spectacles and extravaganzas like *The Devil's Auction* and *The Twelve Temptations* also attracted large audiences. The late nineties ushered in the popular priced (usually about fifty cents) road attractions offering mainly farce-comedies and melodramas. The repertoire players came to the Northwest after the turn of the century. They would remain at a theatre for several weeks and offer two or three productions during one week. In that sense they combined both the characteristics of the traveling roadshow and the stock companies. Vaudeville, an outgrowth of the variety theatre of a previous period, entered the field in earnest after the turn of the century, and had much of its original development in the Northwest. At first the ten-cent show provided entertainment for the entire family, but soon elaborate and lavishly ornamented theatres were erected to house these twice-a-day shows. As a form of theatrical entertainment, vaudeville declined in the late 1920s, to return again a decade later. In general, the trend in theatrical development was not different in the Pacific Northwest from what it was elsewhere.

The movies proved to be ruinous competition for the legitimate stage, but in a few places the "Little Theatre" movement, a product of the twenties, has managed to survive. The Little Theatre idea calls for the production of plays by local talent before small, intimate audiences. The Repertory Playhouse in the University of Washington District, Seattle, is this kind of theatre, as is the Civic Theatre in Portland. Moreover, the experimental Penthouse and the Showboat theatres run by the Drama Department at the University of Washington have enjoyed considerable popularity. Seattle is also regarded now as a leader in the field of play production for children. Under the sponsorship of Seattle Junior Programs, Inc., a nonprofit organization of clubwomen, and in co-operation with the city's public school system, the drama department of the University produces several plays for children each season. Thus, while Broadway comes only occasionally to the Northwest, the theatre movement manages to survive in some places.

Partly to overcome the disadvantages of isolation, and partly, too, because people seek various ways in which to express themselves, the Northwest has established a commendable record for cultural self-service. Portland's symphonic concerts by local talent date back to 1868, and from that time forward, philharmonic and choral organizations have been numerous, though not all have flourished. The first Grand Orchestral Concert in Portland was given at the Masonic Hall in 1875. Playing in the orchestra were such well-known local personages as J. K. Gill, Sigmund Frank, and Edward J. Finck. In 1895 the designation Portland Symphony Orchestra was used for the first time. In 1910 occurred the first Portland Musical Festival in which, under the baton of Adolphe Rosenbecker, the Chicago Symphony Orchestra participated. Recently the Portland Symphony Orchestra, conducted from 1925 to 1938 by the distinguished Willem van Hoogstraten, was disbanded. Meanwhile the Portland Civic Symphony (for students up to the age of twenty-one) has been added to the growing list of Portland's cultural institutions. At present there are in Portland about forty organizations actively engaged in musical programs and musical education for their city.

Much as conservative Portlanders might belittle Seattle's cultural achievements, the city on the Sound has had its own symphony orchestra since 1903. It was organized and for a time conducted by Harry West, a prominent violinist. At various times in its rather unstable career this orchestra has been directed by rather well-known musicians, among them Henry Hadley, John Spargur, Karl Krueger, and Basil Cameron. The present organization, the Seattle Symphony Orchestra, was formally incorporated in 1927. Under the conductorship of Cameron, this organization improved greatly in its performances. The standard set by Cameron was in no way lowered under the brilliant conducting of Sir Thomas Beecham, who succeeded Cameron for a brief period and who has since been replaced by Carl Bricken.

Almost every town of appreciable size has its choral groups and a cappella choirs, its string quartets, brass bands, and symphony orchestras. In addition, the musical offerings presented by visiting artists under the auspices of concert bureaus give Northwesterners an opportunity to listen to the best in musical artistry. The Artists' Service of the National Broadcasting Company and the Columbia Concerts Corporation have both said of Portland, for instance, that it displays a greater musical appreciation than any other city of its size west of the Mississippi River.

Fine Arts and Architecture

The Indians were the first artists and handicraftsmen. The first white artists of any note were nonresident individuals who, like Henry Warre, Paul Kane, and John M. Stanley, found subjects in the Oregon country that were interesting to sketch and paint. Outside sculptors, like the painters, also found in this region new and appealing subjects. One of this group was Hermon A. MacNeil, whose "Coming of the White Man," a well-executed but much over-sentimentalized piece of statuary, now stands in Portland's Washington Park. Equally romantic in their concept are A. Phimister Proctor's "Pioneer" and "Pioneer Mother," placed on the University of Oregon campus.

One need not be a fourth-generation resident to be considered a native Northwesterner, so not all artists considered the region's own are native to the region. Roi Partridge and Thomas Handforth, etchers, and Allan Clark, Mary G. Allen, Paul Gustin, Eustace Zigler, and Edward Espy, painters, are among local artists who helped to pioneer the way for some outside recognition of Northwest art. Others who contributed were Roswell Holt Dasch, who established the department of modeling and freehand drawing at the School of Architecture and Allied Arts at the University of Oregon; Homer Calvin Davenport, who was born at Silverton, but who achieved his fame as a cartoonist for eastern newspapers; and Lucy Dodd Ramsberg. Among the artists who gained more than passing notice in Washington during its first years of statehood were Maria Becket of Spokane, Ella Shepard Bush, Jennie Fisken, and Mary G. Allen, all of the Puget Sound area.

The organization of the Portland Art Association in 1892 was a significant event because for the first time an appreciation of art was expressed by the general public. A modest little museum was established as part of the Association's activities. In considerably larger quarters, thirteen years later, the first public art museum in the Pacific Northwest was opened, and under its auspices instruction was offered to art students. Museums were founded in every large city during the present century and fine-arts organizations were also created to express the growing public interest in local art. Especially beautiful and modern is the Seattle Art Museum.

In 1914, the first Northwest Art Exhibition was held. Since then, the annual showing of the works of Pacific Northwest artists has become an event in the art community, providing an opportunity for budding and mature artists to display their works to the general public. In recent years, Seattle has produced a number of artists who have gained national and even international reputations. Among these are Kenneth Callahan, who has had his paintings and murals exhibited at such places as the Museum of Modern Art and the Whitney Museum in New York. He has been painting for many years, although his earlier works showed a promise that he has not quite fully lived up to. The same comment may be made of Peter Camfferman, whose works may be found in many public and private collections. Morris Graves and Mark Tobey are probably the outstanding artists in the Northwest today. The latter taught for many years in Seattle and was one of the first to introduce the spirit of modernism in art. His influence is felt in the works of many protégés who received their training under his direction. Many references to the work of Graves and Tobey have appeared in national publications dealing with fine arts. Walter Isaacs, director of the Art School at the University of Washington, has also trained many a promising artist. He, perhaps more than any other painter in the region, has earned international distinction through exhibitions of his work in art centers in America and abroad. Other artists who have been producing work worthy of mention are James H. Fitzgerald and his wife, Margaret Tompkins, George Kenyon, George Laisner, Guy Anderson, Patricia Nicholson, and Dorothy Rising. On the whole, the more competent craftsmen in the Northwest are emphasizing the nonrepresentational or abstract approach. Unfortunately, some of the most illustrious painters and sculptors have left the region to work in metropolitan centers of the East and Europe where they felt they could better apply their talents. That the scenery of the Northwest has exerted a great influence upon many an artist is evidenced by the numerous paintings depicting the tall, jagged mountains or the winding, tortuous rivers, or the gently rolling hills.

In the field of architecture, the physical environment is also an important factor in influencing the character of its development; others are climate and the historical background of settlement. Perhaps no other expression of the cultural tastes of a people is more directly related to the nature of the society than architecture. The types of homes constructed reveal the social and economic backgrounds of the residents, their geographical origins and their social points of view. Unlike California or New England, there were no historical precedents in the Pacific Northwest to produce a so-called indigenous and local architecture. In California, the early settlers developed a mission type of architecture adapted from the Spanish Renaissance style prevalent in the mother country, and the colonists who first settled on the Atlantic seaboard patterned their structures along lines of the English Renaissance. But in the Northwest for almost fifty years following the explorations of Vancouver and Gray, the only white people were the explorers, trappers, and traders. Their contributions in this sphere were the crude stockades and blockhouses designed to offer protection against Indian attacks.

The early settlers who began coming into the region during the 1840s soon displayed evidence of their place of origin. Their nostalgic feelings were expressed in the adaptation of the colonial and the Georgian as well as of the Greek Revival which had characterized the dwellings of New England, the South, and the Ohio Valley from which they came. The mild, equable climate of the area west of the Cascade Mountains and the climate prevailing east of the Cascades, which was not dissimilar from New England's, accounted, in part, for the popularity of the modified colonial style. The extensive timber resources of the region led to the wide use of wood in the construction of homes, especially during the early period of settlement. With the later discovery of raw materials necessary for the manufacture of cement and clay products, brick and terra cotta, new kinds of architectural edifices gradually came to replace those of wood. The manufacture of these building materials became an important industry in the Northwest. Tacoma had the first structural-steel building, a type widely used at present.

In general, architectural development has followed a pattern similar to that of other parts of the country. When the Victorian influence made itself felt in this country with its rococo and ornate extravagances, the homes of the wealthy in the Northwest were not immune from its effects. Probably as many as one-third of the buildings which still stand in Oregon were constructed either during this Victorian period of the sixties, seventies, and eighties, or show its influence in one way or another. Many commercial structures with mansard roofs and façades of brick, wood, cast iron, and ornamental plaster still stand and show the evidence of an architectural motif of a bygone era. Toward the end of the nineteenth century, the neoclassical style was introduced into the Northwest as part of a national trend made popular by a group of architects trained in academic institutions. By then the followers of the neoclassical school were devoting more time and attention to planning and to correct proportions and to detail, and the private and public edifices which were constructed during this period generally bore the mark of this new influence. After the turn of the century, school-trained architects and members of the craft whose backgrounds were enriched by travel abroad were becoming increasingly numerous and were steadily replacing the practical builder-designer. On the whole, the absence of any extreme booms such as had occurred in California helped the architects to concentrate more consistently upon the needs of the small homebuilder and be less diverted by more profitable and dazzling opportunities. During the neoclassical period, traditional styles of all varieties were adapted to many kinds of buildings such as Gothic and English Tudor.

That the architectural profession in the Northwest came of age during the early part of this present century is revealed by several isolated events. A Department of Architecture was established at the University of Oregon in 1914 and, five years later, an architect's registration law was passed by the Oregon State Legislature, incidentally making that state one of the first west of the Mississippi River to enact such a provision. Since the end of World War I, the classical influence has been steadily declining, and various expressions of modernism have been freely attempted. The functional approach influenced by Louis Sullivan and the Chicago School has been replacing the more traditional varieties in the Northwest as elsewhere in the nation. Greater emphasis is being given to simplicity and refinement, with considerations of structure and aesthetic quality assuming a paramount place. Regardless of the particular school of architectural thought, planning in the Northwest has always made provision for adequate home gardens, as the climate in the western portion permits an uninterrupted growth for the entire year.

Education

Educational development has come a long way from the time when the subscription schoolhouse flourished during the beginning years of settlement. The necessity of paying a tuition fee for each child attending school was not conducive toward diffusing the benefits of education to all. The next step in the process, taxation of parents according to the number of their children attending school, was an improvement. But the burden naturally was heaviest on those with the largest families, which often happened to be the poorest. During the pioneer period, legislation designed to provide for effective and competent instruction was meager, and where laws did exist, they were often ineffectively applied. Inadequacies were many: ungraded schools, lack of uniformity of textbooks, low standards in the certification of teachers, and lack of proper buildings and school equipment.

As indicated earlier (see pp. 209–14), this inadequacy was not due to lack of interest on the part of the pioneers. All the territorial legislatures adopted measures in behalf of learning. And typical, too, is the message to the first legislature of Washington Territory by Governor Isaac I. Stevens: "Let every youth, however limited his opportunities, find his place in the school, the college, the university, if God has given him the necessary gifts. I will recommend that Congress be memorialized to appropriate land for a university." The work of laying the educational foundations of the new society went on steadily, but, as elsewhere in the nation, opposition to tax-supported schools was voiced by those who feared the prospects of having to bear the financial burden, or those who saw in the trend some sort of ideological specter. First the object of attack was the elementary school and then the tax-supported high school, but each in turn weathered the storm and became a fixed and permanent part of the social structure. And in due time, by appropriate legislation, all schools were graded. Even though a provision for grading had been made some time before 1890, it was not compulsory and not until stringent legislation was enacted to enforce the measure did graded schools become universal. In 1887, for example, the year when the last territorial report was submitted by the superintendent, only thirty-two graded schools existed in the Territory of Washington.

Certification of teachers was also loosely handled. Although laws were passed regularly to provide set standards, the pioneer conditions of society prevented them from being either far-reaching or conscientiously applied. Attempts were steadily made to raise the level of instruction. By 1917, Washington required for a teaching certificate the successful completion of a four-year secondary-school program; and at least one year of professional training in a school of higher learning for a first-grade teacher's certificate.

Perhaps one of the most pragmatic tests in judging the success of educational progress is the extent of literacy among the people. It is of no mean significance, therefore, that, next to Iowa, the state of Oregon has the highest rate of literacy in the country. Only one out of every hundred

Oregonians is illiterate, whereas about four out of every hundred in the total population of the United States is illiterate. The consolidation of school units, an inevitable consequence of population increase, has been effectuated throughout most of the region. And with this development have come the advantages that often go with greater size, such as better-qualified teachers and broader programs of study. By 1940 most children of grade school age, except those in the most out-of-the-way places, were receiving regular schooling unless parents had a way of avoiding the truant officers. At present, roughly thirty per cent of the school population attends high school, while the colleges have recently become one of America's most congested areas.

It will be recalled that the first institutions of higher learning were denominational in character; then came the founding of the state universities and colleges (see pp. 214-17). Since then, academic development has been as far-reaching as the limitations of the region's population and resources would permit. Additional private and state schools were also established during the past half-century, as, for example, the Jesuit Gonzaga University at Spokane in 1889 and the State College of Washington at Pullman in 1892. The organizing of Reed College at Portland in 1911, with funds bequeathed by Simeon G. Reed of Columbia River transportation fame, was an advance step taken in behalf of college education. At Reed College no professional schools exist to make inroads on the curriculum, and students (very much on their own in personal relations) are given a good dosage in the liberal-arts course of study.

At the universities the present century has witnessed a rapid rise and expansion of professional and graduate schools. Medicine, pharmacy, dentistry, law, forestry, business, education, journalism, architecture, and music are among those comprising the list of professional schools which go far to provide the Northwest states with adequately trained professional personnel. Graduate schools, the largest and best of which is the University of Washington Graduate School, founded in 1911, also prepare students for professional work, but the main emphasis is upon advanced training in liberal arts which will ultimately lead to exacting and productive scholarly research and good teaching. Both the professional and graduate schools have been and are staffed by many scientists and scholars with national and even international reputations. Vernon L. Parrington, professor of English at the University of Washington, and author of the three-volume Pulitzer Prize winner, *Main Currents in American Thought,* was such a person. Other eminent scholars at the University of Washington were J. Allen Smith in political science and Frederick Morgan Padelford, a Spencerian authority who for many years was also dean of the University of Washington Graduate School. At the University of Oregon were Thomas Condon, famed pioneer geologist, and Ernest Sutherland Bates, who was not only a brilliant scholar but also a nationally known critic and contributor to nationally circularized magazines. For a period of time the University had the services of Alexander Goldenweiser, a widely known anthropologist. Edmond S. Meany did pioneering work on Washington's state history; Joseph Schafer and Robert C. Clark did the same for Oregon's past. T. C. Elliott and W. S. Kingston have likewise contributed to sound, local historical scholarship (see Bibliography for others). Their names stand as reminders that within the living memory of pioneer settlers, education has advanced from the era of the roving schoolmaster and the ungraded school to that in which outstanding contributions are being made in all fields of the arts and sciences.

From within the region have come many valuable contributions to local history. Among them are the *Pacific Northwest Quarterly,* sponsored by the University of Washington, and edited by Professor Charles M. Gates of the University of Washington history department; and the *Oregon Historical Quarterly,* issued by the Oregon Historical Society (Portland), edited by Lancaster Pollard. Likewise valuable is the *Commonwealth Review,* sponsored and published at irregular intervals by the University of Oregon.

Along with the development of schools went that of the libraries. Resources were naturally meager before the nineties and the few libraries were small and supported by subscription fees. Many, however, served the communities well. Often they were the chief adult educational center of a town, providing a meeting-place and a forum for discussions and debates. The free, tax-supported public-library movement in America was initiated at about the turn of the century. Also during this time, generous gifts by Andrew Carnegie for libraries in the Northwest made possible the greatest expansion of facilities the region has thus far experienced. A number of public libraries had existed before 1900, especially in the larger cities, but the real spurt occurred during the first two decades after that date. Today the Northwest leads all other regions in the extent to which data on its library resources are made available to scholars and research workers.

The first effort to acquaint interested students with the stores of Pacific Northwest materials was made by Charles W. Smith when he was at the University of Washington Library. Mr. Smith compiled a check list of printed sources relating to Northwest history drawn from the combined collections of thirteen libraries of the region. In 1921 he published a revised and enlarged edition which included the bibliographical resources of sixteen libraries. A decade later, under the sponsorship of the Pacific Northwest Library Association, a union check list of the region's manuscript materials appeared. Through the benefaction of a generous Carnegie grant, the University of Washington in 1940 established a Pacific Northwest bibliographical center similar to the one at Denver, with a union catalog of all the holdings of the libraries throughout the region. This makes the interlibrary loan system more effective and eliminates unnecessary duplication and financial waste in the purchase of books or in the acquisition of rare documents and manuscripts.

Outside the field of history, the Pacific Northwest has comparatively limited holdings in books, especially rare books and manuscript materials. It therefore becomes necessary, at least in many cases, for researchers to go to the large repositories such as the Library of Congress, Folger, Harvard, Yale, Henry E. Huntington, and other great libraries to do specialized research work. Even the regional historians find that the Bancroft Library of Western History at the University of California at Berkeley contains more material on certain phases of Northwest history than can be found in local collections. To meet the ordinary needs of undergraduates and of the general public, university, college, and public libraries of the three states are passable, and an effort is constantly being exerted to extend the range of service to an increasingly book-minded public.

Apart from the ever mounting complexities of everyday life, it remains to be said that most people in the Pacific Northwest possess a deep and sincere regard for their region. The great and beautiful outdoors is thrust in upon them and they love it. Many Northwesterners are ardent fishermen and mountaineers, but, like most Americans, they are a car-driving people, and in summers they harken to the call of the open road, the sparkling streams, the moody waters of the Sound, the towering green mountains, the inland deserts, and the hundreds of lakes and thousands of favorite scenic spots which Nature has so generously bestowed upon this — the "farthest reach" of the U. S. A.

BIBLIOGRAPHY

Sixty-six years have elapsed since Hubert Howe Bancroft published his two-volume *History of the Northwest Coast* (San Francisco, 1884), a work which was followed shortly by his *History of Oregon*, 2 vols. (San Francisco, 1886–88), *History of British Columbia* (San Francisco, 1887), and *History of Washington, Idaho, and Montana* (San Francisco, 1890). The actual writing of most of Bancroft's Northwest state histories was done by Frances Fuller Victor of Oregon, but apart from the question of authorship the Bancroft volumes remain to this day the best reference works on Northwest history.

Avid and sustained interest in the region's past has produced such valuable local periodicals as the *Oregon Historical Quarterly*, published by the Oregon Historical Society at Portland, the *Pacific Northwest Quarterly* (formerly the *Washington Historical Quarterly*) published by the University of Washington, *Contributions* published by the Montana Historical Society, and the *British Columbia Historical Quarterly* published at Victoria, B. C. Devoted to the broader Pacific area is the *Pacific Historical Review* issued by the Pacific Coast Branch of the American Historical Society. This periodical literature, contributed to by both local and outside researchers, comprises another invaluable source of informative and interpretive literature covering the full span of the region's history.

Each state, as well as the Province of British Columbia, has produced its own eminent authorities. In addition to Frances Fuller Victor, Oregon claims the late Joseph Schafer, author of *A History of the Pacific Northwest* (many editions) and numerous related articles, and the late Robert C. Clark, author of the thorough *History of the Willamette Valley, Oregon* (Chicago, 1927). Among other Oregon historians is the late Judge Charles H. Carey, author of *A General History of Oregon* (Portland, 1935) in two volumes.

Edmond S. Meany, long the "Grand Old Man" of the University of Washington, served for years as editor of the *Washington Historical Quarterly*, but in addition he wrote a standard *History of the State of Washington* (New York, 1910) and scores of other items focused on his cherished state. Also, T. C. Elliott of Walla Walla, Washington, has contributed fifty or more articles to the regional periodicals on the history of the Pacific Northwest. Clinton A. Snowden's four-volume *History of Washington* (New York, 1910) is another valuable product from the Evergreen state, as is George W. Fuller's *The Inland Empire of the Pacific Northwest* (Spokane, 1928) in three volumes.

Cornelius J. Brosnan has carried the torch for Idaho history. He wrote *Jason Lee* (New York, 1932); also a short elementary *History of the State of Idaho* (many editions). Merrill D. Beal's *A History of Southeastern Idaho* (Caldwell, 1942) is an ably written product from

[463

that state, while one of the better Federal Writers' Projects is the volume on the Gem State — *Idaho, A Guide in Word and Picture* — prepared under the direction of Vardis Fisher.

One of the most reputable, and certainly the most productive, scholars in British Columbia was the late Judge F. W. Howay whose *British Columbia* (Toronto, 1928) is perhaps the most useful book for one interested in a brief historical sketch of the Canadian Province. In collaboration with Howay, W. N. Sage and H. F. Angus published *British Columbia and the United States* (Toronto, 1942) for those seeking an understanding of the past and present relationship between British Columbia and her neighbors on the North Pacific slope.

Northwest biography has not been thoroughly exploited; neither has it been ably executed in many instances. First rate, however, is *The Letters of John McLoughlin from Fort Vancouver to the Governor and Committee*, Champlain Society Publications (Toronto, 1941–46), 3 volumes, edited by E. E. Rich with a scholarly biographical treatise on the Chief Factor written by W. Kaye Lamb. Walter N. Sage, *Sir James Douglas and British Columbia* (Toronto, 1930), is a solid biography, and so too are Clifford M. Drury's lives of the American missionaries: *Henry Harmon Spalding* (Caldwell, 1936), *Marcus Whitman, M.D.* (Caldwell, 1937), and *Elkanah and Mary Walker* (Caldwell, 1940). Interesting, but short of expectation, is Arthur S. Morton's *Sir George Simpson* (Portland, 1944), while excellent are Kenneth W. Porter's *John Jacob Astor: Business Man* (Cambridge, Massachusetts, 1931), 2 volumes, and James B. Hedges, *Henry Villard and the Railroads of the Northwest* (New Haven, 1930).

Limited in scope, but valuable to the specialist and general reader alike, are Washington Irving's old classics, *Astoria* and *Adventures of Captain Bonneville* (many editions). So too are such recent works as Frederick Merk, ed., *Fur Trade and Empire: George Simpson's Journal* (Cambridge, Massachusetts, 1931); W. J. Ghent, *The Road to Oregon* (New York, 1929); Melvin C. Jacobs, *Winning Oregon* (Caldwell, 1938); and Alfred Powers, *History of Oregon Literature* (Portland, 1935).

Useful to teacher and student is a brief source book, *Readings in Pacific Northwest History* (Seattle, 1941), edited by Charles M. Gates. Designed to be a helpful classified guide to the periodical materials is *The Trans-Mississippi West: A Guide to Its Periodical Literature* (Bloomington, Indiana, 1942), compiled by the author of the present volume.

CHAPTER I

MODERN ACCOUNTS — BOOKS. H. H. Bancroft: *The Native Races* (San Francisco, 1882), vol. 1; Otis W. Freeman and Howard H. Martin, eds.: *The Pacific Northwest* (New York, 1942), pt. II; Pliny E. Goddard: *Indians of the Northwest Coast* (New York, 1924); Frederick W. Hodge, ed.: *The Handbook of American Indians North of*

Mexico (Washington, 1907–10), Smithsonian Institution, Bureau of American Ethnology, Bulletin 30, pts. 1–2; A. L. Kroeber: *Cultural and Natural Areas of Native North America* (Berkeley, 1939), University of California Publications in American Archaeology and Ethnology, vol. XXXIX; George Peter Murdock: *Ethnographic Bibliography of North America* (New Haven, 1941), pp. 15–40; Ruth Underhill: *Indians of the Pacific Northwest* (Riverside, California, 1945); C. F. Voegelin and E. W. Voegelin: *North American Indian Languages* (New York, 1944), a map; Clark Wissler: *The American Indian* (New York, 1938), third edition, pp. 224–7, 229–31.

MODERN ACCOUNTS — ARTICLES. Joel V. Berreman: "Tribal Distribution in Oregon," *Memoirs of the American Anthropological Association,* nos. 46–9 (March, 1937); Otis W. Freeman, J. D. Forrester, and R. L. Lupher: "Physiographic Divisions of the Columbia Intermontane Province," *Annals of the Association of American Geographers,* XXXV (1945), 53–75; Rena V. Grant: "The Chinook Jargon, Past and Present," *California Folklore Quarterly,* III (1944), 259–76; Melville Jacobs: "Historic Perspectives in Indian Languages of Oregon and Washington," *Pacific Northwest Quarterly,* XXVIII (1937), 55–74; Georg Neumann: "Migrations and Origin of the Woodland Culture," *Proceedings of the Indiana Academy of Science* (Bloomington, Indiana, 1945), LIV, 41–3; Verne F. Ray: "The Historical Position of the Lower Chinook in the Native Culture of the Northwest," *Pacific Northwest Quarterly,* XXVIII (1937), 363–72; and "Native Villages and Groupings of the Columbia Basin," *Pacific Northwest Quarterly,* XXVII (1936), 99–152; Leslie Spier: "Tribal Distribution in Southwestern Oregon," *Oregon Historical Quarterly,* XXVIII (1927), 358–65.

CHAPTER II

CONTEMPORARY ACCOUNTS. James Cook and James King: *A Voyage to the Pacific Ocean* . . . (London, 1784), III; Charles M. Gates, ed.: *Readings in Pacific Northwest History: Washington, 1790–1895* (Seattle, 1941), pp. 11–18; Frederic W. Howay, ed.: *Voyages of the "Columbia" to the Northwest Coast* . . . (Boston, 1941); John Ledyard: *A Journal of Captain Cook's Last Voyage to the Pacific Ocean* . . . (Hartford, 1783); John Meares: *Voyages Made in the Years 1788 and 1789, from China to the North West Coast of America* (London, 1790); Nathaniel Portlock: *A Voyage Around the World* . . . (London, 1789); George Vancouver: *A Voyage of Discovery to the North Pacific Ocean* (London, 1798); Henry R. Wagner, [ed. and transl.]: *Spanish Voyages to the Northwest Coast of America in the Sixteenth Century* (San Francisco, 1929).

MODERN ACCOUNTS — BOOKS. G. H. Anderson: *Vancouver and His Great Voyage* (King's Lynn, England, 1923); H. H. Bancroft: *History of the Northwest Coast* (San Francisco, 1886), I, chs. 1–10; John C. Beaglehole: *The Exploration of the Pacific* (London, 1934);

Harold W. Bradley: *The American Frontier in Hawaii* (Stanford University, 1942), chs. 1, 2, 5; Charles H. Carey: *A General History of Oregon Prior to 1861* (Portland, 1935), I, chs. 2–8; Hugh Carrington: *Life of Captain Cook* (London, 1939); George S. Godwin: *Vancouver, A Life, 1757–1798* (London, 1930); Frank A. Golder: *Russian Expansion on the Pacific, 1651–1850* (Cleveland, 1914); Sydney Greenbie and Marjorie B. Greenbie: *Gold of Ophir: The China Trade in the Making of America* (New York, 1937); Agnes C. Laut: *Pioneers of the Pacific Coast* (Toronto, 1920); and *Vikings of the Pacific* (New York, 1905); James G. McCurdy: *By Juan de Fuca's Strait* (Portland, 1937), pp. 3–11; Edmond S. Meany: *Vancouver's Discovery of Puget Sound* (New York, 1907); Samuel E. Morison: *The Maritime History of Massachusetts, 1783–1860* (Boston, 1921), chs. 4–6; Kenneth Munford: *John Ledyard* (Portland, 1939); Adele Ogden: *The California Sea Otter Trade, 1784–1848* (Berkeley, 1941), ch. 1.

MODERN ACCOUNTS — ARTICLES. J. Neilson Barry: "Spaniards in Early Oregon," *Washington Historical Quarterly*, XXIII (1932), 25–34; "Broughton on the Columbia in 1792," *Oregon Historical Quarterly*, XXVII (1926), 397–411; "Peter Corney's Voyages, 1814–17," *Oregon Historical Quarterly*, XXXIII (1932), 355–68; Guy Vernon Bennett: "Early Relations of the Sandwich Islands to the Old Oregon Territory," *Washington Historical Quarterly*, IV (1913), 116–26; T. C. Elliott: "Oregon Coast as Seen by Vancouver in 1792," *Oregon Historical Quarterly*, XXX (1929), 33–42, 384–94; F. W. Howay: "The Spanish Settlement at Nootka," *Washington Historical Quarterly*, VIII (1917), 163–71; "Early Navigation of the Straits of Fuca," *Quarterly of the Oregon Historical Society*, XII (1911), 1–32; "Captain Cornelius Sowle on the Pacific Ocean," *Washington Historical Quarterly*, XXIV (1933), 243–9; "The Resolution on the Oregon Coast, 1793–94," *Oregon Historical Quarterly*, XXXIV (1933), 207–15; Horace S. Lyman: "Early New England Exploration of Our North Pacific Coast — The Columbia River," *American Historical Magazine*, I (1906), 52–67.

CHAPTER III

CONTEMPORARY ACCOUNTS. "The Appeal of the North West Company to the British Government to Forestall John Jacob Astor's Columbian Enterprise," *Canadian Historical Review*, XVII (1936), 304–11; Lawrence J. Burpee, ed.: "Some Letters of David Thompson," *Canadian Historical Review*, IV (1923), 105–26; Arthur G. Doughty, ed.: "First Journal of Simon Fraser . . .," *Dominion of Canada Report of the Public Archives for the Year 1929* (Ottawa, 1930), 109–45; T. C. Elliott, ed.: "David Thompson's Journeys in the Spokane Country," *Washington Historical Quarterly*, VIII (1917), 183–7, 261–4; IX (1918), 11–16, 103–6, 169–73, 284–7; X (1919), 17–20; "Narrative of the Expedition to the Kootanae @ Flat Bow Indian Countries, on the Sources of the Columbia River, Pacific Ocean, by D. Thompson . . .," *Quarterly of the Oregon Historical Society*, XXVI (1925), 23–49; "Journal of David Thompson," *Quarterly of the Oregon Historical Society*, XV (1914), 39–63, 104–25; Daniel Williams Harmon: *A Journal of Voyages and Travels* . . . (Andover, 1820). Reprinted editions also available; Milo M. Quaife, ed.: *Alexander Mackenzie's Voyage to the Pacific Ocean in 1793* (Chicago, 1931); Walter N. Sage: "Two North West Company Documents," *Canadian Historical Review*, XI (1930), 129–31; Joseph B. Tyrrell, ed.: *David Thompson's Narrative of His Explorations in Western America, 1784–1812* (Toronto, 1916); William Stewart Wallace, ed.: *Documents Relating to the North West Company* (Toronto, 1934).

MODERN ACCOUNTS — BOOKS. H. H. Bancroft: *History of the Northwest Coast* (San Francisco, 1884), I, chs. 18, 21; II, chs. 11–13; Robert C. Clark: *History of the Willamette Valley, Oregon* (Chicago, 1927), ch. 6; Gordon C. Davidson: *The North West Company* (Berkeley, 1918); George W. Fuller: *A History of the Pacific Northwest* (New York, 1931), ch. 6; F. W. Howay: *British Columbia, The Making of a Province* (Toronto, 1928), chs. 7–10; Harold A. Innis: *The Fur Trade in Canada* (New Haven, 1930), pp. 169–265; and *Peter Pond, Fur Trader and Adventurer* (Toronto, 1930); Agnes C. Laut: *Pioneers of the Pacific Coast* (Toronto, 1920), chs. 5–8; Horace S. Lyman: *History of Oregon* (New York, 1903), II, chs. 11–12; Arthur S. Morton: *A History of the Canadian West to 1870–71* (Toronto, 1939), pp. 463–97, 617–22; Adam Shortt and Arthur G. Doughty, eds.: *Canada and Its Provinces*, XXI, *The Pacific Province* (Toronto, 1914), pt. I, 52–62.

MODERN ACCOUNTS — ARTICLES. T. C. Elliott: "David Thompson, Pathfinder, and the Columbia River," *Quarterly of the Oregon Historical Society*, XII (1911), 195–205; XXVI (1925), 191–202; and "The Fur Trade in the Columbia River Basin Prior to 1811," *Washington Historical Quarterly*, VI (1915), 3–10; Arthur S. Morton: "The North West Company's Columbian Enterprise and David Thompson," *Canadian Historical Review*, XVII (1936), 266–88.

CHAPTER IV

CONTEMPORARY ACCOUNTS. George Verno Blue, ed.: "A Hudson's Bay Company Contract for Hawaiian Labor," *Quarterly of the Oregon Historical Society*, XXV (1924), 72–5; Jane Lewis Chapin, ed.: "Letters of John McLoughlin, 1805–49," *Oregon Historical Quarterly*, XXXVI (1935), 320–37; XXXVII (1936), 45–75, 293–300; *Charters, Statutes, Orders in Council &c. Relating to the Hudson's Bay Company* (London, 1931); T. C. Elliott, ed.: "Letters of Dr. John McLoughlin 1835–37 to Edward Ermatinger," *Quarterly of the Oregon Historical Society*, XXIII (1922), 365–71; "Hudson's Bay Company Claims in the Northwest, 1857," *Washington Historical Quar-*

terly, XIX (1928), 214–27; Frederick Merk, ed.: *Fur Trade and Empire; George Simpson's Journal* (Cambridge, Mass., 1931); E. E. Rich, ed.: *The Letters of John McLoughlin from Fort Vancouver to the Governor and Committee* (Toronto, 1941–44), 3 vols.

MODERN ACCOUNTS — BOOKS. H. F. Angus, ed.: *British Columbia and the United States,* by F. W. Howay, W. N. Sage, and H. F. Angus (Toronto, 1943); H. H. Bancroft: *History of the Northwest Coast* (San Francisco, 1884), II, chs. 14, 20–24; Robert C. Clark: *History of the Willamette Valley, Oregon* (Chicago, 1927), chs. 7–8; George W. Fuller: *A History of the Pacific Northwest* (New York, 1931), ch. 7; Frederick V. Holman: *Dr. John McLoughlin, The Father of Oregon* (Cleveland, 1907); F. W. Howay: *British Columbia, The Making of a Province* (Toronto, 1928), chs. 11, 14–16; Harold A. Innis: *The Fur Trade in Canada* (New Haven, 1930), pp. 152–69, 285–344; Robert C. Johnson: *John McLoughlin; Patriarch of the Northwest* (Portland, 1935); Agnes C. Laut: *The Conquest of the Great Northwest* (New York, 1908), 2 vols.; Horace S. Lyman: *History of Oregon* (New York, 1903), II, chs. 13–14; Douglas MacKay: *The Honourable Company; A History of the Hudson's Bay Company* (Indianapolis, 1936); Richard G. Montgomery: *The White-Headed Eagle, John McLoughlin, Builder of an Empire* (New York, 1935); Arthur S. Morton: *A History of the Canadian West to 1870–71* (Toronto, 1939), pp. 710–32; and *Sir George Simpson; Overseas Governor of the Hudson's Bay Company* (Portland, 1944); Grace Lee Nute: *Caesars of the Wilderness* (New York, 1943); Robert E. Pinkerton: *Hudson's Bay Company* (New York, 1931); Walter N. Sage: *Sir James Douglas and British Columbia* (Toronto, 1930); William Schooling: *The Governor and Company of Adventurers of England Trading into Hudson's Bay during Two Hundred and Fifty Years, 1670–1920* (London, 1920); George P. Scriven: *The Story of the Hudson's Bay Company* (Washington, D. C., 1929); Adam Shortt and Arthur G. Doughty, eds.: *Canada and Its Provinces,* XXI, *The Pacific Province* (Toronto, 1914), pt. I, 62–71; Constance L. Skinner: *Adventures of Oregon* (New Haven, 1920); and *Beaver, Kings and Cabins* (New York, 1933); Robert Watson: *The Hudson's Bay Company* (Toronto, 1928).

MODERN ACCOUNTS — ARTICLES. Charles H. Carey: "Lee, Waller and McLoughlin," *Oregon Historical Quarterly,* XXXIII (1932), 187–213; T. C. Elliott: "The Fur Trade in the Columbia River Basin Prior to 1811," *Washington Historical Quarterly,* VI (1915), 3–10; and "John McLoughlin, M.D.," *Oregon Historical Quarterly,* XXXVI (1935), 182–6; Mary A. Gray: "Settlement of the Claims in Washington of the Hudson's Bay Company and the Puget's Sound Agricultural Company," *Washington Historical Quarterly,* XXI (1930), 95–102; Ralph Richard Martig: "Hudson's Bay Company Claims, 1846–69," *Oregon Historical Quarterly,* XXXVI (1935), 60–70; Aaron Newell: "North West and Hudson's Bay Companies," *Washington Historical Quarterly,* XV (1924), 199–204.

CHAPTER V

CONTEMPORARY ACCOUNTS. Clarence B. Bagley, ed.: "Journal of Occurrences at Nisqually House, 1833," *Washington Historical Quarterly*, VI (1915), 179–97, 264–78; VII (1916), 59–75, 144–67; Charles M. Gates, ed.: *Readings in Pacific Northwest History: Washington, 1790–1895* (Seattle, 1941), 45–66; William S. Lewis and Paul C. Phillips, eds.: *The Journal of John Work, A Chief-Trader of the Hudson's Bay Co. . . .* (Cleveland, 1923); Alice Bay Maloney, ed.: *Fur Brigade to the Bonaventura: John Work's California Expedition 1832–1833 for the Hudson's Bay Company* (San Francisco, 1945); Frederick Merk, ed.: *Fur Trade and Empire; George Simpson's Journal* (Cambridge, Mass., 1931); E. E. Rich, ed.: *The Letters of John McLoughlin from Fort Vancouver to the Governor and Committee* (Toronto, 1941–44), 3 vols.; Charles Wilkes: *Narrative of the United States Exploring Expedition . . .* (Philadelphia, 1845), IV.

MODERN ACCOUNTS — BOOKS. H. F. Angus, ed.: *British Columbia and the United States*, by F. W. Howay, W. N. Sage, and H. F. Angus (Toronto, 1943); H. H. Bancroft: *History of the Northwest Coast* (San Francisco, 1884), II, chs. 20–24, 27–30; and *History of Oregon* (San Francisco, 1886), I, ch. 2; Charles H. Carey: *A General History of Oregon Prior to 1861* (Portland, 1935), I; Robert C. Clark: *History of the Willamette Valley, Oregon* (Chicago, 1927); George W. Fuller: *A History of the Pacific Northwest* (New York, 1931), ch. 7; F. W. Howay: *British Columbia, The Making of a Province* (Toronto, 1928); Alfred L. Lomax: *Pioneer Woolen Mills in Oregon* (Portland, 1941), ch. 1; Mathew Macfie: *Vancouver Island and British Columbia* (London, 1865); Walter N. Sage: *Sir James Douglas and British Columbia* (Toronto, 1930); Constance L. Skinner: *Adventures of Oregon* (New Haven, 1920); and *Beaver, Kings and Cabins* (New York, 1933).

MODERN ACCOUNTS — ARTICLES. J. Neilson Barry, ed.: "Pickering's Journey to Fort Colville in 1841," *Washington Historical Quarterly*, XX (1929), 54–63; Miles Cannon: "The Snake River in History," *Quarterly of the Oregon Historical Society*, XX (1919), 1–23; T. C. Elliott: "British Values in Oregon, 1847," *Oregon Historical Quarterly*, XXXII (1931), 27–45; and "Spokane House," *Washington Historical Quarterly*, XXI (1930), 3–7; William S. Lewis: "Information concerning the Estab[l]ishment of Fort Colvile," *Washington Historical Quarterly*, XVI (1925), 102–7; William S. Lewis and Jacob A. Meyers, eds.: "Life at Old Fort Colville," *Washington Historical Quarterly*, XVI (1925), 198–205; J. A. Meyers: "Finan McDonald — Explorer, Fur Trader and Legislator," *Washington Historical Quarterly*, XIII (1932), 196–208; J. Orin Oliphant: "Old Fort Colville," *Washington Historical Quarterly*, XVI (1925), 29–48, 83–101; Walter N. Sage: "Life at a Fur Trading Post in British Columbia a Century Ago," *Washington Historical Quarterly*, XXV (1934), 11–22; Leonard A. Wrinch: "The Formation of the Puget's Sound Agricultural Company," *Washington Historical Quarterly*, XXIV (1933), 3–8.

CHAPTER VI

CONTEMPORARY ACCOUNTS. Ross Cox: *The Columbia River* (London, 1832), 2 vols.; John Dunn: *The Oregon Territory* (Philadelphia, 1845); Gabriel Franchère: *Narrative of a Voyage to the Northwest Coast of America* (New York, 1854); Charles M. Gates, ed.: *Readings in Pacific Northwest History: Washington, 1790–1895* (Seattle, 1941), pp. 41–4; E. R. Harlan, ed.: "The Lewis and Clark Expedition in Its Relation to Iowa History and Geography," *Annals of Iowa*, XIII, 3rd series (1921–23), 99–125, 163–92; Archer B. Hulbert, ed.: *The Call of the Columbia* (Denver, 1934); Washington Irving: *The Adventures of Captain Bonneville, U.S.A.* (London, 1837); and *Astoria, or Anecdotes of an Enterprise Beyond the Rocky Mountains* (Philadelphia, 1836); Meriwether Lewis and William Clark: "Lewis and Clark Description of Pawnee Nation," *Nebraska History Magazine*, X (1927), 195–200; Reuben G. Thwaites, ed.: *Early Western Travels 1748–1846* (Cleveland, 1905), "Narrative of a Journey across the Rocky Mountains," by John K. Townsend, XXI, 112–369; and *Original Journals of the Lewis and Clark Expedition, 1804–1806* (New York, 1904), 7 vols., atlas; F. G. Young, ed.: *The Correspondence and Journals of Captain Nathaniel J. Wyeth, 1831–6* (Eugene, Oregon, 1899).

MODERN ACCOUNTS — BOOKS. Charles H. Carey: *A General History of Oregon Prior to 1861* (Portland, 1935), I, chs. 12–13; George W. Fuller: *A History of the Pacific Northwest* (New York, 1931), ch. 6; Grace R. Hebard: *Sacajawea* (Glendale, 1933); Melvin C. Jacobs: *Winning Oregon* (Caldwell, Idaho, 1938); Edmond S. Meany: *History of the State of Washington* (New York, 1924), chs. 6–8, 10; Kenneth W. Porter: *John Jacob Astor, Business Man* (Cambridge, Mass., 1931); Maurice S. Sullivan: *Jedediah Smith, Trader and Trail Breaker* (New York, 1936); Olin D. Wheeler: *The Trail of Lewis and Clark, 1804–1904* (New York, 1904), 2 vols.; Charles Morrow Wilson: *Meriwether Lewis of Lewis and Clark* (New York, 1934).

MODERN ACCOUNTS — ARTICLES. J. Neilson Barry: "Astorians Who Became Permanent Settlers," *Washington Historical Quarterly*, XXIV (1933), 221–31, 282–301; and "The Trail of the Astorians," *Quarterly of the Oregon Historical Society*, XIII (1912), 227–39; Alfred A. Cleveland: "Social and Economic History of Astoria," *Quarterly of the Oregon Historical Society*, IV (1903), 130–49; Ramsay Crooks: "Did the Returning Astorians Use the South Pass?" *Quarterly of the Oregon Historical Society*, XVII (1916), 47–51; W. Clement Eaton: "Nathaniel Wyeth's Oregon Expeditions," *Pacific Historical Review*, IV

(1935), 101–13; T. C. Elliott: "The Surrender at Astoria in 1818," *Quarterly of the Oregon Historical Society*, XIX (1918), 271–82; and "Wilson Price Hunt, 1783–1842," *Oregon Historical Quarterly*, XXXII (1931), 130–4; Frederick V. Holman: "Lewis and Clark Expedition at Fort Clatsop," *Oregon Historical Quarterly*, XXVII (1926), 265–78; and "Some Important Results from the Expeditions of John Jacob Astor to and from the Oregon Country," *Quarterly of the Oregon Historical Society*, XII (1911), 206–19; C. S. Kingston: "Sacajawea as Guide: The Evaluation of a Legend," *Pacific Northwest Quarterly*, XXXV (1944), 3–18; P. Koch: "The Story of Astoria, With a Sketch of the Pacific Fur Company," *Magazine of American History*, XIII (1885), 269–76; Andrew T. Lewis: "Meriwether Lewis," *Quarterly of the Oregon Historical Society*, VI (1905), 391–402; Horace S. Lyman: "The Lewis and Clark Expedition," *American Historical Magazine*, I (1906), 329–66, 439–56; Donald M. Major: "Benjamin Bonneville," *Journal of American History*, XXI (1927), 127–36; Grace P. Morris: "Development of Astoria, 1811–1850," *Oregon Historical Quarterly*, XXXVIII (1937), 413–24; Philip Henry Overmeyer: "Membership of First Wyeth Expedition," *Oregon Historical Quarterly*, XXXVI (1935), 95–101; and "Nathanial [sic] Jarvis Wyeth, His First Expedition," *Washington Historical Quarterly*, XXIV (1933), 28–48; James Parton: "John Jacob Astor," *Harper's Magazine*, XXX (1864–65), 308–23; Leslie M. Scott: "Nationalism of Lewis and Clark," *Oregon Historical Quarterly*, XXXII (1931), 101–4; Reuben G. Thwaites: "The Story of Lewis and Clark's Journals," *Quarterly of the Oregon Historical Society*, VI (1905), 26–53; F. G. Young: "The Higher Significance in the Lewis and Clark Exploration," *Quarterly of the Oregon Historical Society*, VI (1905), 1–25; and "The Lewis and Clark Expedition in American History," *Quarterly of the Oregon Historical Society*, II (1901), 410–22.

CHAPTER VII

CONTEMPORARY ACCOUNTS. Jesse Applegate: "A Day with the Cow Column in 1843," *Quarterly of the Oregon Historical Society*, I (1900), 371–83; Theressa Gay: *Life and Letters of Mrs. Jason Lee* (Portland, 1936); John Ewing Howell: "Diary of an Emigrant of 1845," *Washington Historical Quarterly*, I (1906–07), 138–58; Archer B. Hulbert and Dorothy Printup Hulbert, eds.: *Marcus Whitman, Crusader* (Denver, 1936–41), 3 vols.; and *The Oregon Crusade* (Denver, 1935); John Minto: "Reminiscences of Experiences on the Oregon Trail in 1844," *Quarterly of the Oregon Historical Society*, II (1901), 119–67, 209–54; James W. Nesmith: "Diary of the Emigration of 1843," *Quarterly of the Oregon Historical Society*, VII (1906), 329–59; J. Orin Oliphant, ed.: "Letters of Hezekiah Johnson, 1838–1849," *Pacific Northwest Quarterly*, XXXVII (1946), 15–30;

Thomas W. Prosch, ed.: "Diary of Dr. David S. Maynard while Crossing the Plains in 1850," *Washington Historical Quarterly*, I (Oct., 1906–07), 50–62; Robert Robe: "Diary while Crossing the Plains in 1851," *Washington Historical Quarterly*, XIX (1928), 52–63; Oscar Osburn Winther and Rose [Rosa] Dodge Galey, eds.: "The Diary of America Butler," *Oregon Historical Quarterly*, XLI (1940), 337–66; Ina Faye Woestemeyer, ed.: *The Westward Movement* (New York, 1939), 212–19.

MODERN ACCOUNTS — BOOKS. H. H. Bancroft: *History of Oregon* (San Francisco, 1886), I, chs. 4–5, 19–20; William N. Bischoff: *The Jesuits in Old Oregon 1840–1940* (Caldwell, Idaho, 1945); Cornelius J. Brosnan: *Jason Lee, Prophet of the New Oregon* (New York, 1932); Charles H. Carey: *A General History of Oregon Prior to 1861* (Portland, 1935), I, ch. 15; Robert C. Clark: *History of the Willamette Valley, Oregon* (Chicago, 1927), ch. 9; Clifford M. Drury: *Elkanah and Mary Walker* (Caldwell, Idaho, 1940); *Henry Harmon Spalding* (Caldwell, Idaho, 1936); and *Marcus Whitman, M.D.* (Caldwell, Idaho, 1937); W. J. Ghent: *The Road to Oregon* (New York, 1929), chs. 1–7; Melvin C. Jacobs: *Winning Oregon* (Caldwell, Idaho, 1938), ch. 2; Edwin V. O'Hara: *Pioneer Catholic History of Oregon* (Paterson, N. J., 1939), chs. 2–14; Irene D. Paden: *The Wake of the Prairie Schooner* (New York, 1943).

MODERN ACCOUNTS — ARTICLES. John Martin Canse: "Jason Lee: New Evidence on the Missionary and Colonizer," *Washington Historical Quarterly*, VI (1915), 251–63; and "The Oregon Mission — Its Transition," *Washington Historical Quarterly*, XXV (1934), 203–9; Harrison C. Dale: "The Organization of the Oregon Emigrating Companies," *Quarterly of the Oregon Historical Society*, XVI (1915), 205–27; J. T. Dorris: "Federal Aid to Oregon Trail Prior to 1850," *Oregon Historical Quarterly*, XXX (1929), 305–25; Charles M. Harvey: "On the Road to Oregon," *Atlantic Monthly*, CV (1910), 628–39; Edwin V. O'Hara: "Catholic Pioneers of the Oregon Country," *Catholic Historical Review*, III (1917–18), 187–201; and "De Smet in the Oregon Country," *Quarterly of the Oregon Historical Society*, X (1909), 239–62; Nellie B. Pipes, ed.: "Spalding Mission, 1843," by H. H. Spalding, *Oregon Historical Quarterly*, XXXIII (1932), 348–54; Harvey W. Scott: "Jason Lee's Place in History," *Washington Historical Quarterly*, I (1906–07), 21–33; F. G. Young: "The Oregon Trail," *Quarterly of the Oregon Historical Society*, I (1900), 339–70.

CHAPTER VIII

CONTEMPORARY ACCOUNTS. J. Henry Brown: *Brown's Political History of Oregon: Provisional Government* (Portland, 1892); M. P. Deady and L. Lane, comps.: *General Laws of Oregon, 1843–1872* (Salem, 1874); L. F. Grover, ed.: *The Oregon Archives* (Salem, 1853).

MODERN ACCOUNTS — BOOKS. H. H. Bancroft: *History of Oregon* (San Francisco, 1886), I, chs. 12, 16–18; Charles H. Carey: *A General History of Oregon Prior to 1861* (Portland, 1935), I, ch. 18; Robert C. Clark: *History of the Willamette Valley, Oregon* (Chicago, 1927), ch. 10; Caroline C. Dobbs: *Men of Champoeg* (Portland, 1932); George W. Fuller: *A History of the Pacific Northwest* (New York, 1931), pp. 194–203.

MODERN ACCOUNTS — ARTICLES. J. Neilson Barry: "The Champoeg Meeting of March 4, 1844," *Oregon Historical Quarterly*, XXXVIII (1937), 425–32; Marie Merriman Bradley: "Political Beginnings in Oregon," *Quarterly of the Oregon Historical Society*, IX (1908), 42–72; Robert Carlton Clark: "The Last Step in the Formation of a Provisional Government for Oregon in 1845," *Quarterly of the Oregon Historical Society*, XVI (1915), 313–29; Peter H. D'Arcy: "Historical Review, Champoeg, the Plymouth Rock of the Northwest," *Oregon Historical Quarterly*, XXIX (1928), 217–24; T. T. Geer: "Incidents in the Organization of the Provisional Government," *Quarterly of the Oregon Historical Society*, II (1901), 366–80; F. I. Herriott: "Transplanting Iowa's Laws to Oregon," *Quarterly of the Oregon Historical Society*, V (1904), 139–50; also in *Annals of Iowa*, VI (1903–06), 455–63; Frederick V. Holman: "A Brief History of the Oregon Provisional Government and What Caused Its Formation," *Quarterly of the Oregon Historical Society*, XIII (1912), 89–139; C. S. Kingston: "The Oregon Convention of 1843," *Washington Historical Quarterly*, XXII (1931), 163–71; C. J. Pike: "Petitions of Oregon Settlers, 1838–48," *Oregon Historical Quarterly*, XXXIV (1933), 216–35; James Rood Robertson: "The Genesis of Political Authority and of a Commonwealth Government in Oregon," *Quarterly of the Oregon Historical Society*, I (1900), 3–59; H. W. Scott: "The Formation and Administration of the Provisional Government of Oregon," *Quarterly of the Oregon Historical Society*, II (1901), 95–118; Leslie M. Scott: "Modern Fallacies of Champoeg," *Oregon Historical Quarterly*, XXXII (1931), 213–16; Russell B. Thomas: "Truth and Fiction of the Champoeg Meeting," *Oregon Historical Quarterly*, XXX (1929), 218–37.

CHAPTER IX

CONTEMPORARY ACCOUNTS. Robert C. Clark, ed.: "Aberdeen and Peel on Oregon, 1844," *Oregon Historical Quarterly*, XXXIV (1933), 236–40; and "Letter of Aberdeen to Pakenham, March 4, 1844, Concerning the Oregon Question," *Oregon Historical Quarterly*, XXXIX (1938), 74–6; Charles M. Gates, ed.: *Readings in Pacific Northwest History: Washington, 1790–1895* (Seattle, 1941), 107–13; Hunter Miller, ed.: *Treaties and Other International Acts of the United States of America* (Washington, 1931–37), V, 3–101; Allan Nevins, ed.: *Polk: The Diary of a President, 1845–1849* (New York, 1929); Milo M. Quaife, ed.: *The Diary of James K. Polk during His Presi-*

dency, 1845 to 1849 (Chicago, 1910), 4 vols.; Joseph Schafer, ed.: "Letters of Sir George Simpson, 1841–1843," *American Historical Review,* XIV (1908–09), 70–94.

MODERN ACCOUNTS – BOOKS. H. F. Angus, ed.: *British Columbia and the United States,* by F. W. Howay, W. N. Sage, and H. F. Angus (Toronto, 1942); Thomas A. Bailey: *A Diplomatic History of the American People,* 3rd ed. (New York, 1946), ch. 15; Charles H. Carey: *A General History of Oregon Prior to 1861* (Portland, 1936), II, ch. 20; Robert C. Clark: *History of the Willamette Valley, Oregon* (Chicago, 1927), ch. II; Bernard A. DeVoto: *The Year of Decision: 1846* (Boston, 1943); Cardinal L. Goodwin: *The Trans-Mississippi West* (New York, 1922), chs. 6, 9; Melvin C. Jacobs: *Winning Oregon* (Caldwell, Idaho, 1938), ch. 5; Eugene I. McCormac: *James K. Polk, A Political Biography* (Berkeley, 1922), ch. 21; William I. Marshall: *Acquisition of Oregon* (Seattle, 1911), 2 vols.; Oliver W. Nixon: *How Marcus Whitman Saved Oregon* (Chicago, 1895); Richard W. Van Alstyne: *American Diplomacy in Action* (Stanford University, 1944), ch. 33.

MODERN ACCOUNTS – ARTICLES. J. Neilson Barry: "Oregon Boundaries," *Oregon Historical Quarterly,* XXXIII (1932), 259–67; G. Verne Blue: "France and the Oregon Question," *Oregon Historical Quarterly,* XXXIV (1933), 39–59, 144–63; and "The Oregon Question – 1818–1828," *Quarterly of the Oregon Historical Society,* XXIII (1922), 193–219; Robert C. Clark: "How British and American Subjects Unite in a Common Government for Oregon Territory in 1844," *Quarterly of the Oregon Historical Society,* XIII (1912), 140–59; Henry S. Commager: "England and Oregon Treaty, 1846," *Oregon Historical Quarterly,* XXVIII (1927), 18–38; C. T. Johnson: "Daniel Webster and Old Oregon," *Washington Historical Quarterly,* II (1907–08), 6–11; and "Daniel Webster, Lord Ashburton and Old Oregon," *Washington Historical Quarterly,* I (1906–07), 208–16; Frederick Merk: "The British Corn Crisis of 1845–46 and the Oregon Treaty," *Agricultural History,* VIII (1934), 95–123; "British Government Propaganda and the Oregon Treaty," *American Historical Review,* XL (1934–35), 38–62; "British Party Politics and the Oregon Treaty," *American Historical Review,* XXXVII (1931–32), 653–77; and "The Oregon Pioneers and the Boundary," *American Historical Review,* XXIX (1923–24), 681–99; also in *Oregon Historical Quarterly,* XXVIII (1927), 366–88; Charles O. Paullin: "The Early Choice of the Forty-Ninth Parallel as a Boundary Line," *Canadian Historical Review,* IV (1923), 127–31; Julius W. Pratt: "James K. Polk and John Bull," *Canadian Historical Review,* XXIV (1943), 341–9; Joseph Schafer: "The British Attitude toward the Oregon Question, 1815–1846," *American Historical Review,* XVI (1910–11), 273–99; Richard W. Van Alstyne: "International Rivalries in Pacific Northwest," *Oregon Historical Quarterly,* XLVI (1945), 185–218.

CHAPTER X

CONTEMPORARY ACCOUNTS. Charles H. Carey, ed.: *The Oregon Constitution* (Salem, 1926); M. P. Deady and L. Lane, comps.: *General Laws of Oregon, 1843–1872* (Salem, 1874); Charles M. Gates, ed.: *Readings in Pacific Northwest History: Washington, 1790–1895* (Seattle, 1941), ch. 7; W. Turrentine Jackson, ed.: "The Capitol of Washington," *Pacific Northwest Quarterly*, XXXVI (1945), 249–67; J. Orin Oliphant, ed.: "Additional Note on the Constitution of 1878," *Washington Historical Quarterly*, XVII (1926), 27–35; *Statutes of the Territory of Washington* (Olympia, 1854–59).

MODERN ACCOUNTS — BOOKS. H. H. Bancroft: *History of Oregon* (San Francisco, 1886), II, chs. 3–5, 11, 13–14, 17; and *History of Washington, Idaho and Montana, 1845–1889* (San Francisco, 1890), Washington, chs. 2–3, 6, 8–9; Idaho, ch. 3; Charles H. Carey: *A General History of Oregon Prior to 1861* (Portland, 1936), II, ch. 21; Robert C. Clark: *History of the Willamette Valley, Oregon* (Chicago, 1927), ch. 14; Clifford M. Drury: *Marcus Whitman, M.D.* (Caldwell, Idaho, 1937), ch. 19; Sister M. Margaret Jean Kelly: *The Career of Joseph Lane: Frontier Politician* (Washington, D. C., 1942); Horace S. Lyman: *History of Oregon* (New York, 1903), IV, ch. 7; Edmond S. Meany: *History of the State of Washington* (New York, 1910), chs. 16–17, 28; Charles Miles and O. B. Sperlin, eds.: *Building a State: Washington, 1889–1939* (Tacoma, 1940), ch. 2; *Proceedings of the Fiftieth Anniversary of the Admission of the State of Oregon to the Union* (Salem, 1909); Clinton A. Snowden: *History of Washington* (New York, 1909), III, ch. 42; IV, chs. 49, 60; Hazard Stevens: *The Life of Isaac Ingalls Stevens* (New York, 1900), I, ch. 22.

MODERN ACCOUNTS — ARTICLES. Arthur S. Beardsley: "Code Making in Early Oregon," *Pacific Northwest Quarterly*, XXVII (1936), 3–33; "Compiling the Territorial Codes of Washington," *Pacific Northwest Quarterly*, XXVIII (1937), 3–54; and "Early Efforts to Locate the Capital of Washington Territory," *Pacific Northwest Quarterly*, XXXII (1941), 280–87; Samuel F. Cohn: "Martial Law in Washington Territory," *Pacific Northwest Quarterly*, XXVII (1936), 195–218; T. W. Davenport: "Slavery Question in Oregon," *Quarterly of the Oregon Historical Society*, IX (1908), 189–253, 309–73; George H. Himes: "Delegates to the Constitutional Convention of Oregon in 1857," *Quarterly of the Oregon Historical Society*, XV (1914), 217–18; C. S. Kingston: "The North Idaho Annexation Issue," *Washington Historical Quarterly*, XXI (1930), 133–7, 204–17, 281–93; and "The Walla Walla Separation Movement," *Washington Historical Quarterly*, XXIV (1933), 91–104; Ira W. Lewis: "Education in the Oregon Constitutional Convention of 1857," *Quarterly of the Oregon Historical Society*, XXIII (1922), 220–9; Edmond S. Meany: "The Cowlitz Convention: Inception of Washington Territory," *Washington*

Historical Quarterly, XIII (1922), 3–19; Thomas W. Prosch: "The Political Beginning of Washington Territory," *Quarterly of the Oregon Historical Society*, VI (1905), 147–58; Henry H. Simms, ed.: "The Controversy Over the Admission of the State of Oregon," *Mississippi Valley Historical Review*, XXXII (1945), 355–74; George H. Williams: "The 'Free-State Letter' of Judge George H. Williams," *Quarterly of the Oregon Historical Society*, IX (1908), 254–73.

CHAPTER XI

CONTEMPORARY ACCOUNTS. Eva Emery Dye, ed.: "Earliest Expedition against Puget Sound Indians," by Frank Ermatinger, *Washington Historical Quarterly*, I (Jan., 1906–07), 16–29; Charles M. Gates, ed.: *Readings in Pacific Northwest History: Washington, 1790–1895* (Seattle, 1941), ch. 5; W. B. Gosnell, ed.: "Indian War in Washington Territory," *Washington Historical Quarterly*, XVII (1926), 289–99; Waman C. Hembree: "Yakima Indian War Diary," *Washington Historical Quarterly*, XVI (1925), 273–83; J. Orin Oliphant, ed.: "Journals of the Indian War of 1855–56," *Washington Historical Quarterly*, XV (1924), 11–31; Harvey Robbins: "Journal of Rogue River War, 1855," *Oregon Historical Quarterly*, XXXIV (1933), 345–58; Douglas S. Watson, ed.: *The Diary of Philip Leget Edwards: The Great Cattle Drive from California to Oregon in 1837* (San Francisco, 1932).

MODERN ACCOUNTS — BOOKS. H. H. Bancroft: *History of Oregon* (San Francisco, 1886), II, chs. 7–9, 12, 15–16; Charles H. Carey: *A General History of Oregon Prior to 1861* (Portland, 1936), II, 478–85, ch. 22; Robert C. Clark: *History of Willamette Valley, Oregon* (Chicago, 1927), chs. 12–13; George W. Fuller: *A History of the Pacific Northwest* (New York, 1931), chs. 13–14; Edmond S. Meany: *History of the State of Washington* (New York, 1924), chs. 18–22; Joseph Schafer: *A History of the Pacific Northwest* (New York, 1918), ch. 18; Clinton A. Snowden: *History of Washington* (New York, 1909), III, chs. 38–39.

MODERN ACCOUNTS — ARTICLES. Lloyd D. Black: "Middle Willamette Valley Population Growth," *Oregon Historical Quarterly*, XLIII (1942), 40–55; William M. Colvig: "Indian Wars of Southern Oregon," *Quarterly of the Oregon Historical Society*, IV (1903), 227–40; "Early Settlers of Seattle," *Magazine of Western History*, XII (1890), 84–5, 186–90, 243–5; Jonas A. Jonasson: "Local Road Legislation in Early Oregon," *Oregon Historical Quarterly*, XLII (1941), 162–75; James W. Nesmith and Joseph Lane: "The Council of Table Rock, 1853," *Quarterly of the Oregon Historical Society*, VII (1906), 211–21; Nellie B. Pipes: "Indian Conditions in 1836–38," *Oregon Historical Quarterly*, XXXII (1931), 332–42; Thomas W. Prosch: "The Indian War in Washington Territory," *Quarterly of the Oregon Historical Society*, XVI (1915), 1–23; "Settlements on Puget Sound," *North American Review*, II (1815–16), 301–6; Buena Cobb Stone:

"Southern Route into Oregon: Notes and a New Map," *Oregon Historical Quarterly*, XLVII (1946), 135–54; Lon L. Swift: "Land Tenure in Oregon," *Quarterly of the Oregon Historical Society*, X (June, 1909), 31–135; Oscar Osburn Winther: "Inland Transportation and Communication in Washington, 1844–1859," *Pacific Northwest Quarterly*, XXX (1939), 371–86; and "The Roads and Transportation of Territorial Oregon," *Oregon Historical Quarterly*, XLI (1940), 40–52.

CHAPTER XII

CONTEMPORARY ACCOUNTS. Mae Hélène Bacon Boggs, comp.: *My Playhouse Was a Concord Coach* (Oakland, 1942); Samuel Bowles: *Across the Continent* (Springfield, Mass., 1866); Thomas C. Donaldson: *Idaho of Yesterday* (Caldwell, Idaho, 1941); Charles M. Gates: *Readings in Pacific Northwest History: Washington, 1790–1895* (Seattle, 1941), chs. 9–10; Horace Greeley: *An Overland Journey* (New York, 1860); John M. Murphy: *Rambles in Northwestern America* . . . (London, 1879); Wallis Nash: *Oregon: There and Back in 1877* (London, 1878); James F. Rusling: *Across America* (New York, 1874); A. L. Stimson: *History of the Express Companies* (New York, 1858); Charles S. Walgamott: *Six Decades Back* (Caldwell, Idaho, 1936); Henry Wells: *Sketch of the Rise, Progress, and Present Conditions of the Express System* (Albany, N. Y., 1864); E. W. Wright, ed.: *Lewis & Dryden's Marine History of the Pacific Northwest* (Portland, 1895).

MODERN ACCOUNTS — BOOKS. Merrill D. Beal: *A History of Southeastern Idaho* (Caldwell, Idaho, 1942); J. V. Frederick: *Ben Holladay, The Stagecoach King* (Glendale, Calif., 1940); LeRoy R. Hafen: *The Overland Mail 1849–1869* (Cleveland, 1926); Alvin F. Harlow: *Old Waybills; The Romance of the Express Companies* (New York, 1934); Oscar Osburn Winther: *Via Western Express and Stagecoach* (Stanford University, 1945).

MODERN ACCOUNTS — ARTICLES. Frank B. Gill and Dorothy Johansen, eds.: "A Chapter in the History of the Oregon Steam Navigation Company," *Oregon Historical Quarterly*, XXXVIII (1937), 1–43, 300–22, 398–410; XXXIX (1938), 50–64; Thomas W. Prosch: "The Military Roads of Washington Territory," *Washington Historical Quarterly*, II (1907–08), 118–26; Walter M. Underhill: "Oregon's Provisional Postoffice," *Washington Historical Quarterly*, XV (1924), 266–75; Oscar Osburn Winther: "Inland Transportation and Communication in Washington, 1844–1859," *Pacific Northwest Quarterly*, XXX (1939), 371–86; "The Development of Transportation in Oregon, 1843–49," *Oregon Historical Quarterly*, XL (1939), 314–26; and "The Roads and Transportation of Territorial Oregon," *Oregon Historical Quarterly*, XLI (1940), 40–52.

478 The Great Northwest

CHAPTER XIII

CONTEMPORARY ACCOUNTS. Clarence B. Bagley, ed.: *Early Catholic Missions in Old Oregon* (Seattle, 1932), 2 vols.

MODERN ACCOUNTS – BOOKS. H. H. Bancroft: *History of Oregon* (San Francisco, 1886), II, 677–94; and *History of Washington, Idaho and Montana, 1845–1899* (San Francisco, 1890), 372–80; Merrill D. Beal: *A History of Southeastern Idaho* (Caldwell, Idaho, 1942), ch. 21; Angie B. Bowden: *Early Schools of Washington Territory* (Seattle, 1935); Robert M. Gatke: *Chronicles of Willamette* (Portland, 1943), chs. 2–5; John B. Horner: *Oregon Literature* (Portland, 1902); Jonas A. Jonasson: *Bricks Without Straw, The Story of Linfield College* (Caldwell, Idaho, 1938); Sister Letitia Mary Lyons: *Francis Norbert Blanchet and the Founding of the Oregon Missions (1838–1848)* (Washington, D. C., 1940); Edwin V. O'Hara: *Pioneer Catholic History of Oregon* (Paterson, N. J., 1939), chs. 17–20; Alfred Powers: *History of Oregon Literature* (Portland, 1935), pp. 3–229; Charles D. Schreibeis: *Pioneer Education in the Pacific Northwest* (Portland, 1937); Henry D. Sheldon: *History of University of Oregon* (Portland, 1940).

MODERN ACCOUNTS – ARTICLES. John C. Almack: "History of Oregon Normal Schools," *Quarterly of the Oregon Historical Society*, XXI (1920), 95–169; Read Bain: "Educational Plans and Efforts by Methodists in Oregon to 1860," *Quarterly of the Oregon Historical Society*, XXI (1920), 63–94; Henry L. Bates: "Pacific University," *Quarterly of the Oregon Historical Society*, XXI (1920), 1–12; Mirpah G. Blair: "Some Early Libraries of Oregon," *Washington Historical Quarterly*, XVII (1926), 259–70; Frederick E. Bolson: "High Schools in Territorial Washington," *Washington Historical Quarterly*, XXIV (1933), 211–20, 271–81; R. A. Booth: "History of Umpqua Academy," *Quarterly of the Oregon Historical Society*, XIX (1918), 1–26; Julia Veazie Glen: "John Lyle and Lyle Farm," *Quarterly of the Oregon Historical Society*, XXVI (1925), 131–50; John B. Horner: "History of Oregon State College, 1865–1907," *Oregon Historical Quarterly*, XXXI (1930), 42–50; Charles Abner Howard: "A History of High School Legislation in Oregon to 1910," *Quarterly of the Oregon Historical Society*, XXIV (1923), 201–37; Charles E. Lewis: "The History of the Educational Activities of the Protestant Episcopal Church in Oregon," *Quarterly of the Oregon Historical Society*, XXV (1924), 101–35; Ira W. Lewis: "Education in the Oregon Constitutional Convention of 1857," *Quarterly of the Oregon Historical Society*, XXIII (1922), 220–9; Edmond S. Meany: "Early Records of the University," *Washington Historical Quarterly*, VIII (1917), 114–23; Philip Henry Overmeyer: "Villard and University of Oregon," *Oregon Historical Quarterly*, XXXV (1934), 340–7; H. Earl Pemberton: "Early Colleges in Oregon," *Oregon Historical Quarterly*, XXXIII (1932), 230–42; James Rood Robertson: "Origin of Pacific University," *Quar-*

terly of the Oregon Historical Society, VI (1905), 109–46; J. F. Santee: "Early Education in Oregon," *Oregon Historical Quarterly,* XXXII (1931), 65–9; "Thomas Milton Gatch, Educator," *Oregon Historical Quarterly,* XXXII (1931), 114–22; "University of Oregon Admission, 1876–1937," *Oregon Historical Quarterly,* XXX (1929), 129–46; and "University Preparatory School, 1876–1904," *Oregon Historical Quarterly,* XXXI (1930), 152–9; Martin P. Simon: "Lutheran Education in Oregon," *Oregon Historical Quarterly,* XXXIII (1932), 164–8.

CHAPTER XIV

CONTEMPORARY ACCOUNTS. Thomas Donaldson: *Idaho of Yesterday* (Caldwell, Idaho, 1941); William S. Lewis, ed.: "Experiences of a Packer in Washington Territory Mining Camps during the Sixties," by James W. Watt, *Washington Historical Quarterly,* XIX (1928), 206–13, 285–93; XX (1929), 36–53; Philip H. Overmeyer: "George B. McClellan and the Pacific Northwest," *Pacific Northwest Quarterly,* XXXII (1941), 3–60; Paul C. Phillips, ed.: *Forty Years on the Frontier as Seen in the Journals and Reminiscences of Granville Stuart* (Cleveland, 1925), I, 130–40; James C. Strong: "Reminiscences of a Pioneer of the Territory of Washington," *Washington Historical Quarterly,* III (1908–12), 179–85.

MODERN ACCOUNTS — BOOKS. H. F. Angus, ed.: *British Columbia and the United States,* by F. W. Howay, W. N. Sage, and H. F. Angus (Toronto, 1942); H. H. Bancroft: *History of Washington, Idaho and Montana, 1845–1889* (San Francisco, 1890); Merrill G. Burlingame: *The Montana Frontier* (Helena, Montana, 1942); W. P. Morrell: *The Gold Rushes* (London, 1940), ch. 5; Glenn C. Quiett: *Pay Dirt* (New York, 1936); William J. Trimble: *The Mining Advance into the Inland Empire* (Madison, Wis., 1914).

MODERN ACCOUNTS — ARTICLES. Samuel Flagg Bemis: "Captain John Mullan and the Engineers' Frontier," *Washington Historical Quarterly,* XIV (1923), 201–5; Robert L. Housman: "Boy Editors of Frontier Montana," *Pacific Northwest Quarterly,* XXVII (1936), 219–26; and "Pioneer Montana's Journalistic 'Ghost' Camp — Virginia City," *Pacific Northwest Quarterly,* XXIX (1938), 53–9; W. M. Underhill: "Historic Bread Riot in Virginia City," *Washington Historical Quarterly,* XXI (1930), 189–94; Oscar Osburn Winther: "Inland Transportation and Communication in Washington, 1844–1859," *Pacific Northwest Quarterly,* XXX (1939), 371–86.

CHAPTER XV

CONTEMPORARY ACCOUNTS. John T. Condon, ed.: "Washington's First Constitution, 1878," *Washington Historical Quarterly,* IX (1918), 129–52, 208–29, 296–307; X (1919), 57–68, 110–41; Thomas J. Dimsdale: *The Vigilantes of Montana* (Virginia City, Montana, 1866);

James H. Hawley, ed.: *History of Idaho* (Chicago, 1920), vol. I; J. Orin Oliphant: "Additional Notes on the Constitution of 1878," *Washington Historical Quarterly*, XVII (1926), 27–35; Charles S. Walgamott: *Reminiscences of Early Days* (Twin Falls, Idaho [1926]).

MODERN ACCOUNTS — BOOKS. H. H. Bancroft: *History of Washington, Idaho and Montana, 1845–1889* (San Francisco, 1890); Merrill D. Beal: *A History of Southeastern Idaho* (Caldwell, Idaho, 1942), chs. 9–10; Harold E. Briggs: *Frontiers of the Northwest: A History of the Upper Missouri Valley* (New York, 1940); Jennie B. Brown: *Fort Hall on the Oregon Trail* (Caldwell, Idaho, 1932); Joseph K. Howard: *Montana; High, Wide, and Handsome* (New Haven, 1943), ch. 5; Frederic L. Paxson: *History of the American Frontier, 1763–1893* (New York, 1924), ch. 58.

MODERN ACCOUNTS — ARTICLES. Mrs. James D. Agnew: "Idaho Pioneer of 1864," *Washington Historical Quarterly*, XV (1924), 44–8; R. E. Albright: "The American Civil War as a Factor in Montana Territorial Politics," *Pacific Historical Review*, VI (1937), 36–46; Eugene B. Chaffee: "The Political Clash between North and South Idaho Over the Capital," *Pacific Northwest Quarterly*, XXIX (1938), 255–67; John D. Hicks: "The Constitution of the Northwest States," University of Nebraska, *University Studies*, vol. XXIII (1923); Robert L. Housman: "Frontier Society — Cedar Creek, Montana, 1870–1874," *Washington Historical Quarterly*, XXVI (1935), 264–73; Oliver O. Howard: "Outbreak of the Piute and Bannock War," *Overland Monthly*, IX, 2nd series (1887), 587–92; C. S. Kingston: "The North Idaho Annexation Issue," *Washington Historical Quarterly*, XXI (1930), 133–7, 204–17, 281–93; and "The Walla Walla Separation Movement," *Washington Historical Quarterly*, XXIV (1933), 91–104; Lebbeus J. Knapp: "The Origin of the Constitution of the State of Washington," *Washington Historical Quarterly*, IV (1913), 227–75; Austin Mires: "Remarks on the Constitution of the State of Washington," *Washington Historical Quarterly*, XXII (1931), 276–88; Frederic L. Paxson: "The Admission of the 'Omnibus' States, 1889–90," *Proceedings of the State Historical Society of Wisconsin . . . 1911* (Madison, Wis., 1912), pp. 77–96; Stella E. Pearce: "Suffrage in the Pacific Northwest, Old Oregon and Washington," *Washington Historical Quarterly*, III (1908–12), 106–14; W. M. Underhill: "Historic Bread Riot in Virginia City," *Washington Historical Quarterly*, XXI (1930), 189–94.

CHAPTER XVI

CONTEMPORARY ACCOUNTS. S. A. Clarke: "The Oregon Central Railroad," *Quarterly of the Oregon Historical Society*, VII (1906), 133–44; Joseph Gaston: "The Genesis of the Oregon Railway System," *Quarterly of the Oregon Historical Society*, VII (1906), 105–32; and "The Oregon Central Railroad," *Quarterly of the Oregon Historical Society*, III (1902), 315–26; Charles M. Gates, ed.: *Readings in Pacific Northwest History: Washington, 1790–1895* (Seattle, 1941), ch. 11; Eugene V. Smalley: *History of the Northern Pacific Railroad* (New York, 1883); "Subscription List for Railroad Survey Fund," *Quarterly of the Oregon Historical Society,* IX (1908), 305–7; Henry Villard: *Memoirs of Henry Villard, Journalist and Financier, 1835–1900* (Boston, 1904), 2 vols.; Oswald Garrison Villard, ed.: *The Early History of Transportation in Oregon,* by Henry Villard (Eugene, Oregon, 1944).

MODERN ACCOUNTS — BOOKS. Enoch A. Bryan: *Orient Meets Occident* (Pullman, Washington, 1936); Robert C. Clark: *History of the Willamette Valley, Oregon* (Chicago, 1927), ch. 17; August Derleth: *The Milwaukee Road; Its First Hundred Years* (New York, 1948); S. Kip Farrington: *Railroads of Today* (New York, 1949); N. S. B. Gras and Henrietta M. Larson: *Casebook in American Business History* (New York, 1939), p. 421; James B. Hedges: *Henry Villard and the Railways of the Northwest* (New Haven, 1930); F. W. Howay: *British Columbia, The Making of a Province* (Toronto, 1928), ch. 22; Harold A. Innis: *A History of the Canadian Pacific Railway* (London, 1923); Leonard B. Irwin: *Pacific Railways and Nationalism in the Canadian-American Northwest* (Philadelphia, 1939), ch. 4; Frederick H. Johnson: *Brief Record of the Development of the Milwaukee Road* (Chicago [1939]); Matthew Josephson: *The Robber Barons* (New York, 1934), chs. 4, 11; Max Lowenthal: *The Investor Pays* (New York, 1933); Charles Miles and O. B. Sperlin, eds.: *Building a State: Washington, 1889–1939* (Tacoma, 1940), pp. 248–62; John Moody: *The Railroad Builders* (New Haven, 1919); Keith Morris: *The Story of the Canadian Pacific Railway* (London, 1916); Joseph Gilpin Pyle: *The Life of James J. Hill* (New York, 1917), 2 vols.; Glenn C. Quiett: *They Built the West* (New York, 1934); Robert E. Riegel: *The Story of the Western Railroads* (New York, 1926); Hazard Stevens: *The Life of Isaac Ingalls Stevens* (Boston, 1900), I, chs. 15–21, 23.

MODERN ACCOUNTS — ARTICLES. Arthur M. Borals: "The Chicago, Milwaukee, and St. Paul Railroad: Recent History of the Last Transcontinental," *Journal of Economics and Business History,* III (1930), 83–84; D. C. Corbin: "Recollections of a Pioneer Railroad Builder," *Washington Historical Quarterly,* I (Jan., 1906–07), 43–6; John Tilson Ganoe: "The History of the Oregon and California Railroad," *Quarterly of the Oregon Historical Society,* XXV (1924), 236–83, 330–52; Frank B. Gill: "Oregon's First Railway," *Quarterly of the Oregon Historical Society,* XXV (1924), 171–235; Frank B. Gill and Dorothy O. Johansen, eds.: "A Chapter in the History of the Oregon Steam Navigation Company," *Oregon Historical Quarterly,* XXXVIII (1937), 1–43, 300–22, 398–410; XXXIX (1938), 50–64; P. W. Gillette: "A Brief History of the Oregon Steam Navigation Company," *Quarterly of the Oregon Historical Society,* V (1904), 120–38; L. C. Gilman: "The Spokane, Portland, and Seattle Railroad Company,"

Washington Historical Quarterly, XIV (1923), 14–20; C. H. Hanford: "The Orphan Railroad and the Rams Horn Right of Way," *Washington Historical Quarterly*, XIV (1923), 83–99; James B. Hedges: "Promotion of Immigration to the Pacific Northwest by the Railroads," *Mississippi Valley Historical Review*, XV (1928–29), 183–203; and "The Colonization Work of the Northern Pacific Railroad," *Mississippi Valley Historical Review*, XIII (1926–27), 311–42; Dorothy O. Johansen: "The Oregon Steam Navigation Company: An Example of Capitalism on the Frontier," *Pacific Historical Review*, X (1941), 179–88; Winlock Miller, Jr.: "The Olympia Narrow Gauge Railroad," *Washington Historical Quarterly*, XVI (1925), 243–50; Randall V. Mills: "A History of Transportation in the Pacific Northwest," *Oregon Historical Quarterly*, XLVII (1946), 281–312; Frederic L. Paxson: "Pacific Railroads and the Disappearance of the Frontier in America," *Annual Report American Historical Association*, I (1907), 105–18; Irene Lincoln Poppleton: "Oregon's First Monopoly — The Oregon Steam Navigation Company," *Quarterly of the Oregon Historical Society*, IX (1908), 274–304; Robert W. Sawyer, ed.: "Abbot Railroad Surveys, 1855," *Oregon Historical Quarterly*, XXXIII (1932), 1–24, 115–35; Leslie M. Scott: "History of Astoria Railroad," *Quarterly of the Oregon Historical Society*, XV (1914), 221–40; C. J. Smith: "Early Development of Railroads in the Pacific Northwest," *Washington Historical Quarterly*, XIII (1922), 243–50.

CHAPTER XVII

CONTEMPORARY ACCOUNTS. Robert Ballou: *Early Klickitat Days.* (Goldendale, Wash., 1938); U. E. Fries: *From Copenhagen to Okanogan* (Caldwell, Idaho, 1949); John Minto: "Sheep Husbandry in Oregon," *Quarterly of the Oregon Historical Society*, III (1902), 219–47; Clarence W. Gordon: "Report on Cattle, Sheep and Swine," *Report on the Production of Agricultural . . . Tenth Census* (Washington, 1883), III, 1–156; [Daniel Montgomery] Drumkiller: *"Uncle Dan" Drumkiller Tells Thrills of Western Trails in 1854* (Spokane, 1925), chs. 6, 8.

MODERN ACCOUNTS — BOOKS. Harold E. Briggs: *Frontiers of the Northwest; A History of the Upper Missouri Valley* (New York, 1940), chs. 3, 4; Otis W. Freeman and Howard H. Martin, eds.: *The Pacific Northwest, a Regional, Human, and Economic Survey of Resources and Development* (New York, 1942), ch. 19; Howard T. Lewis and Stephen I. Miller, eds.: *The Economic Resources of the Pacific Northwest* (Seattle, 1923), ch. 4; Alfred L. Lomax: *Pioneer Woolen Mills in Oregon; History of Wool and the Woolen Textile Industry in Oregon, 1811–1875* (Portland, 1941); John K. Rollenson: *Wyoming Cattle Trails, History of the Migrations of Oregon Raised Herds to Midwestern Markets* (Caldwell, Idaho, 1948); Andrew J. Splawn: *Ka-mi-akin: The Last Hero of the Yakimas* (Portland,

[1917]), *passim;* Charles W. Towne and Edward N. Wentworth: *Shepherd's Empire* (Norman, Okla., 1945); Edward N. Wentworth: *America's Sheep Trails: History; Personalities* (Ames, Iowa, 1948); Chester W. Wright: *Wool-Growing and the Tariff. A Study in the Economic History of the United States* (New York, 1910); Walker D. Wyman: *The Wild Horse of the West* (Caldwell, Idaho, 1945).

MODERN ACCOUNTS — ARTICLES. Herbert O. Brayer: "The Influence of British Capital on the Western Range-Cattle Industry," *The Tasks of Economic History*, Economic History Association, Supplement IX, 1949, 85–89; Harold E. Briggs: "The Development and Decline of the Open Range Ranching in the Northwest," *Mississippi Valley Historical Review*, XX (1934), 521–36; and "The Early Development of Sheep Ranching in the Northwest," *Agricultural History*, XI (1937), 161–80; L. G. Connor: "A Brief History of the Sheep Industry in the United States," *Annual Report of the American Historical Association, for the Year 1918* (Washington, 1921), I, 89–197; Bernard De Voto: "Sacred Cows and Public Lands," *Harper's Magazine*, CXCVII (1948), 44–55; H. R. Hockmuth and H. R. Franklin: "Sheep Migrate, too, to Follow the Grass," *Land Policy Review*, III (1940), 12–19; Roy G. Johnson: "Some Oregon Grazing Problems," *The Commonwealth Review*, XIX (1937), 261–67; C. S. Kingston: "Introduction of Cattle into the Pacific Northwest," *Washington Historical Quarterly*, XIV (1923), 163–85; Alfred L. Lomax: "History of Pioneer Sheep Husbandry in Oregon," *Oregon Historical Quarterly*, XXIX (1928), 99–143; J. Orin Oliphant: "The Cattle Herds and Ranches of Oregon Country, 1860–1890," *Agricultural History*, XXI (1947), 217–38; "The Cattle Trade from the Far Northwest to Montana," *Agricultural History*, VI (1932), 69–83; "The Cattle Trade on Puget Sound, 1858–1890," *Agricultural History*, VII (1933), 129–49; "The Cattle Trade through the Snoqualmie Pass," *Pacific Northwest Quarterly*, XXXVIII (1947), 193–214; "The Eastward Movement of Cattle from the Oregon Country," *Agricultural History*, XX (1946), 19–42; and "Winter Losses of Cattle in the Oregon Country, 1874–1890," *Washington Historical Quarterly*, XXIII (1909), 3–17; Ernest S. Osgood: "The Cattleman in the Agricultural History of the Northwest," *Agricultural History*, III (1929), 117–30; Edward N. Wentworth: "Eastward Sheep Drives from California and Oregon," *Mississippi Valley Historical Review*, XXVIII (1942), 507–38.

CHAPTER XVIII *

BOOKS. Merrill D. Beal: *A History of Southeastern Idaho* (Caldwell, Idaho, 1942), ch. 17; Arthur P. Davis: *Irrigation Works Constructed by the United States Government* (New York, 1917), chs.

* Beginning with this chapter, the classifications indicated, namely, "Books" and "Articles," will be used. Since periods and topics referred to are all rather recent, the materials listed are all contemporary in character.

7–8, 16–17, 20–21; Harold H. Dunham: *Government Handout: A Study in the Administration of the Public Lands, 1875–1891* (New York, 1941); Otis W. Freeman and Howard H. Martin: *The Pacific Northwest* (New York, 1942), chs. 14–21; Benjamin H. Hibbard: *A History of the Public Land Policies* (New York, 1924); George W. James: *Reclaiming the Arid West* (New York, 1917), chs. 11–13, 15–16, 29–30; Howard T. Lewis and Stephen I. Miller, eds.: *The Economic Resources of the Pacific Northwest* (Seattle, 1923), ch. 5; William D. Miner: "A History of the Columbia Basin Projects," Ph.D. Dissertation, Indiana University, 1950 (unpublished); Richard L. Neuberger: *Our Promised Land* (New York, 1938), chs. 3–4; F. H. Newell: *First Annual Report of the Reclamation Service* (Washington, 1903), pp. 160–95, 272–75, 303–5; S. A. D. Puter and Horace Stevens: *Looters of the Public Domain* (Portland, 1908); Roy M. Robbins: *Our Landed Heritage, the Public Domain; 1776–1936* (Princeton, 1942); Joseph Schafer: *The Social History of American Agriculture* (New York, 1936); Fred A. Shannon: *The Farmer's Last Frontier: Agriculture, 1860–1897* (New York, 1945), ch. 13; Wm. E. Smythe, *The Conquest of Arid America* (New York, 1911); United States Department of Interior, Bureau of Reclamation: *Reclamation Handbook, Conservation Bulletin No. 32* (Washington, 1942) – a pamphlet; Rufus Woods: *The 23 Years' Battle for the Grand Coulee Dam* (Wenatchee, Wash., 1944); *Official Proceedings of the Seventeenth National Irrigation Congress*, held at Spokane, August 9–14, 1909 (Washington, n.d.); *Proceedings of a Conference of Governors in the White House, Washington, D. C., May 13–15, 1908* (Washington, 1909).

ARTICLES.　Rose M. Boening: "History of Irrigation in the State of Washington," *Washington Historical Quarterly*, IX (1918), 259–76; X (1919), 21–45; Robert O. Case: "Eighth World Wonder," *Saturday Evening Post*, CCVIII (July 13, 1935), 23 ff; Stuart Chase: "Great Dam," *Atlantic Monthly*, CLXII (1938), 593–9; David W. Clark: "Idaho Made the Desert Bloom," *National Geographic Magazine*, LXXXV (1944), 641–88; "Columbia Basin Reclamation," *New Republic*, CXIII (1945), 175; Rafe Gibbs: "Million-Acre Boom," *Collier's*, CXIX (1947), 14–15, 58; David James: "America's New Million-Acre Oasis," *Science Digest*, XVIII (1945), 39–42; C. R. Koester: "Grand Coulee of Washington," *Nature Magazine*, XL (1947), 34–7; "Migration and Settlement in the Yakima Valley, Washington," *Monthly Labor Review*, LIV (1942), 405–7; Richard L. Neuberger: "The Biggest Thing on Earth," *Harper's Magazine*, CLXXIV (1937), 247–58; and "To the West, Water is Life and Death," *New York Times Magazine* (1948), p. 15; Louise M. Sill: "Largest Irrigated Tract in the World," *Harper's Weekly*, LII (Oct. 17, 1908), 11–12.

CHAPTER XIX

BOOKS. Charles A. Beard and Mary R. Beard: *The Rise of American Civilization* (New York, 1930), II, ch. 22; Harold E. Briggs: *Frontiers of the Northwest; a History of the Upper Missouri Valley* (New York, 1940), ch. 6; Otis W. Freeman and Howard H. Martin, eds.: *The Pacific Northwest, a Regional, Human, and Economic Survey of Resources and Development* (New York, 1942), chs. 14–21; Howard T. Lewis and Stephen I. Miller, eds.: *The Economic Resources of the Pacific Northwest* (Seattle, 1923), chs. 3, 4, 5, 6, 7; Robert Ray Martin: "The Inland Empire of the Pacific Northwest: A Regional Study," Ph.D. Dissertation, University of Washington Library, 1935; Fred A. Shannon: *The Farmer's Last Frontier* (New York, 1945); Thomas Shaw: *Dry Land Farming* (St. Paul, 1911); Charles W. Towne and Edward N. Wentworth: *Shepherd's Empire* (Norman, Okla., 1945), ch. 7.

ARTICLES. A. Berglund: "The Wheat Situation in Washington," *Political Science Quarterly*, XXIV (1909), 489–503; Leonie N. Brooke: "The Sugar-Beet Industry in Malheur County," *The Commonwealth Review*, XXIII (1941), 54–63; David W. Clark: "Idaho Made the Desert Bloom," *National Geographic Magazine*, LXXXV (1944), 641–88; H. L. Davis, "Back to the Land — Oregon, 1907," *American Mercury*, XVI (1929), 314–23; Rafe Gibbs: "Million-Acre Boom," *Collier's*, CXIX (1947), 14–15, 58; Mary W. M. Hargreaves: "Dry Farming Alias Scientific Farming," *Agricultural History*, XXII (1948), 39–56; David James: "America's New Million-Acre Oasis," *Science Digest*, XVIII (Oct., 1945), 39–42; Oscar Lewis: "Bumper Crop in the Desert," *Harper's Magazine*, CXCIII (1946), 525–28; Robert C. Nesbit and Charles M. Gates: "Agriculture in Eastern Washington, 1890–1910," *Pacific Northwest Quarterly*, XXXVII (1946), 279–302; J. Orin Oliphant: "The Eastward Movement of Cattle from the Oregon Country," *Agricultural History*, XX (1946), 19–43; and "History of the Livestock Industry in the Pacific Northwest," *Oregon Historical Quarterly*, XLIX (1948), 3–29; Louise M. Sill: "Largest Irrigated Tract in the World," *Harper's Weekly*, LII (Oct. 17, 1908), 11–12; Dexter K. Strong: "Beef Cattle Industry in Oregon, 1890–1938," *Oregon Historical Quarterly*, XLI (1940), 251–87; Frank J. Taylor: "An Orchard Became Big Business," *Reader's Digest* (Nov., 1948), 94–6; Oswald West: "Opportunity for Cooperation in Making Vacant Lands Productive," *The Commonwealth Review*, I (1916), 27–46.

CHAPTER XX

BOOKS. Archie Binns: *Northwest Gateway: The Story of the Port of Seattle* (Garden City, N. Y., 1941); Robert C. Clark: *History of the Willamette Valley, Oregon* (Chicago, 1927), pp. 732–4; John N. Cobb: *Pacific Salmon Fisheries* (Washington, D. C., 1911); [Federal

Writers' Project, Idaho]: *Idaho; A Guide in Word and Picture* (Caldwell, Idaho, 1937), pp. 169–71; Otis W. Freeman and Howard H. Martin, eds.: *The Pacific Northwest* (New York, 1942), pp. 255–97; Charles M. Gates, ed.: *Readings in Pacific Northwest History: Washington, 1790–1895* (Seattle, 1941), chs. 12, 14; Carl B. Glasscock: *The War of the Copper Kings: Builders of Butte and Wolves of Wall Street* (Indianapolis, [1935]); Homer E. Gregory and Kathleen Barnes: *North Pacific Fisheries, with Special Reference to Alaska Salmon* (San Francisco, 1939); Stewart H. Holbrook: *Burning an Empire: The Story of American Forest Fires* (New York, 1943); and *Holy Old Mackinaw; A Natural History of the American Lumberjack* (New York, 1939); Howard T. Lewis and Stephen I. Miller, eds.: *The Economic Resources of the Pacific Northwest* (Seattle, 1923); Richard G. Lillard: *The Great Forest* (New York, 1947); Alfred Lomax: *Pioneer Woolen Mills in Oregon* (Portland, 1941); Earl C. May: *The Canning Clan* (New York, 1937); Eliot G. Mears: *Maritime Trade of Western United States* (Stanford University, 1935), ch. 8; Richard L. Neuberger: *Our Promised Land* (New York, 1938); Clinton A. Snowden: *History of Washington* (New York, 1909), IV, ch. 58; Clark P. Spurlock: "A History of the Salmon Industry in the Pacific Northwest," M.A. Thesis, University of Oregon, 1940; [State of Washington]: *A Review of the Resources and Industries of Washington, 1905* (Olympia, Washington, 1905), pp. 48–51; [United States]: *Report on Manufacturing Industries in the United States at the Eleventh Census: 1890*, Part II: "Statistics of Cities"; Part III: "Selected Industries" (Washington, D. C., 1895); and *Report on the Mineral Industries in the United States at the Eleventh Census: 1890* (Washington, 1892); Benjamin MacLean Whitesmith: "Henry Villard and the Development of Oregon," M.A. Thesis, University of Oregon, 1931.

ARTICLES.   Kate M. Archibald: "Selling the Skagit to the People," *American City*, LIV (Nov., 1939), 46–7; Sverre Arestad: "Norwegians in the Pacific Coast Fisheries," *Pacific Northwest Quarterly*, XXXIV (1943), 3–17; R. F. Bessey: "Pacific Northwest States' Economic Potentials," *Proceedings of the First Pacific Northwest Marketing Conference* (Seattle, 1946), pp. 22–26; Iva L. Buchanan: "Lumbering and Logging in the Puget Sound Region in Territorial Days," *Pacific Northwest Quarterly*, XXVII (1936), 34–53; Albert Burch: "Development of Metal Mining in Oregon," *Oregon Historical Quarterly*, XLIII (1941), 105–28; John N. Cobb: "History of Fisheries in the State of Washington," *Washington Historical Quarterly*, XX (1929), 3–11; Nelson H. Darton: "Our Pacific Northwest," *National Geographic Magazine*, XX (1909), 645–63; Herman J. Deutsch: "Economic Imperialism in the Early Pacific Northwest," *Pacific Historical Review*, IX (1940), 377–88; Joseph W. Ellison: "Marketing Problems of Northwestern Apples, 1929–1940," *Agricultural History*, XVI (1942), 103–15; Frederic F. Fish: "Return of Blueback Salmon to the Columbia River," *Scientific Monthly*, LXVI (1948), 283–92; Clinton H. Grattan: "Future of the Pacific Coast," *Harper's Magazine*, CXC (1945), 301–10, 400–9; Homer E. Gregory: "Salmon Industry of the Pacific Coast," *Economic Geography*, XVI (1940), 407–15; Mildred Vera Hayden: "History of the Salmon Industry in Oregon," *Commonwealth Review*, XIV (1932), 84–107; Tim Kelley: "Fishery Conservation in Washington," *Pacific Northwest Quarterly*, XXXVIII (1947), 19–34; and "Program for Stabilizing the Fishery of Washington," *Economic Geography*, XXIII (1947), 256–60; Burt P. Kirkland: "Continuous Forest Production in the Pacific Northwest," *Commonwealth Review*, III (1918), 63–78; Richard G. Lillard: "Timber King," *The Pacific Spectator*, I (1947), 14–26; Leo Livingston: "The Tourist Industry of Washington," *Northwest Industry*, I (1942), 1–7; Alfred L. Lomax: "The Facilities, Commerce, and Resources of Oregon's Coast Ports," University of Oregon *Studies in Business*, no. 14, 11 (1932), pp. 1–53; and "Pioneer Woolen Mills in Oregon," *Oregon Historical Quarterly*, XXX (1929), 147–60, 238–58, 339–43; Gertrude L. McKean: "Tacoma, Lumber Metropolis," *Economic Geography*, XVII (1041), 311–20; Richard L. Neuberger: "The Great Salmon Experiment," *Harper's Magazine*, CXC (1945), 229–36; J. Orin Oliphant: "A Beef-Canning Enterprise in Oregon," *Oregon Historical Quarterly*, XXXIV (1933), 241–54; Roy M. Robbins: "The Federal Land System in an Embryo State," *Pacific Historical Review*, IV (1935), 356–75; Frederick Sempich: "Wartime in the Pacific Northwest," *National Geographic Magazine*, LXXXII (1942), 421–64; Frank J. Taylor: "Northwest, 'Our Promised Land,'" *American Mercury*, XLIX (1940), 168–72; Roy A. H. Thompson: "What's Happening to the Timber," *Harper's Magazine*, CXCI (1945–46), 125–33; and "Timber!" *World's Work*, LX (Nov., 1931), 54–7.

CHAPTER XXI

BOOKS. Howard T. Lewis and Stephen I. Miller, eds.: *The Economic Resources of the Pacific Northwest* (Seattle, 1923), ch. 12; Grant Ridford, ed.: *That Man Thomson* by R. M. Thomson (Seattle, 1950); Clarence E. Rose: "The Development of Utility Districts in Oregon and Washington," M.A. Thesis, University of Oregon, 1941; [United States Department of the Interior]: Bonneville Power Administration: *Pacific Northwest Opportunities* (Portland, [1944]), mimeographed.

ARTICLES. Robert O. Case: "Eighth World Wonder," *Saturday Evening Post*, CCVIII (July 13, 1935), 23, 34, 36; Stuart Chase: "Great Dam," *Atlantic Monthly*, CLXII (1938), 593–9; O. B. Coldwell: "Beginnings of Electric Power in Oregon," *Oregon Historical Quarterly*, XXXI (1930), 25–36; and "Early Days of Electricity in Portland," *Oregon Historical Quarterly*, XLII (1941), 279–94; Carl Dreher: "J. D. Ross, Public Power Magnate," *Harper's Magazine*,

CLXXXI (1940), 46–60; H. J. Gille: "The Contribution of Private Power to the Development of the Northwest," *Northwest Industry,* X (1943), 9–18; "Grand Coulee," *Fortune,* XIV (Nov., 1936), 78–9; XVI (July, 1937), 79–89; C. R. Koester: "Grand Coulee of Washington," *Nature Magazine,* XL (1947), 34–7; C. Edward Magnusson: "Hydro-Electric Power in Washington," *Washington Historical Quarterly,* XIX (1928), 90–8; Maynard O. Williams: "The Columbia Turns on the Power," *National Geographic Magazine,* LXXIX (1941), 749–92.

CHAPTER XXII

BOOKS. James D. Barnett: *The Operation of the Initiative, Referendum and Recall in Oregon* (New York, 1915); Solon J. Buck: *The Granger Movement* (Cambridge, Mass., 1913), chs. 1–3, 9; Ezra S. Carr: *The Patrons of Husbandry on the Pacific Coast* (San Francisco, 1875); Harriet Ann Crawford: *The Washington State Grange, 1889–1924; A Romance of Democracy* (Portland, 1940); Allen H. Eaton: *The Oregon System: The Story of Direct Legislation in Oregon* (Chicago, 1912); Marion Harrington: *The Populist Movement in Oregon, 1889–1896.* University of Oregon Thesis Series, No. 22 (Eugene, Oregon, 1940), mimeographed; Paul L. Haworth: *The Hayes-Tilden Disputed Presidential Election of 1876* (Cleveland, 1906), chs. 9, 11; John D. Hicks: *The Populist Revolt* (Minneapolis, 1931); Claudius O. Johnson: *Borah of Idaho* (New York, 1936); George E. Mowry: *Theodore Roosevelt and the Progressive Movement* (Madison, Wis., 1946); Carlton C. Qualey: *Norwegian Settlement in the United States* (Northfield, Minn., 1938); Edgar E. Robinson: *The Presidential Vote 1936; Supplementing The Presidential Vote 1896–1932* (Stanford University, 1940); Edna A. Scott: "The Grange Movement in Oregon, 1873–1900." University of Oregon Thesis Series, No. 1 (Eugene, Oregon), 1939, mimeographed; Fred A. Shannon: *The Farmer's Last Frontier* (New York, 1945), ch. 13; Lincoln Steffens: *Upbuilders* (New York, 1909).

ARTICLES. Thomas A. Bailey: "The West and Radical Legislation, 1890–1930," *American Journal of Sociology,* XXXVIII (1932–33), 603–11; James D. Barnett: "Reorganization of State Government in Oregon," *American Political Science Review,* IX (1915), 287–93; John E. Caswell: "The Prohibition Movement in Oregon," *Oregon Historical Quarterly,* XXXIX (1938), 235–61; Charles B. Cheney: "Political Movements in the Northwest," *Review of Reviews,* XXXI (1905), 337–41; Chester M. Destler: "Western Radicalism, 1865–1901: Concepts and Origins," *Mississippi Valley Historical Review,* XXXI (1944), 335–68; M. C. George: "Political History of Oregon from 1876–1898 Inclusive," *Quarterly of the Oregon Historical Society,* III (1902), 107–22; Claudius O. Johnson: "The Adoption of the Initiative and Referendum in Washington," *Pacific Northwest Quarterly,* XXXV (1944), 291–303; "The Initiative and Referendum in Washington," *Pacific Northwest Quarterly*, XXXVI (1945), 000–00; and "The Washington Blanket Primary," *Pacific Northwest Quarterly*, XXXIII (1942), 27–39; F. Kelley: "Campaign for Enfranchisement of Women," *Outlook*, LXXXIII (1906), 675–6; K. A. Murray: "Aberdeen Convention of 1912, Republican Party," *Pacific Northwest Quarterly*, XXXVIII (1947), 99–108; Richard L. Neuberger: "Curtain Raiser for '48," *Nation*, CLXIV (1947), 682–3; and "Wayne Morse: Republican Gadfly," *American Mercury*, LXV (1947), 16–24; J. Orin Oliphant: "Legislative Reapportionment in Washington, 1930," *Washington Historical Quarterly*, XXII (1931), 3–25; Roy M. Robbins: "The Federal Land System in an Embryo State," *Pacific Historical Review*, IV (1935), 356–75; Waldo Schumacher: "Thirty Years of the People's Rule in Oregon: An Analysis," *Political Science Quarterly*, XLVII (1932), 242–58; M. Thompson: "Senator on Horseback; Wayne Morse," *Saturday Evening Post*, CCXVIII (Oct. 20, 1945), 20–1 et seq.; Winston B. Thorson: "Washington State Nominating Conventions," *Pacific Northwest Quarterly*, XXV (1944), 99–119.

CHAPTER XXIII

BOOKS. Archie Binns: *Northwest Gateway: The Story of the Port of Seattle* (New York, 1941); John S. Gambs: *The Decline of the I.W.W.* (New York, 1923); William D. Haywood: *Bill Haywood's Book: The Autobiography of William D. Haywood* (New York, 1929); Yamato Ichihashi: *Japanese in the United States* (Stanford University, 1932); Charles Miles and O. B. Sperlin, eds.: *Building a State: Washington, 1889–1939* (Tacoma, 1940), ch. 7; Nard Jones: *Evergreen Land: A Portrait of the State of Washington* (New York, 1947); [Federal Writers' Program, Oregon]: *Oregon: End of the Trail* (Portland, 1940), pp. 102–34; Carlton C. Qualey: *Norwegian Settlement in the United States* (Northfield, Minn., 1938), ch. 9; Joseph Schafer: *The Social History of American Agriculture* (New York, 1936); Marjorie R. Stearns: "The History of the Japanese People in Oregon," M.A. Thesis, University of Oregon, 1937; Charlotte Todes: *Labor and Lumber* (New York, 1931); Sidney Warren: *Farthest Frontier: The Pacific Northwest* (New York, 1949); *Proceedings of the Fifth Pacific Northwest Regional Planning Conference* (Portland, 1939).

ARTICLES. Robert W. Bruère: "The Industrial Workers of the World," *Harper's Magazine*, CXXXVII (1918), 250–7; and "Notes on the I.W.W. in Arizona and the Northwest," *Journal of the National Institute of Social Sciences*, IV (1918), 99–108; Woodrow R. Clevinger: "Southern Appalachian Highlanders in Western Washington," *Pacific Northwest Quarterly*, XXXIII (1942), 3–25; L. S. Cressman and Anthony Yturri: "The Basques in Oregon," *Commonwealth Review*, XX (1939), 367–80; J. C. Cresswill: "Regional Shifts in Our Economy Resulting from War," *The Magazine of Wall Street*, LXXVI (1945), 72–4, 114, 116; Nelle P. Davis: "Out of the Dust Bowl into

'Paradise Valley,'" *New York Times Magazine* (Feb. 9, 1941), 8–9, 23; Katharine F. Gerould: "Our Northwestern States," *Harper's Magazine,* CL (1924–25), 412–28; Herbert H. Gowen: "Problem of Oriental Immigration in Washington," *Annals of the American Academy of Political and Social Sciences,* XXXIV (1909), 329–37; D. G. Hill: "The Negro as a Political and Social Issue in the Oregon Country," *Journal of Negro History,* XXXIII (1948), 130–45; Jules A. Karlin: "The Anti-Chinese Outbreaks in Seattle, 1885–1886," *Pacific Northwest Quarterly,* XXXIX (1948), 103–30; Joe J. King: "Sheltering the Migrating Agricultural Laborers in the Pacific Northwest," *Sociology and Social Research,* XXVI (1942), 259–64; "Migration into Oregon, 1930–37," *Monthly Labor Review,* XLIX (1939), 1106–8; Richard L. Neuberger: "The Cities of America — Portland, Oregon," *Saturday Evening Post* (March 1, 1947), 23 et seq.; George S. Perry: "Seattle," *Saturday Evening Post,* CCXVIII (Oct. 13, 1945), 22–3 et seq.; "They Grow Longer Villages in Idaho," *American City,* LXII (Oct., 1947), 7; Harvey Elmer Tobie: "Oregon Labor Disputes, 1919–1923," *Oregon Historical Quarterly,* XLVIII (1947), 7–24, 195–213, 309–21.

CHAPTER XXIV

BOOKS. V. L. O. Chittick, ed.: *Northwest Harvest: A Regional Undertaking* (New York, 1948); Eugene C. Elliott: *A History of Variety-Vaudeville in Seattle* (Seattle, 1944); Stewart H. Holbrook: *Promised Land; A Collection of Northwest Writing* (New York, 1945); Alfred Powers: *History of Oregon Literature* (Portland, 1935); J. Van Male: *Resources of Pacific Northwest Libraries* (Seattle, 1943); Mary C. Rohrer: *The History of Seattle Stock Companies* (Seattle, 1945); Sidney Warren: *Farthest Frontier: The Pacific Northwest* (New York, 1949); [Writers' Program, Washington]: *Washington: A Guide to the Evergreen State* (Portland, 1941), pp. 120–62.

ARTICLES. Salley Elliot Allen: "The Very Little Theatre of Eugene," *Commonwealth Review,* XIX (1937), 240–46; Frederick E. Bolton and Thomas W. Bibb: "History of Education in Washington," *U. S. Office of Education Bulletin,* IX (1934), 196–250; John H. Bradley, Jr.: "A Voice from the Wilderness," *Saturday Review of Literature,* VII (1930–31), 758; Alice H. Ernst: "Eugene's Theatres and 'Shows' in Horse and Buggy Days," *Oregon Historical Quarterly,* XLIV (1943), 127–39, 232–48; Frederick W. Goodrich: "Oregon Orchestra Music, 1868–1932," *Oregon Historical Quarterly,* XXXIII (1932), 136–42; Charles Hilton: "A Note on Regionalism," *Northwest Literary Review,* I (Sept.–Oct., 1935), 4; Nard Jones: " The Coming Literary Movement," *Northwest Literary Review,* I (May–June, 1935), 4; Helen H. McCandless: "Education in the Pacific Northwest," *Education,* XXXVI (1915), 110–16; Carey McWilliams: "A Letter from the Northwest," *Saturday Review of Literature,* VI (1929–

30), 1193; Edmond S. Meany: "Has Puget Sound a Literature?" *Washington Magazine*, I (Summer, 1883), 8–11; H. G. Merriam: "Tameness in Northwest Writers and Readers," *Northwest Literary Review*, I (Nov.–Dec., 1935), 6 et seq.; "Northwest Authors," *Fortnightly*, Feb. 10, 1933, 5; Feb. 24, 1933, 15; L. E. Rader: "A Washington Literarium," *Pacific Magazine*, II (March, 1890), 11–12; Edward Sheppard and Emily Johnson: "Forty Years of Symphony in Seattle, 1903–1943," *Pacific Northwest Quarterly*, XXXV (1944), 19–28; James Stevens: "The Northwest Takes to Poesy," *American Mercury*, XVI (1929), 64–70.

INDEX

Abbott-Downing Company, 198
Aberdeen, Lord, 147, 148
Aberdeen, 359
Abernethy, Governor George, 135, 137; and Whitman massacre, 153
Abernethy & Clark Express Agents, 194
Academies, 212–14
Acapulco, Mexico, 21
Acequia, Idaho, 308
Acme, 370
Ada County, Idaho, 301 n
Adair, John, 155 n
Adams, Alvin, 194
Adams, Orville, 441
Adams County, Washington, 303 n, 328 n, 329
Adams Express Company, 196
Addington, Henry, 74
Admiralty Inlet, 25
Adventure (sloop), 28
Agricultural Adjustment Administration, 415
Agricultural Wheel, 395 n
Agriculture: North West Co., 43–4; Hudson's Bay Co., 73–82; spread of farmer population, 167–71; pioneer crops, 181; revolution, 322–3; irrigation, 323–6; dry farming, 326–30; diversified, 330–3; livestock, 333–6; marketing problems and cooperatives, 336–9; see also Cattle, Sheep
Aguilar, Martin de, 22
Ainsworth, John C., 205, 263
Ainsworth Dock, 367
Alaska, 22, 344, 348, 349, 350, 351, 352, 362; see also Russian America
Albany, 168, 191, 195, 259, 357
Albany College (now Lewis and Clark College), 214, 215 n
Albatross (ship), 90
Albemarle, Duke of, 50
Alder Gulch, 225
Alexander, Governor Moses, 404
Alki Point, 170, 196
Allen, Mary G., 453
Alta California, 292
Alturas County, Idaho, 301 n
Aluminum Company of America, 379 n
Amalgamated Copper Company, 344–5

American Board of Commissioners for Foreign Missions, 113, 117–18, 122, 123, 208
American Dream, 444
American Falls, Idaho, 308
American Falls Reservoir Project, 308
American Federation of Labor, 433, 437
American Forestry Association, 356 n
American Fur Company, 41, 91
American Legion, 425
American Mercury, 446
American Society of Newspaper Editors, 449
American Tobacco Company, 402
Anaconda, Montana, 345
Anaconda Copper Mining Company (Anaconda Silver Mining Company), 344, 346
Anaconda Mining Company, 280
Anaconda Silver Mining Company (Anaconda Copper Mining Company), 344
Anacortes, Washington, 357, 370
Anderson, Guy, 454
Anderson, J. Patton, 164
Anderson Dam, 308
Anderson Ranch Dam, 320
Andover Theological Seminary, 113
Anglo-American Convention, 139, 140 n
Anian, Strait of, 21
Antelope Hills, 444
Anti-Alien League, 425
Appalachian Mountains, 426–7
Applegate Creek, 221
Applegate Family, 210
Applegate, Jesse, 111, 125, 138; quoted, 126
Applegate, Lindsay, 111
Applegate Pass, 259
Appomattox, 322
Architectural styles, 455–6
Architecture, 218–19; Indian, 13 ff.; pioneer, 218–19; nouveau riche, 219; modernism in, 455
Arctic explorations, 34
Argentina, 401
Arkansas, 395 n, 427
Arrowrock Dam, 307–8
Arrowrock reservoir, 307

[i

Artists' Service of the National Broadcasting Company, 453
Ashland, 169, 169 n, 268, 275, 393
Ashland Normal School, 212
Ashland *Tidings*, 268
Ashley, General William H., 98
Asia, 347
Asotin County, Washington, 303 n
Assiniboine River, 51
Astor, John Jacob, 40, 90–1, 105; *see also* Astoria, Astoria expedition
Astoria, 128, 189, 204, 372, 393, 419; *see also* Fort Astoria
Astoria (book), 97
Astoria and Columbia River Railroad, 273
Astoria expedition, 38; plans for, 90–1; voyage of the *Tonquin*, 91–3; Hunt's Overlanders, 93–4; Astor's achievements and failures, 94–7
Atanum, 300
Athabaska Department, 40
Athabaska Lake, 34
Athabaska Pass, 38
Athabaska River, 34, 57
Atlantic Monthly, 446
Atlantic seaboard, 287
Atomic bomb manufacture, 378
Aurora, Oregon, 418
Australia, 294, 295, 349
Avery, Idaho, 280
"Aymara" head flattening, 10
Ayrshires, 284 n

Babcock, Dr. Ira L., 131
Babcock, Orville, 386
Baboon Gulch, 224
Bagley, Clarence B., 209
Bagley, Daniel, 215
Bailey, Dr. William J., 131
Bainbridge Island, 369
Baker, Dr. Dorsey S., and "Dr. Baker's Road," 257–8
Baker City, 226
Baker County, Oregon, 282, 302 n
Balch, Frederick Homer, 440
Ball, John, 207
Ballard, David, 244
Ballard (section of Seattle), 419
Bancroft, Hubert Howe, *quoted*, 158, 184 n, 244, 442
Bancroft Library of Western History, 462
Banff, 36
Banks, Frank A., 318
Bannack (or Bannock), 225, 291

Bannock Indians, 17
Baptist Home Mission Society, 213
Baptists, 213
Barbed wire, 322
Barkley, Captain Charles William, 23–4
Barlow, Captain Samuel K., 111
Barlow Road, building of, 111
Barnett, Professor James D., *quoted*, 408
Barrell, Joseph, 27
Bashford, Herbert, 441, 445
Basque immigrants, 420
Bates, Ernest Sutherland, 460
Bathurst, Lord, 51
Bear Creek Valley, 259
Bear Lake, Idaho, 332
Bear Lake County, Idaho, 300 n, 301 n
Beard, Charles A., 322
Beard, Mary, 322
Beautiful Willamette, 445
Beaver (steamer), 72, 82, 94, 202, 203
Beaver City, 223
Beaver skins, 44, 55, 66, 71
Beck, David W., 438
Becket, Maria, 453
Beckley Farm, 76
Beecham, Sir Thomas, 452
Beeler, Florence Ashley, 445
Bell, William, 170
Bella Coola River, 34
Belle (steamer), 175
Belle Vue Point, 57, 74
Bellevue, Idaho, 433
Bellingham, Washington, 357, 363, 370, 379
Bellingham Bay, Washington, 333, 346
Ben Hur, 450
Bend, 274, 311
Benewah County, Idaho, 328 n
Benton, Senator Thomas Hart, 143–4; and railroad to Pacific, 256
Benton County, Washington, 168, 169 n, 313
Bering, Vitus, 22
Bering Sea, 350
Bering Strait, 6, 347
Berkeley, California, 462
Berne, 272 n
Bethel, Missouri, 418
Bethlehem Steel Company, 379–80, 402
Beverly Plains, 314
Beyond the Garden Gate, 444
Bidwell-Bartleson party, 122

Big Bend Electric Cooperative, 377
Big Bend region, 38, 302, 311, 316, 326, 328 n; reclamation in, 314–15
"Big Four," 268
"Big Y" apples, 337
Bimetallism, 398
Binns, Archie, 444
Bishop, Anna, 450
Bishop Scott Academy, 213
Bismarck, North Dakota, 88, 257
Bison. *See* Buffalo
Bitterroot Mountains, 88, 224; Northern Pacific Railroad through, 266
Bitter Root River, 70
Blackfeet Indians, 70, 100, 102
Bladridge, Governor H. C., 413
Blaine, James G., 385
Blanchet, Father Francis N., 119, 131 n, 209 n
"Bleeding Kansas," 160
Blethen, Alden J., 448
"Blind Pool," 265
Blue Mountains, 101, 102
Blue River, 109
Boardman and Pope, trading firm, 31
Bodega, Juan, 23
Boeing airplane factory, 379
Boise, 197, 231, 237, 240, 297, 307, 308, 372, 393, 402, 431
Boise, R. P., 157 n
Boise Basin, 235
Boise City, 223
Boise County, 239, 301 n
Boise Project, 307
Boise River, 236, 307, 320, 326
Boit, John, 29
Bombay, 23
Bone, Senator Homer T., 412
Bonnemain, Baron de, 287
Bonner's Ferry, Idaho, 373, 427
Bonneville, Captain Benjamin L. E., expedition, 99–101; estimate, 101; without government support, 105; mentioned, 108
Bonneville, railroad station, 101
Bonneville Dam, 5, 347, 347 n, 365, 368, 374, 377
Bonneville Dam Project, 374 n
Bonneville Power Administration, 368–9, 369 n, 371, 374, 376, 376 n, 377, 378 n, 379, 379 n, 382, 415
Bonneville Project Act, 377
Bonte, Louis L. ("Sailor Jack"), 107 n
Boone, Daniel, 22

Borah, Senator William E., 404, 434
Boren, Carson D., 170
Boston, 26, 31, 47, 123
Bottelfsen, Governor C. A., 413
Bradford, Daniel F., 205
Brady, Governor James H., 404
Breckinridge, John C., 161, 162
Bremerton, 379
Bricken, Carl, 452
Bridge of the Gods, 440
Brigades, 44, 59, 63, 65, 119; Hudson's Bay Co. cavalcades, 67–71; *see also* Cavalcades
Brigham County, Idaho, 300 n, 301 n
Bright Ambush, 446
British Columbia, *passim*, but especially, explorations by sea, 23 ff.; North West Co. fur trade in, 39–40 ff.; Hudson's Bay Co. operations in, 54 ff.; farming in, 75 ff.; mining developments in, 226–9; *see also* Indians
British Isles, 283, 418, 420
Brosnan, Cornelius J., 442–3
Brotherhood of Locomotive Engineers, 433
Broughton, Lieutenant William R., 25
Broughton (sloop), 72
Brown, Aaron V., 191
Brown, Samuel, 27
Browntown Camp, 221
Bruère, Robert W., 435–6
Bryan, William Jennings, 400–1, 402, 403, 413, 443
Bryant, William P., 155 n
Buchanan, James, 148, 160
Buena Vista, Battle of, 154
Buffalo, 18, 42; skins, 44
Buhl-Kimberly Corporation, 301
Bulfinch, Charles, 27
Bullion, Idaho, 433
Bunton, "Billy," 248
Bunyan, Paul, 419
Bureau of Reclamation (Reclamation Service), 305, 306–7, 308, 309, 310, 311, 312, 314, 315, 316, 317, 319, 320, 321, 373
Burley, Idaho, 308
Burlington Railroad, 272–3, 277, 278
Bush, Asabel, 157
Bush, Ella Shepard, 453
Butte, 271, 278, 344, 345
Butterfield, John, and overland mail, 191–2
Butteville, 132, 195

Cadboro (schooner), 72, 82
Calapooya Mountains, 259
Caldwell, Idaho, 444, 446
Calhoun, Senator John C., 143
California, 31, 32, 68, 73, 83, 98, 101, 274, 283, 293, 297, 309, 310, 326, 337, 338, 351, 355, 363, 364, 422, 424, 425, 427, 428, 455; sea otters, 32; gold discovery, 163; gold rush, 155, 169, 220, 283, 294 n
California and Columbia River Railroad, 259, 260
California and Oregon Railroad Company, 259–60 ff., 268
California and Utah Camel Association, 232
California Central Valley Project, 374
California Fruit Growers' Association, 338
California Stage Company, 190–1, 192
Callahan, Kenneth, 454
Camels, use of, for packing, 231–2
Cameron, Basil, 452
Camfferman, Peter, 454
Campbell, Hardy W., 327
Campbell, 329
Canada, 279, 312, 317, 362, 418, 419–20, 427
Canadian fur trade, 33–48
Canadian Northern Railroad, 269
Canadian Pacific Railroad, 269–70, 271, 273
Canadian Rockies, 4
Canby, General Edward R. S., 177
Canby, Oregon, 393
Canneries. *See* Fishing
Canning, George, 141
Cannon, William, 107
Canoes, 14, 44, 45, 46, 56, 69
Canton, trade at, 23, 27, 28, 30, 31, 32, 47, 83; *see also* China
Cantrel, Robert, 445
Canyon Road, 178
Canyonville, 191
Cape Disappointment, 92
Cape Flattery, 424
Cape Horn, 90
Carey Act, 304–5
Cariboo, 78, 235; gold rush to, 228 ff.
Cariboo Road, 232, 235
Carlsbad Caves, New Mexico, 365
Carnegie, Andrew, 461
Caroline (steamer), 190
Carr, Edmund, 215
Carr, Ezra, 393 n

Carrier Indians, 7 n
Carson, Alexander, 107 n
Carteret, Sir George, 50
Cascade Mountains, 3, 73, 272, 272 n, 274, 278, 282, 294, 295 n, 299, 302, 312, 323, 324, 330, 352, 365, 370, 455–6
Cascade Portage Railroad, 258
Cascade Road, 180
Cascade Route, 274
Cascades, Columbia River, 101, 110, 257, 391; the gorge, 5; location, 5, 7
Cascades Dam, 308
Case, Robert Ormond, 445, 446
Case, Victoria, 446
Cass County, Nebraska, 444
Cassia County, Idaho, 300 n, 301 n
"Catholic Ladder," 209, 209 n
Catholics, 60, 184; missions, 118–20; schools, 206 ff.; missionaries, regarding Indian education, 208–9
Catt, Mrs. Carrie Chapman, 407
Cattle: Hudson's Bay Co., 75–8; at missions, 116; over Oregon Trail, 125; imported from California, 182; on the range, 333–6; breeds, 335
Cattle kings, 287–8
Caucasoid race, 9
Caughey, John W., 442 n
Cavalcades (fur trading), 67–71; *see also* Brigades
Cayuse Indians, 70; country, 119; and Whitman massacre, 152–3
Cayuse War, 153, 171–3, 177
Cedar Falls, 370
Celilo Falls, 11, 110, 204
Census, 284 n, 285, 286, 300, 301, 302, 305, 336, 341, 341 n, 342 n, 343, 346, 357 n, 430
Central Pacific Railroad, 259, 268, 285, 421
Centralia, Washington, 436
Centreville, 223, 224, 231
Chadwick, S. F., 157 n, 387
Chamberlain, Governor George E., 403, 414
Champoeg, 133 n; meetings, 132–4 ff.; express office at, 195
Chapman, John B., 163
Charboneau, Indian, 88
Charles II, King, 33, 49
Charlevon, M., 131 n
Chase, Stuart, 318
Chatham (ship), 25
Chehalis Indians, 7 n

Index

v

Chehalis River, 170
Chenoweth, F. A., 204
Cheops, 317
Cheyenne, 285, 286, 291
Cheyenne Club, 291
Chicago, 275, 276, 277, 278, 370
Chicago, Milwaukee, and Puget Sound Railway Company, 279
Chicago, Milwaukee, St. Paul and Pacific Railroad, 165, 275–81
Chicago Northwestern Railroad, 276
Children of God, 444
Chilkat Indians, 14
Chimney Rock, 109
China, 401
China trade, 23 ff., 41, 46–7, 73, 84; *see also* Canton
Chinese, 223; prohibited from voting in Oregon, 159; immigrants, 421–4
Chinese Exclusion Act, 422
Chinook Indians, 7 n; reduced, 9, stature of, 10; upper, 7, 12; lower, 12, 19
Chinook jargon, 11–12
Chittenden, Hiram M., *quoted*, 96, 97
"Choeg" cooperative, 336
Chorpenning, George, 191
Chosen Valley, 440
Chouart, Médard, 49
Christian X, King of Denmark, 444
Christian Advocate and Journal, 114, 115
Christian Church, 213
Christian College at Monmouth, 215 n
Cincinnati, 439
Cities: beginnings of, 168–71; figures, 169 n; growth of, 431–3
City Creek, 300
Civic Theater, Portland, 451
Civil War, 192, 282, 283, 286, 289, 296, 304, 322, 336, 354, 355, 384, 385, 394, 395, 408, 431; Oregon and the, 160 ff.
Clackamas County, Oregon, 169 n, 392, 418
Clark, Allan, 453
Clark, Governor C. A., 413
Clark, Daniel, 392
Clark, Robert C., *quoted*, 135, 185, 356; 460
Clark, William, 86–7; *quoted*, 88; *see also* Lewis and Clark expedition
Clark, William, 344–5
Clark County, 171 n, 214

Clarke, General Newman S., 177
Clarke, John, 91, 95
Clarker, Samuel, 442
Clark's Fork, 278
Clark's Fork River, 5, 37, 88, 232
Clatsop County, 169 n
Clayoquot Sound and harbor, 28, 92
Clear Lake, 310, 370
Clearwater County, Idaho, 328 n
Clearwater River, 222
Cleveland, Grover, 253, 254, 255, 386, 424
Climate: of coastal area, 4; of Inland Empire, 4–5
Clinton, DeWitt, 91
Coast Range, 4
Cobb, John N., 348 n
Coeur d'Alene, 223, 278, 309, 433, 440
Coeur D'Alene, 440
Coeur d'Alene Indians, 176, 178
Coeur d'Alene Mountains, 223, 232
Cold Springs Canyon, Oregon, 309
Collier's, 446
Collins, Mrs. Nat, *quoted*, 290
Colonel Wright (ship), 204
Colonies: English, 292; Dutch, 292; Swedish, 292
Colorado, 129, 309, 427
Colt 45, 290
Colton, Calvin, 256
Columbia (ship), 28, 29–30, 203, 366, 371
"Columbia" proposed as name for Washington Territory, 163
Columbia Basin, 284, 285, 288, 300, 315–19, 383
Columbia Basin Project, 374, 374 n
Columbia Concerts Corporation, 453
Columbia County, Washington, 303 n, 328 n
Columbia Department (North West Company), 36 ff., 72
Columbia District (Hudson's Bay Company), 52; organized, 54–8; fur trading operations in, 59–73; Hudson's Bay subsidiaries in, 73–85
Columbia Indian Reservation, 177
Columbia Intermontane Province, 4
"Columbia Plateau," 4
Columbia River, *passim*, but especially, 102, 109, 189; size of system, 5; discovery of, 21; Lewis and Clark expedition to, 86 ff.; dangers of, 111; respecting Oregon boundary question, 146

Columbia River and Northern Railway, 273
Columbia River Bar, 92; *see also* Gray, Robert
Columbia River Basin, North West Company operations in, 36–8; *see also* Indians, Hudson's Bay Co., Bonneville Power Administration
Columbia River Fishing and Trading Company, 103
Columbia River Highway, 365
Columbia Valley Authority, 382
Colville, 195, 291
Colville Indian Reservation, 177, 251, 311
Commencement Bay, 257
Commerce. *See* Trade
Commission on Tenancy, 430 n
Commonwealth Review, 359, 460
Compulsory Statement Bill, 406
Conconully, Washington, 312
Concord stagecoach, 187, 198, 202
Condon, Thomas, 460
Conestoga wagons, 182, 183, 193
Confederate Gulch, 225
Congregationalists, 113, 214
Congress (U. S.), *passim*; attitude toward Oregon Country, 129; establishes postal service, 189 ff.; petitions to, 239; land grants, 257; reclamation acts, 304–21
Congress of Industrial Organization, 435, 438
Connell, 314
Connolly, William, 70
Conquest, 441
Conquistadores, 292
Continental Divide, 3, 4, 5, 38, 70, 100, 109, 282
Cook, Captain James, 27; voyage of, 23
Cooke, Jay, and Company, 257
Coolidge, President Calvin, 272 n, 414
Co-operatives, 336–9
Cook's Inlet, 30
Coos Bay, Oregon, 6, 221, 363, 363 n
Coos-Curry Electric Cooperative, 377
Coquille, Oregon, 357
Corbett, Henry W., stage lines, 192–3
Corinne, 237
Cornelius, T. R., 263
Corrupt Practices Act, 407
Corvallis, 168, 169 n, 187, 191, 195, 259
Corvallis Academy, 213

Corvallis College, 216
Cosgrove, Governor Samuel G., 404
Cottage Grove, 168
Coulee City, 319
Count of Monte Cristo, 450
Courier and Constitutional Advocate, Madison, Indiana, *quoted*, 145
Cowboys, 286–91
Cowlitz Convention, 163, 164
Cowlitz County, Washington, 427
Cowlitz Farm, 75, 79, 80
Cowlitz Mission, 209 n
Cowlitz River, 5, 189, 200
Cowlitz River Landing, 80, 195, 200, 204, 210
Cowperville, Washington, 393
Cox, Ross, 42, 93, 206; *quoted*, 43
Coxe, John, 107 n
Crabtree, Lotta, 450
Craigflower (or Maple Point) Farm, 76
Cram, Rogers and Company Express, 194
Crater Lake, 363, 364, 365
Crater of the Moon, 365
Crawford, Harriet Ann, 394
Crazy Dog societies, 17
Credit Mobilier, 386, 393
Crescent City, California, 183, 230, 231, 235
Crocker, Charles, 259; *quoted*, 268
Cronin, E. A., 387–8
Crook County, Oregon, 302 n
Crowell, "Old Tex," 248
Cruiser, 441
Culbertson, Paul T., *quoted*, 408–9
Cultural life: among Indians (missionary influences), 206–9; pioneer education, 209–14; higher learning, 214–17; churches, 217–18; architecture, 218–19; recent, 439–62
Cunningham, A. G., 263
Currents, 376 n, 378 n
Curry, George L., 157 n
Custer County, Idaho, 301 n

Dakota, 271
Dakota Territory, 239, 327
Dakotas, 275, 427
Dallas Academy, 213
Daly, Marcus, 344
Danebo, Oregon, 419
Daniel, James, 249
Danish immigrants, 419
D'Arcy, Peter H., *quoted*, 136 n, 401

Dasch, Roswell Holt, 453
Davenport, Homer Calvin, 453
Davies, Mary Carolyn, 446
Davis, Arthur P., *quoted*, 306
Davis, Governor D. W., 413
Davis, E. W., 187
Davis, H. L., 443–4
Davis, Jefferson, 231
"Day with the Cow Column, A," 125–6
Dayton, 195, 218
Deadwood Dam, 308
Deady, M. P., 157 *n*, 159; as regent of University of Oregon, 216
Deady Hall, 216
Dease, John Warren, 58
Decatur (sloop), 176
Deer Flat reservoir, 307
Deer Lodge, 225
Del Norte County, California, 98
Delaware River, 292
Demers, Father Modeste, 119
Democratic Herald, 157
Democratic Party, *passim*; in Oregon Territory, 156–7; Oregon State, 160; in Idaho, 244; Montana, 245; in Northwest, 384–416
Denmark, 418, 444
Denny, Arthur A., 170, 204, 215, 353
Department of Architecture, University of Oregon, 457
Department of the Interior, 305, 319
Derby, Elias Hasket, 26
Derby, John, 27
Deschutes, 320
Deschutes Project, Oregon, 311
Deschutes River, 328 *n*
Desert and the Sown, 440
Desert Land Act, 304
De Smet, Father Pierre-Jean, 119, 128
Desperadoes. See Lawlessness
Devil's Auction, 451
Devil's Gate, 109
Devine and Todhunter, ranchers, 287
Devons, 284 *n*
Dewey, Thomas E., 415–16
"Diamond Brand" apples, 337
Diamond ranch, 287
Dinsmore, William B., 191
Disciples of Christ, 215 *n*
Discovery (ship), 23
Disosway, G. P., 114
Disputed election of 1876, 385, 386–8
Diversified farming, 330–3

Dixon, James, 246
Dixon gang, 246
"Doc Apple" label, 338
Dolly (schooner), 94
Domain, national (public), 334
Dominus, Captain John, 79
Donaldson, Thomas C., *quoted*, 223, 246
Donation Land Law, 157–8, 169, 171; effect upon agriculture, 167 ff.
Dorion, Marie, 107
Dorion, Pierre, 107
Dorr, Edward, and Sons, trading firm, 31
Douglas, James, 58, 84, 227, 229; establishes Fort Victoria, 65
Douglas, Stephen A., 154, 162
Douglas County, Washington, 168, 328 *n*; academy in, 212
Dry Falls of the Columbia, 365
Dry farming, 326–30
Dry Land Farming, 327
Dryer, Thomas J., editor of *Oregonian*, 157; *quoted*, 162
Dubreuil, Jean Baptiste, 107 *n*
Dungeness Point, 25
Durhams (cattle), 284 *n*
Dust Bowl, 427–8
Dutch, investments of, in railroads, 270
Dutch East Indies, 27
Dutch shorthorns (cattle), 284 *n*
Dutch Town, 191
Duwamish League, 175
Duwamish River, 170
Dye, Eva Emercy, 441

Eagle City, 223
Eagle Cliff, 348
Earle, L. B., 194
Earle's Express, 194
Earling, Albert J., 276, 277, 280
East India Company, 24, 47, 55, 71
East Side Company, 260 ff.
Edison, Thomas A., 366
Education: missionary schools, 206–9; pioneer elementary, 209–11; private, 209 ff., 214 *n*; normal schools, 212; academies, 212–13; colleges, 213–14; rise of universities, 214–17; since 1890, 457–62
Edwards, Philip L., 115
Eells, Reverend Cushing, 118, 208
Electoral Commission of 1876, 388
Electron, Washington, 370
Elk City, 223
Elks (B.P.O.E.), 392

Elkton, 168
Ellensburg, Washington, 213, 370, 393
Elliott, Simon G., 259
Elliott, T. C., 460
Elliott Bay, 162, 170, 175
Ellison, Joseph W., 338
Elma, Washington, 393
Elmore County, Idaho, 301 n
El Paso, Texas, 192
Embree, Carey, 209
Empire State Building, 317
Empress of China (ship), 26
England. See Great Britain
English, David, 247
Entertainment, theatrical and musical, 449–53
Episcopal Church, 213
Episcopal Missionary Diocese, 213
Ephrata, 319
Ermatinger, Edward, 58; quoted, 70
Ermatinger, Francis, 58
Eskimos, 12
Espy, Edward, 453
Esquimalt Farm, 76
Eugene (Eugene City), 111, 168, 169 n, 188, 191, 195, 259, 261, 272, 274, 365, 373, 377, 419, 444
Europe 362, 418, 420, 455
Everest, Wesley, 436
Everett, 357, 363, 368 n, 370, 432
Explorations: Spanish, 21–3; Russian, 22; British, 23–6; American, 28 ff.
Exports. See Trade
Express business: origin of, 193–4; in Northwest, 194–5; Adams and Co. and Wells Fargo and Co., 196–8

Fairfield, 195
Fairy (steamer), 204
Falk's Store, Idaho, 393
Far Eastern trade, 361, 362
Fargo, William G., 191, 194
Fargo Lake, Washington, 333
Farley, James A., quoted, 413
Farm Bureau, 394
Farmers' Alliance, 336, 396
"Farmers' Clubs," 391
Farmers' Union, 336, 391, 392
Farming: dry, 326–30; diversified, 330–3
Farthest Frontier, 443
Federal Reclamation Service, 301
Federal Writers' Project, 345 n
Ferguson, Jesse, 353
Ferry, Elisha P., 254

"Fifty-four forty or fight," 145
Fillmore, Millard, 164
Financial affairs, 169
Finck, Sigmund, 452
Fine arts, 453–5
Finnish immigrants, 419
Fish, 73; as Indian food, 13; see also Fishing, Salmon
Fish ladders, 347
Fisher, Vardis, 444
Fishermen, nationality of, 349
Fishing: Hudson's Bay Co. operations, 82–4; and canning, 346–52
Fisk, Dr. Wilbur, 115
Fisken, Jennie, 453
Fitch, George A., 371
Fitzgerald, James H., 454
Fitzpatrick, Thomas, 103, 104
Flathead House, 37
Flathead Indians, 70, 100, 114, 115; origin of name, 7 n; skull alterations, 10
Flint, Timothy, 124
Floradora girls, 450
Florence, 223, 274
Floyd, Sergeant Charles, 87 n
Floyd, Dr. John, 120, 129, 141
Flying Fortresses, 379
Folger Library, 461
Foote, Mary Hallock, 440
Forest Grove, 214
Forests, 5; spoliation, conservation of, see also Lumbering
Forgive Adam, 444
Forsyth, John, 129
Fort Alexandria, 68 n, 76
Fort Assiniboine, 271, 272
Fort Astoria, 38, 41, 45, 67; sale of, 46; founded, 92; fur trade operations centered at, 94–5; respecting restoration to American owners, 141, 142; see also Fort George
Fort Augusta, 36
Fort Bellingham, 227
Fort Benton, 225, 232, 237, 291
Fort Boise, Old, 63, 109, 118, 235, 307
Fort Clatsop, 88
Fort Colvile, 57, 62, 71, 74, 75, 77, 222
Fort Durham. See Fort Taku
Fort Farm, 76
Fort Flathead, 62, 70
Fort Fraser, 39, 62
Fort George (Astoria), 45, 46, 57, 62, 67, 71, 74, 83
Fort George (B. C.), 39

Fort Hall, 63, 104, 105, 109, 111, 112, 122, 123, 237; sold to Hudson's Bay Co., 105
Fort Hall-California road, 112
Fort Hope, 65, 228
Fort Kamloops, 38, 40, 62, 76
Fort Kootenai, 62
Fort Langley, 62, 67, 72, 76, 83, 84, 228
Fort Laramie, Old, 109
Fort Lytton, 228
Fort McLeod, 39, 40, 43, 44, 45, 62
Fort McLoughlin, 63
Fort Mandan, 87
Fort Nakasleh, 39; see also Fort St. James
Fort Natleh, 39; see also Fort Fraser
Fort Nez Percé, 62
Fort Nisqually, 72, 79, 81, 116
Fort Okanogan, 15, 58, 62, 68 n, 95
Fort Redoubt St. Dionysius, 64
Fort Rupert, 65
Fort St. James, 39, 62, 67 n, 68 n, 73, 76
Fort Simcoe, 175
Fort Simpson, 62, 63, 72
Fort Spokane, 78, 96
Fort Steilacoom, 227
Fort Stikine, 64, 72
Fort Stuart, 44
Fort Taku (or Durham), 64, 72
Fort Townsend, 227
Fort Vancouver, 68, 71, 77, 110, 115, 195, 208, 353, 424, 450; founded, 57-8; described, 59-61; skins received at, 66; importance of, 74; Jedediah Smith at, 98-9; school at, 207
Fort Victoria, 65, 76, 110
Fort Walla Walla (also Old Fort Walla Walla), 58, 79, 100, 101, 102, 109, 204, 232, 291
Fort William (Kaministikwia, Grand Portage), 41, 44, 45, 51
Fort William (Wyeth's), 104, 105, 128
Fort Yale, 65, 228
Fort Yamhill, 218, 219
Fort Yuma, Arizona, 192
Fort Vancouver barracks, 101
Fortune, quoted, 318
Foster, Michael, 444
Four Lakes, 176
Fox, Ebenezer D., 92
Franchère, Gabriel, 93, 95
Franck, "Long John," 248
Frank, Sigmund, 452

Franklin County, Washington, 303 n, 329
Fraser, Simon, 34; in New Caledonia, 39-40
Fraser Lake, 39
Fraser River, 84, 184, 197, 228, 235; region, 78; gold rush, 226-8
Free Masonry, 214, 218
Free State Republican Party of Oregon, 159
Freighting, wagon, 182-3, 188
Frémont, John C., 112, 121; and Topographical Engineers, 129; and railroad to Pacific, 256
French, 19; in Northwest; see also French Canadians
French, Peter, 287
French Canadians, 34, 78, 107, 118, 135, 136, 184, 222; politics at French Prairie, 130-1; at French Prairie, 168; see also Voyageurs
French Prairie, 116, 119, 124, 168; school at, 207
Friesach, Dr. Carl, 227
Frobisher, Joseph, 34
Fruit Growers' Union, 336
Fruits, 325
Fur bearing animals, 44, 66
Fur trade, 19; North West in Old Oregon, 34-48; at Hudson's Bay Co. posts, 66-7; cavalcades and expeditions, 67-71; coasting trade, 71-3
Fur traders: early contacts with Indians, 19; in Canadian West, 33-7; Nor'westers in Old Oregon, 39-48; Hudson's Bay men, 54-9 ff.; American, 89-106
Fur trading posts: North West Co., 37-40; Hudson's Bay Co., 59-65; life at, 66-7; see also individual post or fort names, and also Fur trade
Furs, 19

Gaines, Governor John P., 156
Gallagher, Jack, 248
Gallvert, R. G., 449
Garfield, James A., 385
Garfield County, Washington, 303 n, 328 n
Garrison, city of, 266
Gary, George, 117
Gass, Sergeant Patrick, 87 n
Gaston, Joseph, 259, 260
Gates, Charles M., 303, 460
Gaugain, 450
Geer, Governor T. T., 403

Gem, Idaho, 433
General Laws of Oregon, 409
George, Henry, 405
German immigrants, 418
Germany, 418
Gervais, Joseph, 107, 131
"Geyser" Bob, 199
Gibbon, John, 250–1
Gibbs, Governor Addison C., 384
Gibbs, George, 333
Gibson girls, 450
Gila River, 155
Gill, J. K., 452
Gilliam, Colonel Cornelius, 173
Gilliam County, Oregon, 302 *n*
Gilson, Horace C., 241
Glenham, South Dakota, 277, 278
Glidden, Joseph F., 322
Gold Creek, 225, 266
Golden Gate, 362
Goldendale, 273
Goldenweiser, Alexander, 460
Gooding, Governor Frank R., 404
Gordon, Clarence W., 284 *n*
Gordon Report, 286
Gossett, Governor Charles C., 413
Gove, Warren, 204
Government, provisional, 127–38
Governor and Committee at London, 55 ff., 120
"Governor and Company of Adventurers," 33; *see also* Hudson's Bay Co.
Grand Coulee Dam, 315–19, 365, 372, 373, 374, 374 *n*, 376, 376 *n*, 377
Grand Orchestral Concert of 1875, 452
Grand Portage, Canada, 34, 35, 45, 50
Grand Pyramid, 317
Grand Right and Left, 446
Grande Ronde, 109, 250
Grand Ronde region, Oregon, 328 *n*
Grand Trunk Railroad, 269
Granger, Wyoming, 269, 285
Grangerism, 391–5, 396, 397
Granite Creek, 231
Grant, President Ulysses S., regarding Idaho, 244; 385
Grant County, Oregon, 282, 302 *n*
Grant County, Washington, 314, 328 *n*
Grants Pass, 272, 275
Grapes of Wrath, 427
Grasshopper Diggings, 225
Grassi, Father Urban, 209
Graves, Morris, 454

Gray, Captain Robert: and discovery of Columbia River, 21, 25; trading voyages of, 27–30
Gray, William H., 117
Grays Harbor, 6, 11, 23, 139, 359, 370
Great Basin, 98
Great Basin Indians, 12, 17; their food and house types, 17–18; their use of horses, 18–19
Great Britain, 64, 84, 96, 283, 292, 294, 338, 349, 418, 420, 424; Nootka Convention, 25; goods from, 47–8, 72 ff.; grants charter to Hudson's Bay Co., 49–50; merges fur companies, 51–3; political status regarding Oregon Country, 127–8; rights respecting Oregon Country, 139–41; diplomacy regarding Oregon boundary, 146–9; settlement of Oregon boundary, 149–51; immigrants from, 418
Great Circle Route, 362
Great Depression, 273, 318, 326, 335, 394, 414, 415, 428, 437–8
Great Falls, Montana (Territory), 271, 345
Great Falls Power Company, 280
Great Migration, 123
Great Northern Railroad, 165, 270–4, 277, 278, 327
Great Plains, 282, 283, 284, 286, 288, 289, 291, 293, 428, 440
Great Register, 109
"Great Reinforcement," 116
Great Salt Lake, 68, 70, 300
Greeley, Horace, 123, 201, 385
Green, Jonathan S., 114
Green River, 117
Green River rendezvous, 103
Greenaway, Donald, 364 *n*
Greenback Party, 396
Gregory and Company Express, 194
Groseilliers, Sieur des. *See* Chouart, Médard
Grover, LaFayette, 132 *n*, 157 *n*, 387, 389–90
Grug, J. A., *quoted*, 319
Gunn Ditch, 303
Gustin, Paul, 453
Gwin, William M., 161

Hadley, Henry, 452
Haida Indians, 6 *n*, 9; number of, 7
Haines, Governor John M., 404
Halsey, J. C., 94, 95

Handforth, Thomas, 453
Hanford, Seymour, 170
Hanford, Washington, 378, 432
Hanna, Captain James, 23
Hannegan, Senator E. A., 145
Hanwell, Henry, 71
Hapgood, Hume and Company, 348
Harding, Benjamin, 157 n
Harlow, Richard A., 278
Harlowtown, Montana, 280
Harmon, Daniel, 40, 43, 44, 73
Harnden, William F., 194
Harney, General William S., 177
Harney County, Oregon, 302 n
Harper's Magazine, 329, 359
Harriman, Alice, 445
Harriman, E. H., 276–7
Harris, Moses, "Black," 111
Harrisburg, 385
Harrison, Benjamin, 253, 385
Hart, Governor Louis F., 412
Hartley, Governor Roland, H., 412
Harvard University Library, 461
Harvey County, Oregon, 287
Hastings, Lansford W., 122
Haswell, Robert, 29
Hatch, Crowell, 27
Hawaiian Islands. See Sandwich Islands
Hawkins, John, 446
Hawkins, Ward, 446
Hawley, Governor James H., 404
Haycox, Ernest, 445, 446–7
Hayes, Julia Dean, 450
Hayes, Rutherford B., 385, 386–8
Haywood, William D., 434–5
Hearst, William R., 423; papers, 448
Hecata, Bruno, 23
Heinz, Frederick A., 345
Helena, 225, 271, 291
Hendricks, Thomas A., 387
Hensil & Company, express agents, 194
Heppner, Oregon, 297
Hilderman, George, 248
Hill, George D., 369
Hill, James J.: early career, 270–1; and Great Northern Railroad, 271–3; and Northern Securities Company, 273; and Milwaukee Road, 277–8; and irrigation projects, 303
Hillsboro, 168
Hines, Gustavus, 131 n
History of the Pacific Northwest, 442
History of Washington, 442

Hobart, Garret A., 402
Hoecken, Adrian, 209
Hogem (Pioneer City), 224
Hogg, T. Egenton, 274
Hogs: raising of, 74, 78, 79; breeds, 335
Holbrook, Amory, 155 n
Holbrook, Stewart, 445, 446
Holderness, Samuel M., 138
Holladay, Benjamin: "Stagecoach King," 197, 198; Oregon steamship lines and railroads, 261–2; 284 n
Holladay Overland Mail and Express Company, 198
Holladay stagecoach route, 286
Hollywood, 295
Holman, Fred V., 367
Home Guards, 423, 424
Homestead Act of 1862, 134, 171, 304, 306, 354, 356
Honey in the Horn, 443
Honolulu, 208
Hood Canal, 25
Hood River, 332, 424, 425
Hood River Apple Growers' Association, 338
Hood River News, 449
Hoodsport, 379
Hoogstraten, Willem van, 452
Hoover, Herbert Clark, 414
Hopo, 235
Hopkins, Mark, 259
Hopkins & Donald, express agents, 194
Hoquiam, 170
Horner, John B., 442
Horse Fly Lake, 310
Horses, 45, 78, 181; introduced by Indians, 18, 19; breeds, 335
Horticulture, 76
Horton, Dexter, 170, 353
Hoskins, John, 28; quoted, 29
Houser, Indian, 13 ff.; early styles, 218–19
Howard, General O. O., 250, 251
Howay, F. W., 31 n
Howe Sound, 25
Howse, Joseph, 54
Howse Pass, 37, 38
Hudson Bay, 35, 49
Hudson River, 450
Hudson's Bay blankets, 66
Hudson's Bay Brigade Trail, 68 n
Hudson's Bay Company, 33, 40, 41, 48, 122, 123, 135, 140, 169, 182, 202, 222, 282, 283, 292–3, 340, 353; founding of, 49–50; operation in Hudson Bay, 50;

Hudson's Bay Company (continued)
Red River settlement, 50–1; North West Co. merged with, 51–3; the Columbia District organization, 54–9; posts, 59–66; cavalcades and expeditions, 67–71; coasting trade, 71–3; agricultural pursuits, 73–7, 79–83; cattle and sheep, 77–9; industries, 82–5; relations with Nathaniel Wyeth, 104; buys Fort Hall, 106; respecting Oregon Treaty, 150–1; respecting Whitman massacre, 153; regarding education, 206–7
Hudson's Bay Company Charter, quoted, 49–50
Hudson's Bay Company seal, described, 50
Humboldt Bay, California, 230
Humboldt County, California, 98
Humbug City, 195
Humbug Creek, 195
Hundred Day Express, 46
Hunt, Governor Frank W., 404
Hunt, Wilson Price, 91, 93; overland expedition, 93–4, 95
Huntington, Collis P., 259
Huntington, Oregon, 269
Huntington Library, 461
Hunt's Merchants' Magazine, quoted, 121
Hunt's Overlanders. See Hunt, Wilson Price
Hydroelectricity, 366–83
Hermiston, Oregon, 310
Hibbs, Ben, quoted, 446
Higginson, Ella R., 440–1, 445
High schools, 212

Ice Age, 6
Idaho, passim, but especially, 95, 234; mineral development, 222–4; early transportation and commerce, 229 ff.; territorial period, 239–45; lawlessness in, 245–6; achieving statehood, 252 ff.; population of (1880), 253; reclamation in, 304–14, 319–21; population figures (1900–40), 417 n, 430, 430 n; see also Indians
Idaho and California Wagon Road Company, 235
Idaho City, 223, 231
Idaho County, Idaho, 239, 301 n, 328 n
Idaho Direct Primary Law, 407
Idaho Falls, 373

Idaho panhandle, 223, 255
Idaho potatoes ("Bakers"), 222
Idaho Power Company, 372
Idaho Presidential Primary Law, 407
Idaho Territory: created, 164; organized, 239; boundaries of, 239–40; government of, 240; political frauds in, 241, 244–5, 393
Illinois Valley, 231
Immigration (since passing of frontier), 417–18; German, 418; Scandinavian, 418–19; other European, 419–20; Negro, 421; Chinese, 421–3; Japanese, 324–5; figures on, 426 n; from other parts of U. S., 426–31; for early period, see Settlement of Oregon Country
Imperial Eagle (ship), 24
Independence, 195
Independence, Missouri, 108, 125
Independence, Missouri, Expositor, quoted, 121
Independence Rock, 109
India, 401
Indian corn, 74
Indian Mission Manual Labor School, 208
Indian: tribes, 6–9; physical characteristics, 9–11; languages, 11–12; modes of life, 12–19; early contacts with white people, 19–20; trade with North West Company, 41–4; Lewis and Clark and, 87–8; attack Tonquin, 92–3; on reservations, 174 ff.; missionary work among, 206–9; as artists, 453
Indian Wars: Cayuse, 171–3; Rogue River, 173–4; Yakima, 174–5; attack upon Seattle, 175–6; Modoc, 177; Chief Joseph's War, 250–2
Indian wives, of white men, 184
Indiana, 440
Industrial Worker, 436
Industry: Hudson's Bay Co., 82–5; pioneer, 181 ff.; wool, 294; manufactures, 341–3; mining, 343–6; fishing, 346–52; lumber, 352–60; spread of, 360–3; tourist, 363–5; hydroelectric, 366–83
Inland Empire, passim, but especially, 118; geography of, 4; stage-coach service, 201–2; mineral development, 221–6; early transportation and commerce, 229–38; first railroad in, 257–8;

Inland Empire (*continued*)
reclamation, 307–15; the range, 282–6; hydroelectrical developments, 366–83; industries, 341–65
Inland Empire Rural Electric Association, 377
Innis, Harold, *quoted*, 34
Intermountain Power Company, 280
International Congress on irrigation, 305
International Workers of the World, 435–7
Interstate Commerce Commission, 273, 279, 281, 336, 409
Iowa, 458
Iowa Statutes, 133
"Iron Chink," 349
Irrigation. *See* Reclamation
Irving, Louise, 450
Irving, Washington, 97, 121
Isaac Todd (ship), 46, 97
Isaacs, Walter, 454
Isthmus of Panama, 189
Ives, George, 248 ff.
Iwakoshi, Miyo, 424

Jackanut River, 39; *see also* Fraser River
Jackson, Andrew, 129, 145
Jackson, Sam, 448
Jackson, W. Turrentine, *quoted*, 244–5
Jackson County, Oregon, 221, 302 n
Jackson Lake, Wyoming, 308
Jackson's Hole, 99
Jacksonville, 169, 169 n, 190, 191, 221, 231, 235, 259
Jamestown, Virginia, 291
Janet (ship), 155
Japan, 347, 401
Japanese Immigrants, 424–5
Jawbone Railroad, 278
Jay, John, 26
Jefferson, 259
Jefferson County, Oregon, 311
Jefferson Institute, 209
Jefferson, Thomas, 86, 91, 141
Jesuit Gonzaga University, 459
Jewish population, 420, 420–1 n
John Day River, 226
Johnson, President Andrew, regarding Idaho, 244
Johnson, John W., 216
Johnson, William, 131 n
Johnson's Express, 196
Joint Commission, respecting Oregon boundary, 150

Jones, Nard, 444
Jordan River, Idaho, 420
Joseph, Chief, 177; Chief Joseph's War, 177, 250–2
Joseph Creek, 195
Josephine County, Oregon, 302 n
Juan de Fuca Strait, 5–6, 25, 141, 170
"Judge Lynch," 245 ff.
Junction City, Oregon, 419

Kadlec, Lieutenant Colonel Harry, 432
Kaiser, Henry J., 360
Kalama, 201, 257
Kaministikwia, 41; *see also* Fort William
Kamloops, B. C., 95; region, 78
Kane, Paul, 453
Kansas, 297, 398, 427
Kansas City, 275
Kansas River, 109
Kearney, Dennis, 422
Kelley, Hall J., 182; writings of, 102, 121; *quoted*, 120
Kelley, Oliver H., 391–2; *quoted*, 395
Kellogg, Idaho, 343, 434
Kendrick, John, 28
Kennewick Division, 320–1
Kentucky, 426
Kenyon, George, 454
Kerbyville, 221
Kettle Falls, 57, 62, 372
Kicking Horse Pass, 269
King, Ervin E., 394
King, Stoddard, 445
King, Colonel William M., 179
King County, Washington, 171 n, 304, 419
Kingston, Professor C. S., 88
Kingston, W. S., 460
Kirkland, Burt P., 359
Kitsap County, Washington, 419
Kittitas County, Washington, 303, 313, 326, 332
Kittson, Norman, 270
Klamath County, Oregon, 302 n, 310
Klamath Falls, 274, 311, 326, 358, 432
Klamath Indians, 17, 178
Klamath Project, 320
Klamath River, 310
Klickitat County, Washington, 282, 303 n
Klikitat Indians, 175
Klinker boats, 69
Klondike, 344, 362

Knights of Labor, 395 n, 397, 424, 433
Knights of Pythias, 392
Know Nothing Party, 158
Kodiak Island, 350
Koehler, Richard, 263
Kohrs, Conrad, 287–8
Kootenai, 228
Kootenai Falls, 37
Kootenai House, 37, 57
Kootenai Indians (Upper), 16–17
Kootenai River, 37
Krueger, Karl, 452
Kullyspell House, 37, 42
Kwakiutl, Indians, 7

Labor movement, 433–8
La Crosse, 275
Ladd, W. S., 284 n
Lady Washington (sloop), 28
Lafayette, 195
La Follette, Robert, 394
Laframbois, Michel, 107 n
Laisner, George, 454
Lake Chelan, Washington, 282, 365, 371
Lake Coeur d'Alene, 365
Lake County, Oregon, 282, 302 n
Lake Crescent, 365
Lake Indians, 7 n
Lake Michigan, 275
Lake Pend Oreille, 365
Lake Superior, 257
Lake Winnipeg, 55
Lamayzie (Indian interpreter), 93
Lamb, J. and Thomas, trading firm, 31
Lambert and Smith's Express, 196
Lampman, Ben Hur, 446
Lander, Edward, 215
Lander Cutoff, 108
Lane, "Clubfoot George," 248
Lane, General Joseph, 159; orders census, 124; appointed territorial governor of Oregon, 154; war record, 154–5; trip to Oregon, 155; administration, 155; territorial delegate, 156; Oregon Senator, 161; secessionist and Democratic vice-presidential nominee, 161–2; census, 167 n
Lane County, Oregon, 168, 392; early school described, 210
Lane County Electric Cooperative, 377
Langlie, Governor Arthur B., 412
Lanzillotti, Robert F., 364 n
Lapwai Indian Reservation, 178

Lapwai Mission, 118, 122, 152, 299; schooling at, 208
Laramie Valley, Wyoming, 285
Lark (ship), 96
Last Chance Gulch, 225
Latah County, Idaho, 328 n
Latin America, 420
Laurels Are Cut Down, 444
Lausanne (ship), 116
Lawlessness: absence of, in British Columbia, 229; gold rush days in Idaho, 245–6; Plummer gang in Montana, 247–50
Lawyer, Chief, 174
Lease, Jacob, 293
Lease, Mary Elizabeth, 398, 398 n
Lebanon, Oregon, 357, 440
Le Breton, G. W., 131
Ledyard, John, 27
Lee, Daniel, 103, 115; quoted, 115
Lee, H. A. G., 173
Lee, Jason, 103, 124, 128, 130, 131 n, 168, 293; characterized, 114; with Wyeth, 115; establishes missions, 115–17; quoted, 115; mission school, 207–8; see also Methodist missions
Legislation League, 405
Legislative reform, 405–9
Leonard, Zenas, 121
Leschi, Chief, 176
Levinson and Company's Express, 195
Lewis, Meriwether, 86; quoted, 87; see also Lewis and Clark expedition
Lewis, Oscar, 329
Lewis and Clark Centennial Exposition, 368
Lewis and Clark College, 215 n
Lewis and Clark Expedition, 37; plans for, 86, Captains Lewis and Clark, 86–7; membership of party, 87 n; journals of, 87; the march, 87–9; significance of, 89; mentioned, 90, 141
Lewis County, Washington, 214, 427
Lewis County, Idaho, 328 n
Lewiston, 223, 240, 328 n
Lewiston Orchard Project, 320
Libby, 37
Libraries, pioneer, 214
Library of Congress, 461
Lillard, Richard G., quoted, 355
Lillooet Indians, 7
Lincoln, President Abraham: declines territorial governorship of Oregon, 156; Oregon vote in

Lincoln, President Abraham (*continued*)
election of 1860, 162; signs Homestead Act, 171; signs Idaho Territorial Act, 239; appointments, 241; appoints Montana governor, 245; signs railroad acts, 256
Lincoln County, Washington, 328 *n*
Linfield College, 215 *n*
Linn, Senator Lewis F., 120, 142, 143
Linn County, Oregon, 168, 169 *n*, 392
Linnton, 168
Lister, Governor Ernest, 404
Literary productions, 439–46
Little Falls, Washington, 371
Little Rock, Arkansas, 192
Little Sandy River, 122
Little Theatre movement, 451
Livestock. See Cattle
Local elections, 1896–1916: Oregon, 403–4; Washington, 404; Idaho, 404–5. After 1918: Oregon, 411–12; Washington, 412–13; Idaho, 413
London, 362
London Colonial Magazine, quoted, 147
London Missionary Society, 113
London *Times*, quoted, 147
Long Bell Lumber Company, 355
"Long Drive," 334
Long Lake, Washington, 371
Longshoremen's Protective Union, 433
Longview, Washington, 357, 359, 378, 379 *n*, 432
Longview *Daily News*, 378 *n*
Loon Creek, 223; Loon Creek "strike," 223
Los Angeles, 237, 062, 363, 432; irrigation congress at, 305
Lot Whitcomb (ship), 203
Lovejoy, Amos L., 123
Loyal Legion of Loggers and Lumber, 437
Lucier, Etienne, 107 *n*, 131 *n*
Lull, Roderick, 446
Lumbering: Hudson's Bay Co. operations, 84; lumber exports, 6, 84, 183; modern phase, 352–60; pioneer lumber mills, 353–4; exploitation and "barons," 354–5; legislation, 355–6; recent statistics on, 357–9
Lutheranism, 419

Lyle, John E., Institute, 209–10
Lyle, Washington, 273, 440
Lyman, George W., 31
Lyon, Caleb, 241

McArthur, Harriet Nesmith, 209
McCall's, 446
McClellan, George B., surveys in Washington Territory, 164–5
McConnell, Charlie, 199
McConnell, William J., 224
McDonald, Archibald, 58, 75
McDonald, Finan, 37, 38, 42
McDonald, John, 41
McDonald of Oregon: A Tale of Two Shores, 441
Macdonell, Alexander, 51
McDougal, Duncan, 91
McGillis, Donald, 94, 95
McGillivray, Duncan, 36
McGuffey's *Eclectic Reader*, 210
McKay, Alexander, 50, 91, death of, 92–3
McKay, Governor Douglas, 411
McKay, Jean, 107 *n*
Mackenzie, Sir Alexander, 19, 34, 35; and Company, 35
Mackenzie expeditions, 39
McKenzie, Donald, 91, 94
McKenzie Pass, 180
McKinley, William, 401–3, 413, 434
McKinley Tariff, 1890, 298
McLane, Louis, 148
McLaughlin, Frank, 371
McLellan, Robert, 91
McLeod, Alexander R., 58, 69, 99
McLeod, John, 70
McLeod, Malcolm, 69; quoted, 68
McLeod Lake, 39
McLoughlin, Dr. John, 84–5; 137, 140, 202, 292, 353; quoted, 74, 84, 100, 104, 120; early life, 56; appointed Chief Factor, 56; characterized, 66–7; organizes Columbia District, 59–65; in connection with inland fur trade, 66 ff.; coasting trade, 71–3; sponsors agriculture and industries, 73–9; Puget's Sound Agricultural Co., 79–82; host to Nathaniel Wyeth, 103; political powers, 128; Willamette Falls land claim, 134; attitude toward settlers and missionaries, 63, 207
McLoughlin and Old Oregon, 441
McMillan, James, 58, 59, 62, 75; quoted, 83

McMinnville, 213, 215 n, 373
McMinnville College (later Linfield College), 213, 215 n
McMinnville Telephone-Register, 449
McNary, Charles L., 415
MacNeil, Hermon A., 453
McTavish, Simon, 34, 35, 36
Magruder, Lloyd, massacre, 246
Mails: ocean service, 188–90; overland mail service, 190–3
Main Currents in American Thought, 460
Major Tompkins (steamer), 205
Makah Indians, 13
Malheur County, Oregon, 302 n, 420
Malheur Indians, 226
Man with the Iron Mask, 450
Mandan Indians, 87, 88
Manhattan Island, 378
Manifest Destiny, 124, 144–5
Mann, Horace, 212
Manufactures, 341–3
Maple Point Farm, 76
Marching, Marching, 444
Marias River, 89
Mariella; of Out West, 440–1
Marietta College, 443
Marine Transport Workers' Industrial Union, 435
Marion County, 169 n
Marketing, 336–9
Marshall, James W., 220
Marston, Gilman, 244
Martin, Governor Charles H., 411
Martin, Governor Clarence D., 412
Martinez, Captain Esteban José, 25, 206
Mary Dare (ship), 82
Marysville, 168
Mason City, Iowa, 275
Masons, 392
Masset, Stephen C., 450
May, Samuel E., 194
May Dacre (ship), 103, 104, 115
Maynard, David S., 170
Mayne, Richard C., 227; *quoted*, 63
Mead, Governor Alter E., 404
Meany, Edmond S., *quoted*, 440; 442, 460
Meany Hall, 442
Meany Hotel, 443
Meares, Captain John, *quoted*, 24–5
Medal of Freedom, 444
Medford, Oregon, 169, 275, 333
Meek, Joe, 185; goes to Washing-

Meek, Joe (*continued*)
ton, D. C., 153; appointed U. S. Marshal, 155
Meek, S. H. L., 187
Meeker, Ezra, *quoted*, 188
Meek's Cutoff, 226
Meier, Governor Julius L., 411
Meier and Frank Department Store, 411
Meigs, George A., 353
Memphis, Tennessee, 192
Mercer, Asa S., 215
Mercer, Thomas, 170
Merk, Frederick, *quoted*, 137
Merriam, Willis B., *quoted*, 334
Methodist Mission, 130, 131, 182
Methodist missionaries, 113–17; 130, 134; *see also* Jason Lee, Daniel Lee
Methodist Missionary Board, 114
Methodist Missionary Society, 114
Mexico, 6, 73, 230, 289, 295, 420
Meyers, Lieutenant Governor Victor A., 412
Michilimackinac Company, 90
Middle West, 283, 289, 292, 355, 361, 396
Milbanke Sound, 63
Military: Wilkes expedition, 129; expedition against Cayuse Indians, 153; surveys in Washington Territory under direction of Governor I. I. Stevens, 164–5; Cayuse War, 171–3; Rogue River Indian War, 173–4; Yakima War, 174–5; Indian attack upon Seattle, 175–6; renewed skirmishes with eastern Washington Indians (1858), 176; military districts created, 176–7; Modoc War, 177–8; summary of Indian wars, 178; War Department camel experiment, 231–2; Mullan Road, 232–4; Chief Joseph's War, 250–2
Miller, Joaquin, 439–40, 445
Miller, Roswell, 276–7
Milwaukee, 275, 276
Milwaukee and St. Paul Railway Company, 275
Milwaukee and Waukesha Rail Road Company, 275
Milwaukee Road (Chicago, Milwaukee, St. Paul and Pacific Railroad), 275–81
Milwaukie, 168
Mineral development: California, 220; Oregon, 220–1; Inland Empire, 221–6; Fraser River and

Mineral development (*continued*)
Cariboo, 226–9; factors attending, 229–38; in the post-frontier period, 343–6
Mineral frontier, 283
Minersville, 195
Minidoka, 308, 320
Minidoka Project, Idaho, 309
Mining. *See* mineral development
Minneapolis and St. Cloud Company, 271
Minnesota, 275, 355
Minnesota Central Railroad, 275
Mirski, Ilma de, 450
Mission Party, 136, 156
Mission Schools, 206–9
Missionaries, societies of, 113–14; interest in Oregon country, 113–15; Methodists, 115–17; American Board, 117–18; Catholic, 118–20; and Provisional Government, 128 ff.; schools, 206–9; *see also* individual missionaries and groups
Mississippi River, 275, 276, 319, 453, 457
Missoula River, 70
Missouri, 293
Missouri Pacific Railroad, 277
Missouri River, 70, 87, 277, 297
Missouri River freighter service, 234
Modeste (British ship), 450
Modoc, Jack, 177
Modoc Indians, 17, 177
Modoc War, 177
Mojave Desert, 237
Monckton, New Brunswick
Money: trading goods in lieu of, 66; wheat as legal tender, 135
Mongoloid race, 9
Monmouth, Oregon, 393
Monmouth Normal School, 212
Montana, *passim*, but especially, 252, 254; mineral development, 224–6; achieving statehood, 252 ff.
Montana Central Railroad, 271
Montana Post, 230
Montana Power Company, 280, 372
Montana State Department of Agriculture, Labor and Industry, *quoted*, 345
Montana Stock Growers' Association, 288
Montana Territory, 225, 245
Monterey, California, 146, 347
Montesano, 170

Monticello, 163, 195
Montreal, 38, 44, 45, 46, 90
Montreal, Bank of, 270
Montreal Department, 52
Moore, A. W., 210
Moore, Governor Charles C., 413
Moore, "Gad," 248
Moore, Robert, 131 n
Moores, I. R., 260
Morey, P. F., 367, 368
Morgan, 272, 277
Morison, Samuel, *quoted*, 29–30
Mormons, 295, 302; in Idaho, 241, 255; and irrigation in Columbia Basin, 300
Morrill Act, 217
Morris, Robert, *quoted*, 26
Morrison, Governor John T., 404
Morrow County, Oregon, 302 n
Morse, Senator Wayne L., 382
Mortgage Your Heart, 444
Moscow, 217
Moses Lake, 318
Mott, Lucretia, 407 n
Mount Baker, 365
Mount Hood, 110, 111, 365
Mount Idaho, Idaho, 393
Mount Mazama, 364
Mount Olympus, 21
Mount Rainier, 25, 365
Mount St. Helens, 365
Mount Stephen, Lord (George Stephen), 270
Mount Vernon, 370
Mountain Men, 90, 98, 185
Mountain States Power Company, 372
Mud-wagons, 200
Mullan, Idaho, 278
Mullan, John, 232 ff.; surveys in Washington Territory, 164
Mullan Road, 232–4
Multnomah (ship), 204
Multnomah County, Oregon, 404
Murphy, John Miller, 447
Murray, 223
Murray, C. A., 121
Museum of Modern Art, 454
Music, 451–3
Musselshell River, 278

Naches Pass, 165, 170, 175, 180
Nanaimo, 65
Nash, Wallis, *quoted*, 199, 200
Nass River, 62
National Art Exhibition, 454
National Broadcasting Company, 453
National Editorial Association, 449

National Farmers' Alliance, 395 n
National Industrial Recovery Act, 373
National Institute of Social Sciences, 436
National Irrigation Association, 306
National Reclamation Act, 306
National Recovery Administration, 415, 437–8
National Transportation Act, 437
Natron Cut-Off, 274
Nature Stories of the Northwest, 441
Nebraska, 297
Nebraska Territory, 239
Negroes: negroid race, 9; attitude of Provisional Government toward, 135; prohibited from voting in Oregon, 159; recent arrivals, 421, 424
Nesbit, Robert C., quoted, 303
Nesfield, David W., 450
Nesmith, J. W., 157 n
Nevada, 284, 306
New Caledonia: North West Co. in, 39–40 ff.; Hudson's Bay Co. in, 52, 58, 76 ff.
New Deal, 347 n, 414–16
New Dungeness, 170
New England, 330, 352, 455, 456
New Jersey, 407 n
New Market, 170
New Mexico, 254, 365
New North West Company, 35
New Orleans, 91, 268
New Orleans Picayune, quoted, 145
New Spain, 21, 283, 289
New York, 26, 91, 123, 292, 301, 317, 362, 386, 450, 454
New York Evening Post, 435–6
New York State, 91
New York Times, 371
New York Tribune, 201
New Zealand, 27, 84, 294
Newberg, 132
Newell, Frederick H., 305, 306
Newell and Company's Express, 194
Newlands, Francis G., 306
Newport, Oregon, 393
Newport, R. I., 26
Nez Percé Indians, 14, 70, 100, 114, 115, 118, 174; how named, 7 n; stature of, 10; schooling, 208; non-reservation, 250–2
Nez Perces County, Idaho, 328 n
Nez Perces First Book, 208

Nicholson, Patricia, 454
Nisqually Farm, 75, 81
Nisqually River, 189
Noble, T. A., 316
Nootka Sound, 23, 92; discovered, 22; controversy, 25; Treaty, 25
Norblad, Governor A. W., 411
"North Bank Road," 273
North Carolina, 427
North Coast Railroad, 274
North Dairy Farm, 76
North Dakota, 252, 255, 278
North Dam, 320
North West Company, 50, 52, 54, 62, 67, 69, 90, 106, 206; origin of, 34–6; in Columbia River basin, 36–8; in New Caledonia, 39–40; how organized in Oregon, 40–1; the Indian trade, 41–4; communications, 44–6; its overseas trade, 46–8; merger with Hudson's Bay Co., 51–3; purchase Fort Astoria, 96–7
Northern Alliance, 395, 395 n
Northern Department of Rupert's Land, 52
Northern Pacific, Yakima, and Kittitas Irrigation Company, 303 n
Northern Pacific Act, 256, 257
North Pacific Coast Indians, 12; food of, 13; houses, 13–14; arts, 14–15
Northern Pacific Railroad, 201, 238, 252 ff., 271, 272–3, 277, 278, 286, 291, 303, 314, 327, 367, 390, 418, 423, 434; Villard completes, 264–6
Northern Securities Case, 273
Northern Securities Company, 273, 402
Northwest, Old, 330
Northwest Ordinance, 133
Northwest Passage, in search of, 21
Northwestern Alliance, 395 n
Norway, 418
Norway House, 55
Norwegian immigrants, 418–19
Nor'westers. See North West Company
Novelists, proletarian, 444
Nuttall, Thomas, 103

Oakland, Oregon, 191, 274
Oblate Fathers, 300
O'Cain, Captain Joseph, 31
Oddfellows (I.O.O.F.), 392
Ogden, Peter Skene, 58; expeditions of, 69

Ohio, 361
Okanogan, 38, 287, 295, 312; Indian name Okinágen, 7 n
Okanogan County, Washington, 282, 311, 312
Okanogan River, 312
Oklahoma, 427
Olachen oil, 14
Olcott, Governor Ben W., 411
"Old Wyoming Trail," 286
Olympia, 166, 188, 195, 196, 197, 353, 357, 363, 393, 447; territorial capital described (1854), 165; academy at, 213
Olympic Mountains, 4
Olympic Peninsula, 365
Omaha, 225, 268, 297, 396
Omnibus states, 252–5
Oneida County, Idaho, 300 n
Ontario, Oregon, 311
Operation of the Initiative, Referendum, and Recall in Oregon, 408
"Operations Haylift," 335
Orchard, Harry, 434
Ordway, Sergeant John, 87
Oregon, *passim,* but especially mineral development, 220–1, 226; reclamation in, 309–11; politics, 386–8, 403–4, 411–12; population (figures, 1900–40), 417 n; foreign born in, 426 n; *see also* Oregon Country
Oregon Agricultural Society, 391
Oregon and California Railroad Company, 260, 262, 263, 266–8
Oregon and Transcontinental Company, 265, 266
Oregon and Washington, 442
Oregon Argus, 157
Oregon Board of (Tax) Equalization Law, 409
Oregon boundary dispute: Spanish, Russian, British, and American claims, 139; Spanish and Russian withdrawal, 139–40; American and British occupation jointly, 139–41; American public interest in, 144–6; diplomacy respecting, 146–50; Oregon Treaty (1846), 149–50
Oregon Caves, 365
Oregon Central Railroad Company, 260
Oregon City, 111, 155, 156, 169 n, 173, 191, 195, 367, 368; early maritime center, 204
Oregon City College (later called University), 213

Oregon City portage, 262
Oregon Colonization Society, 102
Oregon Country: geography and boundaries of, 3–6; Indians of, 6–20; explorations and sea otter trade, 21–32; fur trade in, 33–106; settlement, 107–26; promotion of, 120–21; Provisional government, 127–38; boundary dispute, 139–51
Oregon Detour, 444
Oregon Electric Railroad, 273, 274
Oregon Electric Steel Rolling Mills, 379
Oregon Farmers' Alliance, 395
Oregon Historical Quarterly, 460
Oregon Historical Society, 460
Oregon Institute, 213
Oregon Journal, 448, 449
Oregon Pacific (Yakima) Railroad, 274
"Oregon Pony" (steam locomotive), 257
Oregon Portage Railroad, 257, 258
Oregon Primary Law, 406
Oregon Railroad Commission, 410
Oregon Railway and Navigation Company, 264, 265 n, 266, 269, 274
Oregon Short Line Railroad, 268–9
Oregon Spectator, 138, 157, 187, 195, 445, 447; *quoted,* 178
Oregon Stage Company, 188
Oregon State College, 212, 216–17
Oregon State Grange, 392
Oregon State Legislature, 212; railroads, 260; land grants to Holladay, 261; progressive legislation, 405–9
Oregon State Planning Board, 428
Oregon Statesman, 157; *quoted,* 189
Oregon Steam Navigation Company, 205, 205 n, 263; holdings, 257–8
Oregon Steamship Company, 263
Oregon Territory, 145; creation of, 153–4; Joseph Lane as first governor of, 154–6; territorial politics, 156–7; Donation Land Law affecting, 157–8; efforts at securing statehood, 158–60; statehood, 161–2; settlement in, 167–9; Indian menace, 171 ff.; pioneer road building, 178–81; social and economic life, 181–6; legislature, 211

Oregon Trail, 94, 98, 236, 237, 284, 286, 293, 297; course of, 108–9; immigrant parties over, 109–12 ff., 121–4; travel conditions on, 124–6
Oregon Treaty, 149–50
Oregonian's Handbook, 354; quoted, 354
Orient, 26, 46, 418; *see also* China, Japan
Oro Fino, 223, 224
Oro Fino Creek, 222, 223
Osaka, 362
O'Sullivan Dam, 320
Oswego, 213, 379
Ottawa River, 44
Otter (ship), 203, 226
Otter skins, 55 ff.
Overland expeditions: Alexander Mackenzie, 34; David Thompson, 36–8; Simon Fraser, 39–40; Lewis and Clark, 86–9; Hunt's Overlanders, 93–4; Jedediah Smith, 98–9; Benjamin Bonneville, 99–101; Nathaniel Wyeth, 102–4; immigrant trains, 108–12, 121–6; John C. Frémont, 129
Owen, John, 224
Owyhee Plateaus, 240
Owyhee Project, 309, 311, 320
Owyhee Valley, immigration to, 240

"P" ranch, 287
Pacific Christian Advocate, 196
Pacific Coast Range of Canada, 4
Pacific Flower, 439
Pacific Fur Company, 41, 141; organized, 91; Astoria expedition, 91–4; operations, 91–6; sale of Astoria to North West Co., 96–7; estimate of, 97
Pacific Light and Power Company, 372
Pacific Mail Steamship Company, 189–90
Pacific Northwest Forest and Range Station, 356
Pacific Northwest Fruit Distributors, 337
Pacific Northwest Fruits, Inc., 338
Pacific Northwest Library Association, 461
Pacific Northwest Public Service Company (Portland General Electric Company), 368
Pacific Northwest Quarterly, 460

Pacific Ocean, *passim*, but especially, 3, 5, 88; sea otter trade and explorations, 21–32; seeking outlet to, 46–7; coasting trade, 71–3
Pacific Railroad Company, 277
Pacific Republic, 161
Pacific University, 214, 215 n
Pack horses, use by fur traders, 45
Pack River, 39
Pack trains, 183; western Oregon, 183; and packing, Inland Empire, 229–32
Paddlewheelers, 202–5
Padelford, Frederick Morgan, 460
Pakenham, Richard, 148
Palisades Dam, Idaho, 309
Palmer, Joel, 174
Palouse country, 328 n
Palouse Indians, 176
Palouse Project, 314
Pambrun, Pierre C., 100, 103
Panama Canal, 277
Parker, Colter and Company's Express, 196
Parker, Samuel, 117
Parliament, Act of (1821), 53
Parochial schools, 212 ff.
Parrington, Vernon L., 460
Parrish, Josiah L., 131 n
Parsnip River, 39
Parsons, Philip A., 428–30
Partridge, Roi, 453
Pasco, 314, 319, 432
Patkanim, Chief, 176
Patrons of Husbandry (Grange), 391–5
Patterson, Governor I. L., 411
Paul Bunyan, 444
Payette, Francois, 107 n
Payette River, 295 n, 308, 320
Peace of Ghent, 47
Peace River, 34, 39, 44
Peel, Sir Robert, 147
Pemmican, 42
Pend d'Oreille Indians, 100
Pend d'Oreille Lake, 37, 230
Pend d'Oreille River, 222
Pendleton, Oregon, 297, 365, 393
Pennoyer, Governor Sylvester, 400, 422
Peoples, William, 247
People's Call, 399
Peoples' Party (Whig party, Oregon), 156; *see also* Populism
People's Power League, 405
"Peoria Party," 121
Pérez, Juan, 22
Perham, Josiah, 256

Perkins, J. and T. H., trading firm, 31, 47
Permanente Metals Corporation, 379 n
Phelps and Wadleigh Company, 287
Philadelphia, 26
Philippine Islands, 21
Philomath College, 215 n
Phoebe (ship), 46
Picked Company, 440
Pickering, William, 385
Piegan Indians, 38
Pierce, E. D., 222
Pierce, Franklin, 164
Pierce, I. Nathan, 398
Pierce, Governor Walter M., 411
Pierce City, 223
Pierce County, Washington, 240, 404, 419
Pierre's Hole, 99, 102
Pintard, John M., 27
Pioneer and Democrat, 196
Pioneer City (Hogem), 223, 224, 231
Pioneer Days of Oregon, 442
Pioneer Line, 187
Pioneer settlers: Willamette Valley (early), 107–8; missionaries, 113–20; arrival of, 1841 and after, 121–4; establish provisional government, 129–35 ff.; spread in Willamette Valley, 167–9; in Washington Territory, 169–71; in Idaho Territory, education, 457–62
Pittman, Anna Maria, 116
Placerville, 223, 224, 231
Plank roads, 178
Plateau Indians, 12; food of, 15; houses, 15; arts, 15–16; cultural traits, 16–17, 20
Platte River, 102, 109
Pleasant Hill, 168
Plummer, Alfred A., 170
Plummer, Henry, gang, 247–50
Pocatello, 431
Point George, 92
Point Grenville, 23
Political developments. See individual territories and states, Grangerism, Populism, Progressivism, New Deal
Polk, President James K., 145, 153, 154, 220; respecting Oregon boundary, 146, 148–9
Polk County, Oregon, 168, 169 n, 392
Pollard, Lancaster, 460

Pond, Peter, 34
"Popocrats," 401
Population: Oregon Territory (1849), 167 n; Census of 1850, 169 n; Census of 1860, 169 n, 171 n; in post-frontier period, 417–21; Orientals, 421–6; westward emigration, 426–31; figures, 417 n, 420–1 n, 426 n, 430 n
Populism, 395–403, 404
Populist Party, 395
Populists, 394
Port Angeles, 363
Port Blakely, 369
Port Orchard, 25
Port Orford, 197
Port Townsend, 25, 195, 197, 210
Portage la Loche, 34
Portaging, 45
Porter, Corydon F., 170
Portland, 169 n, 192, 200, 201, 259, 268, 269, 272, 274, 319, 333, 342–3, 357, 361, 362, 363, 363 n, 365, 366, 367, 368, 369, 379, 404, 420, 421, 423, 424, 431, 432, 433, 445, 446, 447, 450, 451, 452, 453, 459; townsite surveyed, 168; wagon freighting center, 183; staging terminal, 190; express office at, 197
Portland and Valley Plank Road Company, 178
Portland Art Association, 453
Portland Civic Symphony, 452
Portland Electric Power Company (Portland General Electric Company), 368
Portland General Electric Company, 367–8, 369
Portland Masonic Hall, 452
Portland Oregonian, 157, 162, 192, 393, 398, 408, 422, 433, 447, 448, 449; quoted, 340–1, 367–8, 401, 422, 423, 428
Portland Railway Light and Power Company (Portland General Electric Company), 368
Portland Symphony Orchestra, 452
Portneuf River, 104
Post Falls, Idaho, reservoir, 309
Post-Intelligencer, 423
Post Office Appropriations Act, 191
Postal service. See Mails
Potatoes, Idaho ("bakers"), 324
Powder River, 226
Powell, J. W., 305
Powers, Alfred, 126 n

Prairie City, 197
Prairie du Chien Railroad, 275
Prairie schooner, 182; see also Conestoga wagons
Pratt, O. C., 155 n
Pratt, William W., 450
Pre-emption, 158
Prentiss, Narcissa, 117; see also Whitman, Marcus
Presbyterians, 113, 215 n; schools, 214; see also American Board
Presidential Preference Primary Law, 407
Press, 446–9
Preston, Texas, 192
Preston Bench, 320
Prickett, Judge H. E., 246
Priest Rapids Project, 314
Prince Rupert, 50
Prince Rupert, B. C., 269
Prineville, Oregon, 297
Pritchett, Knitzing, 155 n
"Pro pelle cutem," 50
Proctor, A. Phimister, 453
Progressive Era, 405
Progressivism, 405–9
Prohibitionists, 397
Protection Island, 25
Provisional Government: events leading to, 127–32; Champoeg meetings, 132–5; effect of immigration upon, 135–7; final period (1846–49), 137–8; respecting Whitman massacre, 153
Prudential Committee, 113
Public Service Commission, 410
Public Utility Districts (PUDs), 377–8
Public Works Administration, 415
Puget, Lieutenant Peter, 25
Puget Sound, 4, 163, 190, 201, 271, 294, 330, 332, 346, 347, 349, 350, 351, 353, 369, 427, 450, 453; described, 6; served by express, 196
Puget Sound Milling Company, 353
Puget Sound Power and Light, 369, 370–1
Puget Sound Power Company, 370
Puget Sound Traction, Light, and Power Company, 370
Puget's Sound Agricultural Company, 76, 79–82, 292; respecting Oregon Treaty and possessory rights, 150
Pulitzer Prizes, 446, 449, 460
Pullman, 215, 459

Puyallup Indians, 7 n
Puyallup River, 170, 333, 370

Queen Charlotte's Islands, 226; Indians of, 9
Queen Mary (liner), 317
Queen of the Pacific, S. S., 423
Quileute Indians, 13
Quincy, 319
Quincy Plains, 314
Quincy Project, 314–15
Quincy Valley, 314

Raccoon (sloop), 46, 97
Radisson, Pierre Esprit, 49
Rae, W. G., 63
Railroads: projections and surveys, 256–7; short lines, 257–8; in the Willamette Valley, 258–62; Benjamin Holladay and, 261 ff.; and appearance of Henry Villard, 262–4; Northern Pacific, 264–6; completion of Oregon and California, 266–8; Oregon Short Line, 268–9; Canadian Pacific, 269–70; Great Northern, 270–4; Milwaukee, 275–81; reforms, 389–90
Rainier, 195
Rainy Lake, 42
Ralph, Julian, quoted, 291
Ramsberg, Lucy Dodd, 453
Ramsey, George, 107 n
Range cattle industry, 282–6
Range life, 286–91
Raver, Paul J., 382
Ray, Ned, 248, 249
Raymond, Rossiter W., quoted, 225
Reclamation: through private initiative, 299–304; public interest in, 304–7; Reclamation Service in operation in Idaho, 307–9; in Oregon, 309–11; in Washington, 311–14; in Big Bend region, 314–15; Grand Coulee Dam, 315–19; plans for future, 319–21
Reclamation Act of 1902, 306
Reclamation Bureau, 303
Reclamation Fund, 306
Reclamation Program: 1948–54, 319
Reclamation Projects Act, 307
Reclamation Service. See Bureau of Reclamation
Reconstruction Finance Corporation, 281, 414, 415
Red River of the North, 50–1, 270
Red River settlement, 50
Red River Transportation Company, 270

Reed, John, 94
Reed, Simeon G., 205, 284 n, 459
Reed College, 459
Reform movements, 389–91
Religious life, 217–18; of Indians, 16 ff.; *see also* individual denominations
Renton, William, 353
Renton, Washington, 346
"Re-occupation of Oregon and the re-annexation of Texas," 145
Repertory Playhouse, 451
Republican Party: in Oregon Territory, 156–7; Oregon state, 161; in Washington, 162 ff.; in Idaho, 241 ff.; in Northwest, 384–416
Resolution (ship), 23
Reynolds Metals Company, 379 n
Richland, Washington, 432
Richmond, William, 213
Riggs, H. C., 188
Rip Van Winkle, 450
Rising, Dorothy, 454
Ritzville Warehouse Company, 336
"River of the West," 3, 29
River of the West (book), 441
Rivers and Harbors Act, 373
Riverside, Washington, 312
"Road agents," 246 ff.
Roads: pioneer, 178–81; Mullan, 232–4; Inland Empire-California, 234 ff.
"Robber's Roost," 248
Robins, Governor C. A., 413
Robinson, Edgar E., 416 n
Rockefeller, William, 280
Rockport, 370
Rocky Mountain Fur Company, 100, 102
Rocky Mountain House, 39
Rocky Mountains, 4, 40–1, 55, 88, 89, 99, 269, 272, 354, 445, 447; Canadian Rockies, 4; South Pass in, 108
Rogers, Governor John R., 404
Rogue River, 4, 169, 183, 221, 259, 325 n, 332, 365
Rogue River Indian Agency, 195
Rogue River Indian War, 173–4, 177
Rogue River Valley, 111; trade, 230–1
Rollinson, John K., *quoted*, 290
Roman Catholics, 300
Roosevelt, Franklin D., 316, 394, 412, 414–15; *quoted*, 376–7
Roosevelt, Theodore, 306, 356, 405, 409, 413; *quoted*, 315
Roosevelt Highway, 365

Rose Festival, 365
Roseburg, 161 n, 168, 169 n, 191, 259, 275
Ross, Alexander, 45, 55
Ross, Governor C. B., 413
Roza Division, 313, 320
Ruby City, 223
Rupert, Idaho, 308
Rural Electrification Administration, 377
Rural Spirit, quoted, 331
Rusling, James F., 199
Russell, Israel C., 316
Russell, Lord John, 148
Russell, Majors and Waddell, freighting firm, 192, 197
Russia: respecting Oregon boundary, 140; Bolshevik Revolution, 420; immigrants from, 420; *see also* Russians
Russian America, 73; *see also* Alaska
Russian-American Convention, 140, 140 n
Russian American Fur Company, 22; agreement with British, 64
Russian immigrants, 420
Russian revolution, 420
Russians, 19, 40, 76, 81; exploration and trade, 21–2; Czarist ukase, 64
Ryan, John D., 279–80

Sacajawea, Indian woman, 87 n, 88
Sacramento, California, 190, 268
Sacramento River, 98, 259, 348
Sacramento Valley, 235
Sacred Heart Mission, 119
Saddle Mountains, 316
Sage, Walter N., *quoted*, 67
Sailor Diggings, 221, 231
St. Helen's, 168, 195, 363
St. Helen's Hall, 213
St. Ignatius Mission, 119, 209
St. Johns, 168, 357
St. Joseph, Missouri, 125, 293
St. Louis, 87, 88, 91, 95, 102, 114, 191, 192
St. Mary's Academy, 213
St. Michael's College, 213
St. Paul, 270, 275, 297
St. Paul and Pacific Railroad, 270
St. Paul, Minneapolis, and Manitoba Railroad Company, 270–1
St. Paul Mission, 119
Salary Grab, 386
Saleesh Indians, 42
Salem, 396–7, 410

Salem, Massachusetts, 26, 116, 130, 159, 168, 169 n, 191, 195, 259
"Salem Clique," 156, 157
Salisbury, Gilmore and Company, 246
Salish Indians, 10
Salmon, 346–50
Salmon Creek, Washington, 311
Salmon River, 70, 312
Salt Lake-Atchison Stage Line, 197
Salt Lake City, 191, 192, 197, 198, 225, 231, 237, 300, 301, 305, 434; irrigation congress at, 305
Salubria, Idaho, 393
San Antonio, Texas, 191
San Diego, 191
San Francisco, 63, 190, 194, 200, 235, 274, 361, 362 ,367, 423, 441
San Francisco Bay, 146
San Juan Islands, 151
San Pedro, California, 155
Sandalwood trade, 32
Sanders, Helen F., 202
Sanders, Wilbur Fish, 202
Sanders's readers, 210
Sandwich Islands, 31, 32, 73, 79, 83, 84, 104, 113; native from, 92
Santa Fe, New Mexico, 155
Santiam Academy, 213
Santiam River, 221
Sapling Grove, 125
Sarsi Indians, 7 n
Saturday Evening Post, 446
Sault Ste. Marie, 144
Sauvies Island (formerly Wapato Island), 104
Savage, John L., 318
Scammon, J. L., 170
Scandinavia, 418–19
Scandinavians, 394
Scenic, 272 n
Schafer, Professor Joseph, 442, 460
Schirnding, Baron August von, 113
School of Architecture and Allied Arts, 453
Schools, at Fort Vancouver, 60; see also Education
Schumacher, Waldo, 408
Scott, Harvey, 447
Scott, John, 111
Scott, Levi, 111, 112
Scott, Nelson, 247
Scott, Thomas F., 213
Scott's Bluff, 109
Scottsburg, 168
Sealth, Chief. See Seattle, Chief
Sea Otter (brig), 23
Sea otters, 66; trade in, 23–32; described, 24–5, 29; California, 32

Seaside, 88
Seattle, 171 n, 195, 197, 272, 273, 277, 278, 317, 333, 343, 353, 357, 361, 362, 363, 363 n, 365, 369, 370, 371, 373, 377, 379, 399, 404, 419, 420, 421, 423, 424, 431, 432, 436, 438, 445, 446, 448, 451, 452, 454; port of, 6; secures University of Washington, 166; Indian attack upon, 175–6
Seattle, Chief, 170, 175
Seattle Art Museum, 454
Seattle Call, 423
Seattle Electric Company, 370
Seattle Electric Lighting Company, 369
Seattle Junior Programs, Inc., 451
Seattle Post Intelligencer, 331, 369, 448
Seattle Times, 448
Select Committee on Irrigation and Reclamation of Arid Lands, 305
Selkirk, Lord, 50 ff.
Semple, Eugene, 390–91
Seneca Falls, New York, 407 n
Seton, Alfred, 94
Settlement of Oregon Country: Willamette Valley (early), 107–8; missionary settlements, 113–20; immigrant settlements (1841–44), 121–4; spread in Willamette Valley, 167–9; during the 1850's, 167–71; in Washington territory, 169–71
Seven Oaks massacre, 50–1
Seven Years' War, 22, 34
Seward, William H., 161
Seymour, Horatio, 385
Shaftesbury, Earl of, 50
Shanghai, 362
Sharp, Joseph H., 210
Shasta City, California, 190, 195, 230
Shasta River, 259
Shaw, Frank, 353
Shaw, Major Samuel, 26
Shaw, Thomas, 327
She Whaps, 95
Sheep, 78; Hudson's Bay Co., 78; raising, 79; on the range, 291–8; drives, 296–8; breeds, 335
Sheldon, Henry, quoted, 216
Shepard, Cyrus, 115, 207
Shepherds, various nationalities, 295
Sheridan, Lieutenant Phil, 175
Sheridan, Oregon, 393
Sheridan Academy, 213
Sherman County, Oregon, 302 n

Shoalwater Bay, 170
Shoshone County, Idaho, 434
Shoshone Indians, 17, 222
Shoup, George L., 255
Shuswap Indians, 7
Sierra Nevada Mountains, 236
Silver, free coinage of, 398
Silver City, 223
Silver Republicans, 404
Silverton, 453
Simcoe, Governor J. Graves, 36
Simcoe Indian Reservation, 174
Simmons, Michael T., 169, 353
Simpson, Aemilius, *quoted*, 83
Simpson, Governor George, 64, 76, 140, 141; appointed Hudson's Bay Co. governor, 53; early life, 53–4; organizes Columbia District, 54–9; *quoted*, 58, 69, 73–4; opinion on Indians, 207
Simpson, Samuel, 445
Siskiyou Mountains, 69, 230, 268
Sisters of the Most Holy Name of Jesus and Mary, 213
Skagit County, Washington, 419, 427
Skagit River, 373
"Skin Book," 71
Skinner, Eugene, 168
Skookum Packers' Association, 338
Slacum, Lieutenant William A., 129, 182
Slaughter, Lieutenant W. A., 175
Slavery: attitude of provisional government toward, 135; bill to prohibit in Oregon, 154, 160
Smith, A. B., 118
Smith, C. DeWitt, 241
Smith, Charles W., 461
Smith, Delazon, 161
Smith, Donald. See Lord Strathcona
Smith, J. Allen, 460
Smith, Jedediah, west coast expedition, 98–9
Smith, Joseph, 444
Smith, Solomon H., 207
Smith's and Clark's grammars, 210
Smith's *Arithmetic*, 210
Smith's Express, 196
Snake Indians, 17
Snake River, 5, 40, 63, 69, 70, 94, 102, 282, 300, 301–2, 307, 308, 317, 332 420; expeditions 71
Snake River Basin, 41, 55, 68, 101
Snake River Ferry, 235
Snell, Governor Carl, 411
Snipes, Benjamin E., 287
Snohomish County, 371

Snohomish County, Washington, 419, 427
Snoqualmie Falls, 370
Snoqualmie Falls Power Company, 370
Snoqualmie Pass, 165, 278
Soda Springs, 122
Soil Culture Manual, 327
Songs of the Olympics, 445
South America, 73
South Bend, 359
South Coulee Dam, 320
South Dakota, 252, 254, 255, 277, 279
South Pass, 108, 109; discovery of, 95
South Road, 168
South Road Company, organization of, 112
South Sea Company, 24, 47
Southern Department, 52
Southern Methodist University, 215 *n*
Southern Pacific Railroad Company, 267, 268, 274
Southwest, 292; Spanish in, 292
Spain, cedes rights to Oregon Country, 139–40, 140 *n*
Spalding, Reverend Henry Harman, 152; and Mrs., 117, 118, 207; 299; teaches Indians, 208
Spanish, 19; coastal explorations, 21–3
Spanish-American Treaty, 139–40, 140 *n*
Spanish galleons, 21
Spargur, John, 452
Spirit of American Government, 443
Spokane, 272, 273, 274, 282, 328, 328 *n*, 371, 378, 379, 431, 441, 445, 453, 459
Spokane, Portland and Seattle Railroad, 273
Spokane Aluminum Fabrication, 379 *n*
Spokane Aluminum Reduction Company, 379 *n*
Spokane County, Washington, 303 *n*, 328 *n*
Spokane Falls, 371
Spokane Falls Irrigation Company, 303
Spokane Falls Water Power Company, 371
Spokane House, 37–8, 55, 58, 62, 96
Spokane (or Spokan') Indians, 7 *n*
Spokane River, 5, 38, 118, 222
Sprague, Governor Charles, 411
Springfield, Oregon, 357

Squak Valley, 423
"Square Deal," 356
Squire, Governor, 424
Stagecoach: transportation and travel, 187–8; 200–2; overland, 190–3; drivers, 198–200
Stampede Tunnel, 266
Stanford, Leland, 259
Stanley, John M., 453
Stanton, Elizabeth Cady, 407 n
Stanton, Richard H., 163
Star of Oregon (schooner), 293
Stark, Beujamin, 205
State College of Washington, 459
State of California (steamer), 366
State of Idaho vs. Western Federation of Miners, 434
Staten Island, 26
Steamship transportation, 202–5
Steilacoom, 164, 195, 197
Steinbeck, John, 427
Stephen, George. See Mount Stephen, Lord
Steptoe, Colonel Edward J., 175, 176; "Steptoe disaster," 176
Sterling, Donald J., 449
Steunenberg, Governor Frank, 404, 434
Stevens, Isaac Ingall, 174, 176, 177, 180, 232; appointed Washington territorial governor, 164; survey in Washington Territory, 165; delegate to Congress from Washington Territory, 166; railroad surveys, 256; quoted, 458
Stevens, James, 444
Stevens County, Washington, 303 n, 312
Stevens Pass, 165, 272 n
Stinson, Buck, 248, 249
Stone and Webster (engineering company), 369
Stories of Oregon, 441
Strahorn, Robert E., 273–4
Strange, Captain James, 23
Strathcona, Lord (Donald Smith), 269, 270
Stuart, A. B., 195
Stuart, C. W., 170
Stuart, David, 91, 95
Stuart, Granville, 224–5
Stuart, James, 224–5
Stuart, John, 39, 40, 44, 46
Stuart, Robert, 94, 95
Stuart Lake, 39
Stuart's Express, 195, 196
Sturgis, S. D., 251
Sturgis, William, quoted, 28, 30
Sublette, Milton G., 100, 103

Sublette, William L., 102
Sublette cutoff, 108
Sullivan, Louis, 457
Sultana (ship), 102, 103
Sun Valley, 365
Sunday school libraries, 214
"Sunkist" label, 338
Sunnyside Canal, 303, 312
Superfortresses, 379
Sutler's Store, 194
Sutter, John, sawmill, 220
Swamp Land Act of 1850, 354
Swan Land and Cattle Company, 288
Sweden, 418, 444
Swedish immigrants, 419
Sweet Home, 359
Swift Flows the River, 444
Sylvester, Edmund, 353

Table Rock Treaty, 174
Tacoma, 277, 343, 357, 361, 362, 363, 363 n, 370, 371, 373, 377, 378, 404, 419, 423, 424, 431
Tacoma Aluminum Reduction Company, 379 n
Tacoma Mill Company, 369
Taft, William Howard, 413
Taggard, Genevieve, 446
Takagi, S., 424
Take All to Nebraska, 444
Takel'ma Indians, 6 n, 7
Tamsuky Indians, 152
Tappan, W. H., 194
Taylor, Edward, 334
Taylor, Zachary, 156
Taylor Grazing Act, 1934, 334
Teachers, pioneer, 206 ff., 210, 211; scholars, 457–62
Teamsters, 238
Teamsters' Union, 438
"Telegraph Line," 187
Templar Channel, 92
Ten Nights in a Bar Room, 450
Tennessee, 427
Tennessee Valley Authority, 382
"Term Schools," 209
Terry, C. C., 215
Terry, Montana, 278
Texas, 283, 285, 289, 290
Texas Grand State Alliance, 395 n
Texas longhorns (cattle), 283, 284 n
The Dalles, 5, 11, 109, 110, 111, 116, 123, 195, 197, 198, 231, 287, 348
The Dalles and Celilo Railroad, 258
The Dalles-Celilo portage, 257
Theater, 449–51

This Passion Never Dies, 444
Thompson, David, 34, 40, 41, 94; enters Columbia Basin, 36–8; *quoted*, 42; trading operations, 41–2; at mouth of Columbia, 42
Thompson, R. R., 205
Thompson, Roy A. H., 359
Thompson Falls Company, 280
Thompson Indians, 7 *n*
Thompson River, 38, 40; region of, 68
Thompson's *Arithmetic*, 210
Thompson's Falls, 37
Thompson's Portage, 257
Thorn, Captain Jonathan, 92 ff.
Thornton, J. Quinn, 112; *quoted*, 136; in Washington, D. C., 153
Three Forks, Montana, 278
Three Sisters, 365
Three Weeks of Marriage, 450
Thurston, 168, 195
Thurston County, 171 *n*
Tichenor, William, 157 *n*
Tilaukait, Indian, 152
Tilden, Samuel J., 386–8
Tillamook County, Oregon, 331
Timber. See Forests, Lumbering
Timber and Stone Act, 355
Timber Culture Act, 304, 354
Tlingit Indians, 6 *n*, 7 *n*, 14
Tobey, Mark, 454
Tobie, Harry Elmer, *quoted*, 437
Todd, Alexander H., express business, 194
Todhunter, W. B., 287
Tolmie, Dr. William Fraser, 81–2, 292
Tompkins, Margaret, 454
Tongs, 422
Tongue Point, 92
Tonquin (ship); voyage of, 92; disaster, 92–3
Tourist industry, 363–5
Townsend, John K., 108
"Tracking," 45
Tracy, E. W., 195
Tracy and Company Express, 195
Trade: sea otter, 23–32; fur trade, 33–106; Pacific, 141; California Cattle Co., 182; wagon freight commerce, 182–3; pack animal commerce, 183; exports and imports (territorial period), 183–4
Trading posts. See Forts, individual names
Trading ships, statistics, 31 *n*; *see also* individual ships
Trans-Allegheny West, 287
Trans-Mississippi West, 292

Transportation: by foot, horse, and canoe, 44–6; wagon freighting west of Cascades, 182–3, 188; pack animal west of Cascades, 183; stagecoach, 187–8, 190–3; express, 193–8; mail, 188–90 ff.; steamboat, 202–5; Mullan Road, 232–4; wagon freighting and packing (Inland Empire), 229–32, 234–8; railroad, 256–81
Travel, Indian, 14; over Oregon Trail, 124–6; by stagecoach, 198–202; by steamer, 204–5; *see also* Transportation
Treaties and conventions: Nootka Sound, 25; Paris, 33; Ghent, 97; Anglo-American, 127, 139; Spanish-American, 139–40; Russian, 140; Oregon Treaty (1846), 149–50; treaty establishing Joint Commission respecting possessory rights, 150; Treaty of Washington, 151
Treaty of Ghent, 97
Treaty of Paris (1763), 33
Triangle trade, American, 26–32
Trinity County, California, 98
Troutdale, Oregon, 378, 379 *n*
Truman, President Harry S., 382, 415–16
Tshimakain Mission, 118
Tsimshian Indians, 7
Tucker, George, 124
Tucson, Arizona, 155
Tule Lake, 177
Tulips, 333
Tumwater, 162, 170, 204, 210, 353
T'Vault, William G., 138; editor of *Spectator*, 157; express agent and postmaster, 195
T'Vault & Company's Oregon and Shasta Express, 195
Tweed Ring, 386
Twelve Temptations, 451
Twin Falls, Idaho, 301
Typographical Society of Portland, 433

Umatilla, 197, 231
Umatilla County, Oregon, 282, 302 *n*, 332
Umatilla Indian Reservation, 174
Umatilla Indians, 174
Umatilla Project, Oregon, 309
Umatilla River, 309
Umpqua Academy, 212, 213
Umpqua City, 168, 197
Umpqua River, 4, 183, 188, 259, 332

Umpqua River Valley, 68, 69, 111, 168, 259
Union, 231
Union County, Oregon, 282, 302 n
Union Labor Party, 397
Union Pacific Railroad, 268, 269, 274, 276, 277, 284, 285, 291
Union Party, 395
United Brethren, 215 n
United States Alien Property Custodian, 425
United States Department of Agriculture, 335
United States Electric Lighting and Power Company, 367
United States Geographical and Geological Survey of the Rocky Mountain Region, 305
United States Geological Survey, 305, 306, 316
United States government: claims to Oregon Country, 139–41; Congressional opinion on Oregon claims, 141–4; negotiations and final settlement regarding Oregon, 146–51
United States Immigration Act, 425
United States mail. See Mails
United States Shipping Board, 437
United States Steel Corporation, 402
United States Supreme Court, and Northern Securites case, 273
Universities, rise of, 214–17
University of California, 462
University of Idaho, founded, 217
University of Oregon, 217, 359, 408, 442, 453, 457, 460; founding of, 215–16
University of Washington, 166, 215, 438, 442, 443, 451, 454, 459, 460, 461
Updyke, Dave, gang, 246
Uplands Farm, 76
Upper Klamath Lake, 310
Upper Snake River Storage Project, 309
U'Ren, William S., 405
Urso, Camelia, 450
U.S.S.R., 435
Utah, 417

Vale Project, Oregon, 311
Van Buren, President Martin, 142
Vancouver, Captain George, 11, 79; explorations and discoveries, 25
Vancouver, 269, 273, 378, 393, 421, 432; academy at, 213
Vancouver, B. C., 6

Vancouver (schooner), 72
Vancouver Island, 19, 28, 65, 77, 92, 195, 227
Vanport, 421, 432–3
Vaqueros, 289
Vaudeville, 451
Vermont, 445
Victor, Frances Fuller, 441–2, 442 n
Victoria, Queen, 290
Victoria, B. C., 227–8; port of, 6
Vigilance Committee, 249
Vigilantes, 245 ff.
Villard, Henry: donor, 216; rise of 261–2; enters Northwest railroading, 263–4; completes Northern Pacific, 264–6; 366–7
Virginia, 291, 426
Virginia City, Montana, 197, 225, 291
Vizcaíno expedition, 22
Vladivostok, 362
Voyageurs, 7, 44, 185

Waddington, Alfred, quoted, 226
Wagner, "Dutch John," 248
Wagon freighting, Western Oregon, 182–3; Inland Empire, 234–8
Waiilatpu Mission, 109, 118, 122, 208, 299
Waldo, 220, 221
Walker, Elkanah, 118
Walker, Joseph R., 101
Walker, William, 114
Walker's Road, 180
Walla Walla, 195, 197, 231, 297, 393
Walla Walla and Columbia Railroad, 258
Walla Walla County, 171 n, 303 n, 328 n, 332
Walla Walla Indians, 174
Wallace, Idaho, 433–4
Wallace, Lew, 240
Wallace, William, 94, 95, 240, 241
Wallamet (ship), 204
Wallgren, Governor William C., 412
Wallowa County, Oregon, 302 n
Wallula, 5, 231, 232
Walton, Judge Joshua J., 216
Wapato Island (now Sauvies Island), 104
War of 1812, 46, 51, 292
War Relocation Authority, 425
Ward, Henry C., 199
Warre, Henry, 453
Warren, Sidney, quoted, 443

Index

xxix

Wasco, 169 *n*
Wasco (ship), 175
Wasco area, Oregon, 328 *n*
Wasco County, Oregon, 282, 302 *n*
Washington, *passim*, but especially, territorial legislature, 215; mineral development, 222; admission to statehood of, 254–5; reclamation in, 311–14; Grand Coulee project, 315–19; population figures (1900–40), 417 *n*; foreign born in, 426 *n*; *see also* Washington Territory
Washington (sloop), 28
Washington Bureau of Labor, 410
Washington Direct Primary Law, 407
Washington Fruit Growers' Association, 337
Washington Initiative, Referendum, and Recall Amendment, 407
Washington Park, Portland, 453
Washington Power Company, 280, 371
Washington Standard, 447
Washington State College, 215
Washington State Grange, 394
Washington State Grange, 394, 412
Washington State Legislature, 314
Washington Territory, 78; early settlements in, 162–3; Cowlitz convention, 163; creation of, 164; Isaac I. Stevens appointed first governor of, 164; surveys respecting, 164–5; Indian policies, 166; spread of settlement, 169–71; Indian troubles, 171 ff.; pioneer road building, 179–81; pioneer economic and social life, 181 ff.; population of (1880), 253; constitutional convention, 254, 261, 390, 392, 448, 458
Washington (Webster-Ashburton) Treaty, 144
Washington University, St. Louis, 329
Washington Water Power Company, 372
Watauga Association, 129
Watson, Thomas, 400
Watt, Joseph, 293–4
Watts, John W., 387
Weatherwax, Clara, 444–5
Weaver, James B., 396–9, 401
Webber and Slater's Express, 196
"Webfeet," 200
Webster, Daniel, 144
Webster, John, 215
Webster's *Spelling Book*, 210

Weed, 274
Weidler, G. W., 263, 367
Weiser, Idaho, 393
Wells, Fargo & Company, 192; operation in Northwest, 193 ff.; robbed, 246
Wells, Henry, 194
Wells Fargo messengers, 197
Wenatchee, 303, 370, 379
Wenatchee Indian Reservation, 174
Wenatchee (We'natchi) Indians, 7 *n*
Wenatchee-Okanogan Co-operative Association, 338
Wenatchee River, 325, 325 *n*
Wesleyan Institute, 213
Wesleyan University, 115
West, Harry, 452
West, Governor Oswald, 403, 411
West Side Company, 260 ff.
West Virginia, 426
Western Federation of Miners, 434
Western Pacific Railroad, 274
Wetmore, Alphonso, 121
Weyerhaeuser, Frederick, 355; lumber interest, 355, 358
What the Queen Said, 446
Whatcom, 197
Whatcom County, Washington, 333, 419
Wheeler, William A., 387–8
Whidbey Island, 25, 170, 370
Whig Party, 157, 158; in Oregon Territory, 156–7
Whiskey Ring, 386
White, Dr. Elija, 111, 122, 129, 133 *n*, 138
White Bluffs Military Project, 432
"White Headed Eagle." See John McLoughlin
Whiteaker, Governor John, 161
Whitehorse Ranch, 207
Whitman, Dr. Marcus, 117, 118, 122, 123, 128, 293, 299; death of, 152–3; Indian instruction, 208; *see also* Waiilatpu Mission
Whitman County, Washington, 328 *n*
Whitman legend, 123
Whitman massacre, significance of, 152–3
Whitman Mission. *See* Waiilatpu Mission
Whitman-Spalding party, 118
"Whitman's Ride," 123
Whitney, Asa, 256
Whitney Museum, 454
Wigwam Convention, 161
Wilbur Academy, 213

Wilkes, Lieut. Charles, 74, 81; 299–300; visits Fort Vancouver, 60–1; quoted, 75; exploring party, 129; quoted, 299
Wilkes, George, 256
Willamette Cattle Company, 182
Willamette Falls, 133, 167, 168, 204, 367, 368, 391
Willamette Falls Electric Company, 367, 368
Willamette Pass, 180
Willamette-Puget Trough, 4
Willamette River, 5, 84, 94, 274
Willamette University, 213, 215 n; founding of, 208
Willamette Valley, passim, but especially, 47, 68, 111; Astorians in, 94–5; Methodists settle in, 115–16; settlements in, 167–8; railroads in, 258–62, 274
Willamette Valley Cattle Company, 293
Willapa Bay, 6, 351
William and Ann (ship), 71, 72
Williams, William, 53
Willow Creek, 259
Wilmer and Smith's Times (England), quoted, 147
Wilson, John L., 254
Wilson, Woodrow, 405, 413–14
Winchester, 168, 169 n, 188, 195
Windermere Lake, 37
Winnemucca Province, 286
Winship, Captain Jonathan, 31
Winship, Captain Nathan, 31, 90
Winship expedition, 89–90
Winther, Sophus Keith, 444
Wisconsin, 275, 355
Withycombe, Governor James, 403, 411
"Wobblies," 435–7
"Wolf meetings," 131
Women's Suffrage, 407
Wood, Charles Erskine Scott, 443, 445
Woodward, Absalom, 191
Work, John, 55, 58–9, 62, 70; quoted, 75
Workmen's Compensation, 407
Works Progress Administration, 415
World Almanac, 346
World War I, 280, 337, 360, 368, 372, 403, 437
World War II, 281, 318, 338–9, 360, 362, 368, 372, 378

Wrangell, Alaska, 64
Wrangell, Rear Admiral Baron Ferdinand, 64
Wright, Colonel George, 175, 176, 222
Wurdemann, Audrey, 446
Wyckoff, Stephen N., quoted, 356
Wyeth, Nathaniel, 63, 79, 100, 102, 108; 1832–33 expedition, 102–3, 207; 1834 expedition, 104; Fort Hall founded by, 104; failure of, 105; as colonizer, 105–6
Wyoming, 94, 101, 252, 255, 282, 284–6, 290, 291, 308, 309, 407 n, 427
Wyoming Stock Growers' Association, 285–6, 288
Wyoming Territory, 239

X Y Company, 35, 39

Yakima Canal Company, 303, 303 n
Yakima County, Washington, 282, 303, 313, 332
Yakima Fruit Growers' Association, 338
Yakima Indian War, 174–5, 177
Yakima Indians, 176, 177, 178, 222, 299
Yakima Irrigation and Improvement Company, 303
Yakima River, 312, 318, 320, 326
Yakima Valley, 45
Yale University Library, 461
Yamhill, 387
Yamhill County, 169 n, 390, 392
Yaquina Bay, 274
Yaquina (Oregon Pacific) Railroad, 274
Yellowstone River, 89, 278
Yerba Buena. See San Francisco
Yesler, Henry L., 170, 353
Yokohama, 362
Yoncalla, Oregon, 393
York Factory, 55, 57
Young, Brigham, 417
Young, Ewing, 108, 130, 182
Young, Joaquin, 130 n
Yreka, California, 259
Yuman tribes, 10

Zigler, Eustace, 453
Zion's Herald, 114

A NOTE ON THE TYPE IN WHICH
THIS BOOK IS SET

The text of this book is set in Caledonia, a Linotype face designed by W. A. Dwiggins, the man responsible for so much that is good in contemporary book design and typography. Caledonia belongs to the family of printing types called "modern face" by printers — a term used to mark the change in style of type-letters that occurred about 1800. It has all the hard-working feet-on-the-ground qualities of the Scotch Modern face plus the liveliness and grace that is integral in every Dwiggins "product" whether it be a simple catalogue cover or an almost human puppet.

The book was composed, printed, and bound by The Plimpton Press, Norwood, Massachusetts.